3/96

A HISTORY OF MOZAMBIQUE

A History of Mozambique

MALYN NEWITT

INDIANA UNIVERSITY PRESS
BLOOMINGTON AND INDIANAPOLIS

Manufactured in Hong Kong

Library of Congress Cataloging-in-Publication Data

Newitt, M. D. D.
  A history of Mozambique/by Malyn Newitt.
    p. cm.
  Includes bibliographical references and index.
  ISBN 0-253-34006-3. — ISBN 0-253-34007-1 (pbk.)
  1. Mozambique — History. I. Title.
DT3341.N48 1995
967.9 — dc20   93-7477

1 2 3 4 5 97 96 95

PREFACE AND ACKNOWLEDGEMENTS

At the time when the writing of this book was completed, November 1992, Mozambique was just over 101 years old. The country came into existence in its present form as a result of an Anglo-Portuguese treaty of May 1891 and became independent from Portugal in July 1975. This book, however, is concerned with much more than the last hundred years. The Mozambique created in 1891 was not a piece of random map-drawing but an attempt to make sense of the history of the region, grouping within the borders of a single colonial state the major ports between Cabo Delgado and Delagoa Bay with at least a substantial part of their commercial hinterland. In so doing it accepted a partition of the African coast which had been made as far back as the sixteenth century when the Portuguese divided their command in eastern Africa between the captaincies of Mozambique and Mombasa. This work therefore attempts to summarise five hundred years of the experience of the societies that existed within the area that became Mozambique in 1891.

Summarising so much history in such a short space has been an exercise in compression and exclusion. Each one of the chapters could easily be enlarged to become a monograph in itself, and much more could be said about every one of the themes dealt with. I am also conscious of the extent to which this book rests on the research of other writers. Mozambique has attracted a succession of distinguished historians whose work I am only too happy to recognise. Pride of place must be taken by Leroy Vail and Landeg White's *Capitalism and Colonialism in Mozambique*, the outstanding book on the country's history and one that is indispensible for anyone wanting to study it. Close behind in importance come E. A. Alpers' *Ivory and Slaves in East Central Africa*, Allen Isaacman's *Tradition of Resistance*, the notable *História de Moçambique* (a joint production of the talented history department of Maputo University), and Thomas Henriksen's *Revolution and Counterrevolution*. Of fundamental importance also are René Pélissier's *Naissance du Mozambique* and Almeida de Eça's *História das Guerras no Zambeze*. If these might be ranked as the most important seven books on Mozambican history, they in turn would have been impossible without the work of other scholars, some of whose research can be found only in theses or scholarly journals. Chief among these are José Capela, António Rita-Ferreira and Gerhard Liesegang, who is in a very real sense the doyen of modern Mozambican studies.

Barry Neil-Tomlinson's notable work on the Moçambique Company deserves to be more widely known, as does that of Jeanne Penvenne who has almost singlehandedly revolutionised the writing of the social, economic and urban history of the last hundred years.

For the earlier periods, it is important to recognise the definitive achievements of Eric Axelson and Alexandre Lobato who have left little more to be said about the sixteenth and seventeenth centuries and whose work is underpinned by the great archival collections — the nine volumes of G. M. Theal's *Records of South Eastern Africa* and the eight volumes of the *Documents on the History of Mozambique and Central Africa*, which, together with other collections of documents, provide an accessible archive of early documentation almost unrivalled for any other part of Africa.

In some ways this is the wrong time to be writing a history of Mozambique because the riches of the Maputo archives are only just beginning to be exploited by a group of historians who are rewriting the history of the colonial period. I am only too aware that the present work does not do full justice to much of this research. I could certainly have devoted more space to the urban history of Lourenço Marques, and would have attempted to discuss the riches of Mozambican artistic culture from the traditional sculpture of the Makonde and the music of the Chopi to the work of modern poets, writers and painters. That Mozambique has produced in Malangatana one of the world's greatest modern painters should surely earn a mention in a history of the country. To such major gaps in this work I would be the first to draw attention.

In other ways this is a very appropriate moment to be writing. The catastrophe that has overwhelmed Mozambique since independence has attracted much attention from commentators and politicians. What is badly needed is some way of seeing these catastrophic events against a long view of Mozambique's history. I set out to write this book acutely conscious that in many ways the modern period of famine, drought and endemic social violence formed familiar patterns. There have been many similar episodes in Mozambique's history, and the coming together of the ecological, social and political forces which have caused these 'times of trouble' need to be understood. One of the themes of this long view of history I have described with the word 'dis-integration'. The history of Mozambique can be viewed as a dialectic between forces of integration and those of disintegration. Integration is the process of creating larger-scale polities where security is guaranteed by some overarching authority, where economic interdependence grows and related cultural patterns become established over a wide geographical area. This process can be seen in the conquests of the Karanga, Tsonga, Maravi and Nguni chiefs, in the effects of the international trade in gold, ivory and slaves, in the spread of Islam and Christianity, in the influence of some of the spirit cults of the land, and of course in the needs and institutional structures of international capitalism and the colonial state, whether in the earlier form of the *Estado da India* or the later form of the *Estado Novo*.

Against these integrative processes must be seen the forces of dis-integration — drought and famine, banditry and warlordism, the self-sufficiency and survival strategies of the small society of the village and the clan, the low level of technology and the forces within the colonial state that made for dis-integration: the captain's monopoly, the feuding of Afro-Portuguese seigneurial families, the export of labour, and the system of concession companies.

Of course, these ideas are not new. Many able commentators have chronicled the catastrophic history of Mozambique since independence, and the processes of dis-integration and collapse have been laid bare. In particular the refrain of banditry and warlordism is one which no student of Mozambique's past or present can fail to have picked up. I would particularly draw attention to the recent work of Christian Geffray and Michel Cahen and to the article by Gueorgui Derluguian which Cahen translated for *Année Africaine*. In that article Derluguian wrote:

> It is important to note how particularly important for my model of armed violence in postcolonial Mozambique is the tendency, in a context of crisis in precolonial society, for archaic classes to appear in the form of castes of professional fighters who had either been alienated from their ethnic identity (as with the *mabulundlela* of the Gaza empire) or in whom it had been destroyed (as in the case of the *achicunda* of the Zambesi valley). . . . These communities of slave-fighters served the interests of the proprietor of a *prazo da coroa* in the Zambesi valley, or of a dominant lineage in Gaza. This created relations of domination and subjugation previously non-existent which, in their turn, opened the way to power groups and to means for the exploitation of the dependent agricultural communities which were wholly new.[1]

This book tries to examine in twenty chapters what Derluguian managed to say in one paragraph. However, I hope that someone reading this history will be able to say, not that the débâcle of the present is preordained by the happenings of the past, but that it is at least more complicated than any consideration of immediate causes might suggest.

It has not been possible to arrange every chapter in a purely chronological manner, nor do I think this is desirable. Strict chronology may be the best way to order and describe 'events', but it cannot be a successful way of looking at the *longue durée*. There are therefore chapters, notably those on commerce, the fairs, the *prazos* and labour migration, which have dealt with their subjects outside a purely chronological setting. And there are other chapters where the fragmented, dis-integrated nature of the events themselves suggest a regional as well as a chronological framework. Finally, the structure of this book is designed to allow the reader to look through both ends of the historical telescope. There is no relentless movement from the generality of background to the particularity of the actual event — in many instances it is best to start with the vivid record of the individual happening and move outwards through the radiating circles of influence and explanation.

Acknowledgements

I would like to thank the British Academy and Exeter University for research grants enabling me to travel to different archives and libraries. I am very grateful for the hospitality I received from the staff at Eduardo Mondlane University, Maputo, and from the historians at Chancellor College of the University of Malawi and the University of Zimbabwe. I am particularly grateful to David Beach for letting me have copies of his papers and of the Portuguese manuscript collection he compiled, and to Jeanne Penvenne for sending me some of her unpublished papers.

Finally I owe a particular debt to Christopher Hurst, the publisher, for his patience in waiting nearly ten years for the manuscript; to Hilary Earl for reading the draft with such attention; to Sue Rouillard for drawing the splendid maps; and to Joan, Emily, Bernie and Jessie for living patiently with the domestic chaos of books and papers for so long.

Exeter
May 1994

M.N.

REFERENCE

1. G. Derluguian, 'Les têtes du monstre. Du climat social de la violence armée au Mozambique', pp. 95-6.

CONTENTS

MAPS

TABLES

FIGURES

GLOSSARY

Aforamento	Lease (used particularly for *prazo* leases)
Alcaide	Commander of a fortress
Aldeamento	Government strategic village
Aldeia	Village; districts into which Portuguese India was divided for tax purposes which were granted as concessions to Portuguese
Almadia	Canoe
Alqueire	A measure equal to 13.8 litres
Alvará	Writ or order
Aringa	Large fortified stockade
Bandazio/a	Personal attendants of the Afro-Portuguese *senhores* and *senhoras*
Bangwa	Dhow (Portuguese *pangaio*)
Bar (of ivory)	A measure of weight equivalent to *c.* 518 pounds
Bare	Mining camp
Bazo	A slave placed in charge of other slaves
Bicho	Doorboy
Boca	Payment made to obtain an audience
Butaca	Domestic slaves
Cadernete	Pass
Cafila	Trade caravan or convoy
Cafre	Kaffir, black African
Câmara	Town Council (see also *Senado da Câmara*)
Cantineiro	Bar-owner; drink-seller
Capitania	Captaincy
Capitão	Captain (used for leaders of *chicunda* warbands and for those in charge of work gangs)
Capitão-mor	Literally captain-major — widely-used rank conferring military and civil authority
Carta de Aforamento	Lease (used for documents conferring titles to *prazos*)
Cartaz	Safe conduct license issued to a ship by Portuguese authorities in the East
Casa	Household
Chefe do Posto	Local administrator in the colonial government
Chibalo	Forced labour for the government
Chicunda	Slave (used for the armed retainers of the Afro-Portuguese)
Chuambo	Fortified stockade
Cipai	African soldier or armed policeman in Portuguese colonial service

xvii

Circunscrição	Circumscription; rural administrative district
Colonato	Irrigated settlement of small farms
Colono	A member of a *colonato*, also a free peasant on the *prazos*
Commerciantes volantes	Itinerant traders
Conselho	Council; unit of local government in 20th-century Mozambique
Conselho do governo	Government Council; council that advised the governor-general of Mozambique
Conto	A thousand units of currency (*milreis* or *escudos*)
Cooperante	Foreign volunteer worker
Cruzado	Coin worth 400 *reis*
Curador	Term used particularly of official who supervised contracting of labourers
Curva	Payment made by Portuguese captains to Monomotapa
Dona	Lady; title assumed by the female *prazo* holders
Donatário	Holder of a donatory captaincy in the 15th and 16th centuries
Empata	Embargo on trade
Encomendero	Holder of an *encomienda*
Encomienda	Grant of Indians made by the Castilian Crown to *conquistadores*
Ensaca	Company or regiment of *chicunda* soldiers
Entrada	Expedition of conquest made under contract to the Crown
Escravo	Slave
Escravos do Bar	Mining slaves
Estado da India	Portuguese empire in the East
Faraçola	Measure of weight of about 18 pounds
Fato	Trade cloth
Fazenda	Treasury; also trade goods
Feira	Fair
Fidalgo	Gentleman
Filho da Terra	Person of mixed race, locally born
Flechas	Black troops under control of the DGS
Foreiro	Lessee
Frei	Brother (as for a friar)
Fumba	A sleeping sack
Fumo	Chief
Grêmio	Guild
Incube	Village
Indígena	Native
Invernar	To winter (used for ships waiting a favourable monsoon)

Juiz Ordinário	Judge
Junta	Board
Lançado	Afro-Portuguese in Guinea
Liberto	Freed slave
Lobola	Brideprice
Luane	Country house of a *prazo senhor*
Luzio	River boat
Mabulundlela	Tsonga in Gaza service
Machamba	Garden or plantation
Machilla	Palanquin
Machira (Machilla)	African-made cotton cloth
Madzi Manga	Sacred water used at coronation of the Macombes
Mãe de Ouro	Mother of Gold (used to describe Butua)
Mahlatule	Great drought and famine of 1790s
Majobo	Gaza official
Malemo	Pilot
Mambo	Chief
Manilhas	Copper rings
Matical (mithqal)	Measure of gold equivalent to 155 ounces
Meirinho	Bailiff
Metical	Unit of currency in independent Mozambique
Mfecane	Wars and migrations following the establishment of the Zulu kingdom
Mhondoro	Spirit medium among the Karanga and Shona
Mihrab	The niche in the wall of a mosque indicating the direction of Mecca
Milando	Breach of custom or crime requiring payment of a fine
Milrei	Unit of currency under the Monarchy
Misericórdia	Charitable brotherhood
Missonco	Tribute (see also *mussoco*)
Mitical	See *matical*
Mocazambo	Head of the slave establishment
Modus Vivendi	A temporary agreement (used in particular for the temporary labour convention signed between Mozambique and the Transvaal in 1901)
Morador(es)	Settler or resident (used in particular for the Portuguese and Afro-Portuguese of Mozambique Island)
Mtepe	Traditional sewn boat used in the Indian Ocean
Muavi	Poison ordeal
Munhai (Vanhai)	Soldiers of the Monomotapa chieftaincy in the 18th century; descendants of unfree clients
Mussambazes	Professional traders in Zambesia
Mussenze	Free population of the *prazos* (see also *colono*)

Mussito	Fortified stockade used by bandits or escaped slaves
Mussoco	Tribute (see also *missonco*)
Muta-hano	Agrarian custom of working free days for a landlord (used on mainland opposite Mozambique Island)
Muzungo(s)	Afro-Portuguese
Mwanamambo	Chief African official of the *prazos*
Mwenyi	Elected leader of the Muslim community in Zambesia
Não-indígena	Person of non-native status
Nganga	Traditional doctor (witchdoctor)
Nhacoda	Slave in charge of female slaves
Nau	Carrack
Nomi	Societies of adolescents among the Sena people
Obras Públicas	Public works
Ouvidor	Judge
Pangaio	Dhow (see also *bangwa* and *mtepe*)
Panja	A measure of capacity of between 27 and 30 litres
Pardão	Coin worth 360 *reis*
Pasta	A measure of gold, valued in the 18th century at 800 *cruzados*
Pataca	Portuguese name for the Maria Theresa *thaler*
Patamar	African trading agent (used in Mozambique Island and the mainland opposite)
Prazo	Leased crown estates in Zambesia
Presídio	Garrisoned port or town
Provedor	Official
Quinta	Country house or villa
Quintal	Weight equivalent to 4 *arrobas* or 59 kilogrammes
Quissapo	Sack
Quite	Throne
Regedoria	Official chieftaincy
Regimento	Official instructions
Régulo	Chief
Relação	High Court
Residencia	Judicial inquiry
Rios	Rivers (used for Zambesia)
Sachicunda	Leaders of a group of *chicunda* (see also *capitão*)
Saguate	Present
Senado da Câmara	Town council
Senhor(a)	Title used for the *prazo*-holders
Senzala	Shack

Sertanejo	Backwoodsman
Sesmaria	Vacant land
Sharif	Descendant of the prophet
Sul do Save	Region south of the Sabi river
Tanador-mor	Official responsible for the promotion of agriculture
Tanga	Eighth of a *matical*
Tenente-geral	Title of the governor of Zambesia in the 18th century
Termo de Vassalagem	Treaty by which a chief acknowledged Portuguese sovereignty
Terras da Coroa	Crown lands (see also *prazo*)
Terras em Fatiota	Freehold estates in Zambesia
Thangata	Labour service performed by peasants in Nyasaland
Vedor da Fazenda	Chief treasury official
Velório	Trade beads
Xerafim	Coin worth 360 *reis*
Zambuco	Dhow
Zimbabwe	Capital of a Karanga chief

ABBREVIATIONS

AHM	Arquivo Histórico de Moçambique
AHU	Arquivo Histórico Ultramarino
ANC	African National Congress
BNU	Banco Nacional Ultramarino
BSAC	British South Africa Company
CAIL	Complexo Agro-Industrial do Limpopo
CFLM	Caminho de Ferro de Lourenço Marques
CONCP	Conferência das Organizaçoẽs Nacionalistas das Colónias Portuguêsas
DGS	Direcção Geral de Segurança
ENN	Empresa Nacional de Navigação
Frelimo	Frente de Libertação de Moçambique
GD	Grupos Dinamizadores
GE	Grupos Especiais
GEP	Grupos Especiais Páraquedistas
MFA	Movimento das Forças Armadas
MPLA	Movimento Popular de Libertação de Angola
OJM	Organização da Juventude Moçambicana
OMM	Organização das Mulheres Moçambicanas
PAIGC	Partido Africano da Independência da Guiné e Cabo Verde
PIDE	Polícia Internacional e de Defesa do Estado
Renamo	Resistencia Nacional Moçambicana
RNLB	Rhodesia Native Labour Bureau
SADCC	Southern African Development and Coordination Conference
SADF	South African Defence Force
SWAPO	South West Africa Peoples Organisation
UMCA	Universities Mission to Central Africa
UNITA	União Nacional para a Independência Total de Angola
WNLA	Witwatersrand Native Labour Association
ZANU	Zimbabwe African National Union

1

THE MOZAMBIQUE CHANNEL REGION
IN THE SIXTEENTH CENTURY

Prologue

The vast majority of the human race has never recorded in writing any reflections on its consciousness of its own existence. In many societies such individualistic activity would appear unprofitable, pointless or even subversive of the welfare of the community. Even in western Europe where social groups evolved who were able to exploit and live by the art of literacy, there were few people with the leisure or the capacity to depict in words the shifting patterns of human relations. Where such records were made, the passage of centuries, aided by such apocalyptic agents as damp, worms, fire and earthquake, have weeded the record more effectively than any government archivist. The voice that speaks from the past, particularly when carrying the authentic tones of human emotion, is therefore as treasured as it is rare. There is such a document, surviving from 1547, which vividly captures the passions and complexities of a small urban community on the coast of what later became Mozambique.[1] It is a long, impassioned and confused outpouring of resentment, hatred and indignation written by João Velho, the king of Portugal's factor in Sofala. Velho had assumed his post in 1542 and had charge of the warehouses containing the cloth and beads used to buy gold and ivory for the king and provisions for the fort. During his four years in Sofala he lived in the tower of the fort close to the sea with a white slave woman, called Victoria, who cleaned and cooked for him. When the captain of Sofala was absent, he was in charge of the fortress and its personnel and he dealt with the local traders and with chiefs in the interior.

In 1544 the newly-appointed captain, Dom Jorge Teles de Meneses, arrived at Sofala with his retinue and accompanied by his henchman, Francisco Ribeiro. At the time the trade of the region was dominated by a Muslim trader, Mohammed Dao, who was one of Dom Jorge's principal creditors and was clearly putting pressure on the captain to pay his debts. Dom Jorge summoned Mohammed Dao to Sofala and then gave instructions to the sinister Francisco Ribeiro to murder him, with the result that 'one morning he was found all cut to pieces' while his chief wife, Zara, was seized and kept in chains. Dom Jorge intended to hand her over, perhaps as a slave, to his

1

mistress and she was put in a canoe with one of the captain's retainers to be taken out to his ship. On the way the boat overturned. Unable to swim and weighed down with chains the wretched woman clung to her escort and both were drowned. 'God sees evil deeds and punishes them', recorded the outraged factor, 'but, in this world, the just sometimes suffer for the sinners.'

Dom Jorge then joined forces with another Muslim trader, Mohammed Joane, whom he intended to install as 'lord of the river'. Retainers of the captain were sent to 'throw out Changamira who, until then, was king and lord of all those lands', a euphemism which involved the killing 'of the people of the land who were not friends of the said Mafamede Joane'. Changamira himself escaped, 'and if he comes again to rule', reflected Velho, 'it will be hard for the people of the fortress.' Meanwhile 'Dom Jorge sent him [Mohammed Joane] quantities of Your Highness's goods for him to give away so that all the people of the land would obey the said Mafamede Joane.'

Now fully in control of the situation, Mohammed Joane and the captain built a stone warehouse on one of the islands at the mouth of the river and soon had a thriving trade in ivory. Between 700 and 800 merchants visited their trading post in 1546 attracted by the fact that the captain was flooding the market with cheap goods. Poor Velho tried to intervene to stop the diversion of the royal cloth and beads into Dom Jorge's hands, reflecting ruefully that in his fourth year as factor, 'there was only one tooth [tusk] for Your Highness and the factory was left empty and without cloth.' To prevent the factor's interfering, the captain appointed another of his retainers, Jerónimo Rodrigues, as clerk in the factory and when Velho refused to hand over either trade goods or the property of the deceased which was in his care, Rodrigues drew his sword and tried to kill him. Velho was wounded and some of his own men were killed but they managed to arrest Rodrigues and hold him prisoner until Dom Jorge peremptorily ordered his release. Bands of the captain's armed retainers then went round all the houses in the town and Velho had to take refuge in the church suffering the humiliation of seeing Victoria kidnapped and passed from hand to hand among the victors.

Then, as Velho made clear in another letter, Dom Jorge and Francisco Ribeiro proceeded to make their fortunes. The royal trading ship which ran between Goa and Mozambique was brought south to Sofala and filled with 450–500 *bars* of ivory, quantities of the royal ivory being thrown into the sea to make room. The captain, wrote Velho, 'is taking away more money than any captain ever took from these parts and Francisco Ribeiro is making more than 20,000 *miticals*'. In order to cover himself with the king, Dom Jorge agreed to marry a lady of the king's choice, and the factor commented that he was rich enough to be able to marry fifteen wives and should be made to marry at least four as a punishment for his evil deeds. There was little in any of this to cheer the factor who had to derive what comfort he could from the fact that when Dom Jorge eventually left only one person went to the quayside to see him off. Velho wrote:

> If the viceroy Dom Joam de Crasto were alive, this would never have happened. . . . Were he alive he would do me justice for the many injuries and evils done to me by Dom Jorge and Francisco Ribeiro and their men but, now that he is dead, I have no hope of obtaining it. I am keeping everything for Your Highness . . . but woe to those who show any desire to serve you, for their life is empty.[2]

This drama and the personal conflicts it contains are free-standing and comprehensible in purely human terms. However, for the historian the details of the story are so many strands that weave ever more intricate patterns of human relations in time and space. In them one can also find the clues to understanding the social and economic relations of a whole region of eastern Africa, of the Indian Ocean and the burgeoning capitalist world beyond. When the extent of this pattern is fully revealed, the passionate, individualistic actions of these men seem to be locked into a kind of predestination. The rest of this chapter seeks to follow the threads one by one — the historical geography, the patterns of human interaction and the particular events — until the happenings just described are explained.

Sofala

Sofala, the place where these violent events took place, was a town of some antiquity. It was situated on a low-lying sandy coast just south of the mouth of the Buzi, the largest river on the east African coast between the Pungue and the Sabi (Map 1). The Buzi descends from the escarpment of the central African plateau and crosses 100 miles of bush-covered low veldt, becoming sluggish and meandering on its journey and depositing its fertile silt every time the rains cause the flooded river to break its banks. The mouth of the river has been heavily barred with sand and its exact outfall into the ocean has probably changed many times over the centuries. Its silt, together with that of the other rivers that flows from the highlands, has created a string of low-lying islands, sandbanks and bars which leave a network of shallow, sheltered channels and waterways, easy of access for canoes and small sailing craft but dangerous for larger ocean-going vessels.

Settlements have existed on this coast for a thousand years, for it provides the most convenient access to the sea for the people of the high veldt. The dunes and islands south of the Buzi have always been well populated. Fresh water is easily available and coconut groves thrive. In the early sixteenth century it was estimated that there were 10,000 people living around the bay of Sofala and that there were at least two villages apart from the main town.[3] But the sands shift and are impermanent. As fast as the rivers deposit their silt, the sea gnaws at the dunes and during the high equinoctial tides invades the land in all directions. The villages and larger towns have frequently to be rebuilt, and their locations change. The Sofala of the Arabs and the early Portuguese gave way to the Beira of modern times but both settlements lay on the same stretch of coast and provided access to the same interior.

In the sixteenth century the main town of Sofala lay on the northern arm of a wide, shallow, horseshoe-shaped bay.[4] There had been an important trading centre of that name, possibly on or near that very site, since at least the ninth century AD and probably earlier. Over such a long period the life of the sea — trade, boat-building and fishing — had become linked in a complex way with the growing of crops, the ownership of land and the conduct of internal commerce. Sofala was ruled by a sheikh who sat, spider-like, at the centre of this web of relationships. He was Muslim by religion and through his patrilineage was a *sharif* claiming kinship with the ruling families of Kilwa and the Somali coast.[5] The position of the sheikh was not dissimilar to that of the rulers of many of the other east African towns. He had considerable status within the world of Indian Ocean trade, and traders who came to Sofala had to seek his permission to buy and sell. According to the Portuguese, he used to levy a tribute of one cloth in every seven that were imported, and twenty *miticals* on every *bar* of ivory exported.[6] In return for the payment of tribute, he would allow visiting traders access to the networks of internal trade, and provide them with warehouse and storage facilities and the services of pilots (*malemos*), ship repairers and canoemen. However, he was not just the civil authority. He was also, himself, the principal trader, and buying and selling at the sheikh's price was part of local commercial practice.

To be a member of a sharifian lineage was an essential part of the prestige on which success in Indian Ocean trade depended. Kinship ties with African chiefly lineages were of equal importance for the conduct of trade in the interior and for the day-to-day affairs of the town. Through polygynous marriages the sheikh himself, and the other traders of Sofala, were linked with the chiefly families of the immediate hinterland. Some, though by no means all, of these chiefs themselves adopted Islam — located up the rivers that flowed into the bay of Sofala were two or three *reis mouros* (moorish kings), as the

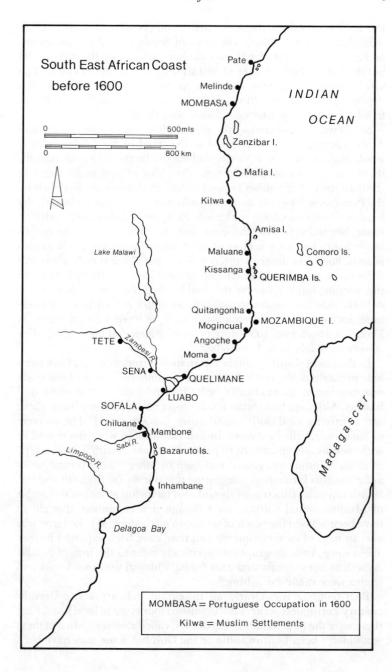

South East African Coast
before 1600

INDIAN OCEAN

Pate
Melinde
MOMBASA
Zanzibar I.
Mafia I.
Kilwa
Amisa I.
Maluane
Comoro Is.
Kissanga
QUERIMBA Is.
Quitangonha
MOZAMBIQUE I.
Mogincual
Angoche
Moma
SENA
QUELIMANE
LUABO
SOFALA
Chiluane
Mambone
Bazaruto Is.
Inhambane
Delagoa Bay
Lake Malawi
TETE
Zambesi R.
Sabi R.
Limpopo R.
Madagascar

0   500 mls
0   800 km

MOMBASA = Portuguese Occupation in 1600

Kilwa = Muslim Settlements

Portuguese described them, as well as others who were merely *reis cafres* (kaffir kings). Round the town of Sofala itself the palm groves and *machambas* (plantations) were probably owned by the merchants, but the town relied for its food and security on the inland chiefs. The safe passage of trading caravans to and from the interior also depended on the friendship of the chiefs and hence on the network of family ties that could be established with them.

Sofala was not, of course, the only trading town on this coast, and Arab geographers often referred to the 'land of Sofala' implying a whole region and not a single settlement. In the sixteenth century there was a string of coastal towns stretching at least as far south as the Sabi river. A few miles beyond Sofala was Chiluane, described by the Portuguese as a *villa dos mouros*, situated on an offshore island, the kind of site favoured for settlement along the whole eastern African coast. Beyond that was Chibuene and then Mambone at the mouth of the Sabi. The most remote of these settlements were the Bazaruto islands, known in the sixteenth century as the Hucicas or Vacicas. All these towns may have participated to some extent in the gold trade of the interior, but Sofala was the gold trading port *par excellence* and it is likely that the smaller coastal towns either traded in other commodities valued in the international trade, or owed their existence, as Duarte Barbosa said, to trading in 'rice, millet, and meat which they convey to Sofala in little vessels'.[7]

In the towns south of Sofala international traders would have been able to obtain ivory, turtleshell, pearls or ambergris, while local trade was conducted in foodstuffs, salt, cotton cloth, woven mats and baskets. Although fine cotton textiles were imported from India, there was a thriving local cloth manufacture along the coast. The weavers of Sofala unravelled coloured Indian cottons and wove the thread in with their locally spun yarn to produce a material with a special type of stripe.[8] Cotton was grown and spun by other coastal communities as far south as Inhambane suggesting that during the fifteenth and sixteenth centuries this region should also be included within the ambit of Muslim coastal culture, even though it is commonly thought to have been beyond the reach of monsoon navigation. Worked iron was also an item of local commerce and may have been exported further afield since Arab geographers specifically refer to the iron of Sofala. As well as hoes, spears and axes for agricultural use, iron hooks and chains were made for fishing.[9]

Boat-building was clearly an important industry and sixteenth-century Portuguese writers distinguished four types of local boat. First there were the large ocean-going dhows, called *zambucos*. Most of these would have been built in India or the Gulf but some may have been constructed in the major boat-building centres of eastern Africa like Mozambique Island or the Comoro Islands. The smaller versions of these were the *bangwas* (called *pangaios* by the Portuguese), which carried the local trade up and down the coast but which were able to make journeys across to Madagascar. These boats were of an ancient and very traditional design. The boards were sewn together and sealed with gum, for which Mafia Island was an important source. The superstructure was made of cane and the sails of matting. The Portuguese were somewhat scathing about the flimsy construction of these vessels and about their sailing capabilities, but until the twentieth century they were to compete successfully on the coast with boats of European design.

In addition to these there were *luzios* and *almadias*. The *luzios* were decked river boats used in the estuaries and inland waterways as far south as Delagoa Bay. They were able to carry sails and sometimes had a deck cabin. The *almadias* were canoes made from hollow trees and were fitted with outriggers in the northern coastal areas, the Comoros and Madagascar, but were used without outriggers in the region of the Zambesi and to the south. *Almadias* could be of considerable size. The largest Zambesi *almadias* carried up to 20 tons and in 1505 Francisco de Almeida's fleet was attacked by ocean-going ones off Madagascar.[10] The different types of boats built and used along the coast reflected the wide variety of maritime activity, from inshore and estuarial fishing to the more specialised catching of turtles and whales, diving for pearls, coastal trading voyages, and finally the longer ocean journeys to Kilwa, Madagascar, the Gulf and India.

It is important to stress the close links that the communities of the Sofala coast had always had with Madagascar. Sofala was often represented as being a dependancy, even a colony, of Kilwa — an isolated trading port acting as a relay station in Kilwa's control of the central African gold trade. This is certainly mistaken, for Sofala was an ancient trading centre whose commercial life was by no means centred on Kilwa. Sofala had always had direct commercial links with various towns in Madagascar and through Madagascar with India and Indonesia. Direct trade from Indonesia to Africa had been common up to the thirteenth century and the spread of Indonesian food crops and outrigger canoes, as well as of other aspects of Indonesian culture and language, to Africa by way of Madagascar has always been inherently more probable than imagining Indonesian influence to have taken a circuitous route round the fringes of the Indian Ocean. During the height of direct maritime trade between Indonesia and eastern Africa, Sofala was at the terminus of an ocean trade route every bit as important as that which came via Kilwa. The links between Sofala and Madagascar were close enough for there to have been a regular flow of migrants from south east Africa, and it seems likely that members of important mainland African lineages may have migrated there, taking with them their characteristic attitudes towards cattle and spirit cults. Sofala, or one of the other towns on the coast, would have been likely ports for these migrants to have used.[11]

Kilwa and East Africa

However, it was not for its trade with Madagascar or for its network of local commerce that Sofala was well known to Arab geographers throughout the literate Muslim world. Its fame rested on its trade in gold, which came from the great granite plateau stretching from the Manica highlands southwestwards towards the Kalahari. It was mined in many scattered outcrops, extracted from the quartz by crushing and washing, and brought for sale to fairs held under the auspices of the various chiefs whose territories lay along the eastern escarpment. These fairs were visited by traders from the coast, and until the middle of the fifteenth century the traders based in Sofala were the main buyers. Although the gold was destined for export to India or the Gulf, merchants from these regions seldom made the journey direct to Sofala. The trade of the Indian Ocean was dominated by the monsoons which allowed ships from India and the Gulf to reach east Africa between October and March. Return journeys had to be made between April and September if shipowners wished to avoid having to wait another six months on the African coast. It was difficult, if not impossible, to reach as far south as Sofala and return in a single season, and towns further north on the 'Swahili' coast acted as staging posts. It was this relative inaccessibility of the southern coast which set it, even at this point, somewhat apart from the northern coastline between Kilwa and Mogadishu which was able to enjoy much closer and more regular contacts with the centres of Indian Ocean trade and culture.

Indian or Gulf merchants reaching Kilwa or Melinde would either base themselves there for an onward journey to the south or, more probably, sell their goods to local merchants who operated the southern trade routes. Kilwa was ideally placed to perform the 'middleman' role. It lay at the parting of the ways, one route leading via the Comoro Islands to northern Madagascar, and the other going south to the Sofala coast. Kilwa's exceptional importance in international trade had attracted many important Muslim trading families, and its ruling sultans claimed to be *sharifs* and hence to have ties with the most prestigious families of the Hadramaut and the Gulf. It is no surprise to find that Kilwa was on the itinerary of the thirteenth-century traveller, part-time merchant and academic, Ibn Battuta, and that impressive mosques and palaces would be built to reflect the importance of its ruling families. However, although they were powerful and important, the merchant families of Kilwa never monopolised the trade of the coast.[12] At various times Mombasa, Melinde and possibly also the towns of the Comoro Islands, like Domoni, were significant independent centres of international trade. The ruling families of these towns acknowledged common lineage ties with the sultans of Kilwa and held the same myths of origin. This belief in a common 'Shirazi' identity merely emphasised the closeness of the lineage networks that operated throughout the region.

Just as Sofala was the centre of a local network of trade, so Kilwa, Melinde and the Comorian towns also had their local commerce and satellite settlements. The smaller coastal towns came into existence in response to commercial opportunity and it is likely that the more successful of them attracted members of the leading trading families to settle and contract local marriages.[13] Others may well have been founded as the result of feuds and rivalries within the merchant families. The traditional histories of the area say much about feuds, and often seem to have been recorded to reflect, or even to perpetuate, such rivalries. To represent kinship networks simply as a basis for co-operation and not also as a source of rivalry would be to fly in the face of everyone's experience of relations within an extended family.[14]

To be able to survive and prosper, the smaller coastal towns needed first of all to be able to attract trade from the African interior or to become the centre of some local industry. Economic activity of this sort would attract external traders to visit the ports and settle in them. Towns also needed to be sited in a favourable geographical location and to have the support of the local peoples whose agricultural surpluses would be needed to supply the urban population. The vigour of the coastal economy in the fifteenth century is apparent from the frequency with which new settlements were founded and from the number of such coastal towns that built coral mosques with carved *mihrabs* or erected pillar tombs to commemorate members of the ruling families. Kilwa itself was an archetypal port-town of this type. It was situated on a coral island lying close inshore, separated from the mainland only by a narrow channel. It had an important agricultural hinterland and was the centre of a local network of smaller trading towns which supplemented and complemented the international trade of the metropolis. Zanzibar was another important centre, and on their first piratical visit to the island the Portuguese recorded the capture of twenty boats taking food for sale in the Zanzibar market.[15]

For 200 miles south of Kilwa runs an almost unbroken chain of islands. These islands are linked by reefs, sandbanks and rocky islets and between them and the mainland runs a protected waterway, ideal for light coasting craft which could pass over the reefs and sandbanks on a falling tide, but dangerous for ocean-going ships which have to seek out the few deep-water channels. Many of these offshore islands are waterless but the reefs swarm with fish, and the larger islands like Mafia, Amisa and Querimba have always supported a settled population. Along this coast a number of specialised industries had developed. Mafia was famous for its production of gum and for the weaving of coir ropes and mats; Amisa was the centre of the important weaving industry that produced 'Maluane' cloth; Mozambique Island was a boat-building centre. Around these important centres were other coastal towns and villages linked to the larger communities by the fine ties of kinship and smallscale commercial transactions.[16]

South of Mozambique Island the nature of the coast changes. Arab geographers knew this region as *Al-Akwar*, the estuaries, for the land is low-lying and swampy. Numerous rivers deposit silt from the highlands in the marshy estuaries, while stagnant lagoons lie behind the immediate shoreline. The copious fresh water discharge kills the coral but helps the formation of sandbars which are drawn out by the strong currents into spits and low sandy islands that are frequently covered with mangrove thickets. The waters of the Mluli, the Moniga, the Mlela and the Lurio all enter the sea by means of channels which wind through muddy islands and salt marshes. The coast is well-watered and fertile and, although it has always been extremely unhealthy for humans and for cattle, there has been a steady movement of population down from the highlands attracted by the fertility of the land.

In the fifteenth century a number of new urban settlements were established along this coast, the most important being Angoche, near the mouth of the Mluli river. The traditions of the ruling family of Angoche link its foundation to the arrival of dissidents from Kilwa and it is known that in the fifteenth century Kilwa was indeed torn by factional strife. The Angoche sultans also acknowledged kinship with the rulers of Mozambique and may also have founded other settlements, including Quelimane near the mouth of the Zambesi, for in 1517 the Portuguese geographer Barbosa was to write of the Muslims of Quelimane that 'these Moors are of the same language and customs as those of Angoya'. However, the foundation of the towns of Mozambique, Quelimane and Angoche was not just the result of factional quarrels in Kilwa. Of far greater importance was the major reorientation of the gold trade of central Africa at the end of the fifteenth century.[17] During the latter half of the century mining activity had increased in the northern part of the granite plateau and new gold fairs came into existence along the Zambesi escarpment. Sofala did not provide good access to this region which was more easily reached by boats from towns like Angoche travelling up the Zambesi. The new coastal towns that grew up, therefore, reflected this reorientation of trade, though their actual location was influenced by the characteristics of the Zambesi as a waterway.

The Zambesi is one of the world's largest rivers but its navigation is not easy nor is most of its valley suitable for agriculture or urban settlement. The flow of the river is highly seasonal. In the dry season it shrinks to become a relatively narrow, winding stream following an unpredictable course through a landscape of sandbanks, islands and shallows: when the rains come from November onwards and the floods pour down from the central African plateau, the torrent sprawls over a bed which, in its lower reaches, is 2 miles wide, and sometimes inundates the countryside for miles beyond that. No settlement on its banks is safe unless sited a long way back from the floodwaters. The river is highly dangerous to navigate. Not only does the course of the main stream change from one year to the next, this year's floods washing away last year's sandbanks, but the mouth of the river also changes. The delta of the Zambesi has a 50-mile sea frontage and the floods find their way to the sea through a tangled network of waterways. The main river does not always use the same channel, and access to the interior via the delta has been a difficult and unpredictable business. This may explain why, since at least the fifteenth century, the preferred point of entry was the Qua Qua river on which the town of Quelimane was situated. The Qua Qua was not one of the mouths of the Zambesi but until the nineteenth century was directly linked to it, at least in the wet season. Only after the disastrous droughts of the 1820s did the river channel silt up and become overgrown with vegetation. Reaching the main stream of the Zambesi along the comparatively safe and narrow channels of the Qua Qua was definitely to be preferred to facing the turbulent floodwaters forcing their way to the sea through Luabo or Chinde or one of the other main mouths of the river.

Quelimane, therefore, grew in importance as the port with the safest access to the Zambesi. The attractions of Angoche, situated among low-lying mangrove-covered islands to the north, are less easy to determine, but there may have been an overland route from the Zambesi which had Angoche as its terminus.

Traders seeking the gold fairs of the northern plateau had to travel 200 miles from Quelimane up the Zambesi before beginning the overland journey. Urban centres therefore grew up along the river itself, which thus became, functionally, an extension of the sea coast and of its pattern of commercial and social relations. By the end of the fifteenth century two river ports had come into existence — one, later known as Sena, serving the Manica and Barue regions and the other, Tete, beyond the Lupata Gorge, serving the fairs of the Mazoe and Mount Darwin. A Portuguese document of 1511 describes how after Muslim merchants entered the Zambesi,

> . . . . they land a good 6 leagues upstream at the house of an honoured Kaffir king, king of that land, and there they pay his duties and . . . he gives them *almadias* to take the cloth up-river. Further up there is a narrow pass through which the *almadias* go after they have been unloaded by him and then they load again and go another 20 leagues or so, where there is a mountain they call Otonga, and there lies a large village where . . . all the Kaffir and Moorish merchants of the land gather together and where they sell and set up their markets.[18]

Angoche, Quelimane, Sena and Tete were no more foreign colonies of alien merchants than were Kilwa or Sofala. Like their older and more famous counterparts, they depended equally on the agriculture of their immediate hinterland and on the commerce brought by the caravans from the interior and fed into the bloodstream of Indian Ocean trade. The traders who operated out of these towns linked themselves by marriage with the important Muslim lineages which controlled the ocean trade and with the territorial chiefs through whose land the trade caravans had to pass. Moreover, as family, trade and religion were always inseparable, Islam began to spread in the Zambesi valley from the trading centres that had been established. Traders linked themselves by marriage with the peoples of the land and shared in the preoccupations of an agricultural society, acknowledging lineage obligations and consulting spirit mediums. They were also linked with the families who conducted the ocean trade, the ships' captains and the rulers of the east coast towns and through them the network of lineages spread throughout the Muslim world. Through these contacts came many external influences. Islamic brotherhoods established themselves on the coast, and new foodstuffs, technologies and fashions in architecture and tomb construction were brought from the Gulf and adapted to meet the needs and tastes of the local élite. On the east African coast and in the Comoros, easily worked coral rag or volcanic tufa encouraged the development of a distinctive east coast architectural tradition, the finest surviving examples of which, apart from Gedi and Kilwa, are found in the Comoro Islands and northern Madagascar. South of Mozambique Island the lack of such materials meant that building was done in pole and dagga with roofs of thatch — the difference of material not necessarily indicating a lack of wealth or sophistication.

For all the importance of local commerce, it was international trade that created the wealth and brought eastern Africa into the orbit of the world economy. The ships that came from India and the Gulf would, on their return, meet Chinese, Persians, Jews and Italians and through the great entrepots of Malacca or Ormuz their trade extended as far as China and Europe. A few Chinese came to eastern Africa in the fifteenth century but no Europeans are known for certain to have done so, and Marco Polo referred to Madagascar in his writings only from hearsay. At the end of the fifteenth century, however, all was to change when Europeans opened a route which gave them direct access by sea to the east and which placed eastern Africa, particularly Sofala, squarely in their path.

The arrival of the Portuguese

Since the time of the pharaohs the Mediterranean world had participated in the trade of the Indian Ocean. There had been Greek trading towns along the Red Sea and the east African coast from which luxury products had been dispatched to Europe, primarily in exchange for bullion. As a by-product of this trade the peoples of the Indian Ocean received the monotheistic religions of the Middle East. Judaism and Greek and Syrian Christianity spread to Mesopotamia, the Nile valley, Ethiopia, Yemen and western India. When a third monotheistic religion, Islam, was brought by traders from the Middle East, it did not in itself herald any major change. Although in the Levant, Africa and India Judaism and Christianity now became confined to isolated geographical enclaves, the silks, spices and perfumes of the East continued to pass through the Red Sea and the Gulf on their way to the markets of Byzantium and northern and western Europe.

In the Mediterranean the Venetians came to monopolise much of this commerce which they protected with a fleet of armed galleys. The land barrier of the Middle East was less secure. It had been occupied successively by predatory bands of Saracens, Crusaders and Mamelukes whose protection had to be bought by high transit tolls. In the Indian Ocean, however, protection costs were relatively low. None of the great land powers which bordered the ocean maintained navies, little is heard of piracy and the shipping which crossed on the monsoons was lightly built and still more lightly armed. Firearms, though known in Asia since the thirteenth century, were seldom used with any effect on land and never at sea. The maritime communities of the East were therefore quite unprepared to meet the armed onslaught of the Portuguese when it came in the early sixteenth century.

Portuguese expansion was a direct byproduct of Portugal's poverty, not its wealth. Medieval Portugal produced wine and olives but was frequently unable to grow enough corn to feed its population of about one million. There was comparatively little good agricultural land, particularly in the north, and the livelihood of the population and Portugal's contribution to international trade lay largely in the catching of fish and the production of salt. With the land yielding poor returns, the nobility had always been inclined to seek its fortunes through armed exploits, first in the wars against the Moors and then in the Hundred Years War when the succession struggle in Castile provided *fidalgos* and unendowed younger sons with opportunities to enrich themselves. When the wars with Castile finally ceased in 1411 the royal princes Henrique (the 'Navigator') and Pedro encouraged the knights and squires of their households to attack the rich coastal towns of Morocco and to plunder Moorish shipping for ransoms, slaves and booty. North Africa was expensive and dangerous to attack, although the enterprises against Moroccan port-cities continued to be popular until well into the sixteenth century, and increasingly individual boats were sent to cruise down the north-west coast of Africa, raiding the indigenous Guanche people of the Canary Islands, hunting seals or bargaining with desert nomads and the black kings of Senegambia for gold and slaves. The traditional 'chivalrous' activities of the Portuguese nobility thus merged inextricably with ever more profitable mercantile activity.

Settlements were also founded on the Atlantic islands which were granted to court noblemen and their followers as feudal captaincies. These settlements attracted the Genoese who invested capital in sugar production and helped to give Portuguese expansion its financial dynamism. At first profitable agriculture developed only in Madeira, while the settlers in the Azores, Cape Verdes and Guinea Islands turned to further exploration in the Atlantic or slaving on the African coast. To run the sugar plantations established in Madeira, slaves had to be brought from West Africa, giving an added impetus to the growth of commerce in that region.

If the interests and expectations of the Portuguese nobility were rooted firmly in their traditional view of themselves as a military aristocracy, the Portuguese Crown had other ends in view. Royal trade monopolies had been created early in the fifteenth century as a way of supporting the high risk of investment in maritime expansion. The Infante Dom Henrique, for example, had been granted a monopoly of the Guinea trade during his life as well as seigneurial rights in the Atlantic islands. After Henrique's death in 1460, monopolistic privileges had been granted in the early 1470s to the Lisbon merchant Fernão Gomes to finance the trade with Guinea, and after that the

Crown was always ready to create a monopoly if this would help it to finance or manage any part of its empire. However, what brought the Crown directly into action as a monopolist in its own right was the threat that Castilians would elbow their way in on the profits of Portugal's West African trade. When a succession war broke out with Castile in 1474 the Crown had to take vigorous action to protect Portugal's prior claim to the Guinea region. From this grew the Infante Dom João's interest in maritime expansion, so that when he became king in 1481 he organised a royal monopoly of the gold trade at Mina, initiated the slave trade with the Congo, and arranged for private monopolists to begin the settlement of the Guinea Islands and trade with the Niger. Encouraged by the success of these ventures he had, by the middle of the 1480s, embarked on his ambitious project for wresting the monopoly of the eastern spice trade from the Venetians.

The planning of this enterprise had begun soon after João's accession to the throne. Agents were sent overland to the East to locate potential allies and report on the markets, and one of these, Pero da Covilham, probably visited Sofala disguised as a Muslim merchant in 1490. Attempts to find a sea route round Africa, which cartographers had foreshadowed as early as the 1450s, proved at first to be unsuccessful. Diogo Cão's two voyages (1482–5) revealed only thousands of miles of barren African coast stretching to the south, while Bartolomeu Dias, although he discovered the passage round the Cape of Good Hope in 1489, was forced by a mutiny of his men to turn back to Portugal. The project was further delayed by the diplomatic contest with Castile over spheres of influence following the discoveries of Columbus in the Caribbean in 1492, the struggle which led to the publication of Pope Alexander VI's Bulls in 1493 and the famous Treaty of Tordesillas in 1494 which partitioned the world between Spain and Portugal. The death of King João in 1495 caused yet further delays, and not until 1497 did Vasco da Gama's four ships set out from Lisbon.

Da Gama's fleet rounded the Cape of Good Hope without mishap and, sighting the coast of Natal on Christmas Day, touched the coast of southern Mozambique and then put into the Qua Qua river, before reaching Mozambique Island in February 1498. From Mozambique Da Gama sailed to Mombasa and Melinde where he obtained the services of a pilot who was later reputed to have been none other than Ahmed Ibn Majid, the greatest Arab navigator of his day and the author of numerous treatises on the Indian Ocean. With his aid the first voyage of the Portuguese to India was safely accomplished.

Vasco da Gama returned to Portugal in 1499 and the following year Pedro Alvares Cabral set out on the second Portuguese voyage to the East. He returned with further detailed geographical knowledge, and a strategy was devised to secure for the Portuguese Crown a monopoly of the trade in Indian pepper. Royal ships, built and freighted by the king, would undertake annual voyages to India where they would make bulk purchases of pepper from the rajas of Malabar with whom they established formal alliances. In Europe the cargoes of pepper would be unloaded on to the market in such a way as to undermine the trade of the Venetians. There has always been some argument about whether this relatively peaceful strategy would have succeeded had it not been for the high-handed and violent behaviour of the Portuguese commanders. In fact the rapid change that took place in Portugal's strategy, from seeking to trade peacefully to attempting to establish military and political domination, had less to do with the personal qualities of the Portuguese commanders than with the realities of Portugal's position as a trading nation.

Soon after the return of the second fleet from India the Portuguese Crown began to experience severe problems in finding the finance to equip the fleets and make payments for the pepper. The Venetians had been able to pay for their large purchases of pepper through the diversification of their commercial activities and the balancing of accounts with middlemen involved in a variety of commercial transactions. However, even Venice had had to meet part of the payment with remittances of silver and gold, and the drain of bullion from Europe to the East had been a major factor in the periodic bullion shortages from which Europe had suffered in the Middle Ages — the resultant loss of liquidity causing difficulties in financing its economy. Portugal had nothing approaching the Venetian network of commercial transactions and simply did not possess the scale or diversity of foreign trade necessary to finance the pepper payments. Since prices for pepper were at exceptionally high levels at the turn of the century due to war between Venice and Turkey, the early Portuguese voyages had been financed by German banking houses, but by the end of the first decade of the sixteenth century, when pepper prices began to fall, Portugal's enterprise threatened to founder, not through the technical difficulties of the voyage to India nor through armed opposition in the East but through failure to raise adequate finance. Forced to try to find goods to export to the East, and to obtain silver in Europe to meet the deficit on payments, the Portuguese were compelled to market their pepper in Antwerp and to try to make the necessary purchases on the Antwerp metal exchange. It is in the light of this urgent and growing problem that the Portuguese Crown decided to establish its political power in the East, a strategy in which Sofala and Kilwa were to play a major role.

If Portugal was finding difficulty in paying for pepper purchases with goods or bullion sent from Europe, and if the cost of equipping and freighting the fleets was beyond the financial resources of what was one of the poorest states in Europe, there remained the option of making the empire in the East pay for itself. Portugal would seek to take part in the lucrative trade which was carried on between eastern countries and thus establish the multilateral trade that would spread the burden of the pepper payments. Not only would trade in these items itself be profitable but it would also give the Portuguese access to sources of bullion, notably Persian silver and the gold of eastern Africa. So increasingly the Portuguese began to trade in Cambay and Coromandel cloths, Persian horses, African ivory, elephants from Ceylon and other commodities not intended for export to Europe.

The decision to enter these markets was quickly followed by an attempt to turn many of the most lucrative of these Asiatic trades into Crown monopolies using Portugal's naval strength to control the sea-lanes of the East. Of course, political power could also be made to yield direct financial profit. The Portuguese Crown devised the original political doctrine that it was lord of the sea in the same way that the kings and sultans of the East were lords of the land; just as these exacted tolls and customs from merchants using their ports and benefiting from their protection, so the Portuguese Crown claimed to do the same on the sea and began to levy customs dues on all cargoes and to grant letters of protection to all merchants taking their goods by sea. In this way the profits of empire supported the overheads of the military and naval establishment and helped to resolve the problem of making payments for the pepper. A third way of gaining entry into eastern trade, and one frequently used in the early days of the empire, was plunder and tribute. Ships sailing without Portuguese protection would be plundered, and coastal states would be forced to pay tribute in foodstuffs, gold or some other commodity. However, once the system of customs dues and passes (*cartazes*) was established, direct levying of plunder and tribute receded in importance although it never wholly ceased.

When this strategy for acquiring political power in the Indian Ocean was first elaborated in the instructions given in 1505 to the viceroy, Francisco de Almeida, eastern Africa was given a central role. The Portuguese believed the volume of the gold trade from Sofala and Kilwa to be much greater than in fact it was, and the expectation that it would cover the payments on their pepper cargoes helped to determine their early actions on the coast. However, eastern Africa was important to them in another way. In the days before the arrival of the Portuguese, Kilwa had prospered as a port of call and trans-shipment for merchants unable to complete voyages to the south in a single season, and Portugal found the African ports useful for the same reason. Ships sailing between India and Europe needed a way-station where repairs could be made, sick men landed and fresh crews taken on board, and where water and provisions could be obtained. Sometimes ships had to wait months on the coast for a favourable monsoon. A port in east Africa would have to be developed as a naval base to meet these practical needs.

The Portuguese come to Sofala

On his first voyage Vasco da Gama had not stopped at either Sofala or Kilwa, but he must have heard news of both, for Cabral, making the second voyage to India in 1500, called at Kilwa and on his return dispatched a Castilian adventurer, Sancho de Toar, on an embassy to the sheikh of Sofala.[19] Presents were exchanged, and Toar discovered, from a hostage he seized, something of Sofala's importance in international trade.

On his second voyage, which began in 1502, Vasco da Gama himself called at Sofala, and when the instructions for Francisco de Almeida were drawn up in Lisbon in 1504 both Kilwa and Sofala were scheduled to play a large part in the strategy that was devised.[20] Both cities were to be occupied and fortified, and factories established to buy gold. The rival Muslim traders with whom the Portuguese suspected they would be unable to compete were to be suppressed. In March 1505 Almeida left Lisbon with a large armada to establish Portuguese power at Kilwa, at the mouth of the Red Sea and on the west coast of India. Shortly afterwards a second expedition left under Pero de Anhaia with instructions to found a fortress at Sofala. Almeida reached Kilwa in July and occupied the city after only a token show of force. A sultan friendly to the Portuguese was installed and a stone tower constructed near the waterfront which was to be the nucleus for the Portuguese factory. The factory was initially stocked with loot taken during the plundering of the city, showing clearly that one of the reasons for establishing political power was to acquire the trade goods necessary to take part in eastern trade. Pero de Anhaia did not reach his destination until September but was able to obtain permission from Yussuf, the sheikh of Sofala, to construct a factory. He proceeded to erect a stockade on a sand spit near to the entrance to the bay on which Sofala stood.

It was not the original intention of the Portuguese to occupy any other part of the coast but, like Muslim shipowners before them, they soon realised the need for a port between Kilwa and Sofala where ships could be repaired and where they could stock up with water and provisions. Moreover, the captains of the large ships which sailed between Portugal and India showed an increasing reluctance to risk grounding their vessels in the sandy shallows near Sofala. In 1502

Vicente Soares had assembled a boat at Mozambique Island and in 1506 Tristan da Cunha and Afonso de Albuquerque had to winter on the coast of east Africa and chose Mozambique Island as their base.[21] In 1507 the decision was taken to found a permanent settlement there. Vasco Gomes was sent to set up a factory and shortly afterwards a hospital, church and fortified battery were built. Mozambique had begun to replace Sofala as both port of call and administrative centre.[22]

The Portuguese planned that a squadron should patrol the coast between Kilwa and Sofala and detain any Muslim ships operating without a licence. At Kilwa and Sofala the factors were to act as crown agents, buying all the gold sent from the interior and selling cloth and other trade goods to the merchants. It is sometimes suggested that the Portuguese were ignorant of the complex network of kin-based commercial contacts that operated the trade of eastern Africa, but initially they tried to fit into the system as they understood it. Their idea was not to drive Muslim traders out of business but to make them and their African associates work as middlemen for the Portuguese who intended that they alone should control the international side of the trade.[23] Even here they did not intend to be too exclusive, and allied themselves with the sultan of Melinde, allowing his ships to continue to trade under permanent Portuguese safe-conduct.

This plan did not work well. The first difficulty was that the Portuguese did not have the right goods to supply the market. European cloth was not in demand and Indian cloth could only be obtained through agents already established in the trade. Some Indian cloth looted from Kilwa or captured on Muslim ships had been taken to Sofala, but the factory could not operate indefinitely on stolen goods, and urgent attempts were made to secure a regular supply of Indian cloth through the good offices of the sultan of Melinde.

A still greater difficulty faced the Portuguese in controlling Kilwa and Sofala. It was inevitable that Portuguese overlordship would conflict fundamentally with the traditional position of the rulers of the two towns who had had the right, to issue trading licences, authorise sales, determine prices, collect tribute and generally control the complex commercial network that operated both within Africa and in the wider world of the Indian Ocean. In Kilwa the Portuguese had hoped to overcome this problem by installing a ruler favourable to their interests, but in 1506 severe disturbances broke out between supporters of the Portuguese nominee and his displaced rival. In spite of attempts to pacify the city, there was a wholesale exodus of the leading merchant families, for whom dynastic quarrels were probably less important than the loss of their trade. By 1513 traders had ceased to call at Kilwa and it was with relief that the Portuguese decided to abandon their factory and allow the old line of sultans to return.

Events in Sofala were no more peaceful, but had a somewhat different outcome. No sooner was Pero de Anhaia established in Sofala than he began to develop his own network of trading contacts, sending presents to chiefs inland, receiving messengers and loaning trade goods. This directly threatened the continued existence of Yussuf's status and authority, and in August he left the town of Sofala and withdrew inland. The following month Yussuf's African allies attacked the Portuguese stockade and in a counterattack the Portuguese captured and killed the sheikh, installing on the throne a new ruler, called Suleiman, acceptable to the Portuguese and to at least some of the Sofala merchants.

In spite of these violent confrontations, it is by no means clear that it was the arrival of the Portuguese and their high-handed seizure of Sofala and Kilwa that led to the decline of these two ancient trading towns. The Portuguese factors soon acquired the goods that the market needed, and built up their own network of contacts to supply the fortress and encourage the traders to bring gold from the inland fairs.[24] In 1506 some 4,000 *miticals* of gold were sent to India — equivalent to 17 kilos — while it is likely that twice or three times that amount was actually traded. In 1508–9, 8,000 *miticals* (34 kilos) were sent to India in an eighteen-month period, and 7,000 *miticals* (31.75 kilos) were traded in eight months in 1512–13. These are by no means insignificant amounts and it is clear that a number of the merchants were willing to trade on Portuguese terms. However, the arrival of the Portuguese had coincided with severe political disturbances among the chieftaincies of the Shona-speaking peoples which had disrupted the mining of gold and the operation of the traditional fairs. This, coupled with the flight of many important merchant families from Kilwa and Sofala, led to a major reorientation of trading activity, the main beneficiaries being the Comoro Islands, Angoche and the trading towns of the Zambesi.

Portuguese occupation of the coast widens

By 1513, when the Portuguese abandoned their Kilwa factory, their activity in the Indian Ocean was increasingly marked by the forcible imposition of monopoly and political control. Such a development was more congenial to the *fidalgos* who served in the East than was peaceful trade. The captains of the Portuguese maritime expeditions were almost all drawn from the minor Portuguese gentry, the men who had traditionally sought their fortunes in the service of the king or one of the royal princes. While at home in Portugal, these men would eat at their patron's table and expected to receive a stipend as a retainer, in return for which they would enlist in any expedition that he organised. As a professional class of fighters, they expected warfare to yield fame and fortune and their services to receive recognition and reward. Increasingly these expectations had to be met in the East rather than in Portugal itself.

Armed with crossbows, swords and lances, and clad in half-armour which they wore even in the hottest parts of the Red Sea, the Portuguese *fidalgos* and their men would have been formidable enemies, though their numbers would have been far too few for them to have dominated the Indian Ocean if they had had to fight solely on land. However, during the piratical expeditions they had undertaken in the fifteenth century, the Portuguese had developed a naval technology which constituted one of the most important 'technical revolutions' of early modern times. Ships had been built which were able to survive the battering of Atlantic gales and endure months without putting into port, while the charts the Portuguese drew and the navigational knowledge they acquired were of an accuracy unequalled until the seventeenth century. Most important of all, however, the Portuguese developed the modern concept of an armed warship. Fifteenth-century cannon were too heavy and immobile to be of much value in land warfare, but mounted on a warship the heaviest guns could be manoeuvred and used to maximum effect — with the result that every town of the Indian Ocean seaboard became exposed to bombardment and destruction from the sea.

Under their first two permanent governors in the East, Francisco de Almeida (1505–9) and Afonso de Albuquerque (1509–15), the Portuguese systematically crushed armed opposition to themselves and built bases at the mouth of the Gulf and on the Straits of Malacca, while their warships regularly patrolled the west coast of India and the approaches to the Red Sea. It was only logical that they should seek to supplement the work of the factories by destroying the rival centres of international commerce that still seemed to prosper in eastern Africa. In 1506 Tristan da Cunha, finding himself delayed at Mozambique by the adverse monsoon, led a raid across the Mozambique Channel, sacking Sada and Langane on the north-western coast of Madagascar and only turning back when headwinds prevented his ships rounding the north cape of the island. In 1507 Da Cunha's second-in-command, Albuquerque, attacked Oja and Brava on the northern Swahili coast before continuing to the capture of Socotra and the systematic sack of the port-cities of the Hadramaut. In 1509 it was the turn of Mafia, Zanzibar and Pemba to be plundered and laid under tribute — or, more accurately, 'protection' — by a fleet under Duarte de Lemos.[25]

If these actions helped to stock the royal factories with looted goods and kept the soldiers happy with their plunder, they apparently did little to help the Portuguese establish a monopoly in the international trade of the region. By 1511, they had come to realise that Angoche was the centre of the clandestine trade that was still flourishing under their noses. An armed expedition burnt the town and captured the leading *sharif*. The same year there was fresh trouble at Sofala, and Suleiman was killed and replaced by yet another sheikh.

Even with the destruction of Angoche and of a great deal of Muslim shipping, the lineage networks which had controlled the Indian Ocean trade from the historic centres of Kilwa and Sofala continued to operate. The ports and fairs of the Zambesi were still free from Portuguese interference as were the Comoro Islands. The towns south of Sofala, like Chiluane, had not been attacked, and regions like the Querimba Islands with their important cloth industry continued to flourish. It might seem illogical that the Portuguese should leave so much of the Muslim trading network intact but the reason is not hard to find. It had never been the purpose of the Portuguese to destroy all Muslim commercial activity; they merely sought to break the hold of the *sharifian* families on the international trade in gold. By the second decade of the century the Portuguese were busy weaving themselves into the existing fabric of the coast's commercial life, and their occasional violent forays against individual towns were less the result of a consistent policy of destruction than a reaction to the circumstances special to each case. Moreover the Sofala factory and the naval base at Mozambique Island were dependent on the local communities for food, and it was this increasing involvement of the Portuguese in the local economy of the region that helped to prevent further violence.

Nevertheless the Portuguese were concerned that the gold trade which was conducted in the Zambesi towns still escaped their control. An attempt to establish a trading factory in the Zambesi delta was made as early as 1513 but proved a failure, and the idea of blockading the mouths of the river was clearly impractical.[26] So a number of reconnaissance expeditions into the interior were undertaken by a convict called António Fernandes, as a result of which a decision was eventually taken in 1519 to try a second time to set up a factory somewhere in the delta. A wooden tower was actually constructed which was to be taken in sections for erection at the chosen site, but the ship carrying it was wrecked and the project had to be abandoned.[27]

In the 1520s there was a brief return to the policy of terror. In 1522 a powerfully armed expedition was sent to Cabo Delgado, prompted by rumours that merchants from Kilwa and Zanzibar had settled in the Querimba Islands. A *casus belli* was found in the refusal of the islanders to sell coir for ropemaking to the Portuguese. In the attack on the islands, the town of Querimba was burnt along with the vessels in the port, and loot worth 60,000 *cruzados* was taken. In 1524 a similar attack was carried out on Mombasa, but with the sack of that city the era of Portuguese violence was closed — for the next forty years at least. The reason is simply that the southern Swahili region was about to enjoy a period of greatly increased prosperity based on the growth of the ivory trade — a prosperity in which the Portuguese were to share to the full. Gold always aroused ugly passions in Spanish and Portuguese *conquistadores*; the successful exploitation of ivory, perhaps by the very nature of the commodity itself, seems to have required co-operation and collaboration rather than violence and extortion.

The rise of the ivory trade

In 1530 a *regimento*, or set of instructions, for the conduct of the fort of Sofala was issued. Influenced by the success of the royal trading factory at Mina in West Africa, this document still envisaged a tightly-controlled royal monopoly of the gold trade. This was an administrator's fantasy of the ideal Portuguese community. It made provision for a permanent force of eighty men — a veritable standing army by the standards of the sixteenth century. These men were to live under military discipline, reporting to their accommodation in the fort by night, receiving their pay from the royal treasury, and severely circumscribed in their contacts with the local population. At best this was a bureaucratic vision of a settlement of military servants of the Crown, not the blueprint for a colony, for there was no provision for wives or families. By 1530 this whole concept was anachronistic and the *regimento* was legislating for a situation that had long ceased to exist.

Between 1506, when the Portuguese had imposed their imperial structure on Kilwa and Sofala, and the events recorded by João Velho in 1547, the Portuguese community had considerably modified its relations with the African peoples in a way that their predecessors as rulers of the coast, the sheikhs and *sharifs*, would fully have understood. Although Portuguese *fidalgos* with a certain pride of family and a position to return to in Portugal could maintain their cultural exclusiveness, the average soldier or seaman had no such desire. Recruited in the fishing villages of the Algarve or in the remote mountain farms of northern Portugal, the men who sailed in the India fleets came from a society not very dissimilar in its organisation and cultural level from the one they found in Africa. In Guinea there had already emerged a class of *lançados* who had preferred to leave the narrow confines the Portuguese community and settle as traders among the coastal African population, marrying into the local lineages and participating in the networks of trust and credit which these represented. The emergence of this class of Afro-Portuguese led to the development of two rival Portuguese empires — a formal and an informal one — wherever the Crown tried to set up an exclusive monopolistic trade structure.

The attempt to operate a trade monopoly from the royal factory at Sofala, as envisaged in the 1530 *regimento*, encouraged the development of informal contacts. The royal monopoly of the gold trade had been cumbersome and inflexible from the first. The prices of goods supplied by the factory were too high, the goods themselves were often of the wrong kind, and the bureaucracy and the general overheads of the fort and factory consumed all the profits. The rewards for royal service appeared meagre and the boredom of garrison life was scarcely remedied by such things as archery contests and religious services, which appear to have loomed large in the communal life of the fort. Already by 1513 there were reports of Portuguese deserters in the interior marrying the daughters of chiefs and helping them in a military capacity. An Afro-Portuguese society was beginning to emerge. The dispersal of Portuguese as private traders gathered momentum as the century progressed. By the 1560s all the islands from Bazaruto in the south to Mombasa in the north had resident Portuguese, trading in local commodities, contracting local marriages and forming their own kinship ties with the peoples of the coast. These traders performed a vital function, bridging the gap of incomprehension between Portuguese officialdom (the captains of Mozambique and the commanders of the Indiamen) and the families who had traditionally operated the trade of the coast.

However, private trade also had its attractions for those ranking higher in the system — the captains and officials of the forts and the commanders of the royal ships. It appears that they were permitted a certain amount of private trade from the very beginning, and they used their access to credit and shipping within the structure of the Portuguese empire to complement the prestige of their official positions, which enabled them to deal directly with sheikhs and chiefs and other local men of importance. It was the initiatives of the captains that expanded Portuguese commercial activity beyond the narrow horizons of the factory at Sofala, sending António Fernandes on his two journeys into the interior between 1511 and 1513, exploring the mouths of the Zambesi and developing the contacts with the chiefs up and down the coast; and it appears to have been the captains who developed the ivory trade and initiated a whole new era of prosperity for the maritime communities of the region.

Although the ivory obtained both from elephants and hippopotamuses was one of Africa's most ancient exports, the pattern of international trade before the Portuguese arrived was wholly determined by the needs of the trade in gold. Ivory appears to have been of much less importance, featuring only as a minor item of commerce from ports on the Mozambique coast. The nature of the gold trade concentrated commercial activity at a small number of places. Gold was obtained in very small quantities and had first to be brought from many different points of production for sale at the inland fairs. From these it was brought, still in small quantities, to one or two coastal ports frequented by the international merchants. The high concentration of international trade at one or two ports suggests that it was gold rather than ivory which was the dominant concern of the traders. There is a second and much more simple reason for believing that ivory was not a major item of commerce in 1500. The Portuguese, when they first explored the coast, appear to have been quite unaware of its importance. However, in 1506 the captain of Kilwa wrote excitedly about the quantity of ivory available on the coast between Sofala and Kilwa, the lack of interest of Muslims in the trade and the immense profits to be had in India:

> . . . . that a great quantity of ivory is to be had between Sofala and Kilwa which is valued at 15 *miticals* of gold the *quintal* and that in time it will be worth 80 and 100 *miticals* the *quintal* in Cambay and that Your Highness may have as much as you want since no king or white Moors are to be found there.[28]

Thereafter ivory is mentioned increasingly frequently in reports from the factories. Pero Pessoa left 76 *quintals* behind in the factory of Sofala when he left office in 1509; during the years 1513–14 the factor shipped 81 *quintals* (the equivalent of 4,762.8 kilos) and in 1519 8,820 kilos were registered. The amounts continued to rise until 26,000 kilos were exported from Sofala in 1545.[29]

A similar development took place at Kilwa. When the Portuguese abandoned the town in 1513 its gold trade was finished. Soon, however, they were back and a factor was installed in the town to buy the ivory that reached the island on the overland caravans. As the ivory boom developed, factors were placed in Mafia, Zanzibar and, temporarily, in Angoche. Ivory was shipped from the Querimba Islands and from the Zambesi, and the Portuguese established a factory at Quelimane around 1530. Large consignments also reached the river mouths in the neighbourhood of Sofala. Annual trading vessels were sent to the mouth of the Sabi, and in 1542 a captain, called Lourenço Marques, made the first successful trading voyage to Delagoa Bay, probably further south than any Muslim trading vessel had ever ventured.[30]

Clearly the ivory trade would never have grown in this way had the Portuguese clung to their narrow monopolistic policy of compelling merchants to buy and sell at one or two designated Portuguese factories. The Crown did, indeed, try to maintain the ivory trade as its own but was forced to allow trade at numerous points along the coast where the ivory could be brought for sale. Once trade was dispersed in this way, however, any hope of maintaining it as a monopoly in the hands of the royal factor disappeared and it became the mainstay of the rapidly growing private trade of the captains of Mozambique, the office held by Dom Jorge Teles de Meneses from 1544-7.

The captains of Mozambique and Sofala

The captaincy of Mozambique and Sofala was one of the major appointments in the gift of the Portuguese Crown. Initially the responsibility for east African affairs had been divided between the captains of Sofala and Kilwa, but the captaincy of Kilwa was abolished in 1513 and thereafter the northern part of the coast came under the orders of the captain of the coast of Melinde whose base was at Melinde in the north. The captain of Sofala had control over the whole of the south and over the ships that were supposed to uphold the royal trading policies in the region. Although he received a generous salary, allowances for himself and his household, and a share in any booty taken on military expeditions, the captain came increasingly to turn his attentions to private trade. During the three years in which he held office he had almost supreme authority over his command. Little could be done to restrain him until his period as captain ended when restraint had become irrelevant.

In the maritime world of the Indian Ocean political and commercial power had always been closely associated with each other. Rulers of the coastal cities had granted licences to traders and had themselves always been the principal merchants and dealers. As the Portuguese captains usurped political power, so they were expected to perform a similar role. The captain of Sofala was expected to deal with ship-owners, territorial chiefs and the Muslim trading families in the same way that the former sheikhs had done. Yet, seen from the angle of the strict operation of the royal monopoly, the captain was only supposed to be a paid agent of the Crown's mercantile bureaucracy. Thus a tension grew up between the idea and the reality — the passage of time and the vast distances between Europe and the East gradually stretching the two further and further out of alignment. As early as 1510 an estimate suggested that three-quarters of Portuguese trade was in private hands. Thereafter more and more of the trade that reached the coast passed through the hands of the captain while the official trade of the factory dwindled until it barely covered the expenses of the fort itself, the garrison and the ships.[31]

The growth of the captain's trade was facilitated by the fact that the gold trade for which the factory had been established was anyway in decline, while the ivory trade was now expanding and involved trading relationships not provided for in the royal *regimento*. With their command over shipping and over the personnel in royal service, the captains were in a position to establish their own private trading network and two competing trading systems began to emerge. Increasingly the captains could reward their personal following of retainers, household servants and clerks more amply than these could be rewarded by serving the fort or the factory. The local traders and their contacts among the African peoples watched the growth of this rivalry within the Portuguese community and prepared to exploit it. It was a dangerous rivalry, for not only was the value of the trade considerable but the personal risks involved were high. The captain and his followers were in breach of the law and knew that retribution might eventually catch up with them: but while the captain held office, it was the royal factor and any royal servants loyal to him whose position was precarious. Among their rival backers in the Muslim trading community the situation was even more deadly. It is these rivalries, exacerbated by deep personal animosities, which erupted in the events of the captaincy of Dom Jorge.

The Portuguese impact on coastal East Africa

The violent events in Kilwa and Sofala, and the evident destruction of much of the old trading system, when taken together with the sharp decline in the gold trade, might lead to the conclusion that the arrival of the Portuguese was largely destructive of the commercial life of the coast. This is far from being so. The growth of the ivory trade encouraged the foundation of new settlements along the Mozambique coast. Trading towns grew up at Moma, Sangage and Bajone as well as at Angoche. With Mozambique Island occupied by the Portuguese and developed as a naval base, the ruling family of the island moved to Sancul on the mainland while other settlements grew up at Cabaceira and Quitangonha nearby. Many of these were involved in the ivory trade, but the servicing of the Portuguese fleets and settlements was to prove still more important to their prosperity.

In the first half of the century the Portuguese garrisons on the coast were quite large and their numbers were often considerably swollen by the arrival of India fleets which sometimes had to 'winter' on the coast.[32] In 1506 there were eighty-five people on the Kilwa pay-roll, while the Sofala garrison fluctuated in the first two decades between forty-one and seventy-four. Although Kilwa and Sofala were to decline, the growth of Mozambique Island helped to maintain the overall numbers of Portuguese on the coast. The arrival of an India-bound fleet or a military expedition could swell the numbers by as much as ten times. For example, in 1548 Francisco Barreto maintained 1,000 men from his fleet in Mozambique, while in 1569 the same commander came to east Africa with an expedition that was maintained at a strength of around 800 men for the next six years. In addition to these, every passing ship left its complement of sick at the royal hospital on Mozambique Island and there were always survivors of shipwrecks straggling into the coastal settlements, passengers awaiting a ship to India and missionaries *en route* to save souls anywhere from China to Ethiopia.

The base at Mozambique injected considerable amounts of capital as well as buoyant demand into the coastal economy which therefore had the opportunity of expanding to meet the demand. The gold and ivory trades employed African labour extensively in extraction and hunting, and encouraged the concentration of effort on the production of commodities for the international market. However, the growth of the elaborate infrastructure of the Portuguese maritime empire had the effect of encouraging a diversity of economic activity, as well as increasing demand and opportunity. Slaves were bought from dealers on the coast and employed as interpreters or as orderlies in the hospital and store-rooms. More often, however, workmen were hired — sawyers to make planks, charcoal-burners, makers of cooking oil, carriers, stonemasons, boatmen, divers and limekiln workers.[33] The arrival of a fleet would always result in high demand for replacement seamen, and the building of forts would increase demand for stone and lime. The African coast has few areas where good stone can be obtained, and for the building of Fort Jesus at Mombasa at the end of the century stone had to be brought from the Comoro Islands. Visiting fleets also needed repairs of all kinds and coir rope and resin were much in demand, becoming the focus of a considerable local industry.

Local artisans were also able to sell a variety of products to the Portuguese, including hats, baskets, matting and objects made of turtleshell and gold.[34] The Portuguese also made extensive purchases of the various local cloths, patronising the weavers of Sofala, the lower Zambesi, Maluane (Querimba) and Madagascar all of whom had their distinctive products.[35] However, it was in the demand for foodstuffs that the Portuguese made their greatest impact on the local economy. The food consumption of the garrisons and visiting fleets involved some extremely large purchases. For example, the Sofala factory bought 287,000 litres of sorghum during 1513–14 and the factor also bought rice, kaffir corn, meat, salt, oil, chickpeas and sugar.[36]

To find this quantity of food was a continual problem. During 1511, for example, rations had to be reduced, and the factor recorded that 'the supplies are now few and there are none to be had in the land'. Although some coastal rulers may have been reluctant at times to sell to the Portuguese, the principal reason for these deficiencies was the inability or unwillingness of the coastal populations to produce significant agricultural surpluses. As a result, the organisation of food supply became a major feature of Portuguese diplomacy. In 1506, for example, the factor of Kilwa, Pero de Fogaça, wrote that four sheikhs had come to make peace with the Portuguese

> . . . . each engaging himself and residents of their islands to pay yearly to Your Highness in acknowledgment certain oxen and sheep and bales of millet and chickens and coconuts and also to sell to all the Portugals both in this fortress and on the *naos* all the supplies available in the said islands for the price that they sell them to one another.[37]

Thereafter the Portuguese were anxious to retain the friendship and goodwill of any community able and willing to supply food, and their trading vessels visited every part of the Mozambique Channel building up a fine network of local contacts to supply food for the Portuguese market. The Africans cultivated rice, wrote Santos, 'to sell to the Portuguese, especially upon the coast of Melinde and Cabo Delgado, where there is an infinite quantity of rice, which is the chief commodity dealt with by many merchants'.[38] Round Sofala the inhabitants of the land 'grew rice which occupies them for the greatest part of the year'. In the Zambesi delta lived many Muslims 'who carry on most of the cultivation and commerce, taking to Sena provisions, coconuts, vinegar and coconut fibres'. North of Quelimane were a number of Islamic and Makua settlements whose 'commerce with the Portuguese is principally in ivory, rice, millet, panicle, yams and many other kinds of vegetables'. Off Quitangonha in 1591 the English captain, James Lancaster, captured some boats 'laden with millio, hennes, ducks, with one Portugall boy going for the provision of Mozambique'.[39] Cattle, fruit and rice were also imported from Madagascar and the Comoro Islands and the latter in particular became the main supplier of food for Mozambique Island. This dependence probably explains why the Portuguese made no attempts to conquer the islands or interfere with their trade.

The supply of food and of locally produced manufactures thus became a most useful supplement to the wealth to be derived from ivory. Because of this prosperity new settlements grew up and the coastal population expanded through immigration from inland. However, this economic growth was not on a scale to constitute an economic revolution. Production still took place using traditional technologies that had existed before the Portuguese arrival. Apart from firearms and European styles of shipping, the Portuguese do not appear to have disseminated European technology, and their small settlements soon adopted local modes of production. They even made use of local shipping and employed local pilots and navigators. Although maize is recorded in the sixteenth century and may have been directly imported from America, the Portuguese do not appear to have introduced other American food crops as they did in West Africa. The demand introduced into the local economies of eastern Africa presented conditions for technological change and for the reorganisation of the social relations of production. The opportunity certainly existed for African weavers or boat-builders or food producers to expand their activities to meet the new demand but, for reasons which must lie somewhere within the structures of African society and thought, the opportunities were missed, and with the decline of the Portuguese empire in the seventeenth century and the rise of a very different pattern of commercial activity introduced by the Dutch and the English, such opportunities were not to occur again until the nineteenth century.

2

THE INTERIOR SOUTH OF THE
ZAMBESI IN THE SIXTEENTH
CENTURY

Geographical setting

Modern Mozambique was created by a series of international treaties signed between Great Britain and Portugal in 1891. Inevitably these treaties were, first and foremost, a reflection of the tensions and political realities of the time, but the frontiers which they delineated were not simply arbitrary lines drawn on a map. Geography and the historical evolution of the peoples of the region played a considerable part in deciding the shape of the modern state. South of the Zambesi, the frontier-line separates the high veldt and the low veldt regions, the line itself sometimes running along the crest and sometimes through the middle of the broken escarpment where the high granite tablelands break down towards the sea. The escarpment and the low veldt are a region of broken hills thickly covered with low trees and bushes presided over by towering baobabs. It is hot and, when not controlled, the bush easily becomes infested with tsetse fly. Stream-water coming off the high veldt is collected by large rivers and carried across the low veldt to the coastal flats. There the rivers deposit their alluvium which mingles with the sea sand to create a world of coastal marshes, sand spits and mangrove forests. Land along these rivers can be very fertile but, especially where regular flooding occurs, the country is infested with mosquitoes which carry malaria and other tropical diseases. The valley of the Zambesi, by far the largest of these rivers, is in many ways like an extension of the coastal zone, a finger of low veldt extending 300 miles into the interior. The river flows through a volcanic fault and is bordered by a narrow alluvial plain and a rather thicker insulating layer of broken escarpment. The climate of the valley, however, is hotter and drier than that of the coast. The heavy perennial rain that falls at Quelimane on the coast becomes an unreliable seasonal rain at Tete, making the valley a region that suffers from extremes of drought and flood.

Beyond the escarpment lies the high veldt, most of which, after the partition treaties, became Southern Rhodesia. This beautiful country has with justice been compared to an island bounded to the west by the desert, and to the east by the low veldt and the sea, and with its

31

northern and southern boundaries marked by the valleys of the Zambesi and the Limpopo. In the north and east this great granite plateau rises to form the mountain ranges of Manica and Vumba with peaks as high as 9,000 feet. There winter frosts and cold, clear air condense the moist winds from the Indian Ocean into heavy seasonal rain. The plateau then slopes gently towards the west until it becomes overlaid by the Kalahari sands. Although very dry towards the south and west, most of the high veldt is favourable to human habitation. Rainfall is regular and plentiful, there are broad areas of fertile uneroded soil, bush is light and the vast savannahs are rich in game and eminently suitable for cattle. Some of the high mountainous area of Manica fell within Mozambique but otherwise all the high veldt lay beyond its frontiers. Nevertheless this region is important in the history of Mozambique, for the high veldt was the heartland of Shona culture and this diverse but distinctive African civilisation at one time penetrated and dominated much of low veldt Mozambique as well.

The Tonga

When the Portuguese first described east central Africa, they clearly distinguished three African peoples. North of the Zambesi were the Makua while to the south there were Karanga and Tonga. The great Dominican ethnographer, João dos Santos, made it clear that the classification was essentially linguistic:

> All these Kaffirs are called Mocarangas, since all speak the Mocaranga language, and for this reason all these lands are also called Mocaranga, except for parts of the kingdoms along the seacoast, where other languages are spoken, particularly the Botonga tongue, for which reason these lands are called Botonga and their inhabitants Botongas.[1]

The term Tonga was applied to people living as far south as Inhambane as well as to those who inhabited the hinterland of Sofala, the Zambesi valley and the escarpment. They carried on mixed farming from stockaded villages, but because of climatic conditions in the low veldt cattle could not be an important part of their economy and they therefore lacked the principal means whereby wealth in Africa is accumulated and redistributed. This lack of easily accumulated wealth may explain why their society lacked dominant élites and large, powerful chieftaincies. The Tonga were fragmented and lacked integration, the basis of their social and political organisation being the village ruled by the lineage head. Lacking the means to build up cattle-wealth, they sought to strengthen themselves and extend their lineages by acquiring additional women through warfare or the purchase of slaves. Indeed raiding for women became an important feature of the life of the Tonga and the other Zambesi peoples. When the Portuguese established themselves in the Zambesi valley they soon found that Tonga soldiers could be readily recruited if the defeat of the enemy was likely to yield female captives. Santos, for example, describes the attack on the 'Mumbos' by the captain of Tete and his Tonga allies after which 'he returned with his men to Tete, taking with him as captives all the women of the enemy', and António Bocarro describes an episode during the wars of the seventeenth century when the Portuguese settlers were persuaded to attack the slaves belonging to the absent Diogo Simões Madeira 'and put the land to fire and sword . . . and made prisoners of many negresses, girls and women, belonging to Diogo Simões who were taken to Sena and other places and sold.'[2]

However, there were chieftaincies among the Tonga. They were ruled by *mambos* whose overrule covered clusters of villages and settlements. Some of these were sufficiently large for the Portuguese to call them 'kingdoms', but they were mostly small and revealed a tendency to further segmentary fragmentation. Language apart, cultural unity among the Tonga was expressed through the rain shrines whose influence frequently extended over wide areas and embraced people from many different polities. Influential also were the spirit mediums of dead chiefs and ancestors. The power of the spirit mediums stemmed from a belief that the ancestors helped to assure the continued prosperity of their descendants. Such spirit cults could be associated with powerful *mambos* and even with prestigious foreigners who had intruded into the Tonga world. The guardians of the rain shrines and the spirit mediums wielded considerable political power, none more so than the Kaguru spirit of Barue without whose consent it was difficult for a new Macombe (ruler) of Barue to establish his authority.[3] The spirit mediums often became in effect surrogate chiefs who could act as a check on a living chief's power or even a rival to his authority. The comparative weakness of chieftaincy among the Tonga can be seen as a direct consequence of the power of the mediums.

Although little is known of the archaeology of the low veldt, the general pattern of settlement on the coast and on the high veldt has been established and this throws considerable light on the historical development of the low veldt peoples. The first Iron Age cultures on the high veldt date from the fourth century AD. These early iron-users did not own cattle in any quantity nor did they entirely displace the Boskop people who preceded them. Two distinct cultural traditions can be discerned, the Ziwa and the Urungwe, the latter possibly having connections with people north of the Zambesi. The Ziwa people, who traded in copper and alluvial gold and used granite to build walls and terraces, may have been the ancestors of the low veldt populations known by the Portuguese as Tonga.

At first the Tonga/Ziwa people probably occupied the most favoured areas of the high veldt but from about the fourteenth century they began to come under pressure from the south and gradually retreated towards the low veldt region óf the Zambesi valley and the seacoast, or took refuge in comparatively remote mountainous regions like Inyanga or in unhealthy areas shunned by their cattle-owning opponents. When the Portuguese arrived, this Tonga retreat from the high veldt was far from complete. Pockets of Tonga population retained an autonomous existence among the Karanga into the seventeenth century, while the stone terraces and walls that cover so much of the hillsides in the Inyanga mountains point to the survival of a well-organised, if somewhat isolated, Tonga population well into the eighteenth century.[4]

Most of the trade routes that at the end of the fifteenth century ran from the coast to the interior were controlled by Tonga chiefs, and in the hinterland of Sofala it was they who had intermarried with the Muslims to create a network of partly Islamised Tonga societies along the coastal lowlands. Along the Zambesi a number of Tonga chiefs played an important role in the river trade. Tolls were exacted by a chief who controlled the Lupata narrows before coastal traders reached a fair which, the Portuguese understood, was called Otonga. There was another fair, which may have been in the Zambesi valley, called Onhaquoro. The river port of Sena was situated in the territory of the Tonga chief Mpangu and became important as a crossroads between the Shire valley and the roads leading to Manica and the high veldt. Control of these trade routes enabled the Tonga to supplement their income by taxing traders, taking presents and selling their services as boatmen and carriers.[5]

When the Portuguese arrived, the Tonga chieftaincies were under pressure from the cattle-owning Karanga chiefs, who made considerable gains at their expense in the course of the sixteenth century. In many ways the Portuguese attempt to conquer the high veldt using armies recruited among the Tonga, which began in 1569 and reached a high-water mark of success in the mid-seventeenth century, should be seen as a counter-attack by the Tonga against their long-standing Karanga enemies.

The Karanga

Although the high veldt region south of the Zambesi has often been seen as a single cultural island, there has always been a marked difference between the north-east and the south-west. In part this is a natural geographical and economic division which separates the areas suitable for mixed farming in the north from the drier grasslands of the south suitable only for cattle. However, in the history of the region this division has taken on a political and even a religious reality.

The early Iron Age peoples who had inhabited the high veldt since at least the fourth century AD had kept few if any cattle.[6] At some time in the tenth century the southern regions of the high veldt were invaded by considerable numbers of cattle-owning immigrants who may have come from beyond the Limpopo to the south. They absorbed, or displaced to the north, the Iron Age peoples they found already in the country. The new culture developed two main strains, one named after Leopard's Kopje (near Bulawayo) and the other linked to Great Zimbabwe (near Fort Victoria/Masvingo). From Leopard's Kopje the culture spread south and west into modern Botswana and Transvaal. The economy of the Leopard's Kopje people was probably based on cattle-owning, and the chief distin- guishing characteristic of its civilisation was the construction of stone platforms on which huts and other buildings were erected. The mining of gold was begun and trade in copper, salt and gold was carried on with neighbours inland or with traders from the Indian Ocean coast.

The civilisation that was based on Great Zimbabwe shared many of the same characteristics. It too was marked by the mining of gold and the development of long-distance trade, and it has been suggested that much of its wealth and importance may have derived from its ability to levy tribute on trade passing from the coast to inland areas. Its influence spread northwards into the area of the older Ziwa culture. Settlements associated with Great Zimbabwe are noteworthy for the evolution of an elaborate tradition of stone wall building which achieved great artistic and technical sophistication and which concen- trated more on the building of walls and enclosures than on the con- struction of platforms.

The exceptional scale and magnificence of Great Zimbabwe might suggest that it was once an urban centre of some importance and the capital of a state of considerable size. Certainly Great Zimbabwe is set apart from other Iron Age settlements by the very scale and magni- ficence of its buildings and by its long history of occupation covering at least 1,000 years. However, excavations have revealed little trace of foreign trade and none of the external influences that might have come with foreign traders. Moreover it is unusual in Africa for a state to maintain its political centre unchanged in one place for any length of time. It is much more common for a chief to build a new capital after the death of his predecessor. The extreme 'longevity' of Great Zimbabwe may therefore be due to its being a centre of religious rather than political and economic activity.

The spread of the Zimbabwe culture northwards is likely to have been the result of junior members of the ruling clans moving with their followers to found new chieftaincies among the Tonga and the Iron Age peoples who had produced the Harare and Musengezi cultures. These migrants from the south were cattle-owners and are the people described by the Portuguese as Karanga. Excavations carried out at some of the settlements they founded in the north show marked cultural contrasts between the inhabitants of the stonewalled settlements and those of the villages that surrounded them. As Peter Garlake suggested, it seems reasonable to think in terms of a ruling élite which

> . . . . must have depended on larger outside communities for labour, for stone and hut building and probably also in the fields and with the herds . . . the assistance that was given took the form of intermittent tribute and generally did not entail a continuous or close relationship.[7]

The mining and washing for gold that took place on a large scale in the thirteenth and fourteenth centuries was clearly of great importance for the Islamic settlements of the east African seaboard, and trade in this commodity constituted one of the main sources of the wealth that allowed the sultans of Kilwa to build the magnificent palaces and mosques that made their island city famous. However, it would be wrong to deduce from this that foreign trade was of equal importance for all the ruling élites of the high veldt. Many of the sites where stone building took place were not near any centre of gold or copper mining. Some of them may have been 'fairs' where gold, mined elsewhere, was concentrated or worked before being sold, but the trade in copper with the interior was probably of equal importance and the wealth and status of the rulers of the plateau states depended far more on cattle than on foreign trade. Santos, indeed, wrote of the southern state of Butua that

> there is a quantity of fine gold, but the natives of the country do not trouble to seek it or dig for it . . . but they are much occupied with the breeding of cattle, of which there are great numbers in these lands.[8]

If this is so, then the long-term weakness of the Karanga chieftaincies of the north would be explained. Although able to mine gold and control trading fairs, theirs was not good cattle country, while the regions to the south and west from which they had originated remained rich in cattle and hence could support political power of a more impressive and continuous nature.

The northward expansion of Karanga dynasties, bringing with them the cultural traditions of Great Zimbabwe, continued throughout the fifteenth century, and shortly after the Portuguese reached the coast, Karanga rulers were actively trying to establish themselves in the low veldt hinterland of Sofala. The northward direction of this expansion was dictated by the fact that to the south and west the country was already occupied while to the north were relatively weak 'stateless' peoples and unexploited goldfields. The establishment of Karanga chieftaincies in the north was reflected in the rapid expansion of the Zambesi trade route and the rise in importance of the coastal towns of Quelimane and Angoche.

In the history of central Africa no two names so powerfully evoke myth and speculation as Great Zimbabwe and Monomotapa. The rapid decline and abandonment of Great Zimbabwe after centuries of prosperity took place in the final years of the fifteenth century, while the rise of the important Karanga paramount chieftaincy of Monomotapa in the northern part of the plateau dates from the same period. This coincidence, of course, suggests that there is a linkage, but historians and archaeologists have been at great pains to muddy over any clear causal connection between the two developments. According to David Beach, the Mutapa traditions by themselves do not show that there was a direct link between the Zimbabwe and the Mutapa states, and certainly do not indicate that the last ruler of Zimbabwe was the first Mutapa. 'Yet inspite of all this, the Mutapa state did derive from the Zimbabwe state, but in a much more generalised and less dramatic fashion.'[9] The coyness and caution of these conclusions are the result of spending too long trying to make sense of oral traditions which, it is sensible to conclude, are not able to show much about chronology. On the other hand there does exist a remarkable document dating from 1506 which gives a perfectly clear and logical account of events, apparently linking the end of Great Zimbabwe with the establishment of the Monomotapa dynasty in the north.

In 1506, shortly after the Portuguese established a permanent presence in Sofala, Diogo de Alcaçova was waiting for a ship to India.[10] No doubt obtaining his information from merchants with connections at the trading fairs, he recorded details of political developments in the interior which may, naturally, have been totally distorted but are far nearer in time to the events they describe than the oral traditions collected centuries later. The story Alcaçova tells deserves to be tested with a *prima facie* assumption that it is accurate.

According to his account, about thirteen years earlier (that is about 1493) conflict had broken out between the Karanga chief, Mucombo, and one of his subordinates who carried the relatively common chiefly title of Changamire, but whose clan name was Toloa. In the conflict which followed, Mucombo, the Monomotapa, was expelled from his stone-built capital and took refuge with a kinsman. His son subsequently killed Changamire, but the Toloa ruling family retained their independence and the dislocations of this civil war were still being felt by the Portuguese in 1506. There seems to be no real reason to suppose that this letter is not giving an account of the actual abandonment of Great Zimbabwe itself; it certainly refers to the displacement of the paramount lineage which moved northwards to find new territory among related clans which had moved earlier in the century.

When the Portuguese next heard of Great Zimbabwe in the middle of the sixteenth century, it was in a report from a Muslim traveller who made it clear that the city had become an abandoned and mysterious ruin.[11] The discovery of stone ruins associated with the Karanga chieftaincy of Gamba at Manekweni between the Sabi and Inhambane shows that, while other Karanga chiefs had been planting the distinctive culture of Great Zimbabwe over the northern part of the high veldt in the fifteenth century, at least one section of the Karanga ruling élite had moved southeastwards.[12] It has also been suggested that some Karanga may have crossed to Madagascar where cultural traits typical of the Karanga chieftaincies are clearly discernible. Early in the sixteenth century, at the time when the Portuguese arrived, the spread of Karanga power into new areas was still continuing. When the Portuguese first reached the coast there were no powerful African states in the low veldt between Sofala and the Zambesi. The region in the neighbourhood of Sofala was ruled by Tonga chiefs who had formed marriage ties with the Muslims of the coastal towns and had become partly Islamised. By the second decade of the sixteenth century, however, the Karanga were everywhere establishing their political control over the low veldt peoples and in particular over the immediate hinterland of the town of Sofala — a process viewed with considerable alarm by the Portuguese in the fort.

Karanga rule south of the Zambesi

Apart from a brief *entrada* in the seventeenth century, the Portuguese never penetrated into the southern part of the high veldt and knew little about it or about its inhabitants. With the northern peoples, however, they soon established contact and began to record details of the states and societies they encountered. However, no systematic account of the African peoples of the region was written by a first-hand observer before the 1570s, earlier accounts being compiled from hearsay by those who lived at Sofala or by men whose experience of the area was even more remote like Duarte Barbosa, the factor of Cochin, or João de Barros, a professional historian who never went to the East at all. Not only are these early Portuguese accounts fragmentary, but it is clear that the writers were to no small extent influenced by the spectacular nature of the Spanish conquests in America and the discovery of the great silver mines of Potosí. Desire to emulate the Spanish made the Portuguese credulous and led to their instinctively embroidering the accounts of the interior that reached them. In this way the myth of the 'empire' of Monomotapa took root in their minds. They imagined, and in this some later historians have copied them, that this monarchy rivalled the great empires of the Aztecs and the Incas, a concept which, if correct, would indeed have entitled the handful of Portuguese who in the seventeenth century harried and plundered the high veldt region to be placed alongside Pizarro, Cortes or Almagro. The reality, however, was somewhat different.

The migration of chiefly families which establish their rule, more or less peacefully, over a more numerous pre-existing population with weak traditions of chieftainship is a phenomenon common enough in Africa, and it is usual in such cases for the chiefly families to preserve traditions of a common origin or even of kinship between themselves, and to accept the ritual paramountcy of the senior lineage. However, such acceptance and the possession of common pottery or stone-building traditions, does not necessarily imply the existence of a single political structure or any central control from a common metropolis.

By the 1510s, the rapid expansion of the Karanga had established their ruling lineages throughout the northern part of the plateau and in most of the low veldt between the Zambesi and the Sabi. Most of the Karanga chiefly dynasties probably derived originally from the same ruling clan and the likelihood is that their founders were claimants who had failed in succession disputes and been forced to move with their followers to occupy new territory. At the end of the fifteenth century they were joined by the senior lineage which had been expelled from Great Zimbabwe during the wars with the Toloa. Wherever they established their power, these ruling families took with them much of the court structure and ritual of the Karanga paramount chieftaincy and they continued to recognise the seniority of the lineage of the Monomotapas. Because of the similarity in the institutions, language and customs of these chieftaincies and because they acknowledged a close relationship with the senior line, the Portuguese came to think of them all as forming different parts of a single feudal state. They called the Monomotapa an 'emperor' and the other chiefs his kings or vassals. Santos distilled this history into a form reminiscent of the symbolic reality of a fairy tale:

This division [of his kingdom] was made by an emperor Monomotapa, who not wishing, or not being able, to govern such distant lands, made three of his sons governors thereof, sending one named Quiteve to govern the lands extending along the river of Sofala, another named Sedanda to govern the lands traversed by the river Sabi . . . and the third, named Tshikanga, he sent to govern the lands of Manica, where there are very extensive gold mines.[13]

There is, in fact, no evidence whatever that a large, centralised Karanga state existed or that there was ever an 'empire' of Monomotapa. When the Portuguese eventually established themselves in the interior and were able to send back detailed firsthand accounts of the African states discovered there, it became clear to them that most were very small in size. At its greatest extent at the end of the sixteenth century, the land actually ruled by the Monomotapa may have covered an area measuring 150 miles by 100 miles — an area little bigger than Devon and Cornwall combined — and much of this region was only precariously under the rule of the chief. The other Karanga states were much smaller — at most two or three days journey across, a distance which could possibly be as much as 50 miles.[14] Yet the Portuguese clung to the belief that there was an 'empire', partly because it was in their interest to deal with, and try to manipulate, a single centre of power, partly no doubt because the existence of vast centralised Indian states had been revealed by the Spaniards in South America, and partly because a hierarchy undoubtedly did exist among the Karanga chiefs, and still more among the spirit mediums, which could easily give the impression that a large and imposing state structure existed or had recently done so.

The Portuguese called the region that came directly under the Monomotapa's rule Mokaranga. It was bounded approximately by the Zambesi to the north, the Hunyani in the west and the Mazoe in the south and east. Even within this restricted area the Monomotapa never seems to have exercised full authority. The Zambesi valley and much of the escarpment was usually effectively outside his control, and João dos Santos, writing at the beginning of the seventeenth century, says that after their conquest the Tete chieftaincies were handed to the Portuguese since they were too remote for the Monomotapa to control.[15] One should therefore think of the fringes of the high veldt from the Ruenha through Mount Darwin to Sipolilo as being the real extent of Mokaranga in the sixteenth and seventeenth centuries.

All the Karanga chieftaincies established in the north either absorbed or made tributary the pre-existing Tonga or Shona-speaking populations with their ancient structure of village headmen and chiefs ruling over clusters of villages. In some of these areas the Karanga language and culture triumphed but in others the Karanga dynasty took on the culture and language of their Tonga subjects. David Beach has identified sixty Karanga chiefly dynasties, but not all of them established stable, independent states. South and east of Mokaranga on the high veldt were the states of Mtoko and Maungwe — mentioned occasionally in Portuguese documents from the seventeenth century — which were small and relatively unimportant chieftaincies but had a stability that enabled them to survive to be incorporated into the colony of Southern Rhodesia when the frontiers were drawn in 1891. Due east of Mokaranga lay the state of Barue, mentioned by name by António Fernandes in the early sixteenth century, which occupied much of the broken escarpment country between the plateau and the Zambesi. The Barue country was unsuitable for cattle and this deprived the rulers of one of the principal sources of Karanga chiefly power. As a consequence, Barue's rulers came to adopt the culture of the conquered Tonga people. The stability of the state depended to a great extent on the powerful Kaguru spirit medium to whom the Tonga inhabitants looked for political advice and without whose endorsement the secular rulers, who bore the dynastic title of Macombe, could not rule. Sandwiched between the Karanga of the plateau and the Portuguese in the Zambesi valley, Barue maintained a precarious independence till the twentieth century.[16]

In the remote, cold uplands of Inyanga, Tonga populations appear to have remained free from Karanga control, preserving their distinctive civilisation till at least the eighteenth century. To the south, however, the Manica highlands saw the emergence of the chieftaincy of Chicanga and the development of the kingdom of Manica which was to survive, albeit with a change of chiefly dynasty, till the end of the nineteenth century, although its size and influence were to fluctuate greatly in the intervening years. Three other Karanga ruling dynasties established important states in the sixteenth century, all in the region between the highlands and the sea later to become part of Mozambique. In the far south near Inhambane was the kingdom of Gamba (or Tonge); between Sofala and the mouth of the Sabi was the Sedanda kingdom, mentioned by the chroniclers but about which little is known; the third is the state of Kiteve which dominated the country between Sofala and the Manica highlands and with which, in the sixteenth century at least, the Portuguese had the closest contacts and of which they had the most detailed knowledge.

The chieftaincy of Gamba was south of the Sabi river, the most southerly of the Karanga states. It was visited by the first Jesuit mission to eastern Africa but is best known from the excavation of the stone ruins at Manekweni which have been convincingly identified as Gamba's capital. Manekweni is clearly related to the culture of Great Zimbabwe but is 250 miles southeast of the nearest comparable stone ruin site. Peter Garlake, who excavated the site, suggested that the earliest building dates from the twelfth century when newly-arrived Karanga chiefs tried to use the local limestone to replicate the granite stonewalling of the plateau. The earliest pottery and walling is that most closely resembling the styles of Great Zimbabwe, distinctive characteristics developing gradually over centuries of separation. The inhabitants of Manekweni were cattle-owners who pastured their stock at a distance from the town and depended heavily on their cattle for food. The continuous occupation of the same site was probably due to the availability of water in the surrounding country, and to its relatively healthy location 35 miles from the sea on one of the main trade routes from the Vuhoca coast to the interior. The Gamba state appears to have distintegrated in the seventeenth century since it was no longer mentioned in Portuguese documents, and Manekweni itself was abandoned.[17]

The rise of the Kiteve state confirms the general picture of the spread of the Karanga chiefly lineages. For nearly ten years after their arrival on the coast, the Portuguese were unaware of any African power of note in the hinterland of Sofala, although they heard rumours of the existence of the Monomotapa and in 1507 received an embassy sent to them by the paramount chief. Between 1511 and 1513 António Fernandes had travelled in the interior and witnessed the building of a new capital by the Monomotapa, suggesting that an 'emperor' had recently been installed. It is likely that one of the unsuccessful factions in the succession struggle was that of chief Inhamunda who moved eastwards with his followers. In 1514 the Portuguese began to experience serious disruption in the trade reaching Sofala and by 1515 they had identified chief Inhamunda as the man whose power lay between themselves and the gold fairs of the interior. At first the Portuguese tried to befriend the chief but relations deteriorated as Inhamunda began to demand guns and closed the roads into the interior. By 1520, however, his authority was firmly established (apparently with the help of some Portuguese mercenaries) and an era of easier relations with Sofala began.

That Inhamunda and his followers were cattle-owners intruding among a non-cattle-owning people is graphically borne out in a letter from Francisco de Brito to King Manuel recounting that attempts to cross Inhamunda's territory secretly to trade in the interior had been frustrated by the fact that Inhamunda's people were always out herding cattle and had found out what was going on. At the end of the sixteenth century the Karanga were still a distinct element in the population of Kiteve, and Santos was consciously making this point when he described the Karanga in general as 'handsome men, especially the Mokaranga who dwell in the lands of Quiteve'.[18]

Much is known from Portuguese accounts about the internal structure of the Monomotapa and Kiteve states, and somewhat less about Barue and Manica. From these accounts it is possible to reconstruct the principal characteristics of Karanga society and government, although it should be stressed that the dominance of the Tonga element in the populations of Barue and Kiteve soon led to marked differences emerging between them and the other Karanga chieftaincies.

The essential characteristic of these polities was that they were decentralised and segmentary — as António Bocarro said, 'the dominion is divided among petty kings and other lords with fewer vassals who are called *inkosis* or *fumos*.'[19] Although in total area they were comparatively small, the chieftaincies were subdivided into smaller units and wards which in turn were decentralised to the level of the village which was ruled by the head of a lineage. The subchieftaincies were frequently of long standing and as they and the village heads had important functions in the agricultural life of the people, it was their influence that tended to be felt most strongly. The subchieftaincies were also strongly connected with the spirit mediums who claimed to speak with the spirits of dead chiefs and whose influence was so decisive in political affairs. Rainmakers were also associated with the subchieftaincies. The Karanga monarchies were a kind of overrule grafted on to these pre-existing institutions with which they tried to form ties in various complex ways. In time of war or civil strife, the Karanga states could rapidly break down into their component subchieftaincies whose rulers either asserted their independence or transferred their payment of tribute (in effect their allegiance) to some other paramount chief or to the Portuguese. Bocarro describes how, during the civil wars of the early seventeenth century, chief Motoposso broke away from the overlordship of the Monomotapa, 'rejoicing that the Monomotapa was no longer emperor, that he might be an absolute monarch and exempt from paying tribute'.[20]

The pattern of society and politics, then, was one of tightly knit and durable village communities and ancient ward- or subchieftaincies which, according to the circumstances of the day, might become grouped under some overlord — a Monomotapa, a Changamire, a Gungunhana, or a Portuguese *sertanejo*. David Beach has vividly contrasted the 'little society' of the villages with the 'great society' of the paramount chiefs, the former durable and lasting, the latter evanescent and kaleidoscopic.

Nevertheless, the Monomotapa, the Kiteve and the other Karanga kings tried to establish stable states and weld the segments over which they ruled into a durable structure. Important in this process — and in regulating relations among themselves — was the ritual position of the chief. In early modern Europe one of the ways in which monarchs tried to unite decentralised collections of feudal lordships into a cohesive state was to exalt their own status above that of their feudal equals through elaborate court ceremonial and the development of rituals which made the king a semi-divine figure, and by the early seventeenth century, exaggerated claims were being made for the divine right of kings and for the peculiar sacredness of their persons. The development of ritual at the court of the Karanga kings seems to have served a similar function. As recently established overlords claiming to rule a variety of ancient and stable chieftaincies, they could make their position more secure by exalting their own sacred and ritual status and developing a court ceremonial that would bind the subchiefs and their families with bonds of interest or kinship to the ruler. Studies of the kingdom of Kongo in west central Africa have shown clearly how power in the kingdom became a struggle between the ruling lineage and families linked to it, and the territorial chiefs with control of the territorial cults as one of the objects of contest.[21] It seems that a not dissimilar struggle took place in the Karanga chieftaincies.

It is clear from Portuguese accounts that the Karanga chiefs tried whenever possible to insist on the ritual and 'divine' nature of their kingship. Within their *zimbabwe* (the chief's capital) was an enclosure which no one but their wives and servants could enter. Here the chiefs lived, mostly unseen by the people; they could only be served by pages who were bound to chastity. When the kings grew ill or feeble with old age, they were reputed to commit ritual suicide. Often they received visitors secluded behind a curtain, and ordinary subjects were not supposed to see them eat or drink or perform any other bodily function. In their more public roles, the Monomotapa and the Kiteve assisted at religious ceremonies to obtain rain or good harvests, although they did not themselves claim to be rainmakers. At one time there had been an annual firelighting ceremony when all fires in the kingdom had to be rekindled from that of the chief himself, and this custom persisted in Barue, where significantly the torch used to rekindle fires was supplied by the medium of Kaguru.

Yet all this apparently impressive ritual has to be set beside the realities of life and political struggle within the real world of central Africa. In practice the chiefs could not remain aloof and exclusive. They hunted and fought, exacted tribute and administered justice, enforcing customary rights over game, levying fines for such things as abnormal births or witchcraft, and taking tribute from subchieftaincies and communities of foreigners. As in early modern Europe, administering justice was no abstract attempt to maintain a just and stable social order but one of the ways in which the central state extracted wealth from its feudal segments. The levying of fines for breaches of customary law therefore became an essential attribute of authority.

Ultimately a state, in Europe or in Africa, survives only as long as the control of force remains with the ruler, and the power of the Monomotapa and the Kiteve ultimately rested on the use of coercion. However, other means were employed to strengthen the paramount chieftaincy, and linking the subject chiefs and their people, whether Tonga-speaking or belonging to earlier Karanga settlers, to the ruling lineage was an important part of Karanga statecraft. Some territorial rulers became court dignitaries and were given ritual functions to perform; others sent their sons to be royal pages and there was a continuous coming and going between the villages and the *zimbabwe*. Power and reward functioned reciprocally. Pages at court were hostages for the good behaviour of their families but they were also the representatives of their families at the source of patronage.

The power of the territorial chiefs and their shifting allegiance can be illustrated by the significant case of the Mukomowasha (called in the Portuguese documents Mocomoaxa). When first heard of in the early seventeenth century, he was described as chief (*régulo*) of Condesaca, in which capacity he had an important function at the court of the Monomotapa, none other than captain general (*capitão geral*) of his forces. Another account confirms that he was the captain general but adds that he was always 'of the Botonga nation'. Later, however, as Isaacman has explained, the Mukomowasha was a leading figure in the Barue kingdom: here too he is described as coming from a Tonga not a Karanga clan, and as the chief councillor of the Macombes he assumed *de facto* power in the kingdom when there was an interregnum. 'The Barue refer to Mukomowasha as their brothers-in-law who originally provided them with wives.' Both the Monomotapa and the Macombe realised the need to have a chief of a senior Tonga lineage as a close adviser; the change of allegiance of Mukomowashas from one Karanga chieftaincy to another underlines the structural weakness of the Karanga states and the real freedom of action which the traditional territorial chiefs possessed.[22]

The Monomotapa dispensed wives and lands to his pages in reward for their loyalty, and the Karanga chiefs themselves married outside their own clan into the ruling families of the territorial chieftaincies, although their chief wives traditionally came from their own lineage. As described by António Bocarro, there were nine royal wives 'who are like queens. Most of them are his relations or sisters, and others are the daughters of the kings and lords who are his vassals.' These chief wives 'have houses and estates of their own . . . and many lands and vassals, and some of these women have kingdoms pertaining to their houses'. The Monomotapa, therefore, was using his own wives to represent his authority, presumably because male members of the ruling lineage tended to break away to form rival Karanga chieftaincies.

One technique for maintaining authority has a very familiar ring to students of early modern European monarchies. At the succession of a new Kiteve, subchiefs were summoned to court when the new Kiteve would take the opportunity to eliminate those he suspected of disaffection.[23] However no chief could rule for long in that way, and chieftaincy, like kingship, usually required considerable resources, followers having to be continuously and expensively rewarded. Resources could be obtained through levying fines or imposing taxes on mining or trade. In Kiteve the peasantry were required to work for certain specified days on millet fields belonging to the chief (a sixteenth-century form of co-operative, it would seem) but in Mono-motapa's kingdom the day-to-day expenses of the *zimbabwe* derived from the field labour of the king's secondary wives. To this extent at least the Karanga chiefs had not developed their state system far beyond that of the smallest village headman.[24]

The larger Karanga states were to prove vulnerable, just as the smaller territorial chieftaincies were to show great durability and strength. Like the early feudal monarchies of Europe, they were crippled by inherent contradictions. First and foremost were the problems of succession. According to João dos Santos, chiefs went to considerable trouble to nominate and install their successors ahead of their own death, and the alleged custom of ritual suicide may perhaps be functionally explained as a way in which the orderly transfer of power was achieved before the reigning chief became incapacitated by age or illness and the chieftaincy was torn apart by factionalism. Succession rules in patrilineal societies were by no means clear, and all the male descendants of former rulers had some sort of a claim to succeed. In Barue and Kiteve, for example, the brothers of a dead chief succeeded in turn before succession moved down a generation to the eldest son of the eldest brother. Even without the complications provided by the existence of children by different wives, this succession law created a number of different descent lines with claims to, and expectations of the throne.

In Barue contested successions were supposed to be avoided by the mediation of the Kaguru spirit. However, in the larger chieftaincies the body of courtiers — the wives, mediums and pages who controlled access to the chief — along with the other court officials — treasurers, *ngangas*, musicians, masters of ceremonies, cooks, guards, praise singers and executioners — all formed a volatile and faction-ridden mass ready to back one of the many candidates for succession. The royal wives played a major role in succession disputes, since a new chief inherited his predecessor's wives and they might reject a candidate they did not fancy by refusing him admission to the royal hut enclosure. Santos tells a story of the chieftaincy of Sedanda where the choice of the dead chief's wives ultimately prevailed over the successor appointed by the chief himself before his demise.[25]

A second cause of weakness in some Karanga states was the inability of the chiefs to build up adequate institutional backing to counter the inherent fragility of the segmentary structure. Although Kiteve claimed to be a rainmaker, the Karanga chiefs in general never gained control over the territorial cults — the rainmakers and mediums remaining closely attached to the territorial chieftaincies. In their efforts to establish the legitimacy of their rule over the Tavara in the north of their kingdom, the Monomotapas allowed the leader of the Karuva cult to have an important position in the *zimbabwe* and to 'select' the ruler's chief wife. Courtiers were frequently members of subchiefly families, and until the Portuguese arrived the Karanga chiefs did not have the support of an independent class of literate administrators. All this might have been of little importance had they been able to sustain their military superiority, but they had no permanent armed force and depended on levies raised by their sub-chiefs for particular campaigns. There was no system, such as the Nguni were to develop in the early nineteenth century, for taking young men and women out of the society of their lineage and enlisting them in age-set regiments which could be controlled centrally by the chief. As it was, the loyalty of the troops that were raised depended on the ability of the chiefs to pay the soldiers with imported goods, plunder or female slaves. The ineffectiveness of these armies was to be amply demonstrated early in the seventeenth century when they had to face well-organised Maravi invaders and the armed retainers of the Portuguese *sertanejos*.[26]

Most African rulers have had to come to terms with the problems posed by the existence of foreigners within their states, and in the six-teenth century the Karanga chiefs had to find some way of accom-modating coastal traders who might be of Portuguese or Muslim origin. The Karanga chiefs were anxious that the foreigners, with their access to prestigious trade goods, should be dependent on themselves and not on any potential rival among the territorial chiefs. Foreigners were encouraged to come to the *zimbabwe* where they were rewarded with gifts of women. They were allowed to establish self-governing communities, and within the fairs they were often expected to keep order in the name of the chief. To symbolise the closeness of the relationship the chiefs frequently referred to the leading members of the foreign communities as their 'wives'. According to Santos the term 'wife' was 'a name which the king bestows upon the captains of Mozambique and of Sofala, and upon all those Portuguese whom he greatly esteems; this name signifying that he loves them, and desires to show them as much courtesy as to his wife.'[27]

The Monomotapa was said by Bocarro to nominate two of his chief wives to supervise the foreign communities. In return the chief received presents and privileged access to foreign trade goods. There is some evidence that by the late sixteenth century the Monomotapa, conscious of his military weakness, had begun to look to the foreign community for military support. 'Captain of the Gates of the Kingdom' was, according to Father Monclaro, the title of one of Monomotapa's principal officials. It was a title which, before the end of the century, was to be bestowed on the Portuguese captain of the fair of Masapa.[28] But chiefs who summoned Portuguese military aid often found they had opened the way for foreign intervention in their domestic affairs.

The existence of small cohesive territorial chieftaincies which formed the segments of the Karanga states, explains how the Portuguese were able to establish their rule in this region. In certain circumstances the Tonga chiefs and their spirit mediums were prepared to submit to Portuguese rather than Karanga rule. It was quite possible that by entering the service of a Portuguese captain or *sertanejo* a chief would enjoy more real independence and find greater possibilities for acquiring booty in women or trade goods. A persistent theme in the history of Mozambique has been the weakness of central authority in the face of the powerful institutions of territorial chieftaincies, spirit cults and the lineage loyalties of the 'little society'.

However, because the inherent weakness of the Karanga chieftaincies did not reveal itself in any disastrous way during the sixteenth century, it is somewhat surprising to find that the tradition of building prestigious stone towns declined in the northern part of the plateau. The reason for the disappearance of stone building may contain the clue to the weakness of the northern Karanga chieftaincies relative to the powerful Torwa state in the southwest. While Great Zimbabwe was still occupied in the fifteenth century, the new Karanga chieftaincies being established in the north continued to draw their cultural strength from this centre of the stone-building tradition. Small *zimbabwes* were constructed in stone throughout the north and one of these was seen actually in the process of being built by António Fernandes in 1511. This is the last that is heard of stone building, and when the Portuguese later spoke about stone structures it was always to indicate that they were abandoned and were to be explained only by some reference to the Queen of Sheba. Portuguese accounts make it clear that by the middle of the sixteenth century the Karanga chiefs lived in towns built of wood, while the Portuguese *sertanejos* themselves used earth, timber and brick, not stone, for their buildings.

So why did stonewalling disappear in the north of the plateau? It has been suggested that there is a lack of suitable stone in this region, but the fact that stone walls were constructed at various times clearly shows that this cannot be the reason. Another possible explanation is the declining wealth of the chiefs — but it is not clear that building in stone is much more costly than building the massive wooden stockades that were characteristic of the *zimbabwes* of the Barue chiefs. It is more likely that the capital sites of the northern Karanga chiefs were frequently moved while there was a tendency for those in the south to occupy the same sites for many years. In the south, the wealth of the chiefs lay primarily in the ownership of cattle. Cattle could be herded far and wide and would not necessarily cause ecological damage in the immediate neighbourhood of the capital. In the north, particularly the low veldt and escarpment areas, cattle were less important and field agriculture formed the resource base of the society. The land round the chief's residence could easily become exhausted and the capital would therefore have to be moved to an area where fertile land was still available. The larger, more stable and stronger the chieftaincy, the more often the capital would have to be moved.

However, there may well be cultural explanations as well as economic ones. Most of the Karanga chiefly dynasties had to adjust to the ideas of their predominantly Tonga subjects. The Tonga were not builders in stone and lived in stockaded villages. Stone-walled villages may have been a symbol of chieftaincy and élitism for the Karanga but they carried no such connotation for the Tonga. A Tonga chief established and maintained his authority in close consultation with the mediums of his ancestors, and by the middle of the sixteenth century the Karanga chiefs had adopted this practice themselves, the spirit mediums of dead Karanga chiefs becoming increasingly powerful in politics. At the same time the Tonga-style stockaded village replaced the old stone *zimbabwes*. The prestige purpose of stone walling had gone and the tradition died out in the north where Karanga culture was increasingly coloured by the values and traditions of the Tonga. In the south and west, where these ecological and cultural factors did not come into play, stone walling survived and new styles continually evolved.

Trade and trade routes

It is difficult to dissociate modern Mozambique from the history of the seaports of eastern Africa. By the early sixteenth century long-distance trade and the economic specialisation that underlay it had already had many centuries of development. It has been argued that even by the time the Portuguese arrived, Africa was already partly incorporated in an international commercial system which it did not control and which was continuously abstracting wealth from the continent. However, the uneven distribution of foreign imports and their total absence from many Iron Age sites suggests that trade with the outside world in gold or any other commodity was probably not the mainstay of commerce. The staples of long-distance trade appear to have been copper, with a major centre of the industry lying near the Zambesi on the Urungwe plateau; cloth, which mostly came from the low veldt regions round Sofala, the Shire and the Zambesi valley; salt and ironware. The routes along which this trade travelled criss-crossed the high veldt and linked its communities with neighbours beyond the Limpopo or north of the Zambesi.

Control of trade routes was not the economic mainstay of the Karanga chieftaincies, which still depended on cattle for most of their wealth, but it was none the less of considerable importance. Trade seems to have been conducted at recognised fairs under the control of the different chiefs. These fairs were not usually held at the chiefs' *zimbabwes*, which probably accounts for the relatively tiny quantity of imported wares found when these are excavated. Instead, they were established on separate sites in the neighbourhood and were supervised by officials appointed by the chiefs for the purpose. The system of fairs grew up primarily because of the desire by chiefs to control the trade routes and tax the merchants. Trade routes leading to well-established fairs would be kept 'open' by chiefs through whose lands they passed — the word 'open' having as many layers of meaning as 'protection' for a Chicago mafioso. At the fairs themselves the trade was regularly taxed and at the end of the sixteenth century Santos reported that the Kiteve levied a 5 per cent tax (one cloth in twenty) on traders' wares. The fair system also enabled the chiefs to tax the gold brought for sale by their subjects — a 50 per cent tax apparently being not uncommon. But the fairs were also functionally necessary as the factor of Sofala, Pero Vaz Soares, explained in 1513:

> Although there is gold in all the land it is spread out throughout the land and there is none who has it in such quantity as to allow him to come so far to trade it, and also because they wait for the merchandise to be taken to them where each one may buy what he wants; so they come to establish fairs where there are sheiks here from Sofala, the factors of these merchants, and where they buy the merchandise that is sent to them from here.[29]

The goods brought to the fairs apparently consisted mainly of cloth and beads, worked metal objects or cowries, and only occasionally porcelain. The societies of the plateau and the low veldt were in no way dependent on imports. The cloths they imported were exotic Indian fabrics, but they had their own textile industry, and cotton was grown and cloth woven throughout most of lowland Mozambique and even in some high veldt regions. Imported beads were also a luxury item, and there was a wide variety of locally made beads to supplement the imports. Other items of trade were of local manufacture and were not imported from outside. Iron hoes and gongs, copper rings and cross-shaped ingots, salt from the sea or from inland saltpans were all of African manufacture. Although contemporary references are sometimes confusing, it seems that goldmining was an occupation that supplemented agriculture and did not replace it. Most of the mining took place during the dry season when the water table fell and hands were not needed in the fields. Ivory likewise was obtained as a byproduct of hunting for meat. Ivory hunting was the work of men; agriculture and, it seems, weaving and mining was women's work.

In the sixteenth as in the twentieth century African societies were liable to be struck by drought and famine, and it has been suggested that the fear of famine led the peoples of the plateau to concentrate so much effort on goldmining, ivory hunting and trade at the expense of agriculture. This, for instance, was the view of António Bocarro early in the seventeenth century. The Africans, he said, 'are so lazy and given to an easy life that they will not exert themselves to seek gold unless constrained by necessity for want of clothes or provisions'.[30] However, there is no evidence of food being one of the items traded from the coast which would in any way have been logistically impossible. The only possibility was for the gold producers to use the cloth and beads obtained from coast traders to buy grain or cattle from neighbours with surpluses. One Portuguese document from the sixteenth century suggests that in Manica imported trade goods were used in just this way. In 1573 an official inquiry was held into the gold trade of Manica, and evidence was taken from three Portuguese who had lived and traded in the country. One witness, Manuel Barroso, explained:

> the land of Manhica has little food. That which does exist is not enough for many of the inhabitants of the land and most of the year they eat food which they go to find outside in the lands of Quiteve and Baroe where there is a lot and which is not far away, and the inhabitants of Manhica are more given to trade than agricultural work.[31]

In this way the fear of famine stimulated the production of food surpluses as well as mining and trading activity. As João dos Santos makes clear, the existence of the trade routes to the gold fairs encouraged African peasants to produce surpluses for sale:

> When the boats are proceeding along this river [Zambesi], the Kaffirs who inhabit the many villages on its banks approach in their little canoes laden with fruits of the land, rice, millet, vegetables, fresh and dried fish, and numerous fowls, which things they sell cheap to the passengers, as these lands are very fertile and abundant, and fowls are very plentiful, which the Kaffirs do not eat, but breed to sell to those who navigate this river.[32]

Trade goods were also used in brideprice transactions. Another witness, Alvaro Fernandes, testified in 1573:

> Every *cafre*, whether king or vassal, who wants to marry gives a certain quantity of *fazenda* [trade goods] to the father of the woman, with whom he is in this way married, and so long as they have given the said *fazenda* they consider that they are married and, after being thus married, if a *cafre* does not want to live with the woman he has married in this way or does not want to continue with her, she returns to her father and he, if he has the *fato* [cloth] which was given to him at the time of the marriage, gives it back.

This otherwise isolated account can be compared with Santos, who says of the people of Kiteve that women were given in marriage in exchange for 'cows, cloths (*pannos*), beads (*contas*) or hoes, each according to his power and the value of the woman'.

The trade concentrated on the central African fairs was handled by professional traders known to the Portuguese as *mussambazes*, who might spend a year or more on a trading expedition and who came to form a distinctive foreign community in the regions in which they traded. The length of these journeys was partly accounted for by the time it took to gather the gold to pay for the goods brought from the coast. The fairs thus tended to become semi-permanent townships, and many of the traders settled there, married and founded families. By the sixteenth century there were already large Muslim communities established among the Karanga and Tonga.

A number of different trade routes connected the fairs to the coastal ports. The best-known routes were those that ran up the Sabi from Mambone, from Sofala through Kiteve to Manica and from Angoche and Quelimane via the Zambesi valley. The traders who used the Zambesi valley followed one of three routes to the interior, either travelling from Sena through Barue to Manica or following the valley of the Shire to Lake Malawi, or taking the route running from Tete up the valleys of the Ruenha and Mazoe. From Tete traders could also travel further up the river into the interior, but next to nothing is known about this route in the sixteenth century. By 1570 Sena and Tete were both important Swahili towns. In Sena there were twenty-five Muslim families with their own *mwinyi*, or leader, and Tete had probably as many. Some of these families had established plantations and maintained large households of slaves and retainers. The situation at the fairs in the interior was probably similar, and the arrival of the Portuguese may have prevented Islam from spreading still more widely in the interior of Africa, a phenomenon which was to occur later in the nineteenth century when the Koran followed the expansion of coastal trade as far as the great lakes and beyond.

Portuguese penetration of the interior

When the Portuguese first arrived on the east African coast, it was with the idea of monopolising the trade in gold which they believed to be concentrated at the two ports of Kilwa and Sofala. The ships' crews and fort garrisons were all paid wages and expected to live under military discipline. However, the coastal fortresses were hot and unhealthy, food was often scarce, pay was low and irregular, and there were few women available within the Portuguese community. From the start some private trade was allowed and, as has been shown in Chapter 1, this soon grew in volume and came to dominate the life of the Portuguese community. In West Africa Portuguese traders (*lançados*) had settled among the coastal populations of Guinea and raised families. Thus it is not surprising to find reports from east Africa of individuals leaving the shelter of the forts and finding their way into the interior where they traded firearms, fought in local African wars, married local women (sometimes the daughters of chiefs) and generally adopted the lifestyle of the Islamic traders who had preceded them. Other Portuguese settled on the offshore islands both south of Sofala and to the north as far as Pemba. Here they could live by fishing and coastal trade. Stragglers from shipwrecked crews were to be found in villages along the coast, while one Portuguese is reported to have fled inland rather than face a charge of heresy. By the middle of the century, small mixed-race communities similar to the *lançados* of Guinea existed in many parts of the east African littoral.

This steady trickle of Portuguese leaving the forts to seek their fortunes in the interior was matched by an increasingly lively official interest in penetrating inland. The first official journeys of exploration were sent in search of food to supply the forts. These explored the inlets, estuaries and coastal villages north and south of Sofala, establishing good relations where possible and, in particular, venturing down the lower reaches of the Pungue. A military expedition went to Angoche in 1511 and the same year an attempt was made to trade up the Zambesi. The first major official journey inland was made by António Fernandes, a former convict who had become interpreter to the fort of Sofala. Between 1511 and 1513 he made at least two journeys overland as far as the court of the Monomotapa. He brought back extensive information about the river routes, fairs, trade conditions and general political situation in the interior. He also seems to have made a favourable impression on the chiefs he visited. As a result of his reports and of the fear that the major trade routes to Sofala would be blocked, the Portuguese authorities made preparations to explore the Zambesi route more fully and to establish factories there which would tap the trade flowing to the Muslim traders of Angoche.

The first expedition sent to the delta in 1511 ended when the crew came to blows with the local Muslim traders. A second expedition was organised in 1518 with the aim of constructing a wooden 'tower' to form the core of a permanent factory. However, the ship carrying the materials foundered, as did the project as a whole, and as late as 1530 there was still no permanent Portuguese presence on the Zambesi. In 1531 Vicente Pegado became captain of Mozambique and the first Zambesi settlements were said to have been founded during his captaincy. It is therefore safe to assume that by 1540 the Portuguese were established in Quelimane which they were to use as their main point of entry to the Zambesi till the end of the nineteenth century. Quelimane appears regularly on Portuguese maps after 1560, but it did not immediately assume great importance for the Portuguese, and at the beginning of the 1570s Father Monclaro found only two or three married Portuguese in the town.

Little is known of the activities of the *sertanejos* at this period, although sometime during the 1550s an unnamed Portuguese helped to organise the invasion of the Lupata region by the Mongas, anticipating the role that many Portuguese backwoodsmen were to play in the region in the next hundred years or so, and in 1570 there were ten Portuguese established at Sena and a number at the court of the Monomotapa.[33] The reason may have been that during the 1530s and 1540s it was the ivory trade that was expanding and much of this was centred on Sofala and the ports to the south. The Zambesi route to the interior was not a matter of major concern to the Crown and became part of the 'unofficial' empire of the *sertanejos*.

It is in the 1560s that the first detailed information about Portuguese activity on the Zambesi becomes available. In 1560 a Jesuit mission arrived, led by a Castilian called Gonçalo da Silveira. Silveira belonged to the heroic school of missionaries who were more concerned to take the Christian gospel to parts of the world where it had never yet been preached, even at the cost of martyrdom, than to set about the tedious and undramatic task of building up a mission that would achieve lasting results. Not surprisingly his efforts achieved little but notoriety, although it was a notoriety that was to have a number of serious political consequences. With six companions Silveira travelled first to Inhambane. Having left two priests there to found a mission, he departed for the Zambesi to try to convert the Monomotapa himself. At the chief's court he found Portuguese and Muslim traders already established and Silveira was received with interest. As he was clearly a foreigner of some standing, he was offered gifts of cattle, land and women which, unlike other Portuguese at court, he refused. After a short stay he was murdered, apparently at the command of the Monomotapa who, the Portuguese believed, had been influenced against Silveira by the Muslims. Silveira's murder had no immediate effect on the position of the Portuguese traders in the interior, and clearly was in no way a result of their activities, but its impact in Europe was considerable.[34]

Accounts of the murder reached Europe in the letters of the Jesuit Luis Frois and coming only shortly after the publication on Barros' *Da Asia* in 1558, helped for the first time to draw the attention of the literate world to central Africa. The murder came at a time when Portuguese imperial strategy was being fundamentally reassessed, and this event probably contributed to the formulation of the expansionist policies pursued for the next two decades. By the 1560s the empire was entering a phase of financial and economic instability. Yields from the sale of spices no longer covered the cost of maintaining the forts and garrisons, and the solvency of the empire was increasingly coming to depend on taxes raised from Indian peasants and other revenues derived from the possession of land. The expansion of a territorial empire was therefore encouraged by the Crown, which was having to look for additional sources of revenue.

However, it seems that the Portuguese were also influenced by the knowledge that between 1545 and 1560 the Spaniards had discovered vast silver deposits in Mexico and Peru. The Portuguese Crown came to believe that similar sources of wealth could be secured in Africa, and it is no coincidence that the rumours of the existence of silver mines at Chicoa on the Zambesi and at the mountain of Cambambe in Angola were being widely believed at the time that the Spaniards had begun to exploit the real silver mountain at Potosí. That the Spanish conquests were uppermost in the minds of the Portuguese is revealed by an interesting symbolic gesture. In 1571 the Portuguese sent an embassy to the Monomotapa which took with it presents for the Karanga king. Among these was a picture made by Mexican Indians out of birds' feathers in the old Aztec style.

The interests of the church were also served by a more expansionist policy. The idea of territorial control appealed to the new generation of missionaries who set out to convert the heathen, firmly stamped with the hallmark of the Council of Trent. Heretics and the heathen were no longer to be wooed by gentle persuasion; instead forcible conversion was to be countenanced and the secular arm was invoked to put pressure on reluctant eastern rulers in a way that had not previously been attempted. The 1560s saw not only Silveira's quixotic mission but also the establishment of the Inquisition in Goa and the viceroyalty of Constantino de Braganza which featured the first Portuguese invasion of Ceylon and the attempt to destroy the sacred relic of the Buddha's tooth. Undoubtedly therefore, ecclesiastical, and more specifically Jesuit, pressure was behind the expansionist policies adopted in Africa in the 1560s and 1570s. Between 1569 and 1575 three large expeditions were assembled for the conquest of central Africa. The first was sent to the Congo in 1569 where it rapidly achieved its fairly limited objective of restoring the king of Kongo, and with him Portuguese influence, to a dominant position south of the Congo river. Then in 1570 Paulo Dias was granted a charter for the conquest of the silver mines of Angola. His expedition set out in 1575 to begin the long saga of the Portuguese wars in Angola. The third expedition, under Francisco Barreto, was sent to conquer the mines of Monomotapa.[35]

Francisco Barreto had been captain of the royal galleys and governor of Azamor in North Africa, and had served as viceroy of the *Estado da India* between 1552 and 1555. He had become well acquainted with eastern Africa when the ship in which he was returning to Portugal foundered and he had to wait on Mozambique Island for six months with his retainers and crew. The importance of the expedition on which he was now sent was made clear when his command was made independent of the control of the viceroy in Goa. He was accompanied by 1,000 veterans of Mediterranean warfare, possibly the largest purely military force ever sent by the Portuguese to the East. Clearly there were great expectations of its success. During the 1550s two accounts had been published of Cristovão da Gama's expedition to Ethiopia to confront the spread of Islam and Turkish power. This expedition had ultimately been successful, although it cost the life of its commander, and the histories of Castanheda and Bermudes made it clear that there were lessons to be learnt about campaigning in the African interior.[36] The battles fought in Ethiopia had been decided by the deployment of firearms, although the campaigns had frequently been lost for lack of horsemen to pursue a defeated enemy, and the movement of cannon had proved an almost insurmountable problem. Barreto determined to overcome these difficulties in central

Africa by using river transport where possible and providing his army with oxen, carts and even camels for transport. Cannon accompanied the expedition and there was also a contingent of cavalry.

Barreto reached east Africa early in 1570. Having waited in Mozambique for stragglers, the commander undertook an expedition northwards along the Swahili coast as far as Pate, taking prizes and seeking supplies. However, the days when such a cruise could make the fortunes of those who took part were long gone; eventually Barreto had to turn his attention to the real object of his expedition and set off up the Zambesi in November 1571. At Sena fever struck men and horses. Barreto affected to believe that the local Muslims were responsible and authorised his men to massacre them. Having impaled the last of the Muslims they could catch, and not having received any embassy from the Monomotapa, the Portuguese expedition, now somewhat depleted in numbers, continued up the Zambesi.

Between Sena and Tete lie the Lupata mountains through which the Zambesi passes along the bed of a narrow gorge. Here the army was met by a hostile force, referred to by the chroniclers as Mongas (this was, in fact, the name of a chief whose people were advance elements of the Maravi invaders who were soon to dominate the whole north bank of the Zambesi). Although they could not resist Portuguese firepower in the one pitched battle that occurred, the Mongas successfully harried the expedition. Horses died, the carts broke and men went down with fever so that even the general surrendered his charger to help carry the sick. By the height of the hot season the whole expedition ground to a halt; the sick were sent down the river by boat and the remnant of the army trailed ignominiously back to Sena. There the commander deserted his men and returned to Mozambique to seek reinforcements.

In early 1573 a fresh expedition arrived with 700 men and new equipment. Barreto returned to Sena where he in turn succumbed to fever. He was succeeded by his second in command, Vasco Homem, a soldier of much greater ability who immediately withdrew the army from the fever-ridden Zambesi valley, took it by sea to Sofala and from there conducted a successful 300-mile march into the Manica highlands. Scarcely half a dozen sentences survive to describe this remarkable expedition. The army captured and burnt the capital of the Kiteve before reaching the gold fields of Manica. But Kiteve's kraal was not Cajamarca nor were the mountains of Manica a Potosí. Having seen the small river-side washings in the highlands, Homem rightly concluded that there was little there to conquer and withdrew to the coast. A final disaster had yet to overtake the expedition. Two hundred men were sent up the Zambesi again to investigate rumours of silver at Chicoa above the Cabora Bassa rapids. After a few months of fruitless endeavour the expedition was overwhelmed and massacred. By 1576 the last survivor of Homem's army had left eastern Africa. The Jesuit chronicler of the expedition concluded: 'To endeavour to conquer these territories is to waste money and Portuguese lives. . . . He who would have all loses all.'[37] For the Portuguese it had proved a tragic failure, only to be matched by the still more tragic failure of their invasion of Morocco two years later.

It is instructive to speculate why such a large Portuguese force failed to achieve any significant conquest in central Africa when the handful of men led by Pizarro and Almagro had been able to overthrow the empire of the Incas in South America. The failure of Barreto's expedition was probably due as much to its size and inability to move swiftly as to any other factor. It remained immobilised for long periods in the fever-stricken bush of Sena and when once it did move, it could not be properly supplied. Other, smaller Portuguese forces were to prove much more effective in central African warfare in the following century. The Spaniards had found that their warhorses and steel weapons were decisive against footsoldiers armed only with weapons of stone, but in Africa the Portuguese could not use horses since these died even more rapidly than men, and they found that their African opponents had finely made iron weapons, comparable to their own. Moreover, in Africa the Portuguese were not confronting the highly organised, centralised monarchies which the Spaniards discovered in Mexico and Peru. The Spaniards had been able to paralyse these states by striking a swift blow at the ruler and his capital, but the Portuguese were fighting relatively small, decentralised segmentary chieftaincies. There were no large armies for them to beat, no major battles to win and no way of bringing the war to an end. In Peru the Spaniards found royal roads, store houses, bridges and a teeming population which could be enlisted to provide carriers. In central Africa there were no roads, no accumulated surpluses of food or treasure to be plundered, and the thinly scattered population mostly lived in small settlements dependent on subsistence agriculture. Finally, just as Napoleon said he had been defeated in Russia by 'Generals January and February', so Barreto was confronted by 'General Malaria'. The Portuguese succumbed to the diseases of the region which totally destroyed their army. In South America the opposite had happened. It had been the diseases which the Spaniards carried, and to which they were relatively immune, that had wiped out the Indian populations. Had there been a great 'empire of Monomotapa', then a ruthless Portuguese conquistadore might have acted the part of Pizarro, overthrown the monarch and seized control of the country, but the small-scale, segmentary nature of Karanga political organisation proved far more resilient than the great military monarchies of South America.

The Karanga chieftaincies survived this onslaught relatively unscathed, and in the diplomacy they employed to ensure the departure of the Portuguese there is a touch of the skill that was to mark Moshoeshoe's dealings with his enemies in the nineteenth century. Once Barreto had returned to Sena after his empty 'victory' over the Mongas, the Monomotapa sent him a courteous embassy which made no material concessions but thanked him for disciplining an unruly vassal. The following year Homem, after burning the Kiteve's capital, was welcomed by the Chicanga of Manica and shown the gold mines, a tactful way of persuading the Portuguese commander that he was wasting his efforts by staying in the country. With expressions of friendship, he was expedited on his way back to the coast.

The Karanga chiefs had seen the Portuguese humiliated and totally defeated in their objective of 'conquering the mines'. Yet the subsequent years were to show that Barreto's army of occupation had fundamentally altered the political, social and economic relations of the Zambesi valley and the escarpment regions. The massacre of the Muslim traders in Sena destroyed the independent Muslim trading community on the Zambesi and with it the last vestige of Angoche's independent role in Indian Ocean trade. A Muslim population survived but, like its counterpart in Sofala, had to live by trading with, and supplying services to, the Portuguese. Indeed many of the Muslims who survived Barreto's massacre, particularly those in the delta region, apparently did well out of the expedition, supplying it with food and transport and being rewarded with grants of land. However, where trade with the outside world was concerned the Portuguese, and more particularly the captain of Mozambique, were now in complete control.

The second major result of the expedition was the establishment of official Portuguese captaincies at Sena and Tete. The first earth-walled forts were raised, garrisons installed and captains appointed with commissions from the governor of Mozambique. These captaincies acquired jurisdiction over a number of the valley chieftaincies and from this time the Portuguese captains were to act, in all important respects, as paramount chiefs over the peoples of the valley and the delta. They also acquired jurisdiction over the chieftaincy of Inhabanzo near Tete with its eleven subchieftaincies. The sovereignty was technically bestowed on them by the Monomotapa in response to an embassy sent by Barreto to his *zimbabwe*, and with it went the honorific title of 'chief wife'. However, the likelihood is that Monomotapa had never had more than the most shadowy control over these Tonga chieftaincies and that the Portuguese were merely acquiring formal recognition of a control they already exercised over the peoples in the vicinity of the fort. Some Tonga chieftaincies, indeed, even maintained a precarious independence sandwiched between the Portuguese on the Zambesi and the Karanga on the plateau. To the Tonga headmen and peasants the imposition of a foreign overlord was no new experience and was not necessarily a disruptive one, for the Portuguese captains continued to perform chiefly functions, attending ceremonies connected with crops, appointing headmen, claiming customary rights over game and administering justice. In particular they took the tribute in kind that the Tonga traditionally paid, and demanded labour and military service from the population.

The Karanga chiefs of the plateau might have survived Barreto's attempt at conquest, and could for the moment look with complacency on the Portuguese overlordship of the Tonga of the valley. However, in the longer term relationships had been fundamentally changed. The Portuguese had acquired control of population and resources and this was to enable them, in the following century, to mount a much more formidable assault on the Karanga chieftaincies and bring about the downfall and subjection of many of them.

3

MOZAMBIQUE NORTH OF THE ZAMBESI TO THE MIDDLE OF THE SEVENTEENTH CENTURY

The Portuguese and the region north of the Zambesi in the sixteenth century

The Dominican friar João dos Santos relates a gruesome tale of events that took place in 1586, the year he arrived in Africa. Two Africans brought a black woman for sale to the Portuguese at Mozambique Island. They offered her to a Portuguese lady who owned one of the plantations on the mainland opposite the island. She, however, thought that ten pieces of cloth was too high a price and offered to pay only half that amount, whereupon the two Africans said 'they would rather eat the negress than sell her at so cheap a rate'. As no other buyer could be found, 'they proceeded to a thicket that was close by and killed the negress, and remained there three or four days eating her flesh boiled and roasted'. The captain of Mozambique laid part of the blame for this horrific occurrence on the Portuguese lady and she was punished for not having saved the slave by purchasing her, but he also punished 'several of the heathen kaffirs who resided in these palm groves as he learnt that they had assisted in eating the said negress'.[1]

There seems, at first sight, every reason to discount such a story. Eating human flesh is as abhorrent in Africa as it is in Europe and the most likely explanation would seem to be that the heated imagination of the friar was willing to accept and embellish picturesque tales of barbarism which he knew would excite his European audience. In this way all the accounts of cannibalism in early Portuguese literature can be written off as figments of a superstitious and ignorant Lusitanian credulity. However, whether the details of this story are true or not, it has a symbolic significance for understanding developments among the peoples who inhabited Mozambique north of the Zambesi in the late sixteenth century.

In the middle years of the century central Africa began to experience one of its periodic phases of climatic instability. Already by the 1560s drought and famine had set in motion a pattern of armed raiding and large-scale migrations that were to affect both the western and eastern parts of the region. With the drought came the locusts.

61

In 1561 locusts afflicted the region south of the Zambesi for the first time in living memory and their swarms were still a plague when the Jesuit Monclaro accompanied Barreto's expedition to the Zambesi in 1571-2. The famine conditions returned in the 1580s. Dos Santos vividly described

> . . . . the cruel plague of very large locusts that passed through these lands in such numbers that they covered the ground and when they rose in the air they formed so dense a cloud that the land was darkened. The damage caused by them was great as they devoured all the crops, gardens and palm groves through which they passed, leaving them dried and burnt up as though consumed by fire, so that for the next two years they produced no fruits, and therefore during this time there was great sterility and famine, of which numbers died. . . . There was so great a scarcity of provisions that the kaffirs came to sell themselves as slaves merely to obtain food and exchanged their children for an *alqueire* of millet, and those who could not avail themselves of this remedy perished of hunger.[2]

With the famine came disease. Smallpox spread along the coast, 'a subtle pestilence, as it kills everyone in a house where it appears, men, women and children alike, and very few escape who are attacked by it.'

Drought was working out its terrible logic on the peoples of Africa, as it was to do so many times in the centuries that followed. A failure of the rains was followed by locusts, famine, disease, war, cannibalism and slavery. In west central Africa the Jaga invasions on the Congo (whoever the Jaga may have been) were accompanied by famine, stories of cannibalism and the wholesale enslavement of sections of the BaKongo population, including members of the chiefly lineages. In east central Africa the immediate consequence was the flight of whole populations, the 'Zimba' raids and the subsequent redrawing of the political map of northern Zambesia. In this context incidents of cannibalism and slavery were only too likely to occur and stories linking the two are, at the very least, symbolic of the catastrophe that had overtaken the peoples of the region.

The Makua

The north of Mozambique is today dominated by peoples who speak languages of the Makua and Maravi groups, but at the beginning of the sixteenth century the Portuguese were only aware of the existence of the Makua speakers. The Makua language is now spoken in dialects sufficiently distinct to suggest that a thousand years may have passed since the break-up of the original Makua-speaking group. Whether the original Makua-speakers entered the country between Lake Malawi and the sea from the north or from the south can only be the subject of speculation.[3] Makua traditions record only that the home of the nation was in the Namuli mountains, and it is likely that initially only the highlands east of the Lake were occupied, the newcomers mixing with the San population whom they found inhabiting the region. Such evidence as there is suggests that even in the sixteenth century the coastal regions may have been quite thinly populated, but that inland the Makua speakers had already spread out to the north and south and the main lines of differentiation between the various groups had been drawn. In the north were the people who today are known as the Medo and Niassa Makua, while in the south were those sometimes grouped under the name of Lomwe. This latter group was also divided, one part occupying the old heartlands of the Namuli mountains the other establishing themselves along the Zambesi valley. This latter section was known to the Portuguese as Bororo, a name now usually rendered as Lolo. In the sixteenth and early seventeenth centuries they occupied the northern bank of the Zambesi as far upstream as Tete. On the southern bank were the Tonga, and the river formed an ethnic and linguistic frontier such that boatmen sailing downstream would steer for 'Bororo' or 'Botonga' to indicate whether they wished to go to port or starboard.[4] Makua-speakers also inhabited the Shire valley but probably did not extend into the highlands west of that river.

The Portuguese had contacts with the Makua on the mainland opposite Mozambique Island and occasionally with groups encountered in the coastal estuaries. Most of the comments made in the sixteenth century stress the simplicity of the social organisation and material culture of the coastal people. Duarte Barbosa in 1517 described the population near Mozambique Island as 'going naked smeared with red clay . . . their lips bored with three holes and in these they place bones with little stones and other little pendants'.[5] The coastal Makua did not have any large-scale political organisation. 'Many of their neighbours', wrote Father Monclaro in the 1570s, 'have more policy and better mechanical arts than they have.' He thought that 'there was no great chief to whom they pay tribute but they live as in a republic.'[6] João dos Santos wrote in 1609 but his information about the Makua seems to have been obtained from Father Thomas Pinto, the Inquisitor of Goa wrecked on the coast in 1585. He was also quite clear that along the coast north of the Zambesi delta there were no great chieftaincies similar to those he had described south of the Zambesi among the Karanga, although 'in the interior of this country live several great and powerful kings, heathen kaffirs with woolly hair, of whom the greater number belong to the Makua nation'.[7] Immediately north of Quelimane was a Makua chief called Gallo. 'He has the title of king, but his dominions are small. He has few vassals and less property.' Five leagues north of Quelimane Makua villages were scattered along the banks of the river Loranga subject to a chief called Bano. With the powerful and sophisticated Karanga chieftaincies in mind, Santos explained:

> The government of these people is very simple. In each village there is a chief who governs them, who is called a fumo. He gives verbal sentence in their differences, which are few; and when the fumo is unable to decide, Bano, lord of the country, settles the question with the advice of the other fumos who assemble for this purpose on a terrace at the door of the house of the said Bano.[8]

One reason why the coastal regions were comparatively thinly populated and why no large chieftaincies existed was the unsuitability of the land for cattle rearing, a fact noted by Santos who, however, explained it by saying: 'These Kaffirs are not fond of work, and are more given to dancing and feasting.'

It seems that in the sixteenth century the Makua-speaking people were politically fragmented and had not evolved any large state systems. Part of the explanation for this lies in the matrilineal descent system and the strong matriarchal tradition whereby not only was control over agriculture and its produce vested in the senior women of the village but inheritance of land and property rights stayed within the mother's clan, passing to children of the mother's brother. Rita-Ferreira describes how matrilineal inheritance related to political power in what he called 'matricentric communities':

> The mother and senior sister of the chief enjoyed a certain political preponderance. The eldest daughter of the latter, the *pia-muene*, was guardian of the customs and was responsible for the burial places of the matrilineage.[9]

Where people who, like the coastal Swahili, practised patrilineal inheritance, intermarried with the Makua, complicated systems of dual inheritance of property and political power evolved. Santos, who liked to translate what he saw into the language of European institutions, observed that, 'although there are many lords who have vassals, yet none of them have the title of king except some Moors who reside on the coast in small towns, who call themselves kings of the towns in which they live.' The lack of political cohesion among the Makua was to open the way not only for coastal Muslims to create their urban communities but also for external conquerors to establish an overrule although, as with the Tonga south of the Zambesi, the social cohesion of the matrilineal descent groups at the village level was to prove remarkably durable, as it has right up to the present.

A vivid and almost affectionate portrait of the coastal Makua is painted by the Jesuit, António Gomes, wrecked on the coast between Quelimane and Angoche sometime before 1645. As he and his companions staggered ashore,

> . . . . we saw a great number of *cafres* who had been watching our plight from far away . . . children, men and women and the grown-ups so badly dressed that the women scarcely had on two fingers' width of cloth and even so not all of them for some only had on the width of one section of a palm leaf and the others, under twelve years, were stark naked.

Clearly at this stage contact with the Portuguese had not led to the widespread use of imported cloth. Father Gomes asked to see the local chief, and

> . . . . there came an old man with parched skin and grey beard who must have dated back to Afonso de Albuquerque's days; I started to complain about the sea that had done us so much wrong and he gave me an answer which I considered very wise. 'Master, if you know the sea is crazy and has no brain, why do you venture upon it.' . . . He had come to meet us, as he had had word that we were on his beach, so that no one would touch anything of ours and this his elders had done many other times . . . and he would not leave there until we did so too.[10]

He goes on to describe the people with their filed teeth 'as sharp as a dog's' and the tattooed faces and bodies as 'pretty as characters out of hell', while 'those who look more distinguished wear a tiger's or lion's claw crown like some plaited trimming which makes them look even more ghostly.' The women wore liprings, 'those who stretch the lower lip the most are the prettiest', while a man decked out for his wedding 'had four beautiful horns on his head artfully arranged one just above his forehead, another behind and one above each ear'.[11] Since it was impossible to sleep in these head-dresses, a carved head-rest had to be used at night. The Makua of this stretch of the coast did not farm but lived on fish caught in the lagoons and dried for storage, supplemented by fruits and roots. Hunting was a major communal effort, in which 'they all get together and surround a big piece of land and then set it alight; as the animals get out, they spear them'.

When the Portuguese were ready to march the chief allowed the people to scavenge the remains of the wreck, 'which was done in a very orderly manner because of the great fear they have of the Portuguese guns'. On their way the party got lost and entered a stockaded village which was empty as the population had all gone down to the fish weirs. The poles of the stockade displayed ten or twelve skulls, including

> . . . . three heads recently cut off. . . . It was a big village with wooden huts all round, most of them big and with an upper floor, with the doors kept closed by means of a small rope and with no other lock. . . . Through the openings of the houses we saw a lot of ivory and great bundles of dried meat and fish.

The Portuguese passed on and spent the night in another 'big village which also had raised huts built on poles with an open lower part where people can take shelter.' They were told that the raised huts were a protection against lions. All along the coast they found that the people had had regular contacts with the Portuguese. One man had served on Portuguese ships and been to Portugal and another showed them a piece of artillery and the relics of old shipwrecks.

In the seventeenth century the Makua of this coastal area had not yet hunted the elephant to extinction, for Father Gomes found that the villages could not maintain palm plantations because of the raids by the elephants on the young trees. Coconut palms, however, grew in profusion inside the stockaded villages, and in villages abandoned after the death of the chief their fruit lay unpicked:

> When someone who is held in great respect dies, they leave him in his house exactly as when he died, put in the house everything he used to use, the bowls in which he ate his food, the *quite* on which he sat, and everything else, close the door, which is made of bamboo or sticks tied together, block it up with kneaded mud, and then they move their village over to a place nearby and the palm-trees are thus abandoned.[12]

The Portuguese castaways, on this occasion, defied local custom and gathered the fruit from the abandoned village. At the next village the Portuguese were asked to stop for a meal, a courtesy much appreciated until one of the party found a human finger in his soup.[13]

The Bororo of the Zambesi valley were considerably more integrated into the central African commercial system than the Makua described by Father Gomes. They were involved in the manufacture of cotton cloth (*machiras*) and profited from the extensive trade in this commodity. Monclaro, otherwise rather contemptuous of the material culture of the Makua, admired the techniques used to thread and weave bead patterns into their textiles. He commented also on their skill in gold and copper working, and he and Dos Santos shared a slightly horrified fascination with the filed teeth, pierced cheeks and lip-rings which 'makes them look like devils'.

In spite of the invasions of this region by the 'Zimba' at the end of the sixteenth century and the subsequent establishment of Maravi chieftaincies, the Portuguese fathers still believed that the coastal Makua they met were a poor population, possibly an outcast element, living on fish and millet with their small village communities concentrated in the river estuaries and thereby escaping the overrule of any powerful chief. However, the growth of Islamic trading towns such as Angoche and the accompanying growth of the ivory trade, all of which took place in the sixteenth century, had led to significant changes for many of the populations north of the Zambesi. António Gomes thought that the Muslims were 'more cultured so that the cafres became more civilised through this contact.'[14] Islam began to spread from the Muslim towns by the familiar processes of intermarriage and economic interdependence. Santos himself records the brother of one Makua chief becoming a 'moor' and mentions that 'black moors' were to be found among the Makua population of the Loranga estuary.[15] Ivory trading brought ships to the river estuaries and these provided a market for food surpluses produced by the local population. In addition an overland route between Mozambique Island and the Zambesi was opened up and was certainly in operation by 1645, when Gomes wrote of the coastal plain north of Quelimane that 'it has plenty of big villages and the cafres (although primitive) give good shelter to the Portuguese by bringing their chickens, rice and meal with what best they have.'[16] This relative prosperity almost certainly led to the movement of more people into the coastal area.

Peaceful cultural and commercial contacts between the Makua and the Muslim and Portuguese maritime communities were brutally interrupted in the middle of the sixteenth century by the onset of drought and the resultant social dislocation which led to the invasion, devastation and conquest of Makua territory by people from the interior.

The Maravi incursions

Sometime in the 1550s an unnamed Portuguese adventurer had enlisted the aid of some people called Mongas 'to revenge himself upon certain people on the other side of the river.' These Mongas mercenaries had then settled and carved out a domain for themselves extending from the Lupata mountains to Tete. They gained a reputation for living by raiding and in the late 1560s carried out a daring and successful attack on Tete during the absence of the Portuguese traders.[17] The Mongas proved formidable opponents for Barreto's army in 1572 and so weakened the Portuguese by their resistance that the conquest of the gold mines had to be abandoned. In the diplomatic exchanges that followed, the Monomotapa made it clear that he was glad the Mongas had been chastised since they were rebellious vassals. Subsequently the Mongas were to be attacked by the Karanga and their power destroyed. The name Mongas was in fact that of a chief whose people seem to have been the advance guard of the migration of the Maravi from central Africa (Map 2).[18]

After the withdrawal of the Barreto expedition in 1576 the Portuguese met other bands harrying the settled population north of the river and were soon to clash violently with the traders of Sena and Tete. According to the chronicler Do Couto, people called the Ambios or Macabires first made their appearance on the Zambesi in 1570. They were led by a chief called Sonza, the 'soft-haired,' and they clashed with the Portuguese of Tete and their African allies. Heavily defeated by the Portuguese the invaders turned aside and marched into the Makua country where they settled. Their invasion, or more probably the onset of the great famine, apparently displaced a Makua chief called Maurusa who moved with his followers into the region immediately inland from Mozambique Island. The Portuguese who had gardens and plantations on the mainland tried to drive the intruder away but suffered a humiliating military defeat in 1585 and had to come to terms with a Makua political authority more formidable than any they had hitherto met, and one that had possibly been called into existence by the initial Maravi invasion of the region.[19] It was about the Makua followers of Maurusa that Santos told his shocking story of cannibalism.

The Portuguese clash with Maurusa occurred in 1585. At the same time armed raiders, referred to by the Portuguese as Zimba, attacked the coast opposite the Querimba Islands, sacked Kilwa and appeared before Mombasa and Melinde. At Mombasa the Zimba played a decisive role in the defeat of the Turkish fleet of Mir Ali Bey; they crossed to the island and allegedly ate the Turks they managed to capture. The raiders were finally destroyed near Melinde in 1587. Whoever these raiders may have been, the Portuguese thought they were the same horde of 'Zimba' warriors who had originated in Zambesia.[20] The devastations of these armed bands are clearly to be associated with the famine of the 1580s, but clashes with the Portuguese in Zambesia continued in the following decade. In 1592 a Portuguese force from Tete crossed the river to help an ally against 'Mumbo' raiders. The 'Mumbo' chief, Quizura, was defeated and his village burnt.[21] Two years later a similar request for help was received by chiefs lower down the river who were being attacked by the Zimba chief Tondo. Two Portuguese expeditions were sent against Tondo, both ending in disastrous defeats for the Portuguese and large-scale loss of life.[22]

Although these events might, on the evidence of later historical

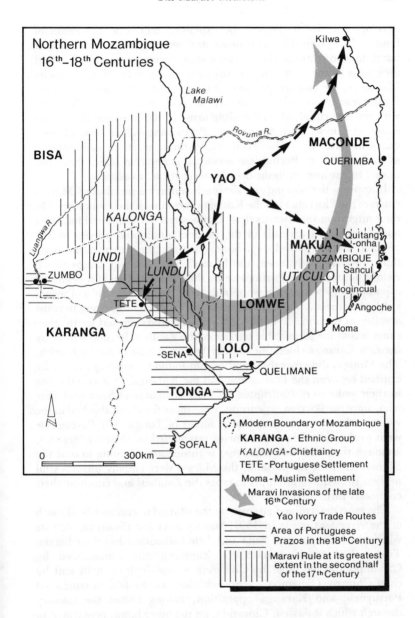

Northern Mozambique
16th–18th Centuries

Kilwa

Lake Malawi

Rovuma R.

BISA

MACONDE

QUERIMBA

YAO

KALONGA

UNDI

LUNDU

MAKUA

Quitang -onha

MOZAMBIQUE

UTICULO

Sancul

Luangwa R.

ZUMBO

TETE

LOMWE

Mogincual

Angoche

KARANGA

Moma

-SENA

QUELIMANE

LOLO

TONGA

SOFALA

0   300km

Modern Boundary of Mozambique

KARANGA - Ethnic Group

KALONGA-Chieftaincy

TETE - Portuguese Settlement

Moma - Muslim Settlement

Maravi Invasions of the late 16th Century

Yao Ivory Trade Routes

Area of Portuguese Prazos in the 18th Century

Maravi Rule at its greatest extent in the second half of the 17th Century developments in the region, be explained merely as the result of famine disrupting the social order and sending fragmented raiding bands in all directions, the Portuguese observers were quite clear that they were witnessing a major invasion by intruders from outside. Moreover, the cannibalism described in so horrific a manner in the Portuguese accounts is, on balance, as likely to have been associated with the war rituals of an invading army as to have been simply the result of famine and destitution. Portuguese writers record with gruesome fascination that even when Maravi warriors were enlisted as mercenaries in Portuguese service a generation later, they continued to eat human flesh. So who were these invaders?

It appears that during the sixteenth century a number of Maravi chiefs of the Phiri clan left the Katanga region with their followers. On their migration southwards these bands attracted additional followers and, possibly as a result of the famine conditions, preyed on the populations they passed — in Santos' words, 'they ate up every living thing.' As they advanced, the Maravi built fortified camps which clearly impressed the Portuguese by their construction and defensive capabilities. These camps were built 'with many high banks of wood, earth and trees . . . and these banks were sufficiently strong to resist a volley of cannon.'[23] As the Maravi war bands pressed south, they came across the formidable barrier of the Zambesi beyond which lay the rich Karanga chieftaincies and the fertile land of the high veldt. The Mongas did cross the Zambesi but found themselves eventually crushed between the Portuguese and the Karanga. Others following in their wake were confronted by the Portuguese of Sena and Tete who, since the Barreto expedition, were more firmly established in the valley and who commanded large forces of Tonga. The Portuguese went to the aid of the chieftaincies threatened by the invaders and, although they and their allies met with disaster in trying to oust the Maravi from the north bank, the Maravi were equally unsuccessful in their subsequent attempts to cross the Zambesi and continue their conquests further south.

The most determined attempt by the Maravi to conquer land south of the river was made in 1597, shortly after the disastrous defeats which the Portuguese of Sena and Tete had suffered at their hands. Two armed bands crossed the Zambesi, one commanded by Capampo and the other by Chicanda — and both of them sent by chief Chunzo. Capampo's army withdrew in the face of combined Portuguese and Karanga opposition, having looted the country through which it passed. Chicanda, on the other hand, penetrated to a position quite near to the *zimbabwe* of the Monomotapa where he diplomatically made peace and was allowed to settle with his men. Two years later, in 1599, he rose in rebellion and withstood a siege by a joint Karanga and Portuguese force. His encampment was described as built of 'very high and thick strong wood; it was surrounded by a trench twenty-five palms in depth and as many in width; and it had a wall of earth taken from the trench banked very high against the wood, with loopholes for arrows with which to molest the Mokarangas.'[24] This was clearly a Maravi fortress of the kind that had defied the Portuguese during their north bank campaigns and the Portuguese experienced familiar difficulties in attacking it.

Chicanda was eventually expelled but there were to be at least two further Maravi incursions into Karangaland in the early seventeenth century. Both of these were blocked by the natural barrier of the Zambesi and by the resistance of the Portuguese and the Karanga, and the Maravi failed to establish a permanent presence south of the river. As new migrations continued to exert pressure in the rear, the advance groups of the Maravi, unable to proceed further south, were forced to turn eastwards towards the sea, overunning the small Bororo chieftaincies and occupying the land between the Shire and Mozambique Island. There they established new chieftaincies among the Makua, while the cult of the rain shrine of Mbona spread with them from the Shire valley into the Mozambique lowlands.[25]

The emergence of the Maravi kingdoms

Early in the seventeenth century the invading Maravi war bands coalesced into a number of powerful chieftaincies in the area north of the Zambesi bounded by the Shire and Lake Malawi to the east and the Luangwa valley to the west. The details of this process of state formation can be pieced together from the fragmentary references in Portuguese documents. During the last quarter of the sixteenth century Portuguese writers used a variety of names to describe the different Maravi groups that invaded northern Zambesia. The map published by Filippo Pigafetta in 1595 marks the Embeoe and the Mozimba, and contemporary chroniclers also refer to the Ambios, the Zimba, the Mumbos and the Cabires. This last name appears also in the viceregal correspondence and possibly refers to the ruling Phiri clan of the invaders.[26] The name Maravi was used for the first time in 1616.

The chiefs mentioned in the sixteenth-century accounts are Mongas, Quizura, Tondo, Sonzo and Chunzo (the last two possibly being one and the same). However, none of these names refers unambiguously to any of the three major Maravi chieftaincies (Kalonga, Lundu and Undi) which had established themselves in the region between the Zambesi and Lake Malawi by the middle of the seventeenth century. Tondo must have fairly convincing claims to being the founder of the modern Zimba chieftaincy of that name, and it has been cogently argued that the Zimba as a whole were the subjects of chief Lundu[27] although Lundu was not mentioned by name in documents till 1613.[28] Undi is also referred to in 1613 but there is no early seventeenth-century mention of Kalonga. Instead a lot is heard of a Maravi chief called Muzura.

In the first three decades of the seventeenth century there was considerable conflict between the rival Maravi chieftaincies, and a number of attempts were made by them to get involved in Karanga politics. In 1608 the Portuguese recruited 4,000 warriors from the chief, called Muzura, for service in the wars in Karangaland. Muzura, we are told, was the leader of a war band who had taken the opportunities provided by the disordered state of the country to build up a power-base for himself — one of a line of Zambesian warlords whose activities have enlivened the history of Mozambique virtually up to the present. Indeed one contemporary account alleged that Muzura was once in Portuguese service before setting himself up on his own. Muzura's mercenaries enabled the Portuguese to triumph in 1608 and the aid was reciprocated when soon afterwards the Portuguese helped Muzura in his wars with Lundu, enabling him to establish his paramountcy over the eastern Maravi. In 1614 the Portuguese again recruited mercenaries for their Karanga wars, this time from both Lundu and Undi.

By the 1620s Muzura had established his power on the north bank of the Zambesi and began to intervene south of the river. In 1620 the Portuguese accused the Monomotapa of having employed Muzura's soldiers in his wars and in 1623 Muzura made what was probably the last attempt by the Maravi to establish their power across the Zambesi when, on the death of the Monomotapa Gatse Lucere, he launched a major invasion of Karangaland and attacked both Sena and Tete. This invasion was defeated, and apart from a final raid into Karangaland in 1628 there appear to have been no further significant incursions by the Maravi across the river, the Portuguese settlements forming an effective barrier between them and the high veldt.[29] However, Muzura did join in the grand alliance against Mavura who had been installed as Monomotapa with Portuguese arms in 1629. The rising took place in 1631 and Muzura took the opportunity of launching a major attack on Quelimane, the only Portuguese settlement north of the river. He failed to take the town and received the brunt of the Portuguese counter-attack in 1632.

The paramount chieftaincy of Kalonga

By the middle of the seventeenth century the chieftaincy of Kalonga was being recognised as the paramount Maravi state. The name

Kalonga appears for the first time in Portuguese documents in 1667 when he is already described as 'emperor' of the Maravi. It has been suggested that Muzura, whose activities are mentioned for the last time in 1632, was the founder of the Kalonga dynasty. Some people might bridle at attributing to the former Portuguese servant and adventurer Muzura the foundation of a chieftaincy which was to acquire great prestige and to which are attached many sacred traditions and rituals. However, there are strong reasons for thinking that this was so. The name Maravi first appears applied to Muzura's capital, and this was sited 'half a league' from the western shore of Lake Malawi where Kalonga's chieftaincy was later to be centred. Manuel Godinho, writing in 1663, only four years before the name Kalonga is first mentioned, still refers to 'the court of Mesura or Marabia.'[30] So, if Muzura was not the founder of the Kalonga chieftaincy, what happened to his chieftaincy and where was the Kalonga all the time that the Portuguese were dealing with the other Maravi chiefs? That the revered chieftaincy of Kalonga should be associated with the power of an upstart need not cause undue surprise. Warlords and usurpers have founded monarchies throughout history and have hastened to legitimise their rule by every device possible, including inventing lineages, seeking the sanction of religious authority, contracting marriages with ancient dynasties and embellishing their rule with all the ritual trappings of the most prestigious courts.

Kalonga, Lundu and Undi had emerged as the three dominant Maravi chiefs by the mid-seventeenth century. Of these Kalonga was recognised to be the senior, and during most of the seventeenth century this chieftaincy dominated the region between the Luangwa and the sea. However, the Kalonga's capital was far from the coast and was sited close to the west shore of Lake Malawi where it is marked on a map of 1677. As a result, throughout much of the Makua region his paramountcy may not necessarily have meant effective rule. It seems that chiefly dynasties of Maravi origin imposed their hegemony over the disintegrated inland Makua communities and that Maravi raids might be launched on the coastal communities at any time. The Jesuit, António Cardim, who was shipwrecked on the coast just south of Mozambique Island in 1649, records that when news of the wreck reached the Maravi, a raid, no doubt in search of plunder, was mounted against the sheikh of Mogincual who was captured by the raiders.[31]

Muzura and the Kalongas who followed him maintained diplomatic relations with the Portuguese on the Zambesi, and Portuguese traders were allowed to operate to a limited extent in Maravi territory north of it. A trade route, travelled by Gaspar Bocarro in 1616, ran from the Zambesi through the heart of the Maravi kingdoms to Kilwa.

However most of the ivory was traded directly with the residents of Mozambique Island and there were good commercial reasons for this. The trade of the Zambesi was, in the seventeenth century, subject to the monopoly of the captains of Mozambique, and Manuel Barreto, writing in 1667, specifically says that private traders were excluded from the Maravi markets when the captain had agents with trade goods ready to sell. At Mozambique Island, however, the trade was in the hands of the residents (*moradores*) and a better price could be obtained.

Trade was clearly important for the Maravi chiefs and they did their best to control the flow of foreign imports into their country so that these valuable and prestigious products would remain in their own hands to enable them to reward followers and allies. Like other similar African monarchies, the Maravi 'empire' was a hierarchical structure with subordinate chiefs linked to the senior or paramount chief by ties of kinship and the distribution of gifts. Tribute exacted from subjects was redistributed as largesse to those who were loyal or who served the interests of the state. The brief summary account of Gaspar Bocarro's journey through Muzura's kingdom shows how loose the structure of government really was. Having been entertained by Muzura in his capital, Bocarro stayed at a town ruled by a son of Muzura and then passed into country where it was not clear whether Muzura ruled or not. Muzura sent presents to the chiefs to let Bocarro pass, and at one town called Manhanga, the chronicler records, the chief 'gave Bocarro an ivory tusk, and sent Muzura a present of cloths, which he obtains from the coast of Melinde, for this Kaffir also obeys Muzura.'[32] The techniques for centralised control and administration did not exist and such monarchies were decentralised and segmentary. António Gamitto only visited the Maravi chieftaincies in the 1830s, but his account contains a classic exposition of the political relationships in this type of state:

> The Mambos or Fumos, according to their rank, receive Chipatas, or presents for safe conduct, from all traders passing through their lands; fees, or costs, for hearing and judging cases; mouths (*muromos*) and tribute from the land, etc. The only way they spend this is by sharing it out among the people about them, and the more liberal they are, the greater the number of followers, the larger the Muzindas, the stronger their cause and the greater their power. . . . The Fumos pay tribute to the Mambos to whom they are subordinate, and the Mambos pay to Undi.[33]

If gift-giving was important in establishing relationships within the hierarchy of chieftaincies, the internal stability of the Kalonga paramount chieftaincy rested on the relations of the Phiri rulers with the

Banda clan, which may have been the dominant group of a pre-conquest population controlling the territorial cults of the area. At some stage an elaborate compromise was reached by the Phiri and the Banda whereby a Banda princess, entitled Mwali, became the wife of a Kalonga and thus legitimised his rule. This was probably more than merely a political compromise, for this 'ritual' marriage with Mwali was also a process by which the Kalongas gained control of the Banda cults, the spirit wife being transformed into Kalonga's wife.[34]

The chieftaincy of Lundu and its relations with Quelimane

In the second half of the seventeenth century Lundu was recognised as being the second most prestigious Maravi chief after Kalonga. The Lundu chieftaincy rose to power as a result of the Zimba wars of the 1580s which enabled it to establish its dominance over most of the southern Makua and over the northern bank of the Zambesi in its lower reaches. If Lundu's state had been founded by his army of Zimba, its survival came to depend on the control over the Mbona rain cult and over the principal areas of cotton cloth production in the Shire region. Lundu's capital and the principal rain shrine of Mbona lay up the Shire river and it was here also that cotton grew in abundance and that the people produced the *machiras* or strips of woven cotton cloth which were valued in the trade of the region.

The only area north of the Zambesi that did not fall under Lundu's control in the early seventeenth century was the town of Quelimane and its immediate hinterland, and it was here that the Portuguese and the Lundu most frequently came into conflict. João dos Santos, describing eastern Africa as he had known it in the late sixteenth century, says that around Quelimane lived Africans subject to the Portuguese fort. In the immediate vicinity were Makua chiefs and Makua were still controlling some of the Zambesi islands. The estuaries north of Quelimane had small Muslim settlements and both the Muslims and the Makua traded ivory and provisions with the Portuguese. In 1595, however, Santos witnessed the activities of the Zimba in the hinterland of the Quisungo estuary, suggesting that Lundu was asserting his authority on this part of the coast at the time. Maravi pressure continued in the seventeenth century following the victory of Muzura over the Lundu, and by the 1630s Muzura was claiming sovereignty over all the land north of the Zambesi as far as the sea, including Quelimane.

Wherever possible the existing Makua population sought Portuguese protection against Lundu's Zimba and against Muzura's armies. This enabled the Portuguese to claim an informal control over the coast 20 leagues to the north of Quelimane 'as far as Licungo and

Casungo' and for 10 leagues or so inland. In 1634 these territories were probably still under the direct control of the captain of the fort at Quelimane but were soon to be organised as land concessions, or *prazos*. When Manuel Barreto described the situation in 1667, the coastlands north of Quelimane and along the Qua Qua river were leased out to individual Portuguese 'who are bound to assist with their kaffirs in the defence of the *chuambo* [fort] when summoned by the captain.'[35] The Maravi who had 'subjected by force' the chiefs of the Bororo Makua had attacked Quelimane a number of times but had always been beaten back from the fortifications. Not for the last time in Mozambique's history, war and banditry in the interior were to send refugees flocking to the comparative safety of a Portuguese coastal town.

Under the protection of the fort and on the *prazos* of the coast, therefore, a section of the Bororo remained independent of Maravi control, calling themselves 'people of the fort', or Chuabo. In time they came to acquire a distinct ethnic identity and dialect. The 'people of the fort' were to have their counterparts among the populations living in the neighbourhood of all the Portuguese trading posts and parallels are to be found particularly in the Tonga who lived around Inhambane and the Sena people of the lower Zambesi who, like the Chuabo, also took their name from a Portuguese town.

The chieftaincy of Undi

The third Maravi chieftaincy of importance was that which carried the title of Undi. Although this chief is mentioned in seventeenth-century documents as early as 1613, little can be discovered about the history of his kingdom until the eighteenth century. According to the traditions of the Cewa people, Undi had been a close relative of the Kalonga and when the split occurred which caused Undi to depart with his followers, most of the royal lineage accompanied him, including Nyangu, the ritual 'mother' of the Kalongas. It appears that after this all Kalongas were born and brought up at Undi's court and that the throne of the Maravi paramount was filled by one of the ruling lineage of Undi's kingdom. This bizarre arrangement, underlining the largely ritual nature of Kalonga's paramountcy, must have militated against the development of any effective state system. Undi is said to have gained possession of Kaphirintiwa, the legendary home of the Maravi, and eventually to have fixed his capital at Mano north of Tete. Like Kalonga and Lundu, his power came to rely on the control of the local territorial religious cults, but if this strengthened his authority over the pre-existing populations it did little in the long run to counter the fragmentation of political authority, as segments of the ruling lineage continued to break away and establish what were virtually independent chieftaincies. The relations of these chiefs with Undi were based on exchanges of gifts and wives, on the redistribution of tribute and trade goods to clients and supporters, and on a formal recognition of Undi's ritual overlordship.[36]

Portuguese relations with the Maravi

During the sixteenth and seventeenth centuries the region north of the Zambesi did not see any serious political interference or any attempt to establish territorial control on the part of the Portuguese — the sole exception being the region round Quelimane. In the sixteenth century the Portuguese had suffered a number of serious military defeats north of the river and they remained fearful of the military reputation of the Maravi well into the following century. However, this respect for Maravi power did not prevent contacts. Traders entered their country travelling certainly as far as Lake Malawi. Maravi mercenaries were regularly recruited for the Karanga wars and the Portuguese in their turn aided Muzura in establishing his hegemony. It was possible for Gaspar Bocarro to cross the whole Maravi territory en route for Kilwa in 1616, for a number of Portuguese to go to Muzura's court in the 1620s — all of whom, we are told, had a sight of Lake Malawi — and for Theodore Garcia to go to the court of the Kalonga in 1679. But only in the eighteenth century was there any permanent Portuguese penetration of the northern interior.

The explanation for this must lie in the fact that until the eighteenth century no gold was known to exist north of the Zambesi and therefore there was nothing to distract the Portuguese from their efforts to control the Karanga gold fields in the south. During this period it was official Portuguese policy to maintain good relations with the Maravi, to trade ivory with them at Mozambique and in Zambesia, to keep open the road along the north bank of the Zambesi for military purposes and to draw on Maravi manpower. Before the eighteenth century the Portuguese had neither adequate resources nor any compelling reason to embark on military enterprises north of the river or south of it.

Portuguese influence on the formation of the Maravi states was probably crucial in two or three ways. It was the Portuguese who prevented the Maravi expanding across the Zambesi, and the coastal populations round Quelimane from coming under Maravi control. At the same time, it was apparently Portuguese aid which enabled Muzura to gain ascendancy over Lundu and thereby to lay the foundations for the power of the Kalonga chieftaincy in the middle of the century.

It has also been claimed that the ivory trade with the Portuguese diverted the energies of the Maravi into activity 'in no way contributing to the economic development of their own societies'.[37] In the sixteenth and seventeenth centuries there is no evidence at all for this assertion. It is known that at one stage the Kalonga tried to control all ivory trading and that the Maravi traders regularly sought out the most favourable market for their ivory, avoiding whenever they could the trading monopoly which the captain of Mozambique exercised in Zambesia and taking their ivory to the freer market of Mozambique Island. It is clear also that transport problems stood in the way of further development of the ivory trade in the interior north of the Zambesi. This suggests that manpower was not necessarily being diverted from other activities to the carriage of ivory. Finally it is clear that the Portuguese traded with the Maravi in commodities other than ivory, buying from them ironware, copper wire and large quantities of locally produced cotton cloth — *machiras* — as well as food.

The Karanga chieftaincies, the Portuguese settlements on the Zambesi and the Maravi chieftaincies to the north were all engaged in commerce, and to a lesser extent in mining, which linked them with the world of international mercantile capitalism. Important as this was, it must not be forgotten that in the sixteenth and seventeenth centuries the state systems of this region, large as well as small, were not primarily dependent on trade. Political authority was based on extracting tribute from peasants who worked the land and on the redistribution of this tribute to clients and followers. The power to tax trade and mining and control the distribution of imported goods was part of the structure of political power but, as in Europe in the early modern era, societies were still overwhelmingly based on village agriculture and political power rested ultimately on the capacity to control and tax such communities. The long-term evolution towards development or underdevelopment had at this stage less to do with international market forces than with the way that ruling élites in Africa and elsewhere utilised the surplus they extracted from the peasantry.

4

THE PORTUGUESE CONQUEST AND
LOSS OF THE HIGH VELDT

The Portuguese conquest in its context

Events in seventeenth-century Karangaland are brilliantly illumi-
nated by the writings of a whole series of chroniclers and missionaries,
fascinated by the unfolding struggle in the interior and by the hope
that conquest in central Africa would turn the tide for a declining
empire. António Bocarro, the last of the great secular chroniclers of
Portuguese India, devoted one whole section of his work to events in
eastern Africa, while the rivalry of the Jesuits and the Dominicans
prompted the production of a series of documents detailing the rival
claims within what had become a fiercely competitive struggle for conversions. Over the course of a century these chroniclers witnessed and
described the confrontation and ultimate disintegration of two state
systems — the Portuguese *Estado da India* and the Karanga monarchy
of the Monomotapa. With the fall of these state systems, the missionary orders lost any hope of achieving major conquests for the
church, for they had depended for their success on the wealth and
patronage of the one to achieve the conversion of the indigenous ruling
élites of the other.

The decline of these two state systems runs curiously in parallel. As
the central authority of the Portuguese *Estado da India* disintegrated,
power passed first to the fortress captains and then into the hands of
local creole communities, which often had little more than their names
to identify them as Portuguese and distinguish them from the local
population. Likewise, as the Karanga monarchies disintegrated they
broke down into the smaller territorial chieftaincies, centres of power
matching the economic realities of a society organised predominantly
for subsistence agriculture and a localised system of exchange.

In western Europe, and to some extent in India, the growth of mercantile capital was leading to revolutionary developments in agricultural production, technology and industry. The changes brought
about were often profound and disruptive but, as central governments
acquired the capacity to dominate local centres of power, they helped
to create larger state systems and larger areas of economic interdependence. During the seventeenth century there was a possibility that
central Africa would be drawn firmly into the field of developing world

capitalism, in which case a Portuguese colonial state or a strengthened and centralised Karanga monarchy might have emerged. However, for reasons which this and subsequent chapters will explore, this economic revolution never occurred and traditional technologies and small-scale localised systems of production and exchange maintained their hold, and with them survived decentralised, segmented political structures. The seventeenth century was certainly crucial in directing Africa on the path of underdevelopment but this was not, as has so often been argued, because international capitalism made it a peripheral area and controlled its economic relationships. Underdevelopment came about because the technologies and institutions needed to create a modern state failed to implant themselves among either the indigenous Tonga and Karanga or the Portuguese and Afro-Portuguese communities.

The instability of the Karanga monarchy

The monarchy of the Monomotapa had successfully faced the challenge posed by the Barreto expedition in the 1570s and appeared powerful and united. The Portuguese attack had been absorbed by the peoples on the fringes of the Karanga state, the Mongas, the Tavara of the Chicoa region, and the inhabitants of Kiteve and Manica on the eastern escarpment. The Monomotapa had not been seriously affected and there is no suggestion in the Portuguese chronicles of any civil war or factional divisions which the Portuguese might have exploited. The impression remains of a united state under a strong chief. In the last years of the century, however, 'fickle fortune turned her wheel against him, and brought him to a miserable condition'. The Karanga state was invaded by Maravi warbands and its internal weakness and the essential brittleness of Karanga political structures were brutally exposed.

The various Karanga monarchies had a segmentary structure. The ruling dynasties maintained a precarious paramountcy over territorial chiefs whose power was securely based on the spirit cults and on a close control over the subsistence peasant farmers of the villages. This paramountcy was maintained by marriages, by the appointment of the territorial chiefs to important ritual positions within the monarchy, and by a control over traders coming from the coast. For much of the sixteenth century Portuguese and Muslim traders were accommodated through ritual relationships with the Monomotapa of the kind that led to the Portuguese captain being described as the Monomotapa's 'wife', and their trade was channelled through official fairs where it could be taxed. However, by the early seventeenth century the Karanga paramountcy was showing signs of increasing weakness. It is clear that the Monomotapas had not gained control over the spirit cults, that many of the territorial chiefs evaded paying tribute to the centre whenever they could, and that no effective monopoly could be maintained over imports from the coast. The Tonga chieftaincies of the Zambesi valley were the most difficult to control, and by 1600 some of them had already ceased to pay tribute to the Monomotapas and were recognising the overrule of the Portuguese instead.

The first Karanga civil war

In 1597 the Monomotapa died and, although nothing is heard of a disputed succession, it is clear that the opportunity was taken for various rivals to challenge the authority of the new chief, Gatse Lucere. In 1628, some years after Gatse Lucere's death, a Dominican friar recorded that the chief had had only one eye and that the weakness of his position, the number of his enemies and the consequent attempts to dethrone him were partly due to this ritual imperfection.[1] It is perhaps more likely that this story is symbolic and reflects the feelings that were held about an essentially weak monarch after thirty years of civil war and strife.

The year of Gatse Lucere's accession saw Karangaland invaded by two Maravi warbands from across the Zambesi. The invaders had come looking for booty and land, and one of the groups had to be appeased by being granted permission to settle. In 1599 the leader of this warband, Chicanda, rebelled and withstood a siege by the Karanga within his stockade before being forced to flee with his followers. Chicanda, like Mongas a generation earlier, is a figure of a familiar type in the history of Mozambique — leader of a tightly-knit warband, moving rapidly about the country, living off stolen cattle, swelling his numbers with captured women, able when necessary to defy conventional means of attack within a stockade but for the most part outmanoeuvring and outwitting the forces of a slow-moving and cumbersome state. Gatse Lucere successfully defeated this invasion but at considerable cost to his future position. In 1597 and again in 1599 he had called on the Portuguese for aid, and on the second occasion had received help from seventy-five Portuguese musketeers and 2,000 of their armed followers recruited from the captaincies of Sena and Tete. It was to be a costly precedent for 'from that time forth the king allowed the Portuguese to enter his country with guns, a thing which was strictly forbidden by him before'.[2]

The war had also brought to the fore a feud within the Karanga hierarchy. According to the chronicler Bocarro, Gatse Lucere was angry with his army commander, Ningomoxa, for having allowed the first of the invading bands to ravage the country and escape unharmed, and as a result had him killed. However, the commander was a person of importance, ruler of one of the minor Karanga chieftaincies, called Daburia, 'uncle' of the Monomotapa and described as 'second person in the kingdom'. Very likely the events of 1597 merely provided a pretext for the Monomotapa to get rid of a man who may have been a rival or have opposed his succession but, as Bocarro said, 'from his death arose all the evils which afterwards fell upon the Monomotapa, brought about by the relations of Ningomoxa'.[3]

The pattern of the coming years was now set. As the feud among the Karanga chiefs deepened, Monomotapa increasingly came to depend on his Portuguese allies. The dependence weakened him still further as the Portuguese demanded rewards for their assistance, and this use of foreign mercenaries alienated still further the basis of traditional loyalty among the Karanga. The principal dissidents were at first the Tavara followers of Chief Chiraramuro, but when he was killed by a chief loyal to Gatse Lucere, leadership of the opposition passed to Matuzianhe, a man who had allegedly begun life as a cowherd but now declared himself 'king of Mokaranga' and was joined by three other chiefs.[4] Faced by this formidable challenge to his authority Monomotapa turned for help to the Portuguese in Tete and at the fair of Masapa. Although the Portuguese were badly affected by the revolt, which interfered with their trade, they were reluctant to intervene. The factor at Sena refused outright and the Portuguese at Masapa had to be threatened by the Monomotapa before they would turn out with their followers, for they had been assured by one of the dissident Karanga chiefs that the rising was not aimed against them. This cautious attitude, however, soon gave way to a vigorous and determined intervention.[5]

The events so far make it clear that it was a crisis within the Karanga monarchy which precipitated the cycle of civil war. However, as so often happens with war, the original causes get lost as the struggle for power brings about shifts of allegiance and provides the opportunities for upstarts and newcomers to promote their interests in a way that would have been denied them in times of peace. The wars among the Karanga were to provide opportunities for Portuguese penetration and eventual dominance of the Karanga state. However, the Portuguese were not a monolithic political grouping and the rivalries within their camp were to prove every bit as important as the rivalries among the Karanga chiefs. Already by 1600 various competing centres of Portuguese power had emerged. The captaincies of Sena, Tete and Masapa had come to take on some of the characteristics of rival chieftaincies. Each contained households of Portuguese traders with their slaves, and the first two at least levied tribute on large subject populations of Tonga. The jealousies and rivalries of the three Portuguese captaincies mirrored those of the rival Karanga chiefs. The balance of forces was soon to be complicated still further by the struggle for the control of the Zambesi settlements between the local Portuguese and the agents of the increasingly powerful captains of Mozambique backed by the awe-inspiring if shadowy imperial authorities of Goa and Madrid.[6]

The decision of the Portuguese actively to involve themselves in the Karanga civil war stemmed from the unwise decision of Matuzianhe to raid the country adjoining the town of Tete, but intervention was soon to revive the Portuguese ambition, abandoned since the end of the Barreto expedition, to conquer the mines. The leader of the Portuguese traders of Tete, Diogo Simoẽs Madeira, was a man of considerable vigour and daring who had originally been chosen because of his influence and standing among the African population. Madeira raised an armed force among the Portuguese in both Sena and Tete and enlisted large numbers of Zambesi valley Tonga. With the backing of this army, which included a number of musketeers, he soon made it clear that his objectives were wider than the mere restoration of peaceful trading conditions.

In August 1607, in return for providing military assistance, he obtained from Gatse Lucere a formal grant of all the mines in Karangaland — a curious foreshadowing of the famous Rudd concession that led to Cecil Rhodes taking control of the high veldt at the end of the nineteenth century, with consequences almost as momentous for the Karanga.[7] Madeira claimed to believe, along with many other Portuguese, that there were important silver mines somewhere in the country and persisted for the next twenty years in his attempt to locate them. In the pursuit of this African Potosí he showed all the determination of the great Spanish *conquistadores* and, like them, had to contend with royal officials intent on the destruction of independent *conquistador* power. However, there was more to Madeira's quest for the silver mines than the deluded lust for bullion. Obtaining official sanction to search for the mines became a means by which he tried to control the trade of Zambesia and sought to build a personal empire for himself. Besides the grant of the mines, Gatse Lucere agreed that two of his sons would be brought up as Christians in Madeira's household. These children would be hostages for the good behaviour of the chief but there was also the clear intention that at some time in the future a Portuguese-educated Christian line of Monomotapas, singularly beholden to Madeira, would attain the throne.[8]

In 1607 all this still lay in the future, with many years of campaigning and guerrilla warfare in which Madeira's talents as leader of a successful warband flourished. The fighting was spread over a huge area of the dry hilly Zambesi escarpment stretching from Chicoa in one direction to Barue in the other. Much of this country is tinder-dry bush, sandy, rocky and barren. Huge baobabs dominate a desiccated landscape, and human habitations and the growing of crops are concentrated in the river valleys or in isolated pockets of fertile land. Madeira, Matuzianhe and the other warlords operated from fortified strongholds, suffering military disasters and dramatic victories, raiding each other's territory, burning villages, driving off cattle and plundering the scanty wealth of the population. Although the fortunes of the leaders of the different warbands fluctuated, Madeira was to emerge as the dominant warlord of the region, his power based partly on a body of Afro-Portuguese musketeers but still more on the Tonga warriors recruited in the Zambesi valley who became the core of his fighting force. As Bocarro wrote,

> The power of the natives is vastly greater than that of the few Portuguese who are found in the country, but the conditions are now very different from what they were in former times, for we fight them with the same kaffirs with whom they formerly fought us.[9]

In Madeira's army the Tonga, after years of subjection to Karanga rule, found the tables turned and seized the opportunity to plunder their former overlords. Bocarro also commented shrewdly that the Karanga had no skill in siege warfare or in attacking the fortified strongholds of their enemies, while Madeira proved as determined and resourceful in breaching a stockade as in defending one.

Before long Gatse Lucere found himself completely dependent on Madeira. After gaining the cession of the mines, Madeira marched to drive Matuzianhe out of the territory of Inhabanzo, 'which is vast and has many vassals, leaving only the natives who then rendered obedience to Diogo Simoẽs'.[10] The Monomotapa for his part, after initial successes against the dissidents, was tempted to attack the Mongas and Barue and so extend his effective authority beyond the Karanga heartland. This policy proved disastrous: his forces were defeated and Matuzianhe took advantage of the situation to overrun and plunder the Karanga kingdom itself. Gatse Lucere was only saved by Madeira who persuaded him to retreat westwards and winter in Chidema where there were supplies and where Madeira hoped the silver mines were to be found. In 1609, when reinforcements had raised the Portuguese strength to 100 musketeers, Madeira marched to restore Gatse Lucere to his throne. The main fighting was around the *zimbabwe* where Matuzianhe was eventually defeated and murdered on the Monomotapa's orders.

Restored to his throne with Portuguese arms, Gatse Lucere might well have become a puppet with the Portuguese effectively ruling

Karangaland. This did not happen because of the skill with which he extricated himself from their toils and exploited the rivalries that became apparent in the Portuguese ranks with the arrival in 1609 of Nuno Alvares Pereira as the officially appointed *conquistador* of the mines. Replacing one *conquistador* with another more powerful had been a device used by the Spanish crown in the conquest of America, and had Madeira been well-read in history he must have feared that he would suffer the fate of Vasco Nunez Balboa. Perhaps he knew what was in store, for rather than wait to receive the new *conquistador* bearing a royal contract, he departed for the south on a trading expedition.[11]

Pereira did not long enjoy his commission and was succeeded the same year by Estevão de Ataide, whose henchman Diogo Carvalho took command of the Portuguese forces and continued to co-operate with the Monomotapa against the last of the dissidents holding out in the hills near Masapa. Before long, however, the Portuguese came to blows with the followers of the Monomotapa. Apparently on Ataide's orders, they refused to pay the customary present (*curva*) to Monomotapa for the right to trade in the country. Gatse Lucere imposed a trade embargo (*empata*) until it was paid, whereupon Carvalho attacked the local Karanga forces. In the fighting that followed, the Karanga carried out some successful raids on the lands round the town of Tete and the Portuguese were confined to their fortifications. Madeira himself was robbed and was fortunate to escape with his life.

Returning to Tete, Madeira resumed control of the Portuguese forces in the town and quickly reconquered the low veldt region, bringing back to Tete 'great spoils and many captives'.[12] He himself had already secured the chieftaincy of Inhabanzo from the Monomotapa in his earlier campaigns, and it was probably on this occasion that the chieftaincy of Marango fell into Portuguese hands as well. The security of Tete was thus re-established but Ataide refused to make peace or send the *curva* to the Monomotapa. Instead he built a fortress on the Zambesi upstream of Tete and installed some soldiers in readiness for an invasion of Karangaland. This fort and its garrison achieved nothing and in 1613 Ataide was removed from his command and Madeira was once again appointed to lead the Portuguese.[13]

Although Matuzianhe had had a broad-based following and briefly been able to occupy the *zimbabwe*, it is not certain that he had tried to establish himself as the Monomotapa. Bocarro says that he called himself 'king of Mokaranga' but not that he tried to usurp the paramountcy. In fact Matuzianhe looks very much like the type of opportunist — the minor chief, bandit leader and warlord — whose careers are so characteristic of the history of Mozambique. Matuzianhe's following had been made up of dissident headmen and bands of robbers and outlaws, some of whom continued to prey on the trade routes and fairs long after his death.

With Matuzianhe dead, the Monomotapa Gatse Lucere had clearly re-established much of his authority among the Karanga. The Portuguese were preoccupied with their own increasingly bitter disputes, while prestige still attached to the holder of the legitimate title, and the firm line which he had taken with the Portuguese over the payment of the *curva* no doubt helped to restore his prestige. However, his position was certainly weaker than it had been at the start of his reign. Not only had he signed the fateful treaty ceding the mines and allowing the Portuguese to enter his lands with their firearms, but the chieftaincies of Inhabanzo and Marango had passed formally into Portuguese possession and the Portuguese were established in strength as far upstream as Chicoa. Moreover any vestigial claims to levy tribute in Barue or in the Mongas country of the Lupata region had had to be abandoned.

Madeira and the search for the silver mines of Chicoa

Only in 1614 was Madeira himself appointed formally as *conquistador* of the mines and was thus in a position once again to try to secure control of the Chicoa silver mines in which he appeared to believe so firmly. Gatse Lucere had made peaceful overtures to his former ally and Madeira welcomed these, sending the *curva*, reopening trade and wooing the chiefs who controlled the roads from Tete with presents. In May Madeira reached Chicoa and there erected a fort which he called São Miguel (Map 3). The chief of Chicoa acknowledged Portuguese overlordship and then disappeared leaving the mines unrevealed. Madeira patiently sent an embassy to Gatse Lucere who appointed a new chief to Chicoa. The new chief also failed to reveal any mines but continued to provide evidence which kept the Portuguese living in hope and friendly enough to maintain the supply of presents. Throughout 1615 Madeira kept up his search for the silver and let it be known that some ore was being found. No mines, however, were revealed and the continuing presence of Portuguese soldiers at Chicoa caused friction with the local inhabitants who harried the fort and cut off supplies.

It is possible that important mines of silver or other precious metals did exist and that the Monomotapa was pursuing a masterly policy in preventing the Portuguese from discovering their whereabouts, isolating them in the hot, desolate Chicoa country far from the Karanga heartland. However, it seems much more likely that no mines existed at all, and that Gatse Lucere deceived Madeira by getting the local chiefs to bury pieces of ore which were revealed at appropriate

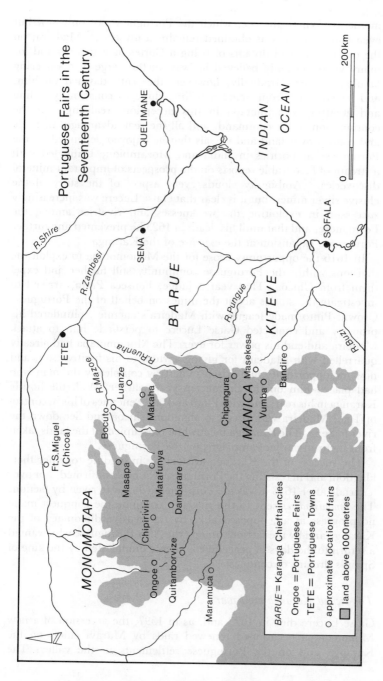

Portuguese Fairs in the Seventeenth Century

200km

INDIAN OCEAN

QUELIMANE

R.Shire

R.Zambesi

SENA

SOFALA

BARUE

TETE

R.Mazoe

R.Pungue

R.Ruenha

KITEVE

R.Buzi

Luanze

Makaha

Bocuto

Chipangura

MANICA

Masekesa

Vumba

Bandire

Ft.S.Miguel
(Chicoa)

Masapa

Matafunya

Chipiriviri

Dambarare

MONOMOTAPA

Ongoe

Quitamborvize

Maramuca

BARUE = Karanga Chieftaincies

Ongoe = Portuguese Fairs

TETE = Portuguese Towns

○ approximate location of fairs

█ land above 1000 metres

moments. Where the ore, which the Portuguese not only saw but even had assayed, was obtained remains a mystery.[14] Madeira, on the other hand had dreams of being a Cortes or a Pizarro and for many years certainly believed he was on the verge of discovering fabulous mines. Gradually, however, the truth dawned on him, and he changed from being a willing dupe to consciously aiding and abetting Monomotapa in this deception, realising that the continuation of his command, and all the real advantages in trade and control over land and vassals that he enjoyed depended on the Portuguese authorities in India and Mozambique being fed with a stream of favourable reports on the prospects of important mineral discoveries.[15] Ambiguity clouds every aspect of the story of the elusive silver mines, but it is clear that Gatse Lucere was increasingly successful in exploiting the weaknesses and rivalries among the Portuguese, and that until his death in 1623 he prevented any further Portuguese expansion at the expense of the Karanga.

In 1616 the opportunity arose for the Monomotapa to exploit the divisions within the Portuguese community still further and expel them from Chicoa. That year a judge, Fonseca Pinto, arrived to investigate the stories about the mines on behalf of the Portuguese Crown. Pinto made league with Madeira's enemies, plundered his property and contacted Gatse Lucere to persuade him to attack Madeira and end his power for ever. The Monomotapa had already quarrelled with Madeira for giving asylum to his fugitive son, and now the opportunity had arisen to destroy completely the man who had placed him on the throne ten years earlier. With the hostile Karanga in his rear, and with Pinto and other enemies of his in control of Tete, Madeira was forced to abandon Chicoa and flee down the river to Sena. The Karanga meanwhile reoccupied all the lands taken from them in earlier campaigns by the Portuguese.[16]

The success of the Karanga aristocracy in holding together their kingdom and in resisting the Portuguese was now confirmed. For over a decade after 1616 it was the Portuguese who were riven by faction. The *conquistadores* sent to the rivers to continue the conquest made no progress at all, opposed alike by the evasive diplomacy of the Karanga and by the factions among the Afro-Portuguese who wanted a return to the days of peaceful commerce unmolested by the king of Spain's dreams of conquest.

The second Karanga civil war

Gatse Lucere died in 1623 and, as in 1597, the accession of a new Monomotapa occasioned renewed raids by Maravi chiefs on the Karanga and on the Portuguese settlements in the valley. The

Portuguese believed this was a bid by the Maravi chief, Muzura, to become Monomotapa and some slight support for this can be found in traditions, reported in the eighteenth century, that the first Kalonga had been born to a daughter of one of the Monomotapas. Muzura, however, did not press home his attacks and in 1624 a new Monomotapa, Inhambo, later called Caprasine 'which signifies the king who flees', was installed.[17]

In 1628 a second war with the Portuguese broke out which was to last until 1632 and was to prove disastrous for the Karanga aristocracy. The war was occasioned by the murder in 1628 of the Portuguese envoy Jerónimo de Barros at the Monomotapa's court, followed by an embargo on trade during which many Portuguese traders were attacked and killed. As might be expected there were deeper reasons for this outbreak. The Portuguese chroniclers maintained that the *curva* had been paid and that the real reason for the war lay in the aggressive activities of the Dominican missionaries. This was indeed a period when the Dominicans were becoming extremely active in the mission field, providing priests for all the Portuguese trading posts and nursing ambitions of spectacular conversions among the Karanga. The struggle which followed did not find a chronicler of the calibre of Bocarro, and records of the events are wildly distorted by the self-glorification of the Dominicans.[18] However, it is clear that the Dominican priests provided the leadership for the Portuguese and that the Portuguese traders and *sertanejos* had to show a common front since they were suffering so severely from the embargo which had been declared on trade. The initiative taken by the Dominicans is best conveyed in the words of the friar, Luís do Espírito Santo:

All the men of that place took advantage of my being in Tete as vicar, and requested me to come to Sena as their representative. . . . I accepted this labour for the love of our Lord and honour of religion. I came to Sena and obtained from the captain and inhabitants the required assistance and . . . went to Masapa where we found the army of the emperor which consisted of a hundred thousand men, and ours not more than fifteen thousand. . . . Our little army attacked this great one, and by the help of God put them to flight. Having obtained this victory we went with our army to Zimbabwe, the court of the king, and there I built a little church and put up a crucifix I had brought with me, and a statue of the Blessed Virgin of the Rosary, dedicating the church to her and calling it 'of the Rosary'. I put an uncle of the conquered king called Mavura in possession of the kingdom, he being the eldest of the other brothers. I made him tributary to the Catholic king.[19]

In a series of campaigns extending into 1629 Caprasine was defeated and driven from his *zimbabwe*, and Mavura, installed as Monomotapa, was duly baptised by the Dominicans who planned through him to achieve the conversion of the whole population. However, not all the Portuguese supported this high-handed kingmaking by the Dominicans and we are told that a faction of the settlers wished to support another Karanga prince against Caprasine. It seems that virtually all the Karanga notables and the Mukomowasha, the prestigious Tonga chief and commander of the Monomotapa's forces, supported Caprasine. There was no repetition of the divisions within the Karanga ruling élite that had precipitated the previous civil war. It is equally clear that the Portuguese won their victory by employing their Tonga vassals and sending cloth to hire mercenary soldiers from the Maravi.[20] Although highly impressionistic, the accounts of the fighting by the Dominican historians, for whom this was a great moment in the history of their Order, suggest that many of the Karanga aristocracy lost their lives fighting for Caprasine.[21] If the natural leaders of the people had indeed been destroyed in this way, it would provide a clear explanation for the Portuguese dominance of the country that was to follow.

Mavura was never universally recognised as Monomotapa and from this time two chiefly descent lines were to claim legitimate right to the title. However, by mid-1629 Mavura was in possession and had been installed on the throne. He submitted to baptism and signed a treaty of vassalage to the king of Portugal. Pieces of paper do not, of course, represent political reality and this treaty stood for nothing if the Portuguese did not physically control the country. However, it did alter the Portuguese attitude to the Karanga chiefs. Up to 1629 the Portuguese had recognised that the Monomotapas were independent monarchs, to be courted by ambassadors, kept sweet by presents and approached for favours. After 1629 the Monomotapa was increasingly treated as a Portuguese client; he was no longer given presents but was expected to pay tribute; there were no more petitions for favours and instead the Portuguese made demands and expected the Monomotapa to conform to their policy. Above all they were now determined to have a decisive voice in the question of succession to the throne.

Yet despite all the Dominican euphoria, the war was far from over. The immediate effect of the treaty had been for a stream of Portuguese traders and adventurers to enter the country. New trading fairs and mining camps were opened, and with their new found freedom of action the Portuguese lorded it over the country. No royal official had been appointed to oversee the vast area that now came under Portuguese control since it was thought this would infringe the trade monopoly of the captains of Mozambique. As a result the captains appointed to command the Portuguese settlements tended to act very much on their own initiative. The Karanga did not accept Mavura, and many of them fled to join Caprasine who appears to have taken refuge across the Zambesi with the Maravi. In 1631 a widespread rising, planned by Caprasine, found the Portuguese and their followers scattered and disorganised. Hundreds of them were killed before the survivors could take refuge within their stockades. This time the rising spread well beyond Karangaland. In Manica the Portuguese were attacked, and more significantly the Maravi, led by Muzura's son, took the opportunity to launch an assault on Quelimane, the Portuguese enclave on the northern shore of the Zambesi whose existence proved so irksome to Maravi prestige.

The Karanga had skilfully exploited the greatest weaknesses of the Portuguese, their lack of any effective central command, shortage of manpower and individualistic and anarchic style of life. Equally skilfully they had built a diplomatic alliance and co-ordinated the attack on all the Portuguese garrisons at once. It is clear also that they singled out the Dominican friars as their principal enemies and two of them, one being Friar Luis himself, were captured and put to death. However, there was one preparation which the Karanga chiefs had omitted to make. They had not acquired firearms or prepared defensive positions. When the Tonga chief, Chombe, had fought Madeira back in 1614 he had made sure he had a large stock of firearms acquired from Madeira's enemies in Sena, and built himself a formidable fortress. Caprasine had no such allies within the Portuguese community and appeared to have no answer to Portuguese firepower once this could be organised against him.

In 1632 Diogo de Sousa de Meneses took over the captaincy in Mozambique. It was a critical time for the *Estado da India* with mounting threats to its survival in Ceylon, Japan, Mombasa and almost every part of the East while the Anglo-Dutch 'fleet of defence' preyed on Portuguese shipping and blockaded Portuguese ports. Sousa de Meneses stated that he would not allow the Rivers of Cuama to be lost as well, and from the depleted reserves of the *Estado da India* brought 200 musketeers. The new governor was to make enemies and would face dismissal. As a consequence there was no chronicler to sing the praises of the man who proved one of the most successful *conquistadores* the Portuguese ever sent to eastern Africa.

Landing at Quelimane he rapidly defeated Muzura's son, then went to Luabo to recruit levies among the Portuguese subjects in the delta. With an army of 2,000 men he marched to Manica, picking up the surviving fragments of the Portuguese community on the way. There he sacked and burnt the capital of Manica, killing the ruling Chicanga and replacing him with a Portuguese nominee. He then marched into Karangaland and, apparently with little loss to himself, utterly destroyed Caprasine's forces there. It is recorded that the battle was fought close to where Caprasine himself had defeated the Portuguese the previous year. Perhaps the chief had remained encamped on the spot, for he apparently made no effort to manoeuvre and his men were shot down by the Portuguese musketeers. Caprasine was not captured and escaped once again across the Zambesi into Maravi territory. However, by the end of 1632 his rebellion had been swept from the field and Mavura once again reigned, even if he did not rule, in *zimbabwe*.

Sousa de Meneses' campaign was undoubtedly a great military triumph but there is an intriguing possibility that in confronting Caprasine Mavura had allies other than the Portuguese. Frey Gaspar de Macedo says that after the campaign the Monomotapa gave the chieftaincy of Entomboe to a Muslim called 'Xarife' (*sharif*) as a reward 'for having helped him in the conflicts'.[22]

The era of Portuguese dominance

The victories of Diogo de Sousa de Meneses opened a period of approximately sixty years in which the Portuguese ruled in Karangaland and dominated the neighbouring chieftaincies. There was to be no further serious military challenge to them till the 1690s. During this time the Karanga chiefs remained officially in charge of their kingdoms and ruled them as vassals of the king of Portugal. The paramount chief, the Monomotapa, paid an annual tribute of three *pastas* of gold and in practice was very much subordinate to the local commanders of the fairs. He had to put up with the presence in the *zimbabwe* of a Portuguese captain and a body of Portuguese troops, nominally there for his own protection but in reality watching and controlling political events at the heart of the Karanga state. He also had to admit the presence of a Dominican priest who acted as his secretary and corresponded with the Portuguese authorities. He himself had to accept Christianity and undergo the ritual of baptism along with his children and members of his household.

When a Monomotapa died, the Dominicans tried to use the presence of Portuguese in the *zimbabwe* to influence the succession to the chieftaincy and make sure that a new Monomotapa favourable to Portuguese interests was installed. On the death of Mavura in 1652, the Dominicans moved quickly to install their candidate, Siti (called by them Siti Domingos) and obtain his official baptism. This succession was not seriously disputed, but when Siti died in 1655 the Dominicans found a problem in repeating their success. Initially their candidate, Dom Afonso, triumphed against his opponent, but he was soon ousted by a rival who came from the other line of Monomotapas and had the backing of a faction among the Portuguese traders as well as the leading Karanga. This succession dispute, in which the candidates were supported by rival Portuguese factions, revealed the powerlessness of the Karanga chiefs, but also represented a high-water mark of Dominican influence. After this the order's pretensions were not only limited by the settlers but frowned on by the viceroys and the Mozambique authorities as well.[23]

The Monomotapas' loss of independence coincided with Portuguese ascendancy in the other Karanga chieftaincies of the escarpment and the northern plateau region. The chieftaincies of Barue, Kiteve and Manica were smaller in size than that of the Monomotapa and were still less able to resist the *sertanejos* with their musketeers and their armies of Tonga and Maravi soldiers.

The chieftaincy of Barue, whose rulers bore the dynastic title of Macombe, was probably already in existence at the time of the Portuguese arrival in eastern Africa. The inhabitants of the chieftaincy were Tonga and their Karanga ruling dynasty appears to have accepted the dominant role of the spirit mediums in the life of the kingdom as the price of retaining power. Barue lay in the escarpment country between Sena and Manica, and throughout its history its chiefs were to become adept at political survival against the ambitions of both the Portuguese and the powerful states of the plateau. Barue's survival was twice seriously threatened in the seventeenth century — in 1607 when Gatse Lucere invaded the country, and in 1657 when it was attacked by the Portuguese *sertanejo*, António Lobo da Silva. On the first occasion the invading Karanga forces were cut off by a rising among the Mongas in their rear, and Gatse Lucere only extricated himself with difficulty. Silva's invasion apparently took place after elephant hunters in his employment had got into trouble. This time Portuguese forces overran the chieftaincy but failed to establish any long-term presence since the captain of Sena supported Macombe and presumably put pressure on Silva to withdraw.[24]

If the Macombes survived, it was less through military prowess than through a policy of co-existence with the Sena Portuguese and the fact that there were no important gold mines or gold fairs within Barue territory and therefore no permanent Portuguese settlements. Barue traded with the Portuguese in ivory, iron, cattle and a little gold, but more significant for their relationship was the fact that the road to the Manica fairs passed through Barue territory and the Portuguese relied on the Macombes to keep it open. The relationship between Macombe and the Portuguese in the early 1630s is described by Bocarro:

He is at peace with the Portuguese, and by a treaty we have made with him, we pay him two *motoros*, or bales of cloth, which we take to his country, and certain cloths which he in courtesy pays for with cows. . . . There is nothing in his kingdom but the said cows, certain *machilas*, which are the cotton cloths of which we have spoken before, and a quantity of iron of which they make hoes, which are used in exchange like small money.[25]

The Macombes, for their part, came to depend on Portuguese recognition to establish their legitimate authority. In the eighteenth and nineteenth centuries a Portuguese ambassador would be present at the installation of a new Macombe, bringing the *madzi manga*, the holy water from Mozambique, without which the ceremony would be incomplete. The origin of this custom is obscure and there is no record of it in the seventeenth century. However, it is recorded that there was a Christian mission in Barue at the end of the seventeenth century. Although it did not make much progress and was severely discouraged by the Macombes, it is possible that it established the practice of ritually baptising the Macombes to which the chiefs found it first expedient, and then essential, to submit, in the same way as the Monomotapas and the kings of Kiteve found similar rituals a *sine qua non* of Portuguese support. For the Barue, however, the *madzi manga* was no alien rite. It was the 'historic medium through which the sacred qualities of kingship were transmitted'.[26]

With Kiteve the Portuguese had had close relations ever since the chieftaincy was established by the Karanga in the early sixteenth century. The Portuguese in Sofala had witnessed the Kiteve establish his rule over the peoples between the Manica mountains and the sea, and had to come to terms with his evident desire to control the trade routes to the interior. The natural disposition of the Sofala Portuguese was to collaborate with the rulers of Kiteve, and Portuguese ambassadors annually took a present to the ruler's court. They regularly attended the important fair at Bandire some 70 leagues into the interior and in the mid-sixteenth century considerable quantities of ivory were reaching Sofala, most of it presumably coming by routes controlled by Kiteve.[27]

In 1575 Vasco Homem's attempt to conquer the gold mines of Manica brought a Portuguese army to Kiteve's country. The chronicler, Diogo do Couto, states that Kiteve believed that if the Portuguese conquered Manica, gold would be sold directly in fairs under Portuguese control; thus he offered resistance and the Portuguese army sacked and burnt his *zimbabwe*.[28] However, Manica had no mines which Homem thought worth conquering, and on his retreat he signed a treaty with Kiteve which was to stabilise relations for the next sixty years. In exchange for an annual payment of 200 rolls of cloth, Portuguese traders would be free to enter and cross the lands controlled by the chief, paying him in addition one bale for every twenty they traded. This identity of interest and close collaboration between the Karanga chief and the Portuguese was sealed by a regular exchange of ambassadors.

Kiteve was not directly affected by the Portuguese wars against the Monomotapa in the early seventeenth century and did not join in the general rising against the Portuguese in 1631. The reason for this may lie in the traditional hostility between the chieftaincies of the Kiteve and the Monomotapa, but more probably it reflected increasing Portuguese influence within the Kiteve state. Already by the turn of the century individual Portuguese were established in positions of importance within the chieftaincy, and in 1631 a report refers in passing to a Portuguese nominee occupying the Kiteve throne in the face of the rightful chief. This intervention in the Kiteve succession must pre-date the 1631 rising and no doubt explains why the Kiteve was quiet when virtually the whole of the rest of the region joined the war against the Portuguese.[29]

This Portuguese nominee was probably Kiteve Peranhe. In 1633 he is referred to as paying tribute to Portugal, and the precariousness of his position was emphsasised when in the 1640s he had to call on the Portuguese to protect him.[30] The protection took the form of armed intervention by the most powerful of the Sena settlers, Sisnando Dias Bayão, who demanded as a reward the cession of Gobira, the whole northern part of the Kiteve kingdom. This vast district, which came to form the *prazo* of Cheringoma, was henceforward lost to the Kiteve chieftaincy which as a result was greatly weakened both in prestige and in material resources.[31] The rulers were now more than ever clients of the Portuguese. The Dominicans established a mission within the kingdom and princes of the ruling lineage were sent out of the country to receive their education. One of these, christened Dom Lanzarote, married a Christian wife and may even have travelled to Portugal before petitioning in 1681 to return to his native land.[32] Further intervention in Kiteve occurred in the 1690s, and once again this may have been a move by the Portuguese to prevent the chief joining in the war on the plateau which was destroying the Portuguese hold on the country. The reigning Kiteve was deposed and a Portuguese nominee was, once again, placed on the throne. This time, however, the legitimate chief rallied support and drove the Portuguese back to their coastal strip near Sofala, thereby re-establishing a modicum of independence. However, Kiteve never recovered the lands lost to Bayão sixty years earlier.[33]

Portuguese relations with Manica followed a somewhat similar pattern, although the existence of rich gold reefs stimulated them to a much more active intervention and to several attempts to exploit the mineral wealth directly themselves. The Manica gold fields had been one of the two major objectives of Barreto's expedition and they had been reached after Homem's march through Kiteve in 1575. Chicanga had showed the Portuguese their simple gold extraction techniques and Homem concluded that unless a major investment was made in machinery and crushing mills, the gold was best obtained by trade. The treaty signed with the Chicanga before the army withdrew allowed the Portuguese traders access to the gold fairs and, in the years immediately following, considerable numbers of them made their way to the Manica mountains. Some of them came to trade at the official fairs, but it is also clear that some obtained concessions to mine for themselves and established private gold fairs or mining camps in the country under their own, not Chicanga's, control.

In 1631 Chicanga had been persuaded to join the rising against the Portuguese and had received the main brunt of Sousa de Meneses' counterattack the following year. An army advancing from Sena, presumably along the road through Barue, burnt the chief's capital and captured and executed the chief himself. The Portuguese then baptised and installed their own nominee and continued their victorious march into Karangaland. The ruler of Manica now had to pay an annual tribute of three *pastas* of gold, and for the rest of the seventeenth century the Chicangas were effectively puppets of the Portuguese.

In the 1630s there were three principal Portuguese settlements in the country and some fifty traders (Map 3). Chipangura, later renamed Masekesa, was the site of the main fair, still nominally under the control of the Chicanga. The fair had a Portuguese captain and a resident priest. The second settlement was in Matuca, reckoned to be the richest of all the gold-producing regions. It was a private mining and trading enterprise established by a *sertanejo* called João da Costa. The third settlement was at Vumba where there was a fair frequented by the traders from Sofala.[34] This fair was later abandoned when Portuguese traders lost interest in attending.[35] Portuguese dominance over Manica was to be spectacularly ended when the victorious Rozvi army sacked Masekesa in 1695. Thereafter trade continued but under conditions that made the Portuguese clearly subordinate to the control of the Manica kings, backed by the ever-present threat of fresh intervention from the Rozvi.[36]

Immediately to the west of Manica was the Karanga chieftaincy of Maungwe ruled by chiefs who carried the dynastic title of Makone. It is likely that after the campaign of Sousa de Meneses, Maungwe became tributary to Portugal. The Dominican Frei Gaspar de

Macedo, one of the priests in Manica, reported that the land was rich in gold, copper and iron and that there were many traders in the chieftaincy exchanging cloth for gold. However, he also says that 'Makone does not want digging to be carried out so much as in the Manica kingdom'. Whatever the reason, Maungwe probably remained marginal to Portuguese interests in the seventeenth century, although it was there that Portuguese armies confronted the growing power of Changamire in 1683.[37]

The impact of the Portuguese on African society

The first Portuguese attempt to conquer the plateau between 1569 and 1575 was made with an army four times larger than the one with which Pizarro overthrew the empire of the Incas. Its failure was complete, and to military failure had to be added diplomatic defeat in the negotiations with Monomotapa and Chicanga. However, the three decades that followed brought important changes in the balance of power in the region. Portuguese commercial infiltration of both the Karanga and the Manica areas grew, and the chiefs of these regions and of the regions through which the Portuguese had to pass became increasingly involved with this commerce and dependent on it. At the same time the Maravi arrived on the north bank of the Zambesi and began their raids across the river and their attempts to settle. The Karanga beat them off but only with Portuguese military help which increased the collaboration and mutual dependence of the Karanga aristocracy and the Portuguese *sertanejos*.

A more important development was the growing Portuguese hold on the Zambesi valley, in particular the lands in the delta and in the immediate vicinity of their trading towns of Sena, Tete and Quelimane. Portuguese rule over the Tonga chieftaincies of the valley never became totally secure but by the early seventeenth century they had established their paramountcy over the majority of the Tonga population. This gave them access to large reserves of manpower and supplies of food, locally-produced cloth and iron implements, all of which they received as tribute from the Tonga villages. Through intermarriage with Tonga women, a class of Afro-Portuguese came into existence and by the middle of the seventeenth century the Portuguese settlements on the Zambesi were largely self-sufficient and had become a relatively secure base from which to mount a fresh, and this time more successful, attempt to conquer the high veldt.

The effect of these conquests on the plateau chieftaincies and peoples was, in the long run, not as revolutionary as could be imagined. Certainly the most important consequence was the irreversible decline in the prestige of the Monomotapa chieftaincy. The

Portuguese had made the control of this Karanga chieftaincy the main objective of their policy, having deluded themselves that the Monomotapa held some kind of imperial sway over the other major kingdoms of the region and that there were silver mines which he could reveal to them. By 1632 they had succeeded in reducing the Monomotapa to the status of a client chief only to see the former prestige and influence of the chieftaincy evaporate before their very eyes. Portuguese interference in succession disputes and their practice of forcing the Monomotapas to be baptised and to allow their children to be educated by the Portuguese alienated the Karanga aristocracy and, perhaps more important, the spirit mediums whose power was so important in the localities. By the end of the seventeenth century it was only the Portuguese who still tried to uphold the paramountcy of the Monomotapa chieftaincy; for the vast majority of the Karanga this role had now passed to the chiefs of Butua in the south who had maintained their independence of the Portuguese *sertanejos*. In the eighteenth century, although the Monomotapa chieftaincy survived, it became still further weakened by perpetual feuding among the rivals for the chiefly title, until it ceased to have any political or institutional significance.

The decline in the Monomotapa chieftaincy was partly economic. Until Mavura was forced to sign the humiliating treaty of vassalage in 1629, the Monomotapas had retained wide economic control over their territory. The Portuguese had had jurisdiction within their fairs, and then only in the name of the chief; they were not free to travel or trade at will, and paid taxes to the Monomotapa. The chief clearly controlled gold production, taxing output and determining which mines were to be worked. He also enjoyed the profits of justice and received a handsome annual present from the Portuguese to oil the wheels of commerce. Similar economic privileges were enjoyed by the Kiteve, Macombe, Chicanga and possibly other Karanga kings. Thus the chiefs were able to maintain the clientship system that cemented the clan-based segments of the 'little society' together into a large state. The chief was able to dispense patronage, providing his followers with prestige imports, wives and lands and so maintained the reciprocal relationships on which chieftaincy depended.

Much of this economic base was damaged or destroyed during the wars with the Portuguese. After 1629 the Portuguese travelled about the plateau and traded at will; they usurped lands, seized women to reward their Tonga followers and forcibly recruited labour. They opened their own gold diggings and the number of fortified fairs and mining camps multiplied, many apparently being privately owned. However, what underlined the economic decline of the Monomotapas most starkly was that the annual present (*curva*) ceased to be sent and was replaced by an annual tribute which they had to pay to the Portuguese.

There is some evidence that the Portuguese appreciated how they were weakening the chieftaincy that they had expended such effort to control. The installation of a permanent garrison at the *zimbabwe*, first provided in 1613, was intended to strengthen the Monomotapa, while there was a proposal to replace the *curva* by giving him the personal right to import cloth duty-free.[38] It is not known how long the Monomotapa had this privilege. If he ever did so at all, it would have made him simply a privileged trader within his own kingdom and no longer the dispenser of gifts and patronage like his ancestors — a subtle but significant alteration in the nature of chieftaincy.

Once the Portuguese had acquired freedom of access to the Karanga, Manica and Kiteve chieftaincies, their main concern was the extraction of gold. By the mid-century they had acquired detailed knowledge of the gold reefs of the plateau. They knew that gold was painfully extracted from small diggings, and no longer expected to find gold mines that could be exploited on a large scale. To obtain the gold they established fairs at many points throughout the country, branching out from the three of Luanze, Bocuto and Masapa originally established under the Monomotapa's control in the previous century. Fairs were set up at Makaha, Quitamborvize, Dambarare and Ongoe all of which, as well as being centres for the trading of gold, were mining camps where the Portuguese tried their hand at the direct extraction of gold, commandeering labour from the Karanga villages to work the reefs (Map 3).

As the century progressed the gold mining and trading frontier moved southwards. Portuguese *sertanejos* began trading for gold in Maramuca and at least one expedition was sent into Butua.[39] These southern expeditions probably stemmed from the realisation that much of the easily worked gold in the north had already been extracted but that gold fields further south were still waiting to be exploited. However, the Portuguese were also following the population, for it seems that many Karanga abandoned the northern areas controlled by the Portuguese to avoid their lawless exactions. As the population moved south, the Portuguese followed.

By the middle of the seventeenth century the Portuguese in the Zambesi valley had already assumed many of the functions of chiefs towards the Tonga population, but it is not clear whether they attempted to do the same thing to the Karanga of the plateau, or whether they succeeded in providing alternative social and economic structures to replace the authority of the chiefs which they had done so much to weaken. The Monomotapa complained in his official letters that his people were being lured away from their allegiance, and there are also records of the Portuguese abducting and marrying women of the chiefly families. In 1645 the Monomotapa protested to the viceroy about the 'great outrage in taking captive his subjects without any just title, and they are not content with taking humble people but even the sons and daughters of chiefs, some by force, others by deception giving them cloth saying that they want them for wives . . .'[40] In the light of their behaviour elsewhere, this suggests that the Portuguese may have been seeking to acquire a sort of chiefly legitimacy to support an authority otherwise rather precariously based on their bands of Tonga warriors. However, the Portuguese Crown never granted titles to any of the private conquests on the plateau and these lands never formed part of the *terras da coroa* like the conquests in the Zambesi valley.

If the exact nature of Portuguese relations with the plateau peoples is somewhat obscure, one thing is clear. No significant number of Portuguese colonisers entered the country and, unlike in the Zambesi valley, no viable Afro-Portuguese community was to evolve. Although they had established political control over large tracts of country with rich gold mines and eminently suitable for agriculture, there was no repetition of the successful Spanish peopling of South America. European institutions were not transplanted, nor did European technology and material culture take root. Indeed the trend was all the other way. Later in the century, the number of Portuguese in the country declined. Portuguese institutions, fostered with some vigour in the early days of the conquest, atrophied and virtually disappeared; European material culture existed in the form of firearms, a few luxury imports and the accoutrements of the churches, but in everyday domestic life and the technology of production it was the Portuguese who largely adopted African material culture and African ways. Moreover, in spite of their vigorous efforts, the Dominican missionaries made few converts, even among the immediate retainers of the Portuguese warlords who lived in the fairs or followed them on their king-making expeditions.

There was no repetition of the conversion of the American Indians or even of the establishment of the royal Christian cult in the kingdom of Kongo. The failure of the Dominicans to establish a local church is in marked contrast to contemporary developments in the Kongo kingdom. There, Christianity was adopted by the kings and the Mwissicongo aristocracy as a rival to the territorial cults which were not under their control. Superficially there seems no reason why a similar development could not have taken place among the Karanga, since the cults administered by the spirit mediums all seem to have escaped effective control by the Karanga chiefs. One reason may have been the deliberate attempt of the Dominicans to keep tight control of the church in eastern Africa. The policy pursued by the order was to secure the education of the young Karanga princes, some of whom were sent to Goa and Portugal, and to make sure that its members had the sole right to serve the churches in Karangaland and act as secretaries to the chiefs. Such a policy, they believed, was necessary to keep at bay the rival order of Jesuits who were well-established in the Zambesi settlements and who were waiting for any opportunity to become active in the high veldt as well. It also prevented the emergence of a local African or Afro-Portuguese priesthood such as existed in the Kongo kingdom. Whatever the reason, the failure of the Dominicans to found a church is part of a wider failure of the Portuguese to establish a permanent presence in Karangaland.[41]

If the failure of the Portuguese to make a significant impact in the interior is partly explained by the peculiar character of the trade monopoly of the captains of Mozambique, it is also partly the result of the social and economic institutions of the African peoples with whom they had to deal. In the Karanga chieftaincies, and still less in the fragmented society of the Tonga, there were no nerve centres of political power which could be paralysed by decisive military action. As the Portuguese discovered, even the capture of the Monomotapa and his *zimbabwe* achieved little towards the control of the country. Nor were there great accumulations of treasure to be plundered, such as would have attracted numerous adventurers and settlers to the country. Indeed the wealth of Africa, whether in the form of gold, ivory, cloth, slaves, skins or base metals, was best extracted by a few traders prepared to work through the long-established trading networks which tapped sources of wealth widely dispersed through central Africa. The gold was indeed there in large quantities but scattered in thin, broken and easily exhausted reefs best exploited by the labour of villagers devoting time in the interstices of the agricultural seasons. Individual warlords could sometimes grow rich by extracting surplus product from subject Tonga peasants, but the African population was too small and its agriculture too poor to support a large class of *encomenderos* as in Mexico or Peru.

At every turn the Portuguese in east Africa conspired to exclude new settlers and royal officials, and sought to monopolise the wealth of the region for themselves. The captain of Mozambique with his trade monopoly, the handful of great *prazo*-owners on the Zambesi, the captains of the trading fairs and the bush traders mounting long expeditions in search of copper or ivory, all had one thing in common; they opposed closer royal control which would have meant regulation and taxation, and had no wish to share the profits of their African enterprise with settlers from outside. In this they could make common cause with the African chiefs and with the peasants and headmen under Portuguese control. These common interests turned gradually into a mutual interdependence between the old Afro-Portuguese settlers and the African population — leading the Portuguese to adopt African economic, social and even religious practices at the expense of the implantation of alien and disruptive cultural forms.

In the Zambesi valley this mutual dependence achieved some stability as the *prazos* gradually acquired the identity and permanence of effective chieftaincies. However, it is clear that by the end of the century there was no such stability on the plateau. The lack of effective royal authority led to Karangaland being divided between a number of warlords who dominated it very much at will, competing with each other and leaving the whole Portuguese enterprise vulnerable and dangerously exposed. This had been the obvious lesson from Caprasine's well-planned rising of 1631, but the Portuguese learned no lessons, and as the southward drift of the Karanga population gradually built up the strength of Butua, the Portuguese were left controlling fairs and mining camps which were isolated settlements in a depopulated and increasingly impoverished countryside. In the eventual struggle with Butua, the Portuguese were hopelessly weakened and no longer had the ability to respond to a challenge as they had in the 1630s.

Butua and the destruction of Portuguese power on the Plateau

Butua was ruled by the Torwa dynasty who were related to the ruling dynasty of the Monomotapa state. The full extent of Butua authority is unknown. The Portuguese sometimes described it as including Manica and certainly it extended south and west through the region later called Matabeleland. It was in Butua that the tradition of stone building survived and entered a new phase of development with the construction of the impressive buildings at Dhlo Dhlo, Nalatali and Khami in the seventeenth and eighteenth centuries. Butua was believed to be rich in gold and was known to seventeenth-century Portuguese as the *mae d'ouro*, the mother of gold. However, it is likely that the power of the Torwa chiefs lay as much in their cattle herds as in the gold trade.

In the early 1640s there had been a major Portuguese incursion into Butua. A succession dispute had led to one of the claimants coming to Manica to seek Portuguese aid. In Manica at the time was Sisnando Dias Bayão, the most powerful *sertanejo* of his day. He had responded to the call, sensing the kind of opening that had led the Spanish *conquistadores* to their dramatic conquests in America, led a force of musketeers southwards and placed his protégé on the throne, building a fort in the country and leaving a garrison. Bayão himself returned north where he was assassinated, and it appears that the Portuguese presence in Butua died with him. A decade later another significant incursion into the south was led by an adventurer called Gonçalo João who seized control of a region called Maramuca, apparently a Tonga enclave bordering on Butua.[42] Like Bayão before him, João built himself a fort but lost out in the bitter settler feuds which were then weakening the Portuguese community. Thereafter the Portuguese made no further incursions into the south and the Butua kingdom probably became a major refuge for Karanga fleeing the anarchy of the northern plateau.

By the 1680s the strength of Butua was such that it was extending its authority northwards and probing with raids towards the area of Portuguese control. According to the Portuguese chronicler António da Conceição, the ruling Torwa dynasty was overthrown by a neighbouring chief with the title of Changamire. The latter was apparently a minor Karanga chief who had been granted land in the south by the Monomotapa and built up an impressive reputation as a soldier and a 'magician'. He and his followers called themselves Rozvi and used the resources of the southern chieftaincy to raid the Portuguese-held regions in the north.[43] In the first of these attacks, in 1684, a Portuguese force was worsted in a battle in Maungwe. There was a further setback when the Monomotapa, possibly urged by the Portuguese, tried to invade Butua and end the threat that this new chieftaincy was posing. Monomotapa's forces were routed and the Portuguese were powerless to come to his aid.

The attack on the major Portuguese strongholds in Karangaland and Manica came in 1693. As so often in African politics, the occasion for this war was a disputed succession, this time to the Monomotapa's title. The Portuguese candidate for the throne, who bore the baptismal name of Dom Pedro, failed to establish himself in the face of his rival, Nhacunimbiri, who managed to occupy the *zimbabwe*. Fifty years earlier such a reverse would have led to a Portuguese military expedition arriving to place Dom Pedro on the throne. However, the Portuguese bided their time, apparently in order not to disturb the activities of the traders in the interior. Nhacunimbiri began to act more and more independently, and the situation in the *zimbabwe* became very tense with the Portuguese captain and his men daily having to confront the hostile chief and his supporters within the stockade. Inevitably Nhacunimbiri sought allies and turned to Changamire for help. In November 1693 the Rozvi invaded Karangaland and struck at the principal Portuguese fair at Dambarare. Taken wholly by surprise, the Portuguese were killed and the fair was destroyed. The other fairs and mining camps were quickly evacuated, and the Portuguese who survived retreated precipitately to the Zambesi settlements.[44]

There a counterattack was organised. As Portuguese reinforcements trickled in, the local settlers combined with Dom Pedro to defeat Nhacunimbiri and to reoccupy the *zimbabwe*. This success did not, however, herald a repetition of the victory of Sousa de Meneses sixty years earlier, and in 1695 there followed a fresh reverse. As the Portuguese prepared to try to reoccupy Karangaland, the Rozvi forces descended on Manica and sacked the Portuguese settlements there, sending refugees scurrying back to Sena and throwing the Rivers again into confusion. Almost simultaneously a rising in Kiteve destroyed the precarious Portuguese control within that state as well. Further disasters were avoided by the death of Changamire but the Rozvi remained in control of the plateau and the Portuguese and their Monomotapa puppets were never to regain a foothold in the area which they had controlled for so long. Rozvi hegemony on the plateau remained undisputed throughout the eighteenth century, and although the Portuguese were able to trade with the peoples of the high veldt through the fairs at Manica, at Zumbo near the junction of the Luangwa and the Zambesi, and through the port of Inhambane in the south, a real barrier had been raised to their expansion. East central Africa became effectively divided into two spheres of influence which for the first time sketched in vague outline the lines along which this part of Africa was to be partitioned in the late nineteenth century.

5

GOVERNMENT OF MOZAMBIQUE

A murder and its reasons

In January 1618 a vivid and violent incident took place outside the fortress of São Sebastião on Mozambique Island. A ship arrived from Mombasa carrying the former captain of Mozambique, Ruy Melo de Sampayo, who had come to reclaim his right to the captaincy. He was accompanied by Diogo da Cunha de Castelo Branco, a judge of the high court in Goa, and had with him some soldiers. Ruy Melo was met by the acting captain, Salvador Vaz de Guerra, who was also accompanied by a guard of soldiers. As the two parties approached one another, Vaz de Guerra was about to hand over the keys of the fortress, whereupon Ruy Melo's son stepped forward and stabbed him. While still living, Vaz de Guerra was dragged away and hanged.[1]

The complex relationships underlying this crime can be traced back to the early years of the century when Ruy Melo bought the position of captain of Mozambique from Dona Beatriz de Castro. Having presumably paid good money for his post, he was then prevented from occupying it by the appointment of Dom Estevão de Ataide in 1609 to the post of General of the Mines of Monomotapa and captain of Mozambique for four years. Ataide's contract conceded to him immense privileges and was highly contentious, emboldening Ruy Melo to claim damages for loss of his office. While the case was still pending, the Crown acted to deprive Ataide of his post and to restore Ruy Melo in 1612.[2] However, Ruy Melo's appointment had been made directly from Lisbon and because he could not sail immediately, the viceroy proceeded to appoint his own brother as a stopgap. Ruy Melo eventually left Lisbon in 1614, and arrived in Mozambique to find himself at the centre of bitter political quarrelling. He brought royal letters which refused the request of the Mozambique residents that their town should be given the status of a city; he also brought decisions unfavourable to the Jesuits in their struggle with the rival Dominican order. However, his biggest problem arose from the fact that he had come direct from Portugal and did not bring trade cloth with him from India. Without cloth Ruy Melo would be unable to run the captaincy and he apparently began to requisition stocks that were in the hands of the residents. There were also rumours that he embezzled the funds of the Misericórdia (an important charitable institution) on a large scale.[3]

To resolve these complaints a judge, Fonseca Pinto, was sent from Goa with an officer, Salvador Vaz de Guerra, who was given a commission to take over the captaincy. Fonseca Pinto sailed from Goa in 1616 and hearing of his imminent arrival a mutiny broke out in the garrison of the fortress. Ruy Melo seized and executed the ringleaders but a number of the mutineers fled the fortress. When Fonseca Pinto landed, Ruy Melo shut himself in the fortress and barred the gate to the judge. Eventually someone inside the fortress opened a postern and the judge made his way to Ruy Melo's quarters and served the papers of dismissal on him. Vaz de Guerra and his men immediately took over the captaincy and sent Ruy Melo back to Goa. Fonseca Pinto had brought a shipload of cloth with him from India and now proceeded to use the authority conferred on him by the viceroy to make a fortune for himself by usurping the royal trade monopoly. His scandalous conduct played into Ruy Melo's hands and it was not long before the viceregal council in Goa was persuaded once again to reinstate him in his captaincy and to send with him another judge, Diogo da Cunha de Castelo Branco.[4]

Castelo Branco reached Mozambique first and used his commission to order the arrest of Fonseca Pinto. The latter, however, bribed the captain, Vaz de Guerra, to have him released and to imprison Castelo Branco instead. The weak and foolish Vaz de Guerra agreed to do this and then accepted a further bribe from Castelo Branco to allow him to escape to Mombasa. There in Mombasa the judge and Ruy Melo tried Vaz de Guerra *in absentia* and condemned him to death. In December they assembled some soldiers, embarked for Mozambique, and the murder already described was perpetrated.

Ruy Melo was at last able to occupy his captaincy, but his troubles were not at an end. The Crown continued to suspect him of massive embezzlement. In 1620 it tried to sequestrate his property in order to recover the balance of the estate of Estevão de Ataide who had died in Mozambique. The viceroy was still attempting to obtain this money in 1626. Eventually in 1622 Ruy Melo served out his term of office and, like all holders of captaincies, had to submit to a *residencia* or judicial inquiry. This investigated the old claim for the property of the deceased embezzled from the Misericórdia and ordered it to be repaid from Ruy Melo's property.[5]

The problems surrounding Ruy Melo's tenure of the captaincy stretched over almost two decades. Such controversies were not unusual and were the natural concomitants of the system of proprietorial office-holding. The murder was somewhat exceptional, but if the Overseas Council in Lisbon might have been dismayed by such an incident, it would not have been wholly surprised, for by the seventeenth century bitter faction struggles between rival captains and their retainers had become commonplace. However, these violent events were not just meaningless personal feuds but evidence of a system of authority that was breaking down or, at least, failing satisfactorily to adjust the interests of the various dominant groups in society any longer. A deep fissure had been revealed in the social and governmental structure of the *Estado da India*, and Mozambique, as one of the richest and most important of the captaincies, lay directly along this fault line.

The captaincy of Sofala

The captaincy of Sofala (later the captaincy of Mozambique and Sofala) had been created in 1505 at the time of Francisco de Almeida's viceroyalty and formed part of a coherently planned system of government established for the newly-created *Estado da India*. On paper the Portuguese eastern empire was to be a unified bureaucratic structure reflecting the centralist tendencies to which rulers in Renaissance Europe were prone. The king of Portugal claimed extensive rights and powers including a trade monopoly over a variety of eastern commodities such as pepper, cinnamon, horses, gold and ivory; the right to issue safe conduct passes to all shipping in the Indian Ocean and levy customs duties; and the complete control over the church in the East even to the extent of making ecclesiastical appointments and levying the tithe. Such sweeping powers were to be administered east of the Cape of Good Hope by a viceroy — an Aragonese title indicating that the holder was the king's *alter ego* in the East.

From 1530 the capital of the *Estado da India* was fixed in Goa where a bureaucracy grew up commensurate with the extensive powers claimed by the king. A high court (*relação*) heard cases on appeal and was used to hold judicial inquiries (*residencias*) into the conduct of higher officials. A Board of Trade handled the increasingly complex commercial affairs of the empire, and a Board of Conscience dealt with ecclesiastical matters. Portuguese who came out to serve in the *Estado da India* were enrolled as soldiers at Goa or took up salaried posts in the Crown's service. Ships were built or repaired in the dockyard and all vessels coming from Europe had to call at Goa, which thus became a substantial commercial, industrial and financial centre. Finally, Goa was also a religious capital; its archbishop was head of the church throughout the East and the city was the centre for the activities of the Inquisition and all the missionary Orders.[6]

However, what at first sight might resemble a modern centralised bureaucracy looks on closer examination more like the personalised rule typical of medieval microstates. Within this formal bureaucratic shell lived forms of social life better described as bastard feudalism or clientship. Those who held real power and provided the motor force of politics were the viceroys, archbishops and senior officials of the empire whose households of retainers were supported by the profits of office-holding, booty and private trade. Things happened if one of the great *fidalgos* of the *Estado da India* willed them to happen and, whatever royal office they might hold, men survived in the East by attaching themselves to the persons of the great.[7] The networks of patronage soon captured all the official posts in the empire, and the factors, secretaries and other officials became clients of the leading Portuguese nobles. Meanwhile, beneath the personalised rule of the *fidalgo* families, the castes of India, the different ethnic trading communities, and the slaves and servants of the Portuguese made Goa into yet another Indian city dominated by militaristic foreign overlords.

Outside the city-state of Goa, the empire was geographically fragmented. Although called a 'state', the *Estado da India* existed largely without population or territory, in some respects almost a metaphysical state, consisting of abstract rights and claims — claims to control trade or the right to navigation, claims to spiritual jurisdiction over all Catholics, claims to sovereignty of the seas — claims often independent of any physical structure of authority. In some areas the *Estado da India* might be simply Indonesian or Indian traders sailing with a Portuguese *cartaz*, or remote communities of Tamil or Moluccan Christians looking to the spiritual authority of a Portuguese bishop in Malacca or Cochin, or a Luso-Asiatic trading community living under the safeguard of treaties made by Goa with local potentates.[8] However, this metaphysical state had some outlying centres of real authority. There were the fortresses established to uphold and protect the commercial monopolies of the Crown, which were often many weeks' voyage from Goa and many months' from Lisbon. Inevitably their captains were accorded extensive authority in practice uncontrolled by the bureaucratic specificities of their *regimentos* (instructions).

In 1530 the captain of Sofala became the captain of Mozambique and Sofala, a change of title recognising the primacy of the former settlement over the latter. He controlled the ships, forts and settlements south of Cape Delgado as far as the Cape of Good Hope. At Sofala he was head of a military establishment officially numbering sixty persons and consisting of an *alcaide-mor* (commander of the fort), a *meirinho* (bailiff), clerks, soldiers, a surgeon, priests, armourers and artisans. He was responsible also for the royal trading factory which was supposed to handle the commerce in the two royal monopolies of gold and ivory. Within the factory he was able to appoint a deputy to act as factor, and there was a hierarchy of clerks and other personnel. There was also a judicial hierarchy with an *ouvidor* (judge) responsible to the captain. After the building of Fort São Sebastião, a similar establishment was created on Mozambique Island which at the end of the sixteenth century had an *alcaide* in charge of the fortress who also acted as factor, a judge (*ouvidor*), a doctor to serve in the hospital, a barber-surgeon, a constable (*condestabre*), two priests, artisans and soldiers, the whole establishment numbering seventy-one. These were all salaried posts, but in practice the establishment came to resemble a nobleman's household administration rather than a permanent bureaucracy, for the offices of the captaincy were filled more and more by the captain's 'men', his relatives or members of his personal following.[9]

When Francisco Barreto's expedition was sent out to east Africa in 1569, Mozambique was detached from the control of the viceroy and became an independent governorship. However, it reverted to the control of Goa when the army was eventually withdrawn in 1575. This was exceptional. The normal practice was for the captains of Mozambique and Sofala, like the viceroy himself, to be appointed only for three years. This was thought to be an essential means of exerting some form of control over these potentially powerful and independent grandees, for any longer period of office created a possibility that royal authority might be completely usurped. At the end of his three-year term a captain would have to seek another posting, and his previous conduct in office would weigh heavily in any decision made by the Crown. Moreover he might have to undergo a *residencia*, or judicial inquiry, into his conduct. A further check on the captain's activities was provided by the long waiting-list of appointees queuing to occupy the office, men not overly sympathetic to the actions or reputation of the incumbent captain. Since Mozambique was one of the most valuable and prestigious captaincies, many influential men were waiting to hold the office.

The system of making appointments for three years may have provided some notional check on the conduct of the captains, but it soon came to have a decisive influence on the whole development of the *Estado da India*, and not least on the development of Mozambique itself. What appeared at first sight to be a bureaucratic and military office transformed itself into a short-lived and venal commercial monopoly — a microcosmic image of the evolution of venal office-holding in the modern European state with all its economic, social and political consequences.

The development of the Captain's commercial monopoly

The captaincy of Sofala had been created in 1505 to administer a royal monopoly in gold. Later, ivory trading also became a royal monopoly, and in theory the trade of these two products had to be carried on solely through the royal factory. After only a decade the factory of Sofala had begun to present the Crown with a major problem. The profits from the trade were not paying the overheads of the establishment, let alone providing the Crown with a reasonable profit. As early as 1511 Afonso de Albuquerque had taken action to cut the losses of the east African operations. He had closed the factory at Kilwa altogether and suggested leasing out the trade of Sofala to the chief collaborator of the Portuguese, the sultan of Melinde.[10] This policy was not followed, probably because of the growing importance of Mozambique and Sofala as ports of call for the Portuguese Indiamen. Instead the captains were instructed to expand the trade in ivory, while the regulations governing the factories were tightened.

The miserable returns of the royal factory at Sofala were officially attributed to the continuation of contraband trade by the Muslims who used Angoche, the Querimba Islands and other ports on the coast. However, in reality it was the growth of private trade within the Portuguese community itself which was to blame. Private trade had always been legal but gold and ivory had been excepted and the right to import cloth from India was also restricted. However, with Sofala, where the royal factory was located, declining in importance and with the rise of Mozambique Island and the growth of the ivory trade from the numerous small ports of the coast, the opportunities to breach the royal monopoly were immense. By the 1540s the captain of Mozambique himself was leading the way as the major private trader, freighting his own ships under the nose of the royal factor and filling the offices of the captaincy with his own retainers.[11]

This process was described in the first chapter, but it is important that it should not be judged in a simple moralistic way. The trend towards private monopolies derived not so much from human greed as from the functional needs of the empire. The *Estado da India* depended for its survival on the personal power of the great *fidalgos* and their willingness to fill offices and represent the Crown in remote and dangerous regions far from Portugal or Goa. For this they needed the support of a body of personal followers and freedom to build up local networks of influence among the indigenous peoples. The captains of Mozambique had to fit into a pattern of commercial practice which the sheikhs of Sofala had filled before them, and because they could not rely on the military support of the state, they frequently had to provide for and defend the Portuguese settlements with their own resources. The Crown's response to this situation was to try to reach a compromise with the captains whereby the lucrative trade in ivory and gold would be shared. In 1548 the captain, Fernão de Sousa de Tavora, was granted the right legally to sell 5,000 *cruzados* of his own goods, but such a concession was clearly inadequate given the scale of the commercial activities of the previous captain, Jorge Teles de Meneses, who had used the royal trading vessel to ship out 450 *bars* of ivory on his own account. In 1552 the *vedor da fazenda* in Cochin wrote to the king explaining that little ivory was coming from Mozambique:

> For the captains there think it injurious to send it, and do nothing but ask for cloth and beads, which have always been sent to them; and if the viceroy sends to Cuama they complain that he is taking away from them what Your Highness has given and that those for-tresses are theirs. If they do this now, what will they do when greater powers are given to them.[12]

It is clear from this letter that the captains were already acting as though the captaincy and its trade were theirs by right.

Further attempts were made at compromise. In 1560, Pantaleão de Sá was told he could export 100 *bars* of ivory on his own account and in 1563 the captain was officially granted 0.5 per cent of the royal trading profits and 5 per cent of the ivory trade. The private profits of the captains in the middle years of the century were enormous. Pedro Barreto, nephew of Francisco Barreto, who died on his way home to Portugal in 1570, bequeathed a huge fortune, some 70,000 *cruzados* of it being left in the hands of the factor of Mozambique. It is significant that the commander of the expedition 'took possession of this money, as funds for the expedition . . . and he very soon spent it' to meet the vast costs of the expedition to Monomotapa.[13] The wealth of a captain, extracted more or less illegally from his command, was thereby reapplied, with no greater legality but perhaps with some moral justification, to the needs of the captaincy.

After the final withdrawal of the Barreto expedition in 1575, the Crown began to make elaborate contracts with the incoming captains by which the profits of trade were to be shared between the Crown, the officers of the fort, the captains and the Mozambique settlers. However, this was merely a period of transition for in 1580 Philip II of Spain had become king of Portugal and measures were being taken to put the affairs of the empire on a more businesslike basis. It is from this time that the major survey of the empire entitled *Livro das Cidades e Fortalezas* was made. According to this,

The captaincy of these fortresses of Cofala and Moçambique is the best and most profitable of all those in India and from which the captains draw most money especially now that they trade in ivory, beads and cloth which is merchandise forbidden by the *regimento* but which is very profitable for them. And because this fortress is so rich and of such great profit, it always has the first place of all those of India and the kings of this kingdom appoint to its captaincy *fidalgos* who have performed the principal and greatest services and who have the greatest reputation in India. Its stipend is four hundred and eighty *milreis* a year and because of the said trade which the captains carry on in forbidden merchandise, it is worth eighty to a hundred thousand *cruzados* over three years; but if the said trade was restricted to the former custom in conformity with the *regimento* he would not draw from the office more than forty to fifty thousand *cruzados* more or less.[14]

This report is significant. It put a figure to the level of private trade and private profit which clearly influenced the Crown in the decisions it was about to make on the future administration of Mozambique. In 1584 the first contract was made whereby the captains of Mozambique acquired monopoly control over large and defined sectors of east African trade in return for a substantial annual payment. Although attempts were frequently made to modify the terms of individual contracts, the system first used in 1584 took root and persisted unchanged in its essentials till 1675. Under this system, for all its shortcomings, Mozambique survived the attacks of the Dutch and the ivory trade of east Africa became by the end of the seventeenth century the most profitable commercial activity that the Portuguese retained in the East.

According to the system instituted in 1584 the captaincy of Mozambique was filled from a list of those to whom the Crown had granted the right to hold it as a reward for their services. A royal letter of 1613 explained:

I have ordered letters to be given to several noblemen, gentlemen and soldiers, that you may provide them with offices and posts of captain in those parts, in satisfaction for their services and some deficiency in their payment, in which letters no time is stated for which they are to fill the said posts and captaincies . . . [and] if any should present themselves to you or in the future to any of the viceroys or governors of that State . . . you are to provide them with these posts for not longer than three years.[15]

In this way grants might be made long in advance of any expectation of actually filling the office, and a 'queue' developed. It became longer and still more complex when, after the loss of Ormuz in 1622, the waiting list for the captaincy of that fortress was transferred to Mozambique.

It appears that captains were not necessarily appointed from the waiting list in order. There was considerable latitude for the viceroy or the Crown to show favouritism among the eagerly waiting prospective captains. There was also considerable scope for confusion as an appointment made in Lisbon would naturally take precedence over one made in Goa. The viceroy Jerónimo de Azevedo, for example, not only made his brother captain of Mozambique but reduced the annual payment from 40,000 to 25,000 *pardãos*. In 1614 the king wrote disallowing this reduction and making his own appointment of Ruy Melo de Sampaio who was to go to Mozambique directly from Lisbon.[16] To avoid the conflict of jurisdiction which might arise from the possible presence of two captains, one with the viceroy's commission and one with the king's, the king sent to the East no fewer than seven copies of his letter of appointment.

An expectant captain might well die before his turn came to occupy the post, in which case he expected to be able to bequeath his place in the 'queue' to a son or leave it as an endowment for a daughter or widow. If a woman inherited the right to the captaincy then she could either use it as a dowry enabling her to make a good match, or she could sell it. Ruy de Melo himself had bought the captaincy from Dona Beatriz de Castro.[17] In 1629 an auction occurred when two influential *fidalgos* bid against each other to purchase the captaincy from the mother of the viceroy, the Conde de Linhares.[18] The proprietorial rights which the captain purchased meant that if he was afraid that he would die in office he could appoint a relative to serve out his term as interim governor although sealed letters of succession were carried by each captain containing the name of the person nominated to succeed.[19]

Once his turn to occupy the office had come up, the captain negotiated a contract with either the viceroy or the Crown to cover all aspects of his rights and duties while in office. The details of these contracts varied considerably and there was constant argument and litigation over them. However, the following privileges negotiated by Jorge de Meneses in 1586 can stand as an example of the kind of matters with which the contract dealt:

— He was empowered to send a trading ship to Ormuz.
— He could take fifty retainers, 'his relations and servants', with him.
— The captain was to receive a year's salary in advance.
— He was granted the right to import ginger from the Comoro Islands for sale in Ormuz.

— If he died in office his property was not to be touched by any magistrate or administrator of the property of the dead.

— He could send as many trading ships as he liked to the Cape of Good Hope 'to reconnoitre the ports and places, and carry on what trade he pleases'. No one was to infringe this right under pain of treason.

— If no royal ship was available he was to be allowed also to send a trading ship to Cape Correntes (that is to Inhambane and Lourenço Marques).

— His expenditures on the fortress of Mozambique were to be registered as a loan to the royal exchequer for subsequent repayment.

— He could make appointments to 'all the posts both in the magistracy and administration of the revenue which he may find vacant'.

— He might arrange annually for a supply boat to come from India but could not use it to trade ivory (this would infringe the rights of the person who had bought the Mozambique-Goa voyage).

— He could appoint a relative to fill the captaincy in case he should die in office.

— He was to undertake a voyage of exploration to Madagascar.[20]

The contracts negotiated by some captains with the viceroy could be highly favourable to their interests. Ruy Melo had originally been appointed in 1608 but his appointment had been superseded by the reappointment of Dom Estevão de Ataide, the man who defended Mozambique against the Dutch in 1607 and 1608. Ataide negotiated a contract which was supposed to be based on one provided for Franciso de Sousa when he went to Brazil, and when its terms became known in Lisbon steps were taken to have it revoked.[21] Ruy Melo de Sampaio was to be restored provided he would drop any claims for damages.

The main concern of the captain was to purchase from the Crown the trading privileges which made his tenure worthwhile. Although there were some variations and frequent disputes, the accepted price of these privileges was early established at 40,000 *cruzados* a year, often paid in a lump sum at the beginning of the three-year term of office.[22] For this sum the captain bought the exclusive right to trade with Sofala and the Zambesi settlements including Quelimane. He had the sole right to import cloth and beads, and he alone could export the gold and ivory purchased in the interior. The captains were always anxious to extend the scope of their monopoly, and in 1635 Felipe de Mascarenhas purchased the trade of Angoche for a further 7,000 *cruzados*. However, important areas of the coast were not covered by this contract. The trade with the regions south of Sofala, including

Inhambane and Lourenço Marques, was still conducted on the royal account by a factor who dispatched trading vessels twice a year. Moreover, although the captain was supposed to reside permanently in Mozambique Island, the island itself did not come within his trading monopoly and its trade remained free for the *moradores* (settlers). This would cause friction because the *moradores* were often in a position to undercut the captain and attract the trade of the interior away from the markets on the Zambesi that were under his control. The captains and the *moradores* also disputed the right to trade with Madagascar. The captain tried to claim this trade as part of his monopoly, but because the food trade with Madagascar was so essential for the survival of Mozambique Island, this was a pretension which the *moradores* were prepared to resist to the last. The Mozambique *moradores* also claimed that the trade of the Cabo Delgado region was free.

The Jesuit, Manuel Barreto, writing in 1667, described the conflict between the captain and the *moradores* of Mozambique and the way it threatened the whole colony with ruin:

> The trade with Macuani [the mainland opposite Mozambique Island], which is carried on from Cape Delgado through the Querimbas, with that of the island of Madagascar and of the other adjacent islands, was granted to the inhabitants of Mozambique by repeated orders of His Majesty, but the governors of Mozambique have prevented it under various pretexts, as they have other trade, even to the very apothecaries' shops of Mozambique, and they usurp everything, so that now only one or two inhabitants have any capital, whereas in years past the town contained many rich merchants. If His Majesty does not put a stop to this, Mozambique will soon be deserted, and the captain will be left alone with the keys of his fortress.[23]

In return for his commercial monopoly the captain was responsible for maintenance of the fortress of São Sebastião, for the payment of the garrison, and for the defence of Sofala and the Zambesi forts. If this was the general condition that all captains had to undertake, there were some more onerous obligations that might from time to time be inserted into the contract. In 1609, for example, Ataide was ordered to build forts and maintain garrisons at the main interior fairs; or the captain might be ordered to go with an army to conquer the mines, a condition imposed on Ataide and later on Nuno Alvares Pereira. There was endless controversy over the extent of the captains' obligations and over allegations of neglect of the fortress and the hospital. Captains sometimes refused to help the distressed crews of ships that put into the harbour. One strict condition laid on the captains was that they should not go in person to pursue their commercial interests in the Zambesi but should stay in Mozambique Island and be on hand to defend the fort in case of Dutch or Turkish attack.

The system of appointing captains who bought the right to exercise the Crown's monopoly for a limited period of three years led to a succession of quarrelsome and lawless noblemen plundering the office for their own gain. In theory they could be held to account, and the Crown made serious efforts to enforce the contracts and exact high standards of conduct from those to whom it granted such privileges. Indeed the Spanish Crown used to encourage complaints to be laid against its officials. If these seemed sufficiently serious there were a variety of actions that might be taken. In extreme cases the contract might be cancelled and a new captain appointed; more usually it was decided to send a judge to investigate the complaints. A number of judicial investigations into the captains of Mozambique were held and Ruy Melo himself was at the centre of a series of such investigations. Another line of conduct was for a judicial review to take place after the termination of the contract when measures might be taken to try to recover damages or revenues owed to the Crown. In 1613, in an attempt to recover damages from Estevão de Ataide, the Inquisitor General in Goa was appointed to hold an inquiry, and orders were issued to sequestrate any property of Dom Estevão that crown officials could locate. In 1607 a *residencia* was held into shipping losses occasioned by the conduct of Sebastião de Macedo who had been captain from 1604 to 1607.[24] In 1632, on the deposition of certain settlers who had come from Mozambique, a judge was sent to dismiss the captain, Diogo de Sousa de Meneses, and only three years later in 1635 Felipe de Mascarenhas, himself a former viceroy of India, was arrested when he gave up the contract and returned to India.[25]

The details of these endless disputes are not merely the story of a narrow aristocratic élite doing battle for political spoils with an increasingly impoverished and ineffective Crown. In these vivid clashes of Crown and nobility the whole pattern of development of central Africa was being decided. The captains who came to serve their three years in Mozambique had made a heavy investment, and the need to service the loans they had contracted and to make the profits which they, their retainers and creditors expected, was to prove one of the most formative influences on the development of Mozambique. The captain's profits were made from the sale of cloth and beads to the merchants of the Rivers and from the subsequent sale of the ivory and gold to other merchants in India, although, in the 1660s at least, the captains were trading directly with the Maravi chiefs on their own account.[26] The captain's trading vessels were therefore eagerly awaited by the commercial community in Zambesia, and if they failed to arrive commercial life would be brought to a standstill. If the captain's tenure of office had been for a longer period, economic rationality might have dictated a policy of encouraging Portuguese settlement so that the growth of a settler community would increase economic activity and hence the trading profits of the captain. However, such policies would have needed time to take effect, and the limited three-year tenure did not allow for this. Instead the policy adopted by successive captains was to restrict the flow of trade goods and force prices as high as they would go. Manuel Barreto, for example, complained that the captain discouraged the trade of the settlers in food so that he could charge high prices for his own stocks.[27] Again and again the complaint was voiced that, under the influence of the captain's monopoly, the turnover of commerce shrank and the land became depopulated.

António Gomes in 1645 explained at length the shortcomings of the captain's monopoly as a way of ordering the economic life of the region. The captains, he said, either arrive having borrowed heavily to equip themselves with trade goods, or they were appointed without any financial resources at all, in which case they requisitioned the goods of merchants in the country and 'there has hardly been one who has not caused loss to someone or other'. He went on to make the classic case, not so much for free trade as for the appointment of more than one contractor:

> If there were a lot of contractors a lot of merchandise would be traded and Your Majesty's customs would yield more revenue and the traders, working in confidence, would not fear nor would they send their merchandise with misgivings and in small quantities as is at present the case. The capital of one man alone cannot buy so much and thus many voyages are not undertaken that would bring profit to many people.[28]

Pedro Barreto de Rezende had made exactly the same point in 1634:

> As the captain of Mozambique holds a monopoly of the commerce in virtue of the tribute he pays to His Majesty, he carries it on alone, with only one small vessel, others thus losing the profit which they might have derived therefrom. And it is necessary to consider well this monopoly and whether the Rivers cannot maintain merchants.[29]

The existence of the captain's monopoly worked directly against the declared policy of the Crown in the seventeenth century, which was to promote Portuguese settlement in the Rivers. Instead of streams of settlers entering the country and turning the healthy high veldt regions, which were conquered in the 1630s, into a central African equivalent of Mexico or Peru, the captains entered into a close collaborative relationship with one or two powerful backwoodsmen who were able to control the mines and trading fairs, and who had the private armies necessary for lording it over the Karanga and Tonga. The high profits which the captains sought from their contracts were to be obtained by engineering high prices for imports and by extortion, in which not only the African peasants but the chiefs and the ordinary Portuguese merchants were almost equally sufferers. In 1633 the Spanish mining engineer, Don Andres de Vides y Albarado, wrote to the king:

> What these lands need most of all is people to populate them and live in them because what they are at present are few and although the land is over two thousand leagues in length and all of it very fertile and abundant in produce and of very good waters and fruit trees and peaceful, where may come and live more people than there are in all the Spains, there are in it only two hundred Portuguese scattered over the territory in such a way that ten or twelve people are the most who live together and having enquired about the reasons for this, they say that everybody does not come to live here for lack of permission and because the Governors of Mossambique, who have entered a contract with Your Majesty to pay in the course of their three years of office one hundred and twenty thousand cruzados, do not allow entry to these Rivers either to people or merchandise apart from what they themselves send.[30]

Various schemes were officially put forward to reform the system of the captain's monopoly. As early as 1593 a brief experiment was made with freeing the gold trade; again in 1618 there appears to have been an attempt to end the monopoly and open the commerce of the rivers. However, it was found that there was no way of getting responsible people to take up the captaincy if the valuable trade monopoly was not added as a bait. There were, on the contrary, other proposals which would have extended the captain's powers. Suggestions were advanced for severing the east Africa command from Goa and making it a governorship or even a viceroyalty in its own right. A separate command had been established for Francisco Barreto in 1569 and the Conde de Linhares recommended a similar plan in 1633 which he hoped would stimulate the settlement and economic development of the Rivers through setting up an effective Spanish-style government.[31] Again nothing was done, and plans to reform the administration, especially those that would have reformed it along Spanish lines, were shelved when Portugal declared its independence from

Spain in 1640 and embarked on a long struggle to win its freedom from Madrid.

However, eventually the decision was taken to end the system and the last contract made with a captain of Mozambique terminated in 1675, the monopoly being replaced by a *Junta do Comércio* (Board of Commerce) operating from Mozambique in the Crown's name. With the end of the captain's monopoly passed a whole phase of European administrative history — a phase when governments were forced by shortage of resources to mortgage their fiscal rights and their very jurisdiction to private contractors. That the latter were usually members of the nobility created an element of continuity with the forms of feudal government surviving from the Middle Ages. In practice, the contracts were being made to a syndicate of moneylenders who financed the captain's heavy investment in his office. The captains of Mozambique were often cast in Lisbon or Madrid for the role of *conquistador*, but most of them were willing enough to exchange the heroics of a Cortes or a Pizarro for the more lucrative and less risky rewards of fronting a syndicate of bankers. The syndicate had to make its profits in the very short span of three years and was therefore only interested in high rates of return. This caused the captains and their backers to act in a way quite different from the joint stock enterprises of the Dutch and English who could work for returns on their investments over a much longer period.

The administration of Zambesia in the seventeenth century

The subordinate stations belonging to the captaincy of Mozambique varied greatly in size and in the formality of the provision made for their government. They ranged from ivory trading stations, where there might be only a factor, to the larger towns that grew up at Sena and Tete in the heyday of the commercial prosperity of the Zambesi during the seventeenth and eighteenth centuries.

Although by the mid-sixteenth century Mozambique Island had become recognised as the capital of the Portuguese possessions on the southern part of the east African coast, the main trading settlements lay further south in the region of the Zambesi valley. Regular contact between Mozambique and the Zambesi settlements was hard to maintain because of the irregular nature of the winds, the dangerous sea conditions and the overall distance — some 200 miles. As a result, effective authority had to be devolved, and the story of Portuguese administration was at first that of the *ad hoc* arrangements made by the Portuguese backwoodsmen for the ordering of their affairs, the authorities in Mozambique merely endorsing their decisions.

Until the systematic conquest of the Zambesi valley by the Barreto

expedition between 1569 and 1575, the Portuguese gold traders operated alongside the established Muslim merchants and depended very
much on the goodwill of the Tonga and Karanga chiefs. It was in the
interests of the chiefs that the foreign trading communities should
have some organisation and that there should be some recognised
authority with which they could deal. Thus the Monomotapa actively
encouraged the Portuguese *sertanejos* at the fairs to elect one of their
number to serve as a captain. In the sixteenth century there were three
river ports (Quelimane, Sena and Tete) and three principal inland
fairs with a Portuguese population. Each of the fairs had a captain,
that of Masapa being recognised as the senior. The captains were
elected by the Portuguese residents and then confirmed in their offices
by the Monomotapa and the viceroy in Goa. Equipped with this dual
authority, they had jurisdiction within the fairs over Portuguese and
Karanga alike and were frequently called on to settle disputes among
the local population, a task they could presumably perform satisfactorily as outsiders with no vested interest in the dispute. The Muslim
community also elected leaders, called *mwinyi*.[32]

The fairs do not appear to have been greatly affected by the Barreto
expedition, but the position of the captains of Sena and Tete altered
considerably. Up till the 1570s a local Portuguese would be chosen
as captain and his appointment would then be confirmed. After
Barreto's expedition they became Crown appointments and had
jurisdiction over considerable areas of land and a numerous subject
population of Tonga as well as over the Portuguese community. The
captain of Tete, for example, had direct jurisdiction over eleven
villages, performing the functions, and enjoying the privileges, of a
chief. Vasco Homem, when he took over the governorship, created a
formal establishment at Sena with an *alcaide* in charge of the fort, a factor, notary, priest, constable, farriers (*ferradoros*) and smiths.

The other official who is heard of in the latter years of the sixteenth
century is the *capitão-mor dos Rios* — an office known through the
activities of its most famous incumbent, Francisco Brochado. He
apparently had a house near Luabo and owned boats which operated
up and down the coast. His official function appeared to be to assist
shipwrecked mariners or ships in trouble along the treacherous coasts
between Quelimane and Sofala.[33]

By the turn of the century the Rivers settlements were divided into
six jurisdictions, Sofala, Quelimane, Sena, Tete, Manica and Mokaranga. At first these were considered royal appointments with any
emolument being a charge on the royal revenues. However, with
the development of the contract by which the captain of Mozambique
purchased the trade monopoly in the Rivers, responsibility for
appointing and paying the subsidiary captains soon fell to him as well.

Saddled with this additional expense, it is no surprise to find that the captains of Mozambique sold these offices, thereby spreading the concept of venal office-holding at the expense of the older idea of a salaried bureaucracy.

The captaincy of the fort at Sofala remained a salaried post paid for by the Crown until the Conde de Linhares (viceroy from 1629 to 1633) transferred responsibility for it to the captains of Mozambique. The captains then sold the position of captain of Sofala, with the right to import certain trade goods, for 400 *cruzados*. By the early seventeenth century Sofala had shrunk in size and importance and was the least of the Rivers settlements. In 1634 there were no soldiers stationed there and only five Portuguese residents. Defence of the fortress depended entirely on the settlers' slaves. The church continued to be served by the Dominicans, but there was no resident pilot and any ships that called at Sofala had to take on board local Muslim pilots (*malemos*) to find their way through the shoals to the fort.[34]

Sena resembled Sofala in that its captain remained a royal appointment until the Conde de Linhares insisted that the post be paid for by the captain of Mozambique, who then became responsible for making the appointment. In 1634 the captaincy of Sena stretched from the mouth of the Zambesi to the river Ruenha, an administrative division which was to remain till the nineteenth century. At Sena was the main warehouse of the captain of Mozambique in charge of a factor. Subordinate to Sena were the settlements in Manica. There is no mention of a Portuguese captain there before the eighteenth century but in the 1630s there were three settlements, two of which, Chipangura (Masekesa) and Mutuca, had earth forts. The Dominicans had three churches there, one of them within the fort of Chipangura.[35]

The Tete captaincy ran from the Ruenha to a point about 10 leagues up river of Tete. According to Resende, 'the captaincy of the settlement of Tete is much coveted by the married men therein, from among whom the captain is usually selected, and who recompenses the captain of Mozambique for it.'[36] In 1634 there were six Portuguese forts in the interior of Mokaranga: Majova (on the Mazoe but still in Tonga country), Luanze, Matafuna, Dambarare, Masapa and Chipiriviri. Each had a captain chosen by the captain of Mozambique from among the settlers and traders. No salary was paid but the captains had the right to sell their goods first in the market. Traditionally the captain of Masapa had been the principal captain and the official representative of the Portuguese in the country. However, Nuno Alvares Pereira had ordered a fort to be built and garrisoned inside Mavura's *zimbabwe*. When Mavura moved his *zimbabwe*, the fort had to be destroyed and the Portuguese soldiers moved with him to the new site. By the middle of the century the fort at Masapa was discontinued and the captain of the *zimbabwe* garrison became the principal Portuguese officer in the interior. Unlike the other captains, he was appointed by the viceroy and not by the captain of Mozambique, and was considered to be the senior captain in the Karanga fairs.[37] Quelimane had a captain, also appointed by the captain of Mozambique.

As far as one can tell, government of the Portuguese and Afro-Portuguese community was in the hands of these captains. They held commissions as military officers from the captain of Mozambique, with the right to summon the settlers and their slaves to defend the settlements, but they were also judges (*juizes ordinários*) from whom there was appeal to the *ouvidor* in Mozambique Island. The captains did not administer the captain of Mozambique's trade monopoly, which was in the charge of his factors. In military matters the captain of Sena took precedence over all the other captains, and even the captain of the *zimbabwe* 'recognises to some extent the superiority of the captain of Sena which is the chief centre and strongest place in the conquest, upon whose captain resolutions respecting peace and war principally depend.'[38] At the beginning of the century the captains of Mozambique had also made appointments to two other administrative posts — *juiz de orfão* and *provedor dos defuntos* whose jobs were to take care of orphans and look after the property of the deceased. However, it proved difficult to find suitable people to fill these positions and by the middle of the century the functions were being performed by the Rivers captains themselves.[39]

The rudimentary nature of Portuguese government was compensated for somewhat by the activities of the church. Mozambique, like all the Portuguese *fortalezas* in the East, was seen as a potential launching-pad for missionary activity. The Jesuits had been the first missionaries active in eastern Africa, sending the Silveira mission in 1561 and providing priests to accompany the Barreto expedition. In the 1560s and 1570s both the Jesuits and Dominicans established houses on Mozambique Island and began to carve out areas of missionary activity for themselves. After their initial attempt to establish missions at Inhambane and at the court of the Monomotapa, the Jesuits became firmly based in the Zambesi valley while the Dominicans took over the missions to the Karanga and had stations at Manica, Sofala and in the Cabo Delgado islands. Thereafter it was the Dominicans who made the running, establishing a mission in Sofala and another in the Querimba islands. In 1614 the two orders divided the coast between them, the Jesuits taking the coast north of Mozambique and the Dominicans the coast to the south. In 1618 a similar arrangement divided the Zambesi settlements. In the 1630s the Dominicans had churches in Sofala, Luabo, Sena and Tete while the

Jesuits had churches in Quelimane, Sena and Tete. The Dominicans, however, controlled the churches in Karangaland and Manica with churches at Luanze, Dambarare, Masekesa, Matuca as well as the all-important Dominican presence at the *zimbabwe* of the Monomotapa. Each of the orders had a house on Mozambique Island.[40]

The missions played an important part in establishing an ordered society among the Afro-Portuguese. For example, in the 1640s the Jesuit priest at Quelimane provided medical care, and the Jesuits maintained a school at Sena. Both orders owned and administered lands in the Zambesi valley and the Dominicans provided secretarial services for the Monomotapas at their court. Both were also important in ensuring that a flow of information reached the decision-makers in Lisbon and Madrid, and on occasion provided political and military leadership for the Portuguese community, their priests giving a new meaning to the concept of the church militant by leading warbands in support of their orders' political objectives.[41]

Although two missionary orders established themselves in eastern Africa, as well as the nursing order of the Brothers of St John of God, Mozambique did not acquire an effective ecclesiastical organisation. In 1612 the church was detached from the see of Goa and made an independent prelacy (*prelazia*) under the charge of an ecclesiastical administrator. This post was usually given to one of the regular clergy, which meant in effect that Mozambique had no secular church establishment or overall church organisation, nor any means of enforcing ecclesiastical discipline.

The administration of Mozambique, 1675–1752

During the period of the captain's trading monopoly there had been a contentious division between the commercial and political adminis-tration of the Portuguese possessions in eastern Africa. Whereas the captain had full military and political jurisdiction over all the factories and settlements, his private trade monopoly covered only Zambesia, Sofala and Angoche. The ending of the captain's monopoly should have ended this anomaly too, but in practice the Crown was not able to create a unified administration and Mozambique continued to suf-fer from a serious confusion of jurisdictions.

At the head of the government was still the captain of Mozambique but he was now simply an executive officer responsible to the viceroy in Goa and was sometimes referred to simply as the *castellão* of Mozambique. Although nominally head of the whole government, in practice he had control only over Mozambique Island and the set-tlements of Inhambane, Sofala and Cabo Delgado, together with a nominal suzerainty over some of the Islamic sheikhdoms of the coast.

In most of these places the administration was vestigial — the captain appointed to the settlements acting also as factor and justice.

Zambesia, now called the Rivers of Sena (*Rios de Sena*), was effectively a separate governorship. With the ending of the captain's monopoly the appointment to the post of chief captain of the Rivers had been made by the viceroy, and the title of *tenente-geral dos Rios* came into use. In 1709 the *tenente-geral* was formally accorded quasi-independent powers, including the right to carry out military operations and to full jurisdiction over Portuguese subjects. He was issued with his own separate instructions (*regimento*) by the viceroy. The *tenente-geral*, whose headquarters were in Sena in the first half of the century, made all appointments to the subordinate captaincies of Tete, Zumbo and Manica; he appointed *capitães-mores* to the mining camps and nominated the officer to command the *zimbabwe* garrison. The subordinate captains all acted as judges in their particular areas. The *tenente-geral* had two important officials to assist him — the *capitão-mor dos Rios*, a local settler who was appointed to act as his deputy, and the *feitor dos foros e quintos* who acted as a sort of treasurer with responsibility for the Crown's fiscal rights to land rents and mineral royalties.[42]

The exact relationship of the *tenente-geral* and the captain of Mozambique was never really defined, and in one important area their jurisdiction overlapped. The port of Quelimane apparently came under the jurisdiction of both officials. If this was a source of obvious confusion, another lay in the fact that for most of the period up to the administrative reforms of 1752 the captain of Mozambique held the separate post of superintendent of the *Junta do Comércio*, which controlled the trade of the Rivers settlements.

In 1675 the commercial administration of eastern Africa had been taken out of the captain's hands. The trade of most of the coast was declared free to all Portuguese citizens, and a customs house was created at Mozambique at which all traders paid their dues. Of greatest concern was the trade of the Rivers and this the Crown initially entrusted to a *Junta do Comércio*, operating from Goa. The *Junta* was not, however, deemed a success and after a period of free trade in the Rivers a company was formed to conduct all commerce with the Zambesi settlements. The company lasted only from 1696 to 1699. The *Junta* was then restored and continued as the main trading agency till 1739 when responsibility was taken over by the *Conselho da Fazenda do Estado da India* in Goa. This council administered the trade of the Rivers till 1752 when Mozambique was separated from the government of Goa and made an independent governorship.[43] During the period when the trade of Mozambique was administered by the *Junta*, the captain of Mozambique, acting in his separate capacity as superintendent, had overall control of commercial policy.

The confusion was obvious. In Zambesia political and military affairs were controlled by the *tenente-geral* independently of the captain of Mozambique, in spite of being nominally his subordinate. However, the captain, in his role of superintendent of the *Junta*, had control over the commercial life of the Rivers, though not of government finances which were handled by the *feitor dos foros e quintos*.

Up till 1752 the Portuguese possessions continued to be administered in a highly personal, almost medieval fashion. Partly because of the remoteness of the settlements from Portugal and Goa, administration consisted of the actions of a few individuals exercising a personal authority, in whom were vested the executive, legislative and judicial powers of the Crown — the Crown, of course, reserving the right to intervene or legislate directly for the settlements at any time it chose. After 1752 faint reflections of the European Enlightenment reached eastern Africa and an attempt was made to create a modern administration with properly organised lines of authority and with provision for the local self-government of the different settlements.

In 1752 the government of Mozambique was separated from Goa, and the governor, renamed captain-general and then governor-general, was made responsible directly to Lisbon. A secretariat was formed as the nucleus of a bureaucracy in Mozambique Island and it was there that the sole customs house was located. However, the practicalities of communicating between the isolated trading stations stretching from Cabo Delgado to Delagoa Bay meant that the subordinate governorships enjoyed a high degree of independence. In the 1760s most of the settlements were officially raised to the status of towns and each was given its own *Senado da Câmara*. However, in most cases the *Câmaras* had few resources and there were barely enough local settlers to constitute a quorum, though perhaps one should not underestimate the amount the *Câmaras* contributed to institutionalising the power of the Afro-Portuguese families.

The governors of the different settlements nominally had troops under their command and there was a skeleton staff, usually a *juiz ordinário* to handle judicial matters and a secretary. Relations with the African inhabitants were entrusted either to some local chief allied to the Portuguese, who was often given a Portuguese title of *capitão-mor*, or to an influential local settler who would be empowered to raise African troops, recruit boatmen, carriers or workmen, hear cases according to 'native' law and conduct diplomacy with neighbouring independent chiefs. For Mozambique Island this official was the *Capitão-mor das Terras Firmes*, for the Rivers the *Capitão-mor das Terras da Coroa*.[44]

The church, missions and Christianity

By the eighteenth century the attempts to establish Christian ruling dynasties in the main Karanga chieftaincies had largely been abandoned, and the two missionary orders settled down to running their *prazos*, and administering the churches in the main Portuguese towns and *feiras*. Missionary work as such largely ceased in the eighteenth century, but in the Zambesi valley at least, Roman Catholicism had established itself as the dominant religious cult of the Afro-Portuguese community. Most *prazo* owners would insist that their personal slaves, even if not necessarily all their *chicunda*, were at least nominally Christian. The parish churches kept statistical records, and these suggest that the official Christian community in the Zambesi valley in the eighteenth century continued to number between 2,000 and 3,000. In 1824 the total was officially given as 3,541, most belonging to the parishes in and around Mozambique Island.

As a result the orders did much as they pleased, and the Dominicans in particular, who since the sixteenth century had always been the more enterprising of the two orders, experienced some spectacular scandals.[45] Remote control of church matters by the Goan Inquisition or by visiting ecclesiastics did little to encourage the spread of Christianity or tighten up on the religious practice in the settlements.[46]

The dissolution of the Jesuits in 1759 gave an opportunity to create a secular church in eastern Africa but not until 1775 did secular clergy begin to be appointed to the African parishes. In practice most of these were Goan priests and it was frequently impossible to fill vacancies. When the Dominicans were also expelled in the 1830s the church in eastern Africa had become reduced to a vestigial state. In 1782 the prelate of Mozambique was granted the status of bishop but generally the post continued to be bestowed on absentees.[47]

6

AFRO-PORTUGUESE SOCIETY
AND TOWN LIFE

Muzungo society

The peoples of east central Africa had traded with countries across the Indian Ocean since at least the beginning of the Christian era. As already indicated in Chapter 1, this trade led to the growth of Islamic trading towns along the coast whose inhabitants had ties of family and commercial interest with the Muslim lineages of the wider Indian Ocean world as well as with the local African populations. Many of the townsmen of Kilwa, Melinde and Sofala were of mixed ethnic origin, and had a varied cultural inheritance. Through them economic activity in Africa became part of the wider economy of the Indian Ocean. They were a trading class who commanded credit, shipping resources and access to overseas markets, while at the same time mediating the outside world to Africa. Through them Africa acquired access to the products of the East, its technology, religions and many aspects of eastern culture that helped to fertilise the growth of African civilisation. The introduction of cotton, rice and bananas, the use of outrigger canoes and looms, the building of square houses and the use of coral cement in construction, and of course Islam — these and other cultural imports blended with traditional African technologies and cultural practices.

To a large extent the Portuguese who arrived on the coast assumed the same role. If the captains of Mozambique and the senior officials of the forts and factories perhaps never acquired family ties with the local population, this was not true of Portuguese of other ranks. Early in the sixteenth century Portuguese renegades were contracting local marriages and founding the Afro-Portuguese families that were to dominate Mozambican affairs locally until the twentieth century. By the end of the sixteenth century this *mestizo* class was well established from the Querimba islands in the north to the Bazaruto islands south of Sofala.

This Afro-Portuguese population was of very varied origin. Although most of them claimed some connection with European Portuguese, there were some of Indian origin, and António Gomes refers to a Chinese who led a warband of 4,000 men during the wars in Karangaland. Most of them retained the surface attributes of

127

Portuguese culture, were nominally Catholic and retained Portuguese names. They continued to seek office within the Portuguese imperial establishment and in many respects operated as members of the Portuguese community. However, it would be a mistake to dismiss them simply as a collaborating class propping up an alien imperial system. The Afro-Portuguese of Mozambique — known locally from at least the seventeenth century as *muzungos* — were as much African as Portuguese. Many were indistinguishable in physical appearance from the local population; they contracted marriages, some more and some less formal, with African women and established ties of kinship with chiefly lineages. Their lifestyle was frequently more African than Portuguese. It is one of the much misunderstood curiosities of Portuguese colonial rule that apparently little in the way of European 'civilisation' or technology was introduced into Africa over a continuous period of four to five centuries. The reason is that the *muzungos* adopted an African way of life, farming, mining, travelling, ruling and fighting according to local African custom, because they ultimately had to fit into patterns of inheritance, land use and reciprocal obligation that would satisfy their African kin and their African retainers and clients.

If most of the *muzungos* owned muskets, their armed retainers fought in African style; if some of them had Portuguese town houses in Sena, Tete or Sofala, in the rural areas they lived as African chiefs; if in the eyes of the Portuguese establishment they were nominally Catholic, they also consulted *ngangas* (witchdoctors), practised rainmaking ceremonies and after death were in their turn represented on earth by spirit mediums.

The Afro-Portuguese dominate the history of Mozambique. They enabled Portugal to retain its east African territories when almost all the other settlements of the *Estado da India* were lost. Through them Portugal remained an imperial power. In collaboration with professional African traders, they were the medium through which trade with the outside world was carried on and African isolation was penetrated, even if they reflected the outside world in a highly prismatic way. Above all, it was these *muzungo* families who prevented the growth either of a strong colonial state or the emergence of a powerful African monarchy in their area of influence. *Muzungo* influence was the influence of wealthy families with access to European and Indian commercial capital, but was also tied into the networks which linked the chiefs, caravan leaders and elephant hunters, in short the power-brokers of the interior.

Muzungo society was essentially fragmented, factional and disintegrated. It encouraged the upstart and the entrepreneur. It was a society where people who were outcasts either from the formal world of colonial society or from the equally formal world of African chiefly lineages could make their way. A Portuguese deserter or an exiled convict could be an influential member of Afro-Portuguese society, while African slaves or refugees from war or famine who were uprooted from their own societies could establish a position for themselves in the private armies or trading caravans of the Afro-Portuguese. In this way the *muzungos* formed a parallel establishment which challenged the formal authority of Portuguese officialdom and of traditional African chieftaincy. They were the local instruments of expanding mercantile capitalism but they were also one of the instruments by which Africa resisted for so long the economic domination of the outside world. They put up the most formidable resistance to the new imperialism in the nineteenth century, but were also the agents through which conquest and domination were eventually achieved. They were one of the pathways whereby Portuguese language and culture were transmitted to the population but they were also the heart of the nationalist movement that sought the end of Portuguese rule in the mid-twentieth century. Understanding the history of these *mestizo* families is therefore essential for understanding the uniqueness of Mozambique's history.

The *muzungos* operated through a variety of formal or semi-formal institutions. They were an urban class participating in the urban culture of the Iberians; they were traders and gold diggers; and they held land (*prazos*). The exactions of tribute and service that they made from their peasantry gave them wealth and military power. Their influence, therefore, can only be assessed in detail by looking at the evolution of the formalised institutions of town, fair and *prazo* — the subject of this and the two following chapters.

Towns

Urban life was a major characteristic of Mozambican society for centuries before the coming of the Portuguese, and a number of these towns, notably Angoche, maintained a continuous and independent existence up till the nineteenth century. The Portuguese too were heirs of an urban culture. Iberians in the fifteenth century were primarily townsmen who sought status through the occupying of municipal office and looked to towns as the focus for a vigorous local democracy. The marriage of these two urban traditions took place almost as soon as the Portuguese established themselves on the coast. Two of the existing towns on the Mozambique coast, Sofala and Mozambique Island, were taken over within a few years of the Portuguese arrival and in the course of the next fifty years, three more Muslim urban settlements — Quelimane, Sena and Tete — also became Portuguese towns. These five towns provide the focus for much of the historical development of Mozambique before the twentieth century.

At the time of Mozambique's independence in 1975, Mozambique Island was one of the most remarkable ancient towns in Africa, singled out by UNESCO for its historical importance and the richness of its architecture to be declared part of the Cultural Heritage of Mankind.[1] The island is in a wide bay at the point where the southerly trend of the African coast veers to the south-west. It lies at the narrowest point of the Mozambique Channel and is the nearest point of mainland Africa to Madagascar. It was a natural stopping place for shipping bound from Kilwa and the northern cities to Sofala and the south, and in the fifteenth century a settlement grew up specialising in the building and servicing of ocean-going shipping. In 1517 it was described as

> . . . a very good port, which all the ships of the Moors that sail to Sofala and Cuama made the station for repair, where they took in water fuel and food. Among the Moors of this island of Mozambique there was a *sharif* who governed them and carried out the laws. These Moors are of the same language and custom as those of Angoya [Angoche].[2]

Vasco da Gama visited the island early in 1499 and in 1502 the Portuguese established a trading factory there, building a small fortress tower in 1508 where they installed an official (*alcaide*). With the growth of the Portuguese community a chapel called Nossa Senhora do Baluarte was constructed in 1522. By this time Mozambique was growing rapidly in importance as a trading station and naval base where the Indiamen could call to leave their sick, take on fresh crews and supplies, and even undertake repairs. This importance was confirmed when the viceroy Dom João de Castro was instructed in 1546 to begin the construction of a major fortification.

The fortress of São Sebastião was to be one of the largest constructed by the Portuguese in the East. It occupied the whole of one end of the island and was planned on such a massive scale that its completion proved a problem. Not till 1583 was the bulk of the work finished, and additions and modifications continued to be made in subsequent years — the great cistern in the fort was not constructed till the seventeenth century. The other end of the island was protected by the fort of São Lourenço built on a small rocky island protecting the sea passage, and a third fort, Santo António, was added on the island itself in the eighteenth century.

The island was twice attacked by the Dutch, and after the second attempt a moat was dug separating the fortress from the rest of the island. Later in the seventeenth century Mozambique Island was threatened by Arabs and English but its massive fortifications deterred any attacker and helped to persuade other Europeans to seek bases for themselves elsewhere. Nevertheless, the foreign threat made it necessary to maintain a large garrison, 300 men constituting the payroll in 1688. Officers and men of the garrison were therefore always the largest single element in the Portuguese population, and the garrison's need to obtain supplies was always a major factor in the relations of the Portuguese with neighbouring peoples.

Alongside the military establishment grew the naval base. Mozambique's dockyard was important but never became very efficient. Although good local timber was available, visiting ships often had to depend on artisans whom they brought with them to do repairs. As well as structural work, Indiamen needed replacement crews, provisions and fresh water. The water had to be brought from Quitangonha to the north since the meagre supplies on the island were inadequate, and food supplies for the fleets and garrison were brought from as far away as the Zambesi and the west coast of Madagascar.

The royal hospital was perhaps the most important part of the naval base. As early as 1507 a building was erected to serve the sick, and the first regular hospital was established in 1538 to be maintained by the Misericórdia, a voluntary body of laymen which received a grant from the Crown. It was destroyed by the Dutch in 1607, and not fully rebuilt till 1637, when for a time it was run in a highly unsatisfactory manner by the Jesuits. Eventually in 1680 a new building was put up and the care of the sick was transferred to the Brothers of St John of God.[3] The arrival of a fleet to 'winter' (*invernar*) in Mozambique not only filled the hospital but frequently caused epidemics to break out in the narrow confines of the tiny, overcrowded island so that thousands of Portuguese soldiers, seamen and others died and were buried there. The handling of their affairs was in itself a major task and one which provided the Misericórdia with huge disposable resources of property. In 1576 Father Monclaro described the island as he had known it during the Barreto expedition of the early 1570s:

> The island of Mozambique is very small, being scarcely a league in length, and so narrow in the middle that a stone may be thrown from one side to the other. It is of sand, and covered with palm groves. There is no fresh water, except in some pools which they call fountains, where it is brackish. That used for drinking is brought from a distance of five leagues. It has an ancient fortress, but a very fine new one is now being built, on which large artillery which we brought from the kingdom will be mounted. There is a ruined Moorish village. The Portuguese village has about a hundred inhabitants, and of people of that country, namely kaffirs and

Indians mixed, there are about 200. It is about a league distant from the mainland. It is healthier at present, because of different refreshments which are sent from the gardens on the other shore, and a certain quantity of oranges and lemons. Many deaths take place from the ships that arrive from the kingdom.[4]

As well as the naval base the island became an ecclesiastical centre. Although not made a see, Mozambique had an episcopal administrator (or prelate) and the island became the local headquarters of Dominicans and Jesuits, while hermitages, garrison churches and parish churches added to the profusion of ecclesiastical institutions. The Dominican João dos Santos described Mozambique Island as it was before its destruction by the Dutch in 1607:

> In the centre of the court of this fortress is a new church, not yet finished, which is to serve as a cathedral and close by is another church belonging to the Misericórdia. . . . Outside the fortress of Mozambique, at the extremity of the island, is a hermitage called our Lady of the Bastion, which name was given to it because formerly this church was a bastion, where the artillery was placed to defend the entrance before the church was built. This church is a favourite place of pilgrimage, not only for the residents of the island but also of the sailors from Portugal and India who touch at this coast. Adjoining this fortress towards the interior of the island is a very fine square about the length of a good musket shot and of the same width, at the extremity of which is the convent of St Dominic, newly built and very beautiful. There is no other house on it except for the hermitage of St Gabriel. . . . Beyond the convent of St Dominic lies the town in which reside the Portuguese and other Christians of the island numbering two thousand persons. In this town is the old fortress containing the ancient cathedral and the Misericórdia which is used at the present day. In one of the curtains of the wall of this old fortress is a fine tower of two stories, with other dwelling houses close by where the chief factor and *alcaide* of Mozambique reside while he holds office. Flanking this tower is a good cistern and in the lower part of it is the public prison. Close to this old fortress is a hospital, where all those who fall sick in the country are tended. . . . Close to this hospital is a hermitage dedicated to the Holy Ghost and at the extremity of the island is another to St Anthony.[5]

This town, already of considerable size and sophistication, was largely destroyed by the Dutch and when it was rebuilt after the two sieges, the last traces of the old Muslim town disappeared. It was also attacked, plundered and badly damaged by a fleet from Oman in

1671. From these vicissitudes Mozambique re-emerged more magnificent than before, its prosperity assured not only by the continuation of the naval base but also by the rise in importance of the ivory and slave trades which provided its permanent residents with an important source of commercial wealth.

In 1688 a visiting Jesuit left a detailed account of the city. Ships approaching the island fired their guns, at which local pilots (*malemos*) were sent out to bring the ships into port. The pilots, he noted, had their own chapel dedicated to Nossa Senhora da Saude. On his arrival there were some seven ships lying at anchor in the harbour. The town was impressive:

> In the court of our cloister I saw lemon, orange and fig trees like those of Portugal. . . . It has a very good fortress with four bastions and a rampart against the sea; there is a customs house which yields 50,000 *cruzados* a year by the export of ivory, with which I saw the shores covered, of ambergris and of gold. It has also a royal hospital, served by the religious of St John of God — of whom seven or eight reside there, to whom the king gives 250 *reis* a day and clothes and 5,000 *cruzados* for the expenses of the hospital. . . . It has a Misericórdia and a collegiate church, which they call a cathedral. . . . There is also a parish church of St Sebastião which is within the fortress, a beautiful chapel of our lady of health and another of St Anthony who protects the health and safety of the Indian ships.[6]

The eighteenth century saw the prosperity of Mozambique Island reach its peak with a number of important public buildings, including a new customs house, added to the town. The Jesuit College, rebuilt in an elegant classical style, became the palace of the governors after the Order was expelled in 1759. In 1812 a British frigate, the *Nisus*, was despatched by the governor of the Cape on an official visit to Mozambique. The frigate's captain, James Prior, took the opportunity to gather intelligence about every aspect of the Portuguese colony and in the published version of his diary gave a detailed account of the city as he saw it during August and September 1812.[7] He was taken on a tour of Fort São Sebastião and though he found the courtyard overgrown with long grass, some of the buildings in bad repair and many of the hundred pieces of artillery unusable, he was impressed in spite of himself. 'Even in the present day, neither the colonies of the French nor Dutch in the East have a fortification equally good, and, except the three presidencies, perhaps few of our own.' The soldiers of the garrison were all 'natives of the adjoining territories, and having become slaves by war or purchase, are retained in this capacity'. He was impressed by the troops, describing the guard on duty near the quay as 'a body of tall, well-dressed African soldiers, who in figure bore a strong resemblance to the finest of the Bengal sepoys, though in general stronger men. The uniform was white [and] some pains seemed to have been bestowed upon it. . . .' Not appreciating the architecture of eastern Africa he described

> . . . the narrow streets and high houses, the former not remarkable for cleanliness, and the latter partly of a dirty yellow colour, impaired by neglect and decay. The windows seemed barred with lattices as if the town abounded in thieves. This, though formerly intended as a jealous precaution, is retained to obviate the heat by the free admission of air; but as few are light or neat in appearance, the eye is continually reminded of the bars of a prison.

The governor's palace did not impress him,

> . . . . part of the exterior appearing more like an old storehouse than the mansion of the first personage of the settlement. We were first led to it by the clashing of billiard balls and the confused clamour of contending voices, so that we at first took it to be a tavern or gambling house.

Prior noted that the only form of transport was the palanquin, and he did not think much of the island as a commercial centre as 'there is neither the noise nor bustle of busy life', but he thought the hospital 'capacious' and did not subscribe to the view that the island was particularly unhealthy there being 'no specific diseases, as far as I can learn peculiar to the settlement; I might perhaps except ennui. Were I to remain here, I should die of it in three months.'

Prior is one of the few visitors to have described the African quarter. 'It consists of a line of huts, formed of hurdles, or bamboos, fixed in the ground, and connected by wicker-work, with sod or dry grass for the roofs'. He was surprised to find the huts 'filled by strong, healthy, active inhabitants, whose numerous children, gambolling to and fro, naked as they were born, displayed ample proofs of health and vivacity'.

The bishop, Bartolomeu dos Martires, called Mozambique ten years later in 1822 '*uma bela e linda cidade*' (a fine and beautiful city). He described the open square outside the fort where the soldiers drilled, the inhabitants came to promenade and the artisans of the island made their coir ropes. From the square three streets ran through the town off which were 'noble houses, some of them so vast and well constructed that they could rival the fine palaces of large cities'. The houses all had flat roofs where the inhabitants went to enjoy the sea breezes but which were also used to catch rainwater to supply the cisterns which each house possessed. In a second square a food market was held and public punishment was inflicted on slaves and malefactors.[8]

Thereafter the city seems to have been little altered, and when Lourenço Marques was made the capital at the beginning of the twentieth century, it sank into a charming decay, although the fortress remained a prison and a garrison was installed there during the wars of independence. Fort Santo António became a refuge for the poor and destitute. The baroque churches, lofty thick-walled public buildings and ochre-washed houses with verandahs and shady courtyards decayed in a graceful way. As a city Mozambique linked together the Iberian, Islamic and Indian architectural traditions, encapsulating in stucco and stone the whole history of the *Estado da India*.

As well as being a commercial, administrative and ecclesiastical centre, Mozambique was the focus for the lives of a heterogeneous population, made up of peoples from eastern Africa and the western Indian Ocean, who created an individual urban culture from the peculiar tripartite nature of the town. Distinct from the holders of ecclesiastical or government offices were the *moradores*. The Mozambique *moradores* were traders and their battles with the captains and their struggle for a corporate existence of their own marked the first two and a half centuries of Portuguese presence in the city. The *moradores* were not granted the right to establish a formal town government with a *Senado da Câmara* until the separate government of Mozambique was created in 1752. On the other hand the *moradores* did establish a *Misericórdia* which became a focus for their institutional life. There was a similar reluctance on the part of the imperial authorities to establish formal church institutions. Mozambique was not made a bishopric, and the church in the region was left under the direct control of Goa, occasionally attracting the attention of the Goan Inquisition. The failure to create a formal town government or a body of cathedral canons undoubtedly prevented the *moradores* institutionalising their power in a way that, for example, the creole families of São Tomé were able to do.[9]

Mozambique became in the eighteenth century a dense urban settlement, but like most of the Swahili cities which in so many ways it resembled, it was always closely dependent on the mainland communities. During the sixteenth century the *moradores* established agricultural settlements on the mainland. These helped supply the island capital with food and provided a supplement to the incomes of the settlers. On their rural properties the *moradores* maintained large slave establishments and lived in close co-operation with the neighbouring Muslim population and the Makua chiefs. It was here that their society became less that of traders whose interests were focussed on the Indian Ocean and more that of landowners and chiefs, African in their

lifestyle and orientation. So Mozambique Island became a European
city supported by a rural African hinterland with the Afro-Portuguese
moradores the connecting link between them.

Sofala

Mozambique Island acquired the appearance and character of a
European-style Portuguese town, and in the eighteenth century some
fine colonial buildings were erected. Sofala on the other hand, though
the first town in which the Portuguese settled, developed in an entirely
different way. After the first thirty or forty years of Portuguese
presence it ceased to be an important establishment for the imperial
bureaucracy or military. That it survived as a Portuguese town at all
was because a fort was built there soon after the Portuguese arrived
with stone sent from Portugal. This fort was sited on an isolated sand
spit away from the Muslim town as though making a symbolic statement that this very European construction was never going to become
a major part of the life of the urban community.

Sofala was the site of the royal trading factory till the mid-sixteenth
century and a number of Portuguese soldiers and officials lived in the
fort or in houses nearby. There was a church and a Dominican mission which continued till the end of the seventeenth century. However, when the active centre of the captaincy moved to Mozambique
Island in the mid-sixteenth century, Sofala became an increasingly
isolated outpost. Its few buildings hardly amounted to a town at all;
the African bush encroached and Santos recorded at the end of the sixteenth century that hyenas dug up the corpses in the graveyard.
According to an account of the town in 1634, there were no soldiers
at all and the captain lived alone in the fortress. There were three married and two unmarried Portuguese *moradores* whose slaves, the report
said hopefully, 'could serve as soldiers in the fortress on occasion'.[10]
That the town was not abandoned altogether was due to the fear that
the fort might be occupied by enemies of Portugal. So for the rest of
the century Sofala remained a semi-forgotten trading post. At the end
of the seventeenth century,

> . . . . the fort of Sofala also is in bad need of help for at present it
> has no more residents of respect than Joseph da Fonseca Coutinho
> and one *filho da terra* [*muzungo*] . . . and a few others who besides
> being so few are so poor that they can hardly subsist and for this
> reason trade is stagnant and the village diminished.[11]

In the eighteenth century the old Portuguese town virtually disappeared as the sea encroached on the sand dunes on which it was built.
In 1758 Inacio Caetano Xavier wrote:

Sofala lacks *moradores* and the fort is surrounded by the sea so that in many parts it is beaten by its waves. The church which is inside the walls is ruined and needs rebuilding.[12]

In 1783 the sea inundated the old fort for the first time although it somehow remained standing for another hundred years.

Long before this time Sofala had become, in effect, a trading station for a few Afro-Portuguese ivory and gold traders, some of whom owned *prazos* in the vicinity of the port. It had always been the maritime outlet for the trade of Kiteve and through it links with the chieftaincy continued to be maintained. At the end of the sixteenth century ambassadors of the Kiteve came there every year to bring a gift symbolising close friendship with the Portuguese: this was presented to the representative of the captain of Mozambique, and Friar João dos Santos thought of it as a tribute paid to the Portuguese state.[13] However, the reality was that by the beginning of the seventeenth century both the Kiteve and the captains of Mozambique had become dependent for their dealings with each other on the *muzungo* families of Sofala. By the end of the sixteenth century Portuguese *sertanejos* had acquired lands and had positions of importance within the Kiteve kingdom. Rodrigo Lobo had been given the island of Maroupe by Kiteve, 'who was a great friend of his together with the title of his wife. . . . In this island Rodrigo Lobo had many kaffirs, his slaves, and all the other inhabitants were his vassals.'[14]

In the seventeenth century the *muzungo* families established their chiefly control over a considerable territory and population in the hinterland of Sofala. They registered their land titles with the Portuguese authorities but the reality of their power rested on their role in the Kiteve kingdom and the control they exerted over the lives and economic production of the Tonga peasantry. By mid-century the *muzungos* of Sofala were able to act as kingmakers in Kiteve, extorting huge land concessions from the chief so that the territory they directly controlled now adjoined the *prazos* of the Sena Portuguese.

The town of Sofala continued to play a role in the lives of this community. A small group of Portuguese houses and a church existed among the palm groves — a cannon shot from the crumbling fort. Sofala continued as a subsidiary port for the trade of the captains of Mozambique and it was kept supplied with cloth and trade goods through regular voyages from the capital. But the Sofala *muzungos* wore their European culture lightly. Like the *moradores* of Mozambique they had no official town government till 1753, they had no *Misericórdia*, and the church was frequently without a priest and was only spasmodically the centre of active missionary activity.

As an urban centre Sofala remained primarily Muslim. The old

Islamic trading families, headed by a sheikh, survived and retained their religious traditions and kinship ties with the local families inland and down the coast to Chiluane. The Muslim traders of Sofala and Chiluane continued to conduct an independent trade making use of the old port of Mambone and the route up the Sabi to trade with the Karanga states of Butua and Maungwe. Not only was Muslim trade active throughout the seventeenth century but probably Muslim political influence in the interior even grew at this time the chieftaincy of Entombue near Maungwe is described as having a Muslim chief in the 1630s, while it was to counteract supposed Muslim political influence that Sisnando Dias Bayão led his expedition to Butua in the 1640s.

Chiluane lay between Sofala and the mouth of the Sabi and was the site of another small Islamic trading town. The only official notice taken of the port of Chiluane was a proposal in 1635 to establish a fort there as part of a hopelessly ambitious plan for the settlement and colonisation of central Africa. However, already by that time the influence of the Sofala *muzungos* had spread down the coast. Ampara became a *prazo* and south of that were the lands of Molomone belonging to the *muzungo* Luís Pereira. Pereira's lands included Chiluane.[15] However, the importance of the Sabi route was such that sometime in the early eighteenth century the Sofala *muzungos* set up their own base of operations in Mambone, registering it as a *prazo* and maintaining there an isolated outpost of Afro-Portuguese culture and economic activity.[16]

As an urban settlement, therefore, Sofala had unique characteristics. The fort remained and the Portuguese official establishment continued to be represented by a captain and sometimes a few soldiers and a priest. Then there were the houses of the *muzungo* families whose wealth lay in their trade with Kiteve and in the tribute they derived from their subject peasant populations. Some of them also ran plantations in the immediate neighbourhood of the town. But Sofala was also the town of the Muslims whose family histories stretched back far beyond Vasco da Gama, whose mosques and family tombs testified to the town's role as an ancient seat of culture and whose trade and political influence extended to the south and into the interior. With its dense palm groves and modest clusters of buildings Sofala may not have resembled the European idea of a town, and indeed Europeans continually denounced Sofala scornfully as decadent and decrepit. But it was typical of so many towns of eastern Africa where the urban life and culture shaded imperceptibly into, and was intricately bound up with, the life of the rural agricultural communities.

Quelimane, Sena and Tete

Quelimane, Sena and Tete formed a trio of urban settlements linked to each other through the conduct of trade on the Zambesi. Sena and Quelimane had been Islamic towns before the arrival of the Portuguese, and Tete had possibly been one as well. Quelimane was some 10 miles up the Qua Qua river (the Rio dos Bons Sinais which Vasco da Gama had visited in 1499). The river was tidal as far as the town, and further upstream it was linked to the river system of the Zambesi delta whenever, in the wet season, floodwater from the Zambesi used the river as one of its escape channels.

The Qua Qua was protected by a dangerous bar and access to the port for ocean-going vessels, though possible, required a lot of local knowledge. Throughout the seventeenth century trading ships from Mozambique would trans-ship their cargoes for passage up the river. The settlement was guarded by a fort described in 1634 as 'a wooden pallisade of thick strong stakes, with a trench outside, made so that the defenders may be able to fight under cover.'[17] A fort of this kind was known as a *chuambo*, and this name came to be applied to the town by the local population. In the seventeenth century the Maravi chief Muzura made a sustained effort to gain control of Quelimane, and as a result of his attacks a number of the local chiefs sought the protection of the fort. By the middle of the seventeenth century the country north to the Lurio river and inland to the Shire had been divided into *prazos* under the jurisdiction of the captain of Quelimane, and the people living on the *prazos* in the vicinity of the town had acquired a distinct identity and were calling themselves Chuabo.

The town of Quelimane depended very much on its role as a functional sea-port. Santos, who visited it probably in the 1590s, describes the palm groves and gardens where Francisco Brochado, the *capitão-mor dos Rios*, had a house, and he recalls that visiting Portuguese were entertained in the houses of the settlers while nearby 'there is a little village inhabited by cafres and poor moors . . . where the sailors who are usually moors also find protection'.[18] In 1634 it had 'ten or twelve straw houses along the river in which, among others, live four Portuguese and the captain placed there by the captain of Mozambique'. There were no regular troops and 'upon any intelligence of war the married Portuguese go into the fort with their slaves and as many of His Majesty's subjects from the surrounding territory as can be assembled and defend themselves until they can communicate with the captain of Mozambique.'[19] Contemporary descriptions make it clear that the buildings in the town were mostly of the *quinta* variety favoured by Portuguese colonial society and functionally determined by the slave-holding social pattern. Large houses belonging to the traders and *prazo*-holders were surrounded with their own stockades, outbuildings and cultivated gardens, and stood widely separated from each other. The town merged with the plantations of the countryside and these in turn shaded into the pattern of African villages and traditional agricultural settlements.

In the seventeenth and early eighteenth centuries Quelimane seems to have provided little in the form of services or amenities: the passage across the bar was not buoyed and the only medical services available were offered by the Jesuits who served the parish church. Like Sofala, it was controlled by one or two powerful *prazo*-holders whose private armies defended the settlement and who dabbled in African politics in the interior and sold provisions to passing ships. The remarkable continuity of commercial life in central Africa and the growing prosperity of the trade of the region meant that this urban society changed little in the next hundred years. António Pinto Miranda described Quelimane in 1766:

> The houses are made of wood and clay and are covered with straw. Apart from the wasteland and bush (*mattos*) which the town has, there are immense groves of palms, orange trees, lemons and mangoes and other non-fruiting trees which serve to draw the gaze away from the ruined houses. . . .[20]

This was a European of the Enlightenment looking at a town of the Afro-Portuguese, and his description of the society of the town complemented his view of its physical amenities:

> The town of Quilimane which is totally a wasteland where tigers, *ticas* and hippopotamuses roam, is full of native concubines who serve some Portuguese scattered in the town, the men who have deserted from the garrison to the moors, and heathens who come in the ships from Mozambique as well as their European owners.[21]

Quelimane only acquired the right to establish a town council in the eighteenth century when it was officially named Vila de São Martinho de Quelimane. Towards the end of the century it began to enjoy an unprecedented prosperity based on the development of agriculture for export. In the course of the eighteenth century the Portuguese largely abandoned their old trade with Madagascar and the Comoro Islands and began producing food surpluses round Quelimane and in the Zambesi delta region. This may have been linked, as will be discussed later, with the rise of the trade in slaves and the demand of slaving ships for provisions.

Be that as it may, the town described by João Baptista Montaury in 1778, while still recognisably the old riverside settlement of the Afro-Portuguese, was distinctly prosperous:

It is composed of some twenty European residents, well-established and rich and some Canarins from Goa and mulattos of the country; all the houses are thatched with straw although they are sufficiently large, and have such considerable areas of land enclosed round them that they are large *quintas*; the walls are of mud (*taipa*) and the roofs are lined underneath with canes laid close together of a yellow colour which makes a very agreeable sight; there are others lined with beams and painted to resemble our ancient houses; the houses are furnished with rich and luxurious furniture. The town does not have any regularity nor streets of any kind and it is more a mixture of *quintas* and houses near to each other than a town; round about are various small villages of cafres which are called *senzalas*.[22]

Ten years later the town had at last begun to take on a more European colonial appearance. In 1788 it had a stone factory house, a building for the *Câmara*, a prison and a *pelourinho*, used customarily as a flogging post.[23]

Sena and Tete were river ports and the points of departure for trading and military expeditions bound for the interior. Sena lay on the flat alluvial plain more or less opposite the confluence of the Zambesi and the Shire. It had been selected by Muslim traders doubtless because it was convenient for exploiting the trade of the Shire — especially that in *machiras* (locally produced cotton cloth). In 1571 Sena was a 'town of straw huts' but there were twenty substantial Muslim merchants who did business in the town. The Portuguese had their own village a gunshot distant. Barreto took over Sena following the massacre of the principal Muslim merchants, and it became the centre of the government of the Rivers. Barreto built the first stone fort there, dedicated to São Marçal, Homem appointed the military establishment, and by the end of the sixteenth century Sena was spoken of as a town of some size with fifty Portuguese residents and 800 'Christians'. In the 1590s the Dominicans arrived in the Zambesi, a mission field hitherto a preserve of the Jesuits. The Dominicans built a new church at Sena dedicated to St Catherine of Siena, from whom they assumed the town's name derived. Santos, mindful of the earlier evangelistic work of the rival order, records that the Dominicans found a chapel where a painting of the naked figure of the Roman, Lucretia, was being venerated as a saint above the altar. They also established confraternities at Sena and Tete.[24]

In 1634 the Sena Portuguese lived in thatched, mudwalled houses. The fort had been destroyed and the only substantial building was the factory which stored the annual consignment of imported cloth. It was not only the largest house in the town but also one of only two with tiled roofs. There were some thirty or forty Portuguese residents, by which should be understood heads of households, suggesting a total Portuguese community of perhaps 200, to which should be added the slaves, servants *et al.* of the Sena settlers and the large body of soldiers and officials who were always passing through.[25] It had a *Misericórdia* and a parish church, a Dominican convent, and a Jesuit college and school 'to teach reading and writing and a chapel master who teaches music to the children of the Portuguese and some others of all races, the children of Chinese, Javanese, Malabareso, Ceylonese and some natives more of coloured blood than *cafres.*'[26]

Despite the size of its population, Sena in the seventeenth century had little resemblence to a European town. The inhabitants lived in spacious houses, 'each one surrounded by its courtyard; and each house forms a fortress as well as if it had been a stockade.'[27] This type of settlement seems to have been typical of Portuguese Zambesia. It resembled the general layout of Quelimane and reflected the functional needs of the Afro-Portuguese with their large households of slaves and dependants which could never have been accommodated in the narrow confines of a European style of town.

As well as being an administrative and ecclesiastical centre, Sena was the point of departure for caravans bound for the Shire and for the goldfields of Manica. The trade of Manica depended on the passage of traders through Barue, and the Portuguese were always anxious to have friendly relations with this chieftaincy or else to control it. Throughout the seventeenth century the Sena settlers gradually enlarged their political power at the expense of Kiteve and Barue, annexing many of the Tonga chieftaincies on the south bank and eventually extending their rule throughout the whole region between Sena and Sofala. The delta was also a dependency of the Sena captaincy, and the food surpluses grown in the fertile delta region provided food for the towns on the river and Mozambique Island. The Tonga inhabitants of the lower Zambesi region, like their counterparts round Quelimane, acquired an identity from their close association with the Portuguese town and came to be called Asena.[28]

In 1704 the fort at Sena was rebuilt and given a carved stone gateway. Its upkeep depended on the settlers, each of whom was allotted a bastion or a part of the wall to maintain. The extreme factionalism of the Sena settlers meant that this work was seldom efficiently done. Indeed a quarrel, allegedly between the wives of two of the Sena settlers, led to the town being burnt sometime before 1718. The *Misericórdia* was consumed in the blaze and not rebuilt for half a century.[29]

Throughout the eighteenth century Sena maintained its primary purpose, which was to be the point where goods imported from the coast were distributed into the central African trade networks.

Descriptions suggest that little commerce actually took place in the town itself. Instead, agents of various trading enterprises obtained the stocks of cloth, beads and other imports which were then taken by porter to the fairs in Manica or by canoe up the Shire or along the Zambesi to Tete. The latter was another distribution point from which goods were dispatched to interior fairs or further up-river to Zumbo. If Sena was not a major centre of trade in its own right, it remained the seat of the government of the Rivers till the 1760s; it was also an ecclesiastical centre and had a fort and garrison. If these functions meant that it always remained more than just a landing-place with warehouses for trade goods, what constituted its real character as a town was that all the great Afro-Portuguese *prazo*-holders maintained town houses surrounded with huts for their considerable retinue of *chicunda*.

Descriptive accounts of Sena differ greatly. Those coming to Zambesia looking for flourishing European settlements were frankly appalled at the churches and public buildings; those who understood the way social and commercial relations worked in Zambesia saw a large, flourishing and, in its way, dynamic Afro-Portuguese town.

In the mid-eighteenth century, Sena had four churches: the Sé Matriz (so called although Sena was never a bishopric), usually served by the Dominicans; the Dominican church of São Domingos; the Jesuit church of São Paulo, closed after the expulsion of the order in 1759 but rededicated in 1770 as São Salvador and turned over to the use of the newly reconstituted Misericórdia; the Dominican church of Remédios at Macambura outside the town; and the ruins of the old church of the Misericórdia.[30] The Dominicans also had a large conventual house in the town. At least one of the leading Afro-Portuguese *Donas* had a private chapel.[31] Within the fort there was accommodation for the captain and soldiers of the garrison and two warehouses, apparently owned by the Jesuits till their expulsion and let out to the *Junta do Comércio* and the *Feitor dos Quintos e Foros*. After the reconstruction of the fort in the 1760s a chapel was built inside.[32]

In 1766 there were at least eighteen town houses belonging to *prazo*-holders, all with considerable establishments of slaves and other retainers who lived in a huge African settlement surrounding the Afro-Portuguese town estimated by one writer at 3,000 huts.[33] These were probably only the largest establishments because in 1778 João Baptista Montaury, whose father had governed the Rivers, estimated that there were at least seventy houses 'including those of European residents, Indians (Canarins) and those born in the country without mentioning the habitations of the cafres which surround the town'. Although the houses were all mudwalled and mostly thatched, Montaury said they were 'richer and more luxurious' than those of

Quelimane.[34] With riches and luxury went other aspects of Afro-Portuguese life, usually censoriously dismissed by European observers as vice. 'They do not deny themselves living in sin with the slave women which their vicious characters require,' wrote António Pinto de Miranda.[35]

If Sena was facing a crisis in the mid-eighteenth century, it was not lack of population or trade, as some observers claimed, but the extreme unhealthiness of the site. This was generally realised and variously explained by writers as due either to the low hills on each side of the town casting shadows morning and evening; or to the corpses of dead elephants putrefying and poisoning the atmosphere.[36] Others more realistically attributed it to the stagnant water which lay in the large, crocodile-infested pits from which mud was extracted for constructing houses and public buildings in the town.[37] Apparently it was commonplace for the inhabitants of Sena to boil their water before drinking it. One might well wonder in how many European towns of the period such precautions were understood, let alone taken.[38]

Sena was made a municipality in 1753, but in the second half of the eighteenth century its importance declined and in 1767 the seat of government of the Rivers was tranferred to Tete, no doubt reflecting the increasing importance of the gold trade of Zumbo and the new fairs in Maravi territory. The town only survived at all because it housed the factory where the trade goods imported via Quelimane were stored, and retained a small garrison, officially numbering fifty soldiers, which could be used to help maintain the security of the river and a modicum of law and order on the *prazos*. It also remained the base from which caravans set out for the fairs in Manica.

Reflecting on the decline of Sena in a report written in 1806, Vilas Boas Truão recalled that the town had once housed 'a great number of the richest families in the land and [was] the centre of all the commerce of this colony. . . . Nothing can be seen in this unhappy settlement except ruins and each house that falls into ruin is never rebuilt again'. He also attributed the decline to the extreme unhealthiness of the site, saying that infant mortality at Sena was at least four times that at Tete.[39]

Between Sena and Tete were 150 miles of river and the dangerous passage of the Lupata gorge. Tete was near the confluence of the Ruenha and the Zambesi and was the point of departure for caravans and military expeditions to Monomotapa and the Karanga fairs. In the seventeenth century it became the focal point of an ever expanding domain as Portuguese *conquistadores* acquired control of most of the northern part of modern Zimbabwe. Like Sena it was a commercial town but also the centre for all the tortuous diplomacy that surrounded the control of the Monomotapa chieftaincy. Santos said that it had a stone fort but at the end of the seventeenth century it was described as surrounded by a wall in which were three bastions.[40] Stretches of the wall were still to be seen late in the eighteenth century and it was rebuilt in 1837 when the town was threatened with attack by the Nguni. Parts of the town wall were still standing as late as 1880.[41]

In the 1630s the town had twenty Portuguese heads of households and 'with the half-breeds there are about thirty firelocks, without counting the married kaffir slaves, who are very numerous and very good soldiers'.[42] It had a factory and religious houses of the Dominicans and Jesuits.

Tete's fortunes fluctuated much more than those of Sena. As a town it grew rich or declined along with the trade of the interior. Its prosperity was severely damaged by the loss of Karangaland at the end of the seventeenth century. With no significant commercial hinterland and few *prazos* dependent on it, it seems that the Portuguese even contemplated abandoning the town. Early in the eighteenth century, however, it took on a new lease of life with the opening of the fair at Zumbo and the expansion of gold mining north of the Zambesi for which it became once again the natural base and point of departure. However, with few *prazos* of any size within its jurisdiction, it lacked the large town houses and establishments of Sena. The town and lands round it were also exposed to frequent raids and to extortionate 'protection' by the independent chiefs whose lands were nearby.[43] In 1766 it had eight large establishments, three of them owned by Indians; most of the traders operating out of Tete were Indians also. The town itself was built on a rocky outcrop near the bank of the Zambesi. All its buildings used the local stone and it had a stone-built fort described as 'without any form as such, for the houses lack any order and there are outcrops of rock in it.[44]

Because of the growing importance of the gold mining north of the Zambesi, the insecurity caused by the raids, and the unhealthy state of Sena, it was decided in 1767 to move the seat of government of the Rivers to Tete. Two companies of soldiers were posted in the fort and suitable public buildings were built there: a hospital (which actually had a surgeon in 1788), a building for the *Senado da Câmara*, an arsenal, prison, factory house and a *boa casa de residencia* for the governor.[45] After two centuries of fluctuating fortunes, it had begun to grow as a centre of urban life.

Sena, Tete and Quelimane must be considered important African towns. At their height they were centres of commercial, administrative and ecclesiastical life and had churches, schools, government and church buildings, and artisan workshops. Moreover, particularly in the case of Quelimane, their fortifications offered substantial protection to the surrounding peoples. However, their morphology reflected the social and economic dominance of the great Afro-Portuguese *prazo* families whose power was as much rooted in the rural communities of their tributary peasantry and private armies as it was in commerce. The agents of international commerce, first the agents of the captain's monopoly and thereafter the Indians, found that they could only operate through the collaboration of the great *muzungo* families, and by the eighteenth century a working partnership had emerged which linked government officials, landowners and Indian financiers. But as with so many early east African towns, political power was located on the land and not in the towns themselves, a fact brutally demonstrated in the nineteenth century when the towns once more declined and were replaced by the great feudal strongholds of the leading *prazo*-owners.

7

SOUTHERN MOZAMBIQUE

Shipwrecks

The coast of Africa south of the Sabi river has always been inhospitable to seafarers. Although it contains some large rivers like the Limpopo, the characteristic pattern of low sandy islands, lagoons and sheltered inlets on the coast north of the Sabi and the steady and relatively benign regime of Indian Ocean monsoons gives way below the latitude of southern Madagscar to an increasingly barren shoreline with few natural harbours and beaten by a heavy surf and Antarctic storms. The overloaded Portuguese Indiamen repeatedly foundered off these southern coasts as they struggled homeward in heavy seas.

The ships often left Goa late in the season, as they had delayed to await the best pepper coming onto the market in India and to take on the last ton of cargo. The vessels themselves had grown to be anything up to 2,000 tonnes, but their design had not kept pace with the increasing weight. They were still basically giant tubs, like the medieval cogs of the Hansa, with a castle of four or five stories built fore and aft, leaving a low, shallow waist which had to take the full leverage of the main mast. In heavy seas the mast often had to be cut down and in a storm it was not unknown for the castles to break free from the main part of the vessel and be washed away. Although built of Indian teak, the carracks often leaked badly and were allowed to sail with rotten timbers. In 1593 the rudder of the *Santo Alberto* broke away in a storm. The ships were overloaded, with cargo cluttering the decks and preventing the guns from being mounted and obstructing the handling of the sails. Sodden pepper blocked the pumps and sometimes the water level below decks could only be kept down by baling with barrels raised and lowered with a pulley.

In the second half of the sixteenth century these great ships foundered along the shores of southern Africa with increasing regularity. Each wreck was a concentrated drama, a catastrophe in which the savagery of nature was compounded by the corruption of the *fidalgos* whose religiosity was often a more prominent characteristic than their ability to lead, and by the quarrels of an inadequately trained corps of navigators and seamen. These great wrecks appealed to the contemporary mind as a warning of divine wrath and as a vivid and awful illustration of the human soul *in extremis*. The written

accounts, often put together by professional writers, emphasised the
human drama — the terror of imminent death, cowardice and noble
heroism, sanctity, greed, cruelty and chivalrous self-sacrifice. They
were also manuals of survival, charting the path of the survivors along
the coasts of southern Africa, detailing their relations with the African
peoples, describing the country and disseminating useful information
in the best tradition of practical seamen's guides. Few texts from the
sixteenth century describe so vividly both the mentality of these reluctant explorers and the land through which they travelled.[1] Historians
have reason to be thankful to their authors.

The land

The region between the Sabi and the Limpopo that later became part
of Mozambique can best be described as a vast lowland of dense bush,
undifferentiated by major geographical features. The area is dry and
the soil generally sandy and poor. Drought recurs at frequent intervals
and the region has been affected by the tsetse fly from quite early
times. It appears always to have been sparsely populated and consequently rich in game. Although the Limpopo valley has much rich
alluvial soil and parts of it form a floodplain uniquely favourable for
agricultural settlement, the forest along the river is deeply infested
with tsetse fly which has discouraged the movement and settlement of
cattle-owning people.

South of the Limpopo the character of the country changes significantly. The Lebombo mountains, the northernmost extension of the
great South African coastal ranges, rise to 2,500 feet and form a
natural barrier only 50 miles from the coast. The rain that falls on
them pours off in a series of major rivers that empty into Delagoa Bay.
This deep, protected sea inlet, from which the tentacles of eight navigable rivers snake their way inland, is a geographical feature which
has powerfully influenced the whole development of south-eastern
Africa. People have settled round its shores and along its rivers,
fishing, hunting the whales which every year came to the Bay to give
birth, trading ivory, and maintaining a rich and diversified economy
of cattle-keeping and agriculture. Moreover the influence of the Bay
has stretched far to the south and across the mountains to the interior,
drawing trade and providing a natural focus for communications and
migrations.

South of the Bay lie the well-watered coastal foothills of Natal and
the Transkei, backed by the high Drakensberg range which traps the
seasonal rains. These regions are relatively fertile and have always
sustained dense populations, but they lack any natural point of focus
like Delagoa Bay. The coast has no good harbours and apparently the

immediate coastal area was largely avoided by the inhabitants of the region who had no need for fish to provide protein in their diet. Moreover, the width of the coastal foothills created no natural bottlenecks to force communication to take certain routes. Human settlement spread out in scattered homesteads that made full use of the rich varieties of microclimate and vegetation, while further south still there was room for expansion into regions occupied only by San hunters and Khoi herders.

The scattered populations of the dry bush country north of the Limpopo and the inhabitants of the richer country of Natal and the Transkei alike found the motor of their history to lie in the region of the Bay, whose geographical location and natural riches exerted a powerful influence. To these natural advantages the Portuguese came to add the factor of external trade, and Delagoa Bay became the doorway through which the peoples of southern Africa had their first sustained experience of direct contact with the trans-oceanic world.

People

The Sabi river has been a historic frontier separating a region to the north dominated mainly by the culture of Shona speakers from one to the south where the clusters of ethnic groups, culturally related to the Nguni and Xhosa, have been classified as 'south-eastern Bantu'. It is clear that as early as the sixteenth century, from which written records of the peoples of this region survive, the dominant social formation was the patrilineal lineage. Settlements were made up of family heads with their wives, children and other dependents. New settlements would be created by a son acquiring a wife and moving from his father's homestead to establish one of his own. Cattle ownership was the key to wealth and hence to political and social power. Cattle accumulated in the hands of the lineage heads were used to control production and reproduction, and were indispensible for the payment of *lobola* (brideprice) which would enable young men to marry and establish homesteads for themselves. Through cattle ownership the leading males of the community maintained their dominance and the leading lineages acquired political control over neighbours who owned less cattle.

Cattle were acquired through trade and warfare, but also through natural increase so that cattle husbandry became the most important economic activity of the region. Specialist knowledge was built up about the best summer and winter pastures, how to keep the dreaded tsetse fly at bay, and how to survive drought. Over the centuries, the suitability or otherwise of certain areas for cattle-keeping came to determine the pattern of human settlement, the density of population, the size of political units and the relations between the various ethnic groups. Where cattle-keeping was difficult and unrewarding, populations were thinner, political units smaller and other forms of economic activity asserted themselves. People fished to obtain protein, metalware might replace cattle in economic and marriage transactions, and trade and hunting might play a more important role in economic life. Where the country favoured cattle, as it did in the Natal region and round Delagoa Bay, denser populations could be maintained and powerful chieftaincies had the opportunity to develop.[2]

Before the sixteenth century, economic relations based on trade appear to have been rudimentary. Apart from the rivers that flowed into Delagoa Bay, there were no easily navigable waterways in the south. Trade by porterage was costly and few commodities were of sufficient value to make long-distance trade profitable.[3] Such trade as there was appears to have been in metalware, with copper from the Transvaal high veldt being worked and sold in the coastal regions. In the extreme north of the region the Sabi was an important highway to the interior and one of the routes for trade between the Karanga cultural area and the coast, but the influence of Sabi trade was probably not felt further south than Inhambane and the Vuhoca coast opposite the Bazaruto Islands.

Between the Sabi and Delagoa Bay the relatively poor agricultural conditions and sparse population led to the development of small, isolated but distinct ethnic groups. The earliest populations related to the south-eastern Bantu were the people the Portuguese encountered all along the coast south of the Zambesi, whom they called Tonga. The Tonga practised matrilineal descent and their society was characterised by the small size of its political units which were sometimes no bigger than individual villages. North of the Sabi the Portuguese saw the Tonga gradually dominated by the expansion of Karanga chieftaincies and confined to the coasts and river valleys. Karanga invaders had also pushed south of the Sabi, and there were Karanga chieftaincies as far south as Inhambane — one of them, probably Gamba, leaving the impressive hallmark of Karanga culture in the ruins of Manekweni. Karanga cultural influence was felt on the Limpopo and some of the chieftaincies of Delagoa Bay even had traditions of a Karanga origin. However, although the conquering Karanga chiefs left a tradition of strong chieftaincy among the Tonga of the south, as they did among the Tonga of the Zambesi valley, their language did not survive and throughout most of the coastal lowlands of Mozambique the Tonga and Tsonga languages reasserted themselves and diluted the significance of the Karanga expansion.[4]

By the sixteenth century the original Tonga population south of the Limpopo had been overlaid by various groups, in later years often

classified by the Portuguese as Tsonga or Thonga. This broad cluster
of ethnic groups contained people who spoke many different dialects
and called themselves by many different names. Although some of the
Tsonga chieftaincies of the Bay were to grow to an impressive size, it
is clear that no central authority ever imposed a common political
identity in the way that the Karanga chieftaincies had done over the
peoples of the Zimbabwe plateau. The heartland of Tsonga culture
consisted of the Limpopo valley, Delagoa Bay and the fertile valleys
of the rivers that led into it. South of Delagoa Bay, Nguni-speakers
were predominant, while westwards beyond the mountains were the
Venda and Sotho. However, although political fragmentation and the
existence of various dialects always gave the impression of a wide
diversity of different peoples, it is perhaps more important to stress
the essential cultural unity of this region where the cattle-owning
patriarchs provided a cultural mould that fashioned the lives of all the
peoples.

The coast

The influence of Indian Ocean trade and the activities of the Muslim
seafarers stretched a considerable way south of Sofala. The Sabi was
used as a port of entry to the interior, and south of the Sabi were the
Bazaruto Islands where pearls were fished and a maritime community
flourished. That the influence of Indian Ocean culture extended south
to Inhambane can be inferred from the existence there of cotton-
growing and a cloth industry. South of Inhambane the Portuguese
recorded the existence of a 'sheikh' at Inhapula in 1589, which may
indicate that Islamic influence had spread even further south.[5] However, there is no evidence for Muslim commercial contacts with the
Limpopo or with Delagoa Bay itself.

Although they may not have been engaged in maritime commerce,
the peoples of Delagoa Bay had taken to the sea for other purposes.
The whales that bred in the bay were hunted, and ocean-going canoes
capable of carrying up to fourteen people were used for fishing and
for general transport, linking the communities of the different river
estuaries.[6] In 1589 *luzios*, a kind of *mtepe* (or sewn boat), were being
used in Delagoa Bay but their introduction probably followed in the
wake of the Portuguese.

The arrival of Portuguese ivory trading ships in Delagoa Bay in the
middle of the century was to prove a definite point of departure for
the further evolution of the south-eastern Bantu communities. Ivory
trading did not constitute a dramatic revolution, but rather added a
significant variable to the factors which balanced the lives of these
peoples. The fluctuations of foreign trade had now to be taken into

account along with the vagaries of climate and ecology. Imported foreign consumer goods supplemented, but did not replace, the accumulation of cattle by the patrilineages. However, diplomatic and commercial relations with the Portuguese did require the development of a whole set of skills quite different from those hitherto valued in Tsonga or Tonga society.

The Portuguese ivory trade

Although some of the earliest Portuguese exploratory voyages touched on the southern coast of Mozambique, and Delagoa Bay appears on the Cantino map of 1502, the region was not thoroughly explored till the 1540s when the trading voyages of Lourenço Marques revealed the potential of trade with the peoples of the southern river estuaries. Lourenço Marques' semi-official voyages were complemented by the drift southwards of independent Portuguese and *mestizos* intent on developing trade or escaping from the jurisdiction of the forts. At the same time accounts of shipwrecks on the southern coast threw the character of the whole region into vivid relief. Then in 1560 the area south of the Sabi was opened up in another way. The first Jesuit mission to eastern Africa, led by Gonçalo da Silveira, decided to make Inhambane the centre of its activities. For a year the mission tried to establish itself, and detailed reports of the region were sent back to the officials of the Order in Europe.

Portuguese began to desert the garrison of Sofala almost as soon as it was established. They set themselves up as traders or took their firearms and became mercenaries in the service of chiefs in the interior. Within a few years an Afro-Portuguese community began to emerge participating in the commercial life of the local communities and bound to them by kinship as well as by economic opportunity. In 1554 the survivors of the wreck of the *São João* found evidence of Portuguese trade well south of the Bay. They came across one chief who had acquired a Portuguese nickname, presumably from ivory traders, and found a red mark scored on a tree by the crew of a ship that had visited the river of Boa Paz.[7] In 1589 the survivors of the wrecked carrack, *São Tomé*, came ashore near a river on the coast of modern Natal that was called 'the river of Simão Dote' after a Portuguese ivory trader who frequented the area. Subsequently on their march north they came across a Portuguese with a *luzio* 'which is a kind of boat used in those parts, with which he had come there to trade'. Near Inhambane they found 'a half-caste named Simão Lopes, a native of Sofala, who had fled to this place on account of matters concerning the faith', while on the Bazaruto Islands they found a 'native of Sofala named António Rodrigues', although the islands were principally inhabited by Muslims.[8] These were the unofficial Afro-Portuguese, found everywhere along the coast involved in trade and forming part of the local commercial community.

However, by 1589 there was an official Portuguese presence as well. Following Lourenço Marques' successful reconnaissance in 1545, there were regular ivory trading voyages to a number of river mouths and coastal settlements. Soon the ivory trade settled into a pattern. Every year ships from the royal factory in Mozambique were sent to Delagoa Bay and Inhambane to trade for ivory. It is not known how long a stop was made at Inhambane but the same ship also probably visited the mouth of the Limpopo. The vessel that went to Delagoa Bay usually stayed four months, although Santos records the case of a ship staying nearly a year.[9] The length of the stay is at first sight remarkable but it is explained by the structure of the trade that grew up in the Bay.

Delagoa Bay is an extensive system of waterways and estuaries into which four major rivers and a number of minor ones flow. The rivers are navigable for some considerable distance into the interior and no one chief ever controlled all the rivers and all the shores of the Bay. The Portuguese built no permanent settlement, which would have forced them into a complex and difficult political relationship with one of the chiefs. Instead they used their stay of about four months to visit different points in the Bay to trade with the different chiefs. The crew of the trading ship built semi-permanent encampments on Inhaca island in the south and Xefina island in the north and from these points sent their boats to trade in the various rivers (Map 8).

The Portuguese were able to use the flexibility provided by their boats to play off one chief against another. The trade of the Bay was hardly comparable to the silk trade conducted by the Great Ship that operated between Macao and Japan, but the commercial principles were the same. As Japanese *daimyos* vied with one another and granted favours to the Portuguese to attract the Great Ship to call at their ports, so the chiefs of the Bay had to compete for Portuguese favour to obtain the all-important trade goods on which their authority increasingly depended. On the southern shores of the Bay the Portuguese dealt with the chieftaincy of Inhaca through whose land traders from the south had to pass. Inhaca cultivated good relations with the Portuguese and gave much assistance to the shipwrecked parties struggling north from the coasts of Natal, for which he was amply rewarded with gifts of beads and cloth. The survivors of the *São João*, for example, were 'ransomed' for forty beads each.[10]

Imported goods could be used either to acquire more cattle within the traditional economic and social structure of the region, or to reward followers directly and establish bonds of obligation between

rival patrilineages. However this economic advantage was employed,
Inhaca acquired considerable political power, pushing his control as
far inland as the Lebombo mountains and dominating all the access
routes from the south.[11]

In the sixteenth century Portuguese trade with Inhaca put the other
major chieftaincy of the Bay, Tembe, very much into the shade. The
Tembe chieftaincy had traditions of owing its origin to a Karanga
invasion, and claimed some kind of paramountcy in the region.
However, trade was more potent than tradition, and Tembe had to
take second place, often venting his hostility in gratuitous violence
towards shipwrecked Portuguese who struggled round to the northern
shores of the Bay. However, in 1621 a dramatic quarrel with Inhaca
made the Portuguese look to Tembe as their principal trading partner.
Trade with Tembe was conducted from Xefina island from which
Portuguese boats made expeditions to the mainland for supplies of
ivory. In 1647, for example, the Portuguese held five ivory trading
fairs in the various rivers of the Bay, appointing to each one temporary factors who communicated with the main ship anchored off
Xefina. Contact with the Portuguese enabled Tembe to reassert
its paramountcy round the Bay, while Inhaca suffered from being
ignored by the Portuguese. Possibly as a result of the disruption of its
trade, the Inhaca chieftaincy split into two parts, which came to be
called Inhaca and Machavane.[12]

Most of the ivory, in which the Portuguese were principally interested, had to be brought from considerable distances and, as a commodity that repaid transport, it was presumably the growth of this
ivory trade that expanded the long-distance commercial networks
which previously had only existed to handle copper artefacts. Ivory
was sent to the Bay from as far south as Natal, and the evidence suggests that it was mainly the route to the south that was opened up by
Portuguese trade. It seems probable that ivory trading was strictly
controlled by the chiefs. The hunting would have needed the sort of
communal effort that only the lineage heads could organise, while the
transport of the ivory required the permission of chiefs through whose
territory the caravans had to pass. Nevertheless ivory trading did not
lead directly to economic specialisation to the detriment of other
aspects of the local economy. The dominance of cattle wealth was
apparently not seriously affected, and the Portuguese were sometimes
asked to aid in cattle raids. Moreover, their trade was more diversified
than might have been imagined. They bought food for their own consumption and, according to Santos, bought 'ambergris, ivory, slaves,
honey, butter, horns and hoofs of the rhinoceros, and tusks and hoofs
of the hippopotamus'.[13] In return two commodities were imported,
beads and cloth. Ironware was clearly also a valuable commodity,

particularly for the coastal peoples, since the shipwrecked sailors found little difficulty in obtaining supplies and even cattle in exchange for iron retrieved from the wrecks. However, official Portuguese trade in the sixteenth and seventeenth centuries does not appear to have included metalware in any major quantity. Indeed it was the Portuguese who purchased copper artefacts, and the trade in metals was all the other way, from Africa to the Portuguese.

Trade undoubtedly strengthened the lineage heads, enabling them to reward followers and purchase cattle to enhance their economic position relative to other lineages. Both Inhaca and Tembe developed powerful centralised chieftaincies, the first extending as far south as St Lucia Bay and the latter covering all the country as far as the Lebombo mountains. It is difficult not to conclude that these large Tsonga states with their provinces and subchieftaincies, which were larger than the Karanga states of Monomotapa or Kiteve, came increasingly to depend for their political cohesion and strength on the trade of Delagoa Bay. However, both chieftaincies suffered from rivalries within the chiefly families which the system of competing lineages seemingly inevitably encouraged. They showed a tendency to fragment as rival lineages competed for the privileges of trade. The lineage structure of south-eastern Bantu society was too segmentary for centralised institutions to survive for long, and their history emphasises how important the emergence of the dominant Karanga élite had been for the growth of states such as Barue, Kiteve and Monomotapa.

The eighteenth century

The second half of the seventeenth century witnessed two developments: the Portuguese interest in the ivory trade waned, and the Tsonga began a period of vigorous expansion to the north.

After about 1660 the Portuguese began to call less and less often at the Bay. Sometimes years elapsed between the visits of their trading ships. The Portuguese eastern empire was under severe pressure from the Dutch and English, and resources may simply not have existed to provide a regular trading ship. Moreover the rise in the importance of the ivory trade with Kilwa and with the Makua people of the region north of the Zambesi was a far greater attraction, since traders from Mozambique were spared the long and dangerous voyage to the south. Indeed it may be assumed that northern ivory simply priced Delagoa Bay out of the market in what was clearly a highly competitive situation which saw even the Zambesi Portuguese at an increasing disadvantage.

Of course, it is possible that the decline of trade at the Bay was what prompted the Tsonga to move further north to try to re-establish commercial contacts with the Portuguese at Inhambane, the Sabi or even Sofala. However, it is unlikely that foreign trade so dominated the lives of the people of southern Mozambique as to cause a massive migration when it was disrupted. More likely, the expansion was part of the natural process of lineages breaking away from the parent stock and expanding to find new space for themselves. The dryness of the region north of the Limpopo, which can only support a sparse population at the best of times, no doubt encouraged the unusual rapidity and geographical extent of this expansion. It also seems that there may have been pressure from peoples from the high veldt moving into the region of Delagoa Bay. Whatever the reason, by the early eighteenth century Tsonga chiefs, originating in the neighbourhood of the Bay, were migrating northwards with their followers and establishing their control throughout the country inland from Inhambane. Some were even moving northwards towards the Sabi. As they formed political units much larger than those of the native Tonga population, the latter were put under increasing pressure, either moving to the protection of the coastal swamps and sand dunes or staying put and suffering absorption by the conquerors. The details are lacking, but the whole process is clearly reminiscent of the later expansion of the Nguni in the nineteenth century.[14]

Trade at Delagoa Bay, meanwhile, did not die. In the 1680s private English traders operating under the auspices of the East India Company began trading in the Bay. In 1685 the Portuguese reported sighting five of their ships at once in the Bay 'trading ivory and amber with trade goods better than our own'.[15] Their regular visits meant that ivory was once more attracted from the interior, but it also meant that the chiefs were able to trade with two European partners, a factor which restored the balance of competition in favour of the African seller. In 1688 it was recorded that English, Dutch and Portuguese ships were all at anchor in the Bay at the same time.[16] Nevertheless the principal feature of international trade at the Bay remained its spasmodic nature. English traders were mostly opportunistic interlopers anxious for short-term profit, not the long term development of trade. An account of English trading methods in the Bay in 1686 records that the English seized 'six or seven of their captains [headmen?] who came aboard to see the ship and eight or ten more men . . . so that they were forc'd to bring down some more [ivory] before they were released'.[17] This was hardly the approach of people who wanted to build up a long-term commercial relationship.

The *Little Josiah*, commanded by Captain Derring, spent from April to November 1693 trading in Delagoa Bay, exchanging among other things 'tinn barrs' and beads for ivory — 'these people love most large yallow & purple but take little black & white Beads, & no green'. He found the 'peoples in generall are all very civill & honest (with good care taken) from ye highest to ye lowest', though he also commented that 'Mettolo & his people [are] knavishly inclined'. His ship's boats visited fairs in a number of the rivers and as well as ivory found 'some white ambragrese & much plenty of provisions, as cattle corne fruit etc.' He refers to Minissa, thirty-five leagues inland, as the 'greatest towne' with at least four other trading centres on the river before it was reached.[18]

For reasons not entirely clear, but possibly connected with the systematic attempt to root out the pirates who operated in the western Indian Ocean, English traders called less frequently after 1700, while it appears that the Portuguese abandoned the trade entirely after one of their ships was attacked by pirates in 1703. As a result chiefs were left with stocks of ivory and could no longer distribute trade goods to their clients. When European ships did arrive, there was a feverish rush to supply the market but with no guarantee that the trading bonanza would continue even beyond the single year. The dislocation to local trade caused by the irregular visits of European ships to the Bay seems to have encouraged the growth of an overland trade route linking the Bay to Inhambane and Sofala where Portuguese goods were still regularly available.[19]

The Dutch

In 1721 the Dutch East India Company decided to found a trading factory at the Bay. The Dutch settlement at the Cape had initially been made in 1652 for the supply of their Indiamen, and trade had been discouraged. Even so the Dutch had cut ebony wood in Mauritius, had traded for slaves on the coast of Madagascar and frequently, if unsuccessfully, sent exploratory expeditions to the various trading ports on the east African coast. In 1721 the Dutch believed that the time was suitable for developing the trade of the Bay and they decided that this could best be done from a permanent factory.

In March 1721, on the site of the present city of Maputo, a Dutch expedition consisting of 113 men, forty-four of whom were soldiers, built a fort for which 200 African women are said to have been engaged to carry the earth. The Dutch suffered from fever and their numbers rapidly became depleted even though eighty recruits were sent to strengthen the garrison. In 1722 English pirates attacked and destroyed the settlement but the Dutch rebuilt it, building houses, keeping herds of cattle, and planting gardens and plantations in which they grew sugar and indigo. The accounts of the Dutch factory show that it traded ivory totalling about 5,000 pounds a year (an extremely modest amount), copper, aloes, slaves and gold dust — all in small quantities. Over the nine years of its occupation of the Bay the factory cost ten times more than it earned. It failed partly because it could not supply the local market with the type of beads required, while it was handicapped by Company policy which tried to establish monopoly trading conditions and pay low prices. The Dutch traded tobacco but refused to sell firearms. The local population responded to the pretensions to monopoly by withholding ivory supplies. As the settlement's failure became more evident, the Dutch tried the device of inviting local dignitaries to visit the Cape. They sent an expedition inland to explore for gold mines, and agreed to take part in some local wars, but their German mercenaries were reluctant colonists and many of them deserted. In December 1730 they abandoned their fort and withdrew.

Delagoa Bay was a good place for a European colony — better even than the Cape as it had a safe deepwater harbour and a rich hinterland suitable for cattle keeping and tropical agriculture. That the Dutch were unable to make a success of it is evidence of their inefficiency and general mishandling of their opportunities, but it also strongly suggests that the economy of the Bay's hinterland was not large enough at that time to sustain the level of international commerce that a permanent factory would demand. Although ivory could accumulate in the hands of chiefs, enabling individual ships to trade profitably from time to time, a permanent factory probably exhausted the capacity of the local economy to maintain supplies to the market. The Dutch purchases of gold, copper and slaves give the same impression. The market supplied only small quantities of these commodities, the byproducts of the comparatively low level of surplus production in what were still predominantly subsistence economies. Although the Dutch failed to supply the market with the goods it wanted, the English and Portuguese had done so but could not sustain profitable trade over a long period. The African economy did not have the capacity to respond to market forces beyond small marginal increases that could be achieved within the parameters of a traditional subsistence economy. Moreover high transport costs made any increase of production difficult to move over long distances. A breakthrough could only result from major technological innovation (an unlikely eventuality) or a major reorganisation of manpower resources. In the words of David Hedges, 'hunting was a production process susceptible of modification by the aggregation of greater manpower; but there is no sign of such changes resulting from participation in the ivory trade before 1750.'[20]

The existence of the international market had the effect of producing political rivalries as the chiefs sought to increase their share of imports by competing for political control rather than by increasing production for which they did not have the technology. The main political changes in the immediate hinterland of the Bay in the eighteenth century concern the chieftaincy of Tembe. Civil war in the 1730s led to the emergence of a large Tembe chieftaincy under the rule of Mangobe whose political control extended to the mountains. However his dominance coincided with a period when comparatively few Europeans visited Delagoa Bay, and when Mangobe died in *c.* 1765 the chieftaincy once again broke up into smaller units.

Economic expansion at Delagoa Bay

By the end of the eighteenth century the level of economic activity at Delagoa Bay had enormously expanded and in the nineteenth century something akin to a commercial revolution with profound social and political consequences was under way. What happened is easier to describe than to explain. From 1750 English ships from India were once again trading at the Bay and the leading merchant, Edward Chandler, was using Indian commercial agents to buy ivory from the chiefs; how much he bought is not known. Then in 1778 William Bolts, an English adventurer in Austrian service, arrived to found another permanent trading factory. Bolts had found backing for his enterprise in Austrian Trieste and planned a major East India trading company. Delagoa Bay was to be a refreshment station and agricultural settlement as well as a trading factory. Bolts' expedition brought 155 men and an unspecified number of women to help found the colony, and although he himself abandoned the settlement, it continued in existence till 1781 when it was expelled by a Portuguese military expedition. In 1781, after more than two centuries of contact, the Portuguese established their first permanent trading station in Delagoa Bay.[21]

The Austrian factory was by no means unsuccessful, trading on average 75,000 pounds of ivory a year, vastly more than the unsuccessful Dutch station fifty years earlier. However this is not the only evidence for the expansion of commercial activity. English ships continued to visit the Bay in the late 1770s, and one is known to have shipped 100,000 pounds of ivory. The ivory trade continued at this level until it was severely disrupted by French corsairs during the Revolutionary wars.[22] In 1796, as a result of French raids, the Portuguese temporarily abandoned their settlement and the trading ships ceased to call.

It seems clear that one aspect of the ivory boom was the willingness of the Austrians and the English to pay much higher prices, but it is also likely that other factors had begun to influence the internal economy of the region. One of these was the unsettled climate. Although periodically the rains were liable to fail in this region, little can be said about the pattern of rainfall till the end of the eighteenth century when drought became increasingly regular. The 1790s saw the great drought known as the *mahlatule*, which lasted many years and in some regions continued into the new century. The drought naturally strained the traditional social relations and political structures of the chieftaincies. Pressure on good land, water supplies and food reserves intensified, and hunting, a traditional strategy for coping with food shortages, increased. At the same time European traders themselves had begun to enter the market for foodstuffs.

Although European whaling ships are recorded in the seventeenth century, it was from the 1780s that whalers began to use the Bay in large numbers. Their crews were not traders interested in playing a sensitive market, but were simply concerned to purchase cattle and fresh food, for which they were prepared to pay a high price if necessary. At the height of the drought Tembe is reported to have continued to sell food to the whalers while his own starving people came to the shores of the bay to feed on the carcasses of dead whales.[23]

By the end of the century, therefore, the level of economic activity had risen but it had also changed in nature. Imports in much larger quantities were entering the country and this seems to have promoted an increasing flow of ivory and a large-scale movement of cattle on the hoof towards the Bay. The impact of such developments on the economies and social structures of the cattle-owning peoples of the hinterland was considerable, while back along the trade routes and cattle trails the powerful demand of the Delagoa Bay market was to influence the development of people hundreds of miles inland. Perhaps the greatest impact was felt in the south and south-east among the Nguni. The rich, well-watered country of Swaziland and Natal was a region where cattle could be raised in large numbers and with a labour surplus that could be employed in the hunting of ivory. European ships visiting Delagoa Bay looked to traders from the south to meet their demands since the poorer, more barren northern regions could not respond in the same way and do not appear to have been affected by the economic expansion to the same degree. It was this demand, coming at a time of drought and scarcity, which stimulated political change among the Nguni and led indirectly to the great Nguni diaspora of the early nineteenth century.

Inhambane

Inhambane was to become one of the major port cities of Mozambique and the capital of a province. Its history is not very different from that of the other coastal towns except that much less is known about it before the eighteenth century. The settlement of Inhambane owes its existence to a deep sea inlet into which flows the small and unimportant Matamba river. The bay is formed by two protective sandy headlands that create a sheltered harbour across which lies a sand bar. It is reasonable to assume that Inhambane's history as a port pre-dates the arrival of the Portuguese.

Coastal dhows had traded to the Bazaruto Islands attracted by the pearls and ambergris for which they were renowned. Imported Islamic and Persian wares dating from no later than the eleventh century have been found at Chibuene just to the south, and probably these were brought by Muslim seafarers who would also have traded at Inhambane.[24] Naturally cotton cloth was the major item traded with the Tonga inhabitants, and a local cotton spinning and weaving industry developed for which Inhambane became well-known. Sometime well before the arrival of the Portuguese the region inland from Inhambane was invaded by Karanga who had established a number of chieftaincies which dominated the local Tonga inhabitants and probably traded with Muslim merchants through Inhambane.

Just south of Inhambane is Cape Correntes where the African coast changes direction, bending sharply south-westwards, and where ships heading for the ports of the Mozambique coast frequently made their first landfall before heading north along the coast to Sofala. In 1505 one of Francisco de Almeida's ships was wrecked there and the crew made its way along the coast to Chiluane.[25] Freelance Portuguese traders made contact with the Karanga chiefs near Inhambane, and sometime in the 1550s the son of one of these paid a visit to Mozambique Island. As a result Inhambane was chosen as the destination for the first Jesuit mission to eastern Africa in 1560. This mission only survived a short time and after its departure the Portuguese developed Inhambane as an ivory trading port. A ship freighted by the royal factory in Mozambique called once every year or so to buy ivory, and the trade was conducted on much the same basis as the trade at Delagoa Bay. With the development of the contract between the Crown and the captains of Mozambique, Inhambane was included within the area of the Crown's monopoly and by the end of the sixteenth century all the ships trading there were sent on his account.

During the seventeenth century Inhambane, Delagoa Bay and to a lesser extent the mouth of the Limpopo became the points to which the peoples of the interior south of the Sabi came to trade with the outside world. Imported goods circulated through the trade and redistribution networks of the interior, and in spite of rivalries between chiefs for control of this trade, an overland route linking the ports grew up. The survivors of the *São João Baptista* followed this road in 1623, and during periods when Portuguese ships failed to visit one or other of the ports, imported wares continued to be traded along overland routes. It seems that towards the end of the seventeenth century the Portuguese increasingly concentrated their activities at Inhambane, partly no doubt because it was closer to the base of their operations and partly because it was less exposed than Delagoa Bay to the risk of armed confrontation with foreign ships. However, more important than these factors, there is clear evidence that Inhambane proved better able than Delagoa Bay to supply the Portuguese with profitable trading opportunities.

At the end of the century the trade of Inhambane was still conducted by a factor visiting the port at irregular intervals. However, early in the eighteenth century the decision was taken by the *Junta do Comércio* to lease the trade of Inhambane to an Indian named Calcanagi Velabo. He was also to lease the trade of Angoche, and paid 11,000 *cruzados* for the two monopolies.[26] Although the Portuguese Crown refused to sanction this lease and ordered it to be revoked, it is probable that Velabo was responsible for the beginnings of Indian commercial interest in the region. Throughout the eighteenth century Indians were to be the dominant influence in the 'Portuguese' settlement at Inhambane.

The beginnings of a permanent Portuguese settlement dates from 1727 when Bernardo Castro Soares, the commander of the Portuguese trading vessel, found a Dutch ship, the *Victoria*, anchored in the bay and busy trading with the local Tonga chiefs. When the Dutch departed, Castro Soares remained in the bay and sent an urgent message to Sofala for military reinforcements. When the Dutch returned the following year, they found a permanent Portuguese encampment and heard rumours that an army had set out from Sofala to punish the African chiefs who had traded with the Dutch.

The march of the Sofala army, under the command of Domingos Lopes Rebello, was a remarkable undertaking. Its activities are typical of so many episodes in the history of Mozambique where bands of armed men on the move through the bush have been able to terrorise and dominate fragmented and dis-integrated peasant communities almost at will. Rebello's army reached Inhambane after a march of 200 miles which included a crossing of the Sabi. In the words of the historian, Alan Smith,

> Rebello immediately set about the task of making the guilty pay for their misdeeds and heresies. Villages and gardens throughout the area were set afire, a large number of cattle were confiscated and many of those who were unable to escape to safety were either killed or imprisoned as slaves. Among the many people

who died during the *razza* were the chiefs of Tinga Tinga and Nialingue.[27]

The Portuguese settlement founded by Castro Soares at Inhambane was situated twelve leagues above the bar. It was difficult of access as ocean-going ships had to negotiate two other sand banks and could only safely enter or leave the port on the monthly full tides. The settlement had a fort constructed of earth and stakes 'which also served as the residence of the captain; outside its walls was the church, the house of the priest and some other small houses in which live some *mestizos* and christian blacks who form the garrison of soldiers.'[28]

The garrison was supposed to number fifty but seldom approached anywhere near that number. The fort itself would not have protected the settlement from an attack by Europeans. As Pedro do Rego Barretto said in 1745, 'it would have been enough for them to have laid eyes on it to capture it'.[29] In practice the port was protected from external attack by the difficult entrance and the inaccessibility of the Portuguese settlement. In 1763 the governor-general, Pereira do Lago, made Inhambane a town, gave a building for the *Câmara* and endowed the council with the income from a palm grove, but apparently there were seldom enough Portuguese subjects to fill the municipal offices.[30] Census figures from the last two decades of the century show a Christian population of 203 for the parish of Inhambane.[31]

However, modest as the town may have appeared to outside observers, it began to have considerable influence among the surrounding people. Tonga headmen living in the vicinity recognised, in an informal way, the hegemony of the fort and sought its protection. The Portuguese did not encourage the establishment of crown lands or *prazos* as they did in Querimba, Sofala and the Zambesi settlements, so there was not a mediating class of Africanised Portuguese chiefs with whom to deal and there do not appear to have been any major African chieftaincies to reckon with as at Delagoa Bay. Instead the captain of the fort came to acquire a quasi-chiefly position, being the person through whom the valued imports were channelled and who could offer some protection from the hostile attentions of peoples from the interior. The Portuguese distrusted the established Islamised trading class which was established on the coast and began the practice of employing African traders, somewhat like the *mussambazes* of Zambesia and the *patamares* of the Mozambique mainland, to conduct their trade with the interior.[32]

By the mid-century the protective role of the Portuguese was becoming increasingly important. The rise and evident prosperity of Inhambane was accompanied by the large-scale northward movement of sections of Tsonga-speaking Hlengwe (called by the Portuguese Bila and Landins). This invasion, as we have seen, was probably caused by internal stresses, by the need to find good land on which to settle and found new villages, and by the pressures of Sotho-speaking people entering the hinterland of Delagoa Bay from the Transvaal high veldt. The Hlengwe invaders used ruthless methods to subdue the small Tonga chieftaincies, carrying off cattle and women, burning villages and executing Tonga headmen.[33] However, their arrival in the region as a group subjugating the less well-organised Tonga undoubtedly gave the fort captains of Inhambane the opportunity to expand their role and for the fort's sphere of influence to grow accordingly.

By the middle of the century Tsonga invaders had reached the Bazaruto Islands where they interrupted the age-old trade in pearls.[34] So to keep the Tsonga away from Inhambane, the Portuguese captains raised auxiliary forces and successfully mounted counter-raids against the new Tsonga settlements.[35] Considerable numbers of Tonga settled under the protection of the fort, acquiring in this way a separate identity from those who came under Hlengwe rule. However, Portuguese influence could not extend far inland, and the Tsonga chiefs were able to retaliate almost at will by severing the inland trade routes.

Commerce at Inhambane was controlled by Indians trading from their mother houses in Mozambique. In the mid-eighteenth century the dominance of the Indian community was such that a priest of Indian extraction was usually appointed vicar of the parish. He maintained a school for the local Christians but in addition accepted the children of the Muslim traders who also appear to have been prominent in the commerce of the port. The Indian school at Inhambane seems to have acquired a considerable reputation throughout the whole east African coast and even in India.

The principal item of commerce was ivory and that alone might have accounted for the prosperity of the port. However, the rise of Inhambane was also due to its being the first Mozambican port to develop a significant slave trade. This was almost certainly an offshoot of the wars accompanying the Tsonga conquest of the peoples of the coastlands round Inhambane, and early in the 1760s slaves were an important item in the trade of the port, their destination being the French Indian Ocean islands. Inhambane also developed a trade in foodstuffs, becoming one of the major suppliers for the naval base at Mozambique Island. In 1758 the secretary to the Mozambique government, Inácio Caetano Xavier, listed the products of the country round Inhambane which included millet, vegetables, cattle, goats, fish, hens, various sorts of oil, honey, butter

Table 7.1. EXPORTS FROM INHAMBANE, *c.* 1762

Commodity	Quantity	Value in xerafins
Ivory	50 bars	60,000
Pitch	50 candis	15,000
Mafura	60 candis	10,000
Fat	20 candis	6,000
Amber	1 arroba	5,000
Rice	1,000 panjas	4,000
Slaves	400	20,000
Pearls		
Total		120,000

Source: A.A. de Andrade, *Relações de Moçambique Setecentista*, pp. 219–20.

and wooden mortars, as well as ivory, ambergris and slaves (see Table 7.1).

In 1768 the annual average exported was estimated at 90–100 *bars* of ivory and 1,500 slaves.[36] However in 1783 the factory traded only thirty-eight tusks, and the official view was that trade was stagnant — which was variously blamed on the customs regime, the lack of Portuguese settlers, the shortage of transport and the wrong type of trade goods. Pereira do Lago blamed the decline on the Indians and tried to prevent their agents from trading in the interior. However, these so-called *commerciantes volantes* were probably the most successful part of the trading community and were spreading the market economy widely in the interior.

The northward migrations of the Tsonga-speakers into the region of Inhambane meant that by the mid-eighteenth century Mozambique had become broadly divided into three cultural areas — the predominantly Makua region north of the Zambesi, the Zambesi valley and the region south to Manica and Sofala which were influenced by the Afro-Portuguese, and the Tsonga-dominated region to the south of that. Each of these broad cultural areas was linked to the outside world by commerce channelled through Portuguese-controlled ports and financed by Indian capital. However, although by the end of the eighteenth century this pattern of international trade was several centuries old, the traditional subsistence economies of the vast majority of the people remained largely unaffected. In particular there was no significant modification of the traditional technology. Contact with Indian and European capital may have led to an intensification of traditional modes of production but it had not revolutionised the means by which this production was carried on. In 1768 a vivid illustration of this was given by the governor-general, Pereira do Lago. He noted that there were ironwood trees near Inhambane and that he had ordered saws to be sent so that these could be cut into planks to form a useful export. However, he noted, the local Portuguese had adopted the African way of preparing wood, which was to cut a single plank from each tree using the laborious methods of shaping it with an axe.[37]

The Portuguese had even been successful in restricting the importation of firearms and had therefore prevented the political revolution that might have resulted from the possession of firearms by chiefs. Yet in Europe this was the century of the Industrial Revolution and the failure of African societies of Mozambique to adopt new technologies is certainly the most important single factor in the development of underdevelopment in the region.

8

INTERNATIONAL RELATIONS AND THE COMMERCE OF COASTAL MOZAMBIQUE, 1600–1800

Turks, Dutch, English and French

Before the 1590s very few Europeans had made the sea voyage to the East except those who went in Portuguese service. The major maritime threat to Portugal's position in eastern Africa had taken the form of Turkish raiders. Between 1538 and 1553 ships based in ports in the Red Sea or the Gulf had regularly challenged Portugal's maritime supremacy in the northern part of the Indian Ocean, and the threat of a Turkish attack on Mozambique Island had convinced the viceroy, Dom João de Castro, of the necessity of fortifying the island. In 1546 plans were drawn up for the building of the fortress of São Sebastião on the northern tip of the island. Work on it continued for the rest of the century and into the next, but eventually São Sebastião became one of the most formidable of European defensive positions in the East.

In 1583 and again in 1585, Turkish galleys commanded by Mir Ali Bey raided the east African coast as far south as Kilwa, and convinced Lisbon of the need to build a major base on the northern sector of the coast as well. In 1593 work began on Fort Jesus at Mombasa, and a captaincy was created with a customs house to levy dues on commerce in that region. The division between the two captaincies was fixed at Cabo Delgado, making this one of the first of Africa's modern frontiers to be demarcated. By that time, however, the Turkish threat was already past. The treeless geography of the Middle East made it difficult for the Turks to build ships in the ports of the Gulf and the Red Sea, and Portuguese seapower had prevented the Ottoman empire from becoming a maritime power in the Indian Ocean. However, the cost had been heavy. The Portuguese military and naval establishment had had to be greatly increased, at huge expense to the exchequer of the *Estado da India*. This policy gave the Portuguese formidable land bases from which their enemies were to find it difficult to oust them, but it left them without the naval capacity to protect the sealanes and maintain their monopolistic pretensions. The English and Dutch were to make such a rapid impact in the East because they found the Portuguese already weakened, and there was no Asiatic power, like Turkey, in a position to challenge them.

The English and Dutch made their first voyages to the East in the 1590s. The Dutch had been stimulated to undertake this empire-building by their war of independence with Spain, which threatened to deprive them of access to the trade of America and the Orient. The English, less endangered by Spain, were nevertheless anxious about the fate of their woollen cloth industry and were prompted to establish Merchant Adventurer companies to seek export outlets for an industry on which the economy had come to depend to a dangerous degree. Both Dutch and English were conscious imitators of the Portuguese. Initially their enterprises drew heavily on the information provided in the writings of the Dutchman Jan Huyghen van Linschoten, who had written an account of the Portuguese empire after travelling to the East in Portuguese service. Their knowledge of navigation, markets and Asiatic trading methods were all heavily influenced by the Portuguese experience, and the Dutch even tried to take over the Portuguese monopolistic trading structure and to capture the fortified bases from which the system was operated.

However, the Dutch and English were also innovators. They built faster, better armed and more sea-worthy ships than the Portuguese, but the secret of their impact in Asia was to be found in the financial organisation of their enterprises. The Portuguese empire had developed as a monopolistic structure in which the right to exercise the monopolies was sold to individuals or syndicates. These were short-term investments of one to three years, carrying high risks and ending in what can best be described as asset-stripping activities by the holders of offices and commands in search of maximum profit. The English and Dutch experimented with joint stock enterprises, attracting capital from a wide range of investors and eventually carrying their risk over numerous enterprises spread over an increasing length of time. Not only were the Dutch and English companies in this way better financed than the Portuguese, but they could operate at lower risk and on smaller profit margins. Moreover, they could afford to nurse markets and build up profitability over long periods of time.

The French were slower to embark on commercial ventures in the East, but speculative French voyages were sent out as early as 1601 and in 1619 François Pyrard published in French a major account of the Portuguese empire and its commercial and political structure. The first French East India Company was established under royal protection in 1634.

Initially both Dutch and English showed considerable interest in the coast of east Africa. Sailing in the wake of the Portuguese, pioneers like Sir James Lancaster used the inner passage between Madagascar and the African mainland and explored the possibility of using Mozambique, Zanzibar or the Comoros as ports of call. In September 1591 Lancaster had the

> . . . lucke to overshoote Mozambique and to fall with a place called Quitangone, two leagues to the northward of it. And we tooke three or foure barkes of Moores (which barkes in their language they call pangaias), laden with millio, hennes, and ducks, with one Portugall boy, going for the provision of Mozambique.[1]

In Zanzibar the Portuguese were hostile, spreading rumours that the English were 'cruell people and men-eaters'. They decided to make their trading settlements inaccessible to the Dutch and English from the very start. Foreign ships were refused revictualling rights at Mozambique, and the Portuguese traders and factors stationed at other points along the coast did their best to stimulate local hostility to rival Europeans. Three men from the East India Company's fourth voyage were killed in an ambush in Pemba, believed to have been instigated by the local Portuguese, and in 1609 the *Union* lost a man while trying to obtain water in Zanzibar. The Company soon attributed all local hostility, even in Madagascar, to the machinations of the Portuguese, and Edward Dodsworth, writing in 1614, even claimed to believe that the Portuguese deliberately drew their maps wrongly in order to mislead the English who relied on them.[2]

It was the Dutch, far better financed and equipped than the still somewhat tentative English, who decided in characteristically forthright manner to oust the Portuguese from their main African stronghold and make Mozambique the westernmost pivot of the new Dutch empire. The first Dutch entrepreneur to show a strong interest in Mozambique was De Moucheron who sent three fleets to the East between 1598 and 1602. The third of these, under Joris van Spilsbergen, cruised along the Mozambique coast visiting Sofala and the mouth of the Zambesi. The same year the Dutch East India Company, the VOC, was founded.

In June 1604 twelve ships, commanded by Admiral Steven van der Hagen, appeared off Mozambique, seized a ship loaded with ivory and landed on the island. This seems only to have been a reconnaissance and the fleet sailed in August without any attempt to take the fort. The Portuguese took no effective measures to strengthen Mozambique, and São Sebastião was in a pathetically weak condition when Paulus van Caerden launched his systematically planned attack in 1607. Between the end of March and 16 May, when the Dutch finally weighed anchor and left, São Sebastião endured a major siege carried out with all the skill and determination of soldiers trained in siege warfare in the Low Countries. However, the Dutch failed to take the fort, which they found too strong to assault and which could not be damaged with artillery. The attackers were greatly affected by disease but the decisive factors in the successful resistance to their attack proved to be the high morale of the defenders of the fort, most of whom were civilians and many of them women, and the fact that the Portuguese could rely on supplies reaching them from the mainland where they maintained contacts with the African population. Van Caerden revictualled in Mayotte in the Comoro Islands and returned to the attack in August, only to find that three Portuguese warships had arrived to help the defence. After a few weeks blockading the port the Dutch departed to make sure of catching the last of the monsoon winds for Asia.

In 1608 the Dutch made a second attempt to take Mozambique with a fleet of nine warships under Admiral Pieter Verhoeven. This time they persisted with the siege until 23 August when they were once again forced to catch the monsoon for India having devastated the island for the second time. Once again they had been defeated by the massive strength of the fortress which they had been unable to breach even with the help of a siege train. It appears too that morale remained high on the Portuguese side while the Dutch suffered from indiscipline and desertion.[3]

After the failure of the third Dutch attack, no European power seriously tried to capture Mozambique again. However, the naval struggle continued. The Dutch and English concentrated on ousting the Portuguese first from Indonesia and after that from northern India and the Gulf area. In 1621 the two Companies formed a joint 'fleet of defence' and in 1622 English warships forced the surrender of Ormuz tilting the struggle for naval supremacy — permanently — in favour of the Protestant powers. The English and Dutch ships sought to waylay the Portuguese Indiamen and isolate the Portuguese settlements in India from Europe. They chose the Mozambique Channel to lay their ambushes because of the relatively narrow strait through which the Portuguese carracks would have to pass, and because the ports of Madagascar and the Comoros formed useful bases for their operations. A number of naval engagements were fought, the most spectacular being the attack by four English ships on the carrack of the viceroy, Dom Manuel de Menezes, in 1616. Rather than surrender the ship, the viceroy ordered it to be driven ashore on Grande Comore, from which he and most of the crew subsequently escaped.[4]

Further prizes were won in 1617 and 1619 when a Portuguese carrack was stopped off Grande Comore and forced to pay 90,000 *reales* as ransom. In June 1622 the 'fleet of defence' fought a major sea battle with a Portuguese armada off Mozambique Island in which three

Portuguese warships were sunk, and in 1628 English ships blockaded Mozambique Island and raided the mainland plantations.[5]

This was to be the last major hostile engagement. In 1635 the Portuguese signed a peace with the English and in 1640 they also came to terms with the Dutch. Thereafter a new pattern of relations developed. The Portuguese allowed English ships to call at their ports to take on water and to revictual, a facility of which the East India Company was prepared to make full use. As early as 1643 the Company ships were being ordered to make a regular stop at Mozambique Island. Here they were confronted with Portuguese authority in the form of the captain, the proprietor of his office who had paid heavily for the privilege. He was only too willing to trade with the English and by the 1650s a clandestine commerce was flourishing. Good commercial relations were promoted by the ability of the English to offer shipping space to the Portuguese for whom the provision of shipping was rapidly becoming a major problem.[6]

Eric Axelson suggested that the successful Portuguese defence of Mozambique Island was one of the decisive military events of southern African history. Had the Dutch taken it, they would almost certainly have established the main naval base and way station for their Indiamen in the island. The Portuguese would never have been able to recapture it and would eventually have had to abandon their other coastal and interior settlements. Not only would Mozambique have developed within the Dutch, as opposed to the Portuguese, imperial system but also the Dutch settlement in the Cape might never have been made, with incalculable consequences for the history of the region. It is probably dangerous to engage in too much speculation on so narrow a base as two military engagements. In Angola and in São Tomé the Dutch did take the main Portuguese town and fortification but were only able to hold on to them for eight years before being forced by the climate and the continued Portuguese retention of the interior to withdraw. The same might well have happened in eastern Africa.

However, there is one curious aspect of this early phase of the European struggle for Africa. During the early seventeenth century the trade of the Zambesi region made the captaincy of Mozambique one of the most valuable of the whole *Estado da India*. Moreover the Portuguese were making major efforts to open up the gold and silver mines of the interior and in the middle years of the century were achieving some success. The Dutch and English appear to have been little interested in this trade. Although both Companies were aware that ivory fetched a high price in India and were even prepared to buy it in Europe to take out to the East, for most of the seventeenth century they showed almost no interest in the east African ivory trade. It was the same with gold. Shortage of bullion was a serious problem for both the Companies and they tried a variety of means to obtain adequate supplies. However, they did not make any concerted effort to wrest the gold mines of eastern Africa from Portugal. The Dutch, in particular, were famous for their acute sense of the market and their willingness to explore and exploit every commercial opportunity. During the early years of the century they continually searched for commodities which they could export from the western Indian Ocean, carrying on an extensive trade in seal oil, ebony from Mauritius and slaves. One can only conclude that the Portuguese defence of their settlements, combined with the difficult navigation of the east African coast, was successful in convincing the northern Europeans that further explorations were not worthwhile.

However, the northern Europeans were not without their effect on the commercial world of the Mozambique Channel, and their rivalry moved the coastal communities of this area much nearer to the centre of the international commercial system which was rapidly evolving under the influence of Dutch, English and Indian merchant capital.

Mozambique, Madagascar and the Comoro Islands

Although in the sixteenth century ambitious Portuguese captains had occasionally drawn up plans for the conquest of Madagascar or the Comoro Islands, Portuguese relations with these countries remained on a purely commercial footing. Trading vessels from Mozambique made the short crossing to the islands in search of timber, palm cloth and building stone, but chiefly in search of food to supply the enormous consumption of the naval base on Mozambique Island. The trade with Madagascar and the Comoros was of great importance to the Mozambique *moradores* since they were progressively excluded from most of the trade to the south by the growth of the captain's monopoly. Francisco Barreto had revived the project for conquering the Comoros in the 1570s, and the *moradores* had further reason to fear that their access to this local commerce was in danger when in 1585 the captain, Dom Jorge de Meneses, acquired the exclusive right to trade in ginger between the Comoros and Ormuz and attempted to set up a factory on the Madagascar coast at Masselage. As late as the 1650s the captains of Mozambique were still trying to negotiate to lease of the trade with Madagascar.[7]

The boats which carried this trade were, for the most part, locally built *pangaios* (dhows) operated by the Muslim seafaring community which inhabited the small coastal ports on each side of the Mozambique Channel. They were freighted by the Mozambique *moradores* and frequently had one or two Afro-Portuguese on board. The extent of the trade between Mozambique and the islands impressed early European visitors. Sir James Lancaster in 1591 used a Portuguese interpreter in the Comoros; in 1602 the French interloper Martin found '*plusieurs individus qui parlaient portuguais*', and the same year the Dutch fleet under van Spilbergen captured a boat full of Portuguese *mestizos* carrying rice, cloth and slaves. Sir Thomas Roe commented in 1615 on the large vessels which carried on the trade with the Portuguese and remarked on the 'few Portuguese, trading to Mosombique in junks of 40 tonnes made of Cocor, sowed instead of Pinns, Cawked, tackled and wholly fitted, victualed, and fraighted with that Vniversall tree'. The situation was summed up by François Pyrard who wrote that 'these islands [Comoros] are of the utmost convenience to Mozembic and to the Portuguese who dwell there for the supply of provisions'.[8]

It is likely that the Mozambique *moradores* found that trading with the Comoros and Madagascar was a convenient way of circumventing the captain's monopoly and carrying on a contraband trade with the ports of the Red Sea, the Gulf and northern India. It is known that early in the seventeenth century there was extensive trade between the islands and these countries to the north, and the Portuguese vessels coming from Mozambique carried Spanish silver coin which was used in the islands to finance international commerce.

In the late sixteenth century the Comoro Islands were rapidly becoming one of the principal clearing houses for the slave trade, and slaves were brought from the coast of Mozambique as well as from Madagascar. There is little indication that slaves were being exported in large numbers from Mozambique during this period, although there may well have been considerable numbers available on the market as a result of the famine of the 1580s and the Zimba wars. Portuguese traders were actively involved in the slave trade in the Comoros. In 1615, for example, Portuguese were reported buying slaves in the islands for 9 or 10 *reales* each, expecting to sell them for 100 *reales*. Although the Portuguese certainly employed slaves themselves in eastern Africa, the major slave markets were in India and the Gulf, and the Portuguese and Swahili merchants were suppliers of these markets rather than being themselves major consumers.[9]

When the French, Dutch and English fleets began to arrive in the Indian Ocean, they started to use the Comoro Islands as regular ports of call for the supply of fresh food and water. The demand for foodstuffs increased rapidly and it became difficult for the islands to meet the heavy demands being made on them. So the European ships called also at St Augustine's Bay on the south-west coast of Madagascar. Here they were able to barter for cattle, and local Malagasy settlements grew up around the bay to service the visiting ships. The activities of these ships so alarmed the Portuguese that they began seriously to develop a policy of political interference in Madagascar. In 1613 a Jesuit, Luis Marianno, was sent to try to establish relationships with the rulers of southern Madagascar and incidentally to search for survivors of shipwrecks. Two years later Marianno returned with another priest and tried unsuccessfully to establish a permanent mission on the coast. These two missions, however, were not followed up. Apart from occasional suggestions that the captain of Mozambique might establish a fortified post on the Madagascar coast, there was no further official Portuguese interest in the great island, and the eastern side of the Mozambique Channel was left to the exploitation of the other Europeans.[10]

The English, French and Dutch were all looking for permanent bases from which to operate their fleets and were tempted to see in the islands opportunities to establish plantations similar to those being exploited in the Caribbean. The Dutch formed a base in Mauritius in 1639 and the French settled on Île de Bourbon (Réunion) in 1642 and at Fort Dauphin on the coast of Madagascar in 1649. The English were mostly content to profit from their friendly relations with the sultan of Anjouan in the Comoros and used the island for revictualling and as a post office for handling communications between their ships. However, in the 1630s, Madagascar attracted the attention of various entrepreneurs at the English court who were trying to breach the East India Company's monopoly. A rival company, the Courteen Association, was established in 1635 with the avowed object of trying to exploit the commercial opportunities offered by Madagascar and the western Indian Ocean. Courteen sent various ships and eventually there was an attempt to found a colony on the coast of Madagascar. The English persisted with their ambitions in this direction until the 1650s when disease and commercial losses finally forced them to abandon their colonising efforts.[11] The Dutch meanwhile had formed a permanent settlement in Table Bay in 1652 and in 1658 abandoned their colony in Mauritius. As Cape Town slowly developed as a naval base and settler colony, the Dutch demand for slave labour grew and they developed a regular trade with the eastern coast of Madagascar.

The first half of the seventeenth century, therefore, saw a huge increase in the commercial activity of the Mozambique Channel area. Just as the founding of the naval base at Mozambique had injected demand into the economy of the region in the sixteenth century, so the arrival of large English and Dutch and French fleets every year in the early seventeenth century stimulated demand throughout the whole region from the Cape of Good Hope northward. However, most of the foodstuffs purchased by the companies were produced as a byproduct of traditional agricultural practices. Only in the Comoro Islands is there some indication that the growing of food for the market using slave labour developed during this time. If European trade had little effect on methods of production, it certainly appears to have had political repercussions in Madagascar where the expansion of the Sakalava in the eighteenth century is thought to have been connected with economic stimuli deriving from the trade in slaves and firearms.

The Portuguese continued to base their commercial activities on ivory trading, developing their networks of suppliers and extending their commerce deeper into the interior. The policy of discouraging other Europeans from trading with their coastal possessions appears to have been effective. Although there were rumours from time to time of Dutch or English ships snooping up and down the coast, almost no significant commercial activity is recorded. Eastern Africa was largely excluded from Dutch and English trade and escaped the market stimulus which the companies' ships might have provided. What was significant for the economic development of this region was not its integration into the world economic system but its insulation from this system by the successfully implemented monopolistic policy of the Portuguese.

Muscat and the Portuguese

Throughout much of the sixteenth century the Portuguese had controlled the main trading ports of the Gulf, but early in the seventeenth century their grip was gradually prised loose. In 1622, as part of the prolonged war between the Dutch and English Companies and the Portuguese *Estado da India*, Ormuz was taken by Persian and English forces. This did not immediately end the dominance of the Portuguese in the Gulf or the importance of their trade, but the loss of Muscat to the rulers of Oman in 1650 proved much more of a blow. The port of Muscat, with its powerful Portuguese forts, became a base for Omani maritime expansion in the direction of India and eastern Africa. The Omani appear to have wanted to replace the Portuguese as the principal traders on the east African coast and to receive the tribute from the Swahili cities which the Portuguese had been accustomed to levy. After the capture of Muscat, they set their sights on driving the Portuguese from the whole of their east African empire.

Omani ships first appeared on the northern part of the coast in 1652, attacking Zanzibar and reputedly receiving much support from factions within the ruling élites of some of the Swahili towns.[12] The next known visit of Omani warships was in 1660–1 when they attacked Faza, raised a considerable body of support along the coast and then boldly entered Mombasa harbour itself, burning and plundering the Portuguese town. Throughout the next decade Arabs and Portuguese carried on desultory warfare in northern India and on the east African coast where the sultan of Pate emerged as the principal supporter of the Omani interest. In 1671, however, a large Omani fleet of eighteen ships sailed south to Mozambique, sacked the town and attacked the fortress. The fort of São Sebastião was once again too strong to be taken but the Arabs were able to plunder the town more or less at will.[13]

The attack on Mozambique was not repeated although sometime in the 1670s the Portuguese had to beat off an Omani attack on the Querimba Islands. In 1675 it was reported that they tried to halt the growth of Omani power by sending a guard fleet to the Gulf paid for by the customs receipts of the factory at Kung, their last commercial station in the Gulf region.[14] However, Omani influence, continued to spread and in 1678 a Portuguese fleet attempted to regain control of Pate but was defeated after Omani intervention. In 1694 Pemba transfered its allegiance to Oman and in 1696 the Omanis landed once again on Mombasa Island and began the epic siege that ended only with the fall of Fort Jesus in 1698.

By the early eighteenth century, Portuguese influence had been virtually eliminated north of Cape Delgado. The trade of Mombasa had gone and the sovereignty of Oman was established as far south as Kilwa and Mafia. However the Omanis never succeeded in loosening Portugal's grip on the southern coastal regions. Islamic sentiment had certainly been a factor in the establishment of Oman's influence in the north, but Islam was weaker in the south and the Portuguese presence more strongly entrenched. Moreover it soon became clear that the Omani presence severely interrupted the trading network which the Portuguese had established. The rapidly growing ivory trade was a factor which bound the coastal communities of the south with ties of self-interest and commercial interdependence to the Portuguese and the Portuguese Indians who handled the trade. Once again Cape Delgado had proved a frontier between north and south, a geographical point at which real political, cultural and economic interests divided.

The ivory trade

It had been gold that first attracted Muslims and Portuguese to the east African coast and although the trade in gold continued to be important for the economy of the Mozambican people, as a source of bullion in world trade the declining output of central Africa in the sixteenth century was insignificant compared with what was produced in Mexico, Peru or Japan. By the eighteenth century the rest of the world thought of east Africa, if it did so at all, as the producer not of gold but of ivory. Over two centuries, therefore, the major commodity exported from east Africa changed, bringing with it major alterations to social and economic institutions, to the pattern of settlement particularly in the north of Mozambique, and to political relations in the region as a whole.

At the beginning of the seventeenth century the external trade of eastern Africa was largely controlled by three individuals. The ivory trade in Delagoa Bay was administered by the royal factor based in Mozambique; from Inhambane to Angoche the trade was in the hands of the captain of Mozambique who purchased the monopoly on obtaining nomination to the captaincy; and north of Cape Delgado international trade in gold and ivory was effectively a monopoly administered by the captains of Mombasa. Commerce depended on the arrival of ships from India bringing trade goods. The right to ship cloth from India to Mozambique was sold by the Portuguese Crown to another monopolist, although it appears that the captains of Mozambique were entitled to bring cloth with them when they arrived to take up office. The annual Mozambique voyage had to load with ivory for the return voyage to India. Once in Mozambique the cloth was distributed among the various trading factories along the coast or up the Zambesi. Because the ship sometimes did not arrive at all and, even during the best years, there were often long delays before supplies could arrive, much of the trade was done on credit. Before the arrival of the Portuguese, credit had been provided by the Muslim trading families whose members owned the ships and formed the ruling élite in the coastal towns. During the sixteenth century there was a gradual breakdown of credit arrangements since the Portuguese Crown did not have the financial resources to replace those provided by the Muslim trading houses. The growth of the private monopolies injected private capital into east African commerce, which in turn brought in new sources of capital from India.

The only region that lay outside these monopolies was the stretch of coast from Angoche to the northern border of the Mozambique captaincy at Cape Delgado, together with the trade of the Comoro Islands and Madagascar. At the end of the sixteenth century this was an area of 'free trade', claimed as the preserve of the *moradores* of Mozambique Island. The *moradores* claimed the historic privilege of trading with the mainland opposite the island (where many of them had plantations), with the Querimba Islands and with Madagascar and the Comoros where they had close commercial ties with the indigenous merchant class. Indeed the northern Mozambique coast and the islands constituted the last area where the independent Muslim trading families still maintained their networks largely unbroken by Portuguese interference.[15]

The privileges of the *moradores* had originally been granted at a time when there was no trade in gold or ivory with the Makua population of the mainland, and the need to develop the trade in food for the supply of the Mozambique naval base was all important. It had probably never been intended that the *moradores* should be able to claim the right to free trade in any of the monopoly commodities. However, the conquest of the Mozambique lowlands by the Maravi at the end of the sixteenth century had established powerful chieftaincies over the country opposite Mozambique Island. Early in the seventeenth century most of the territory between the Island and the Zambesi came under the sway of the Maravi chief Kalonga, who was intent on expanding the ivory trade. By the 1630s the Maravi were bringing ivory for sale to Mozambique Island as well as trading it at the traditional fairs on the Zambesi. The reason for taking the ivory to Mozambique may well have been that it was possible to obtain a better price from the *moradores* and so circumvent the monopoly of the captain of Mozambique whose objective was to keep prices paid for ivory as low as possible.

It was with considerable frustration that the captains of Mozambique saw their expensively purchased monopolies undermined by the competition of the *moradores*. In 1632 this free trade was challenged, the captain alleging to the Crown that trade was being siphoned away from the Zambesi fairs. A prohibition was issued against purchasing ivory direct from the mainland opposite the island — the area later called Macuana. The *moradores* in their turn protested that the Maravi had openly threatened to invite the Dutch in to trade if their commerce was interfered with. The privileges were reaffirmed and ivory continued to be brought to Mozambique Island providing an element of free trade and market competition.[16]

The ivory trade was to lead to an unprecedented growth of commercial activity along the coast from Angoche north to Kilwa. Kilwa and Angoche had both originally owed their prosperity to the gold trade of the Zimbabwean plateau. Between the two towns there had only been the settlements of Mafia, Querimba and Mozambique Island itself, all of which owed their prosperity to the development of local industries. When the gold trade dwindled and became a monopoly of the Portuguese captains of Mozambique, Kilwa and Angoche both declined considerably in importance. By the second half of the sixteenth century, however, Kilwa was beginning to revive as an ivory trading port. Unlike gold, ivory could be obtained in Kilwa's own hinterland, and the merchant families of Kilwa began to develop trade links with peoples in the interior, notably the Yao who inhabited the region north-west of Lake Malawi. The ivory encouraged the Portuguese to return and the captain of the Coast of Malinde (later the captain of Mombasa) maintained a factor at Kilwa and Mafia.[17]

Kilwa's revival as a commercial centre faltered as a result of the Maravi invasions following the droughts and natural disasters of the late 1570s. In 1588 the town was sacked and destroyed by a 'Zimba' army which supposedly killed and 'ate' 3,000 people captured in the island.[18] Slowly the ivory trade revived, and by 1616, when Gaspar Bocarro made his famous journey overland from the Zambesi to Kilwa, the town was once again a prosperous trading centre, though clearly under the control of the captain of Mombasa's factor and his agents.

The return of the ivory trade to Kilwa must have been partly the result of the wars in Zambesia which made this an unsafe trading area. It is likely that Kilwa attracted traders from deep in the interior, for Bocarro made it clear that the immediate hinterland of Kilwa itself was uninhabited and barren. He himself travelled along what was apparently a well-trodden trade route running from the southern end of Lake Malawi through Yao territory. Along this route it was possible to obtain guides and provisions, as well as ivory and slaves.[19]

During the struggle for supremacy between the Portuguese in Mombasa and the Omani, Kilwa remained a relatively secure and prosperous port and probably continued to attract most of the ivory from the northern end of Lake Malawi and from the Yao country, while Mozambique Island and the factory at Angoche, in competition with the Zambesi fairs, traded ivory from the Maravi chieftaincy of Kalonga (Map 2). It was the Omani capture of Mombasa in 1698 which appears to have had the greatest long-term effect on the ivory trade. When this happened, the trading network of its captains was destroyed and the various factories and customs houses disappeared to be replaced by Omani garrisons. In particular the Kilwa factory was ended. The Omanis apparently did not adequately replace the Portuguese, and trade goods ceased to come regularly to the coastal ports under their control, or came only in the most haphazard manner. Kilwa's trade once again declined which brought it nearly to extinction, and the other coastal towns suffered in consequence. However, the merchants of Diu continued to import Indian cloth into Mozambique Island, and to that port in the early years of the century ivory dealers began to come in increasing numbers. By the early eighteenth century Mozambique Island had become unquestionably the most important port on the whole east African coast and the Yao ivory caravans were being diverted south away from Kilwa.

In 1675 a *Junta do Comércio* had been formed in Goa to operate the trade which was formerly part of the captain's monopoly. The *Junta* had to recognise the rights of the Mozambique *moradores* to free trade but soon challenged, as the captains had done, what they considered the abuses of these privileges. The *Junta* alleged that ivory was being brought clandestinely along the coast to Sancul, a small Muslim town on the coast opposite Mozambique Island, where it was bought by the *moradores* under the protection of their privileges. The privileges were challenged in 1712 but once again the Crown refused to rule firmly against the rights of the settlers, and the competition between Mozambique Island and the Zambesi fairs continued for a part at least of the ivory trade of the interior.[20]

During the first half of the eighteenth century, ivory dominated the foreign trade of eastern Africa and was the sole commercial *raison d'être* of the settlement on Mozambique Island. Some ivory was traded in the south and on the Zambesi, but perhaps 70 per cent of the total exported came to Mozambique Island. The official organisation of this commerce continued to be a matter of controversy. The *Junta*, based in Goa, had its enemies and between 1720 and 1722 the captain's monopoly was briefly restored. The *Junta*, however, returned, was reorganised in 1739 and survived subject to the *Conselho da Fazenda* till 1752 when it was abolished as one of the measures severing Mozambique finally from the control of Goa. After its abolition trade was declared to be free although a royal monopoly on the import of Venetian glass beads (*velório*) was established. Free trade led, predictably, to intense rivalry between the various Portuguese settlers and between themselves and the Indian community, and it prompted the governor-general, Pereira do Lago, to establish a locally-based company with monopoly control of the ivory trade in 1766. Two years later this was abolished as a result of protests from both Lisbon and Goa, and free trade was restored.

Free trade meant that the state raised its revenues from customs duties and not from the profits of conducting trade itself. Originally there had been a 2 per cent duty on goods entering and leaving Mozambique Island and this was eventually consolidated as a 4 per cent duty on ivory being exported. A very heavy tariff was, however, fixed for the Zambesi area and, after the *Junta* was wound up, a general tariff of 41 per cent was imposed. One of the effects, and maybe one of the intentions, of this tariff was to make the trade in ivory in Zambesia uncompetitive and to divert the flow of ivory to Mozambique Island — an ironic reversal of the situation a century before when the trade of Mozambique Island had been discouraged in favour of that of the Zambesi settlements (Fig. 8.1).[21]

The rise of Indian merchant capital

During the eighteenth century the prosperity of the ivory trade attracted many Indian merchants to Mozambique and by the end of the eighteenth century the Indian and Afro-Indian community had

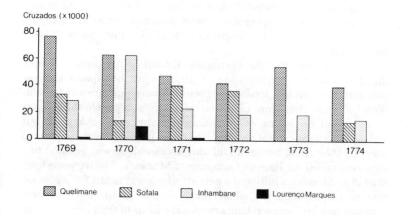

Fig. 8.1. CUSTOMS REVENUES FROM MOZAMBIQUE PORTS, 1769–1774

Source: F. Hoppe, *Portugiesisch Ost-Afrika in der Zeit des Marques do Pombal*, pp. 135–6.

become the dominant élite in much of Mozambique. The Indian connection grew over a long time. Muslim traders from Malabar had, of course, been part of the commercial establishment long before the arrival of the Portuguese, and there had also been Hindu traders at Mozambique Island when Vasco da Gama visited it in 1499. With the establishment of Portuguese power in Malabar, Goa and the northern ports of Cambay, numerous channels were opened for Indians to come to east Africa. Indians from Goa, who were usually called Canarins by the Portuguese and many of whom were Catholic, might come to east Africa as administrators, traders, soldiers or ecclesiastics, but there were also Indians from the northern ports who, if Hindu, were usually generically termed Banyans. They almost always confined themselves to commerce.

Relatively little is known of the activities of Indians in Mozambique during the monopoly regime of the captains. Clearly there were Indian traders in Manica in the 1560s, when they were allegedly maltreated by the Chicanga.[22] Indian soldiers fought in the wars in Zambesia in the 1640s,[23] and there were Canarin doctors in Zambesia in the

1680s.[24] There is reference to a Brahmin involved in Zambesi trade in the 1660s,[25] and Indian traders were active at the gold fairs in the second half of the century. It was Indian traders escaping from Karangaland who founded the first settlement at Zumbo in the 1690s, and Canarins trading in the Rivers were present at the Monomotapa's court and helped raise troops to defend the Portuguese Rivers settlements.[26]

It is remarkable that the Portuguese Crown clearly came to favour the idea of Indian migration to east Africa. After the captain's monopoly had been ended, various suggestions were put forward for sending Indian settlers from Goa who would help to people the Rivers. In the event no migration of Indian peasants ever took place but Indian merchant capital did begin to make itself felt in an important way. In 1686 trade between Diu and Mozambique was granted to a company called the Banyan Company of Mazanes. Twelve years later the fall of Mombasa initiated a period, which was to last for a generation or more, when the whole northern part of the coast became unstable and Indian merchants moved the focus of their operations to Mozambique Island where they settled in ever increasing numbers.

The expansion of Indian merchant capital in the early eighteenth century was a phenomenon which affected Hindu and Muslim communities alike, and both were represented in Mozambique. The rise of the Indian merchant class had been a feature of the Mughal empire at its height in the seventeenth century; Indian bankers had financed the Mughal state and operated its tax system, and by the end of the century were seeking outlets for their vast accumulations of capital. One of the areas where they sought to invest was in traditional overseas commercial enterprises in the Red Sea, the Gulf and eastern Africa. Another route which may have brought them to Mozambique was as financiers to the Portuguese *Estado da India*, which had become sadly diminished and impoverished by the end of the seventeenth century and therefore depended greatly on its Indian bankers.[27]

As the import of cloth and beads was the monopoly of the *Junta*, the Indians who settled in Mozambique Island either entered trade in competition with the *moradores*, or imported commodities which were not part of the *Junta*'s monopoly or confined themselves to putting up the finance for Portuguese trading enterprises. The establishment of the Indians at Mozambique gave rise to considerable tensions which had their origins in commercial rivalry but found a characteristically Lusitanian expression in religious hatred. In the 1720s the Inquisition tried to use its authority to interfere with the trade of Muslims with the mainland, and the Banyans also subsequently complained of harassment by the authorities. Anti-Indian sentiment appears to have increased sharply after the ending of the *Junta*'s monopoly when

Indians were free to import cloth as well as export ivory. In 1758 a determined effort was made by the *moradores* to get Indians excluded from direct access to the mainland and to restrict their activities on the island to only twelve merchant houses. These measures were immediately rescinded by the viceroy, but in 1763 a fresh attempt was made to restrict the direct access of the Indians to trade on the mainland.[28]

In 1777, perhaps in an effort to break the hold of the Indian cloth importers over the trade of Mozambique, the Portuguese government ended the monopoly of the Company of Mazanes over the trade with Diu. The result was a great increase in the volume of Indian business, and by the 1780s there were five ships a year arriving from Diu and some 300 Indians resident in Mozambique Island with twenty or more trading houses active on the mainland. This prompted further measures in the 1780s to exclude the Indians, which foundered on their control of the import of cloth on which all the trade of Mozambique depended.

Meanwhile Indian traders had become active in all the ports of the Mozambique coast. Inhambane, as we have seen, was largely an Indian settlement, as was Zumbo on the Zambesi. In the older Zambesi towns Indians were to be found not only as traders but increasingly also as *prazo*-holders and the heads of households of slaves and retainers.

The commercial networks of Mozambique

Although the Indians are often represented in the documentation as rivals of the *moradores*, both groups were part of a complex network of commerce and exchange which stretched far into the interior. The ivory trade had called into existence a whole new system of social relations, whole communities whose fortunes were closely interdependent. One end of the network was to be found far in the interior of Africa where bands of elephant hunters tracked down the herds, singled out the tusk-bearing adults and killed them employing a variety of dangerous and highly skilled methods. Elephants might be hunted by the males of a village who devoted their surplus time to this lucrative activity, incidentally providing their families with meat, but there were also professional elephant hunters, some of whom would be directly employed by chiefs, traders or *prazo*-holders.

By whatever means the elephants were killed, the territorial chief of the area would claim one of the tusks — the ground tusk — as his right. In this way the chiefs became major partners in the sale of ivory, and their role was enhanced as they usually tried to control the fairs at which ivory was sold to the professional caravan-leaders. Ivory was seldom taken to the coast by the people who hunted it, unless they lived within a few days march of the sea. Instead ivory was bought in the interior by the leaders of caravans. North of the Zambesi in the eighteenth century the caravan trade was dominated by the Yao. The Yao chiefs continually widened their search for ivory, gradually dominating the trade throughout the old Maravi empire from the sea westwards to the Luangwa. By the mid-eighteenth century the Yao were opening up ivory trading west of the Luangwa and south of the Zambesi as well.[29]

The Yao caravans, sometimes with as many as 1,000 porters, brought the ivory to the coast negotiating a free passage through the territories of Makua chiefs who thereby became participants in the profits of the commerce. As they neared the coast the Yao entered a region where the ivory trading network became more dense and complex. When still some distance inland they were met by agents of the Portuguese *moradores*, called *patamares*, who were authorised to buy the ivory. However, there was considerable rivalry among the *patamares* which could boil over into violence and raids on the Portuguese coastal plantations and villages. Moreover there were illegal buyers of ivory who operated through the good offices of the Swahili sheikhs of the coast. These would try to smuggle ivory from small ports to avoid paying duties at the Mozambique customs house. The *patamares* in their turn were linked to the *moradores* or, increasingly, to Indian trading houses which provided them with trade goods and took the ivory that they purchased. Between these trading houses there also existed elaborate bonds of credit and debt, mutual co-operation and rivalry.[30]

The expansion of the coastal communities

During the eighteenth century the coastal area from the bay of Fernão Veloso south to Angoche became dotted with little ports and coastal communities that lived in one way or another from the ivory trade — receiving coastal traffic, smuggling out contraband slaves or ivory, and sending foodstuffs to the large market provided by Mozambique Island (Map 2).

The maritime communities inhabiting these ports were descended from the Muslims who had traded from the ports of the east Africa coast before the arrival of the Portuguese. When the Portuguese had first occupied Mozambique Island, Quelimane and the Zambesi towns, the Muslim community had remained for a time co-existing with the newcomers. The separate Muslim town at Sena was destroyed only in 1571 by Francisco Barreto, and on Mozambique Island there was still a separate Muslim suburb called Mogicate at the end of the sixteenth century. However, by that time the ruling family of Mozambique Island had already moved to the mainland and founded a town at Sancul on a promontory which formed the southern shore of the bay, close to the Portuguese settlements — which was to remain the centre of their influence till the nineteenth century. The Mozambique Portuguese depended on Sancul to provide a satisfactory guarantee for the security of the southern shore of the bay until a disastrous incident in 1753 when, after an unsuccessful joint raid on the Makua, a drunken Portuguese soldier shot the sheikh.[31] Along the coast to the north and south a string of small Muslim villages and towns grew up which were clearly very much within the economic orbit of Mozambique Island but looked to Sancul for political and religious leadership.

Although the territory immediately opposite Mozambique Island was nominally under the control of the Makua chief of Uticulo, the Murimuno, the bay in which Mozambique Island lay, was ringed with the plantations of the Mozambique *moradores* and the villages of their slaves and retainers, precariously defended by a stockade (*chuambo*).[32] There were two Portuguese parishes on the mainland, at Cabaceira and Mossuril, interspersed with Muslim villages. Many of the *moradores* lived permanently on their plantations, and in the eighteenth century the governor-general built himself a fine country house at Cabaceira, while the *chuambo* was replaced with a fort in 1809.[33]

Immediately north of Mozambique was Conducia Bay off which lay the island of Quitangonha where there was a Muslim town, while on the mainland opposite was the settlement of Matibane. South of Sancul was the bay of Mocambo with coastal settlements at Kivolane and Kissanga. Immediately south of that was a swampy, inaccessible coastline with no important settlements till Mogingual, situated in a wide shallow estuary protected by a sand spit. South of Mogincual the coastal peoples tended to look towards Angoche rather than Sancul. The most important towns were Sangage, Angoche itself and Moma, all at or near the entrance to major rivers.

During the seventeenth and eighteenth centuries the Portuguese developed a working relationship with the sheikhs of the coastal communities based on reciprocal self-interest. The Portuguese were anxious for the sheikhs to discourage other Europeans from trading on the coast — which, on the whole, they seem to have done. In 1727, for example, some French ships arrived in the bay of Quitangonha and began to take soundings. The sheikh 'sallied out to encounter them with more than two hundred negroes armed with bows and arrows and a few guns and put a stop to their proceedings.'[34] The Portuguese also looked to them to help travellers shipwrecked along the coast. For their part the sheikhs wanted to trade with the Portuguese while both parties recognised their need to co-operate against possible hostile moves by Makua or Maravi chiefs from the interior. Indeed it seems to have been the fear of Maravi raids that led the sheikhs to recognise Portuguese overlordship and seek their protection.[35]

One of the few documents that deals with the coast south of Sancul is the account of the wreck of the galleon, *São Lourenço*, which went ashore in 1649 on the coast near Mogincual. Most of the crew and passengers were rescued and while messengers were sent to Mozambique Island, the party looked to the sheikhs of Mogincual and of another community called Moxingli (difficult to identify) to provide food and shelter, care for the sick and boats to help carry the Crown property rescued from the wreck. From the account written by the Jesuit, António Cardim, it is clear that, while the sheikhs were willing to help, they were also prepared to profit from the situation and charged high prices for the food and services they provided. Neither sheikh possessed boats larger than oceangoing canoes.

They may have been relatively small communities but they took religious observance seriously:

> Without fail they said their prayers three times a day, and the sheikh who served as *cacis* washed before entering the mosque, and leaving his shoes outside on a stone which was by the entrance he entered the mosque because they consider it sacrilege to enter with shoes on or with feet not clean.[36]

There was no regular road along the coast since there were numerous river estuaries to cross, nor were conditions secure. The coastal villages lived in fear of the Makua and still more of Maravi raids. When the Maravi heard of the shipwreck they sent a raiding party to the coast which among other things took the sheikh prisoner.[37]

During the eighteenth century the Portuguese formalised their relations with the coastal sheikhs giving them the title of *capitão-mor*, intervening in succession disputes, and seeking to co-operate with them in the all-important matter of keeping open the trade routes into the interior. When military action had to be taken, it was expected that the sheikhs would provide contingents to accompany whatever soldiers the Portuguese put into the field. The Portuguese also appointed one of the leading Afro-Portuguese as *capitão-mor das terras firmes* with jurisdiction over the mainland territories. In practice, however, the peoples of the coast formed what was largely a self-regulating commercial community of Afro-Portuguese and Swahili traders and plantation-owners with their retainers and slaves which lived under the law dictated by the need for commercial co-existence — the law that gave everyone an overriding interest in the safe passage of the ivory caravans from the interior and the satisfactory exchange of goods when they arrived.[38]

Angoche

Some 100 miles south of Sancul, halfway to the Zambesi delta, was the ancient town of Angoche. Early in the sixteenth century it had enjoyed considerable prosperity since its ruler attracted Muslim traders wanting to profit from the Zambesi gold trade and avoid the Portuguese monopoly at Sofala. However, by mid-century Quelimane had developed as the main port of access to the interior and Angoche declined in importance, though it continued to enjoy a modest trade in ivory. The Portuguese maintained a factor there who bought ivory first on behalf of the Crown and then for the captain of Mozambique. Angoche is little mentioned in the literature of the seventeenth century and by the eighteenth the Portuguese factory there had closed. Over a period of forty years no official Portuguese trading ship went there.[39]

However, a close relationship existed between the Angoche sultans and the Portuguese on Mozambique Island. The sultans looked to the Portuguese for recognition and were granted the honorific title of *capitão-mor*, while as part of the special relationship the sultans paid no customs dues on trading vessels sent to the Island. The trade of Angoche in the eighteenth century was mostly in foodstuffs which were sent to Mozambique Island, and in the elaborately made mats for which the town had been famous since the sixteenth century. However, dhows from Angoche visited some of the coastal settlements to the south where they traded in amber and ivory.[40]

A Portuguese judge, Francisco Moraes Pereira, who visited Angoche in 1752, left an agreeable account of this independent outpost of Islamic culture. Angoche had recently been rebuilt on a fresh site after disputes with the Makua of the mainland had led to the abandonment of the old town:

> The new settlement is a short distance from the beach towards the east where it is sandy. The houses are made of wood and thatched with straw but are suitable for living in as they are properly partitioned, though they have no windows looking out on the street as is usual with all houses built by the moors. The houses of the king are large and are distinct from the majority in their fabric and size, in the large fence which surrounds them and in the garden adjoining which has many citrus trees, palms and shrubs which are used as remedy for all the complaints which they suffer. The king has a throne from which he speaks to the

people. He wears robes of different silks richly ornamented and a
gold-fringed head-dress.[41]

There was a Koranic school in the town with the result that Arabic was
widely spoken by the population and the ruling house had close relations with Mombasa and Pate as well as with Mozambique Island.

Moraes Pereira makes it clear that the Portuguese maintained close
links with the settlements along the coast road which ran past Angoche
from the Zambesi to Mozambique Island. This road was frequently
used by couriers carrying letters when coastal shipping could not
operate. It is also clear that ships were frequently wrecked along the
coast and the Portuguese depended on the goodwill of the locals to
help in rescue and salvage. Their language was spoken by many of the
people along the route and they were sometimes asked to intervene in
succession disputes or other internal quarrels. The judge found that
chief Mataya was anxious for a close alliance with the Portuguese, and

> . . . . would like to renew with them the treaty which his prede-
> cessors always had with Mozambique from where one or two boats
> every year came to that place to trade cloth for ivory for Your
> Majesty's royal treasury and provisions for the succour of this fort.
> There would be honey, amber and other commodities besides for
> individual trading. . . . The factory which formerly existed at this
> place should be restored and with a small garrison it would greatly
> benefit the commerce which always redounded to the advantage of
> Your Majesty's treasury.[42]

Angoche and Mozambique were clearly the two centres of political
and economic power to which the coastal Makua villages looked.
However, neither of them was very strong or in a position to dominate
and impose a political order on the region. An uneasy balance was
maintained in which the small Makua chieftaincies squabbled among
themselves. Moraes Pereira was impressed by the dense population
along the coastal plain but he equally makes it clear that political
fragmentation opened the way for *ad hoc* political units to emerge and
for bandits to establish their power. Banditry is a major theme in the
history of Mozambique and nowhere were the opportunities for bandit leaders to make good greater than among the fragmented matrilineal communities of the Makua. Here is Moraes Pereira's classic
description of the rise of a bandit chief. The date is sometime before
1750 but it might almost be a description of a Renamo warband of the
1980s:

> Macambe's village is two days' journey from that of Matanda and
> was founded in Matanda's own country. Macambe fled there when
> he was ordered to surrender by António Cardim Froes [governor

of Mozambique]. About him there gathered some fugitive kaffirs from Mozambique. For some years he was a vagabond but swelled his following with other fugitive kaffirs, fortified himself in the lands I have mentioned and built there a settlement which I was told was very strong and impregnable. From here he makes himself feared by assaults and robberies on the neighbouring settlements. His daring reached such heights that, hearing that the king of Angoche . . . wanted to attack him, he surprised his village one night, killed the king and put two hundred men, women and children to the sword. . . . This insolent action made him proud and daring and greatly feared by the neighbouring peoples who, though not at peace with him, yet did not dare to make war on him.[43]

In general, however, it seems that during the eighteenth century Portuguese influence was strong enough to prevent this area from playing any independent role in the valuable international trade in ivory or slaves. Although there are records of isolated Dutch voyages to Angoche, this ancient Muslim town, so important in the gold trade of the sixteenth century and later a centre for the slave trade in the nineteenth, never participated to any great extent in the prosperity of the ivory trade. Ivory was still concentrated for sale in Mozambique Island and there is little record of a clandestine slave trade on this coast before the nineteenth century.

The Querimba Islands

The Ilhas do Cabo Delgado, or Querimba Islands, stretch south from Cape Delgado for some 200 miles. The archipelago is made up of a dozen or so large islands and numerous islets and rocky outcrops. The islands are close to the coast with which they are partly linked by sandbars, coral reefs and mangrove forests. To navigate among them, even small craft with a shallow draft need an intricate knowledge of the channels. Many of the islands are waterless but the larger of them, like Querimba, Ibo, Matemo and Amisa, have always supported human habitation.

When the Portuguese arrived on the east African coast there was already a considerable Muslim population in the islands which were an important centre of cloth manufacture. The cloth was known as Maluane cloth, apparently from the name of the place on the mainland where it was made, and for the first twenty years of their presence in eastern Africa the Portuguese knew the islands as the Maluane Islands. The name survived in use into the seventeenth century in various maps and reports, although the exact whereabouts of

Maluane itself remains something of a mystery. Do Couto thought it was the name of a river on the mainland — possibly in the modern Bahia do Quipaco. As a result of the Zimba invasion of the mainland opposite the islands in the late sixteenth century, the Muslim community of Maluane took refuge on Matemo island where 'Maluane' cloth continued to be woven in the seventeenth century. Both silk and cotton cloth were woven and dyed with locally-grown indigo. These textiles were highly esteemed in the trade of Sofala and Zambesia.[44]

The Muslim inhabitants of the islands had their closest ties with Kilwa, Zanzibar and Melinde and it is likely that at first they were major beneficiaries of the Portuguese occupation of Sofala and Kilwa. Muslim merchants fleeing from the violent faction struggles in the two cities occupied by the Portuguese would have brought their households and their trade with them. Recognising that the islands had become important centres of independent Muslim trade, a large Portuguese expedition raided Querimba in 1522. The town on the island was destroyed, ships in the harbour were burned and the Portuguese made off with considerable booty. The commander recorded that cannon had been found on the island. Although there can be little doubt that the main Portuguese objective was to destroy the independent commercial existence of the island merchants, the immediate cause of the raid was the alleged refusal of Muslims to sell coir to the Portuguese, suggesting that the islands were an important centre for the manufacture of this commodity as well.[45]

In the course of the sixteenth century a number of Portuguese obtained land grants from the Crown and settled in the islands. By 1590 all the major islands but one had a Portuguese *senhor* who received tribute from the local population. On Querimba Island there was a fortified plantation house and a Dominican church serving as a centre for missionary work in the area.[46] A description in 1609 indicates that there was a fortified settlement on Ibo which in 1630 apparently had some artillery, while ruins of large Portuguese plantation houses can still be seen on Quisiva and Matemo. Because of the shortage of water the Portuguese built large cisterns to store rainwater, and this allowed the islands to be stocked with cattle, pigs and goats. As well as Maluane cloth the region produced amber and jet, ivory, turtleshell, ambergris and manna (a sort of edible gum which grew on Amisa and on Mafia further to the north). The region also developed as a major source of food supply for Mozambique Island. Meat, millet, rice, beans and palm products were all exported, and food was sent by the *senhores* of the islands as payment of the quitrents on their island leases. The *senhor* of Matemo, for example, paid thirty 'loads' of grain to the fort of Mozambique.[47] It was probably because a large part of the food supplies of Mozambique came from the archipelago that in 1609 the viceroy, Lourenço de Tavora, decided to winter with his fleet there rather than at Mozambique Island, the usual port of call. The importance of the provision trade to Mozambique Island was such that the *senhores* of the islands tried to claim a commercial monopoly, and in 1663 the *moradores* of Mozambique had to obtain a direct order from the captain confirming their historic freedom to trade in the islands.[48]

When the captaincy of Mombasa was created in 1593 Cabo Delgado formed the division between the new captaincy and that of Mozambique and Sofala. The Querimba Islands thus became part of the Mozambique captaincy, their destiny now linked firmly with the peoples of the south rather than the north. Almost nothing is known of conditions on the mainland opposite the islands in the sixteenth and seventeenth centuries. Santos becomes lyrical in describing the agricultural and natural riches of the north where he had briefly served as parish priest. The islands produced rice and millet, coconut and many different kinds of fruit as well as large numbers of pigs, goats, fowls and pigeons which were hunted in large quantities. Much of this food must have been grown by the mainland communities, and the ivory certainly came from the continent of Africa, so that the impact of Portuguese trade in Querimba would have been felt some way into the interior. Santos described the coastal African population as 'painted' and 'barbarous' but he had heard that inland there existed a large kingdom of Mongallo. Gaspar Reimão, writing about his stay in the islands in 1609, says that the mainland Africans used on occasion to raid the islands, crossing the shallows at low tide, and it was for this reason that the settlements had to be fortified.[49]

In the eighteenth century the islands were all held by Portuguese as *prazos* on three emphyteutic or life tenures similar to those in Zambesia. They formed an isolated community, cut off from regular contact or support from Mozambique Island and left very much to its own devices. A captain-general was appointed, usually one of the principal Portuguese of the archipelago, who had nominal command of local forces and access to government supplies of firearms, but in practice each island was like a little republic, dependent on its household slaves and on the trade with the mainland. The islands were dominated by two powerful Afro-Portuguese families, the Meneses and the Moraes. The former originated with the procreative activities of the Dominican friar João de Meneses, who bought Querimba early in the century and resided there partly in the role of parish priest and partly as *senhor*. Meneses had an armed force of slaves and successfully defied attempts by the viceroy and the superior of his own Order to bring him to justice. He appears to have developed the slave trade with the French who first began to visit the islands to trade for slaves in the 1740s. The Moraes family already held the lease of four islands in 1744 but their principal settlement was on Quisiva in the far south of the archipelago with a trading base on the mainland opposite at Arimba. In the second half of the century the Moraes became king-makers among the Makua peoples of the mainland and in 1790 it was said that 'there are chiefs who only sit on their thrones because Moraes has placed them there.'[50]

In the middle of the eighteenth century, trade between Querimba and Mozambique still depended on the monsoons and was carried in dhows 'which the blacks of the country used before our discovery'.[51] They carried slaves, ivory, rice, maize, manna, turtleshell and cowries. The 40 *bars* of ivory sent to Mozambique in 1762 formed a relatively small part of the estimated 600–700 *bars* exported from the island but the sale of slaves was another matter. By mid-century the Querimba Islands were beginning to emerge from their obscurity. Their maze of coastal waterways, creeks and sheltered dhow harbours were ideal for clandestine activity, and the rise of the illegal slave trade stimulated this commercial life as had the contraband gold trade in the sixteenth century. Arab ships from Zanzibar and Kilwa came south to sell provisions and buy the slaves who were readily available in the islands; in 1762 it was reported that no less than seven Arab ships were to be seen in Querimba. It was feared in Mozambique that the pro-sperous but illegal trade of the Querimba Islands was not only escap-ing the payment of customs dues but risked falling into the hands of Arabs or French. In 1765, following a dispute with the governor, the Afro-Portuguese families in Amisa in the far north apparently tried to place themselves under the protection of the sultans of Kilwa.[52]

After the government of Mozambique was separated from that of Goa in 1752 the governor-general began building a fort at Ibo which in 1763 was raised to the status of a municipality. In the 1770s the fort was completed and a new district of Cabo Delgado was created with its own governor. A church and warehouses were built and in 1786 the islands acquired a customs house. In 1791 António de Melo e Castro began work on a new fort. This fine star-shaped building rose on the mudflats guarding the narrow shipping channel through the reefs into Ibo harbour.[53] The slave trade brought Ibo great pro-sperity. Streets of houses were laid out and fine public buildings were erected round the plaza. By the early nineteenth century Ibo had become second only to Mozambique itself as a prosperous centre of mercantile life.

9

THE GOLD FAIRS

Dambarare

Soon after the arrival of the Pioneer Column in Southern Rhodesia in 1890, gold prospectors found fragments of Portuguese and oriental pottery near the site of old mine workings in the Mazoe valley, and reported them to the archaeologist J.T. Bent. In 1944 another archaeologist, Mrs E. Goodall, located an area near the Marodzi river, a tributary of the Mazoe, where old imported ceramic sherds could be picked up on the surface, and it was here that Peter Garlake conducted excavations during the dry season of 1967. With the help of aerial photography he was able to map an extensive but unusually planned settlement. He discovered five large earthworks scattered over 1.5 square miles of country — a layout very different from the stone-walled chief's towns of the Karanga or the Zambesi towns of the Portuguese with their streets of houses and relatively compact pattern of settlement.

The earthworks were large — the one excavated having sides of 465 and 540 feet with a width of 270 feet. They were made of sun-dried bricks which formed a foundation for a palisade and earth bank, and inside were brick buildings, including a church. Here the burials, undisturbed for 250 years, revealed the social and religious distinctions of a clearly hierarchical society. Inside the church were European males buried with their arms crossed like good Christians and carrying with them in death gold rings or other jewellery. Outside it were buried women (all of them negroid), children, European males without any jewellery and a solitary negroid man. All these were buried with their arms by their sides.[1]

Here was a society distinct from that of the Karanga surrounding it, a society where women were of local origin but the males predominantly European or of mixed race, observing among themselves even in death a racial and cultural stratification. But it was clearly also a society which did not cluster together within the narrow confines of a town wall but whose elements stood proudly apart within hailing distance but independent behind the earth defences of their private strongholds.

Peter Garlake identified the site as that of the Portuguese fair of Dambarare — the most important of the central African gold fairs.

The Central African fairs

The gold trading fairs of central Africa provide one of the elements of continuity in the violent and dis-integrated history of the region. The mining of gold on the Zimbabwean plateau goes back to the eleventh century at the latest, and probably fairs, or some similar institution, developed along with gold mining because of the need to concentrate gold dust for sale. Most gold was produced by peasant farmers panning in the rivers or working small dry diggings where there was an outcrop of gold-bearing quartz. It was a dry season occupation since the miners had to wait for river levels to fall or the water table to drop sufficiently for deeper-level mining to become possible. It was usually a part-time occupation for people whose principal livelihood was farming. The small flakes of gold obtained by this method were traditionally stored in quills which would be brought to the fairs for sale since the coastal merchants would not have found it worthwhile to tour the villages to make many minute purchases.[2]

Most of the fairs were held either near the capital of a chief or under his close supervision. Although there was never any question of chiefs trying to establish trade monopolies as such, there is little doubt that they saw the fairs as providing a convenient opportunity to tax the trade that was taking place and to obtain some control over imported goods. The existence of established fairs also gave them a means of controlling the activities of foreign traders. The permanence of these fairs gave them a character rather different from the seasonal fairs that were common in medieval Europe, although the Portuguese did not hesitate to use the term *feira* to describe both. As permanent settlements the fairs might well have been towns in embryo, but the fact that they were kept separate from the capitals of the chiefs and the shrines of the spirit mediums prevented them from developing that unique mixture of religious, administrative, military and commercial activity which created the cities of medieval Europe.

A few of the central African fairs, like the famous one at Masekesa in Manica, remained in approximately the same place for centuries, despite all the political and social changes that affected the surrounding peoples. Such fairs were not necessarily sited near gold diggings and were therefore unaffected by the exhaustion of individual mines and the discovery of new outcrops. However, temporary fairs were also established near some particularly rich outcrop being worked, and these would be abandoned when mining in the area ceased. Thus, although there were a number of ancient and traditional gold fairs, others were always acquiring a temporary importance, flourishing and disappearing according to the fluctuations of production. The

Portuguese use the term *bare* to describe these gold diggings and the temporary fairs that grew up in their vicinity.

António Fernandes, travelling inland from Sofala in 1511, is the first Portuguese known to have visited the gold fairs. He is reported to have said that a chief, called Ynhacouee, held

> . . . . fairs [*feyras*] on Mondays which they call the fairs of Sembaza where the Moors sell all their merchandise; the kaffirs also gather there from all the lands and thus they have quantities of supplies; it is said that the fair is as big as that of the Vertudes, and the only coin is gold by weight.[3]

In the following decades a number of unofficial Portuguese traders reached the fairs and by the middle of the sixteenth century information about them becomes more illuminating. There were two major groups of fairs, those in the Manica mountains and those in the Mazoe and Ruenha valleys. There were almost certainly others further south, accessible from the Sabi, but little or nothing can be said about these.

The first detailed information about the Manica mines and fairs dates from 1573 and is contained in sworn testimonies from traders who had visited the country, one of them having lived there for six years. The testimonies refer to individual mines by name and to 'rivers where there is gold'. One of those mentioned was 'Macequece', a name that later became famous in Mozambique's history. The testimonies also refer to caravans (*cafilas*) of Muslims from Sofala who carried trade goods for the Portuguese.[4] In the 1630s the main Manica fair was at Chipangura, later called Masekesa, where a large Portuguese and Christian community numbering twenty-five heads of households maintained a mud-walled fort. There was a second fair frequented by the Portuguese at Vumba and in addition a private fair at Matuca where a Portuguese, João da Costa, had his residence and had built himself a fort. All were said to be sited near the mines,[5] and according to a rather unreliable Dominican report of the period, all had churches and three Dominican priests worked in the region. The Portuguese captain of Sena appointed a *capitão* at the main Manica fair, but during the seventeenth century the private fairs, or *bares*, belonging to individual Portuguese were clearly of equal if not greater importance.

The Portuguese who resided at the fairs were able to acquire considerable political influence and in the mid-seventeenth century they repeatedly acted as king-makers in the chieftaincy. However, the fairs of Manica never became centres for formal Portuguese political power. Manica was not divided into *prazos* and the fairs continued to be commercial centres only, dependent on the arrival of regular caravans from Sena.

In the early seventeenth century there was at least one important fair in Kiteve, called Bandire. This was frequented by the traders of Sofala, unlike the Manica fairs which were the preserve of the Sena Portuguese. Little is known of the history of Bandire and probably it operated only spasmodically — one picturesque tradition holding that the original fair was closed because of the adultery of a Portuguese with a queen of Kiteve.[6]

The history of the fairs in Karangaland was somewhat different. Towards the end of the sixteenth century there appear to have been three major gold fairs, Masapa, Bocuto and Luanze. Masapa was close to the capital of the Monomotapa near Mount Darwin and clearly under his direct control. The commercial community at Masapa was ruled by a Portuguese captain who received his authority alike from the Portuguese captain of Mozambique and from the Monomotapa who conferred on him the office of Captain of the Gates, traditionally held by a senior Karanga chief, and the status of a royal 'wife'. The captain of Masapa's authority extended to the two neighbouring fairs. The fairs were fortified early in the seventeenth century during the succession wars in Karangaland, and became bases for the increasingly frequent Portuguese intervention in Karanga affairs.[7] When the Monomotapa formally surrendered his kingdom to the Portuguese in 1629, the captain of Masapa became what would have been described during a later phase of European imperialism as a 'resident'. He now resided in the capital itself and commanded a guard of Portuguese soldiers; also, he was supported by a Dominican mission. With this change in status and with the formal establishment of the *zimbabwe* garrison, the old independent trading fair at Masapa dwindled in importance, although it was still occasionally mentioned in reports at the end of the century.[8]

Luanze and Bocuto also appear to have declined in the second half of the seventeenth century — new fairs, all under direct Portuguese control, replaced them. Quitamborvize, Dambarare and Ongoe are the best known of these, but there were also fairs at Makaha, Chipiriviri, Matafuna and Maramuca (Map 3). Dambarare was mentioned as a fair as early as 1631 and by 1667 was described as being 'a good-sized town in the heart of Mokaranga [which] has grown to be the centre of that conquest with many rich inhabitants'.[9] During the 1670s Dambarare was in decline but in 1684 a new fort was built there on a site overlooking the Marodzi as part of an official attempt to rebuild Portuguese power in the interior.[10] Meanwhile the centre of gold mining activity had shifted to Quitamborvize. After the Portuguese had been expelled from Karangaland at the end of the seventeenth century a report described Quitamborvize as the place 'from where in all those past years came the greatest quantity of gold because the said place . . . is so rich in it that anywhere you dig you find it'.[11]

These fairs usually had a captain appointed from among the local residents, a priest and a small permanent community living in a number of scattered brick-built fortified residences and surrounded by earth banks and ditches. Ongoe had at least three such structures and five were discovered at Dambarare. The scale of Dambarare suggests that at the height of their prosperity the *feiras* may have had a considerable resident population. In different circumstances they might well have formed the urban base from which, as in Spanish America, the surrounding countryside could have been conquered and settled.

However, as the seventeenth century neared its end, it became clear that the fairs would not grow into regular townships. The number of Portuguese residents dwindled and when Dambarare was attacked by the forces of Changamire in 1693, it had only two Portuguese residents, the captain and the priest, who lived within the fortifications.[12] The explanation for this decline in the Portuguese presence at the fairs lies in the activities of the *sertanejos* and the sources of their power. As their political dominance over the Karanga states of the north had grown, the Portuguese became less interested in trade and turned to the extortion of tribute from subject populations or to carrying out direct mining operations themselves. For this they recruited armies of Tonga warriors and aimed to reduce the Karanga chiefs and their people to a tribute-paying subservience. These Portuguese backwoodsmen did not want to live at fairs where they might be subject to influence or control from a Portuguese captain, nor did they want to encourage the settlement of other Portuguese who might become rivals. This comes out clearly in a letter written by João de Sousa Freire in 1673 in which he tells the Crown that

> . . . . it is imperative that all those who live outside the *feiras* come to live in them because their residence in the bush is the cause of the non-existence of mining *bares* and because of the many injustices committed by them. And there are some men here who say that they will not obey His Highness in handing over the lands I have ordered to be handed over in Mocaranga in accordance with the Government ruling.[13]

Another reason why the fairs failed to evolve as towns was because, in the words of a report of 1687, 'it is difficult for the residents to live together in the *feiras* in houses close to one another because those men have many *cafres* among whom there is continuous strife.'[14] However, it was not just the quarrels of the Portuguese that were to blame: the internal operation of the fairs encouraged the Portuguese to build their residences at some distance from one another. Apparently the

African traders liked to visit each Portuguese separately, and on different days, to bargain for favourable prices. Clearly they preferred to visit individuals in complete privacy, which would have been impossible had everyone been living close together within a fortified township.[15] An epitaph on the old Karanga fairs was written by Custodio de Almeida e Sousa at the end of the century. All that the residents were interested in, he wrote, was trade,

> . . . . although even here they did not show much ability. Although the security of the trade resided in the fortification of the *feiras*, where they came every year with merchandise for the exchange of gold, they never bothered to build them when it would have been very easy to do it in the old times when they enjoyed wealth and the power of their captive *cafres*, and no little respect from all those kings and chiefs, thinking that the times would never change, and with great confidence in their own power they kept all those *feiras* open without ever considering any time of danger. However, as the most powerful gradually died and the *cafres* gradually got bolder and lost respect, everything went from bad to worse.[16]

The fairs both in Manica and Karangaland were destroyed in the Changamire wars of the 1690s. Although the fair at Masekesa was successfully re-established within a short time and prospered throughout the eighteenth century, the Karangaland fairs remained closed. They had ceased to be used by the African chiefs of the region and in the eighteenth century they were not re-established. Most of the centres of gold production were now under the control of Changamire, and the Portuguese traders were not permitted to visit his gold fairs further to the south and west in person. Of the Portuguese expulsion from the plateau, S.I. Mudenge wrote very aptly:

> Just as the Portuguese settlers had exploited the weakness and divisions among the Africans in the seventeenth century in order to increase their power, so also the Changamires were to profit from the disorganised nature and lawlessness of the Portuguese settlers.[17]

Not for the first time, and certainly not for the last, the dis-integrated nature of Mozambican society was to lead to political fragmentation and economic collapse.

It would be wrong to think of the fairs as having been operated solely by, and in the interest of, Portuguese traders or African chiefs, although these were often the principals in the trade and wielded the political power which created stable conditions for trade. As centres of commercial enterprise the fairs depended on the caravans which brought supplies of trade goods from the coast and on the Indian or

African traders who conducted much of the business. Indians are mentioned in connection with the trade of Manica in the sixteenth century but they only became a dominant influence at the fairs in the last quarter of the seventeenth century when Indian merchant capital was being invested in eastern African trade on a large scale. Indian traders largely controlled Quitamborvize at the time of its extinction and were also at Dambarare and Ongoe.

More important even than the Indians were the professional African traders, or *mussambazes*. In the seventeenth century individual Portuguese had themselves organised trading expeditions but in the eighteenth century trade was increasingly carried out by the *mussambazes* on behalf of Portuguese or Indian trading houses. Their leaders were able to organise porters and negotiate their passage through the lands of different chiefs. They knew the best routes to the fairs and what goods the market required. The explanation for this change of practice is to be found in the political problems which had beset the fairs at the end of the seventeenth century. The powerful Rozvi chiefs who dominated the plateau after 1693 were adamant in refusing to allow the Portuguese to have direct access to their country, and their exclusion from the interior meant that trade had to be entrusted to African agents. This enabled the principal *mussambazes* to become increasingly influential as middlemen in central African commerce. From being primarily caravan leaders they now had opportunities to become active traders on their own account.

Restoration of the feira of Manica

The war with Butua, which had begun so disastrously in 1693, had led to the expulsion of the Portuguese from all the Karanga fairs. However, this was not at first thought to be irreversible. Reinforcements were sent from Mozambique and it was hoped that the lost territory could be quickly reconquered. Indeed a force made up of the Portuguese and their African allies won a considerable victory the following year and installed their nominee, Dom Pedro, as Monomotapa. However, in July 1695 Changamire's army attacked the *feira* of Manica and expelled the Portuguese residents from there also. A counterattack by Portuguese forces was ruled out by the death of their commander, and there were fears that the Rozvi army would attack the Zambesi towns. However, as the Portuguese waited in trepidation for news of the enemy's advance, they heard that Changamire Dombo had died shortly after the attack on Manica. Thereafter hostilities ceased, although formal peace was not concluded till the end of the 1720s.[18]

The power of the Rozvi, as the élite which rose to power with

Changamire Dombo called themselves, extended over most of the plateau area where the goldfields were located, and in the first two decades of the eighteenth century the northern Karanga chieftaincies were forced to pay them tribute.[19] The Chicangas of Manica recognised Rozvi overlordship and the Changamires also intervened in the Monomotapa kingdom, placing Samutumbu on the throne in 1702 and remaining in occupation till the Monomotapa's death in 1704. After this the Rozvi made no further attempts to control the Monomotapa state, and although occasional Rozvi armies were sent to the north for specific purposes, after 1704 the Portuguese reinstated the *zimbabwe* garrison and restored their influence in the kingdom.[20]

From 1704 the Monomotapa kingdom was torn by almost continuous strife. This was the result partly of the existence of two lineages, Boroma and Nyamhandu, each of which claimed the Monomotapa title, and partly of the virtual independence which many of the sub-chiefs had acquired in the course of the wars with Changamire. Parts of the kingdom, like Dande, almost split away as independent states. One Monomotapa, Mupunzagutu, reigned from 1735 to 1759 but thereafter claimants to the title followed each other in bewildering succession and the Portuguese were neither able to stabilise the state nor even to secure their principal interest, namely the safe passage of their trade caravans up the river to Zumbo. For nearly a decade from 1759 the middle Zambesi suffered from drought and locust swarms. This had a predictable effect on social relations, as banditry increasingly replaced agriculture and commerce as the resort of communities unable to support themselves in other ways. All stable political authority broke down. The overrule which at different times had been exercised by the captains of Tete, the Monomotapa and the Changamire now became ineffective. The *prazos* between Tete and the Monomotapa's lands were also made increasingly insecure and by mid-century had been all but abandoned; social and political organisation became a reality only at the level of the sub-chieftaincy. As ever, the fundamental causes of this banditry lay in the lack of cattle-wealth and the poor soils and dry climate of the Zambesi escarpment area. As David Beach has pointed out, once the Karanga chiefs of the old Monomotapa state had lost control of the plateau country with its gold fields and good agricultural land, they had to resort to warfare and raiding to obtain the only other significant resource of value to an African society, namely women. It seems that during the eighteenth century increasing numbers of slaves were acquired by the chiefly families. The women were valued for their agricultural labour and for the children they bore, but the male slaves and the sons of the women thus acquired were organised into bands of professional fighters (*vanhai*) and used in further wars. This was a replication by the independent chiefs of the middle Zambesi of the Afro-Portuguese society — the Portuguese *chicunda* having their counterparts in the *vanhai* who served the Monomotapa and the other chiefs. Raids by *vanhai* became so serious that the *tenente-geral* ordered any who were captured to be summarily killed.[21]

Thus the social and political dis-integration of the peoples of the Zambesi valley, ever prone to ecological disaster and the predatory culture of raiding, destroyed the ancient and once prestigious paramount chieftaincy of the Karanga.

Despite their military defeat in the 1690s, the Portuguese retained a strong position in eastern Africa. They kept their towns on the Zambesi and the port of Sofala. They also had a *prazo* at Mambone at the mouth of the Sabi, and in 1727 set up a permanent factory and fort at Inhambane. If the Changamire controlled the gold mining areas, the Portuguese controlled most of the routes whereby imports could reach the interior, and this balance of economic and political power south of the Zambesi was to change little till the nineteenth century. Portuguese relations with the Changamire remained distant. Occasional embassies were sent south to the Rozvi capital and for two or three decades there was official concern over the fate of Portuguese captured during the wars of the 1690s who, it was believed, were being held there. However, the ambassadors sent by the Portuguese were always Africans and there appear to have been no direct contacts between the Portuguese themselves and the Rozvi paramount.

With the return of peace to the communities on the high veldt after about 1702, it was in the interest of all parties for trade relations to be re-established, but on what basis this could be done was not clear. The Portuguese wanted to return to their old fairs in Karangaland, but the rulers of Butua were determined not to allow Portuguese backwoodsmen with their private armies ever again to cause the sort of disorder that in the seventeenth century had torn the old Karanga chieftaincies to pieces. Moreover it seems probable that foreign trade was only of minor concern to the Butua rulers. From their impressive stone-walled towns in the southern part of the high veldt, the Rozvi aristocracy based their rule on cattle-ownership, and imports of Indian cloth, Venetian beads, Dutch gin or Chinese porcelain were of only marginal significance to them. The Changamires were content with the long-distance trade routes which linked them to the *feira* of Manica, to Inhambane and to the Zambesi towns. Sufficient imports reached Butua in this way and the further development of trade contacts seems not to have concerned them.

In Manica and Kiteve the situation was different. The immediate result of the Changamire's attack on Chipangura/ Masekesa had been the movement of the centres of trade to Kiteve. The Sofala Portuguese began to be very active in Kiteve, acquiring *prazos* and reopening gold trading centres in the kingdom. As a result the Portuguese at Sena, feeling themselves excluded from their traditional trade in gold, had despatched a mission to reopen the fair at Masekesa in 1719. An account written some fifty years later claimed that the Chicanga had been unwilling to allow the Portuguese to build a permanent *feira*, whereupon the Portuguese had approached Changamire for support. The Rozvi sent an army which protected the Portuguese party while a fort was built again on the old site of the fair of Chipangura. Be that as it may, by 1720 the fair was once again in operation with a *capitão-mor* and a small garrison of soldiers.[22]

The founding of Zumbo

The newly reopened fair of Manica was one route whereby the Rozvi might exchange gold for foreign imports but there was another which served their purpose better still. In 1715 the Portuguese established a new fair at Zumbo at the confluence of the Luangwa and the Zambesi. It had taken shape over a long period. In the last quarter of the seventeenth century Portuguese and Indian traders had increasingly explored the opportunities for trading gold and ivory on the middle reaches of the Zambesi. In the 1690s they were trading regularly to Mburuma and Orenje where considerable stocks of ivory could be obtained. The confluence was the natural point for a permanent base since it formed a meeting-point for river-borne traffic from the central African interior.

According to tradition, the *feira* of Zumbo was founded by a Goan trader, Francisco Pereira, who fled from Dambarare when it was attacked by Changamire. He obtained land concessions from a local chief in payment for a debt and as a reward for services rendered — a story which, whether true or not, is wholly typical of the process by which the Portuguese acquired land and mining concessions throughout Zambesia. Little is known of Pereira but in later years the Changamires used to call all the captains of Zumbo by this name — to the Rozvi they were all 'Pereira'. The first permanent site occupied by the Portuguese traders was on the Zambesi island of Chitakatira and the *feira* was formally established there in 1715. At different times during the next century the Portuguese were to maintain trading establishments on both banks of the Luangwa and use the island as a refuge in times of trouble. Although in the eighteenth century the term *feira* and the name Zumbo were used indiscriminately for the various sites of Portuguese settlement, in the nineteenth and twentieth centuries the names were used more specifically, Zumbo applying to the settlement on the east bank of the Luangwa, and Feira to the west bank settlement which eventually found itself within the frontiers of Northern Rhodesia/Zambia.[23]

Therefore, in the five years 1715–20 the Portuguese had re-established two important trading fairs to tap the gold of the interior. Zumbo and Manica were, however, very different types of settlement. Manica was situated inland in the territory of the Chicanga and was always very much under his control. Portuguese traders travelled to Manica and, although they did not own land round about, they did from time to time take some part in opening and exploiting the gold diggings. Access to Manica could only be obtained by passing through the territory of Barue where the proudly independent Macombes were always asserting their right to levy tolls on the traders or close the roads altogether. Zumbo on the other hand was really another river port like Sena and Tete. Trade goods reached it by river, with porterage round the Cabora Bassa rapids, and from there were despatched to fairs and mining areas in Butua. Portuguese traders never travelled far inland from Zumbo and entrusted their trade goods to the *mussambazes*, whose activities depended very much on the protection afforded them by the Changamires.

The *feira* of Manica, like its trade, remained relatively small. Although the gold was of fine quality, the quantity exported rarely seems to have exceeded 100 *pastas* (1,650 ounces) in any year, and the level of business never attracted more than a score or so of traders or settlers. Moreover the settlement of large numbers of Afro-Portuguese was discouraged by the Manica chiefs. Zumbo, however, was different. From the start the *feira* was recognised as sovereign Portuguese territory and the access it gave to areas which were relatively unexploited commercially attracted a large community of traders and their slaves. Early in the the century Zumbo's trade annually produced 300–400 *pastas* (4,950–6,600 ounces) of gold and the population of the fair rose rapidly. In 1734 Zumbo had 262 Christians and in 1749, when at the height of its prosperity, it had a Christian population of 478, eighty of whom were Europeans.[24] In a short time Zumbo had become the largest of the Zambesi towns and may possibly, have been the largest and most wealthy Portuguese settlement in eastern Africa at that time. A century later, in 1859, Richard Thornton visited the ruins of old Zumbo and wrote in his journal that 'these were very extensive. . . . It is said there are ruins of 200 stone houses extending in a line 2 miles long.'[25]

The prosperity of Zumbo in the thirty years after its foundation was always associated with the person of the Dominican friar who acted as its priest and governor. *Frei* Pedro da Trindade dominated the *feira* through the wealth he accumulated and his prestige among the

African population far into the interior. When he died the governor of Mozambique, Balthasar Pereira do Lago, described him as 'a man so ambitious and so wicked that he died in the midst of a veritable mountain of more than thirty concubines'. His name was given to a medicinal root and to one of the largest of the goldfields in northern Zambesia. Here were the ingredients of prestige in any African society. A man of power would clearly be expected to have many wives and be a powerful medicine man as well as an operator of gold mines. When he died in 1749 he had a personal following of 1,600 clients and slaves and allegedly had a fortune of 100,000 *xerafins*. After his death a spirit cult became associated with his memory and it was still possible at the end of the nineteenth century to find the spirit of *Frei* Pedro invoked in time of famine.[26]

At the time of *Frei* Pedro's death, Zumbo was at the height of its wealth. A report from that time states that the annual trade of Zumbo stood at 500–600 *pastas* (8,250–9,900 ounces) — a figure indirectly substantiated by the information that when Zumbo was raided in 1756 the Portuguese traders lost 1,000 *pastas* of gold.[27] Ten years later Zumbo was said to have imported 400–500 *bares* of cloth and 2–3,000 packets of beads.[28] In 1764 it was given the status of a municipality with a *Senado da Câmara* operating like a diminutive republic. In practice, however, the leader of the community remained the *capitão-mor* whose title changed to *governador* and then to *commandante* before reverting to the more familiar *capitão-mor* again in the last days of the fair.

By 1764, however, Zumbo's wealth was waning and its community was about to enter on a time of troubles. Although sovereign Portuguese territory and hence different from Manica, it was nevertheless just as dependent as Manica on the goodwill of the African chiefs through whose territory trade caravans had to pass. The river route from Tete to Zumbo was blocked by the Cabora Bassa rapids and most of the journey from Tete to Chicoa was made by porters over land. From Chicoa the trade goods proceeded by river but the banks were controlled by the Monomotapa who demanded presents (*bocas*) or levied fines for breaches of custom (*milandos*) on passing boats.[29] This might have caused little problem but for the almost perpetual conflict within the chieftaincy, made worse by the dislocation caused to agriculture by drought and banditry. In 1751–66 no fewer than six Monomotapas came and went and the losses involved in sending trade goods to Zumbo grew to a point where traders were not prepared to take the risk. The latter part of this period was also one of serious drought on the Zambesi, usually a circumstance that led to violence and brigandage as people threatened with starvation took to robbing trade caravans in order to survive. The violence eventually became such that it was seriously suggested that Zumbo be evacuated.

However, in 1769 the Portuguese and Changamire agreed to take measures to restore the fortunes of the fair. The Portuguese sent troops from Sena to secure the river passage and Changamire also sent forces to help Zumbo.

As a result, a report in 1770 was able to refer to Zumbo as 'the metropolis of the whole trade of the Rivers and the fountain of the large profits that the subjects of Your Majesty realize from the trade'. The 1770s saw Zumbo briefly regain some of its prosperity, but in 1779 the town was sacked by a local chief and the fair had once again to be rebuilt under the protection of the Changamire, a fort being built for the first time to defend the settlement.

The slow decline of Zumbo was due partly to the general insecurity of the journey up the Zambesi from Tete but also partly reflected the fact that as an actual trading fair Zumbo itself was of only minor importance. Although gold was mined in the vicinity, so that in 1786 Manuel Galvão da Silva was able to obtain samples from mines on the Revue and Sanhate as well as from two sources which he called Abutua and Muzezuros, the main function of the settlement had always been to act as the base from which the *mussambazes* were organised for their trading journeys to the interior.[30] It was not uncommon for these to last three or four years, during which time the money invested in their trading stock earned no return. Not surprisingly the small traders could not sustain this level of risk and as the century advanced, the ones who remained in the trade were those with powerful backing from Indian commercial houses in Mozambique. Indians had been prominent in the founding of Zumbo and had always played a major role in the town's life. In the last quarter of the century they were running the town as an adjunct to the general trading dominance they had established throughout Mozambique.

For the first three-quarters of the century, Zumbo's prosperity derived largely from trade with the Rozvi which appears to have been conducted at fairs in the interior, some of them sited near the gold diggings. Although this trade was controlled by local chiefs, there seems little evidence that it was a royal monopoly. Neither the Changamire nor the Rozvi aristocracy depended on Zumbo since they could import goods also via Manica on the eastern border of their empire, as well as from distant Inhambane. Therefore, although they were willing and able from time to time to protect the fair at Zumbo, they do not seem to have been much concerned when its trade was routinely interrupted by conflict among the chiefs controlling the Zambesi valley.

In the latter part of the century Zumbo traders began to diversify their activities and to expand their trade into other areas. In 1761 four-fifths of their trade had been with Butua but thereafter traders increasingly speculated in the ivory that came from Orenje (the Lenje country) in the interior to the north-west, and by 1796 this ivory trade surpassed the trade in gold, confirming the radical shift in the orientation of Indian commercial activity in eastern Africa as a whole.[31] However, the growth of the ivory trade was not enough to counter the accumulating problems affecting the fair. During the 1790s the stability necessary for commercial activity seems to have disappeared almost completely, and in 1795 began the great cycle of drought which created unsettled ecological conditions until the 1830s. The first drought lasted from 1795 till 1801, and during this time not only was the Zumbo settlement repeatedly attacked by neighbouring peoples anxious to plunder its wealth but the kingdom of Butua itself dissolved into civil war, cutting the flow of gold and preventing the free movement of caravans. To try to create an element of stability, a permanent garrison was established at Zumbo in 1801, and in the following decade both Zumbo and Feira were fortified with town walls. Those of Feira were investigated by the archaeologist Desmond Clark in August 1960. He found that they had been made of coursed stonework two feet thick and up to eight feet high, strengthened with bastions, observation posts and some sort of inner citadel. The walls had protected the landward side of the angle of land formed by the Zambesi and Luangwa. Although much effort was expended on the fortification of Feira, the settlements were plundered again in 1804, and in 1813 the residents moved out and both fairs were abandoned. The Portuguese continued to appoint a person to the post of *capitão-mor* of Zumbo, and in 1820 the *feira* was formally re-established. However, trade continued there only irregularly, and the terminal decline of the gold trade from Butua meant that the prosperity of Zumbo could never be recaptured.[32] In 1836 as a result of renewed drought and the final destruction of the Rozvi monarchy, Zumbo was once again abandoned.

There is little doubt that during the great period of its prosperity, Zumbo had depended on the gold trade of Butua. Its fortunes rose and fell with the Rozvi dynasty; turmoil in Butua meant danger for Zumbo and a contraction of its trade. The story of Zumbo is instructive. It was no dynamic spearhead of European commercial expansion from which the conditions of the world market imposed themselves on traditional African economies. Neither the Portuguese nor the Africans were able to create the settled conditions essential for long-term growth of trade. Commerce was repeatedly interrupted when drought and famine turned African peasants and their chiefs into bandits who sought a living by preying on river traffic and trade caravans. Thus insecurity of trade was a consequence of the fragile agricultural economy of the valley and the escarpment. The

Rozvi state, when not itself afflicted with civil war, certainly had the capacity to impose order but it did not do so in any systematic way because the trade of Zumbo was just not sufficiently important to the power and prestige of its ruling élite. The professional traders who went to Butua were neither Rozvi nor Karanga. All originated in the society of the Zambesi valley and although they may have established kinship ties in the countries where they traded, they only occasionally succeeded in invoking the active intervention of the Rozvi chiefs.

Already by the end of the eighteenth century the fragility of the economies of the region was being exposed. Without a more sophisticated technological base, there could be little growth within the subsistence economies and therefore only a limited response to the severities of drought once they occurred. The trade of Zumbo proved a victim of ecological change just as surely as the economies of the smallest villages. The great droughts of the early nineteenth century swept away the *mussambazes* and the gold fairs as surely as they destroyed the societies based on subsistence village agriculture.

Gold fairs north of the Zambesi

One reason why the Portuguese never made a serious effort to regain their gold fairs south of the Zambesi was that soon after the beginning of the eighteenth century they began to develop new gold-mining areas north of the river. During the previous century only a few individual Portuguese had explored the land north of the Zambesi and no settlements had been made there. The Maravi chiefs had long posed a serious military threat to the Portuguese towns on the Zambesi, culminating in the great rebellion of 1631. Thereafter relations had become more peaceful as the Portuguese and the Maravi chiefs had developed the ivory trade to their mutual profit. However, up till 1675 the trade had operated under the terms of the captain's monopoly and the captain deliberately retricted the settlement of Portuguese in Zambesia and discouraged the opening of new trade routes north of the river.

By the end of the seventeenth century the captain's monopoly had ceased and the power of the Maravi empire was visibly waning. The prestige of the paramount Kalonga chiefs had never been sufficient to create a centralised political system, and in the eighteenth century proved insufficient to counter the centrifugal forces represented by the territorial and rainmaking cults that underpinned the chieftaincies of Undi and Lundu. Undi's state was based on his capital at Mano north west of Tete, while Lundu's capital was in the Shire valley. Neither chieftaincy was much centralised and as political power was increasingly devolved to subordinate chiefs, so opportunities began to present themselves for the Portuguese to penetrate the territory of the old Maravi ascendancy.

Maravi country was not, of course, entirely unknown to the Portuguese. Traders and missionaries had journeyed up the Shire to Lake Malawi, and in 1616 Gaspar Bocarro had travelled through it to Kilwa. Portuguese warlords had recruited mercenaries in Maravi country and Diogo Simoẽs Madeira had opened up a regular highway along the north bank, while at different times the Portuguese had attacked the chiefs on Mount Morrumbala with the object of incorporating them within the captaincy of Sena. In 1678 Theodósio Garcia travelled on a semi-official mission to the Kalonga's court. However, it was Changamire's expulsion of the Portuguese from the Karanga plateau that indirectly stimulated the gold rush in the north. Portuguese and Indian gold traders fleeing from the Karanga fairs began to look for alternative commercial and mining opportunities, following up the old stories of silver mines and prospecting for gold in the rivers flowing off the escarpment north of the Zambesi. By the early eighteenth century stories of gold strikes had begun to attract the more adventurous elements from the Zambesi settlements.

It appears that gold had not been mined by the African population north of the Zambesi before the eighteenth century, and the Portuguese consequently found untouched alluvial deposits and outcrops of unworked reef gold near the surface. None of these gold sources was very rich but they were unexploited and afforded great wealth for those who first worked them. The Jesuit Mauriz Thoman records one such find:

> A black woman noticed some glittering nuggets of gold in passing an anthill. At once she went for her wooden bowl and, filling it with earth from there, went down to the water and obtained the most beautiful gold dust in considerable quantities. She continued with the work until other women noticed her; they then all dug at this hill with their combined effort and dug it away completely. A value of several thousand gulden was obtained from it. Some thousands of this my predecessor obtained and wiped out the glaring debt of the Residence.[33]

Parties of armed slaves raised on the *prazos* began to cross the river and establish mining camps (*bares*) in the lands of the Maravi chiefs. The chiefs were powerless to prevent them and anyway probably hoped to gain from the presents they were given and from the access to imported goods traded by the Portuguese. The major gold strikes led to the establishment of communal mining camps which in turn grew into semi-permanent fairs.

The only contemporary account of the great gold rush in Maravi country is that of the Dominican Francisco de Santa Caterina written in 1744; most other reports date from the 1760s and 1770s when gold output was already declining and some of the diggings were being abandoned. However, it appears that at the height of the gold rush of *ca.* 1740–60 there were as many as twenty-three mines being worked. The diggings at Pemba were operated by *Frei* Pedro da Trindade from his base in Zumbo and were subsequently worked by the Dominicans, but otherwise Mano, Michonga and Cassunça were to be the best known. Mano, which was presumably near to the capital of chief Undi, was typical of the most productive goldfields. One account suggested that it originally produced up to 400,000 *cruzados* of gold a year but that after this initial high output it declined to a regular 60,000 *cruzados*. However, in 1758, as a result of a severe drought which led to the desertion or death of many of the slaves in Portuguese service, the *bare* was abandoned.[34] A similar story is told of the other mines: very high yields immediately after the first discovery of gold, followed by rapid decline. In the 1770s only two mines — Cassunça, mined by the Tete Portuguese, and Michonga, worked from Zumbo — were still producing. However, from time to time new diggings were opened. Machinga was worked by the slaves of Dona Francisca de Moura e Meneses from 1777, and at the beginning of the nineteenth century was allegedly yielding 40 *pastas* a year. However, when Gamitto visited the area in 1831 he found groups of slaves digging desultorily and entirely unsupervised and he thought the total yield was barely 2 *pastas* a year.[35] In 1786 Manuel Galvão da Silva sent back specimens of gold from a mine near the Zambesi at Cabora Bassa. Java goldfield began operations in 1790 and became the preserve of the Caetano Pereira family, although by 1831 it was producing no gold and was only occupied by a few of Pereira's slaves because of the fruit trees there.[36] The furthest the Portuguese settled north of the river was at Missale on the edge of Cewa country. There, in 1831, a community of *chicunda* lived under their *mwanamambo*, maintaining a residence for their nominal owner but making their living by trading to the north rather than by mining gold.[37]

The northern goldfields were worked by women miners in Portuguese service. Apparently men were not employed and the local Maravi inhabitants took little part in the enterprise. At Mano, now once again in operation, Gamitto found the women miners organised in groups of six under an *nhacoda* who had to see that each miner delivered six *tangas* of gold a week. The working week was considered to be four days, and once the requisite amount of gold had been delivered the women could work on their own account. The owner of the *bare* usually maintained a store and sold goods to the miners in exchange for any additional gold they acquired.[38] Lacerda, who had

had experience of the goldfields of Brazil, was contemptuous of the
primitive practices of the women miners, and described them attempting to bale out the water from the diggings with baskets![39] According to Gamitto, goldmining at Machinga consisted either of digging
pits at random and taking the spoil to be panned in the rivers, or of
bringing gold-bearing quartz to be crushed in mortars. In either case
only the most primitive tools were used.[40]

Like gold rush camps all over the world, the northern Zambesian
bares were lawless. The slaves of the rival settlers fought each other,
and the Portuguese authorities tried to establish order by appointing
capitães-mores with judicial powers. However, in the late eighteenth
century, those *bares* that remained in production and were not just
exploited for a few seasons, fell into the hands of individual Afro-
Portuguese and the feudal forms of authority, represented in
Zambesia by the powerful *prazo* families, asserted themselves. By
1831, when Gamitto described the goldfields, each digging was
operated by the slaves of a single owner.

In the seventeenth century the Portuguese traders and gold prospectors south of the Zambesi had turned their economic power into
territorial authority. Men who had originally gone to east Africa as
traders had gained authority over people and land by the traditional
Iberian process of conquest, patronage and tribute. The *encomiendas* of
Spanish America had crossed the world and reappeared as the *prazos*
of Zambesia. In the eighteenth century a similar process inexorably
gathered momentum north of the Zambesi. The large bands of slaves,
assembled to exploit gold outcrops, enabled the *muzungos* to intervene
in African politics. Supporting one side or another in local conflicts,
they gradually acquired the realities and ultimately the legitimacy of
power. In 1754, for example, a combined force of slaves from the
prazos attacked the minor Maravi chief Bive and drove him from the
lands immediately north of the river.[41] By mid-century the *muzungos*
were looking to the Portuguese Crown to have their conquests confirmed with official land titles. The titles granted for these north bank
lands were different from the leases of the historic Portuguese Crown
lands: they were known as *terras em fatiota*, and were held on heritable
leases which paid no quit-rent to the Crown and came nearer than
the restrictive leases of the *prazos da coroa* to the concept of freehold.
Eventually all the land on the north bank between the Lupata and
Cabora Bassa gorges as divided into some forty *terras em fatiota* and
leased to Afro-Portuguese.

From this powerful territorial base the control of the Afro-
Portuguese feudal class extended ever further over the peoples of the
old Maravi empire. Chiefs were made or unmade and came to hold
their offices by the goodwill of the *muzungos*, and one Indian family,

the Caetano Pereiras, married into the chiefly dynasty of Chicucuru
and eventually held the title to that chieftaincy themselves. It was the
Caetano Pereiras also who used their base in the territory north of the
river to pioneer trading journeys to the north-west, enterprises far
more ambitious than anything the Portuguese had attempted since
Bayão's march into Butua in the early seventeenth century. Their
plan was to tap the ivory and copper wealth of the Lunda and possibly
establish direct trading links with Angola.

As a result of the pioneering trading journeys of Manuel Caetano
Pereira to the Lunda country, *mussambazes* in the service of Dona
Francisca de Moura e Meneses also made the journey, returning with
ivory and with invitations to the Portuguese to open a regular trade
route to the court of Kazembe. Meanwhile Bisa traders anticipated
this development by themselves opening a regular trade route to the
Zambesi. In 1798 Francisco de Lacerda e Almeida, the *tenente-geral* of
the Rivers, took advantage of the presence of the Bisa at Tete to
organise an expedition into the interior, enlisting the support of Dona
Francisca and the Caetano Pereiras.[42] Although Lacerda died on the
journey to the Lunda country, his expedition has usually been seen
as an important landmark in the development of European contacts
with the African interior.

Manica in the eighteenth century

The *feira* at Masekesa had been re-established, probably in 1719, and
throughout the eighteenth century Portuguese trading activity on the
escarpment south of the Zambesi was concentrated there. It had an
official status as a Portuguese government fair with a *capitão-mor* and
a garrison, and it was the means by which official diplomatic contact
was maintained with the Chicanga and, rather more important, with
Changamire. The captaincy had significant diplomatic and ritual
functions. The captains were asked to recognise new Chicangas and
were present at their installation. The anonymous author of the
Descripção Corografica describes a coronation ceremony which any
European monarch might envy:

> For his coronation, apart from many other extravagant cere-
> monies, they catch a live crocodile of which there are some very big
> ones in the rivers Ruanga and Hosa, tie it by the neck and make
> a bed on top of it on which the king had intercourse with a princess,
> one of his daughters, and afterwards sits on the same crocodile and
> has a little water poured on his head by a Portuguese envoy that
> has been requested by the king for that purpose.[43]

The *feira* was a curious hybrid, an official establishment in the control of private individuals. Up till 1771 the captains did not receive a salary and therefore had to maintain their position and make the customary tribute payments from their private resources. Masekesa became, in effect, the private *feira* of the person who held the captaincy at any one time.[44] After 1771 an official salary was paid but this does not seem to have greatly altered the nature of the Portuguese presence at the fair. The captains made a number of payments to the Chicangas, and through them to the Changamires, which were sometimes construed as tribute payments but were clearly important for the chiefs who wanted to acquire the goods which the Portuguese imported and thereby gain implicit recognition of their authority. These payments, according to the *Descripção Corografica*, amounted to 800 pieces of cloth.[45] In return for this recognition and present-giving, the Portuguese expected to be able to trade in relative peace and security.

In practice matters seldom worked smoothly. To reach Masekesa the road had to be kept open from Sena through the chieftaincy of Barue. The Barue chiefs had long been used to Portuguese trade caravans crossing their territory and expected to receive presents in return for the protection they afforded. The Macombes also looked to the Portuguese for recognition following the accession of a new chief. Manuel Galvão da Silva, who left a detailed account of an expedition to Manica in 1788, took nearly a month on the journey, including a stop of nine days on the *prazos* to assemble fresh porters. He was approached by official representatives of Macombe to whom presents were given and he had to camp overnight in the village of a local chief and reward him handsomely for his hospitality before the caravan could proceed. On the return journey, the caravan with which he travelled was subjected to continued demands for *milandos* and eventually had a running fight with Manica soldiers trying to impede its passage.

The safety of the caravans could also be jeopardised if there were disorder on the Sena *prazos* or in Barue itself. This frequently happened and banditry was endemic along the road to Manica. Bandit attacks on the traders might be made by escaped slaves from the Sena *prazos* or dissident Barue headmen building themselves strongholds in the broken escarpment country from which they could raid the trading caravans or plunder the villages of the *prazos*. These fortified stockades (known in the seventeenth century as *chuambos*, in the eighteenth as *mussitos* and in the nineteenth as *aringas*) were a seemingly permanent factor in the history of the lower Zambesi region, allowing bandits to establish their power over quite wide areas of country. Banditry also became endemic in Barue, as in the Monomotapa kingdom, because of the poverty of agricultural resources, the lack of cattle wealth and the perennial need to obtain trade goods and women through raiding more fortunate neighbours. Banditry always increased in periods of economic distress and was particularly serious in the 1760s and again in the 1790s when harvests were bad and people turned to raiding to make good their lack of food. In the late 1760s the whole border region between the Sena captaincy, Barue and Kiteve was in a state of anarchy. Portuguese *prazo*-owners seized land in Barue and the Barue chiefs responded by raiding Sungue and closing the roads to Manica. Both sides accused the other of harbouring fugitives and supporting dissidents, and peace was only restored in 1769 after an official exchange of ambassadors and gifts.[46]

What can only be described as banditry also occurred while the succession to a chieftaincy was being settled. It was common on the death of a chief for widespread violence and looting to break out, directed most of all against foreigners. Trading was stopped throughout the kingdom for a month while 'along the roads there are various gangs collecting a certain amount from travellers and all the *cafres* who want to go along those same roads must have their hair shaved . . .',[47] The Portuguese believed that this was in some way seen by the local people as a legitimate form of mourning, although it was probably just the natural result of the breakdown of authority. An interregnum in Barue could also result in the Sena Portuguese trying to seize control of land on the borders of Barue.

In these circumstances the Portuguese had to try to maintain commercial contacts with their community in Masekesa. The trade goods reached the merchant houses at Sena by means of river boats and from there were consigned in the company of the *mussambazes* to an assembly point on the borders of the Sena *prazos*. In the eighteenth century the favoured spot for the caravans to assemble was Sungue which bordered on Barue territory and appears to have developed into a commercial centre in its own right. There fresh porters could be taken on and the caravans, often accompanied by armed slaves and usually by some Afro-Portuguese or Indian merchants as well, made their way as best they could to Masekesa.[48] The caravans were sometimes large — Manuel Galvão da Silva returned from Manica in 1788 in the company of one numbering over 400 men. The kingdoms of Barue and Manica were separated by the river Aruangoa, and on the Manica side of the river the Portuguese maintained a fortified post which sometimes also functioned as a *feira*.[49]

According to Galvão da Silva, the site of the *feira* of Manica itself, which was near the site of the seventeenth-century *feiras*, had been given to the Portuguese by the Changamire at the time when his writ ran powerfully in Manica. Like Dambarare in the seventeenth century, the fair occupied a wide area of land, described as being 2 miles in circumference. It had a captain and fifteen African soldiers under a lieutenant, and in 1788 its fort was

> . . . . a square construction of stone and clay, with straw-covered walls which partly crumble away during the winter, so that they continually need rebuilding. There is not a single piece of ordnance, no embrasure, not even the least loop-hole from which to fire a gun. Barely in the corner does it have a mast on which to raise our flag. The only use this fortification has, if any, is that it provides an enclosure for a little church, likewise built of stone and clay and straw-thatched.[50]

According to the *Descrição Corographica*, there were never more than three or four Portuguese or Afro-Portuguese resident at Masekesa. The fair itself was run much as had been the practice since the fifteenth century. Essentially it was a place where foreign traders could be properly controlled by the chiefs and where the highly valued imports could be concentrated so that they could be bought by the Chicanga himself or at least made subject to his tax.

In the eighteenth century the Manica chiefs continued to exert tight control over the rate at which gold was extracted. The Portuguese were not allowed to open gold diggings under their own control. In 1750, for example, the then captain of Manica apparently discovered a gold outcrop and employed some local people to dig there. When Chicanga discovered this, the *bare* was closed down and the workmen were punished.[51] Manuel Galvão da Silva, who was able to visit a number of the gold diggings, reported that these were mostly pits up to twelve feet wide and dug down as far as the water table, but that the miners, who were usually women, preferred to obtain alluvial gold in the river beds after the passage of floods.

Manica gold was of fine quality and Masekesa was always primarily a centre for gold trading. But other commodities — high-quality iron hoes, copper, rubber, cattle, crystal and ivory — were also traded at the fair, which suggests that it may have served much more as a centre of regional commerce than might otherwise have been assumed. The Portuguese for their part brought a variety of Indian cloths, white and blue glass beads, Indian tin and pewter and *machiras*, the traditional African-woven cloth of the Zambesi and Shire region.

Masekesa was equidistant from Sena and Sofala and sometimes merchants from Sofala tried to send their *mussambazes* to Manica to trade. However, convention aided by self-interest kept the two spheres of influence separate. The Kiteves maintained their *feira* at Bandire and in the middle of the eighteenth century about 50 *pastas* a year were being exported from Sofala, about half the amount regularly traded at Manica. It was the policy of the Kiteves to prevent

Portuguese from Sofala passing through to Masekesa, though this did not prevent them from occasionally making a bid to control the *feira* there themselves. The Chicangas likewise wanted to monopolise the trade of Sena, while the Sena Portuguese had no desire to compete with rivals from Sofala even though they were nominally fellow-countrymen.

The other Portuguese trading posts, even Zumbo and the northern mining camps, either belonged formally to the Crown of Portugal or were informally under its control. Masekesa was always different. For all that the Portuguese had a fort and maintained a garrison on land given them by Changamire, the fair existed on sufferance from the chiefs of Manica. At any time the Chicangas were in a position to close the fair and end the Portuguese presence in their country. The fair existed because the Chicangas wanted it to exist and they dictated the terms of trade and the conditions under which it was transacted. If the Portuguese had some influence on the general conditions of the market, profiteering could be, and frequently was, countered by the demand for presents, fines and other legal exactions made by the chiefs. One estimate suggested that anything up to a third of all the cloth brought by the Portuguese into Manica was disposed of in ways that were not strictly commercial.[52]

Naturally this subordinate status of the *feira* did not pass unnoticed by contemporary commentators. The contrast with the rapidly expanding trade of Zumbo and the growth of the mining *bares* on the north bank stimulated a number of plans to make Masekesa the base for Portuguese expansion on the southern plateau. Such plans were regularly dusted off whenever the Portuguese got wind of Dutch proposals for penetrating the interior of southern Africa. In the event, however, there was never a serious effort to expand Portuguese dominion from Masekesa. Not only did the Portuguese lack the resources to attempt such a move but the local Afro-Portuguese community much preferred to operate in the traditional way, commanding the services of their slaves and the tribute of their peasants and dealing with the Tonga and Karanga chiefs to the satisfactory exclusion of the government, the avowed enemy of both.

The only threat to the Chicangas, control over the trade came from internal divisions within the chieftaincy itself. If a new chief could succeed relatively unchallenged, the transition would not weaken the control over the fair. However, if there were a prolonged succession dispute, as in 1795 on the death of Chicanga Gowera, then the Portuguese would have an opportunity to sell their recognition dearly and even interfere directly, by military means on the side of one of the contestants.

Manica in the early nineteenth century

In 1795 Manica entered a time of political instability. That year Chipunza was installed as the new Chicanga and reopened the fair at Masekesa to attract back the traders who had retreated to Aruangoa on the borders of Manica at the death of his predecessor. However, Chipunza lasted less than a year, being ousted by his brother Nyarumwe in March 1796. Nyarumwe was not able to establish any kind of order in Manica without the backing of the Portuguese, and for the next three years desultory conflict ensued between the Chicanga, backed by the Portuguese from the *feira*, and various dissident headmen. In 1807 another Manica prince, Nyangombe, tried to seize the throne and he, Nyarumwe and another claimant, Nyamutota, disputed control of Manica for the next six years.[53]

During all this time disorder spread throughout the region and trade became increasingly paralysed. In 1813 the Portuguese traders moved from Masekesa to Vumba but stability did not return to Manica and in 1818 an attempt was made to reopen the *feira* at Aruangoa. Shortly after this Nyarumwe regained control of the kingdom, probably with Portuguese backing, and thereafter banditry gradually declined, although the first effects of the great Mozambique drought were felt in Manica after 1822 and prevented a complete return to normality. It was at this time that the new dynastic title of Mutasa (Umtasa) was adopted.[54] During the 1820s the Portuguese kept both the fairs of Aruangoa and Masekesa in operation but in 1830, at the height of the great drought, the Nguni raids began. Between 1830 and 1835 the fairs were attacked five times and although attempts were made to reinforce them, there was no escaping the fact that gold mining had virtually ceased and with it any prospect of profitable trade.[55] From 1835 the Portguguese abandoned the fairs, and although trading and mining activity was resumed in Manica later in the century, the fairs themselves were never reopened.

10

THE PRAZOS

Origins of the prazos

The *prazos da coroa*, so inseparably linked with the fortunes of the Afro-Portuguese, provide one of the most distinctive features of the history of Mozambique. Their existence can be traced from the sixteenth century to their eventual abolition in the 1930s, and they were one of the most durable and influential of the country's institutions. The name only came into use in the eighteenth century although the institution itself had already been a reality in the lives of Mozambicans for two centuries and had evolved considerably. It is not easy to say in simple terms exactly what a *prazo* was, indeed part of the interest of the *prazos* is that they are like holograms, presenting a different image according to the angle of vision. To the Portuguese they were land grants held under Roman Law contracts of emphyteusis, but from the African point of view they were essentially chieftaincies and as such part of a complex system of social and economic relations bounding together all the peoples of the region. This dual character is typical of the social and political culture of the Afro-Portuguese that enabled them to live and operate in two (or even three) worlds at the same time. Their society was a unique interface between Africa, Asia and Europe and led to the growth of syncretic cultural and social forms which, like the *prazos*, evidently had considerable vitality.

The *prazos* were not, like the Castilian *encomiendas*, initially legal concepts introduced by foreigners bent on conquest and colonisation. They had their origins in Africa itself and their beginnings are to be found in the positions of influence which individual Portuguese, and before them individual Muslims from the coast, were able to acquire within African society, either by marriage or as traders or mercenaries. Information about renegades serving with African chiefs comes from the earliest reports by the captains of the fort at Sofala and throughout the sixteenth century; and from the Bazaruto Islands in the south to Cabo Delgado in the north and inland to the Karanga kingdom of Monomotapa, examples can be found of individual Portuguese adventurers establishing niches for themselves within African society.

At the courts of the Karanga chiefs and at the fairs operating under their supervision, it had long been the custom to grant special status to foreigners and allow them to elect leaders who would maintain order among the foreign community and mediate between it and the African population. In the 1570s a Captain of the Gates (*capitão das portas*) was being appointed by the Monomotapa to have jurisdiction over the Portuguese at the fairs. We are told that the captain administered justice not only among the Portuguese but, in the name of the Monomotapa, adjudicated disputes between all parties within the fairs. He received an appointment and insignia of office from the chief and had his position confirmed by the captain of Mozambique — confirmation of status within the two worlds in which the Afro-Portuguese lived. A somewhat different case is that of Rodrigo Lobo, a Portuguese from Sofala who became a favourite with the Kiteve and was made by him lord of some of the swampy islands near the coast.

Concession or gift from African chiefs may have been one way the Portuguese acquired private jurisdictions in Africa, but an important stage in the evolution of the *prazos* took place as a result of the Barreto expedition of 1569–75. Although it failed in its major objectives, the expedition did occupy the lower Zambesi valley and take over the private plantations and urban settlements of the Muslim community. As part of the peace settlement arranged with the Monomotapa, the Karanga chief handed over to the Portuguese captain of Tete some of the rebellious Tonga chieftaincies of the valley. We are told that the captain assumed the role of chief, carrying out religious ceremonies, raising military levies and tribute and rewarding his warriors with distributions of women and booty after successful campaigns. By the early seventeenth century most of the Tonga in the lands along the right bank of the Zambesi had come into such a relationship with the captains of either Sena or Tete.[1]

At the same time the Portuguese Crown was trying to accommodate the competing bids for office, land and pensions increasingly being made by religious orders, *fidalgos* and superannuated soldiers. The Pope had granted to the Crown of Portugal the right of patronage over the Catholic Church in the East, the so-called *padroado real*, but this laid on it the obligation to provide for the maintenance of the clergy and religious orders. The Jesuits were the first order to work in eastern Africa and their mission had achieved great fame and notoriety in the 1560s. The Dominicans arrived only in the following decade but established themselves much more firmly and negotiated for concessions of property on Mozambique Island. Early in the seventeenth century both Jesuits and Dominicans competed with each other to establish missions in the Zambesi valley, and looked for grants of land and tribute-paying peasants to support their endeavours. As a way of fulfilling its obligations to the missions, the

Crown was prepared to make grants to them under Portuguese law and thus the ecclesiastical *prazos* came into existence.[2]

Meanwhile *prazos* were being granted in the Querimba Islands. These diminutive, barren islands were centres of cloth manufacture and had a thriving trade with the mainland. They were also of some strategic importance. Individual Portuguese had settled there, founded trading establishments and in the second half of the sixteenth century successfully petitioned the Portuguese Crown to grant them legal titles to their islands.[3]

The Crown wished to retain as much control over the lands in central Africa as it could, and was not prepared to tolerate the sort of quasi-independence exercised by the Spanish *encomenderos* in Peru. As in Peru, it was expected that rich mines would be discovered and it would be important to prevent these from falling into private hands. So when in 1607 the Monomotapa made a formal gift of the gold mines, it was to the Portuguese Crown and not to any individual *conquistador* that the gift was made, while in 1629 it was to the Crown that Monomotapa granted the sovereignty over his whole kingdom. Jurisdiction and regal authority were supposed to be wielded by the captains of the fortresses and fairs in the name of the king of Portugal. This policy was sustainable while the Crown had enough troops under the control of an officially appointed *conquistador* to maintain its authority, but as the wars of conquest proceeded, the Crown had to rely more and more on the private armies of the most powerful settlers. The captains of the fairs and the Zambesi towns were, by the middle of the seventeenth century, almost invariably chosen from the leading Afro-Portuguese families.[4] These used their official commissions to recruit and arm their private armies, so making themselves at the same time more indispensable to the Crown and less controllable.

Increasingly these private armies were used to obtain land concessions from chiefs. Diogo Simões Madeira is the earliest, and perhaps best known, example. He won control of the chieftaincy of Inhabanzo, persuaded Monomotapa to cede it to him, and then petitioned the Crown to grant him a title to it. However, Madeira was only the first of a succession of powerful warlords who used their private armies to expand the area of Portuguese control. There was João da Costa who had a private fair in Manica in the 1630s, and Gonçalo João who seized land for himself in Maramuca high in the Karanga plateau. The most important of these warlords was Sisnando Dias Bayão. His private army was used to subdue Manica and then to invade Butua to intervene in a succession dispute. The most enduring of his conquests, however, was to secure the formal submission of Kiteve to the Portuguese and the concession to himself of a large part of the kingdom of Kiteve which he turned into a vast private domain.[5] He was succeeded by his son-in-law António Lobo da Silva, who consolidated the family holdings and extended his personal power over the kingdom of Barue as well.

At the height of Portuguese power in Karangaland between the 1650s and 1670s private armies were repeatedly used to extort land concessions from the Monomotapa until much of northern Karangaland had been partitioned among the *muzungo* warlords. The objectives of these conquerors was not, of course, to populate the land with a thrifty Portuguese peasantry but to extort tribute from a subject population and obtain control of the gold diggings in the hope that these would eventually yield the kind of wealth that the Spanish had found in South America.

The ability of the Portuguese to recruit fighters among the Tonga of the lower Zambesi has already been described. As long as the leader could maintain the flow of booty, particularly the distribution of women captives, he could be assured of large bodies of supporters. However, the leading Afro-Portuguese warlords also recruited Maravi fighters from north of the river who were greatly feared by the Tonga and Karanga because of their reputation as cannibals. Many of these fighters were not recruited only for a single campaign but became a permanent armed force in the pay of the warlord, and it was these men, misleadingly called slaves (*escravos*) in many Portuguese documents, who formed the basis of the formidable *chicunda* warbands of the eighteenth and nineteenth centuries.

For the Tonga of the Mozambique low veldt, overrule by the Afro-Portuguese could sometimes appear more attractive than that by Karanga or Maravi. Portuguese overlordship not only brought a ready supply of female captives but had the added attraction of giving access to large quantities of imported goods which presumably could not be obtained so easily from Karanga overlords. The private armies were used to enforce the payment of tribute and bring extensive new tribute-paying areas of land under control. As the northwards expansion of the Karanga in the fifteenth century had pushed most of the Tonga from the plateau into the hot dry valley, so the Portuguese wars of conquest of the seventeenth century were, to some extent, a return of the Tonga — an act of revenge by an oppressed group to whom the Afro-Portuguese had given a brutal but sometimes effective military leadership.

Although the private armies of the Afro-Portuguese greatly increased the area of land nominally under Portuguese control, their lawlessness was a major problem for the Portuguese authorities. The continual warfare and factional strife destroyed any hope of establishing peaceful colonies or of systematically developing the region. In a

long and detailed complaint sent to the Portuguese viceroy in 1645,
the Monomotapa urged that all the Portuguese should reside at
Dambarare

> . . . .because from the fortifications which are built by individuals
> and are garrisoned by their cafres and by other natives who rebel
> against their chiefs and collect together under their shadow, they
> do great damage to the natives, killing and wounding them and
> stealing their sons and daughters and their cattle.[6]

Twenty years later, Manuel Barreto explained that if the Africans of
the Zambesi region increased their production of gold,

> . . . .there comes immediately some powerful man . . . and com-
> mits such thefts and violence against the poor gold diggers that they
> think it better to hide the gold than to extract any more as a further
> incentive to our greed and their misfortune.[7]

The Crown repeatedly issued orders for the settlers in Karangaland
to be made to surrender their conquests and for land titles to be
refused them. However, after Sousa de Meneses' campaign of 1632,
the Crown was never able to send regular troops in any numbers to
the Rivers and the existence of Portuguese authority came to depend
increasingly on the private armies. In his report written in Goa in
1667, Barreto urged the Crown to recognise the reality of its position:

> The Portuguese deprived of their lands and their vassals would be
> scattered and powerless, and of no service. Besides which, having
> bought the lands with their own money, it was unjust to oblige
> them to give them up without compensation and without some evi-
> dent public necessity.[8]

It was a repetition of the sixteenth-century debate between the New
World *encomenderos* and the Spanish Crown which had not been
resolved until a bloody civil war had been fought.

Nevertheless the Crown always refused to grant land titles to the
conquistadores for their conquests in Karangaland, and this may have
had something to do with the fact that the Portuguese never acquired,
and apparently never sought, the chiefly position among the Karanga
that they had among the Tonga. The Portuguese were preoccupied
with gold mining and trading and did not amass the herds of cattle
which were the basis for chiefly power on the plateau. Without any
legitimation of their position, they remained simply predatory bandit
leaders or warlords, and indeed their intense factionalism led to a
dwindling of the Portuguese population on the high veldt and the
region's eventual conquest by Changamire in the 1690s.

In the Zambesi valley, however, the Afro-Portuguese established effective control over extensive sections of the Tonga and the Crown was willing to grant them titles and allow a systematic colonial regime to emerge. Here royal policy was to try to make the power of the warlords serve imperial purposes by employing legal forms and contracts to create a populous and productive colonial settlement based on plantation agriculture and trade. The *prazos* were to enter the second major phase of their development.

The idea of turning Zambesia into a colony of settlement was first clearly set out in the instructions (*regimento*) which Nuno Alvares Pereira brought with him in 1618. The king ordered him to

> . . . .grant to the new settlers such privileges and exemptions as the viceroy of India will empower you, with the declaration that afterwards they must seek confirmation of them from me so that I will limit the duration; and you will distribute them in such a manner that not everyone shall live near Chicoa [where the silver mines were reputed to be] but there shall be in each part the people necessary for the increase of the settlements and cultivation of the lands.[9]

A further attempt to promote the settlement of Zambesia was formulated after the campaigns of Sousa de Menezes in 1632. In the immediate aftermath of the reconquest a group of miners was sent to the Rivers under the leadership of a Castilian mining expert, Don Andres de Vides y Albarado. Their reports emphasised the potential riches of the mines but insisted that a substantial population was needed for their successful exploitation.[10] In 1635 a scheme was drawn up for sending to the Rivers 200 married couples who would be settler soldiers. They were to be skilled people who would take the tools of their trade, and their numbers were to be supplemented by sending women from the poorhouses of Portugal. The trade of the Rivers would be opened and the captain's commercial monopoly ended. The scheme was never implemented because of the lack of resources available in Lisbon during the struggle with the Dutch, and because of the vested interests, ranging from the captain of Mozambique to the religious orders and the Afro-Portuguese settlers and traders, which presented a united front in opposition to such an invasion of their privileged world.

A further attempt was made in 1677 to send settlers to Zambesia, and this time some ships left for eastern Africa with soldiers, artisans and married couples on board. It seems that some 100 of these eventually reached the Rivers, but there was no follow-up and such a small number of settlers, most of whom were women and children, did little to alter the character of the Zambesi settlements.[11]

Legal formulae

If formal settlement schemes were a failure, the Crown's lawyers did try to achieve the same ends through the conditions attached to the titles which the Afro-Portuguese acquired for their lands in Zambesia. Apparently the Crown's lawyers had three legal models in mind — the laws which had regulated the cession of vacant lands in medieval Portugal and the traditional Iberian institutions of *capitania* and *encomienda*, and those connected with the leasing of property and rents in Portuguese India.[12] In medieval Portugal vacant lands, or *sesmarias*, were granted on long leases, known in Roman law as contracts of emphyteusis. The normal length of a lease was three lives, and the grantee paid the Crown a quitrent. He was also obliged to put the land to use within a specified time, since the object of these grants was to populate empty lands and attract settlement. The term *sesmaria* was frequently used in connection with *prazo* grants in Mozambique, making it clear that the objective of the grant was indeed economic development.[13]

Rather different were the ideas underlying the grants of *capitania* and *encomienda*. The captaincies had originally been granted in the fifteenth and sixteenth centuries to important servants of the Portuguese Crown to organise the settlement of the Atlantic islands, Brazil and Angola. The captain had a wide-ranging jurisdiction which required him to raise taxes, administer justice and undertake defence. In return he could assume commercial privileges, amounting to monopolies on certain forms of commerce. He also had seigneurial rights over the land, although he was restricted in the amount of property he could own himself, and had obligations to introduce settlers and found towns and missions. *Encomiendas* had developed during the time of the *reconquista* in Spain and were introduced into the New World by the first conquerors. There they took the form of grants of Indians whose tribute and labour the *encomendero* could utilise in exchange for a general obligation to christianise and protect the population. The *encomienda* was not supposed to carry with it any title to land. Captaincies were hereditary, whereas *encomiendas*, in theory, were not. The *prazos* shared many of the characteristics of these two institutions — the term *prazo* itself deriving from the word *emprazamento* which indicated the length of time a lease was granted.

In the Portuguese territories in India and Ceylon the Crown had made grants of the revenues of villages (*aldeias*) either to endow the local church of the religious orders, or to provide an income to support some Crown office, or simply as a gift to individuals who had served the Crown. These were not grants of land as such but sometimes carried with them the obligation to provide armed men in case of need (a sort of Indo-Lusitanian scutage) as well as the responsibility for raising revenues.

The first clear statement that three life-tenures were being used in Zambesia comes in a royal letter in 1646 which orders the viceroy

> . . . .to divide the lands of the Rivers of Cuama equally among the married men which you are to send, so that with the fruits of the lands they can maintain themselves . . . and I instruct you that of the lands which are given to individuals in lives, a third shall on their death go to their heirs and two thirds shall be divided among married couples sent to that conquest.[14]

In 1667 Manvel Barreto gives much fuller details of the land contracts:

> All the lands of these Rivers are held from His Majesty for the term of three lives, with the obligation to pay a certain quit-rent and to perform service. . . . The service is that every holder of lands is obliged to assist with his people when it is necessary to make war in any part, or perform any other duty for the common good. The holders of these lands have the same power and jurisdiction as the kaffir *fumos* from whom they were conquered, for the deeds were passed in that form and therefore they are like the potentates of Germany, and can pronounce sentence, put to death, declare war, and impose tribute.[15]

A large number of *prazo* contracts survive from the eighteenth and early nineteenth centuries and in them can be seen, as if inscribed on tablets of stone in their legal language, the ambitions of the Portuguese for their east African colony. The *prazos* were leased for three lives and could not be alienated to the church. The grantee undertook to develop them and pay a quit-rent and not to be absent without leaving someone in charge. In 1760 an attempt was made formally to limit the land area of the grants. The most unusual aspect of the *prazos* was the set of laws governing inheritance. The *prazos* were to be granted to women on condition that they married a Portuguese, and would descend from mother to daughter. No mention is made by Barreto of grants to, or inheritance by, women and it is thought that this condition was borrowed from the practice common in Portuguese India where offices, commands, lands and revenues had frequently been granted to widows of deserving Crown servants or as dowries to orphan girls sent from Portugal to enable them to make a good match. In this way the Crown made provision for the maintenance of its dependants and, through the use of wardship, was able to determine who should hold the offices concerned. However, there is little doubt that the main objective of the *prazo* inheritance laws was to encourage Portuguese men to seek wealthy marriages and settle in east Africa.

In addition to the formal conditions included in the contracts (*cartas de aforamento*), there were customary obligations attached to being the *senhor* of a *prazo*. You had to keep order within the *prazo*, administer it and keep the roads clear; you had to provide soldiers, boatmen or carriers for the government and bear your part of the expense of maintaining the forts and government buildings. Sometimes there were specific obligations to support the church, permit mining activity or rent land to small farmers. In the later eighteenth century stipulations about the need to attract people to cultivate the land become more emphatic. A *prazo* concession of 1772 imposes the

> . . . obligation to receive onto the said land whatever family His Majesty shall send to this conquest, free residence shall be granted on it, and the *donatário* shall be paid from the cultivation half the *missongo* or *chipua* which the kaffir *mussenzes* [peasants] are accustomed to pay on the lands of the *donatários*; on the understanding that the said families shall not make use of the above mentioned lands except for the profits of agriculture without interfering with the free commerce of the *donatários*.[16]

Failure to fulfill these obligations could be used as a pretext to end a lease or not to renew it on the death of the holder.

Although some *prazo* grants were made as endowments to institutions — the religious orders, *Misericórdias* or *Câmaras* (town councils); as official correspondence in the eighteenth century makes clear, the *prazo* grants were primarily supposed to achieve the settlement and general economic development of the Rivers. However, as every single person who wrote about the problems of eastern Africa made abundantly clear, the huge extent of the *prazos*, the length of the leases, and the fact that they involved control over a subject peasantry all combined to frustrate these intentions and reinforce the feudal relationships of the Afro-Portuguese families with their clients and peasants on the one hand and with Crown on the other.

By the eighteenth century, the *prazos da coroa* had become well-established divisions of the land and population and included all the land that had been made subject to the four captaincies of Sofala, Sena, Tete and Quelimane. The fifteen *prazos* of the Quelimane captaincy extended along the banks of the Qua Qua river and up the coast into Makua territory. Four of these were owned by the Jesuits (till 1759) and one by the Dominicans. The Sena captaincy included most of the delta, the right bank of the Zambesi from the Lupata gorge to the sea and the two extensive *prazos* of Cheringoma and Gorongosa which had been conquered by Bayão and which extended south to the

Pungue. In 1763 there were twenty-two Sena *prazos*, three owned by the Jesuits until their expulsion and two declared to be 'disobedient'. There were eight *prazos* dependent on Sofala including Mambone, at the mouth of the Sabi river, which was geographically detached.[17]

The Tete *prazos* were different. Dionizio de Mello e Castro, in his report of 1763, lists fifty-four on the right bank, the remnants of the extensive conquests of the seventeenth century. However, nine of these were listed as 'invaded' or 'deserted', six were confiscated properties of the Jesuits and two belonged to the Dominicans. On the left bank were the lands which the Portuguese had begun to acquire in the eighteenth century as concessions from Maravi chiefs. These were granted on different tenures and known as *terras em fatiota*, the main difference being that they were hereditary. In 1763 there were fifty-one of these, of which the Jesuits had owned no less than twelve.[18]

Because many of the *prazos* originated in Tonga chieftaincies or traditional groupings of villages, they were of greatly varying size, wealth and importance. The Portuguese never carried out a proper survey of the *prazos* before the twentieth century and adhered to the traditional boundaries of the lands they had taken over, occasionally adding additional villages (*incubes*) that were made tributary but were always distinguished from the original *prazo*. The numbers of the *prazos* leased out fluctuated considerably. While those fronting the river and in the immediate neighbourhood of the towns had a kind of permanence and were always sought after and occupied, more remote ones were often added as a result of conquest by an energetic Afro-Portuguese *senhor* or *dona*, only for the inhabitants to regain their effective independence later. This created a sort of penumbra of *prazos* often referred to as 'deserted', 'invaded' or 'disobedient' — the lack of permanent political control underlining the dis-integrated nature of Zambesian society. Some of the *prazos* were very small and might be left with almost no population at all if, as a result of famine, war or oppressive rule, the headmen moved their villages to another *prazo*. On the other hand, some of the largest ones — like Cheringoma and Gorongosa which had been carved out of the old Kiteve kingdom; Marangue at the confluence of the Ruenha and the Zambesi; or the large *prazos* of Mirambone, Licungo and Quissungo that spread out along the coast north of Quelimane — were hundreds of square miles in extent.

The prazo-owners and their relations with the government

The *prazos* were the basis for the wealth and power of the Afro-Portuguese élite. Although no one was supposed to hold more than one *prazo*, in practice large family groupings emerged through the complex pattern of intermarriage. The ethnic origin of the *prazo*-holders and their husbands was diverse. António Pinto de Miranda, writing in 1766, listed the most prominent heads of households (*casas*) in the Rivers, and described them as follows: twenty were Portuguese, eleven Indian, seven mulattos and one was Chinese. In twenty-nine cases he gave the origin of the marriage partner — thirteen Portuguese and six Indians were married to mulattas, and five Portuguese were married to Indians. Afro-Portuguese society was clearly dominated by the locally born *muzungo* (mulatta) women who married Portuguese or Indians, the former often either convicts or men involved with the military or commercial administration, the latter usually Christian Indians from Goa who had arrived as traders or soldiers.[19] The wealth of the larger of the *prazos* meant that there were always Indians and Portuguese soldiers or officials who were anxious to marry an heiress and enter the narrow circle of the *muzungo* families.

The statistics contain no examples of African partners in the official marriages of the *prazo*-holding élite, or of all-white Portuguese marriages. On the other hand, all commentators agree that the males of the Afro-Portuguese community (and, they hint, the females as well) had numerous unofficial partners taken from the African community, and their offspring were accepted as part of the *muzungo* population.

The overall size of the Afro-Portuguese community of Zambesia is difficult to calculate because of the varying and imprecise nature of the categories used. Figures for 1722 record 300 Portuguese, 178 Indians and 2,914 baptised Africans. This is the highest estimate of the eighteenth century. Over the twenty-year period 1780–1800 the average total of all Christians (including Christian Africans) was given as 2,142.[20]

At the height of the eighteenth century the *prazo*-holders formed a feudal aristocracy that effectively dominated the affairs of the Rivers. Without their aid the government of the *tenente-geral* could not function. The major Afro-Portuguese families filled most of the administrative posts and one of their number was usually made captain of Manica, another captain of Zumbo. They also filled the position of captain of the Monomotapa's guard. They provided personnel from whom the increasingly influential *Capitaēs-mores das Terras da Coroa* were selected. These officials were, broadly, in charge of what would later be called 'native policy', their main function being to hear cases involving African law.[21] As the *tenente-geral* seldom had reliable troops at his disposal or bodies of slaves owned by the government, he was dependent on the *prazo*-holders to provide labour for all state purposes — boatmen, carriers, labourers to cut timber or repair public buildings — but principally he relied on them to provide soldiers for any planned military operation.

So dependent did the government become that it had to turn a blind eye to the misconduct and deliberate flouting of the law as long as the *senhores* of the *prazos* would do its work for it.[22] The knowledge that there was little that could be done to bring them to justice allowed the *muzungo* families to pursue personal vendettas with scandalous openness, so that the Zambesi towns often became lawless and violent places torn by the rival armed bands of feuding retainers.

If there was little the Crown could do directly to control the *muzungo* families, there were more devious ways of keeping them loyal. The *prazo*-holding families needed the co-operation of the authorities to secure legitimate titles to their *prazos*, and they were anxious for official recognition which would class them among the Portuguese gentry. The women adopted the title of *dona* and the men sought to obtain commissions in the armed forces or even membership of one of the Portuguese military orders of chivalry. At a more humble level they wanted municipal office or government appointments. Contemporary accounts of the Rivers settlements show them to have been as full of 'colonels' as Cheltenham or Kentucky. It was this desire for status within the Portuguese world which caused them to uphold traditional Catholicism and observe the religious offices of the church. The *tenente-geral*, if he played his cards astutely, was in a position to make the attainment of these social ambitions dependent on loyalty and good behaviour.

The Zambesi donas

Perhaps the most remarkable aspect of the history of the Afro-Portuguese families was the extraordinarily prominent and powerful position of the women who held the titles to the *prazos* and were often the effective heads of the *muzungo* families. This example of matriarchal power can be seen from a European or an African perspective. As already described, ever since the sixteenth century the Portuguese Crown had sought to make provision for orphan girls and for the widows and daughters of those who died in its service by endowing them with official appointments — on condition that they married someone of the Crown's choosing. In this way captaincies of ships and fortresses and ownership of land might be granted to women, although they were not expected to perform the functions of the office themselves. The *prazos* were awarded on the same basis. A man would petition for the grant of one for his daughter citing his own services to the Crown in support, or, if his wife had died, he might petition for his daughter to inherit. Thus, in a surprising number of cases, the legal titles were granted to women, although many men also acquired them in their own names. As it was always difficult to persuade Portuguese women to travel to eastern Africa and few of those who did survived for long, a bizarre plan was concocted in the mid-eighteenth century to send Chinese women from Macao to the Rivers to provide wives for Indians and Portuguese.[23] However, it was not the original grants of *prazos* that gave women their prominent position but the regulations whereby the *prazos* should pass to the eldest daughter on the death of the original grantee.

The Afro-Portuguese families were able to exploit this law to their own benefit. A marriagable girl succeeding to a *prazo* was a valuable asset and could be used to attract a husband of wealth and position or one who would bring with him control over other *prazos* and slaves. As in most parts of the Iberian world, young women were closely supervised by their menfolk, and in practice the affairs of the *prazos* were often controlled by the husbands and fathers of the *donas*. However, the fact that it was the women who held the legal title to the land gave them an opportunity for independence which the more resolute among them were able to seize and exploit. Moreover, because of their tendency to live longer on average than men, women were often left widows many times over and accumulated *prazos* and slaves by a succession of judicious marriages.

There were some notable examples of this. Ursula Ferreira married three times uniting the large and wealthy *prazos* of Gorongosa and Luabo. Her last husband outlived her and married the notorious *Dona* Ines Gracias Cardoso who subsequently married twice more, accumulating by her death altogether four major *prazos*. Even more striking were the cases of *Dona* Ines de Almeida Castellobranco, who made four marriages and eventually combined control of Gorongosa and Cheringoma, and *Dona* Caterina Faria Leitão who married for the fourth time at the age of eighty and held extensive lands in Bororo for which she never obtained legal title.[24] *Dona* Francisca de Moura e Meneses organised her slaves to exploit the gold diggings of Michonga north of the river from where she became one of the pioneers of trading expeditions to Kazembe. In 1798 she was the main provider of carriers for the expedition of Francisco de Lacerda.[25] A final example might be *Dona* Luiza Michaela da Cruz, sister of the notorious Bonga. She rented the *prazo* of Guengue 'where she disposed of a large number of armed slaves and, endowed with a manly spirit, resolute and energetic, she succeeded in capturing the good graces of the government by the antipathy which she said she professed for her brother Bonga'. However, it was not only the good graces of the government that she won. She married three Portuguese soldiers in succession, the second of whom she was accused of poisoning. In 1874

the government tried to take action against her and drew up an indict-
ment listing no less than eighty murders for which she was held
responsible. According to Augusto de Castilho, she used to have her
victims bound and thrown to the crocodiles which infested a lake near
her *aringa*, her chief executioner being 'a corpulent and cruel negro
called Rapozo'.[26]

Clearly, women frequently exercised their own choice in obtaining
a husband, and it is well documented that many acted also as their
own heads of households and controlled their own slave armies. Once
married, they could enjoy a considerable independence. António
Pinto de Miranda gives a colourful if disdainful, picture of the *donas*
in the 1760s. All of them, he says, 'whether Europeans, mulattas or
having their origin in Goa are usually haughty and of a proud disposition'. They have forty or fifty household slaves who amuse them with
'frivolous and indecorous dances'. Morning and evening they send
their female slaves round to neighbouring houses to greet their friends
and to 'inquire what is going on in the neighbouring households'.
Their Christianity, he says, is little different from that of their slaves
and they turn up in church with 'fifty or more female slaves, most of
them heathen':

> Some mistresses inquire about the supposed husbands of their
> slaves and if they satisfy them . . . and the major part of these
> impure conversations take place in the most sacred place and at
> times during the celebration of Mass.[27]

The Zambesi *donas* have their counterparts in the Afro-Portuguese
nharas of Guine and the powerful women landowners of São Tomé and
Príncipe. Their peculiar position, with defined roles in a patriarchal
Iberian tradition as well as a matrilineal African society, enabled them
to bridge one of the divides of incomprehension that have marked
Europe's relations with Africa.[28]

The power of the Zambesi *donas* must, therefore, also seen from its
African angle. Although on the Portuguese side they belonged to a
patriarchal culture that practised patrilineal succession, the Portuguese of the Zambesi were living among, and ruling over, matrilineal
peoples. True, the Karanga were also patrilineal but the Tonga, the
Makua and the various ethnic groupings that made up the Maravi
empire were all matrilineal. It is widely recognised that in matrilineal
societies it is frequently difficult for male-dominated lineages to establish patriarchal regimes. Indeed the power of the mother's lineage is
often translated into power for the female members of that lineage.
Among the Makua, women established close control over land and
crops; in the Maravi states and among the Tonga of the south bank

of the Zambesi, women played crucial political roles, often being installed as chiefs over segments of the population.

The influential position of the Zambesi *donas* and the descent line from mother to daughter has to be seen in the context of the matrilineal societies over which they ruled. It is clear that among the Afro-Portuguese a dual system of inheritance had emerged in which traditional Portuguese patrilineal succession was grafted on to local notions of the primacy of the mother's clan. The result was a curious hybrid system of social and property relations which placed women in positions of great wealth and influence as inheritors of land and slaves and forced men to seek advancement and social status by holding office in the Portuguese establishment or by the practice of taking 'secondary' or 'slave' wives whose offspring would belong to the father's family. Close parallels to this system of gender relations can be found among matrilineal peoples like the Makua or the Yao where husbands, excluded from the ownership or control of the means of production, established their own male-dominated hierarchies through hunting, trade and the purchase of female slaves.[29]

The male heads of the *muzungo* families were frequently polygynous but there appears always to have been a distinction between the official 'Portuguese' wife and the other wives. José Anselmo de Santanna apparently had two official wives at the time when he settled in the Luangwa valley in the middle of the nineteenth century. The relations of his wives formed a separate group within the *chicunda* community and were known as *kamfumu*. Most of them used Portuguese names and considered themselves *muzungos*. The other wives lacked this status, while among the ordinary *chicunda* elements of matrilineal and patrilineal descent seem to have been mixed, with both sides claiming inheritance rights.[30]

Many aspects of Afro-Portuguese culture were to extend along the trade routes far into the interior, but it is nevertheless remarkable to find what is recognisably a 'Zambesi' *dona* at the court of Msiri in Garanganze in 1884. Maria Lino da Fonseca was of mixed race and had apparently been sold to Msiri when aged twelve. Whether she had really been a slave or whether she was the involuntary victim of a marriage of convenience is impossible to say. She had then acquired considerable wealth and influence within the state and, according to Capello and Ivens, behaved very much as she liked, imposing 'by her demeanour and proud behaviour a feeling of admiration in one meeting her for the first time'. On her visit to the explorers' camp she arrived strikingly dressed

> . . . .in an ample coloured cloth from Mozambique, her wrists and toes ornamented with ringlets of ivory and gold, her head

covered with a long, well-woven blue tissue, from the sides of which
hung two embroidered ribbons that were joined below the jaw by
large button of wrought gold, a chain of the same metal around her
throat.[31]

Social relations on the prazos

Most of the *prazo senhores* and *donas* maintained town houses in one of
the Rivers settlements or in Mozambique Island. Some of them even
owned houses in Goa and were absentees. However, the majority also
had country houses on their *prazos* known as *luanes*, large houses surrounded by walled *quintas* and by the villages of their retainers. The
realities of life in Zambesia made it unlikely that they would be able
to control their *prazos* unless they were present in person for much of
the time, for these were not abstract creations of Portuguese law but
institutions fulfilling a vital function in the lives of the African peasantry and in the ordering of the commercial, industrial and agricultural
life of the lower Zambesi region. In short, the most successful of the
prazo-holders also filled the role of chief for the inhabitants of the *prazo*.

The structure of society on the larger *prazos* had all the intricacy of
the hierarchies of feudal and manorial relations in medieval Europe.
There were three overlapping systems of authority which interacted
with each other with a bewildering complexity. Any description will
tend to give the impression that relations were formalised and stable
over a long period whereas in fact they were continually adapting to
the changing political, economic and social conditions in the Rivers.
At the head of the *prazo* was the *dona* and her husband and family.
There might be a number of other Portuguese or Afro-Portuguese
associates, particularly on the larger *prazos*, where agents, called *pro-
curadores*, were frequently employed as business managers. On the
prazos belonging to the religious orders, the role of *senhor* was performed by a Dominican or Jesuit priest, sometimes with spectacular
success. In the eyes of Portuguese law the holders of the *prazos* owed
the state the duty of providing, carriers and boatmen, arming their
followers for the defence of the colony, paying an annual quit-rent and
developing the resources of their lands. They, in their turn, exacted
tribute and labour services from their peasants and performed various
ritual chiefly functions.

The free populations of the *prazos* were known as *colonos*, and they
continued to live in traditional village communities under headmen,
whom the Portuguese called *fumos*. They were expected to pay an
annual tribute in kind, called *maprere* or *missonco* (or *mussocco*), and
payable in grain, *machiras*, ivory or gold dust. In addition the *fumos*
had to make some customary payments in respect of game hunted and

consumed on the *prazos* and as fines for certain untoward events like an occurrence of leprosy or the birth of deformed children. The agents of the *prazo*-holders thus collected large quantities of produce which represented the basic income of the *prazo* and is reminiscent of the tribute lists of the Spanish *encomenderos* in the early days of the conquest in America.

The *prazo*-holders had jurisdiction in cases involving *colonos*. Although routine matters were dealt with by the headmen, the *senhor* would appoint an African official, called a *mocazambo*, to hear more difficult cases in his name. The outcome of these was frequently a fine — for example, one would be levied when it was discovered that the *muavi* poison ordeal had been practised — and such fines were a major source of income for the *senhor* as they were for neighbouring independent chiefs. Against the justice of the *prazo*-holder, the *colono* could appeal to the *Capitão-mor das terras da coroa* who was supposed to review cases, with experts in African law to advise. However, because he was almost invariably one of the leading members of the Afro-Portuguese community himself, this restraint on arbitrary power cannot have been very effective.

As well as receiving tribute and administrating justice, the *senhores* intervened in the appointment of headmen and sometimes appear to have performed certain ritual functions connected with sowing and harvest. The extent to which a *senhor* assumed the role of chief varied from person to person. Some were content to be absentees drawing an income from their *prazo*, but others took their role seriously. There are a number of cases of *prazo senhores* taking wives from African chiefly lineages and at least one clear case of an Afro-Portuguese family successfully usurping an African chiefly dynastic title — that of Chicucuru assumed by the Caetano Pereiras. There are also cases of *prazo senhores* who after their deaths had their own spirit mediums. However, the chiefly role of the *prazo*-holders is more explicit when their relationship with the other element in the population of the *prazos*, the 'slaves', is considered.[32]

The chicunda

As well as the free *colonos* who were their subjects on the *prazos*, the Afro-Portuguese *senhores* had large numbers of clients and retainers directly dependent on them.[33] These dependents were often generally referred to as the 'slaves' of the *prazo*-holders but people who knew the realities of the Zambesi world distinguished between different categories of dependant. Slaves, in the sense of unfree chattels, had been acquired by the Portuguese to serve in the fortresses and fleets almost as soon as they had arrived in the East. They are recorded in the account books of the Sofala factory, and black slaves were taken from Mozambique to other parts of the East where they served the Portuguese in various capacities. However, the institution of 'slavery' that grew up in the Afro-Portuguese community of Zambesia was of a quite different character.

In Africa it was common for lineages to add to their productive and reproductive power by acquiring 'slaves'. Women might be acquired by capture or purchase and males could also be acquired through various clientship arrangements which might involve the exchange of labour service for the eventual acquisition of cattle or wives. It is, therefore, not surprising to find that the Afro-Portuguese families acquired large followings of 'slaves' of both sexes, linked to the *senhor*'s family by a system of reciprocal obligation. These clients performed a wide variety of functions, providing the *prazo*-holders with craftsmen, boatmen, *machilla*-bearers, field-hands and concubines, but more importantly providing professional traders, soldiers and the effective administrators of the *prazos*.

The last three categories had a rather separate status and should probably be distinguished from the slaves whose jobs were frankly more menial or more personal and who were described by a different name. The personal slaves of the Zambesi *donas* were called collectively the *butaca*, while male household slaves were *bandazios* and *bichos*. These were attached to the person of the Afro-Portuguese *senhores* and *senhoras* and not to the *prazo* itself. If their masters or mistresses married or moved residence, their personal slaves would expect to accompany them.[34]

Slaves could be obtained as booty in war or by direct purchase but by the eighteenth century the great *prazo senhores* acquired their households of retainers and clients in a way that involved reciprocal contracts of service and protection formalised by well-established rituals. Many observers, not least among them Livingstone in the mid-nineteenth century, were perplexed at the sight of Africans voluntarily selling themselves into slavery, but by then this had become a common practice in Zambesia.[35] Becoming attached to one of the great Afro-Portuguese households might be a survival strategy in times of famine or war, but it might also be a way of seeking prosperity and advancement as the Zambesi *senhores* employed 'slaves' to run their households, collect tribute from the *colonos*, go on diplomatic missions, command armed forces, and undertake trading expeditions. Part of the expectation of becoming a 'slave' of a *muzungo senhor* was that sooner or later one would be provided with a wife and be able to establish one's own village and acquire slaves. There is an inescapable irony in the fact that it was not uncommon for the 'slave' of a Portuguese to have his own slaves and even be richer than his master.

Moreover someone who became the 'slave' of a Portuguese *senhor* was protected, in theory at least, from being sold abroad as a slave.

By the eighteenth century the clients of the Portuguese *senhores* were usually called *chicunda*. The *chicunda* were organised in small companies under an official called a *sachicunda*. The *chicunda* of a *prazo* came under the overall control of the *mocazambo* who might command them on a military expedition or be placed in charge of a fortified village in some remote part of the *prazo*. In the nineteenth century this term tended to be replaced by the Portuguese term *capitão*. The *prazo senhores* also appointed senior figures called *mwanamambos* to deputise for them on the *prazo* when they were absent. This elaborate hierarchy of slaves and officials bears witness to the strong identity that the *chicunda* came to acquire. They came to think of themselves as attached to a particular *prazo* rather than a particular *senhor*, and as a result it was crucial that whoever was granted a *prazo* should be able to establish control over the *chicunda*. This obedience might well be withheld if the *mocazambos* had reason to distrust or despise the *prazo senhor*. Frequently the *chicunda* would revolt or run the *prazo* in their own interest, taking tribute from the *colonos* and establishing a sort of independent republic.[36] When a *prazo senhor* died, the occasion was taken for widespread plunder and loot to make the population 'weep' for the dead *senhor* — a practice also observed in neighbouring chieftaincies. As sons succeeded fathers and grandfathers in the *chicunda* community they acquired a distinct ethnic identity with their own villages and their own social and political organisation — a separate caste, as it were, among the lower Zambesi population. In the twentieth century colonial administrators recognised the Achikunda as a distinct ethnic group in the valley population, while often remaining ignorant of the origin of this name.

Accurate estimates of slave numbers are difficult to obtain. António Pinto de Miranda gave details of the slave establishments of all the major *prazo senhores* in 1766, but his round numbers are suspiciously high. The detailed inventories of the Jesuit *prazos* in 1759 indicate quite small numbers of slaves attached to the Jesuit establishments. The residence of Tete had 314 slaves in total, of whom eighty-eight were described as *escravos do bar* and were employed in gold mining, seventy-five were employed in field work and forty-eight were domestic slaves while thirty were recorded as 'fugitive'[37]. Marangue had 396 slaves, 185 of them employed in mining operations. A large majority of the slaves employed in mining and field work were women and when these were auctioned on the dissolution of the Jesuit *prazos*, the lot was interestingly referred to as 'a hundred and twenty black women miners . . . with the male kaffirs associated with them'.[38] The Jesuit *prazos* of Tete and Marangue had fifty-two armed slaves

Table 10.1. SLAVE ESTABLISHMENTS OF
CHERINGOMA AND GORONGOSA

Slaves	Cheringoma		Gorongosa	
	Number	Value*	Number	Value*
Male	*761*	*2,266*	*605*	*1,810*
Mocazambos	28	280	28	140
Bazos	3	15	5	25
Goldsmiths	4	80	16	320
Saramálas	6	105	7	105
Barbers	1	20	1	10
Fishermen	6	30	31	155
Washermen (*mainatos*)	1	5		
Cooks	5	125		
Musicians	4	200		
Chicundas	703	1,406	510	1,020
Blacksmiths			5	25
Traders (*tendeiros*)			2	10
Female	*185*	*537*	*290*	*1,097*
Blackwomen	176	407	226	452
Bakers	4	60	9	135
Cooks	4	60	10	150
Washerwomen (*mainatas*)	1	10	1	5
Sweet-makers (*doceiras*)			7	140
Pot-makers			1	5
Concubines (*nunas*)			6	60
Bandazias			30	150
Total	*946*	*2,803*	*895*	*2,907*

*Values in *maticais*.
Source: Luiz Fernando de Carvalho Dias, *Fontes para a História, Geografia e Comércio de Moçambique*, pp. 345–57.

who constituted the police force of the *prazos*. The actual total of slaves attached to the Jesuit residences was 710 although Miranda would boldly declare that the Jesuits in Tete had 2,500 slaves. Inventories of Gorongosa and Cheringoma, which were not owned by the Jesuits but were two of the largest *prazos*, show that they had 895 and 946 slaves respectively.[39]

Whether the *chicunda* acted as a police force collecting tribute and maintaining order, or whether they became anarchic groups of bandits preying on the *colono* villagers and river settlements, depended partly, as has been suggested, on the personality of the *senhores* and *donas*, but it was also a function of the general prosperity of the Rivers.

When the rains came and crops were plentiful, the valley became relatively peaceful, trade caravans could proceed in safety to and from the fairs, and river traffic could move unmolested. But if there were famine, flood or epidemic, a chain reaction began. The *chicunda* began to act as bandits attacking and robbing the *colonos* and each other, the trade routes were closed, agriculture was disrupted, and social and economic disaster could quickly engulf the Rivers settlements.

The *prazo* system in the eighteenth century, therefore, though often with the appearance of having created a prosperous world of great households and benevolent feudal paternalism (or maternalism), was in reality little more than institutionalised banditry. Although the *prazos* provided the sort of overlordship that the Tonga and Makua populations had not previously known, they did not achieve the necessary social and political integration for a stable state system to emerge.

There was another class of 'slave' on the *prazo* — the *mussambazes*. These have already been described in connection with the fairs, but it should be pointed out that as a class of professional traders these 'slaves' were entrusted by their masters with the conduct of trading caravans which might be absent in the interior for years on end. African traders were likewise employed by the Portuguese based at Inhambane and Mozambique Island.

Neither *chicunda* nor *mussambazes* ever detached themselves completely from their nominal masters. It seems that they needed the identity and ultimately the support which a *senhor* guaranteed them. In the world of eighteenth-century Africa it was impossible to be a kinless or lordless person, and in the nineteenth century it was highly dangerous, since slavehunters seldom hesitated to ship such individuals abroad. When African traders acknowledged a master, they were no longer stateless men. Their caravans could not be molested, with impunity; their credit had more solid backing; they could not themselves be enslaved by anyone else — in short they had diplomatic status. In this respect their Afro-Portuguese masters acted as the Sultan of Zanzibar did for Muslim traders in the east African interior in the nineteenth century.

Economic activity of the prazos

In the seventeenth and eighteenth centuries it was ivory and gold that constituted the wealth of central Africa in the eyes of Portuguese and Indian traders. However, during this time the existence of the Afro-Portuguese society of the Rivers was underpinned by the agricultural production of the peasant population which provided the taxable surpluses to support the *prazo* establishments. The importance of peasant agriculture needs to be stressed because whenever there was

Table 10.2. TRIBUTE PAID BY COLONOS
ON JESUIT PRAZOS, 1759

	Tax-paying colonos	Tribute paid Panjas of Maize	Machiras	Amount per colono
Tete prazos				
Marabue	90	1,620		18
Nharupanda	58	508		8.8
Ponde	51	630		12.4
Nhancenge	28	504		18
Micombe	19	304		16
Chunga	7	112		16
Nhatanda	6	96		16
Sub-total	*259*	*3,774*		*14.6*
Panzo	47		47	1
Marangue prazos				
Camacoppe	141	1,861.2		13.2
Nhampende	50	660		13.2
Nhamedima	40	528		13.2
Mattanbahama	34	448.8		13.2
Macheso	18	237.6		13.2
Marangue	16	124		7.75
Nhacome	8	103.6		12.95
Domoe	4	39.6		9.9
Sub-total	*311*	*4,002.8*		*12.9*
Domoe	4		1	.25
Nhampende	50		60 *pastas* of tobacco	1.2
Total	617	7,776.8	48 60 *pastas* of tobacco	

Source: W.F. Rea, *The Economics of the Zambezi Missions, 1580–1759*, pp. 93–5.

drought and famine, the whole social and economic structure of the society would rapidly disintegrate.

Most production took place within the traditional organisation of the village, and the *prazo senhores* simply levied a tax in kind. The figures in Tables 10.2 and 10.3 give some indication of the amounts actually collected. The taxable unit was the household and the figures that have survived, for example for the Jesuit *prazos*, suggest very small populations of *colonos* on many of the *prazos*. On the eight *prazos*

Table 10.3. TRIBUTE FROM THE PRAZOS OF
GORONGOSA AND CHERINGOMA

Commodity	Gorongosa		Cheringoma	
	Quantity	*Value*	*Quantity*	*Value*
Maticais of gold	155.5	1,555 *cruz.*		
Machiras	1,235.5	617 *mat.*	1,257	623 *mat.*
Bares of ivory	4	320	10	800
Pots of honey	56	54	48	48
Faraçolas of wax	4	48	15	180
Pots of oil	20	14	21	15
Chickens	1105	15	560	9
Quissapos of salt	80	13		
Canas of *machiras*	18	18		
Wooden mortars	100	3.5		
Loads of wood	80	3.5		
Panjas of maize	430	36	5,000	416
Faraçolas of sugar	36	108		
Pots of meat			28	28
Dried Fish			6,000	10
Fumbas			100	3
Total		1,250 *mat.*		2,132 *mat.*
		1,555 *cruz.*		

Source: Luiz Fernando de Carvalho Dias, *Fontes para a História, Geografia e Comércio de Moçambique*, pp. 345–57.

attached to the Tete house there were altogether 306 taxed households
(259 paying their taxes in maize) and on eight attached to the church
of Marangue there were 311. The taxes paid by these free tenants may
give some idea of the general level of production of peasant agriculture. The Tete *prazos* officially produced 3,774 *panjas* of maize which
is approximately 113,220 litres or 437 litres per household, while
the Marangue *prazos* paid 4,004 *panjas* or 120,120 litres or 386 litres
per household. There is no way of telling whether this amounted
to more or less than the ecclesiastical tithe, but that it may have
amounted to a tenth of annual production seems a reasonable estimate
(Table 10.2)[40] In addition to grain, the *colonos* had to pay in other
goods according to the nature of the local economy. The Tete *prazos*
thus were charged 47 *machiras* a year while the Marangue *prazos* paid
a single *machira* but 60 *pastas* of tobacco.[41]

Two factors made the populations of the *prazos*, and hence their tax-
yield, irregular. The climate of the Zambesi valley is harsh and
unreliable. Some areas, like those round Tete, are suffocatingly hot,
dry and infertile, but others like the delta and the lower Zambesi

islands are well watered and productive. Harsh climatic conditions forced the peasant population to move often, a tendency increased by the erratic rule of the *senhores*. The peasantry would frequently desert the *prazos* when the violent exactions of the *chicunda* and their masters or mistresses became intolerable. However, the free peasants of the *prazos* were not the only peasant producers. On many *prazos* there were also numbers of *chicunda* villages, which produced crops for their own consumption and paid a percentage for the maintenance of the *prazo* establishment.

Some agricultural production took place by direct labour which might be called plantation production, and it seems that in the eighteenth century there may have been significant growth of this sector of the economy. When the Portuguese first arrived on the coast they depended for the support of their garrisons and towns on being able to buy food from the African or Islamic-African communities. Madagascar and the Comoro Islands were an important source of food and some was even imported from India. The authorities in Mozambique were anxious to develop local sources of supply and to establish proper government granaries. Early in the eighteenth century they tried to secure a regular food supply for Mozambique Island from the delta *prazos* but ran up against resistance from the *prazo* interests. In the eighteenth century there were many paper schemes to promote agriculture in the Rivers, and in 1759 an official called *tanador-mor* was appointed to promote agricultural production.[42]

The success of these policies was patchy. There were experiments with sugar production, and some sugar mills were built in the delta and round Quelimane. There was also some direct food production on the Jesuit *prazos* which produced both rice and wheat. One hears of palm groves near the coast and orchards of fruit trees, while most of the *prazos* maintained smallscale production in the immediate vicinity of their *luanes*.[43] However, further development of commercial agriculture was probably prevented by problems over labour. The unsettled conditions of the Rivers made it difficult to maintain any slave labour force against its will. It was so easy for slaves to abscond either to other *prazos* or to the nearby territory of independent chiefs that largescale slave-run plantations were impossible. Even so, the Jesuit *prazos* had slaves — mostly women — specifically described as field-hands, the Tete *prazos* having seventy-three and the Marangue *prazos* seventy-five.[44]

With the growth of the slave trade towards the end of the eighteenth century, the situation appears to have changed. Large supplies of slaves began to reach the coast, and the risks that escaping slaves ran of being captured and sold abroad made it easier for *prazo*-holders to maintain a field labour force of slaves. Recurring drought in the inland regions also forced the valley population to migrate towards the coast and the delta. Moreover the purchases of provisions by the slave ships increased the market demand, so that in the early nineteenth century there was a considerable increase in the commercial produc- tion of food, particularly in the *prazos* near the coast and in the delta. The *tenente-geral*, Vilas Boas Truão, wrote in 1806 in his description of the economic state of Mozambique: 'The principal commerce of the inhabitants of Quelimane consists of agricultural products, and prin- cipally rice in which the lands of that District abound.' He went on to say that much more could be produced were it not for the lack of shipping.[45] That year over 14,000 *alqueires* (193,200 litres) of rice were exported and more than 6,000 *alqueires* (82,800 litres) of wheat, along with smaller quantities of maize, millet, various vegetables and groundnut oil.[46]

However, it is clear that the profits of agriculture or the tribute in agricultural products extorted from the peasantry would never have supported the Afro-Portuguese society of the Rivers. There were three other sectors of the economy on which the feudal ruling class depended — trade, mining and what one might describe as service industries. Trade and mining have already been described and were clearly important. The service sector was also not insignificant. The large *prazo* establishments, the river towns, the activities of the military and the coming and going of trade caravans and mining expeditions all generated a demand for the services of various skilled personnel. A list of the slaves with specialist skills employed on the *prazos* gives an idea of the variety of these occupations. The Jesuit *prazos* employed, cooks, bakers, barbers, tailors, washerwomen, masons, fishermen, seamstresses, carpenters, tilers, ironsmiths, boat- builders and gold miners as well as household and garden slaves (the slave establishments of Gorongosa and Cheringoma are listed in Table 10.1).[47] Two crafts were particularly characteristic of the lower Zambesi peoples — cloth-weaving and goldsmith work, both of which not only survived the flood of imports that came with overseas trade but continued to find a ready market in the region. The Zambesi boatmen were also a significant class, manning the canoes that plied the hundreds of miles of river, carrying passengers between the Rivers settlements and trade goods from the coast to the factories.

No existing figures give a truly accurate picture of the balance bet- ween these various sectors of the local economy. However, the income returns for some *prazos*, as well as the inventories of the Jesuit *prazos*, have survived and these indicate a spread of economic activity. Table 10.3 lists the tribute payable from two of the largest *prazos* which paid wax, honey, oil, ivory, gold dust, salt, fowls, meat, dried fish, sugar and substantial amounts of grain, as well as manufactured items such as *machiras*, wooden mortars and timber. Tribute on this scale was used partly to support the *prazo*-holder and his or her immediate household, and partly to distribute to various categories of client; it was also partly sold in support of the trading operations of the *prazo*.

The *prazos* had been created by warlords who in the seventeenth century had undertaken major expeditions of conquest. In the eighteenth century the Portuguese colonial state had benefited from the fact that the power of the Changamires on the southern plateau and the relative solidity of the Maravi chieftaincies to the north meant that the *prazo senhores* were peculiarly dependent on it to maintain their position. There was some success in distributing the *prazos* among a number of different holders and preventing the growth of monopolies of power. However, the system was inherently unstable and any disruption of the precarious local economy and any weakening of the central authority would open the way for the warlords once again to gain control of the valley. This is what was to happen in the nineteenth century.

11

TIME OF TROUBLES:
DROUGHT, THE SLAVE TRADE
AND THE NGUNI INVASIONS

Raiders from the sea

In 1800 three strange ships appeared off the island of Amisa at the extreme northern end of the Querimba archipelago. They were different from any boats previously seen on the coast, being 30-foot-long canoes, each made from a single massive tree, carrying a sail and strengthened for an ocean voyage by boards along the sides and a single outrigger. Each warboat carried twenty armed men, and from the first they struck terror into the inhabitants of the coast. The raiding fleets were assembled by the Betsimisaraka chiefs of north-east Madagascar whose main objective was to obtain slaves. In 1795 these 'long ships' raided the prosperous, well-populated and almost undefended Comoro Islands, returning every year for nearly a decade and plundering the towns, carrying off slaves and cattle, and driving the inhabitants into the mountains or forcing them to put up town walls and strange fortifications around the rims of the volcanoes. In 1800 they carried out their first attacks in eastern Africa and in the following years their ferocious raids struck the coast from Kilwa almost as far south as Mozambique Island, harrying the small island communities, dispersing their fishing populations and leading to the abandonment of the coastal regions and the lesser islands. In 1808 the raiding fleet amounted to 500 warboats carrying 8,000 armed raiders.

The fragmented Afro-Portuguese community assembled under the protection of the guns of the Ibo fort, and there the raiders received their first check in 1816. In 1817, however, a Portuguese ship was captured and plundered at sea, and the pirates returned again in 1820, but this was the last of the raids. Urged on by Britain which was thoroughly alarmed at the dominance of this sector of the Indian Ocean by pirates, the Merina of central Madagascar had invaded the northern coastal regions and put an end to the independence of the pirate chieftaincies.[1]

The twenty years in which northern Mozambique had been harried by sea-raiders is full of ironies for the historian. The coastal communities of Afro-Portuguese, Indians and Swahili, which had become used to living off the slave trade and believed themselves immune from the misery and war which generated the supplies of slaves in the interior, now themselves experienced the ferocity of slave raiding pirates. Their communties had been desolated, marginal economic activities like farming or coastal trade were all but wiped out. Thus the slavers themselves became the victims and the slave trade began devouring its own children. The veins of irony run deeper into the geological strata of Mozambique's history. The matrilineal societies of Mozambique had never been able to create the large political units which could assure stable conditions. Warlords and bandits had preyed on the Makua, Maravi and Tonga society. Now banditry and warlordism had taken to the sea, threatening the survival of the coastal culture and the very existence of the international commercial ties which had been the main integrating factor in Mozambican life. The sea-raiders were soon to be followed by the Nguni warbands invading from the south, raiders whose impact was to be far greater than that of the Betsimisaraka because of the permanent polities that they created.

However, the raids of Betsimisaraka and Nguni were not simply the intrusion of outside events; they were related to developments within Mozambique itself, for these were the years when the slave trade came to dominate the commercial life of the country and when a cycle of drought and famine first undermined and then threatened to destroy totally the old societies based on subsistence agriculture, gold digging and ivory trading. Thus the slave trade and the drought played in dreadful harmony with each other. The desolation of famine filled the baracoons with the starving and the destitute. Whole communities were ruined by the drought and its economic consequences. Agriculture and trade contracted, artisan communities were dispersed, and the only form of commercial life was slaving. The violence and destruction of slaving merely compounded the ecological disaster and prevented full recovery. The ability of communities to defend themselves collapsed and only the warlords and the militarised society of their followers were able to survive in a world of increasing violence and endemic banditry.

That these profound, almost revolutionary, changes took place at a time of unprecedented growth in European commercial and industrial capitalism adds one more strand to the complicated causation of events.

Rise of the slave trade

Before the middle of the eighteenth century there had been remarkable stability in the relationships of production and commerce throughout the whole central African region. Commercial activity followed a pattern so deeply worn that if a Swahili boat captain who had known the run between Kilwa and the southern gold ports in the fourteenth century had been able to return four centuries later, he could have resumed his commercial activities without any appreciable problem. However, by the middle of the eighteenth century the European Industrial Revolution was about to change the world economy more profoundly than any development since neolithic times.

The Industrial Revolution happened far from the Indian Ocean, and its impact was to be felt more as a series of shock waves than as the direct impact of an explosion. The most immediate effect, not directly related to the process of industrialisation itself, was a strongly rising demand for slaves. This was followed by a growing interest in African markets and raw materials, and finally by the arrival of surplus capital in search of investment opportunities in Africa. Long before this occurred, however, the old structures of African and Indian Ocean production and commerce, which had easily accomodated themselves to the lazy mercantilism of the Portuguese, had broken down and been replaced by a more direct exposure to the forces of European capitalist enterprise.

The rise in the demand for slaves was first noticeable about the mid-eighteenth century, and came from French sugar producers in the Indian Ocean islands. The French Compagnie des Indes began the settlement of Ile de France in 1721 and during the governorship of La Bourdonnais in 1734-49, its plantation economy and that of the neighbouring island, Ile de Bourbon, grew rapidly. At first the French imported slaves from Madagascar but they soon began to look for opportunities on the African mainland. French commercial agents explored various sources of supply in both the Omani and the Portuguese spheres of influence on the coast. Portuguese official policy was to prevent any Europeans apart from themselves from trading on the Mozambique coast and to prohibit foreign ships from even entering Portuguese ports except in cases of extreme emergency. However, the profits to be made from selling slaves to the French were such that soon a large-scale illicit trade was underway. When a governor of Mozambique was favourable to French traders, the commerce was conducted almost on an official basis, as happened during the governorships of Tolentino de Almeida (1737-40) and Pereira do Lago (1765-79). If the governors were unfriendly towards the French, then the trade tended to move to the northern port of Ibo where the Afro-Portuguese of the Querimba Islands were ready to trade with all comers.

Ibo was the capital of the district of Cabo Delgado, the almost forgotten Portuguese outpost far to the north of Mozambique Island. The Afro-Portuguese community of the islands had lived by

establishing intimate commercial relations with the Swahili population of the coast. They had traded foodstuffs, cowries and some ivory
south to Mozambique Island and they were the main point of contact
between the Portuguese in the south and the Omani-dominated
regions to the north. They were a listening post where the Portuguese
obtained intelligence of northern developments and they were an ideal
base of operations for those who wanted to avoid both the exactions
of the Omani authorities and the monopolistic tendencies of the
Portuguese colonial government. Cabo Delgado was a 'frontier' area
where government authority was weak and where peoples of varying
cultural and ethnic origins survived or prospered through developing
local institutions of mutual co-operation. It is therefore not surprising that this region was where French interlopers were able to
gain almost unrestricted access to the east African coast with the
ready co-operation of the Afro-Portuguese traders and Portuguese
officials.[2]

Trading in slaves with the French was, therefore, an illegal operation from the start. The governors either did not tax the trade at all
or diverted the license fees and capitation charges into the pockets of
themselves and their officials. However, trading with Ile de France
made good economic sense for Mozambique. In exchange for slaves
and cowrie shells from Querimba, which the French needed for their
commercial activities in India, Mozambique could import foodstuffs
and coin. Mozambique Island had always imported large quantities
of foodstuffs and the famine that followed the smallpox epidemic of
1744 provided the French with an opportunity to establish a foothold
in this market. Trade with the French, therefore, brought an important diversification to the trade of Mozambique and made a multilateral settlement of payments possible. The inflow of silver enabled
the Portuguese to settle their accounts with suppliers of Indian cloth
and loosened somewhat the grip which the Banian merchants had
acquired over the region's economy by advancing goods on credit.[3]

Before the 1760s the slave trade out of Mozambique Island appears
never to have risen much above 1,000 a year, but in 1769 the commercial monopoly of the Compagnie des Indes was ended and the 1770s
saw a considerable expansion. Governor Pereira do Lago, reconciled
to the prospect that he would receive no further appointment from the
Crown, embarked on a systematic process of self-enrichment. He
issued trading licenses and charged capitation fees on the slaves
exported, received sweeteners and charged the French rent on property they used on the island. All this he pocketed, reserving for the
Crown only a paltry capitation tax of 2 *patacas* on each slave. A similar
arrangement enabled the French to trade at Ibo. A large payment was
made to the governor of the district who then passed a percentage on

to local traders who supplied the slaves. In the 1770s the French were exporting about 1,500 slaves a year from Ibo and Mozambique.[4]

Aware that attempting to prevent French ships trading would be fruitless, the Portuguese tried to preserve something of the mercantilist structure of their empire by encouraging the export of slaves in Portuguese owned ships. This apparently had some success since slaves exported in Portuguese vessels regularly made up between a third and half of the total for the rest of the century. In 1785 the Portuguese at last made the French slave trade legal provided that it was carried on at Mozambique and not at Ibo or any other port.[5] A customs house and fort were indeed constructed at Ibo to put an end to the heady days of contraband.

During the period 1784–94 French slavers from the Caribbean injected fresh demand into the market. Numbers exported and prices both rose dramatically. Average prices for a slave rose from 120 *cruzados* in the 1770s to between 200 and 240 *cruzados* in the 1780s and over 400 *cruzados* by 1790. During this same period prices for Mozambique ivory also rose sharply and there is little doubt that the end of the eighteenth century saw the international commerce of Mozambique more diversified and more prosperous than at any time since the arrival of the Portuguese in the early sixteenth century.

Not much can be said about the source of the slaves sold to the French or how they were obtained. They were obtained from all areas of the coast, and at mid-century about half came from Sofala, Inhambane and Zambesia. However, northern Mozambique seems to have been the biggest area of supply. The treaty made by the French with Kilwa in 1776 and the vigorous trade at Mongallo (between Kilwa and Cabo Delgado) in the 1780s all point to a concentration of effort on the region round the present-day border between Mozambique and Tanzania.

The trade in slaves developed quite separately from the ivory trade. The days are long gone when the ivory and slave trades were thought of as necessarily being connected. In Mozambique the reverse was true. Ivory was brought primarily by the Yao who obtained their supplies from the Maravi, Lunda and Bisa peoples in the interior. Slaves were apparently obtained nearer to the coast and were generated among the Makua who were the main suppliers. Indeed, far from there being a causal connection between the expansion of ivory and slave trading, it seems that the rise of slaving interfered with the ivory trade. In the 1780s ivory caravans were frequently impeded by the wars among the Makua, and it is not difficult to see these wars as having arisen as a result of the demand for slaves.

The rise of the Mozambique slave trade led to another innovation. Until the arrival of the French, the Portuguese had refrained from trading in firearms. The French, however, made the sale of muskets and ammunition a major item of their commerce, and the effect of the Portuguese embargo on this form of commerce was greatly weakened. As in West Africa, the import of firearms was to change the political relationships between various groups — power came to rest increasingly with those who obtained guns through trade rather than those who controlled the resources of the land.

The growth of the slave trade was interrupted by the Napoleonic wars. British and French warships competed for dominance in the Indian Ocean, and the ports of Mozambique were closed to French commerce. French corsairs retaliated by attacking shipping in the Mozambique Channel and raiding the Portuguese settlement at Lourenço Marques. Exports of slaves from Mozambique to the French islands continued only precariously, and after the final severing of diplomatic ties between France and Portugal in 1808, illegally and only from clandestine ports along the coast. When James Prior visited Mozambique in the *Nisus* in 1812, he commented that although Britain had gained the ascendancy in the naval struggle, and its occupation of Ile de France and Ile de Bourbon in 1810 had considerably reduced the slave trade, French dealers were still frequenting Mozambique where they were 'in high favour at present, owing to speculations in slaves, a trade which still flourishes in these islands, notwithstanding all our vigilance'.[6] The slave trade, briefly legalised and open, had once again become a contraband commercial activity — trade in 'black ivory' being the archetypal black economy.

Nevertheless, if the French connection declined in importance, the two decades 1790–1810, during which occurred the first of the disastrous droughts and famines, saw the trade in slaves continue to grow in volume and importance. In the early nineteenth century the West African slave trade was increasingly disrupted. Britain abandoned the trade altogether in 1807 and most of the French- and Dutch-owned outlets were closed down as a result of the war. Would-be buyers turned to the neutral Portuguese, and the trade from São Tomé and Angola grew rapidly. Portuguese slaving interests working out of Brazil had already appeared on the Mozambique coast in the 1790s, and other New World dealers began to look to Mozambique which, despite the French trade, was a region relatively untouched by slaving.[7] The trade continued to grow when the Napoleonic wars ended. British harassment of the West African trade led eventually to the signing of agreements with Portugal in 1815 and 1817 that limited the slave trade to ports south of the Equator. The effect of these treaties was to bestow a sort of international legality on the Mozambique trade which was now proving an increasingly attractive option for buyers from Cuba and the United States as well as Brazil.

The weak and outdated structures of Portuguese mercantilism which had continued, more or less, to channel the central African ivory trade through Portuguese hands were quite unable to contain the great expansion of the slave trade that now took place. Before 1800 all Mozambique's overseas trade, imports as well as exports, had been taken to Mozambique Island to register cargoes and pay customs dues. Non-Portuguese could trade only with licenses. Moreover tariffs were notoriously high (trade with the Rivers, for example, carrying a 40 per cent duty) and shipping regulations were restrictive — ivory exported from the Rivers having to be shipped to Mozambique in the official ivory trading vessel.[8] These closed, mercantilist policies discouraged all but the wealthy operators who could afford to trade with relatively narrow profit margins, and were clearly designed to maximise profits for the controllers of the trade by means of restricting competition.

The development of the slave trade made such antique regulations unworkable. The best source of slaves was rapidly becoming the Zambesi, with Quelimane the port of departure. Slavers arriving from Cuba, the United States or Brazil wanted to load where the slaves were most plentiful and where they could obtain food supplies. They resented the necessity of beating up the Mozambique Channel in order to conform to outdated Portuguese commercial regulations. Strong voices were raised in Portugal for a revision of the restrictive procedures and in 1811 a royal decree permitted Brazilian vessels to trade directly with the minor ports of the coast. In 1812 Quelimane was made a separate captaincy with its own customs house. Further measures lowered the tariffs, the effect of which was to subject the economic life of the coast to the direct effect of market demand. The slave trade from Mozambique as a whole, and from Quelimane in particular, grew spectacularly (Fig. 11.1).

The arrival of appreciable numbers of slave ships had implications for the area's economy. The slave ships made large purchases of food, each one taking on some 5 *panjas* of meal for the sustenance of each slave. The settlers at Quelimane might have to supply a dozen such slavers while at the same time meeting the food requirements of the slaves in the barracoons waiting for the ship's arrival. Local producers were the first to benefit, the *prazos* round Quelimane experiencing a considerable boom in their food production and general economic activity. However, the free trade regulations soon brought competitors to the scene. Small boats owned by the Muslim coastal traders based as far away as Zanzibar and Madagascar began to visit the Portuguese ports with cargoes of foodstuffs, undercutting the local producers and trading directly with the slave ships.[9]

To try to counter this competition demands were made by the

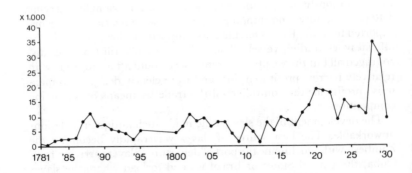

Fig. 11.1. SLAVE EXPORTS FROM MOZAMBIQUE, 1781–1830

Source: E.A. Alpers, *Ivory and Salves in East Central Africa*: G.L. Liesegang, 'A First Look at Import and Export Trade'.

Afro-Portuguese of Quelimane for the reintroduction of controls. These demands were complicated by political developments in Portugal itself. The revolution of 1821 had introduced an era of doctrinaire economic liberalism, but by 1826 the Miguelist conservatives had regained the initiative and were calling for a return of general economic controls. In 1826 the regulations were amended so as to require the shipping visiting the coast once again to call at Mozambique to register cargoes and pay customs dues. The independent captaincy of Quelimane was discontinued and the old structure of a single subordinate Rivers captaincy was resurrected. The immediate impact of this was to persuade slave traders and boat owners with cargoes of foodstuffs to avoid Portuguese ports and meet their clients at one of the small Islamic trading towns which had continued to exist outside direct Portuguese control since the sixteenth century.[10]

This shift of the slave trade from ports flying the Portuguese flag to the less known coastal harbours not under direct Portuguese control was speeded up by the actions of the British government, which persuaded first Brazil and then Portugal to sign treaties outlawing the slave trade. By the terms of the treaty with Brazil no more slaves would be imported after 1830. The immediate response of traders was to step up purchases in the years immediately before this treaty would become effective and slave exports from Mozambique rose dramatically to 30,000 in the two years preceding 1830. Thereafter a further impetus was given to the clandestine trade as slavers continued to buy slaves for illegal sale in Brazil. The compliant sheikhs of the Mozambique coast were only too happy to be the local agents of the trade, and by the 1830s towns like Angoche had begun to experience unaccustomed importance and prosperity.

The rise of the slave trade, and the ill-managed economic experiments that accompanied it, had served to alienate the commercial community and its far-reaching network of contacts from the Portuguese administration. This divergence of interest became more pronounced than at any time since the end of the Captain's monopoly in the seventeenth century, and in the political climate of the early nineteenth century it took the form of political dissidence and the beginnings of a separatist movement. During the 1820s successive Portuguese regimes had sent shiploads of convicts to Mozambique, many of them the political victims of changes of regime. In 1829 a mutiny occurred among troops in Mozambique and there was another mutiny in Ibo. A governor had to be removed when the full extent of the clandestine trade he had been carrying on was revealed. Complaints were openly voiced at the continued connection with distant Portugal and many of the slaving community sought to establish a connection with Brazil and even talked of a change of allegiance — of becoming a colony of Brazil instead of Portugal. However, these political disturbances died down in the 1830s when the Mozambique slave trade re-established itself as vigorously as ever.

In the years immediately after the official end of the slave trade to Brazil, the Portuguese government in Mozambique stuck by the letter of the law and refused to countenance slaving, but by the late 1830s it had become reconciled to the need to look after the interests of the Afro-Portuguese commercial community without which there would be no Portuguese presence in east Africa. The governors and other officials stood to gain extensively from the bribes and backhanders, while the traders were happy to pay these small additional costs in order to return to using the best ports of the coast. While makers of colonial policy in Lisbon espoused the causes of abolition and free trade, the whole Portuguese official establishment in Mozambique became enmeshed in a black economy which linked it through ties of self-interest with the coastal sheikhs and the powerful suppliers of slaves in the interior.

There is little contemporary information on how the steadily increasing demand for slaves was met. Indeed the only detailed account from a contemporary who had actually been in a position to see how the trade operated at source was António Gamitto whose experience covered the period 1826-40. He described how the Afro-Portuguese sent their *mussambazes* with a caravan of trade goods into the interior; they passed from settlement to settlement until they found a chief who could supply slaves and then established a market. Captives were produced who were examined physically, and after much bargaining a price was agreed together with a gift in payment for the 'blood of the slave'. He was emphatic that although war captives, criminals and the offspring of slaves were regularly sold, a quarter of all slaves were people accused of witchcraft. The strangest aspect of his account concerns the sale of people 'by deception'. The victims appear to have been people of slave status in African society who had no idea that they were to be sold. After the initial haggling the chief would secretly point the slave out to the buyer as he mingled with the general population. A price was then agreed and the '*moçambaz* takes possession of him, securing him by surprise and putting him in chains.' However, this process could lead to bizarre results, as Gamitto recalls:

> On one occasion an argument broke out between the slave and the vendor over whether he had the right to sell him and as a result of the dispute it was the vendor who ended up in chains and he who had been sold received the price.'[11]

In general the agents of the coastal merchants obtained slaves by purchase, although the slaving caravans were not above kidnapping children or isolated individuals they came across. It was the chiefs in the interior who generated the supply by warfare or by exploiting the unsettled conditions created by drought and migration. The rise of the slave trade from the 1760s was made possible by the recurrence of acute drought and migratory pressure. In the 1760s the northward movement of the Tsonga chiefs and their conquest of the low veldt between the Limpopo and the Sabi generated a large supply of slaves at Inhambane. In the same decade drought, locusts and banditry severely disrupted normal economic life in Zambesia. Drought and civil war returned in the mid-1790s, fuelling the expansion of the slave trade. The beginnings of the great Mozambique drought around 1820, with the subsequent banditry and social dislocation, again helped to fill the baracoons.

The slave trade cannot, therefore, be treated in isolation from contemporary ecological disasters and political changes. However, it is clear that, whatever its cause, the slave trade was not simply an export trade. Slaves were sold internally in Africa and accumulated in the hands of chiefs and warlords, and many of them were used to build up private armies, to increase the number of productive women in a community, or to support the status of chiefs and other leading males within matrilineal societies. As will be seen in the next chapter, the slave trade led to the emergence of large protected settlements, militarised societies and larger-scale political organisation, particularly among the matrilineal peoples north of the Zambesi. The losers were the small, scattered disorganised communities which often had to abandon whole areas of countryside and gather under the protection of some warlord or retreat into more easily defended regions. The depopulation created a vacuum and encouraged migration, so that whole chieftaincies relocated in the early nineteenth century. These in turn helped to reshape the political geography of Mozambique in the period immediately before the colonial partition.

The great Mozambique drought

The climate of southern Africa is notoriously unstable. Although the rains may fail randomly in any year, a well marked pattern of longer wet and dry periods can be detected from the scientific and historical records. Dry periods may last for many years, building up into droughts of fierce intensity which almost always severely disrupt the normal life of the societies in the regions most affected. Traditionally the African population of Mozambique had many ways of coping with drought. The first response would be to intensify hunting, gold mining and trading to provide an alternative to subsistence agriculture. Then, if the drought persisted, populations might have to move from the drier areas to better watered and more fertile regions. This could involve uprooting whole communities, and inevitably led to competition with other groups for available land and water. More prolonged drought seems to have led to great social instability, to war, banditry and an increase in slaving. Drought was frequently accompanied by locust swarms and was followed by epidemics which swept through the weakened population causing numerous deaths. The coming of drought and locusts leading to disease, migration, warfare, and slaving, therefore, created a cycle of violence and social anarchy which has recurred many times in Mozambique's history, from the events of the 1580s described by João dos Santos to the catastrophes of the 1980s.

From 1794 to 1802 southern Africa suffered severe drought as far north as Lake Malawi, acquiring in folk memory the name of *mahlatule*. On the Zimbabwian plateau drought seriously weakened the Changamire state, and it may have been the *mahlatule* which began the political, social and economic changes among the Nguni which led to the emergence of the Zulu kingdom.[12] Early in the nineteenth century ecological conditions recovered but in 1817 drought began again. At first it affected the Natal area but its impact spread north and in 1823 it was reported as severely affecting the Zambesi valley. In the following years all the regions of Mozambique from Cabo Delgado to Delagoa Bay experienced what was apparently the severest drought ever recorded.

The most immediate consequence of the drought was to disrupt traditional agricultural communities. In most regions the routine production of crops became impossible. In the Zambesi valley people moved to the islands in the river or to areas of the delta known to be fertile and well-watered. North of Tete were some mountainous regions which seemed to have escaped the worst of the drought, but in most of lowland Mozambique and throughout the Zambesi valley settled peasant life was abandoned. The population died or fled from the ravages of hunger and smallpox. To the drought were added locusts, which appeared for the first time in 1827. The eccentric governor of the Rivers, Vasconcellos e Cirne, described how

> . . . .day after day the sun was covered by the passage of clouds of these insects and they destroyed even the virgin bush, the most extensive fields and the interior for league upon league so that even the herds of wild animals died for lack of food.[13]

Large numbers of destitute people ended up in the slave barracoons on the coast and still larger numbers must have died.

The drought destroyed the economic basis on which the rule of the Afro-Portuguese and the independent chiefs was based. Like the chiefs, the *prazo senhores* depended on the availability of peasant agricultural surpluses to maintain their clients and their bands of armed *chicunda*. With no peasant agriculture and with peasant communities dispersed, there were no surpluses and nothing to support the slave households. The *chicunda* increasingly deserted along with the *colonos*, and the Portuguese *prazos* were overrun by bands of armed men looking for plunder and for some means of survival. In 1829 a report told the governor-general:

> The town of Sena is in a deplorable state of decay because of the great famine which has reigned there for four successive years, but principally now. It cannot be endured because even if there were sufficient rain, there are no hands to do the cultivating since all the slaves of the inhabitants are scattered through various lands not in

the district of this town; and when the settlers do not exist in the town because of the famine, how much less the slaves. . . .[14]

The African chieftaincies suffered as much as the Portuguese *prazos*. The ancient Karanga and Maravi states either disintegrated entirely or went through a prolonged period of chaos. Both Barue and Kiteve suffered interminable and inconclusive wars of succession. The Monomotapa chieftaincy all but disappeared, while the old Maravi paramountcies of Lundu and Undi ceased to have any effective power and became little more than empty titles. In the 1830s the Rozvi chieftaincy of Changamire was battered by successive Nguni invasions and effectively ceased to exist.

A similar fate befell the *prazos*. The Afro-Portuguese families, deserted by their slaves, fled as their *prazos* were invaded by the *bandidos*. With the *senhor* no longer resident and the slaves leaderless and dispersed, the elaborate social and political structures of the *prazos* disintegrated. The government could no longer call on the *prazo* families to provide manpower and resources to maintain the forts and public buildings or defend the towns. Transport became impossible. The dry river beds of the delta became overgrown with dense mats of vegetation and canoes carrying trade goods could no longer pass. Carriers and boatmen could not be recruited from the deserted villages along the river, and trade caravans, even if they could find porters, could not travel safely. The fair of Zumbo was totally abandoned, all commercial life ceased at the Manica fairs, and the trading community dwindled almost to vanishing point.[15]

Elsewhere in Mozambique the effects of the drought were equally disastrous. A report from Inhambane in 1827 stated that 'the famine is so great that . . . many fall dead through weakness, even on the beaches where they go to find shell fish'.[16] In 1831 the governor-general wrote from Mozambique Island:

I can simply say that it appears that in the whole vegetable kingdom nature has died. Palm groves of great size with innumerable old trees have totally dried up and nowhere are there to be found fruits or green plants of any kind.[17]

The commander of the detachment of Portuguese troops in Fernão Veloso bay reported in the same year that

. . . .the famine has caused a mortality that is almost universal among the apathetic people of the hinterland, so much so that in order to avoid an epidemic, it is necessary almost daily to order the burial of the bodies which are found in the fields.[18]

Although the Afro-Portuguese communities of the port towns suffered severely, they could be supplied by sea and were always going to survive. It was the African and Afro-Portuguese societies dependent on agriculture that faced ruin and starvation. The effects of the great drought of the 1820s was intensified by the fact that it followed earlier droughts which had already weakened the economic infrastructure, both agricultural and commercial, of the whole region. Moreover it occurred at a time when the slave trade was spreading violence widely among the peoples of the interior and had begun to effect the coastal communities as well.

The Portuguese authorities tried to take some remedial measures, which might be seen as the last gesture of the old mercantilist state or the first steps towards a newer type of colonial exploitation. The government in Mozambique tried to organise relief supplies; controls on the movement of Muslim traders were lifted in the hope that boats would arrive to trade provisions; embassies were sent to the rulers of the islands and coastal states to the north to try to persuade them to send food aid. More practically the government sent ships loaded with grain to the ports of the coast with instructions for it to be sold by the local authorities at a fixed price. Although this aid only amounted to small quantities, it may have been enough to enable the Portuguese garrisons and communities to survive, even if only barely and with much depleted numbers.

Significant also were the measures the government took to try to re-establish the traditional trading fairs. Official expeditions were mounted to bring relief to Manica, reopen the fair at Bandire and try to restore commercial activity on the middle Zambesi by reopening Zumbo. An expedition was even sent in 1827 to try to establish a new fair west of the Luangwa (called Aruangoa do Norte to distinguish it from the fair of Aruangoa in Manica) which would attract the ivory of the Bisa traders,[19] and a major expedition set out in 1831 to the Lunda court of Mwata Kazembe. These attempts to restore normal commercial activity did not succeed since they could not counter the social and economic effects of the drought which were everywhere apparent. The Manica expedition became embroiled in Barue politics and that to Bandire in the politics of the Kiteve kingdom. The *feira* at Aruangoa failed because the local population fled the famine, while the Kazembe expedition experienced fearful problems finding porters in the regions devastated by the drought and no follow-up caravans were ever organised.

The Nguni migrations

The third major development which was to transform the political world of Mozambique in the first part of the nineteenth century was the arrival of migrant Nguni warbands. Not since the conquests of the Maravi chiefs in the sixteenth century had there been political change on such a revolutionary scale.

The rise of the Zulu monarchy and the dispersal of the Nguni throughout central and eastern Africa have often been seen as an event without precedent in African history. So it is important to place it within the broad spectrum of the historical experience of the peoples of the region. The Nguni-speaking peoples occupied the region south of Delagoa Bay. Their territory immediately abutted on to that of the Tsonga and the two groups were closely interconnected and clearly influenced each other's development. From as early as the sixteenth century the Tsonga chiefs in the neighbourhood of the Bay had begun to create large unified kingdoms, based at least partly on their lucrative trade with the Europeans. Then in the late seventeenth century, for reasons which are not clear, warbands made up of Tsonga-speakers began to move north, conquering and incorporating the native Tonga of the low veldt and threatening the Portuguese settlements at Inhambane and on the Sabi. The Tsonga conquest of the Mozambique lowlands as far north as Kiteve was barely complete when similar developments began among the Nguni who lived immediately south of the original Tsonga chieftaincies.

The Nguni were patrilineal mixed farmers who had always supplemented their agriculture with artisan activities and trade. They had been traditionally grouped in small chieftaincies whose component lineages were heavily reliant on cattle surpluses and cattle exchange. The rapid changes that began to effect the Nguni peoples in the late eighteenth century were almost certainly resulted directly from the onset of the *mahlatule* period. The dry periods that began in the 1790s placed increasing strains on the ability of the economy to sustain the population. The traditional movement of cattle between sweet and sour veldt became impossible and competition for well-watered land became more intense. Early in the nineteenth century there is evidence of increasing warfare among the Nguni chieftaincies, that was to lead to explosive results.

While the onset of drought was putting strains on the traditional economy, the rise of the slave trade and the growth of whaling and other forms of commerce in Delagoa Bay (the port through which the Nguni experienced the demands of the world economy) were exerting pressure of a different kind. The Europeans who came to the bay were demanding cattle as well as the traditional ivory in return for the manufactured imports that were the staple of the trade. To satisfy the market demand for cattle would anyway have presented severe difficulties, but in times of drought and ecological dislocation the problems soon proved insuperable and the Nguni chiefs took to cattle raiding to replenish their herds.[20]

Clashes between the various Nguni chieftaincies led to the elaboration of age-set groupings and the traditionally organised hunting bands into a system of war regiments that gave the chiefs a means to weld their decentralised lineages into centralised, militaristic states. Such military chieftaincies began to be organised by the Ndwandwe, the Swazi and the Mthetwa/Zulus. Not only did these chieftaincies become organised for military purposes, they discovered in the system of age regiments a means of resource control and a way of incorporating conquered people into the fabric of the state. Through them marriage and human reproduction were regulated and royal cattle herds were managed more effectively. That such a system should emerge at a time of ecological pressure is no coincidence. Drought led not only to warfare but also to the development of new socio-political institutions which allowed the rulers to control economic resources in a new way. The effectiveness of the new organisation in warfare, politics and economic control was soon to be made evident.[21]

The Ndwandwe chieftaincy was feeling the effects of the drought and may already have been disintegrating when Chaka, king of the Zulus, inflicted a disastrous defeat on it in 1819. The defeat was followed by the dispersal of Ndwandwe warbands. Groups led by various commanders moved north away from the sphere of Zulu power and found that the clearest path open for them passed through the relatively thinly populated lowlands Mozambique where there were no chieftaincies well enough organised to resist. However, they were moving into an area increasingly in the grip of drought, and the pressures of famine compounded their own rivalries to bring nearly twenty years of social and political chaos. Once again, because of the dis-integrated nature of the societies of Mozambique, relatively small armed bands were able to raid, plunder and dominate the peasant communities of the countryside. But whereas the Tsonga raids of the eighteenth century had not extended far north of the Sabi, the Nguni invasions were to reach the Zambesi and beyond (Map 4).

In 1821 two Nguni groups, led respectively by Nxaba and Ngwana Maseko, moved through the northern Transvaal and on to the Zimbabwe plateau. At some stage the two groups split, and while the Maseko Nguni tried to establish themselves among the Karanga, Nxaba moved into southern Mozambique.[22] Nxaba's original Nguni followers increased their numbers by taking recruits from the Tsonga, and with his regiments thus strengthened, Nxaba turned northwards attacking Inhambane in 1824 and conquering the ancient chieftaincies of Madanda and Quissanga north of the Sabi in 1827.[23] The advancing forces rounded up the cattle of the conquered people and seized young men and girls to boost their numbers still further. By 1830 Nxaba's hostile presence was noted in Kiteve, where his

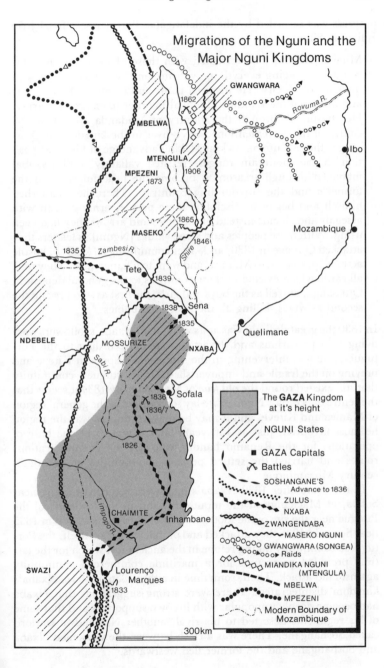

Migrations of the Nguni and the Major Nguni Kingdoms

progress was recorded by the indefatigable Portuguese official João
Julião da Silva:

> Muava [Nxaba] . . . retreated with those of his party into this
> country, ravaging everything with fire and sword as well as with
> unheard of cruelty. He inspired panic and terror in these people
> and uprooted the Landins [Tsonga] in order to enlarge his army.
> He continued through the country of Madanda and along the
> course of the aforementioned Save river to the kingdom of Quis-
> sanga: there Mutema its king, taking advantage of his good posi-
> tion in the mountain ranges, resisted valiantly until [Nxaba]
> managed through treason to become the peaceful ruler of the
> former's and the surrounding countries. There he established
> himself and began to discipline these people, arming them with
> assegais and shields instead of the bows and arrows they had been
> using. With these peoples and some vatuas [Nguni] as leaders they
> attacked Quiteve in 1830, and, after committing all kinds of hostile
> actions, passed on to Manica, and went to Changamire. They took
> all cattle which existed in these countries to the general deposit in
> Quissanga; as well as the boys and girls, the first as soldiers and the
> second as wives, killing all the rest, even babies.[24]

In 1830 the great drought was at its worst, and Nxaba's followers were
living in a precarious and devastated land. According to the Portuguese, he was intervening in the succession dispute in Kiteve and
preying on the fragile and impoverished Afro-Portuguese community
that still existed round the old *feira* of Masekesa. By 1834 it seems that
the centre of Nxaba's Nguni state lay somewhere in the general region
of Manica and Kiteve, and it may be that Gorongosa was the region
he most favoured, just as 150 years later it was to be the base of
operations for the Renamo bandits who cut the communications
routes and harried the settled peasant communities of twentieth-
century Mozambique.

In the years after 1830 Nxaba's men were recorded raiding near
Sofala, at Machanga at the mouth of Sabi, in the lowlands of the
Pungue near the site of the modern town of Beira/Sofala, and in 1835
near Sena. In 1836 they attacked and plundered Sofala itself, the Portuguese community taking refuge in the ancient fort which for the last
time provided protection for a maritime commercial community
against land attack. Then, sometime in either 1836 or 1837, Nxaba's
kingdom disintegrated. There were strong suggestions that Nxaba
had become deeply unpopular with his own supporters and that some
of his regiments deserted to his rival, another Ndwandwe warlord
called Soshangane. There was a clash between the weakened Nxaba
and Soshangane and the former fled westwards.[25]

Nxaba is a major figure in Mozambique history. He established the first Nguni-style tributary state and for ten years brought the region between the Zambesi and the Sabi under the control of a single ruler. He was to create a type of overlordship which would be imitated by others and transform itself gradually into the tributary state of the semi-feudal Moçambique Company at the end of the century. He began the process by which the fragmented lineage-based polities of lowland Mozambique were welded into a large, powerful and cohesive unit.

Two other Nguni warbands, those of Zwangendaba and of the Maseko Nguni commanded by Magadlela, play a less important role in Mozambique history since their battles were fought and their fates decided on the Zimbabwe plateau. Zwangendaba had begun his career as an associate of Soshangane and left him sometime in the early 1820s to invade the Zimbabwe plateau. His followers and those of Maseko ravaged the rich cattle country of the Rozvi chiefs, weakned as they were by the years of drought, and a Nguni warband led by Nyamazana captured and killed Changamire Chirisamhuru and burnt his capital at Khami.[26] However, the two main Nguni leaders fell out. Defeated by Zwangendaba somewhere in the northern part of the plateau, the Maseko Nguni formed an alliance with Nxaba, by then firmly in control of the Manica region. Together they turned the tables on Zwangendaba some time before 1835, when he and his defeated followers crossed the Zambesi at Cachombo and headed north. This victory was short-lived, for the advance of Soshangane from the south drove both Nxaba and the Maseko on a destructive flight through upper Zambesia in 1837 or 1838. Both groups crossed the river and went northwards. Neither the Maseko nor the Zwangendaba Nguni remained long in the area immediately north of the Zambesi, but later in the century their followers were to return to play an important role in northern Zambesia.

Meanwhile, in the south a new Nguni leader had established his authority. Breaking away from the Armageddon that pitted Ndwandwe and Zulu against each other, the followers of Soshangane had entered the area south of the Limpopo. Soshangane was to found a state that was far more durable than the ephemeral power structures of the other Ndwande warlords, and would outlast the Zulu monarchy itself. At first the Gaza kingdom, as Soshangane's conquests were called, had its centre of operations south of the Limpopo, its ruling élite collecting tribute from the Tsonga and building up extensive herds. When the drought broke in the early 1830s Soshangane's cattle empire was able to increase its power and collect tribute over a wider area. However his state was exposed in the south to the attacks of Swazi and Zulu. Swazi raids into the region of the Lebombo mountains were frequent and the Zulus crossed a number of times into what is today Mozambican territory, sacking the Portuguese trading settlement at Lourenço Marques in 1833. Threatened by both Zulu and Swazi, Soshangane moved his capital north of the Limpopo and began to raid into the region loosely controlled by Nxaba. By 1837 he had decisively defeated his rival and had secured a hegemony over the whole region between the high veldt, the Zambesi and the Limpopo.

After his defeat of Nxaba, Soshangane (now usually calling himself Manucusse) returned to build a capital on the Limpopo, leaving his son Umzila to place the area north to the Zambesi under tribute.[27] This northern peripheral region was only loosely incorporated. As with other African paramount chieftaincies, a distinction has to be made between the central core of the chieftaincy under the direct rule of the Gaza king, where his regiments were recruited and where the royal cattle herds were managed, and the peripheral region which paid tribute to him. Every year armed regiments were dispatched to collect tribute, a procedure which David Livingstone graphically described taking place when he visited Sena in 1858. By that time the Gaza state had become an impressive example of overlordship beneath which ancient chieftaincies and Afro-Portuguese *prazos* were able to continue their existence.

The Gaza state was in many ways a typical Nguni polity. Manpower resources were organised into regiments and cattle were seen as the principal means of wealth accumulation of the ruling élite. Like the Zulu monarchy, Gaza allowed pre-existing lineage groups, or even minor chieftaincies, to survive provided they paid tribute and recognised Gaza overlordship. The Gaza monarchy was unique, not in the way it provided an umbrella of sovereignty over tribute-paying subjects, but in the sheer extent of its operations. At the height of its power in the 1850s and 1860s the direct authority of its rulers extended over the whole of what is today southern Mozambique (with the exception of the ports of Inhambane and Lourenço Marques and their immediate hinterland) and large parts of western Zimbabwe and northern Transvaal. It provided a state structure and a kind of political unity far greater than the Portuguese had ever succeeded in creating from their isolated coastal and river settlements.

The Nguni north of the Zambesi

The Gaza monarchy was not, however, the only Nguni state to be permanently established in the future Mozambique. After Zwangendaba's defeated army crossed the Zambesi in 1835, his first conquests north of the river were among the Nsenga, the extreme western group of Maravi peoples. After four years he appears to have moved into the area between the Luangwa and Lake Malawi, effectively destroying the last vestiges of Undi's authority. After another four years Zwangendaba moved on to the shores of Lake Tanganyika where he died in 1845. By this time his army had become a sort of mobile, migrant nation gathering recruits from every ethnic group between Natal and the great lakes but all welded into a cohesive society by the Nguni institutions of patrilineal household and regiment serving the interests of a powerful cattle-owning monarchy.

On Zwangendaba's death, his followers split up. One group followed Zwangendaba's son Mpezeni who returned to the valley of the Luangwa and by the 1860s had formed a Nguni state among the Nsenga. Another group led by Mbelwa occupied the highlands west of Lake Malawi, and a third, which came to be known as the Gwangwara, was led east by Zulu Gama and established a new state based on the Rovuma valley. Raiding by the Gwangwara reached the coast opposite the Querimba Islands and in 1868 extended as far as Kilwa. Other raids scoured the east side of Lake Malawi and reached the Namuli mountains in the southern part of the Makua country. Before the Gwangwara could establish themselves with any permanence, however, they had to confront and defeat yet another Nguni group. The Maseko Nguni had crossed the Zambesi somewhat after Zwangendaba and, having resided for some years among the Maravi, had moved up the east shore of Lake Malawi. It was the Maseko who first moved into the Rovuma valley from where raiding regiments are said to have reached the shores of Lake Victoria. Once defeated by the Gwangwara, however, the Maseko Nguni returned down the eastern side of Lake Malawi, crossed the Shire and established themselves in the highland country of what later became southern Malawi, overlapping into the territory north of Tete known in the twentieth century as Angonia.[28]

Historians have understandably admired the Nguni achievement. The Nguni social and military organisation clearly constituted a powerful political idea, which allowed small bodies of organised fighting men to establish political control over vast regions and gave them the means to incorporate conquered people into a strong, flexible and integrated state structure. But the Nguni states were not really of a radically different type from those they replaced. Although there were elements of centralisation in the powers exercised by the monarch over the fighting regiments and in the national cohesion provided by the first-fruits ceremonies, the structure of society remained segmentary, based on lineage and the subsistence village economy. The Nguni did not bring with them a new technology, nor did they organise production on a radically different basis — they merely had a more effective way of managing resources and creaming off surplus production. Moreover the Nguni states may, in the long run, have served to isolate their peoples from the changes rapidly overtaking central Africa. Because of their fierce reputation and their proud economic self-sufficiency, they effectively prevented a ready intercourse with the outside world.

Over a period of half a century, central Africa underwent major changes associated with the spread of Christianity and Islam, and with the increasing integration of the region into the economy of the Indian Ocean. This happened first through the slave trade and then through the development of commodity and ivory trading. The Nguni kingdoms, however, remained economically and culturally isolated, fossils preserving the forms of the original conquerors but making scanty provision for any kind of change. The Nguni traded with their neighbours but very much on their own terms, not allowing their traditional economic organisation to be modified by market forces or by the new corrosive ideas of the various men of God. When the challenge of colonial rule arrived, they were ill-equipped to cope with it. They were prepared to provide the colonial authorities with mercenary troops during the campaigns of pacification, a function the Nguni of Zambesia were to perform for the last time during the Barue rebellion in 1917, but beyond that they found it difficult to adapt to the changed circumstances and their societies came to seem increasingly archaic. The immediate post-colonial period almost universally saw an eclipse of the Nguni peoples as others proved more ready to accept the changing circumstances and produce new forms of leadership.

Political change in the early nineteenth century

By the 1840s the slave trade, the great droughts and the coming of the Nguni had already produced important political and economic change for the peoples of Mozambique. Gold production and gold trading all but ceased throughout the region, and the mining *bares* and fairs disappeared one by one until not one was operating by 1840. Ivory trading continued but it too changed in important ways. The old trade of the Bisa and the Yao, whose caravans had wound hundreds of miles through the bush and along the river valleys to reach the Mozambican ports, was largely diverted north to Zanzibar where commercial conditions were much more favourable. By the mid-nineteenth century, however, a new ivory trade was developing based on a more systematic hunting of elephants by professional hunters armed with firearms. It was part of an intensified exploitation of Africa's resources that was beginning and would be a powerful instrument of expansion into the interior.

The old pattern of territorial chieftaincies, locally rooted in the lineage structures and supported by the rain cults and spirit mediums, survived but the structures of overlordship, whether Karanga, Maravi or Afro-Portuguese, were profoundly altered. Of the historic Karanga chieftaincies that had ruled the peoples south of the Zambesi, only Barue and Manica survived as effective states, Barue greatly weakened by interminable contests for power, and Manica shrunk to a tiny territorial chieftaincy. North of the river the Maravi kingdoms of Kalonga, Undi and Lundu remained little more than names, while the predatory Nguni states of Mpezeni, Maseko and Mbelwa occupied much of the best cattle country, incorporating conquered Maravi populations and raiding in a wide arc beyond their borders.

On the Zambesi the overlordship of the Afro-Portuguese families also underwent profound change. The effects of the great drought on the *prazos* is graphically described by the judge Joaquim Xavier Diniz Costa in a report to the governor-general in 1831:

In general the *foreiros* [*prazo*-holders] of that district have not paid their tithes, giving as the reason the condition of the *prazos* which are almost totally invaded and devastated by the kaffirs of the interior; they are stripped of their own *colonos* and slaves, some of whom are still wandering about in various parts. It will be very difficult for them to return to live in the lands that belong to them unless force is used to end the invasion, to recover the lands that have been overrun, to impose respect on the barbaric invaders and to defend and protect the new *colonos* and slaves. The state of decay to which the *prazos* have progressively arrived is extreme. Some of the time they are covered with the corpses of those who have perished from the violence of the famine, at others they are full of different kaffir tribes who have invaded and have devastated them through the effects of their natural brutishness and ferocity, driven on by the great famine which has reigned in the countries where they have come from. And finally, even when they were not invaded, the people fled and they became entirely deserted because of the fear of imminent new invasions and incursions. These lands which were once prosperous and highly productive present a wholly calamitous picture. They have become sterile through the irregularity of the seasons and especially through the lack of rain; and if by chance in some areas a small amount of work in the fields, coupled with the fertility of the land appears to be bringing recovery, at once these new crops are devoured by the mouths of the locusts which in vast, dense clouds swarm over the fields and strip them of all vegetation. In view of this picture it can well be appreciated what has been the income from the *prazos* of this district.[29]

By 1840 many of the old Afro-Portuguese families had emigrated. Taking what assets they could, they had departed for Brazil or India. With their departure the Zambesi towns had dwindled almost to the point of extinction, and the old *luanes* with their establishments of *chicunda*, their tilled fields, orchards and busy commercial life were all in ruins. Their place was taken by a handful of powerful individuals, mostly of Indian origin, whose influence rested on the firearms of their private armies and on the powerful fortifications they built to dominate the country. By mid-century they had effectively divided Zambesia into five feudal kingdoms whose ruling dynasties pursued bloody and inconclusive vendettas with each other and whose *chicunda* captains engaged in ivory hunting and raided for slaves in the country beyond their borders. These successor-states to the old *prazos* (to be described in more detail in chapters 12 and 13) were the counterpart in Zambesia of the militaristic states of the Nguni, of which two had their territory within the borders of Mozambique and another five had Mozambican territory within the arc of their raiding and tribute-collecting activity. On the coast the slave trade had also given birth to an expansive tendency among the coastal Muslims. The small sheikhdoms, for so long insignificant and poverty-stricken, also began to recruit private armies and to profit from the chaos in the interior to embark on territorial expansion.

After 1840 all these new centres of power would enjoy an era of political expansion — the phase of African sub-imperialism which preceded the scramble for Africa — and be responsible for servicing the development of a more penetrative Indian and European merchant capitalist activity.

12

EXPANSION IN THE
NINETEENTH CENTURY

Trade and political power

As the nineteenth century progressed, a connection became increasingly apparent in eastern Africa between commercial penetration by outsiders and the appearance in the interior of new political structures. This process can be clearly seen in the development of Zanzibar under Omani rule. As the demand for slaves, ivory and plantation products grew early in the century, traders were attracted to the island, and Indian financiers serviced the trade caravans and provided goods on credit. Zanzibar's commercial community, carefully nurtured by Seyyid Said, rapidly attracted much of the inland trade that for three centuries had been brought to Mozambique Island and the Zambesi towns. However, where the development of Zanzibar differed from the earlier growth of the Portuguese towns was in the rapid penetration inland of its commercial enterprise and in the spread of its political influence.

The traders of Mozambique Island had never organised their own caravans, and had been content to deal with African traders coming from the interior. The Zanzibar merchants, however, organised their own trading expeditions. Way-stations were founded along the main trade routes and the leaders of the larger caravans soon moved from the exercise of commercial influence to the wielding of political power. A large caravan, well supplied with trade goods and guarded with perhaps 100 men carrying firearms, constituted a concentration of wealth and armed might more formidable than could be achieved by any but the largest and best organised chieftaincies. Spheres of political influence and informal political structures grew up, controlled by the great caravan leaders like Tippoo Tib. Under their influence Islam spread and towns reminiscent of the coastal Swahili cities were established, linked externally with the commercial world of the Indian Ocean and through marriage and clientship with the African peoples round them. By the 1850s Swahili caravan leaders had established communities in their own image as far inland as the Congo basin and the shores of the great lakes. On Lake Victoria, at the north-western edge of their area of operations, they were to meet Egyptian-based ivory and slave traders creating similar political spheres of influence on the upper Nile, and to the south they were to come up against the Afro-Portuguese who were planting their own distinctive traditions and institutions in parts of the interior they had never previously penetrated.

Expansion of the illegal slave trade from Mozambique

At the end of the eighteenth century commercial activity along the Mozambique coast had been thriving. Slaves were being shipped in increasing numbers, ivory was being brought from far in the interior, and the cattle trade of Delagoa Bay was expanding year by year. The official expedition of Francisco de Lacerda to Kazembe in 1798 even suggested that the Portuguese were about to embark on a period of commercial expansion in the interior. However, this commercial development was severely disrupted by the Napoleonic wars and then by the onset of drought and the consequent migrations of the Nguni. In the far south the opening of the British trading station at Port Natal in 1824 siphoned off much of the commerce that might otherwise have come to Lourenço Marques from the expanding Zulu monarchy, while further north Zanzibar unequivocally seized the initiative from Mozambique Island in attracting the ivory trade of the east and central African interior.[1]

Perhaps the biggest threat to the trade of Mozambique, however, was the campaign against the slave trade. Under pressure from Britain, Portugal had agreed in 1817 to limit it to the region south of the equator, while Brazil had officially banned the import of slaves from 1830. From 1832 the liberals held the ascendancy in Portugal and began a series of major reforms designed to liberalise commerce, bring about economic development, and put an end to the slave trade. However, trade links with Brazil remained strong and many Portuguese had invested heavily in Brazilian plantations and the slave trade that supplied them.[2] The meagre nature of Portugal's trade with its African colonies, the slave trade always excepted, meant that there was no real backing for the development of an alternative colonial economy, with the result that the abolitionists among the liberal politicans found they had little support. As the historian José Capela expressed it,

> Portugal was the country with the greatest colonial tradition and, partly because of this, found itself in a paradoxical situation: possessing extensive colonial dominions, it had not, in the century of industrialisation, produced a metropolitan class capable of concerning itself with the trade in its products. It is in the light of this that some explanation can be found not only for the anachronisms

in the method of exploiting the colonies which continued into the 60s of the twentieth century, but, more immediately, for the reactions, procrastination and opposition to the abolition of slavery.[3]

It was the bullying of the British government that forced Portugal to try to head off an ultimatum by passing in December 1836 a decree that 'totally abolished' the slave trade.[4] In practice this decree abolished nothing. It became clear that the government did not intend it to apply to Portuguese plantation owners moving slaves they owned in Africa to and from their plantations, and it was not accompanied by any measures of enforcement. Britain continued to press for a treaty that would declare the trade to be piracy and establish mutual rights of search.

Although pessimists among the Mozambican slavers had anticipated the end of their profitable commerce and there had been talk of attaching Mozambique to the newly-independent state of Brazil, the trade in slaves prospered throughout the 1830s.[5] With world sugar prices high, demand for slaves was buoyant and no government in Mozambique was prepared to enforce the anti-slave trade legislation.

Then, in the early 1840s' the price of sugar fell and with it the demand for slaves, prices falling by as much as two-thirds. In 1839 the British government had authorised its ships to stop and search Portuguese vessels' and in July 1842, after an ultimatum from Britain, Portugal signed a treaty declaring the trade to be piracy and legalising the right of search. British warships now actively patrolled the east African coasts and were regular visitors to the ports of Mozambique. By the middle of the decade, however, it was becoming apparent that the slave trade was not to be suppressed by treaty or by the activities of a few British warships. In 1846 there was once more a sharp rise in sugar prices, ironically as a response to British free trade measures

Table 12.1. SLAVE EXPORTS FROM MOZAMBIQUE
PORTS, 1836–41

	Quelimane	Mozambique and minor ports	Total
1836	1,700	4,400	6,100
1837	4,300	10,600	15,000
1838	2,100	5,400	7,500
1839	4,900	12,200	17,100
1840	3,500	8,300	11,800
1841/2	2,000	5,400	7,400

Source: Gerhard Liesegang, 'A First Look at the Import and Export trade of Mozambique, 1800–1914', p. 464.

which equalised import duties and did away with preference for imperial sugar, while the boom in coffee production revived the plantation sector of the Brazilian economy. The work of decades of diplomacy was undone as the price of slaves soared and imports into Cuba and Brazil rose, with one estimate suggesting that as many as 450,000 slaves were imported into Brazil between 1840 and 1847.[6] In 1856 Britain tried to increase the pressure by establishing a consulate in Mozambique with a brief to watch the activities of the slavers, and Livingstone was given vice-consular status when he led his expedition to the Zambesi in 1858. However, throughout the 1850s the clandestine trade in slaves maintained its volume. Although Brazilian markets were finally closed in 1851, Cuba and the United States continued to import large numbers of slaves for another ten years before they also shut the slave markets in the early 1860s.

As diplomatic pressure closed one market after another, the resourceful slavers of Mozambique found alternative outlets for their 'product'. Fresh markets opened up in Madagascar and in the new sugar-growing islands of Nossi Bé and Mayotte, acquired by the French in the 1840s, as well as in the *vieille colonie* of Réunion. To evade the provisions of the anti-slavery treaties, the French introduced the *engagé* labour system in 1854 whereby slaves entered into contracts which turned them technically into 'free' labour. The system of *engagé* labour was openly practised till 1864 when the French officially agreed to discontinue it and the trade in slaves was once again driven underground. Thereafter the main European slave dealers withdrew from the business leaving the Muslim dhow trade to Zanzibar and Madagascar as the dwindling but still important rump of what had once been the principal livelihood of the coastal peoples.

Although after 1842 the slave trade had officially ceased to exist, all indications are that in the 1840s and 1850s the volume of slaves exported equalled or exceeded that of the 1820s and 1830s. Visitors to Mozambican ports were aware that the trade was still going on around them and that everyone they met was involved in it in some way. British naval officers from the anti-slave trade squadron who called at Quelimane or Mozambique were treated with warmth and hospitality, taken on shooting parties and made honoured guests at social functions. Outwardly they saw nothing of the trade but the more observant of them were aware of the secret signals, the movements at dead of night, the large sums of money changing hands. They saw the capacious barges moored in the rivers and were suspicious of the number of well-equipped 'whalers' and 'brigs' that arrived empty on the coast. The trade was like an elaborate game of chess. On one side were the captains of the slave ships and their financiers, the suppliers on the Mozambique coast, the chiefs and leaders of armed slaving parties in the interior and all the numerous people who made their living from the trade; while on the other side were the British naval officers with a wallet full of treaties, a few missionaries and a pathetic handful of honest French and Portuguese officials.

The presence of the British squadrons on the Mozambique coast and their regular visits to Quelimane, Mozambique and Ibo may not have stemmed the flow of slaves, but it did have a considerable impact on the way the trade was conducted. Slaves were brought from the interior and kept in barracoons well away from the Portuguese towns to await the arrival of slavers. The slaving ships approached the coast with caution knowing that British cruisers could have them condemned not only for carrying slaves but also for carrying the equipment of a slaver. Most of them made for deserted river mouths north or south of the main Portuguese ports where they could lie up, hidden by mangrove thickets and protected by shallows and dangerous bars. Messages would then be sent to suppliers and the slaves either marched overland or ferried in the large barges moored on the main rivers.

For the system to work it was necessary for a network of contacts to be maintained along the coast and this was a role for which the Islamised coastal communities and the Afro-Portuguese backwoodsmen were ideally suited. The Afro-Portuguese slaving network was fronted by wealthy landowners, some of them owners of *prazos* and able to utilise the old hierarchies and networks of the *prazo* system. Usually the governors of the towns were bribed into silence, or in the rare event of their attempting to impede the trade, were hounded from office or even murdered. Lieutenant Barnard, who frequently visited Quelimane in the early 1840s, describes how he gradually discovered the full extent of the slaving network although on the surface the town showed no sign at all of any slaving activity. He described slaving as a form of gambling for the wealthy Afro-Portuguese: they would venture 20 per cent of their capital in a slaving voyage, and if it was successful they would double their capital. If it failed, they still had a stake left for a further game.[7]

However, Barnard knew it was no game. While he mixed socially with the Portuguese slavers and enjoyed their lavish hospitality in order to obtain intelligence, he was forced to maintain a diplomatic silence when his sources revealed to him the atrocities of the trade — 300 slaves burnt alive in a baracoon; 700 drowned when a slaver drove on to the reef of the Bassas da India; hundreds dead of disease before being loaded, half the consignment dying on board and the slaver returning to port with the remainder past help. And the horrors were not always ameliorated by liberation. He describes the capture of a slave ship which was followed by the liberated slaves raiding the ship's spirit kegs, large numbers dying an agonising dealth from alcohol poisoning in the orgy that followed.[8]

Twenty years later the trade still seemed as vigorous as ever. William Devereux entered the harbour of Mozambique Island in July 1861 and saw

> . . . .two or three dhows, miniature junks, alias slave-coffins, and a French barque ready for their living freight; also a Portuguese schooner of war (which will do a stroke of illegal traffic at a pinch), and a rakish-looking schooner, the property of a merchant of Mozambique.[9]

The governor, he believed, had

> . . . .the utmost hatred of slavery and the slave trade; but I believe, like all other Portuguese governors, however well-intended, he is sure to be overcome finally by the great temptations the inhuman traffic offers, especially as his pay depends nearly on it.[10]

The governor's advice was that 'in capturing dhows we cannot make a mistake, all of that kind of craft are slavers', but Devereux continued, 'perhaps he wants to draw our attention from the large rakish barque in harbour by sending us after the small fry'. And he went on to describe how one

> . . . .celebrated Portuguese slave company have a small man-of-war schooner as a blind; it carries all the money for the purchase of slaves, and generally leads our cruisers off the scent.[11]

Portuguese relations with the Islamic coastal communities

Because it was diplomatically embarrassing for the Portuguese to trade slaves openly from their principal ports after 1840, a number of clandestine slave trading centres grew up, notably along that part of the Mozambique coast where the Muslim sheikhdoms had survived. Slaving brought renewed commercial prosperity to these parts of the coast while slave traders developing new trade routes carried with them into the interior the political influence of the Afro-Portuguese and Islamic coastal communities. Once these minor ports had begun to develop their slave trading networks, they provided alternative markets for the increasing number of foreigners coming to the Mozambique coast, a situation which not only challenged Portugal's commercial dominance but also threatened to disturb the easygoing political relations that had traditionally existed between the Portuguese and the sheikhs.

Throughout the first half of the eighteenth century the Portuguese had had generally good relations with the sheikhs of Sancul and Quitangonha whose lands lay south and north respectively of the wide bay of Mozambique (Map 2). Relations with the mainland peoples in general had been entrusted to the *Capitão-mor das terras firmes* who was appointed by the governor, usually from among the important local Afro-Portuguese families. Mozambique claimed a nominal sovereignty over the sheikhdoms which was symbolised by granting to the sheikhs themselves, or to leading members of their families, the titles of *capitão-mor*. In practical terms, the Portuguese required the sheikhs to help keep open the trade routes, to provide food and water for the town on Mozambique Island and to lend assistance if military action in the interior proved necessary. Mozambique also expected the sheikhs to discourage foreign traders and generally to observe the Portuguese restrictions on trade.

The system worked well while the interests of the Portuguese authorities and the ruling Muslim families coincided.[12] However, the growth of the slave trade led to a divergence of interest. Slaving was so profitable that in mid-eighteenth century Muslim traders began to deal privately with foreign ships prepared to sell firearms. Once the trust between Mozambique and the sheikhs was broken both sides competed for political influence among the coastal communities, the Portuguese seeking to install rulers favourable to themselves while the sheikhs in their turn exerted pressure for the appointment of a compliant *Capitão-mor das terras firmes*. In the background was the powerful influence of the Makua chiefs, the principal suppliers of slaves, and the French traders, the principal buyers.[13]

Hostilities between the Mozambique authorities and Quitangonha occurred in 1775–6, in 1786 and then more frequently in the 1790s. The Portuguese sought to control the coastline of Fernão Veloso Bay, while the Quitangonha sheikhs tried to expand their territory inland at the expense of the Makua. In 1829 the Portuguese moved to occupy Fernão Veloso and sent a detachment of troops to build a fort. The isolated post existed till 1834 when, following the extreme hardships of the famine years and a mutiny of the troops, the little colony was wound up.[14]

Sancul and Quitangonha were so close to Mozambique that neither was ever likely to grow into an independent Islamic state. However, Angoche was different. Until the mid-eighteenth century the Portuguese had maintained informal relations with the sultanate, appointing a leading local figure to the post of *Capitão-mor dos Rios de Angoche* but interfering little in the sultanate's internal affairs. During the later eighteenth century it appears that Makua migrations in the interior brought a powerful new group, the Imbamella, into the immediate hinterland of the town. Each of the principal lineages of

Angoche — the Inhanandare, Mbilinzi and Inhamilala — had traditionally held the public offices in turn (there was a similar arrangement in Sancul) while forming ties of marriage with Makua chiefs in the hinterland whose influence thus became important in town affairs. The rise of slave trading appears to have increased the tensions between the lineages, and between the town and the Imbamella.

Angoche was difficult of access for oceangoing sailing ships but with the signing of the agreements for the suppression of the trade in 1836 and 1842, American and Cuban vessels began to frequent the shallow river estuaries on that part of the coast. Portuguese and Afro-Portuguese traders also established themselves and Angoche soon became the most important port conducting clandestine trade in contravention of official Portuguese trading policies, just as it had in the sixteenth century. In 1843 British naval captains were issued with orders to enter the minor ports of the Mozambique coast in search of slavers. The political implications of this order were considerable. Although the Vienna treaty of 1815 had recognised Portugal's position on the east African coast, it was by no means clear that Portugal could claim direct sovereignty over all the peoples of the region. The Portuguese government feared that British ships entering ports like Angoche would be followed by the signing of bilateral treaties between the British government and the local rulers such as had already occurred in West Africa.[15]

This threat apparently spurred the Portuguese into action and a warship was sent to Angoche early in 1847 to force an anti-slave trade treaty on the sultan. However, pro-slaving elements in the town drove the Portuguese away and the clandestine trade in slaves continued. The result of this was that the British admiralty reluctantly agreed to mount a joint expedition with the Portuguese, and in November 1847 Angoche was bombarded by gunboats, but no permanent occupation of the town followed and at this stage the only concern of the Portuguese seemed to be to to head off independent action by the British.

In the early 1850s, the end of the Brazilian slave trade meant that arrivals of slaving ships from the Americas became intermittent. Slaves, however, continued to be obtained in the interior and were still being brought to the coast for sale. Contractors and dealers would frequently be forced to wait for some considerable time before a ship arrived, and the accumulation of large numbers of slaves in their hands, and the uncertainty over when and how profitably they could be sold, had predictable consequences for coastal society. Many of the slaves were turned into soldiers to form standing armies with which the rulers sought to supplement their trading incomes through territorial expansion and conquest.

In the 1850s the ruling families of Angoche, for so long content with their role in seaborne trade and localised urban politics, began to recruit slave armies and intervene actively in the politics of the interior. This expansionism was associated with one man in particular — Mussa Momadi Sabo, called by the Portuguese the 'Napoleon' of east Africa, but more commonly known by his sobriquet 'Mussa Quanto'. Mussa was half-brother to the ruling sultan, was well-connected with the leading Muslim families of the coast and had travelled to Zanzibar and Madagascar. He had reputedly accompanied trading expeditions inland as far as Lake Malawi. Early in the 1850s he settled in Angoche and was given command of the armed forces of the sultanate which he built up by recruiting slaves and acquiring modern firearms. In a series of campaigns Mussa Quanto attacked the Imbamella and launched raiding parties as far as the Shire, acquiring slaves and bringing the Makua of this region to recognise the overrule of Angoche. This rapid expansion of Angoche power soon brought conflict with the Afro-Portuguese of Zambesia whose own private armies were being swollen with unsold slaves and who were also looking to compensate themselves for the uncertainties of the slave trade by political expansion.[16]

The major conflict of interest took place between Angoche and the Alves da Silva family, slavers who had bought themselves into the old *prazo* aristocracy by acquiring the abandoned *prazo* of Licungo situated along the coast north of Quelimane. In the 1850s the family was headed by two brothers, João Bonifácio and Victorino Romão, who, after suffering raids from Angoche, began to build up their own private army. The militaristic society created by the Alves da Silva brothers survived the demise of its Afro-Portuguese chiefs and became a sort of republic run by the captains of the regiments (*ensacas*). It was yet another of those bandit states of which Mozambique history furnishes so many examples. In 1861 João Bonifácio, accompanied by a small Portuguese detachment with some field-guns, led eight of his *ensacas* to attack Angoche. Although he died in the fighting, the town fell to the Zambesian army and the Portuguese installed a small garrison and created an administrative district to be controlled from the newly conquered town. However, the effects of the victory were nullified when Mussa Quanto, who had escaped from the battle, reappeared in 1864 and established his military ascendancy along the whole coast from Angoche north to Mozambique Island.

This overland march by one of the Afro-Portuguese armies may perhaps be compared with the *entrada* made by the governor of Sofala south along the coast to Inhambane in the eighteenth century. It was a moment of psychological importance, for never before had the

Portuguese tried to wield political power in this part of northern Mozambique nor had the influence of the Afro-Portuguese *muzungo* families ever extended so far along the coast. It was a moment when another small step was taken towards creating a single state with a single destiny. The slave trade had led to the emergence of Afro-Portuguese and Islamic warlords whose private armies, carrying guns bought with the profits of slaving, were able to dominate the fragmented and musket-less Makua chiefs. Although not apparent at this time, the future of northern Mozambique was to ride on the back of these bandit leaders. In the following decades they were to provide conditions first for the commercial penetration of Indian traders and ultimately for the expansion of the Portuguese colonial authorities once these had learnt to form alliances with one or other of the warlord factions.[17]

Expansion from Portuguese Zambesia

During the great drought of the 1820s and 1830s the sphere of influence of the Zambesi *muzungos* contracted. The *feiras* of Zumbo and Manica, and the hinterland of Sofala, were abandoned, while the trading expeditions to Kazembe failed to develop after the much-publicised initiatives of Lacerda in 1798 and Gamitto in 1831. However, the slave trade continued to prosper and by the 1840s the networks of Afro-Portuguese power began to grow once again. During the mid-nineteenth century Zambesia was dominated by five powerful feudal families — Da Cruz, Caetano Pereira, Vas dos Anjos, Ferrão and Alves da Silva, with Manuel António de Sousa rising to prominence in the 1860s to form a sixth. By the 1850s the armed followers in the service of these dynasties were widening the range of their activities in three directions: the Shire valley, the valleys of the upper Zambesi and Luangwa, and Manica and Barue.

The Shire highlands and the rise of the Yao chieftaincies

The valley of the Shire was not unknown territory to the peoples of the Zambesi. The manufacture of cotton cloth (*machiras*) had attracted traders, and in the seventeenth century a number of Portuguese, including Jesuit priests, had ascended the river and even reached Lake Malawi. However, through most of the seventeenth and eighteenth centuries political control of the valley had been in the hands of the Maravi chief Lundu, and even Mount Morumbala, triumphantly dominating the horizon north of Sena, had been outside Portuguese control and notorious as a refuge for dissidents and escaped slaves. The most important cultural influence on the Shire peoples had been the Mbona rain shrine, and the support of this cult and its priests had been one of the foundations of Maravi power.[18] However, by the mid-nineteenth century the power of the Lundu chieftaincy was disintegrating from the effects of the drought and the Nguni invasions. The Shire valley and the highlands were becoming a political vacuum which attracted the attentions of slavers and led to large-scale migrations which brought Yao from the north and Lomwe and Sena speakers from the Mozambique lowlands.

It seems that, during their passage east of Lake Malawi, Maseko's Nguni had repeatedly attacked the Yao who had also been subjected to raids by various Makua warbands in search of slaves. Traditions that severe drought and famine accompanied these attacks is certainly consistent with what is known about the pattern of Mozambique history where famine and warfare are inextricably, almost causally, linked.[19] When Livingstone travelled down the valley of the Lugenda to Mwembe, the centre of the powerful Yao chieftaincy of Mataka, in 1866, he crossed 50 miles of country which had been almost completely depopulated,

> . . . still bearing all the marks of having once supported a prodigious iron-smelting and grain-growing population. The clay pipes which are put in the nozzles of their bellows, and inserted into the furnace, are met with everywhere — often vitrified. Then the ridges on which they planted maize, beans, cassava, and sorghum, and which they find necessary to drain off the too abundant moisture of the rains, still remain unlevelled to attest the industry of the former inhabitants.[20]

In response to war, famine and slaving, some of the Yao began to migrate south while others were organised into large defensive settlements by the more powerful and warlike of the Yao leaders.

Before the nineteenth century it seems that the Yao resembled the Makua and the Makonde in their social and political institutions. The matriclan was the most important focus for the loyalties of the individual, with the result that territorial chieftaincies were small and generally weak (although there were clearly exceptions to this, like the Makua chieftaincy of Maurusa). A number of circumstances, however, led to a reversal of this situation and the development of major chieftaincies among the Yao in the nineteenth century. First, the physical uprooting of many matriclans from the land caused by drought, the passage of the Nguni and the raiding of the Makua weakened the position of social institutions for which attachment to specific areas of land and to the spirit cults of the ancestors was all-important. Secondly, the experience of war and migration gave the opportunity for the growth of chiefly institutions. The population needed to be protected from raiders, and the ready availability of male and female slaves enabled chiefs to build up their personal followings at the expense of the matrilineal clans. The subsequent spread of Islam offered the chiefs the opportunity to develop a chiefly cult in opposition to the dominant spirit cults, a cult which would encourage trade and help them gain control of the initiation rituals.[21]

Livingstone's journey in 1866 was not emulated by any European traveller until the missionaries of the Universities' Mission to Central Africa (UMCA), who had left the Shire on the death of Bishop Mackenzie in 1862 and relocated to Zanzibar, organised an exploratory journey in 1875 resulting in the establishment of a mission station at Mwembe.[22] The missionaries found that Islam was in the process of establishing itself in Mwembe, and from their description one gets the clear impression that the Islamisation of the Yao followed and did not precede the establishment of the centralised chieftaincies, and that it was closely connected with the maintenance of the slave-trading network.[23]

These new chieftaincies, which were to dominate the region to the south and east of the Lake till well into the twentieth century, were the Yao equivalent of the Afro-Portuguese warlords and, like them, based their political power on building defensive strongholds from which they could offer a sort of feudal protection to the local population. In time some of these grew into considerable urban settlements imitating many aspects of Islamic coastal culture, while the rest of the countryside remained insecure and depopulated (Map 5).

If some Yao chiefs, like Mataka, consolidated large states in the country east of the Lake, others migrated south into the Shire highlands. Eyewitnesses saw them as predatory slavers and there is no doubt that the Yao, armed with muskets and maintaining close ties with the Islamised traders of the Swahili coast, actively plundered the populations of the highlands for the benefit of the coastal trade. However, the Yao were not just slavers; they were also settlers and by 1861, when the UMCA mission arrived, their chieftaincies were established throughout the highlands with the Manganja population reduced to tribute paying status.

From the east also came increasing numbers of Lomwe-speaking settlers. It is difficult to know whether this movement was new or whether there had always been a tendency for Makua from the lowlands to move to the more healthy uplands, but bearing in mind the flood of 'Anguru' (Lomwe-speaking) migrants who entered Nyasaland during the colonial period, it is worth recording that this movement certainly predated the establishment of colonial control. The movement of the Makua was very different from that of the Yao. They did not come as conquering chiefs with large numbers of armed

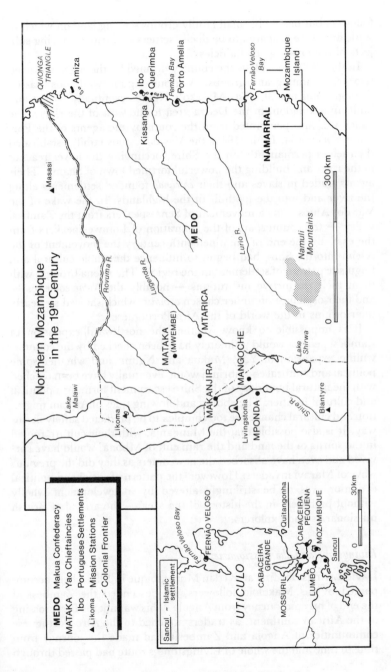

followers but moved in small family groups seeking land on which to settle and were prepared to be docile settlers and tribute-paying subjects of the existing chieftaincies.[24]

In the 1830s and 1840s the country drained by the Shire attracted two other immigrant groups. Various Nguni warbands passed through, and one at least, Maseko's Nguni, eventually settled and built up a kingdom in the Dedza area to the west of the river. The valley was also penetrated from the south by the agents of the Portuguese *muzungos*. In the 1840s the Vas dos Anjos family established themselves permanently on the Shire, occupying the lower reaches of the river and building the powerful fortified town of Shamo. Their agents traded in slaves and their *chicunda* founded settlements along the river and into the foothills of the highlands. In the wake of the Vas dos Anjos came a movement of Sena-speakers from the Zambesi valley — the counterpart of the migration of Lomwe-speakers from the east. By the end of the nineteenth century the movement of the Asena into the Shire had begun to influence the whole cultural and linguistic pattern of settlement in the region. The Asena brought with them their distinctive institutions — notably the *Nomi* societies — and their organisation under chosen *capitães*, which showed so clearly their origins in the world of the Afro-Portuguese.

It is impossible to know whether the northward expansion of Zambesi peoples would ultimately have been checked by the countervailing expansion of Yao, Makua and Nguni, and whether some political and cultural equilibrium would eventually have been reached with the natural boundary of the Shire escarpment forming a political and cultural frontier. The ebbing and flowing tides of African migration and cultural change are too complex to be predicted saftely in this way. It is also possible that the Manganja, with their culture rooted in the spirits of the land and the rain cult of Mbona, would have survived and even have absorbed the newcomers as they did the previous wave of Maravi invaders. However, the pattern of social and political evolution was to be strikingly altered by a development wholly without precedent in the history of the area — the arrival of British missionaries and explorers.

Livingstone and the missionaries

David Livingstone first arrived in Mozambique in 1856 when, accompanied by his Makololo followers, he descended the Zambesi at the end of his epic journey from Angola. This was not the first crossing of the African continent, as traders attached to the Afro-Portuguese communities of Angola and Zambesia had made the journey from time to time and the whole of Livingstone's route had passed through country already penetrated by the trade of the Afro-Portuguese. The expedition was nevertheless of major importance in the history of central Africa. Livingstone was a brilliant publicist, able to attract the full limelight of public attention on himself and on the causes he supported. His book *Missionary Travels*, appearing in 1857, was a bestseller and highly influential in forming public opinion in mid-Victorian Britain. It was not the first account of Mozambique to have been written in English since a number of important works had been published by naval officers attached to survey ships or anti-slave trade squadrons, but it was the first detailed account of the interior and of the Afro-Portuguese settlements on the Zambesi.[25]

On his descent of the Zambesi Livingstone had made a detour which prevented him from seeing the Cabora Bassa rapids, and as a result he had persuaded himself that Portuguese reports of the river being impassable above Tete were exaggerated. He convinced an enthusiastic British public that the Zambesi could be a highway into the interior where Christian missions and the benevolent influence of free commerce would strike at the roots of the slave trade. The British government was persuaded to support an official expedition to the Zambesi, and the London Missionary Society was talked into sending a mission to Barotseland. In May 1858 the 'Zambesi Expedition' arrived at the mouth of the great river and, with the help of a small and very inadequate steamer, proceeded to carry out survey work, which it was hoped would open the navigation of the Zambesi. By 1859 Livingstone had become aware that no vessel could pass Cabora Bassa and he turned his attention to an investigation of the Shire. He took his steamer, itself an innovation unprecedented in Zambesian history, up as far as the Murchison cataracts and then proceeded to 'explore' the shore of Lake Malawi.

One of the most important consequences of the publicity surrounding the expedition was the stimulus it gave to missionary enterprise. Already in 1857 Livingstone's influence had led to the founding of the UMCA and in 1861 the first UMCA mission arrived under Bishop Mackenzie, travelled up the Shire and established itself at Magomero in the Shire highlands.[26] After less than two years the mission was to fail and its members were withdrawn, but in the early 1870s the missionary path to the Shire highlands was kept open, first by an expedition under Edward Young to search for the missing Livingstone and then in 1875 and 1877 when two Scottish churches, inspired by Livingstone's death in the African interior, established stations in the highlands. These missions proved more durable than Bishop Mackenzie's and created a Christian community with a powerful and distinctive culture. The political influence which the Scots acquired over the peoples of the highlands was soon to interfere with the slaving activities and natural expansion of the Afro-Portuguese, the Nguni and the Yao.

However, Livingstone's influence on the Shire region was not done yet. When the Zambesi expedition was finally disbanded in 1864, it left behind some of Livingstone's Makololo assistants whom he had provided with guns. They had been, in effect, part of the Zambesi world of the Afro-Portuguese since Livingstone had first left them there in 1856, and they had survived by adopting the role of the typical Zambesi *chicunda*. With Livingstone's departure they were left without a *muzungo* chief to serve. So, like other *chicunda* in similar circumstances, they set about creating their own chieftaincies, attracting personal clients and bringing sections of the peasant population into a tribute-paying relationship. During the 1850s the power of the Vas dos Anjos family on the lower Shire had been broken and the fall of their fortress at Shamo had left a power vacuum in the region. It was there that the Makololo established their own fortified villages and expanded their political influence.

Although the rise of the Makololo chieftaincies should be seen as part of the more general expansion of the Zambesi *chicunda* and Asena, the Makololo were always to think of themselves as possessing a special status through their earlier association with Livingstone. This association allowed them from time to time to try to invoke British aid in order to maintain their independence of Portugal. It ultimately decided that the largest part of their territory would be included in the Protectorate of Nyasaland and would thrust a wedge of British territory into an area which all the logic of history had made part of the socio-economic world of the Afro-Portuguese of the lower Zambesi.

Livingstone's presence had its effects on the Portuguese as well. His reports and the stream of publications emanating from his associates cast Portuguese Zambesia in a very unflattering light and revealed the full extent of the slave trade in the interior. One effect of this hostile publicity was to persuade the Portuguese authorities of the need for a much more active and effective colonial policy. Within two years of Livingstone's departure the Portuguese had begun to prosecute their disastrous wars against the Da Cruz in Massangano.

Expansion on the upper Zambesi

Zumbo had been abandoned by the Portuguese in 1836, apparently with finality after years of chaos and decline. At approximately the same time the Rozvi monarchy in the south of the plateau, the old *mãe d'ouro*, was overwhelmed by Nguni warbands. The passage of the Nguni also fatally weakened the Maravi chieftaincies to the north of the Zambesi and disrupted the trade routes into the interior. It seems that for perhaps two decades gold mining both north and south of the river virtually came to an end.

Among the immediate beneficiaries of this political confusion were the Caetano Pereiras. North of the Zambesi, Macanga the chieftaincy founded by the Pereiras, was to be the most important successor-state — by the 1840s controlling much of the interior between the Shire and the Luangwa. The Pereiras were an Indian family which rose to prominence at the end of the eighteenth century as ivory traders and operators of gold-mining *bares*. It is indicative of the emerging new order that they never leased *prazos* and therefore never really formed part of the elaborate hierarchical world of the Zambesi *muzungos*. The Pereiras assisted the official Portuguese expeditions to Kazembe in 1798 and 1831 and were the main beneficiaries of the opening up of regular trade with the Lunda and the Bisa. When the Portuguese tried to establish a fair in the Luangwa valley in 1827, it was to the Pereiras that the commandant of the rivers applied for advice. The fair was eventually established within a settlement which Pedro Caetano Pereira had built for his elephant-hunters who were exploiting the herds in the Luangwa valley and selling their ivory to Zanzibar.[27] However, although by the 1820s the power of the Pereiras was firmly established as far west as the Luangwa, there is no indication that the family occupied the old site of Zumbo or tried to revive trade at the fair.

During the 1840s Chissaca, the head of the Pereiras, was pursuing his vendetta against the Da Cruz family on the middle Zambesi, and little is known of his activities in the interior, but by 1858 when he died Macanga's power was in decline and the Luangwa valley was once more a no-man's-land. Its inhabitants lived uneasily between the Nguni states which were being formed in the highlands to east and west, and the Zambesi Portuguese and Ndebele to the south. The decline of the power of the Pereiras had encouraged traders from the lower Zambesi once more to expand their activites. In the 1850s Livingstone came across a number of Afro-Portuguese ivory traders busy on the Zambesi above Zumbo and in 1859 the geologist Richard Thornton, after being temporarilly dismissed by Livingstone, accompanied one such expedition into the valley of the Luangwa.

The expedition was organised by two Tete *prazo*-holders, called by Thornton Senhor Clementina and Senhor Manuel. They were accompanied by five other black traders all of whom had Portuguese names. Above Tete the expedition moved by land through the territory of numerous small chiefs who required presents to allow the trading party to pass. 'He has paid already 11 chief men,' wrote Thornton in his diary on 18 August, 'and has 6 more to pay on the way to Zumbo.'[28] Ivory was bought from the chiefs, usually after long sessions drinking *pombe* and haggling over the price. Thornton records that the two principal traders had with them £1,800-worth of trade goods while the five black traders had a further £1,000-worth.[29] Ivory was expensive, a 14 lb. tusk costing 15 yards of cotton cloth, but the expedition was also buying iron hoes, unworked iron, iron and copper wire and copper *manilhas*. When they reached the confluence with the Luangwa the traders bought canoes and hired boatmen from the neighbouring villages, but after proceeding a few days up the river the party returned precipitately on hearing news of a Nguni raiding party. The expedition then proceeded up the Zambesi and through the Mpata gorge before turning back while still below the confluence with Kafue.

When Thornton visited Zumbo, the site was still deserted and in ruins, but early in 1861 the governor of Tete had received an invitation from Bruma, the most important chief in the neighbourhood, to re-establish the *feira*. As trade was growing and relatively settled and prosperous conditions had returned, and perhaps also as a consequence of the activities of the Zambesi expedition, the Portuguese decided that Zumbo should be officially reoccupied. An expedition was organised under Albino Manuel Pacheco and in 1862 the Portuguese flag was raised once again over the old *feira*. One reason for the re-establishment of the *feira* of Zumbo was that Mzilikazi had now advanced the power of the Ndebele to the Zambesi and was anxious to trade with the Portuguese, exchanging his ivory for guns and slaves as well as the traditional imports like cloth. Later the Shona chiefs (the term Karanga was no longer much used in the latter half of the nine-teenth century) also bought guns from the Portuguese which by the 1880s enabled them effectively to resist Ndebele attacks.[30]

It has been suggested that the expansion of the Afro-Portuguese in the 1850s and 1860s was a consequence of the peace which had reigned in the Tete district after the wars between the government, Chissaca and the Da Cruz in 1853–5. *Chicunda* from the Da Cruz fief of Massangano, finding no employment at home, took service with José Anselmo de Santanna (Chikwashya) and carved out a domain near the confluence of the Zambesi and the Luangwa.[31] Whatever the truth of this story, from the early 1860s Zumbo became the base for the rapid expansion of the influence of the Zambesi *muzungos*, San-tanna chief among them, and by 1863 their agents were buying ivory at the capital of the Litunga of Barotseland.[32] The pattern of their activities presents a picture familiar enough in the history of Mozam-bique. Armed bands of ivory hunters and slavers would move into a region and establish a stockade. They would then send out hunting and raiding parties, and terrorise the local chiefs into ceding land and paying tribute. While boatloads of ivory were sent down the tributaries to collecting-points on the Zambesi, and quantities of slaves were dispatched to various markets on the coast or in the interior, the *chicunda* in the service of the Afro-Portuguese warlords established permanent villages for themselves, populated Zambesi-style with the women captured in the raids.

Thoroughly alarmed by the arrival of a British mission on the Shire in 1861, and knowing that Livingstone was intending to establish further missions among the Barotse of the upper Zambesi, the Portuguese were now anxious to extend their control over as much of the interior as possible. Hitherto the authorities had always been reluctant to encourage indiscriminate conquests and the emergence of over-mighty subjects; indeed, in the mid-nineteenth century they were struggling to control the *prazo* dynasties of the lower river and suffering humiliation at the hands of the Da Cruz. But in the region of Zumbo and the tributary valleys of the Luangwa and the Kafue they seemed prepared to give official recognition to any conquests by the Afro-Portuguese and their *chicunda* bands, provided it was done in the name of Portugal and accompanied by the hoisting of a Portuguese flag. Indeed the Portuguese established a form of submission, known as a *termo de vassalagem*, which the Afro-Portuguese warlords were supposed to observe, such submissions being formally recorded in the newly-established *Boletim Official*.[33]

From the 1860s onwards the *chicunda* leaders played the Portuguese game. As they advanced into new regions, so they raised the Portuguese flag and sent official notification of a new conquest to the Portuguese government. The new area was then made a *prazo* which, as emphyteutic tenures had been abolished, was rented out to its conqueror who was granted the title of *capitão-mor* and wielded jurisdiction in the name of Portugal. In this way the *prazo* system, which had been officially abolished thirty years earlier, received a new lease of life and became once more the instrument for Portuguese advance and for the incorporation of further conquests.

Between 1860 and the formal partition of the region in the 1890s the *chicunda* occupied both banks of the Zambesi between Tete and Zumbo, a region never previously incorporated into the *prazo* system. Beyond Zumbo the peoples of the south bank of the Zambesi generally recognised the overlordship of the Ndebele, but the Afro-Portuguese traders regularly visited the Gwembe valley, usually building encampments on the Zambesi islands but, at some time in the 1860s, constructing a permanent trading town at Inhacoe just above the Kafue confluence (Map 5).[34] The Afro-Portuguese were principally interested in buying ivory, and contemporary observers in the 1860s and 1870s stress that their slaving activities were largely aimed at acquiring women to exchange for ivory with the Tonga or Ndebele.

North of the Zambesi, the *chicunda* war bands dominated the lower reaches of the Kafue and Luangwa rivers, extending Portuguese territory as far as the borders of the Nguni kingdoms of Mpezeni and Maseko. The main instruments of this expansion were two Afro-Portuguese families — Rosário Andrade (Kanyemba) and Araujo Lobo (Matakenya). These families were related by marriage and between them controlled much of the Zambesi valley beyond Zumbo. Like their counterparts on the lower river, they operated from large fortified camps which acquired the dimension of small towns. They cultivated a fearsome reputation for savage cruelty and British visitors to the region at the time of the scramble readily admitted the extent of their power and influence.

The advance of the *chicunda* was at the expense of African societies that had already partly disintegrated. The Maravi chieftaincies had broken up and the peoples of the region had been subject to Nguni raids and long periods of Nguni occupation. The *chicunda* were moving into a region where there was no organised opposition and where effective African state systems had ceased to exist. The *chicunda* themselves were able, up to a point, to fill the gap, setting up their own brand of bandit state centred around large fortified encampments which sometimes grew into urban settlements.

In time the whole region might well have become assimilated into the distinctive, syncretic *chicunda* culture — a blend of the cultures of the lower Zambesi peoples and Catholic Portuguese social ideas and organisation. However, there were natural limits to the advance of the *chicunda*. To the north the Nguni of Mpezeni and Maseko and to the south the Ndebele monarchy were too formidable to be attacked, while further up the Zambesi the Barotse kingdom also had the capacity to resist *chicunda* banditry. Even so, the region effectively conquered by the *chicunda* was considerable and bore comparison with the expanding power of the Swahili warlords in the Manyema or on the northern shore of Lake Malawi. As elsewhere in Africa, the formal partition between the European powers in the 1890s abruptly severed the lines of Africa's own development. The partition treaties limited Mozambique's boundaries to an area far smaller than that already effectively penetrated by Mozambican *chicunda* culture.

Expansion into Manica and Barue

Since the sixteenth century the kingdom of Barue, situated in the dry, mountainous and inhospitable country inland from the Lupata gorge, had remained independent of Afro-Portuguese domination. Barue had controlled the roads from the Zambesi to Manica which had also remained largely free from direct Portuguese control. The isolated

Portuguese fairs in Manica had survived into the nineteenth century as the focus for the traditional commerce of the region, but as a result of the drought and the Nguni invasions, they had been finally abandoned in 1835. Barue meanwhile dissolved into chaos with warring factions disputing the succession to the Macombe title, Nguni armies crossing and recrossing the kingdom and starving bands of armed men surviving as best they could in the desolate escarpment country.

However, by the 1840s both Barue and Manica had been brought to acknowledge the overrule of the Gaza king, Soshangane. Like other Nguni states, the Gaza kingdom had a centrally controlled and administered nucleus and a much larger 'penumbra' of territory where tribute was collected and Gaza overlordship was loosely acknowledged under threat of being raided by Gaza *impis*. On its fringes, therefore, the 'state' was very loosely organised. Subject chieftaincies retained their identities and their traditional ruling dynasties, but they had to accept the presence of representatives of the Gaza state at their capital. These chieftaincies were affiliated to one or other of the great aristocratic 'houses' among which the patrimony of the Gaza monarchy was distributed, and it was armed tax-collecting parties representing these 'houses' which periodically visited the outlying areas.[35] In the 1840s and 1850s the Portuguese *prazos* of the Sena district and the chiefs of Barue and Manica were regularly forced to pay this tribute. Manica paid 100 head of cattle as its acknowledgment of Gaza overlordship and it seems that there was a brief period when some Nguni settled in Manica and married Manyika women.[36] However, it has been claimed that the Gaza kings never intervened successfully in the succession of Manica chiefs.

For the development of modern Mozambique the most important characteristic of the Gaza kingdom was the fact that throughout much of the 1840s, 1850s and 1860s, its overlordship produced relatively settled conditions in the interior, the best evidence for which is the revival of trade. Once it was clear that trade caravans could again move in safety, the Portuguese were anxious to revive the Manica *feiras* and re-establish the old system of privilege and control which had restricted the activities of traders in the common interest of the chiefs and the Portuguese captains. Embassies were exchanged, and in 1854 the Portuguese even went as far as to nominate Izidro Correa Pereira to the post of *capitão-mor* of Manica. However, the *feira* itself was never revived, and indeed could not be revived in the old form because of the wholly different trading conditions now prevailing.

The old fairs had flourished because the trade in alluvial gold necessitated the concentration of tiny quantities of gold dust at one spot for sale. However, during the great drought gold production seems largely to have ceased, and when trade revived it was in response to market conditions in which ivory enjoyed the highest premium. Now it was not gold traders who journeyed inland but the professional hunters and ivory traders in the service of Portuguese or Indian merchants. In the 1840s ivory traders from Zambesia began to send expeditions south into the hinterland of Barue and Manica and as far as the Shona chieftaincies of the plateau. These expeditions were manned by the traditional Zambesian *mussambazes* but they were not undertaken simply to trade, for in the middle of the nineteenth century the traders in ivory had increasingly become its hunters as well. The reason for this may lie in the disordered conditions of the interior which had disrupted the hunting of elephant by traditional means. Effective firearms were now being used by the elephant hunters whereas previously ivory had been hunted, even by the Afro-Portuguese and their *chicunda*, in traditional African fashion. More likely it was the increased demand that now made it possible for hunting parties to pay chiefs the various fines and *saguates* which would permit them to hunt in their own right and so increase the amount of ivory available.

Huge quantities of ivory were exported from Zambesia in the middle years of the century — José Anselmo de Santanna exported 40,000 pounds from the Zumbo area in 1860 — and some of the leading ivory hunters and traders were employing 150 to 200 hunters equipped with firearms.[37] Afro-Portuguese were also buying ivory from Mzilikazi and Soshangane. In their search for ivory, hunters and traders from Zambesia penetrated further on to the high veldt than at any time since the seventeenth century and 'Portuguese' ivory hunters and traders were encountered by Carl Mauch as far south as Great Zimbabwe in the 1860s.[38] It is not surprising, therefore, to find that it was the organised bands of armed elephant hunters in the service of the leading Afro-Portuguese who were to spearhead the expansion of Portuguese political control south of the Zambesi.

In the 1830s and 1840s Sena was the base for the commercial activity of Izidro Correa Pereira and the Ferrão family, but by the 1850s a new name was beginning to be heard: Manuel António de Sousa. He was to become in some ways the greatest of the *muzungo* warlords, but he did not belong to a traditional Zambesian family and cannot strictly be called Afro-Portuguese. In Portuguese parlance he was a Canarin, an Indian from Goa. Born about 1835, he came to Zambesia in 1853 to help administer the property of an uncle. He married his uncle's daughter and successfully set himself up as a trader in the Sena region. Sousa quickly made a fortune in ivory trading and his armed elephant hunters formed the nucleus of a private army which he was repeatedly to make available to the Portuguese authorities during the Zambesi wars. One of the most significant features of his career was the reputation he acquired for working with the government and being a loyal subject of Portugal while ruthlessly building up his own private empire on the fringes of the Portuguese colony. For this 'loyalty' he was amply rewarded. In 1858 he leant soldiers for the campaign against the Vas dos Anjos and sent contingents to accompany most of the expeditions against the Da Cruz during the years 1867 to 1869. From these disasters Sousa emerged stronger rather than weaker, since after its repeated defeats the government came to rely ever more heavily on his support to maintain its position in Zambesia. The government also began to look to him to protect Zambesia from the raids and tribute collecting forays of the Gaza *impis*.[39]

In 1856 the Gaza king, Soshangane, died and Sousa took advantage of the ensuing succession dispute to establish himself in the interior of Gorongosa. There, deep inside territory that had been accustomed to pay tribute to the Gaza kings, he built a powerful stockade and concentrated his armed forces. By 1862 Umzila had defeated his rivals for the Gaza throne, and although he had been backed by the Portuguese he came north, and in 1863 raided the territories of the fort of Sofala and attacked and destroyed Sousa's stockades on the Pungue and in Gorongosa. When his *aringas* were attacked, Sousa had been in Sena to receive his commission as *capitão-mor* of Manica and Quiteve. In appointing him *capitão-mor* in succession to Izidro Correa Pereira who died in that year, the Portuguese authorities intended that he should act as a buffer against further Gaza raids and stabilise the interior in their interest. To achieve this he was allowed to lease most of the *prazos* between the Lupata gorge and the delta.

Gradually Sousa recovered his authority in Gorongosa, and as his position there strengthened he drove a wedge between the centre of Gaza power to the south and access to Manica, Barue and the middle Zambesi. Gaza *impis* could still raid the delta but they had to travel by the coast and found it increasingly difficult to exert any sort of consistent authority in this area. It was Sousa's presence in Gorongosa which probably prevented any serious Gaza interference in the wars between the government and the Da Cruz in the 1860s.

In 1875 Sousa intervened in a Manica succession dispute and in return for his support to the successful candidate received tokens which he claimed constituted the submission of the Manica kingdom to his overlordship.[40] This was later to be disputed by both the ruler of Manica and by the British South Africa Company but, whatever the truth, it was a clear sign that Sousa had by that time become as important a figure as the Gaza king in the politics of the area. He probably never installed any armed force in Manica or exercised formal control in the territory, but in Gorongosa he had already begun to create a formidable organisation based on a line of *aringas* and had cast his eye on the chieftaincy of Barue whose internal disorder suggested it was ripe to be added to his growing empire.

Portuguese expansion in the south

Within the traditional society of the Afro-Portuguese *muzungos* Sousa rose to a position of pre-eminence. He held *prazos* and received from the Portuguese authorities his title of *capitão-mor* which conferred on him the right to exercise official authority and the much-valued access to supplies of firearms which reached him via the Zambesi ports. However, ultimately Sousa's wealth derived from the sale of ivory. It was his need to find fresh reserves of ivory that pushed him into annexing ever greater areas of the interior, and it was his elephant hunters who increasingly came to form his private army, an army which was able to face and soon outface the Gaza *impis*.

If elephant hunting was carrying the Portuguese frontier ever further into the interior of Zambesia, the same process was taking place on the frontiers of the other Portuguese enclaves in the south — the dynamics of the ivory trade creating ties that were gradually binding together the different parts of what was to become Mozambique. South of Zambesia the Portuguese held three garrisoned enclaves or *presídios* — Sofala, Inhambane and Lourenço Marques. At the beginning of the nineteenth century the ancient fortress of Sofala with its captain and garrison still presided over a trading port of some significance. In the immediate hinterland of the town were a few *prazos* in the hands of Afro-Portuguese families but the principal importance of Sofala lay in the trade conducted with Kiteve. Sofala's fortunes tended to reflect the fortunes of that chieftaincy, and from time to time its traders pressed for the privilege of establishing a *feira* comparable to those in Manica to fend off the competition of the Sena settlers.

During an interregnum in Kiteve in 1803–9 the Sofalans demanded the right to set up a *feira* but with the accession of Kiteve Tica in 1809 they were able once again to re-establish their influence and maintain traders permanently at the Kiteve's court. The famine of the 1820s once again badly disrupted trade, and following the death of the Kiteve in 1830 Nxaba was invited by various of the factions to intervene in the kingdom's affairs. In the next few years the Nguni launched three raids on Kiteve, while the Sofalans sent an expedition in 1831 to re-establish the old *feira* at Bandire; this was done but in the event it only lasted a single year. The following years saw Sofala's trade with the interior collapse. The town itself was attacked and plundered by Nxaba in 1834 and again in 1836, and was barely able to survive.[41]

With the defeat of Nxaba and the establishment of the Gaza kingdom, trade revived as it did throughout the whole of the southern interior. Kiteve began to send trade caravans again in 1840 and in 1842, after receiving tribute from the Afro-Portuguese in the Sofala *prazos*, Soshangane also sent ivory to Sofala for sale. The gold trade briefly revived and in 1857 Portuguese traders began to exploit alluvial gold at Nyaoko in the interior. In 1855 an expedition was sent to establish a Portuguese settlement at Santa Carolina in the Bazaruto Islands with a trading post on the mainland. In its first two years it traded 8,000 lb. of ivory and, significantly for the future, some rice and sesame bought from the local population.[42] As a result of the civil wars following the death of Soshangane in 1858, the centre of the Gaza kingdom was moved further north so that the southern hinterland of Sofala came more directly under Gaza influence. The immediate result was a great increase in the quantity of ivory sold to the Portuguese, and the trade of Sofala reached new heights of profitability attracting Indian merchants to the region. However, already the days of the old town were numbered. The fort was regularly awash at high tides and the harbour was silted up and unapproachable. In 1860 the Portuguese finally moved their seat of government to Chiluane, the old Muslim port a few miles south.

The trading port of Inhambane, established in the 1720s, had attracted Indian traders and throughout the nineteenth century its population was to remain predominantly Indian and Muslim. Although the intention had been that the settlement would merely provide a focus for the trade of the region, it had increasingly attracted a client population of coastal Tonga who settled near the town and who recognised Portuguese overlordship. The Portuguese rule in these crown lands (*terras da coroa*) was very informal and resembled the type of influence that the Portuguese had been accustomed to exercise over the Swahili populations of the northern coastal areas, so that in some ways Inhambane can be seen as a southern extension of the Swahili cultural area.[43] Francisco Maria Bordalo estimated that in 1858 there were fifty-five villages and a total of 56,444 people subject to the *presídio* and that

> . . . .in all there are still twenty-two minor chiefs who are subject to the government of Inhambane. They pay a small amount of tribute to the treasury and supply any manpower which is needed for various purposes. Formerly these chiefs used to come together once a year in the town but today they assemble, for a festival which they call *banza*, only when a new governor arrives; on this occasion they are lavishly entertained and given presents by the newcomers.[44]

In 1834 the town had been sacked by Soshangane's army and almost all the trading community had been killed or dispersed. Following this disaster the town was involved in serious hostilities with local Tsonga chiefs in 1849 and in 1850 with a mutiny of the garrison. However, Inhambane gradually recovered and in 1858 had a population of 810 free persons (120 of whom were military personnel) and just over 3,000 slaves.[45]

The traders of Inhambane retained a considerable interest in the clandestine slave trade and, as in the eighteenth century, this reflected the supply side of the trade. The Nguni armies which invaded southern Mozambique and the high veldt in the 1820s, accompanied as they were by the onset of drought and famine, generated huge numbers of captives. In 1824 the glut was such that the price of a slave had fallen to only a few shillings. Brazilian and French slavers came south, and by the 1830s prices had begun to stabilise and Inhambane was exporting about 1,000 slaves a year. By the 1840s, however, the slave trade was clearly becoming less important as more settled conditions in the interior and the opening of alternative markets in the Transvaal caused the flow of captives to dry up. Inhambane's rise and decline as a slaving port show clearly the importance of supply rather than demand in the history of the trade.[46]

In addition to slaves Inhambane exported ivory and became a point of departure for ivory hunters whose activities gradually widened the commercial hinterland of the port. In the late 1840s traders from Inhambane were resident in the Zoutpansberg, but although one formal mission was sent in 1855 to try to open regular trade routes, Inhambane traders were effectively excluded from trade with the Transvaal.[47]

Inland from Inhambane, beyond the *terras da coroa*, were the Chopi who were increasingly the object of raids by the Gaza regiments. The Gaza king, Umzila, saw the Chopi as an unassimilated and unassimilable group and in the 1870s repeatedly raided and attempted to subdue them. As a consequence the Chopi and the Inhambane Portuguese saw each other as allies and the Chopi were pulled into the orbit of influence of the *presídio*, being armed and organised in their resistance to Umzila by the celebrated Portuguese *sertanejo* João Loforte.[48]

The southernmost Portuguese settlement was Lourenço Marques which was to have an altogether more stormy and significant impact on events than its northern neighbour. Since the sixteenth century Delagoa Bay had been the trading port for a huge hinterland extending west to the Transvaal and south to Zululand and Natal. This hinterland had shrunk somewhat with the opening of the British trading port at Port Natal (Durban) after 1824, but Lourenço

Marques was still seen as the major trading port for the Swazi and Zulus, for the Tsonga chieftaincies to the north and, after the Great Trek, for the Transvaal Boers as well. The permanent Portuguese settlement was only founded in the 1790s, and in the early nineteenth century a tiny Portuguese garrison defended the stockaded town situated on the north bank of the Maputo river. The fortunes of the settlement were somewhat chequered. With the rise of the Zulu monarchy the port came increasingly under Zulu influence, and Dingane certainly considered that the Portuguese were his tributaries. In 1833 the town was sacked by a Zulu army and the governor was abducted and murdered.[49] However, as Zulu power contracted after the battle of Blood River in 1838, Lourenço Marques became the object of jealous rivalry between the Swazi and Gaza who competed to control the import trade of the port.

During the wars of the *mfecane* and the expansion of Gaza power in the 1830s and 1840s, large numbers of slaves found their way to Delagoa Bay and the export of slaves was to continue almost throughout the century in spite of emphatic denials by the Portuguese and claims that the trade had definitely ceased by 1845.[50] Yet if it is clear that slave trading continued, it is also clear that in the mid-century the most important form of commerce was the export of ivory.

Although by the 1850s the Gaza state controlled the country between the Limpopo and the Zambesi, Soshangane had resided since 1839 principally at his capital in Bilene in the south. Ivory began to be traded in ever growing quantities and came to form an important source of income for the monarch. This ivory was hunted by the Gaza themselves and Portuguese hunters were largely excluded. However, further to the northwest, the region of the Lebombo mountains and the Zoutpansberg, which was situated on the edge of the area from which Swazi and Gaza took tribute, beckoned adventurers. The Zoutpansberg has usually been seen as a frontier region where the advancing Transvaal Boers could buy slaves and enjoy a certain anarchic freedom but it was also the destination of professional elephant hunters based on Lourenço Marques. Expeditions to the interior, organised by Portuguese like Diocleciano das Neves, were becoming common in the 1850s and 1860s. The hunters operated in a manner reminiscent of the traders and hunters of Zambesia. The Portuguese *senhor* maintained contact with the traders of the port, who supplied the arms and other necessities for the expedition and advanced the capital. The *senhor* then engaged professional African hunters who usually went alone in pursuit of the elephants but who were on occasion accompanied into the interior by the *senhor* himself.[51]

As ivory hunting grew in importance, considerable numbers of the local population came to depend on it for a living, and the Portuguese were able to call on large bodies of men skilled in the use of firearms for their wars in the interior. It might be imagined that the pattern of Zambesia would repeat itself with the most powerful Portuguese becoming warlords controlling large areas of land and a numerous population. In one case this clearly happened.

João Albasini, first heard of as a trader in Lourenço Marques in 1831, pioneered a trade route on to the high veldt in the late 1830s. He attracted a number of Tsonga followers and established a settlement in the interior on the Sabie river. In 1846 he accompanied a Portuguese embassy sent to the newly established Boer Republic in Ohrigstad and in 1853 moved with his followers north to the Zoutpansberg.[52] He apparently established good commercial relations with the Boers, and was clearly involved in supplying the Boer community with slave children (*inboekselings*), building up his own following from the same source. He was appointed Superintendent of Kaffir Tribes (reminiscent of the Portuguese office of *capitão-mor* in Zambesia) in Schoemansdal and married the grand-daughter of Jan van Rensburg. Albasini became Portugal's official consul in the Zoutpansberg and it was at his fortified trading establishment, Goedewensch, that Umzila took refuge in the early phase of the Gaza civil war after 1858. In 1860 Albasini with his private army of Tsonga tried to enforce his overlordship on 'Chinguine' which had previously paid tribute to the Gaza king, but he was defeated by Mawewe, Umzila's rival for the Gaza throne. In 1864, when Umzila was at last victorious, the screws were turned on Albasini and the whole of the hunting area in the low veldt to the east was declared closed unless Albasini agreed to hand over his Tsonga followers. Although Albasini was willing to do this, the Tsonga deserted and the confusion that followed led to the collapse of the Schoemansdal settlement in 1867. Albasini's lands were declared Portuguese territory and christened the *Colónia de São Luis*, but they were shortly afterwards incorporated within the Transvaal in the frontier treaty of 1869.[53]

Albasini's career was rather exceptional and it seems that the Portuguese patrons of the ivory hunters mostly did not seek to wield individual political power. However, the availability of bands of armed elephant hunters did provide the Portuguese governors of Lourenço Marques with the means to intervene in African politics, and in the late 1850s and early 1860s, when the Zambesian government was winning notable victories against the Vas dos Anjos family and the Angoche sultans, it seemed as though similar successes would be registered by the southern governors as well.

The crisis in Gaza

The most powerful monarchical state can be made unstable by a succession crisis — a problem of government that has not been solved by the substitution of elective presidencies for hereditary monarchies. The polygamy practised by African monarchs was a highly successful means of integrating conquered peoples and binding together different elements in the society but it made succession disputes all the more difficult to resolve as the lines of succession became that much more complicated.

Soshangane's conquest of southern Mozambique in the 1830s had brought some stability to an area which for decades had been torn by war, famine and migration. Moreover his state, large even by modern standards, covered an area far greater than had ever previously been united under one ruler. The expansion of commerce in the 1840s and 1850s was the clearest indication that the situation in the country was widely perceived as having changed. In 1858, however, Soshangane's considerable achievement was threatened when his death plunged the state into a bitter civil war. Mawewe, Soshangane's son by a Swazi wife, seized the initiative driving out his brothers and establishing close links with Mswati, king of Swaziland — creating a sort of Nguni axis for the domination of the low veldt. Mawewe also received some support from the Portuguese traders of Inhambane, though not, it was soon apparent, from Lourenço Marques or from the British in Natal.

Umzila was Soshangane's son by a Tsonga wife and had been the effective governor of the northern part of Gazaland since 1839 when his father had returned to his capital in the south. On his father's death Umzila had fled south looking for allies to contest the succession. He took refuge in the Zoutpansberg with João Albasini who tried to create an alliance linking the Transvaal Boers, the Portuguese of Lourenço Marques and Umzila's supporters to seize control of Gaza from Mawewe. Albasini was trying his hand at the kind of African diplomacy at which the Natal Native Secretary, Shepstone, believed himself to be such a master. However, the Transvaal Boers never co-operated and in 1861 Umzila moved down into the district of Lourenço Marques and was joined by large numbers of the Tsonga elephant hunters in Portuguese service.

The fighting of the next two years was bitter and confused. In November 1861 Mawewe was defeated after his Tsonga *impis* deserted to Umzila. Umzila then signed a treaty acknowledging Portuguese sovereignty over the land as far north as the Incomati and recognising, so the Portuguese claimed, Portuguese lordship over Gaza as a whole.[54] The Portuguese, in return, provided Umzila's forces with 2,000 rifles. Together Umzila and the Portuguese then overwhelmed

Mawewe in a battle near the Limpopo, immense booty being brought back to Lourenço Marques as the spoils of war. Mawewe fled to the Swazi court, and early in 1862 a Swazi army descended on the area south of the Limpopo overrunning the whole country, defeating both Portuguese and Tsonga. Umzila was forced to retreat north with his followers while the Portuguese retired behind the walls of their *presídio*. In August 1862 Umzila and the Portuguese counterattacked, and the Swazi withdrew in anticipation of the beginning of the rainy season. There were further Swazi raids into the south in 1863 but the army suffered from famine and disease in what had become a wasted land, and with the death of Mswati in 1865 any further Swazi attempts to replace Mawewe on the Gaza throne were abandoned.[55]

This period of nearly seven years of warfare devastated the south of Mozambique, the Tsonga chieftaincies south of the Limpopo receiving the brunt of the fighting. War and pillage were accompanied, as always in Mozambican history, by famine and a virulent epidemic of smallpox, remembered as 'the smallpox of Mawewe', which ravaged the population of the south.[56] If a boom in the slave trade did not follow war and famine, as it had in the 1820s, this was because the slave trade from Lourenço Marques was definitely in decline. However, the first largescale movements of migrant labour to South Africa date from this period and are clearly connected to the chaos of the civil wars.

Between Delagoa Bay and Swaziland the country had been repeatedly fought over and it was possible to travel for four days without meeting a living person. The Swazi had not extended the boundaries of their kingdom but had contented themselves with creating the sort of waste that the Zulus had created on the high veldt in the 1820s. The Portuguese in Lourenço Marques had not been able to stop the Swazi raids, but inevitably they had attracted a mass of refugees who settled near the town so that the population that thus came under the formal or informal influence of the *presídio* was greatly increased and included most of the chieftaincies in the valleys of the Maputo and lower Incomati.

As a result of the famine and the Swazi raids, Umzila was forced to retreat north, attacking Sousa in Gorongosa in 1862, sacking Sofala in 1863 and finally establishing a new capital at Mossurize on the eastern slopes of the Chimanimani mountains. Despite the losses suffered during the civil war, he was still monarch of the largest of all the Nguni states and under his rule Gaza achieved its most impressive size — its raiding parties exacting tribute from the Portuguese *prazos* on the Zambesi as well as from the Tsonga south of the Limpopo, while his regiments were able to strike into south-eastern areas of Zimbabwe and into the northern Transvaal.

The sheer size of the Gaza monarchy and its ability to survive pressures that would have made other monarchies collapse raise questions about how this state was governed. The core of the state consisted of a number of aristocratic Nguni 'houses' associated with past Gaza monarchs and their near relatives. These houses were endowed with the tribute from sections of the population, and it was they who had the responsibility of collecting tribute and administering relations with subject peoples. The 'administrators' of the houses were the most powerful of the Nguni aristocracy and had the right of attending the king's council. The regimental structure was superficially similar to that of the Zulu. Some twenty-four age sets were formed during the existence of the state, but unlike the Zulu regiments they were not stationed in barracks and did not have their own headquarters or stocks of cattle. Many of them were recruited from among the *Mabulundlela* (the conquered Tsonga who were incorporated in the monarchy) and the Ndau who were the original population of the Mossurize area. It was indiscipline among the regiments that was to become the fatal weakness of the state in its final days.[57]

From the start there were two centres of the kingdom — Bilene south of the Limpopo which was favoured by Soshangane, where his 'house' was located and where he himself was buried, and Mossurize on the eastern slopes of the Zimbabwe plateau, good cattle country favoured by Umzila. Much of the rest of the country was not fully incorporated but, like the Zambesi *prazos*, was considered to be tributary to the various Nguni 'houses'.[58]

It has been suggested that during Umzila's reign the economic base of this great state was steadily weakening. Although its heartland in the Chimanimani mountains was healthy cattle country, the Gaza never achieved the prosperity and economic self-sufficiency of the Zulus. Indeed the Gaza suffered, as one historian has put it, from 'severe crises and blockages in the production and distribution of food'.[59] The ever-widening area that was raided indicated a continued dependence on plunder, while in the 1870s the growing scarcity of elephant in the low veldt made it difficult for the Gaza to pay for imported goods. It was in this economic context that the Gaza chiefs began to encourage the movement of migrant workers to South Africa and to replace them in the domestic economy with slaves. However, migrant labour undermined the social and economic structure of the kingdom in a way which wars had never done, and began the rapid absorption of the people of southern Mozambique into the modern world economy.

13

ZAMBESIA AND THE ZAMBESI WARS

Background to the wars

The Afro-Portuguese families who had established themselves along the Zambesi in the late sixteenth century and made this dry, inhospitable region of sand, dusty bush and mosquitoes the centre of their world, had never been easy subjects of the Portuguese Crown. Throughout the seventeenth and eighteenth centuries there were many incidents of rebellion, violence and outrageous lawlessness. Nevertheless, the interests of the Crown and the *muzungo* families had always broadly coincided and, without any independent means of exerting its authority, the Portuguese government had had to rely on the private armies made available to it by the far from disinterested Afro-Portuguese *prazo*-holders. The symbiosis proved effective. Although the fairs of the Zimbabwe plateau had been irretrievably lost at the end of the seventeenth century, new territories had been opened up at Zumbo and north of the river in Maravi country, and the lower reaches of the Zambesi valley itself remained securely part of the Portuguese colonial domain.

In the nineteenth century, however, the interests of the government and the major Afro-Portuguese families began to diverge and the result was a series of fratricidal wars in which the leading families fought for control of Zambesia, and the government tried to assert its authority in ways which went counter to the traditional interests of the Afro-Portuguese élite. While these obscure struggles, often a grotesque mixture of savagery and farce, were fought out within the cultural context of traditional Zambesi society, the world outside was rapidly changing. The explosive industrialisation of Europe and the United States spread its influence until eventually the armed stuggles on the Zambesi became absorbed and transformed by the global economic revolution of nineteenth-century imperialism. The *muzungo* families embarked on the conflict in a world relatively little changed since the sixteenth century, only to find that the outcome of their wars would find a place in the formation of the industrialised twentieth century.

In the eighteenth century the Afro-Portuguese families and their armed *chicunda* had lived from the services and tribute of the free peasantry of their *prazos* and from the profits of trade. The two occupations interlocked in such a way that the *muzungos* were usually able to maintain their position even if their trade suffered heavy losses or their peasantry rose in revolt and deserted. The fortunes of these families had been underpinned by the offices they held in Portuguese service, while intermarriage between the families created networks of interest that sustained their position against rivals, newcomers or officious bureaucrats.

However, the severe drought and famine of the 1820s undermined the agricultural base of the *prazos*, and created unstable social conditions and widespread banditry which interrupted trade with the fairs of the interior. Many Afro-Portuguese families abandoned Zambesia during this period, leaving *prazos* depopulated and untenanted and the old symbiosis of trade and agriculture in ruins. The severity of the social dislocation led to thousands of starving and destitute people being sold as slaves so that when the drought broke in the 1830s and more stable social conditions began to return, the patterns of economic activity had changed.

Gradually the Tonga population returned to the villages along the river but the surviving Afro-Portuguese families no longer looked to their peasantry to support their status. Instead they depended for their wealth and position on the links they had formed with the slave-traders. If during the height of the drought and the rule of the bandits, slaves had been obtained from anywhere and everywhere, by the 1840s most were being brought from areas further inland than the Zambesi valley. Slaving expanded up the valleys of the Luangwa and the Shire, and the lucrative nature of the trade ensured that the Portuguese governors and officials could be safely and profitably included within the network of those who shared the profits. However, the local governors were not being left to run things their own way and various forms of external pressure were increasingly being felt.

During the 1820s and 1830s Britain insistently demanded that the Portuguese put an end to the slave trade. The apparently high-minded British policy was made that much more acceptable to British opinion in that slavery was ceasing to be profitable for an industrial country, and economic common sense pointed to the much greater advantages that would accrue from the opening of Africa to legitimate forms of trade. In the seventeenth and eighteenth centuries the Portuguese had successfully excluded other Europeans from a share in the trade of eastern Africa, but Britain was now determined that this would cease. The campaign against the Mozambican slave trade would become a campaign to open up Mozambican markets. The British believed that the Portuguese officials in eastern Africa were all in league with the slavers and were without exception corrupt and untrustworthy. In general this may have been true, as officials brought up in the old mercantilist traditions sought to preserve what they saw as the life-blood of the commerce of the Portuguese community. However, some officials were beginning to reflect the liberal ideas that predominated in the metropolis. Now that Brazil was independent, the liberals believed that the African territories of Angola, São Tomé and Mozambique had great potential as settler colonies where plantation agriculture could help Portugal replace its lost Atlantic empire. By the 1840s coffee growing had begun in São Tomé and in the highlands inland from Luanda, and experimental plantings of sugar and cotton were being made in the south of Angola.

As early as 1829 the government had tried to establish a colony on Fernão Veloso Bay where the garrison was supposed to grow crops as well as control the slave trade, and a similar experiment was launched in November 1857 when thirty-six settlers were granted land concessions at Pemba on the northern coast where the city of Porto Amelia was eventually built. Both settlements ended quickly in disaster but they bore witness, however feebly, to the faith that enthusiasts still retained in the empire.[1]

Naturally the Zambesi valley, which continued to enjoy a largely unearned and undeserved reputation for being highly fertile, was also seen as having great potential for agricultural development. Successive liberal administrations passed laws intended to end the old emphyteutic *prazo* tenures and substitute for them a system of landholding which would encourage owners of capital to rent land and develop the region's agricultural resources. A decree of 6 November 1838, published in Lisbon, had forbidden the government to make any new *prazo* grants. Referring to the Rivers as 'uncultivated and almost depopulated', it declared that the '*prazos* have usually been granted through patronage to persons without the capital to be able to cultivate such vast territories'.[2] The decree of 22 December 1854 stated even more clearly that, 'far from producing the benefits expected from them, the *prazos* have, on the contrary, powerfully obstructed the development of agriculture in the most important districts of this province'.[3] The decree went as far as to abolish the *prazos* altogether, replacing the old feudal obligations of the peasantry with a straightforward obligation to pay tax, and granting freehold rights to those who actually farmed the land, with penalties if such land was left undeveloped. This freeing of the land from the old seigneurial regime was to be accompanied by putting an end to slavery, but here the government moved with great caution and the decree of April 1858 merely declared that slavery would be formally ended in twenty years' time.

British pressure, coupled with the ideological concern of the metropolitan liberals for legitimate commerce, land reform and agricultural development, was gradually driving a deep wedge between the interests of the Portugese government and its officials on the one hand

and those of the Afro-Portuguese families and their allies among the coastal Islamic trading communities on the other.

If one consequence of the war on the slave trade had been to alienate the government from its traditional supporters in the Afro-Portuguese community, a second consequence was that the slave-trading families came increasingly to recruit the slaves whom they found difficult to sell into their own private armies. The Afro-Portuguese and their Muslim counterparts along the northern coasts used these armies not only to pursue traditional feuds and rivalries, sometimes giving these the character of full-scale wars, but also to bring new and larger areas under their control. A vicious spiral twisted its way through the politics of Zambesia. As the government gradually intensified its measures against the slave trade and tried to introduce alternative economic strategies, so ever greater numbers of the unsold slaves accumulating in the hands of the traders were transformed into private armies which increased the capacity of the Afro-Portuguese and Muslim families to resist reform and change. The more the Portuguese government tried to improve its effectiveness, the stronger became its opponents until the government found itself confronted not with rebellious *prazo senhores* but with rebel chieftaincies ruling formidable militarised states.

The Aringa

At the heart of these slave-owning, slave-hunting and, in some cases, slave-dominated and slave-run states was usually to be found a fortified urban settlement called an *aringa*. This was a natural development from the traditional stockaded village common in the Zambesi valley area. Tonga villages had always been surrounded by stockades to protect them from wild animals, and in time of war these stockades had been further strengthened by earthworks to form a combination of palisade, ditch and bank that was formidably difficult to attack. There are many descriptions of such fortified strongholds dating from the wars of the seventeenth century, and the Portuguese themselves adapted this style of building for the defence of their *feiras* and other establishments.

The *aringa* which featured so dramatically in the Zambesi wars was in essence the traditional fortified stockade of the chief, but greatly increased in size. On 11 September 1858 Richard Thornton, geologist to Livingstone's Zambesi expedition, described the recently captured *aringa* at Shamo near the junction of the Shire and the Zambesi. The outer stockade was about a mile in circumference and enclosed a 'fine patch of trees':

[It] had been strong, about 15 feet high, of poles about the thickness
of one's leg & thicker. At the bottom a clay wall about 3 feet high
was built up to shelter the musket man. Facing the river were brick
earthworks.[4]

There was a second palisade and 'in places strong outworks of earth
hide the commencement of a third line of brick and mud defense'. The
walls of an *aringa* were frequently made of green timber cut in such a
way that the posts took root and formed walls of living trees which proved extraordinarily difficult to burn, cut down or even breach with
artillery. Frequently the walls were strengthened with earthwork
bastions on which cannon would be mounted — four brass cannon
were recovered when Shamo was captured.

Within the stockade there was usually a walled inner enclosure containing the house and other buildings of the chief. This replicated the
fencing-off of the chief's house which was common in traditional
Tonga villages, but in the *aringas* the houses would usually be of a Portuguese design reflecting the European life-style to which the chiefs
aspired. The *aringa* at Muchena, forming the capital of the Pereira
chieftaincy of Macanga, was built along the banks of the Revubwe
river and consisted of five enclosures, one containing the private
quarters of the head of the Pereira family together with his family
mausoleum and another being set aside for the chief's wives.[5]
Although the *aringa* was always associated with the great Afro-
Portuguese families of Zambesia, its essential forms were adopted by
important traditional chiefs like the kings of Barue, and by the
Muslim sheikhs of the northern coast whose style of government came
increasingly to resemble the traditional rule of the *prazo senhores*.

Massangano, the most famous *aringa* and centrepiece of the dramatic events of the Zambesi wars, was described by Castilho after its
final capture in 1888 as being 1,300 metres long and 150–180 metres
wide. It was built along the bank of the Zambesi just below the confluence with the Ruenha. Its perimeter wall consisted of a row of living
trees connected with poles laid crosswise between them and bound
with fibre cords. The site of the *aringa* was overlooked by a low rocky
outcrop and on that side the fortifcations were strengthened with an
inner stockade and one or two wooden towers. Almost in the centre
of the *aringa* was a raised knoll on which had been built the house of
the head of the Da Cruz family and the family mausoleum.[6] The rest
of the interior was filled with huts arranged roughly on each side of
a central street, and during the final phases of the siege of 1888 the
defenders made dugouts beneath the floors to protect themselves from
the fire of the Portuguese army.

The *aringas* tend to be represented as bandit strongholds. They were often besieged and became the focus for bloody struggles for the control of the surrounding regions. However, during the years of peace which interspersed the Zambesi wars, they served as urban centres of some importance. To the *aringa* were brought the slaves and other booty captured on expeditions. There were storehouses where the trade goods were kept and stockpiles of food and arms were accumulated. Thornton described how the defenders of Shamo abandoned 'great heaps of stores' including 'an enormous quantity of grain, rice, peas, beans etc., goats, fowls, several head of cattle etc.'[7] Cattle might be moved into the *aringas* for safety. Often the *aringa* was the centre of a more or less intensive agricultural activity which brought the surrounding countryside into production to support its inhabitants.

As well as the *aringas* that grew to be sizeable towns and which housed the entourage of the *muzungo* chiefs, the *aringa* system was developed to hold down the outlying parts of the countryside or subdue newly-conquered territory. Small stockades could be rapidly erected and garrisoned, and from these makeshift strongholds tribute could be levied over an area of the countryside. In this way the domains of the *prazo* chiefs could expand and new areas be brought into a state of tribute-paying obedience. When José Anselmo de Santanna first moved into the lower Luangwa valley, he built a stockaded camp where his family and *chicunda* were housed, Santanna's head wife supervising the distribution of food. Soon the *chicunda* were provided with wives of their own captured from the local population, and the requisitioning of food gave way to agricultural activity. The stockade was the embryo of a small *chicunda* state.[8]

The rule of the prazo chiefs

The large chieftaincies which thus grew up were dominated by the Afro-Portuguese families whose status depended on the rank and wealth they obtained within the Portuguese community and at the same time on the position they came to acquire *vis-à-vis* their African subjects and their *chicunda*. Within the Portuguese community the Afro-Portuguese families used their Portuguese names and maintained their nominal adherence to Roman Catholicism. They were married in church and summoned priests to baptise their children. They took part in the affairs of the Zambesi towns and aspired to hold office and be given ranks and titles. They relied on their Portuguese connections to dispose of their slaves and ivory and to import firearms and other trade goods. A few of them had pretensions to some education, possessing libraries or displaying other aspects of European culture. The Vas dos Anjos house in the stockade at Shamo had a

'quantity of very good furniture, also wine, decanters etc.'[9] According to Emile Durand, Sacasaca, head of the Pereiras in the 1880s, had
received the beginnings of an education at Quelimane, and a female
cousin of Joaquim José da Cruz lived for twenty-two years with her
husband in Paris before returning to Zambesia accompanied by their
son who had been brought up and educated as a Parisian.[10]

Looking back on the sway which the *muzungo* families held throughout Zambesia in the nineteenth century, the colonial statesman Ayres
d'Ornellas, who served in Mozambique in the 1890s, was outspoken
in his views:

> The almost constant state of war in which Zambesia has lived is
> principally due to the system of appointing natives or mulattos and
> *mestizos* as the sole authorities in the interior. The vicious product
> of whiteman and black woman or of Canarin and black woman,
> these individuals establish themselves with a brutal energy in dif-
> ferent parts of the country, setting themselves up with absolute
> authority like independent bandits. Around them, with the expec-
> tation of plunder, collect all the natives or *mestizos* who are
> discontented for whatever reason. Organising real robber bands
> they terrorise the rest of the population establishing a barbarous
> and despotic government. Impotent to conquer them and too weak
> to oppose them, the government considers it political skill to win
> them over with gifts, honouring them with titles, giving them
> official positions and on them founding the so-called dominion of
> the Portuguese Crown.[11]

As warlords, the heads of the families had to be successful in war
and in trade. They needed to keep the loyalty of their followers by
assuring a steady flow of booty, women slaves and imported luxuries,
and they had to be able to provide land on which their *chicunda* could
settle and found villages of their own. Many of them acquired a fearsome reputation for cruelty and for the barbarous punishments they
meted out. Although this reputation for savagery was no doubt frequently well-deserved, it is worth noting that to cultivate it served
them in good stead, enhancing the respect with which they were held
in a world of slavers, elephant hunters and *chicunda* mercenaries, and
frequently inducing panic among government soldiers at the mere
mention of their names.

As traditional chiefs, the heads of the *muzungo* families would
administer justice, exact services and tribute, and claim the chiefly
rights over ivory or other commodities. They would perform
ceremonial rites connected with sowing and harvesting of crops and
they had a well established role within traditional religion. They
themselves frequently consulted spirit mediums to obtain advice or

to legitimise their activities, and after death many of them became in their turn the object of active spirit cults. The mediums of past *prazo senhores* rose to be important and influential figures at the same time no doubt as the priests in the churches of Sena and Tete were saying masses for their souls.

Although all the stress has been on the importance of the chiefly families, the complexity of the networks of authority meant that a chiefly dynasty was not essential to the operation of the predatory *chicunda* states which by mid-century had largely replaced the old *prazos*. Increasingly the *chicunda capitães* themselves became an independent political force exercising power in parallel with the surviving traditional chiefs of the free population of Zambesia. On the death of the Alves da Silva brothers, for example, control of their domain passed to the captains of the *ensacas* of their private army who formed a sort of *chicunda* republic which marginalised the future role of the Alves da Silva family.[12] Similarly, when Manuel António de Sousa was suddenly removed from the scene following his capture by the Rhodesian police in 1890, the huge territory he had controlled was in effect divided between his leading *capitães*, who continued to control the population and to govern after a fashion for the next ten years.[13]

The leading Afro-Portuguese families and the Zambesi wars

The *prazo* families of the seventeenth and eighteenth centuries had probably mostly been European in origin, although their connections had often been with Goa rather than Portugal. By the second half of the eighteenth century the number of Indians entering Mozambique was increasing and by the early nineteenth century almost all the most important families on the Zambesi appear to have had their origin in India. Whatever their family background, however, intermarriage with numerous African wives meant that subsequent generations rapidly became physically indistinguishable from the local African population.

Four *muzungo* families were particularly involved in the early stages of the Zambesi wars. The Caetano Pereiras are first heard of in the eighteenth century as Indian gold traders and speculators in the country north of the Zambesi. They acquired the diggings at Missale and Java and began to send trading expeditions into the interior to the north; one of them, led by Manuel Caetano Pereira, reached the court of Mwata Kazembe in 1796. The Pereira dominance north of the Zambesi grew in the first half of the nineteenth century. The family built up its following among the Zimba and at the expense of the declining chieftaincy of Undi, and through marriage the Pereiras were eventually recognised as legitimate holders of the chieftaincy of

Chicucuru. Pedro Caetano Pereira (known as Choutama) held the rank of captain in the Tete militia and was entrusted by the Portuguese with helping to establish and defend the trading fair at Aruangoa do Norte in the Luangwa valley. Choutama was described by the Portuguese officer at Aruangoa as an illiterate, 'living like the kaffirs and chiefs, not only going about clothed like them but even resembling them in their customs and superstitions'.[14]

By 1840 the Pereira empire had come to dominate most of the country between the Luangwa and the Shire and the family sought to control the trade in ivory and slaves that reached the Zambesi by those routes. To achieve this supremacy they had not only to force the Zimba and Nyanja chiefs of the north bank to recognise their sovereignty but they also had to confront the power of more formidable rivals. For by 1840 another powerful *muzungo* dynasty was seeking to establish its dominance in the lower Shire valley.

The Vas dos Anjos family were also of Indian origin. Early in the nineteenth century they held land at Maruro near Quelimane, and at Mussembe, and rented the fertile and valuable *prazo* of Luabo where they provided a refuge for fugitives during the great drought. A marriage alliance with the powerful Goanese slave owner and trader, Galdino Faustino de Sousa, brought them trading interests in the Shire while other marriages linked them to António Cruz Coimbra, the leading financier of the slave trade on the lower River. On Sousa's death in 1853 his trading interests and his *aringa* on the Shire passed into the hands of his son-in-law, Paul Marianno Vas dos Anjos, who began to exploit the slave trade of the Shire with considerable effect, building for himself the formidable fortress at Shamo (already described).[15]

The third of the great Afro-Portuguese families of nineteenth-century Mozambique was that of the Alves da Silvas. António Alves da Silva came from the province of Beira in Portugal and established himself in the ivory and slave trade in the early nineteenth century. He married one of the *prazo*-holders of the Quelimane district and his daughter and two sons, João Bonifácio and Victorino Romão, were to make the family a power to be reckoned with in nineteenth-century Mozambique. The two brothers cashed in on the great expansion of the slave trade early in the century leading expeditions to the Luangwa and the Shire. With the banning of the official slave trade they, like so many of the other traders, were no longer able to use the port of Quelimane, so they began to ship their slaves from their own anchorage at the mouth of the Moniga river which they fortified with an *aringa*. However, it was in the interior of what became known as Maganja da Costa that the Silva brothers built their principal stronghold and assembled their *chicunda* army.

The standing army of the Alves da Silva brothers was made up of *ensacas* of 250 men, each under their own captains. The *ensacas* were stationed in fortified stockades in the interior while the headquarters were located in the large fortified encampment at Errive. The *aringa* of Maganja da Costa, called M'Passue after the African title assumed by the family head, was reputedly the largest ever built in Mozambique and later became the capital of a sort of *chicunda* military republic. Through marriage the Silvas were connected with most of the principal *muzungo* families of the Quelimane area including that of Nunes, one of whose members later in the century acquired the position of honorary consul to the British government in Quelimane.[16]

Finally, one must turn to the Da Cruz, by far the most famous of the Zambesi dynasties of the nineteenth century. Nicolau da Cruz came originally from Siam and entered Portuguese service as a soldier, arriving in the Rivers in 1767 with a detachment of Portuguese troops. Unlike the other families that have been mentioned, the Da Cruz made their way not in trade but through the more orthodox route of acquiring *prazos*, marrying heiresses and holding government office. Nicolau da Cruz married into one of the Zambesian families, held various Portuguese offices in Tete district and had numerous progeny who also married locally and extended the network of the Da Cruz interests. It is highly characteristic of the nature of Afro-Portuguese influence that one of his sons, António José, married a daughter of the Monomotapa, thus establishing a family connection with one of the most prestigious chiefly dynasties of the valley.[17]

In 1807 António was allegedly involved in the mysterious events surrounding the death of the governor of the Rivers, Vilas Boas Truão — a crime of which he was probably innocent but for which he was executed in Mozambique in 1813. This contretemps did not, however, prevent the continued growth of the family's influence in the Tete region. Hitherto, with the exception of António, the family had remained closely connected with the Portuguese settler world of Tete and showed no signs of the independence and rebelliousness that later made them a by-word throughout Zambesia. The transformation in their fortunes came with the career of Joaquim José, one of António's sons.

Joaquim, described in later life as 'thin to the point of looking like a mummy . . . with features pronouncedly Chinese', was born about 1810 into a respected and widely connected family of *prazo*-holders.[18] At first, like his great rivals the Pereiras and the Vas dos Anjos, he made his career in trade, since the basis for the wealth of the surviving Afro-Portuguese families had shifted from agriculture to the slave trade as a result of the great famine of the 1820s. Joaquim accompanied Gamitto, a relative by marriage, to Kazembe in 1831 and worked for two other Zambesian traders, José Vicente Aquino and an Indian, João da Costa Xavier. With his commercial wealth he began to acquire *prazos* of his own and in 1849 rented Massangano from the government. There, at the juncture of the Ruenha and the Zambesi, where Manuel Paes de Pinho had dominated the Zambesi in the seventeenth century, he built the great *aringa* of Massangano which was to be one of the most fought-over and bitterly contested few acres in the whole of Africa (Map 6).

These four great families dominated the early stages of the Zambesi wars, but it should be emphasised that they were only the most prominent of a number of Afro-Portuguese dynasties whose family connections formed a web of commercial interest and political power throughout the valley in the nineteenth century. Of considerable importance, not least because they remained largely loyal to Portugal, were the Ferrão family of Sena. They were also of Indian origin and by the 1820s had acquired *prazos* and extensive commercial influence throughout the delta and along the trade routes to Manica and Kiteve. Francisco Henriques Ferrão was governor of the Rivers in the 1820s and it is clear that he used his position as a Portuguese official to obtain extensive influence for his family throughout the whole of the lower Zambesi. In 1829 he was replaced in this post by Vasconcellos e Cirne, his bitter opponent, but when the latter died Ferrão returned to power, briefly becoming Governor of Mozambique itself when that post was put into commission in 1830.[19]

The Ferrão family continued to dominate the Sena area, remaining closely associated with the government but also acquiring links with the Gaza kings and apparently acting as their agent in the Sena region. Later in the century they were able to raise soldiers from the Gaza Nguni for use in the Zambesi wars — not the least of the services they rendered the government.

The Zambesi wars

As has been described in earlier chapters, the peoples of the Zambesi valley and neighbouring regions failed to acquire a political stability to match the social stability of the family homestead. The area was prone to the depredations of armed bandits who sometimes established themselves as a parallel political system overarching the traditional chieftaincies but seldom achieved the same level of continuity over long periods. In the 1820s the great famine had led to the re-emergence of banditry and at its height armed bands of former Portuguese slaves or destitute peasants from surrounding chieftaincies had roamed the Zambesi region at will, their depredations matched

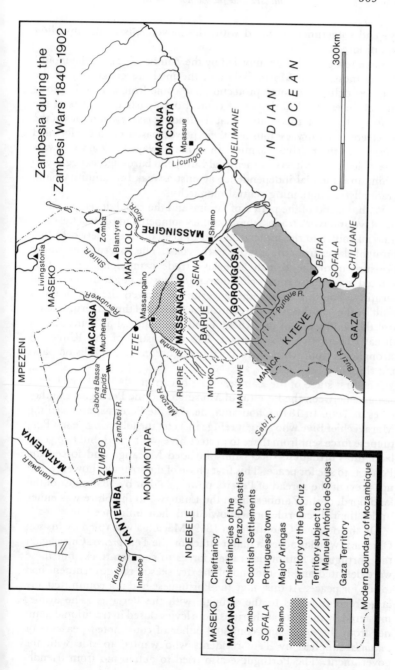

Zambesia during the 'Zambesi Wars' 1840–1902

MASEKO — Chieftaincy
MACANGA — Chieftaincies of the Prazo Dynasties
▲ Zomba — Scottish Settlements
● SOFALA — Portuguese town
■ Shamo — Major Aringas
— Territory of the DaCruz
— Territory subject to Manuel António de Sousa
— Gaza Territory
— Modern Boundary of Mozambique

by, and sometimes confused with, the movements of the invading Nguni forces.

Some refuge had been afforded by the Zambesi islands, the mountain fastnesses like Morumbala and the intricate geography of the Zambesi delta, and some protection had come from warlords strong enough to establish a degree of control over particular parts of the country. It was in this context that the leading *muzungo* families of the nineteenth century established their power based on their fortified *aringas* and their private armies. In so many ways the Zambesi wars resemble the activities of a medieval European baronage struggling to maintain its feudal independence against a weak but ambitious and gradually strengthening central monarchy.

With the end of the period of famine and the rapid development of the slave and ivory trades, these families competed to control the commercial routes to the hinterland and to keep open the networks that brought slaves from the interior to the coast. The government, under pressure from the British anti-slave trade campaign, for its part wanted to see these routes closed or at the least brought under official scrutiny. For this reason the government viewed the fortifications built by the Vas dos Anjos to control the Shire and the Da Cruz to control the confluence of the Ruenha and the Zambesi as being such a threat. These two *aringas* stood, like the castles of the Rhine, as strongholds from which Afro-Portuguese barons levied tolls on passing shipping.

The first stage of the Zambesi wars began in 1840 and involved a struggle between the Pereiras of Macanga and the Portuguese authorities in Tete. In 1840 Choutama, head of the Pereiras, attacked the Maravi chief Bive who sought refuge in Tete; the following year a Portuguese force sent from there to protect Bive was routed, but two years later the Portuguese successfully invaded Macanga and forced the Pereiras to sue for peace. This first phase of the struggle, however, did not prevent the spread of Pereira power, so that by 1850 most of the land north of the Zambesi from the Luangwa to the Shire was either under their direct rule or acknowledged their influence.[20]

On the death of Choutama in 1849, Macanga was ruled by his son Chissaca, who launched a major attack on the Tete *prazos*. Once again the Portuguese authorities raised forces to counterattack, but these were defeated and by the end of the dry season the government had to sue for peace. At this stage the Portuguese had not committed any large regular forces to the struggle with the Pereiras. The armies mustered by the Tete authorities were levies raised in traditional manner from the *prazos* and consisted either of conscripted peasants or *chicunda* supplied by Tete residents who wanted to side with the government. The Portuguese also tried to obtain aid from friendly chiefs and the 1849 attack on Macanga included a contingent of warriors supplied by Chibisa, one of the Nyanja chiefs of the Shire, who felt threatened by the growing power of the Pereiras.

For their part the Pereiras were clearly becoming increasingly worried by the growing influence of the Da Cruz family whose network of *prazos* spread threateningly throughout the whole district. It is significant that it was in 1849 that the Da Cruz were allowed to lease Tipue and Massangano, which gave them effective control of the river below Tete. Chissaca's attack in that year was clearly levelled at them, and many of their *prazos* were raided. Augusto de Castilho suggests that the origin of the quarrel between the two families can be traced to a present of six bottles of gin sent to Choutama by an Indian trader called Francisco João Xavier who was related to the Da Cruz. Choutama died after drinking the gin (hardly surprising if he had consumed all six bottles), and his successor accused Xavier of witchcraft and demanded that he be surrendered to justice.[21]

The threat posed to the Pereiras by Massangano was explicitly the reason for the next attack launched by Chissaca on the Tete district. In 1853 the Pereiras struck up an alliance with the Macombes of Barue who also felt themselves threatened by the Da Cruz, crossed the Zambesi with a large army and laid siege to Massangano. For the first but not the last time, this famous fortress was the object of concentrated attack. However, it resisted Chissaca's assaults and by October the investing army had begun to disintegrate. Famine and disease worked havoc in its ranks and the approach of the rains provided the final persuasion for the fighters, who were also peasant farmers, to return to their own country for the sowing. The first phase of the Zambesi wars had become a stalemate. The Pereiras ruled in Macanga and their influence extended far up the Luangwa, while the power of the Da Cruz on the Zambesi grew ever greater, their *aringa* at Massangano enabling them to exert a real control over river traffic passing from Tete to the sea.[22]

Further down the river, the slave trade of the Shire and the delta area was controlled by a network of slaving interests at the heart of which was the Vas dos Anjos family which also felt itself threatened by the rising power of the Da Cruz. In 1852 António Cruz Coimbra, a relative of the Vas dos Anjos, was robbed of ivory worth 4 *contos* as it was being taken by river to Quelimane.[23] As a result it was a combination of the trading interests of the lower Zambesi that launched the next assault on the Da Cruz. An army raised on the lower river *prazos*, including a contingent supplied by the Alves da Silvas, marched up-river in April 1853 and was joined in May by Portuguese troops sent from the metropolis — and by the slaves of Galdino Faustino de Sousa, until their master's death caused them to desert.

The whole expedition was eventually put under the command of Livingstone's friend, Major Tito Araujo Sicard. Sicard's army advanced through the heat of the dry season but its morale was low and eventually it disintegrated and fled after a brief encounter with the forces of the Da Cruz at Bandar.

Joaquim da Cruz, known as 'Nhaude' (the spider), the man who more than any other had built the fortunes of the family, died in 1855 and for the next twelve years there was peace between the Da Cruz and their enemies. Joaquim's successor was António da Cruz, called 'Bonga' (the wild cat). António had some trouble establishing control of his *prazos* and asserting his mastery over his own followers. At the same time he appears to have tried to re-establish his position in Portuguese society, sending his children to be baptised and seeking for himself military rank in the Portuguese militia.[24]

In the mean time government attention became focussed on the Vas dos Anjos whose power had come to seem more threatening even than that of the Da Cruz. In 1855 and 1856 *chicunda* in Paul Marianno's service raided the *prazos* round Sena, their object almost certainly being to obtain slaves and assert the family dominance over rivals. From 1855 the area between the Shire and the coast had also been raided by Mussa Quanto at the head of his private army built on the profits of the Angoche slave trade. The disorder on the lower river was becoming a great embarrassment, with the British anti-slavery cruisers increasingly investigating the nature of the trade from Mozambique ports and a British expedition under Livingstone on its way to the Zambesi.

In 1857 the government moved again to try to exert some control over the interior of its Zambesian territories. In that year Paul Marianno came to Quelimane on business and the authorities took their courage in their hands, arrested him and had him transferred to Mozambique. His brother, also confusingly called Bonga, at once took the main body of the family *chicunda* to Shamo near the mouth of the Shire and proceeded to fortify the great *aringa* there. In May 1858 the government launched its attack on the Vas dos Anjos, a body of Portuguese troops acting as a nucleus for the forces raised from other Afro-Portuguese friendly to the government.[25]

The campaign was witnessed and graphically described by the members of Livingstone's Zambesi Expedition who arrived at about the time of the start of the campaign. As they advanced the government troops fired the bush to prevent ambushes and wiped out the villages and food reserves of Marianno's peasants. Eventually on 9 September Shamo was abandoned by its defenders before any serious attack was launched. Kirk and Thornton both speculated that this was due to shortage of ammunition.[26] The Vas dos Anjos and their followers now escaped up the Shire carrying with them the seigneurial institutions and predatory life-style of Afro-Portuguese society. In 1861 a further government expedition was sent to dislodge Paul Marianno from Morumbala mountain from where, after his release from Mozambique, he was once again threatening to dominate the river.

Meanwhile another military expedition was being assembled to attack the slavers in Angoche. If it was successful it would strike a blow at the main base of the illegal slave trade and bring the whole coastline between Quelimane and Mozambique Island firmly under Portuguese control — something that was becoming increasingly necessary as the growing rivalry between Britain and France in Zanzibar and in the Comoro Islands made the international scene ever more threatening. The attack on Angoche was the pet project of João Bonifácio Alves da Silva and it proved a triumphant albeit bloody success. João Bonifácio was killed and his principal opponent, Mussa Quanto, fled into the interior, but the stockades of Angoche were stormed and the island and port were taken and garrisoned by the government.

The taking of Angoche, coming so soon after the fall of Shamo, was a significant success. Although no effective Portuguese administration was established in the Angoche region till the twentieth century, Portugal's claims to sovereignty along the coast were now secure and there was never to be any serious challenge to them during the scramble for Africa. Moreover, the death of João Bonifácio and the subsequent turmoil among the Alves da Silva family and their followers was an unforeseen blessing since it meant that there was no powerful Afro-Portuguese dynasty to threaten Portuguese control of the region. Mussa Quanto, however, had escaped and the independent line of Angoche sultans inevitably became a focus for various forms of resistance to Portuguese colonialism.

Between 1861 and 1863 the Portuguese also watched the British depart. In 1861 the UMCA mission was established in the Shire Highlands, threatening to establish a permanent British presence in the interior. However, the mission was withdrawn after little more than a year and Livingstone himself departed finally in 1863, much to Portugal's relief. The Portuguese responded to the challenge presented by Livingstone with the reoccupation of Zumbo in 1862, completing a trio of successful enterprises undertaken since 1858.

The military disasters at Massangano

The success of Portugal's more forward policies seemed to warrant another attempt to bring the Da Cruz to obedience. Relations with

Massangano had been gradually deteriorating and with the confidence derived from the success of the attacks on Shamo and Angoche, the government turned its attention to eliminating the threat of Massangano. Although the governors of Mozambique had not been able to deploy effective metropolitan troops and had to rely on local resources to maintain their authority, their confrontations with the slavers had not been unsuccessful. They had been able to play the powerful interest groups off against each other and had enlisted the private armies of one group of Afro-Portuguese families to take on those of another group. These resources had been deployed to humble first the Pereiras, then the Vaz dos Anjos and finally the over-powerful sultan of Angoche. There remained the enigmatic but undeniably powerful clan of the Da Cruz whose *prazos* spanned both banks of the Zambesi and who dominated the approaches to Tete and the high veldt to the south. It must have seemed that a successful campaign against the Da Cruz only awaited a commander with enough patience and determination to raise an alliance among the Zambesi *senhores*, and that a few metropolitan troops with the necessary supplies would create the atmosphere of confidence necessary to bring the local *chicunda* over to the government's side.

In July 1867, at the height of the dry season, the governor of Tete, Miguel Gouveia, assembled a force from the surrounding *prazos* and advanced on Massangano which lay only a few day's march away. His motley force was ambushed and massacred and the governor himself was executed by the victors. Bonga's victory had been fortuitous and did not result in any massive Da Cruz counterattack. That the war with Massangano turned into a major tragedy was due to the over-reaction of the Portuguese metropolitan authorities, determined to avenge the defeat and assert a direct authority in Zambesia which their predecessors had mostly been wise enough not to attempt.

In November 1867, 400 regular troops arrived under the command of Oliveira Queiros. Local auxiliaries were recruited on the Sena *prazos* and a contingent was supplied by Manuel António de Sousa, who first rose to prominence in Mozambican affairs in connection with this campaign. Queiros attempted to take Massangano in the rainy season and actually blockaded the *aringa* until his force ran short of supplies and ammunition. Having failed to make a spectacular capture he found his auxiliaries melting away and he was able to retreat in relative good order down-river where he was relieved of his command. In May 1868 a third expedition set out, accompanied by 500 regular troops. Once again the Portuguese reached Massangano and laid siege to the stockade, causing considerable loss of life and privation among Bonga's followers. However, sorties by the Da Cruz warriors overran the Portuguese positions and the army was routed in lurid and spectacular fashion leaving hundreds of dead and massive booty in the hands of the victors.[27]

A major military effort was now made by the Portuguese to avenge these disasters. An expedition was raised over the following year with contingents recruited in Portugal and in Goa. Some 850 regular troops, a sizeable army for any European campaign in Africa at this time, arrived in Zambesia in May 1869 to form the basis of an army of conquest. Once again, however, the sheer size of the military force guaranteed failure rather than success. It proved impossible to provide adequate transport or supply the troops who had to pass through country infested with fighters in the service of the Da Cruz. Although Massangano was reached, the commander was unable to sustain a siege and resolved on a retreat. During the fatal night when the retreat began, Bonga's men sallied out and the retreat rapidly became a rout with the army disintegrating and scattering in fragments down-river or up-river in the direction of Tete.[28] Thereafter, for nearly two decades, the Portuguese left the Da Cruz alone, and the formation of the colonial state proceeded around this proud and independent bandit enclave.

The rout of four Portuguese expeditions in three years provides a spectacle of military disaster almost without parallel in the history of Europe's relations with Africa. Zambesi warfare was not a pleasant affair, and the fighting was accompanied by violence and atrocity that made the events still more lurid. The whitening skulls of Portuguese soldiers adorned the stockade at Massangano for decades to come — an awe-inspiring sight for those passing along the river. António da Cruz became the apotheosis of the Zambesian warlord — that three-headed monster, one of whose heads wore a Portuguese military hat reflecting his status as *prazo*-holder, officer of the militia and pillar of the Portuguese establishment, one the insignia of an African chief, and one simply adorned with the trophies and booty of a successful bandit. However, the political power of the Da Cruz was never as great as their military victories led contemporaries to suppose. They never ruled over a cohesive or well-organised state and dissent within the ruling family was always rife. The stockade of Massangano was essentially the centre of a bandit operation and the outlying parts of the Da Cruz domain paid tribute to the family only when their power and prestige was in the ascendant. Massangano itself was a formidable fortification made in traditional Zambesi style with a stockade of living trees which could not be breached by the sort of light artillery which accompanied Portuguese expeditions. Yet the *aringa* was sited by the river and overlooked by a low hill, which in fact made it extremely vulnerable. It was Portuguese military incompetence and not the inherent strength

of the *aringa* which caused the Portuguese such severe military problems for so long.

Massangano was situated in a strategically important area where
tolls could be levied on river traffic and where access to the interior
via the Ruenha valley could be controlled. However, it was not a
region of great agricultural wealth or dense population. Da Cruz
power was never rooted in a large and obedient group of subjects, and
the limitations of their position were always seen most strikingly after
they had inflicted some sensational defeat on a luckless Portuguese
expedition. These victories were not followed by great extensions of
Da Cruz power. The family never controlled nearby Tete, let alone
the more remote settlements of Sena or Quelimane. Moreover, the
humiliating defeats of the Portuguese military had surprisingly little
long-term effect on the development of Mozambique. They neither
brought forward, nor significantly delayed, the expansion into the
interior that was just about to begin and in which other Afro-
Portuguese families were to play a major part. Nor did the Da Cruz
and their activities have any long-term influence on the development
of commercial capitalism, which had already begun to spread rapidly
into the coastal areas in the 1870s.

14

MOZAMBIQUE AND THE SCRAMBLE
FOR AFRICA, 1879–1891

Introduction: emergence of a coherent modern state

As Livingstone and his companions steamed up the Zambesi in 1858, bumping on sandbanks, stopping every mile or so to cut wood, and spending hot irritable evenings on the little *MaRobert* quarrelling, medicating each other and writing their voluminous diaries, they were witnessing a world recognisably the same as that described by the Jesuit observer Manuel Barreto in the 1660s and not dissimilar from that seen by Father Monclaro in the 1570s. But the *MaRobert* was itself a portent — a steam-powered boat from the world of the industrial revolution packed with hardy pioneers from Calvinist Scotland, carrying with them not only their scientific instruments and their Bibles but also their Protestant work ethic and the ideology of modern capitalism. The tensions that developed between them and the Catholic Afro-Portuguese of Zambesia provide an endlessly fascinating study in Weberian social analysis.

However, behind the old forms of Mozambique's existence — the *prazos* of Zambesia, the faded ochre-washed grandeur of Mozambique Island and the slaving port of Ibo, the palm groves and mosques of the coastal sheikhdoms — economic changes were about to erupt like so many subterranean volcanoes to create the new political landscape of twentieth-century Africa. Change in Africa has never been mono-causal, and in the late nineteenth century the peoples of what was to become Mozambique experienced economic change from four main directions. First, economic change came from the steady penetration of eastern Africa by Indian merchant capital. Second came the pressures of British-inspired free trade liberalism with its attack on the slave trade and its promotion of 'legitimate' commerce. The third factor was the slow but important transformation in the metropolitan Portuguese economy which began to effect Lisbon's policy towards its colonies. The fourth and probably the greatest instrument of change was the South African mining revolution and the rapid creation of a major industrial economy in one of the economically most primitive parts of the continent. For the first three, economic change occurred over a sufficiently long period to allow for social adjustments to the old regime and the avoidance of violent political change. However, the mining revolution and the demands of mining capital transformed the economies of the region with great rapidity and led to equally rapid and far-reaching changes in its political fabric.

Taken together, these changes were to create new economic structures more productive than anything that had existed previously, which helped to weld the numerous small societies, with their centuries-old self-sufficiency, into large interdependent regions. The new level of economic activity needed a government which could provide the necessary infrastructure and guarantee security for fixed investments, and by the end of the century a new political system had come into existence to meet these needs.

Indian capital and economic growth in the nineteenth century

Indians had traded with the peoples of eastern Africa for hundreds of years, but only in the late seventeenth century did Indian merchant capital begin to look to the western Indian Ocean as a major area of investment. Indian merchant houses based in Bombay or Gujarat began to open branches under the protection of the Omanis in Zanzibar and of the Portuguese in Mozambique Island. From these centres they spread out along the coasts, establishing agencies in many of the smaller coastal ports under local Swahili rulers or Portuguese governors. Indian merchant houses conducted a number of operations — they traded in ivory and other international commodities, owned ships and acted as bankers or financiers entering into partnerships or advancing credit to other merchants. They also took a major role in state finance and provided the credit to underpin the Omani sultanate, running its customs service and treasury.[1]

By the end of the eighteenth century, the activities of Indian merchant houses were beginning to extend inland. Indians were prominent in the Zumbo trade when that *feira* was for a brief period the foremost trading station of eastern Africa, and during the early nineteenth century Indian merchant houses established branches along the main caravan routes from Zanzibar to the great lakes.

Although Indian merchants themselves did not play a prominent part in the Mozambique slave trade, they provided the financial resources which enabled commerce to grow in volume in the post-slave trade era. Before the nineteenth century there had been no coherent commercial infrastructure in the Mozambique interior. Apart from the ancient gold fairs and a few large well-established markets where caravans halted to meet the agents of coastal dealers, there had been no systematic attempt to develop commercial outlets, and imported goods had been distributed within the context of traditional society. It was to be the role of the Indian commercial community to create a new infrastructure for trade and so stimulate the subsistence peasant economies to produce for the market.

The most successful Indian merchants were prepared to deal in a wide variety of products as well as the items of high value such as ivory or gold. Their mode of operation was to establish stores where imported goods could be exchanged for local products — often in small quantities. Each merchant thus became his own *feira*. Just as the old fairs had concentrated the tiny quantities of gold, produced in river washings by peasant miners, thereby creating a major international commerce, so the Indian store was to concentrate the tiny surpluses of groundnuts, maize, cashew, sesame, hides, wax, honey and other items of peasant production. Once collected at an Indian store, these items could enter into the mainstream of international commerce which previously isolated peasant communities could never hope to achieve. The UMCA missionary W.P. Johnson described the sort of commercial infrastructure the Indians had created in an account of a journey from Lake Malawi to Quelimane in 1884. He records that when only three days from the coast

. . . .we found a man . . . who knew the Portuguese, but not one of them was seen. We reached the place to which caravans are allowed to come and trade. Here coconut palms, cashew-nut trees, and limes were abundant. A man, son of an Indian and a Makua woman, who has become a christian, presides, and was very attentive to us. Several Indians had goods-stores there, and already had news of a caravan we had passed on the way. . . . A long road led to a place where there was an office with a Goanese clerk, and Indian helper; and there we got a boat . . . we did not see a Portuguese till we were in Quelimane.[2]

The effects of Indian trading methods were first visible in the growing trade in foodstuffs. There is little doubt that the great drought of the 1820s promoted the production of food crops in the relatively unaffected areas. The scale of the trade in provisions led the Portuguese authorities in Zambesia to complain that the coastal *mujojos* (Muslim shipowners who often had Indian backers) were undercutting the Portuguese *prazo*-owners in the markets.[3] The continuation of the clandestine slave trade along the coast in the 1840s and 1850s may have held back agricultural development, and high freight costs certainly discouraged potential exporters.[4] Nevertheless the 1850s saw the beginnings of a commercial revolution which was to transform economic conditions on the coast and, in the long run, to have a profound effect on political perceptions of the region.

In 1853 the liberal government in Portugal introduced a series of measures designed to open up trade in the colonies. The experiment of the 1820s was repeated with new customs houses being established at Ibo, Quelimane, Inhambane and Lourenço Marques, so that goods no longer had to go to Mozambique Island to pay duties. Tariffs were lowered and the trade of the colony was opened to foreigners. At first the implementation of these radical measures was suspended by the governor-general and they did not become fully operative until 1857. However, in 1853 a commercial treaty had been signed with France and this appears to have attracted the Marseilles firms of Fabre et Fils and Régis Aîné to establish themselves first on Mozambique Island and then at all the major coastal towns.[5] At first the French concentrated on the shipping of contract *engagé* labour to the Indian Ocean sugar islands, but in 1855 the Portuguese outlawed this traffic and the French firms turned increasingly to the shipment of agricultural products, in particular oilseeds purchased for them by Indian agents. In 1862 tropical raw materials from Mozambique were shown at the London Exhibition and in 1867 in Paris, and the opening of the Suez Canal in 1869 lowered freight costs — all of which helped promote commerce.[6]

For twenty years the French retained a position comparable to that of the Indian merchant houses in the overseas trade of the Mozambique ports. The French also became important in coastal shipping, and their warehouses and installations represented some of the first private capital investment to be made in Mozambique. Fig. 14.1 shows the proportions of Mozambique's trade carried on with each of its main trading partners in the mid 1870s, while Table 14.1 shows the nationality of the major trading agents.

The combined effect of French and Indian commercial entrepreneurship and Portuguese liberal legislation brought major changes to trade and hence to agriculture throughout lowland Mozambique. Exports registered at the new customs houses indicate the extent of the economic revolution that got underway barely twenty years after the end of the great Mozambique drought. Total customs receipts rose from 87,554$000 in 1856 to 182,550$000 in 1873–4.[7] This growth was primarily export-led and now at last it was exports produced by Mozambican peasants rather than commodities plundered by slave and ivory traders. Sesame exported through Mozambique Island rose from 6,841 *panjas* in 1861–2 to 88,847 in 1871–2; from Quelimane in the same decade amounts rose from 38 to 13,191 *panjas*. Exports from Ibo in the decade 1859–69 rose from 4,477 *panjas* to 27,388 *panjas*. The export of groundnuts expanded too, and in 1870–1 Quelimane registered exports of 25,174 *panjas* and Inhambane 164,980.[8] Such a huge growth of exports naturally sucked in additional imports. Whereas Indians traditionally imported cloth, the French specialised in iron hoes and firearms — the hoes being much in demand from an

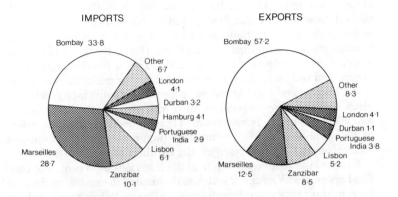

Fig. 14.1. MOZAMBIQUE'S TRADING PARTNERS, 1876 (%)

Table 14.1. NATIONALITY AND BUSINESS TRANSACTED
BY COMMERCIAL AGENTS, 1876 (*in milréis*)

Nationality	Imports	Exports
Banyans and Pathias	220,635	305,342
French	209,353	100,631
Portuguese and Indo-Portuguese	76,476	34,229
Muslims (incl. Swahili)	76,087	95,113
Dutch	20,396	20,871
Parsees	3,630	20,072
English	1,143	—

Source: A. Rita-Ferreira, 'A Sobrevivência do mais Fraco. Moçambique no 3
Quartel do Século XIX', p. 309.

expanding agricultural sector but helping to displace a local artisan
production and regional commerce, and the firearms finding their
way to embattled African chieftaincies in the interior and to the
elephant hunters on the rapidly receding ivory frontier.[9]

In the 1870s the beginnings of the mining revolution led to a great
expansion in the South African market, and the export of foodstuffs
and raw materials produced within the Mozambican peasant economy expanded once again. To encourage this development, João de
Andrade Corvo, the minister with responsibility for the colonies, had
declared the Zambesi open for foreign trade and introduced a new

tariff in 1877 which drastically reduced the duties on exported food-crops. As a result Dutch, French and British trading houses established branches in Zambesia, and Indian store-owners greatly widened the scope of their activities.[10] The boom in the export of peasant-grown cash crops lasted till the 1890s. By that time South Africa's own production had increased to meet the demands of the mines, and Indian traders, ever sensitive to changes in market conditions, had turned their attention to providing consumer goods and alcohol for the mineworkers returning with their accumulated pounds and *xelims* (shillings). It was recorded that immediately after the defeat of Gungunhana in 1895, some 900 Indian merchants established themselves in Gaza to cream off the earnings of the miners.[11]

North of the Zambesi, in spite of slaving, raids by Nguni, and conflict between the Yao chiefs which so dominated the middle of the century, peasant agricultural production and the collection of wild rubber continued to develop rapidly and provided good business for coastal traders. Between 1873 and 1883 the duty paid on rubber exported from Mozambique rose from £443 to £60,000 (exports rose from 42 tons in 1874 to 447 tons in 1887). In the 1880s Henry O'Neill, the British consul, described 'hundreds of thousands of acres which are now under cultivation', all cleared by peasant hoes and axes and producing sesame and groundnuts. These, after harvest, were

> . . . .packed in baskets of native manufacture and carried on the heads of blacks, in some cases a distance of eighty or a hundred miles, to the house of the coast-trader, there to be bartered for cloth, beads, powder, and the rest, and to be stored until an opportunity occurs for shipment.[12]

When the Nyassa Company sent an expedition to explore its concession north of the Lurio river in 1893, it reported:

> We were always meeting traders in the villages from Ibo and Mikandani, and met many caravans loaded for the coast with ivory, bees-wax, gum copal, indiarubber, oil nuts, rice etc. although we were very little on the true caravan trail.[13]

A description of the charter territory written for the Company in 1899 frankly admitted that the culture of oil seeds and the collection of rubber were 'the only two industries which can be said to be firmly established, and they are entirely due to spontaneous native effort'.[14]

The undoubted commercial success of the Indian merchant community produced very different reactions in contemporary observers. R.C.F. Maugham, who held various consular appointments in east and central Africa, wrote in somewhat romantic vein about the typical Indian trader:

Not only is he wonderfully impervious to the effects of the climate, but he possesses the inestimable facility of easily acquiring a fluent knowledge of native tongues. . . . No profit is too small or inconsiderable; no time too long to devote to the successful driving of a bargain. His manner of life, domestic in the extreme, is nevertheless so thrifty, so frugal, and his wants . . . are so inexpensive, that few there are who cannot remit a few rupees to India at the end of the year.[15]

However, the Portuguese high commissioners, António Ennes and Joaquim Mouzinho de Albuquerque, made little secret of their desire to eradicate Indian influence from Mozambique entirely. While Ennes had tried to hamper their activity in Zambesia by restricting trade on the *prazos* to specific centres, for Mousinho the Indians were people who 'trade without civilising . . . defrauding the black in every way they can'. He wanted to prevent them building stores in the interior and to insist on properly constructed buildings near the military command posts. Above all, he wanted to prohibit Indians from selling alcohol and firearms, the principal items that attracted Africans to the stores.[16]

Indian merchants not only financed traditional trade and shipping and bought peasant surplus production in the interior but they also created much of the infrastructure of early modern Mozambique. Outside the usually crumbling walls of the *presídios* and governors palaces, the building of residences, warehouses, stores etc. was usually the work of Indians; they provided most of the coastal shipping and financial and commercial services; and the Indian rupee circulated widely in the colony. Moreover, by no means all Indians were destined to return home. Many Indian men married African women, and Indians or Afro-Indians provided much of the skilled manpower — literate clerks, accountants and administrators.[17]

British influence on the development of Mozambique

Many of the Indians who traded in Mozambique came from British India and by their presence closely involved the British Indian government in the affairs of eastern Africa. However, Britain was becoming involved with Mozambique for other reasons. The East India Company had largely ignored the east African coast and used the Comoro Islands as a way station, and it was not until Britain acquired control of South Africa in 1806 and Mauritius in 1810 that London became at all interested in the south-west corner of the Indian Ocean. In the 1820s Commodore Owen's survey ships visited the Mozambique coast, and Owen raised the British flag on the southern shore of the

Maputo river in 1823, realising how important this great natural harbour was for the future of the area. The following year British commercial interests established themselves permanently at Port Natal, and Britain's stake in the trade of the southern hinterland of Delagoa Bay began to grow rapidly.

Britain's war against the slave trade, which began to effect events in the Indian Ocean soon after the end of the Napoleonic wars, involved diplomatic initiatives and a naval patrol along the coast. The campaign soon became a conscious attempt both to suppress slaving and to promote a new economic and social order. However, it was not until Britain forced Portugal to sign a treaty guaranteeing rights of mutual search in 1842 that British warships regularly began to patrol the Mozambique Channel and hunt for slavers in the swamps and estuaries of the Mozambique coast. In the 1840s British ships were frequent visitors at Quelimane and Mozambique Island and British warships were involved in actions against Angoche and the slavers who used its port. The anti-slave trade campaign had long been associated with the promotion of free trade and with the activities of Protestant missions, and the idea that Britain was conducting a moral crusade coincided with, and provided an ideological justification for, the pursuit of a variety of British interests in the western Indian Ocean.

The British were particularly alarmed at the apparent revival of French influence in Madagascar, the Comoro Islands, Zanzibar and Mozambique itself. In 1843 a period of great activity by the French culminated in the formal occupation of Mayotte, one of the Comoro Islands, and the drawing up of plans to turn it into a naval base. Britain had reacted by establishing a consulate in Zanzibar in 1841, while in 1850 William Sunley, an English planter in Anjouan, was made consul in the Comoro Islands.[18] In 1856 Britain decided to establish a consulate on Mozambique Island and appointed Lyons McLeod to hold the post. McLeod's appointment was partly a measure against the slave trade that still continued along the coast, but much more it was an extension of a wider duel between France and Britain in the Indian Ocean and did not necessarily have implications for the future of the people of Mozambique.[19]

Of a different order was the appointment of Livingstone as vice-consul on the Zambesi in 1858. The idea of the Zambesi expedition was very much Livingstone's own, but he successfully sold the idea to the British government which saw that a number of national interests would be served if it were successful. As a consular official Livingstone was to report to the British government on the state of the slave trade in Zambesia, but he was also to chart the river, explore a route to the interior, and investigate the opportunities for trade, for the growing of cotton and for the planting of missions. This expedition therefore encapsulated Britain's three major interests in the African continent — opposition to the slave trade, encouragement of Protestant missions, and promotion of free trade.

The Zambesi expedition failed in most of its objectives, but Livingstone returned to Mozambique in 1866 and before 'disappearing' made the first crossing of northern Mozambique by any European since Gaspar Bocarro in 1616. Of the expeditions mounted to search for Livingstone, that of Edward Young entered the Zambesi and used the old route up the Shire to Lake Malawi.[20] However, it was Livingstone's death in 1873 that led to the revival of British interest in the region of the Shire and the Zambesi. Between 1875 and 1877 missions were established by the Church of Scotland and the Free Church and from then onwards there was to be a strong British presence on the Lake and, with the founding of Blantyre, in the Shire Highlands — both of which regions were very much part of the commercial hinterland of the Portuguese coastal and river ports.

From the end of the 1870s a constant stream of missionaries, traders and explorers used the river route to the glens of the Shire Highlands. In 1878 Fred Moir founded the Central Africa Company (later the African Lakes Company), with the result that British commercial interests rapidly increased and the Portuguese authorities on the coast were faced with demands for the free passage of goods in transit. However, a still more thorny issue — brought to a head in 1877 when the British consul in Mozambique, Frederick Elton, visited the Shire Highlands — was the question of who had jurisdiction over the ever-increasing European community which, one way or another, had become attached to the Scottish missions.[21]

In the early 1880s Britain was to become embroiled with the affairs of the quarrelsome missionaries and their commercial associates in the African Lakes Company. In 1880 a Church of Scotland commission, backed by the government, had to be appointed to investigate scandals in the Blantyre mission and, following the reoccupation of Massingire on the lower Shire by Portuguese forces in 1882, the British consul, Henry O'Neill, made a semi-official visit to the Shire and recommended the appointment of a consul to oversee what was happening in the area. In 1883 one was appointed, accredited to 'the territories of the African kings and chiefs in the districts adjacent to Lake Nyasa'.[22] In spite of this, the Foreign Office repeatedly refused to entertain the idea of a British protectorate in the Shire Highlands or on the Lake — partly on general financial grounds but also from an awareness that any protectorate would be wholly at the mercy of the Portuguese who controlled access to the Zambesi and the Shire. Friendly agreement with the Portuguese seemed a wiser course. As late as March 1888 the Foreign Office was still telling representatives of the African Lakes Company that it could take no responsibility for protecting British settlements which were not officially authorised, and in May of that year Lord Salisbury wrote a very clear-headed minute on the position of the British consul on the Lake:

> To please the missionaries, we send a representative of the Government; to spare the taxpayers, we make him understand that he will in no case be supported by an armed force. The only weapon left him is bluster . . .[23]

The truth was that, although the African Lakes Company was busy trading ivory and some of its agents had started to grow coffee on the slopes of Zomba mountain, the total volume of British trade with the Mozambique interior in the early 1880s was still very small, much smaller than that of the French. The suppression of the slave trade and the energetic burst of exploratory activity by Livingstone and his followers had not in itself led to an economic revolution.

Britain, Portugal and the Boers

While the diplomatic activity of Britain and the commercial penetration of Indian traders was providing a stimulus for commerce along the Mozambique coast, the development of plantation agriculture and mining was about to involve the southern areas of Mozambique ever more closely with the development of Natal and the Transvaal. There is a geographical logic to the relationship between the long coastlands of Mozambique and the high veldt of the interior plateau. The rivers which rise on the plateau flow through the escarpment to the Mozambique coast, not the sort of highway into the interior that rivers provide in some continents but important lines of communication nevertheless. The ports and river estuaries of Mozambique therefore provide the natural access to the interior for half of the eastern side of the African continent. In the immediate hinterland of these ports had grown up the Muslim and Afro-Portuguese communities which had serviced the international trade and whose commercial networks had linked Mozambique inwardly to the peoples of central Africa and outwardly to Europe and Asia.

The logic of geography was especially strong in the case of Delagoa Bay. The high veldt lies barely 50 miles inland from the Bay and at least from the sixteenth century the ivory of the interior, and later cattle and slaves, had been brought to the port to exchange for cloth and metalware. As one of their first acts after their initial settlement of the Transvaal in the late 1830s, the Boer trekkers had tried to open a road to the sea. In 1838 Louis Trigard and his companions had reached the

Bay after suffering extensively from malaria and sleeping sickness, his epic journey having served to demonstrate the difficulties of using oxen and horses along this route infested with tsetse fly.

In the 1840s the trekkers made further attempts to open trading stations in the neighbourhood of the Bay and in 1848 their Volksraad even voted money to build a road, but such moves were discouraged by the British, and by the Portuguese who feared active British intervention.[24] So for two decades the Boers had to look to the ports of Natal and even the Cape for their commercial outlets as the routes to the east were blocked for them not only by disease and international hostility but also by hostile Swazi, Pedi and Tsonga chieftaincies. By the 1850s, however, a hunting and slaving frontier community, barely controlled by the Republican government, had established itself in the Zoutpansberg and begun to form links with the Portuguese traders and ivory hunters from Inhambane and Lourenço Marques, chief among whom was the increasingly rich and powerful João Albasini. For two decades the region north-west of the Bay saw a mixed community of Boer and Afro-Portuguese traders and elephant hunters, together with their armed followers, co-operating to a greater or lesser extent with local chiefs and with the more distant Gaza monarchy in developing a trade in ivory, slaves and cattle which made use of the Portuguese ports.[25]

However, the Transvaalers continued to harbour ambitions of establishing their own route to the coast which would free them from British control, and they were thoroughly alarmed at the renewed attempt by Britain to claim sovereignty in the Bay in 1861. It was this, coupled with a growing shortage of land, which in 1868 prompted President Pretorius to claim that the Transvaal's frontiers extended to the coast. The British and Portuguese governments both protested and Portugal retaliated by confirming its sovereignty over the whole of Delagoa Bay including the northern and southern shores and by recognising as Portuguese territory the *Colónia de São Luis* (the grandiose name which Albasini had given to the land he had acquired in the interior).[26] It was an unreal rivalry which the Boers had no desire and no means to prosecute further. In July 1869 they and the Portuguese signed a treaty which was the the first official recognition of what was to be one of the closest but most uneasy of international marriages. The treaty recognised Portugal's possession of Delagoa Bay and of the coast as far south as latitude 26° 30′, and drew the eastern frontier of the Transvaal along the ridge of the Lebombo mountains. However, this was not just a partition treaty concerned with the demarcation of frontiers, for Portugal and the Transvaal also agreed to the building of a road to link the high veldt and the port. The Portuguese were so pleased with the outcome that the consul in Cape

Town, Alfredo Duprat, who negotiated the treaty was granted the title of *visconde*.[27]

Clearly the Transvaal recognised that, provided there were no tariff barriers, Portuguese possession of Delagoa Bay served its purpose as well as if it owned the port itself. The treaty also signalled the end of freedom on the frontier. The government of Pretoria was now increasingly to exercise itself over the communities of the Zoutpansberg, and the easy days of slaving and hunting were coming to an end. It proved also to be one of the treaties which defined both the physical composition and also the future relationships of the modern state of Mozambique. Although the agreements confirmed Delagoa Bay in Portuguese possession, the frontier that was drawn severed the port politically from much of its trading hinterland, although the effects of this were somewhat mitigated by the signing of a free trade agreement in 1873 allowing for the closest possible economic relations with the Transvaal.[28]

When the Portuguese-Transvaal treaty was published, Britain itself immediately challenged Portugal's possession of the southern shores of Delagoa Bay. Britain's case rested on the fact that the Bay was a wide area into which flowed four rivers whose courses were controlled by different chieftaincies. Portugal had established a fort on the north shores of the Bay in the late eighteenth century but had never prevented other powers from using it as an anchorage or for trade. In 1823 Commodore Owen had raised the British flag on the south shore and this claim had been reasserted twice in the 1860s. The British government was concerned at any diplomatic initiative that would link the Boers to a Portuguese port, as it feared that its hegemony in the region might be threatened. It was also reluctant to accept frontiers which Portugal and the Boers had drawn in the hinterland of Delagoa Bay as a result of negotiations from which Britain had been excluded.

The move was clearly linked to Britain's traditional policy in southern Africa. After the Great Trek Britain had tried to maintain its paramountcy over the Boer republics and their trade, not through direct rule but by controlling the seaports with access to the interior. The successful opening of a road to the Bay would completely undermine the whole foundation of British policy. Britain and Portugal were also in dispute in West Africa and it was at Portugal's suggestion that in 1871 the dispute in both areas was referred to the President of France for arbitration.[29]

However, while Marshal MacMahon was still pondering his adjudication, work had begun on a road to the interior, and a transport company had been formed to connect the Bay with the newly-discovered goldfields at Lydenburg. When MacMahon made his award in 1875 he granted full control of the Bay to Portugal. The judgment ended years of uncertainty and enabled plans, not only for the opening of the road but also for the building of a railway, to go ahead. Britain saw its whole policy in southern Africa begin to disintegrate.

Meanwhile, economic development in the interior of southern Africa was producing other revolutionary forces of change. It is usually held that the discovery of diamonds in the Vaal river in 1867 and of gold at Lydenburg in 1869 initiated an industrial revolution in an economically backward and fragmented region. However, as far as the southern African region as a whole is concerned, the development of a regional economy centred on capital enterprise had begun rather earlier. In the 1850s sugar growing on a large scale had got under way in Natal and resulted in a demand for labour which the local African population was unwilling or unable to satisfy. Labour recruiters began to visit the Mozambique ports to the north, and traders who penetrated the Gaza kingdom at this time came looking for the right to contract labourers as well as for opportunities to buy ivory. In 1870 Umzila, the Gaza king, had sent an embassy to Natal offering to supply contract labour, and this in turn occasioned a number of visits to Gazaland by St Vincent Erskine between 1871 and 1875.[30] Labour migration to the south in search of wages had begun.

The mineral discoveries of the late 1860s, and in particular the development of the dry diggings at Kimberley in the early 1870s, began to attract large-scale industrial investment, not only to work the mines themselves but also for the building of railways and for the development of other aspects of the South African economy. When the great gold reef was discovered on the Witwatersrand in 1886, South Africa embarked on massive industrialisation that was to involve transport, construction, dynamite manufacture, coal mining and the development of all the service and consumer industries needed by the mining community.

The industrialisation of South Africa speeded up the creation of a regional economy into which southern Mozambique was to be inexorably drawn, especially as a supplier of labour. The growth of diamond mining and the prospect of the rapid development of Delagoa Bay as the main highway to the interior encouraged the British government to undertake the political unification of southern Africa so that the many problems, not least those associated with the supply of labour, could be tackled regionally.[31] In 1874 the colonial secretary, Lord Carnarvon, launched his confederation scheme and began a series of discussions with the colonial governments and Boer republics, discussions which became all the more urgent with the French President's declaration in 1875 that the whole Bay rightfully belonged to Portugal.

Meanwhile President Burgers of the Transvaal and the Portuguese pressed ahead with their railway. The first concession was granted to George Moodie but he sold out to the Transvaal government, and in 1876 Burgers began to raise funds to construct the line, travelling with a prospectus to Europe, buying rolling stock and trying to persuade sceptical European financiers to back the project. To make the idea of a railway more credible, Burgers also attempted the final pacification of the Zoutpansberg, and he even appears to have contemplated buying the Bay from Portugal, as so many others were to do later. Portugal meanwhile had transferred the concession to build the section of line in their territory to the Lebombo Railway Company.

Containing the Boer republics now seemed more and more problematic, and the British government concluded that a wiser strategy might be to seek to incorporate them once again into the empire. If Britain itself could not control the Bay, and if the Transvaal were to build a road or a railway, the only means by which Britain could maintain its position would be to bring the Transvaal itself under some form of British rule. In April 1877 Theophilus Shepstone entered the Transvaal with thirty Natal police and occupied Pretoria, and within weeks he had annexed the territory as a British colony. The annexation cut short the developing independent Transvaal-Mozambique economic axis and radically transformed political and economic relations in the region. On the one hand the annexation was a giant step towards the short-term objective of creating a Confederation but it also contributed to the longer-term aim of integrating the economies of the southern part of the continent. It now became possible to organise transport and labour supply across the whole region. Moreover the idea of the Lourenço Marques railway, which had seemed so contrary to Britain's traditional policy in South Africa, suddenly became all-important for its rational development, and British and Portuguese negotiators began to draw up a treaty in which the commitment to build the railway was the central objective.

While these events had been taking place in the south, the two Scottish missions established in the Shire Highlands and on Lake Malawi had begun to raise very urgently the question of whether they and the traders who attached themselves to the missions should have free access to the Shire highlands via the Zambesi. The discussion of this issue coincided with, and was to some extent replicated by, the question of the navigation of the Congo, where Portugal had longstanding local ties but Britain had commercial and missionary interests which it was concerned to protect. It was in this situation that Britain, through its ambassador in Lisbon, Robert Morier, began bilateral negotiations with Portugal aimed at creating an ordered structure for the development of commercial activity in the interior of the Congo and the Zambesi — a traditional line of British foreign policy, and the logical extension of the free trade policies Britain had pursued throughout the century. At the same time the negotiators tried to secure conditions for building a railway from Delagoa Bay to the high veldt (now safely under British control), a development inspired not by the world of commerce but by the needs of the new industrial revolution.

The Portuguese minister who conducted the negotiations, João de Andrade Corvo, belonged to the class of Portuguese liberals anxious that the colonies should develop along free trade lines. He wanted to reach agreement with Britain and anticipated the conclusion of negotiations by unilaterally introducing a new 10 per cent tariff on the Zambesi which significantly altered the high tariff structure which had traditionally protected Portuguese commerce. He also tried to introduce the first regular steamer services on the river, and in 1878 concluded an agreement with Britain which halted the trade in firearms through the port of Lourenço Marques.[32]

By 1879 a series of agreements had been negotiated which Morier incorporated into a treaty whereby Britain would co-operate with Portugal in building the railway and in return the Portuguese would guarantee free navigation of the Zambesi, a lowering of tariffs on transit trade and the use of the port of Lourenço Marques by British troops. This treaty, usually known as the Lourenço Marques Treaty, was signed in May 1879 but never ratified. It was initially opposed by Portuguese interests which saw Britain as the sole beneficiary of the treaty; then, after the Portuguese political establishment reluctantly agreed to its implementation, the British abandoned it when Gladstone's government decided in 1881 that the Transvaal should be handed back to the Boers. The vital clauses over free navigation of the Zambesi (which incidentally fixed the confluence of the Ruo and the Shire rivers as the limit of Portuguese jurisdiction in the interior) were then incorporated into the Congo Treaty which the British and Portuguese finally completed in February 1884. This treaty, not concerned at all with the Transvaal railway, bore even more strikingly than the Lourenço Marques Treaty the hallmarks of the era of free trade and slave trade suppression. Portugal was recognised as sovereign of the lower Congo in return for guaranteeing free trade, freedom of worship and free navigation on both the Congo and Zambesi rivers. This treaty also was opposed by extreme interests in Britain and Portugal, and had not been ratified when it was overtaken by the summoning of the Berlin Congress in October 1884.[33]

In these bilateral treaties Britain had effectively recognised Portuguese sovereignty in the interior subject to the provisions of effective occupation. The modern Mozambican state was emerging from the ill-defined hinterland of the coastal ports, criss-crossed by the routes followed by the trade caravans, and being given a coherent shape by the work of the treaty-makers. However, the treaties negotiated with Britain envisaged a state very different from the one that eventually emerged. Portugal believed that the whole central African region was its sphere of interest by virtue of its long-established commercial presence, and politicians in Lisbon were talking of a new Brazil — a new empire on a truly continental scale that would unite West and East Africa. The bilateral treaties would have gone far towards making this a reality — they did not draw the frontiers of a modern transcontinental state but were a sort of modern Tordesillas Treaty which demarcated a sphere of influence within which Portugal could expand as it wished at its own pace.

The bilateral treaties are tantalising for historians. Had they been ratified they might have pre-empted the scramble for southern Africa, since they would have effectively prevented the competition for central African territory between Germany, Leopold II of the Belgians, Britain and Portugal. Moreover, it is difficult to imagine Cecil Rhodes casting such a giant shadow over southern Africa if most of what later became the Rhodesias had fallen within an internationally accepted Portuguese sphere of interest. However, the treaties were not ratified. The Portuguese parliament believed that Britain had secured control of Delagoa Bay by the back door through its control over the proposed railway, and it resented the free navigation, freedom for Protestant missions and lowering of the tariffs, all of which seemed to detract from Portuguese sovereignty and to expose the 'new Brazil' to a British commercial domination as complete as that experienced by the old Brazil. The failure of the treaties coincided with Britain's abandonment of its confederation policy. Drought, war and finally the rebellion of the Transvaal Boers threw British policy-makers on to the defensive. The Transvaal was once again granted effective autonomy and Britain withdrew its support for the Delagoa Bay railway. Portugal and the Transvaal resumed their private negotiations for the construction of the line.

The failure of the bilateral treaties had other consequences. It convinced the government in Portugal of the reality of the international threat to the informal Afro-Portuguese commercial empire, and in the formation of colonial policy it confirmed the supremacy of the committed imperialists over the free traders. Imperial thinking was moving away from the relaxed liberalism of the mid-century and was beginning to create a stronger line of policy which sought more direct exploitation of the African territories. Hitherto Mozambique had not been a state in the modern sense, but a collection of peoples linked by commerce to a string of Portuguese-controlled ports. Now this loose and largely formless relationship was to have various more or less rigid institutional forms imposed upon it.

Portugal and its African empire

As the people of Mozambique began to be drawn more into the rapidly flowing stream of the world economy, Portugal itself started to take a new interest in its African territories. Following the end of the Napoleonic wars it had been plunged into twenty-five years of almost constant civil conflict. It was a war which saw the final independence of Brazil and the ultimate triumph of the urban bourgeoisie of Lisbon and Oporto supported by liberal elements of the aristocracy — a class alliance anxious to liberalise the country's institutions and adopt the doctrines of laissez-faire and free trade which Britain was so powerfully advocating. Major changes to land law and the conduct of commerce and industry were introduced. As for the colonies, the liberals believed that their principles would transform the old slave-trading domains of the Angolan and Mozambican Afro-Portuguese into prosperous capitalist enterprises. It was under their auspices that the slave trade was abolished, trading monopolies were ended and the old feudal tenures of crown land were replaced with a system of freehold and rent.

The vision emerged of an Africa that would grow to replace Brazil — rich in resources, attracting Portuguese emigrants, providing markets for Portuguese products and helping to generate the capital that Portugal itself so signally lacked. Africa would help Portugal free itself from British domination. The liberals, once firmly installed in power in the 1850s, began a hopeful policy of reform in Africa, encouraging investment and organising settlement schemes to promote the new liberal imperialism. These ambitions had only modest success. The powerful alliance of the coastal slaving interests, which were strongly linked with warlike chieftaincies inland in Angola and the *prazo senhores* and Swahili sheikhs in Mozambique, proved more than a match for the weak resources that the government was able to deploy. The disasters of the wars against the Da Cruz between 1867 and 1869 were the culmination of a decade of failure to organise economic expansion in Africa on a satisfactory basis.

Meanwhile the economy of metropolitan Portugal itself was beginning to expand. Important industries were developing, notably textiles, and this was accompanied by the rise of the banking sector. In the 1860s Portuguese capital had at last found in the tiny West African colonies of São Tomé and Príncipe a profitable area of the empire in which to invest, and had begun to lay out coffee plantations. Portuguese banks began for the first time to take a more positive view

of the African empire, and interest was further stimulated when
Europe felt the effects of the depression in the 1870s and tariff barriers
began to rise.

The new generation of imperialists who came to the fore in the
1870s did not advocate expansion in Africa from the moralistic,
idealistic standpoint of the liberals. They too saw Africa as a potential
new Brazil but realised the need for a concerted and coherent government policy of expansion before Africa's wealth could be realised.
They were to be advocates of organised exploration, government protection for shipping and trade, colonisation schemes and coercive
labour policies. The government was to be an active partner of commerce and banking in making Africa pay for the economic regeneration of Portugal.[34]

The new generation found its forum in the Lisbon Geographical
Society, established in 1875 and from the first a vehicle for the ideas
of the imperial party. While Andrade Corvo was following the classic
policies of laissez-faire liberalism and negotiating for freedom of commerce and religion, and low tariffs, the leaders of the Geographical
Society, José Barbosa du Bocage and Luciano Cordeiro (who, as
the Society's secretary, was to be the official geographical expert
attached to the Portuguese delegation to the Berlin Congress in 1884),
were calling for a more nationalistic approach to Africa. They were
pressing for Portugal to organise an effective response to British
explorers like Livingstone and Cameron and to challenge the reputation they had acquired by writing literate accounts of the African
interior to which they had largely been guided by Afro-Portuguese
traders.

In the decade following its formation the Lisbon Geographical
Society, in conjunction with the government, organised a number of
major journeys of exploration into the African interior — journeys
not concerned, like those of Lacerda and Gamitto, with establishing
trade links but reflecting the late nineteenth-century passion for
detailed scientific knowledge, which would provide satisfactory
evidence of the need of Africa for civilisation. Traders in the service
of the Afro-Portuguese *senhores* had crossed and re-crossed the central
African interior before David Livingstone but seldom with notebook
in hand or with the idea of revealing its commercial networks to potential rivals. Now Portuguese explorers were to remedy this situation
and prove to the world that central Africa was indeed Portuguese.[35]

Most journeys of exploration at this time had primarily 'public relations' motives. The inland areas of central Africa were already well
known to their inhabitants who usually provided guides for the so-
called explorers from Europe. Moreover the interior of central Africa
was also well known to the Afro-Portuguese and to Muslim and Indian

traders from the coast. All the famous British and German explorers of central Africa — Mauch, Holub, Livingstone, Cameron, Erskine, Kerr, Young, Elton, O'Neill — met Afro-Portuguese traders or traders based on the Portuguese east or west African ports. However, these European travellers, conscious of the expectations of their public whose appetite for books of African adventure seemed insatiable, deliberately gave the impression that they were discovering new lands and that the conditions in the interior needed the civilising attentions of the northern Europeans. It was usually in the atrocity stories, no doubt exaggerated for effect and to meet the tastes of a slightly prurient reading public, that the Portuguese were allowed to feature, and much English writing took on a stridently anti-Portuguese tone. For the Portuguese the most sinister aspect of the activities of these explorers was the fact that many of them, like O'Neill, Elton and Livingstone himself, held semi-official or consular status and had to be treated as to some extent the agents of the British government. It was the hostile image generated by these writers that the Portuguese explorers and the Lisbon Geographical Society set out to counter.

Plans for an expedition to open up the area between Angola and Mozambique for Portuguese interests were developed during 1876 by the Geographical Society and the Geographical Commission of the Ministry of Marine (later to merge). They were approved by Andrade Corvo, who believed in their scientific value even though he always thought that the idea of an empire stretching from coast to coast was hopelessly beyond Portugal's capacity to achieve.[36] A confusion of aim, therefore, dogged Portuguese exploration from the start. In July 1877 Hermenegildo de Brito Capelo and Alexandre de Rocha Serpa Pinto, accompanied by Roberto Ivens, set out to lead the expedition. After reaching Angola the explorers parted company and Serpa Pinto returned to Portugal in 1879 having crossed the African continent travelling from Benguela to Barotseland and then south over the Kalahari to Durban. It was a journey of little intrinsic scientific or geographical interest but it served the patriotic purposes of the Geographical Society which, after the subsequent return of Capello and Ivens in 1880, published a map showing the whole of central Africa as Portuguese territory — the earliest version of the Rose Coloured Map. The Society also opened a public subscription for the construction of a line of 'civilising stations' across Africa — a project which the government did not publicly support.[37]

Of more importance for Mozambique was the second expedition undertaken by Capello and Ivens, commissioned by the Society and the government in 1883 and given the same general instructions as the previous one. This time the two explorers were away between May

1884 and June 1885, making a relatively rapid crossing of central Africa from the Atlantic to the Indian Ocean. They were able to follow existing trade routes for most of their journey which gave the first semblance of reality to Portugal's ancient dream of linking their west and east African possessions. While this expedition was making its way through the interior, the Portuguese minister of marine and the colonies, Pinheiro Chagas, took up the idea, suggested by the Geographical Society as early as 1881, of organising an expedition to explore the route from Ibo to Lake Malawi. This expedition set out under the command of Serpa Pinto in September 1885, apparently with secret orders. As well as exploration it was to make treaties with chiefs in the area of the Lake and continue west to the Luangwa and the Kafue.[38] In the event Serpa Pinto was taken ill; the expedition continued under the inexperienced leadership of a naval lieutenant, Augusto Cardoso, and was abandoned in February 1886 after reaching the Scottish mission stations in the Shire Highlands, though not before important treaties had been signed with chiefs to the east of the Lake.[39]

However, it was realised that exploration and the publication of an attractive book of travels would not be enough to counter what was increasingly seen as a British offensive. The Portuguese therefore planned a diplomatic campaign and a fresh drive for the practical occupation of what they saw as their commercial hinterland in Africa. The 1869 treaty with the Transvaal and the MacMahon arbitration over Delagoa Bay had shown how successfully diplomacy could achieve national objectives, and while Andrade Corvo and Robert Morier were negotiating the bilateral Lourenço Marques and Congo treaties, the Portuguese government hoped that this diplomatic initiative would achieve their aims. However, the Congo Treaty failed to secure ratification or, more important, international recognition, and the Berlin Congress of 1884–5 had introduced Leopold of the Belgians as a major contender for central African trade and resources. Moreover 1884 had seen Germany establish itself on many sectors of the African coast. Although none of these areas was very near to existing Portuguese possessions, it soon became necessary for Portugal to negotiate with the Germans over spheres of influence north of Cape Delgado and in the south of Angola.

Moreover the German activity had stimulated the British in South Africa to annex the vast tracts of the interior that were eventually to become Bechuanaland, an area from which missionaries, gold prospectors and traders soon began to stream northwards.

Seeds of a new colonial order on the Zambesi

While diplomats and explorers were trying to give shape and substance to Portugal's informal empire in eastern Africa, some initial steps were being taken to create a coherent colonial administration. In 1875 the institution of slavery had formally been abolished and a labour code adopted which reflected the government's liberal intentions rather than any real economic or social change in Africa itself. The Portuguese wanted to replace slavery and the old semi-feudal obligations of the *prazo* regime with citizenship rights, legal equality, freedom for peasants to sell their labour, and the duty to pay taxes and perform military service for the state. The African peasants, however, were ambivalent about the proposed changes. In 1878 attempts to take a census on the lower Zambesi *prazos* before the introduction of a poll-tax led to widespread rebellion.[40] Once this was put down, the government pressed ahead with implementing a new law abolishing the *prazos*.[41] Plans were also developed to improve the infrastructure of the lower Zambesi settlements. There was talk of a railway to run from Quelimane to Sena and possibly up the Shire valley, and in 1880 a Portuguese officer actually surveyed the route and appeared at the Scottish mission station at Blantyre.[42]

However, in the early 1880s the reality of power on the Zambesi had changed little. The great Afro-Portuguese families — Ferrão and Sousa in Sena, Da Cruz and Pereira near Tete — still controlled the river and did very much what they liked. Zambesia in the 1880s saw a classic confrontation between feudalism (the Afro-Portuguese families and the traditional African chieftaincies deriving their status from their private armies and tribute levied on the peasantry) and capitalism (represented by plantation concessionaires and trading houses increasingly backed by a bourgeois state apparatus, still feeble but rapidly strengthening itself).

The partition of Central Africa

The train of events that was to lead to the partition of central Africa goes back to 1878. In that year Joaquim Carlos Paiva de Andrada, a relatively unknown officer attached to the Portuguese embassy in Paris who happened to be a friend of the prime minister Fontes de Mello, obtained for himself a huge concession of timber, mineral and land rights in the region defined as within a 38-league radius of Tete and Zumbo.[43] The concession was granted at a time when Corvo was negotiating with Robert Morier the treaty that would confer freedom of navigation on the Zambesi. A concession on this vast scale was clearly an attempt to pre-empt any foreigner using the right of access to the Zambesi to establish a foothold in the interior, as the Scottish missions had done.

Andrada, sometimes referred to as the Portuguese Cecil Rhodes, seems to have been influenced mainly by the atmosphere of speculation that flourished in financial circles in Paris during the heady days of bondholding in Egypt and the Middle East. Between 1879 and 1881 he and his French backers made a number of surveys in Zambesia which resulted in French withdrawal from the projected enterprise. It took Andrada three years to put together another concession company, the *Companhia de Ophir*, for which he even achieved some support from Sir William Mackinnon. However, the Ophir Company, which in February 1884 was given a concession of mining rights in Manica and Kiteve, also failed to find backers, and the British consul Henry O'Neill pointed out that there was little possibility of floating a company to exploit land or mineral concessions in areas where effective control lay with the Da Cruz or the Gaza Nguni. Andrada's failure to find backers is hardly evidence that a massive weight of speculative European capital was poised to rape a virgin Africa — but on the other hand it is significant that Andrada chose to operate through concessions of land, minerals and timber rather than through the establishment of a company to trade in ivory, rubber or wax. The attraction of Africa's commercial potential was clearly giving way to the more predatory interest of the concession broker.

Andrada's feeble attempts to raise capital would certainly not by themselves have led to the scramble for central Africa; to the watchful O'Neil they appeared little better than a farce. However, during his early visits to Zambesia, Andrada had made contact with Manuel António de Sousa and had come to realise how wealth and political power were acquired in Zambesia. For Sousa was about to implement plans which would make him the most powerful figure in central Africa, comparable to the rulers of the Gaza or Ndebele kingdoms.

In 1880 Sousa, who had married a woman of the Barue royal house, took advantage of the death of the Macombe to occupy this chieftaincy. It was a move wholly logical to anyone who knew Zambesian history. The Macombes of Barue had lived in close proximity to the Portuguese of Sena but always stoutly maintained their independence, taxing the trade caravans that had to cross their territory to Manica. While Barue remained independent there could be no safe communication with Manica or even between Sena and Tete. Moreover the Portuguese became increasingly fearful that Barue might form a combination with the Da Cruz in Massangano whose territory it adjoined. Indeed when the great Bonga died in 1879 and there was a disputed succession in Massangano, one faction had sought refuge in Barue. In 1880 the reverse happened when Barue chiefs, resentful of Sousa's usurpation, sought aid from the Da Cruz. Sousa never handed Barue over to the government, and had pretensions of setting himself up as an independent African king. As late as December 1890 the governor of Manica, J.J. Fereira, could write:

> Manuel António's people today reside almost totally in the former kingdom of Barue, a land which he calls his own, exalting his vanity to the point of calling its inhabitants his vassals. And he even now wants to be crowned *king of Barue* which he has only not done because someone has advised him against it.[44]

Sousa's occupation of Barue was ruthlessly efficient and his captains built and garrisoned thirty *aringas* throughout the chieftaincy. His lands now stretched from the Zambesi to the Pungue, the largest concentration of wealth and power in the hands of any *sertanejo* since Sisnando Dias Bayão in the mid-seventeenth century. Clearly Sousa's aid would be vital to any policy that Andrada or the Portuguese government might want to pursue in central Africa but he was an overmighty subject who had to be handled with care. Sousa for his part saw considerable value in an association with Andrada and the government. Like so many Zambesi *senhores* before him, he was anxious to secure the gains of his bandit activity. He wanted official Portuguese recognition of his title to land, so that he could pass his vast territories on to his sons whom he was having educated in Portugal. Moreover, he needed to be able to obtain firearms and to launder his wealth through acquiring respect and status in Portuguese society.

In 1884 the lower Zambesi was violently disrupted by an uprising on the old Vas dos Anjos *prazos* of the Shire and the right bank of the Zambesi. Bands of fighters from Massingire plundered Portuguese military posts and trading establishments, threatening to block the Shire route to the interior and cut Quelimane off from the Zambesi settlements. Unable to deploy troops of its own, the government turned to Sousa for aid. Sousa advanced on the Shire with a force alleged to number 10,000 men, drove the rebels before him and re-occupied the area on behalf of the government. It was on this campaign that he and Andrada drew up their plans for the occupation of central Africa.[45]

Sousa's objectives were to expand his domain from Barue and Gorongosa on to the high veldt, absorbing the Shona chieftaincies of Rupire and Mtoko and making himself master of the Mazoe goldfields — in effect, restoring the old dominion of the seventeenth-century Portuguese over the Karanga. Andrada's ambitions were different, but co-operation with Sousa was the only practical way to realise them. Andrada wished to place his Ophir Company in a position to exploit the natural resources and commercial opportunities of

the region south of the Zambesi which included the northern part of
the kingdom of Gaza. It was a strange alliance of nineteenth-century
speculative capital with a *conquistador* whose mode of operation
belonged more to the seventeenth century. The Portuguese government saw and approved Andrada's schemes. It had no funds or
military resources of its own to occupy Mashonaland or Manica and
was concerned with multiple threats to its trans-African empire coming at it from every direction. Sousa was an ally not to be despised and
Andrada an imperialist who apparently knew how a late nineteenth-
century empire was to be built.[46]

In February 1884 Andrada at last floated his Ophir Company, and
the Portuguese government established a formal district of Manica
and Sofala to include all Andrada's concession. Andrada spent the
rest of the year travelling to Manica and then exploring the Pungue
to its mouth where he established a base for future expeditions to the
interior, a base that later grew into the city of Beira. From there he
tried unsuccessfully to visit Gungunhana to obtain Gaza aid for the
establishment of the Company in Manica.

Meanwhile the occupation of Mashonaland went ahead smoothly.
In May 1886 Sousa overwhelmed the Shona chieftaincy of Rupire and
established his garrisons on the lower Mazoe, while Andrada busied
himself with exploring the Sabi and Pungue and consolidating his concessionary rights in the northern part of Gazaland. Early in 1887,
however, Sousa received a major setback when the forces which he
himself was accompanying were routed in a fight with the Shona of
Mtoko. It was a humiliating but comparatively minor defeat and
Sousa would probably have launched another attack on Mtoko but for
a resurgence of war with the Da Cruz. Since the catastrophes of the
1860s the Portuguese had left the Da Cruz alone in their river stronghold, but the growth of Sousa's influence and his occupation of the
territory of Barue left the Da Cruz all but surrounded. It seems that
an alliance was formed between them, the exiled Barue princes and
Mtoko to oppose the advance of Sousa and the forces of a more formal
colonial rule which their family had successfully opposed for forty
years.[47]

In 1887 the decision was taken by Andrada, Sousa and the governor
of Manica to deal with Massangano once and for all. An army was
raised on the Zambesi, largely from Sousa's warriors, and a swift and
decisive attack was launched on Massangano, which fell into the
government's hands almost without a struggle. This signal victory
seemed to extinguish the last vestige of feudal independence among
the lower Zambesi *senhores*.[48] Nothing now seemed to stand between
the Portuguese and the realisation of their central African dreams. In
March 1888 Sousa and Andrada, forgetting about Mtoko, went to

Lisbon where the new Moçambique Company was set up and granted a concession. They were some six months ahead of Cecil Rhodes whose British South Africa Company was founded only in October 1888.[49]

The Rose-Coloured Map

These developments in Zambesia had been accompanied by a major change in political orientation in Lisbon. The failure of the bilateral treaties with Britain had discredited the idea that, in an age of increasing European competition and entrepreneurial activities by explorers, missionaries and prospectors, it would be possible to maintain the old regime whereby Portugal controlled the coastal ports and allowed Afro-Portuguese influence to percolate along the ancient trade routes into the interior. The Berlin Congress appeared to establish the principle that effective occupation rather than prior discovery would be the criterion for international recognition of African claims; certainly this was the interpretation given to it by the British government. The Portuguese had tended to stress that their rights were based on prior discovery but it is often forgotten that they were much better placed than Britain or any of the other powers then interested in Africa to make realistic claims of effective occupation as well. In central Africa Afro-Portuguese traders and backwoodsmen were hoisting the Portuguese flag in the hinterland of the Luangwa and the Kafue and were present at the Barotse court, while British interests were only occasionally represented by a passing traveller or ivory hunter.

The Berlin Congress also appeared to demonstrate the existence of a Franco-German alliance which could thwart British pretensions and might therefore be favourably disposed towards Portugal. In 1885 the Foreign Ministry in Lisbon had produced a map setting out the extent of Portugal's claims in central Africa (Map 7). This famous Rose-Coloured Map showed a band of Portuguese territory stretching all the way from Angola to Mozambique and including Barotseland and the Ndebele kingdom as well as the valleys of the Kafue and Luangwa and the shores of Lake Malawi. This represented a dramatic extension of Portugal's claims, since only five years earlier, when the Lourenço Marques treaty was being negotiated, Lisbon had recognised the Ruo river as the limit of Portuguese jurisdiction north of the Zambesi. It now became the objective of Portuguese diplomacy to gain international recognition for the Rose-Coloured Map.

Following the end of the Berlin Congress, Portuguese diplomats conducted a series of successful negotiations with France and Germany. In May 1886 a Franco-Portuguese accord was signed that settled the frontiers of Guinea and allowed for the cession of the

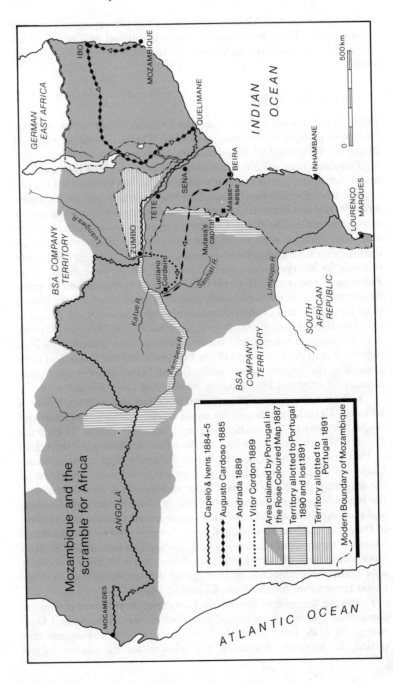

Mozambique and the scramble for Africa

— Capelo & Ivens 1884–5
♦ Augusto Cardoso 1885
— · Andrada 1889
···· Vitor Cordon 1889

Area claimed by Portugal in the Rose Coloured Map 1887

Territory allotted to Portugal 1890 and lost 1891

Territory allotted to Portugal 1891

— · · Modern Boundary of Mozambique

Casamance river to France. To it the Portuguese sought to attach the Rose-Coloured Map. The French were prepared to recognise Portugal's 'right to exercise its sovereign and civilising influence in the territories that separate the Portuguese possessions of Angola and Mozambique, subject to the rights previously acquired by other powers', but would not undertake to recognise any specific boundaries.[50] The French did, however, agree that the Rose-Coloured Map might be attached to the treaty '*à titre d'information*'.[51] In December 1886 a similar boundary convention was signed with Germany settling the northern borders of Mozambique and the Cunene frontier of Angola. The northern frontier of Mozambique was fixed on the Rovuma although the Germans were later allowed to acquire possession of the small disputed enclave south of the Rovuma mouth called the Quionga triangle. Drawing the frontier of Angola along the Cunene river left vast tracts of the southern interior on the Portuguese side of the border, but clearly cut off much of the ivory-trading hinterland of Mossamedes. By making significant concessions to Germany the Portuguese had hoped for recognition of their claims as set out in the Rose-Coloured Map, but Germany, like France, while allowing the Map to be appended to the treaty, would only recognise Portugal's rights in the interior in a general way which did not specify any definite boundaries.

The treaties were not ratified by the Cortes till June 1887, and when they were published Britain made it clear that the Map was not acceptable and reiterated its claim that actual occupation alone could constitute international title to territory. During 1887, however, it seems that private discussions indicated that Britain might sign a frontier convention which would give Portugal substantially what it wanted. The British were anxious to provide protection for the missions at Blantyre and Livingstonia but so far there was no access to them except across territory recognised as Portuguese. The Foreign Office was apparently well aware of the weakness of Britain's position and the strength of Portugal's, and opinions were divided about whether Britain should cut its losses in east central Africa. In October 1887 proposals were put forward informally by the British minister in Lisbon which would have recognised the Zambesi as the northern frontier of Britain's sphere of interest. This would have cut in half the central area claimed by Portugal in the Rose-Coloured Map but still allowed it to claim continuous territory between Mozambique and Angola.

Throughout 1888, however, Portugal believed it still had the upper hand in central Africa. Gungunhana, the Gaza king, continued to recognise his treaty relationship with Portugal and to maintain a Portuguese resident at his court, Afro-Portuguese were busy planting

Portuguese flags on the Luangwa and the Kafue, and plans were in hand for the occupation of Manica. Portugal saw no reason to make concessions to Britain and rejected the proposal.[52] A major reason for the rejection was that in July 1888 the Portuguese government had completed plans for a three-pronged advance from Zambesia. António Maria Cardoso, a former governor of Quelimane, was to make treaties in the region of the Shire, and Andrada and Sousa were to occupy Manica. Meanwhile a Portuguese engineer called Vitor Cordon had been sent, nominally under Andrada's authority, to survey a road by-passing the Cabora Bassa rapids and to occupy the Zambesi above Zumbo as far as the Sanhati confluence.[53]

A German ivory hunter in Portuguese service, Carl(os) Wiese, had meanwhile gone on an embassy to Mpezeni's Nguni state in what later became the Fort Jameson area of Northern Rhodesia. All the way he had witnessed the country under the occupation and control of the *chicunda* captains who seemed already to have secured the Kafue and Luangwa valleys for Portugal.[54]

Once again, however, the Da Cruz were to play a decisive role in Mozambican affairs. In 1888, while Sousa and Andrada were in Lisbon establishing the Moçambique Company, the head of the clan, Motontora, reoccupied the old stockade and raised the middle Zambesi against Sousa and the Portuguese government. An archaic vendetta rooted in the Zambesian past was to intrude a violent subplot into the unfolding drama of the Scramble. With the reappearance of Motontora, like Napoleon returning for his 'Hundred Days', the Portuguese advance was crucially delayed. Another major expedition had to be raised and Massangano endured a long siege before finally falling into Portuguese hands. This time a strong stone fort was built on the low hill behind the stockade to ensure that the Da Cruz would never again occupy the site. The old *aringa* was burnt and remained overgrown with grass and trees on the banks of the river, the square stone house of the family a bleak ruin. Eventually the fort itself was abandoned and, although the *aringa* was occupied briefly during the Barue rising in 1917, the site gradually reverted to the bush.[55]

The fighting around Massangano delayed both Andrada and Vitor Cordon. Cordon took a long detour round the territory controlled by the Da Cruz and only reached Zumbo in January 1889, six months after receiving his orders in Lisbon; it was not till June 1889 that he set off westwards. By the beginning of August he had traversed the country as far as the mouth of the Sanhati where he erected an *aringa* called after Luciano Cordeiro and, like some sixteenth-century *conquistadore*, founded a *villa* (town). On 7 November a new administrative district centred on Zumbo was formally created, setting in place another large piece in the jigsaw of the Rose-Coloured Map. Cordon then returned to the coast in search of fresh supplies.[56]

Andrada meanwhile had been travelling to and fro in the region south of the Zambesi in a style that can only be described as frenetic. He visited the governor-general, Castilho, near Massangano in September 1888, then travelled to his base at the mouth of the Pungue; in November he visited Gungunhana and at last obtained Gaza cooperation in the opening of a route to Manica; in February 1889 he was back at Beira; and in July had joined Manuel António de Sousa in Manica whence he set out in September to join Cordon. Andrada crossed the whole of northern Mashonaland making treaties and distributing guns and Portuguese flags, reaching the Luciano Cordeiro *aringa* eight days after Cordon had left. In spite of the delays which had beset the Portuguese enterprise ever since 1886, Andrada was still ahead of British interests in establishing the Portuguese presence throughout Mashonaland. However, strange as it may seem for such an experienced Africa hand, Andrada did not obtain his treaties with the Shona chiefs in writing, nor did he inform Lisbon of what was happening, an omission that was to make most of his work fruitless.[57]

Meanwhile in November 1888 António Maria Cardoso had set out with a large force of *chicunda* and Nguni to make treaties among the peoples east of the Shire and along the eastern shore of Lake Malawi. Although Cardoso ran into difficulties and had to ask for help, the expedition was a spectacular success in obtaining the submission of the Yao chiefs in the region. It was followed by the establishment of a mission of the White Fathers at Mponda's capital in December 1889.[58]

Diplomacy and confrontation on the Shire

While the war with the Da Cruz had been in progress, the Portuguese had tried to control the import of firearms and ammunition. This very reasonable measure had embroiled it with the African Lakes Company, supported by the British government, which had wanted to import artillery as well as small arms in order to fight a war at the north end of Lake Malawi. The argument hinged on whether there could be freedom of navigation on the Zambesi when Portugal controlled the mouth as well as both banks. The British Foreign Office was eventually forced to recognise that as oceangoing ships could not directly enter the Zambesi, there could be no question of establishing the principle of its being a free international waterway.[59]

Despite the evident progress made by Cardoso and Andrada, the Portuguese foreign minister, Barros Gomes, was apparently willing in

April 1889 to accept an agreement which would have abandoned the
territory linking Mozambique and Angola in return for recognition of
the Shire Highlands as falling within Portugal's area of jurisdiction.
This time the proposals were rejected by Lord Salisbury, against the
advice of his officials, since he had sensed an extremely hostile reaction from Scottish interests.[60]

The failure of these talks and the very public activities of Rhodes
in seeking a charter for his British South Africa Company took the lid
off competition in central Africa. Diplomacy appeared to have failed
and an open season for prospectors and concession-hunters was now
declared. In April 1889 Daniel Rankin officially announced to the
Foreign Office that it was possible for ships to enter the Zambesi
directly, thereby reawakening the old dispute over freedom of navigation.[61] In May 1889 Harry Johnston was sent out as the new British
consul to the Nyasa region and Salisbury, who had previously been
so critical of Portugal's secret expeditions, consented to secret instructions authorising Johnston to make treaties with chiefs north of the
Zambesi.

However, it now began to look as though Portugal would establish
'effective occupation' in the Shire and Lake regions, the very possibility of which had so often been scornfully dismissed by the British.
In April 1889, responding to disturbances between the African Lakes
Company and the Makololo and an appeal to the Portuguese resident
in Massingire for help, a large armed expedition with two steam gunboats sailed up the Shire under the command of the ardent imperialist
Serpa Pinto.[62] Events now moved out of the hands of the diplomats
as the men on the spot competed to establish actual possession. In
August Buchanan, the acting British vice-consul, declared the
Makololo to be under British protection, while Johnston sent Alfred
Sharpe ahead to make treaties on the Luangwa — both of them
actions which certainly exceeded his instructions and dragged Britain
deeper into a conflict with Portugal. There followed three months in
which the tiny British community in the Shire highlands tried every
device to prevent Serpa Pinto's expedition proceeding beyond the
Ruo. A farce of flag-raising and spurious treaty-signing tried to buy
time and commit the British government to the recognition of a protectorate. More seriously, the British in the Highlands encouraged the
Makololo to attack the Portuguese and were partly responsible for the
disastrous attempt by the Makololo to attack the Portuguese camp on
9 November. Following this battle, Serpa Pinto's expedition invaded
the Makololo country and quickly received the submission of the
chiefs. A British steamer on the river was ordered to lower its flag, and
complied. Pinto then crossed the Ruo, which ever since the Morier-
Corvo treaties had acquired an unofficial status as the frontier

between Portuguese and British interests, and by December 1889 had occupied much of the Makololo territory to the north.

On 29 October, however, the British government had granted a charter to Rhodes's British South Africa Company in terms which allowed it to claim not only Mashonaland and Manica but the Zambesi valley above Zumbo as its sphere of influence. Clearly a crisis was in the offing, even though the Portuguese were the only party that could claim effective occupation in any part of the disputed region. At the same time the Foreign Office in London was absorbing the implications of what they chose to see as a highhanded action by the Portuguese in unilaterally annulling the McMurdo concession for building the Lourenço Marques railway.

The vigour and direction being given to Portugal's colonial policy seemed to London so unprecedented and out of character, and the success being achieved by its military in Africa so unwonted, that the Foreign Office came to believe that a conspiracy was afoot which would end with Britain being more or less publicly humiliated by the despised Portuguese. Early in January 1890 the Foreign Office prepared a comprehensive memorandum on the misconduct and deviousness of the Portuguese, and on 8 January Salisbury demanded that their forces withdraw from the disputed area beyond the Ruo. On 11 January Salisbury presented the Portuguese with an ultimatum and issued orders to mobilise the fleet.[63]

The ultimatum of January 1890 and the confrontation of Kitchener and Marchand at Fashoda in 1898 were the only occasions during the partition of Africa when European powers nearly came to blows. Looking back, it is not clear why the differences between London and Lisbon could not have been solved by negotiation, since settlements acceptable to the claims of both sides had twice been worked out by junior diplomats. Much of the blame must lie with Lord Salisbury whose diplomatic good sense abandoned him temporarily in December 1889 and January 1890. Presenting an ultimatum which might have resulted in a war with Portugal over territorial disputes in the hinterland of Africa must qualify as one of the major blunders of British policy in the nineteenth century. However, it was brinkmanship from which the Portuguese inevitably backed away, and this was to encourage Britain to defy France in the same way at Fashoda in 1898 and — fatally — to try the same bullying tactics against Kruger in 1899.

Although the whole Scramble for Africa now appears as an irrational aberration which served no well-defined interests for any of the European powers, and can be seen as nothing more than the use of naked force to rob native Africans of their land, wealth and rights, there is no denying that, among the European scramblers, Portugal's claims to the disputed areas were far superior to those of Britain. The British had always maintained that historic claims had to be supported by effective occupation before sovereignty could be recognised, yet when Portugal established what was clearly effective occupation, Lord Salisbury switched tack and condemned the occupation of areas where Britain had claims, even when these were unsupported by any presence. Moreover Salisbury had acted without taking into account any wider or longer-term interests — the stability of the Portuguese monarchy, for example, endangered by rising republicanism, or the interests of the Berlin Congress powers to whose arbitration Portugal had been willing to submit the whole issue.

For the future Mozambique, the evening of 11 January 1890 was to be a moment when the growth and evolution of its frontiers were suddenly frozen. During the previous two decades there had been a steady expansion of the societies of coastal Mozambique. Now this expansion was suddenly checked, and although two years of diplomacy were to follow, the Mozambique that emerged was very much Mozambique as it existed on that fateful January day.

Gaza

After securing the victory over Mawewe in the civil wars that followed Soshangane's death, Umzila had established his capital in the foothills of the Chimanimani mountains, virtually abandoning the area south of the Limpopo which had been devastated by Swazi raids. From this more northerly position he reimposed his authority on the Zambesi delta, Manica and the hinterland of Sofala. His regiments also raided south-westwards as far as the northern areas of the Transvaal.[64] The extent and power of the Gaza monarchy had already attracted attention from European adventurers of all sorts. The low veldt of southern Gazaland was increasingly visited by elephant hunters from Lourenço Marques and the Zoutpansberg, and by labour contractors and arms dealers from Natal. In 1879 a party of Jesuits had entered Gazaland from the west, and in nearly two years of wandering had visited Manica and the Gaza capital before reaching the coast at Sofala. In 1880 an exploratory expedition, with sponsorship from the Royal Geographical Society in London, set off to explore Gaza entering the country via the Sabi. An English member of the party, William Mayes, visited Umzila and prospected for gold before returning to Natal in the company of Gaza envoys.[65]

Alarmed at what appeared to be a growing British interest in Gazaland, an official Portuguese embassy was sent under António Maria Cardoso in 1882, but Umzila cold-shouldered the Portuguese and was still maintaining his complete independence at the time of his death in October 1884. During the final years of Umzila's reign the direction of Gaza policy was weak and confused. The remoteness of the capital, deep in the interior, made it difficult for the king to retain any real control over the coast or over the populous regions in the south, while the inexorable growth of the power of Sousa and his European backers weakened Gaza's hold on the north.

Umzila's successor was Gungunhana, who quickly won control of the kingdom from other potential heirs and so avoided the debilitating civil war that had followed the death of Soshangane. Gungunhana was determined to defend his independence as best he could by military as well as diplomatic means. Early in his reign he began to assert his supremacy over regions which had slipped from Umzila's grasp. He launched a series of attacks on Manica and extended his raiding among the eastern Shona.[66] However, he probably realised instinctively that the British and Boers posed a greater threat to him than the Portuguese and that the official protection of Portugal was likely to leave him with the greatest freedom of action. On the other hand he feared the expansion of Manuel António de Sousa's personal empire, well aware that Sousa had close relations with Andrada and the Portuguese authorities in Zambesia who had established a formal administrative district of Manica in 1884, the very year of his accession.

It is not surprising, therefore, that Gungunhana decided to negotiate with the Portuguese governor of Lourenço Marques rather than the Zambesian Portuguese.[67] A Portuguese embassy under J.C. Alegria Rodrigues was favourably received in 1885, and Gaza envoys travelled to Lisbon where they signed an agreement by which they consented to fly the Portuguese flag, to permit only mineral prospectors with concessions granted by Portugal, and to allow the appointment of a Portuguese resident. In return Portugal recognised Gungunhana's jurisdiction and agreed that no Portuguese armed force should enter the kingdom without the chief's consent.[68] It seems that Gungunhana also pressed unsuccessfully for the Portuguese to make him a payment for each of the labourers leaving the Portuguese ports for South Africa. In requiring the appointment of a resident, who was to undertake various forms of 'civilising' activity, the Portuguese wanted to be in a position to claim that they had some form of effective occupation of Gaza. Rodrigues, the first resident appointed, reached Gaza in May 1886.

Although he had accepted a Portuguese resident, Gungunhana let it be known that he still intended to enforce his overlordship of the chiefs of the Inhambane region and over the Zambesi delta. He roundly refused to acknowledge that he had ever granted William Mayes mineral rights, and refused Andrada permission to prospect in

Gazaland. In September 1886 Gaza regiments attacked chiefs in the region of Inhambane but were beaten off with the help of Portuguese forces. However, during 1887 Gungunhana continued to maintain his sovereignty over the coast and the lower Zambesi region, and sent emissaries to Natal to try to maintain some political freedom of manoeuvre.[69]

The new Portuguese administrative district of Manica, established in 1884, had been designed to drive a wedge of territory between the Gaza kingdom and the sea and prevent Gaza *impis* raiding or collecting tribute in the Zambesi delta. It was also to secure the isolation of the Da Cruz in Massangano and provide a bridgehead for the occupation of Mashonaland. However, in the late 1880s the district was little more than a front for the personal ambitions of Sousa, and the historic chieftaincy of Manica became the focus of rivalry between Gungunhana and the Portuguese. The sensational discoveries of gold on the Rand in 1886 made prospectors take an interest once again in regions like Manica where ancient gold diggings were known to exist. The rulers of Manica were skilled survivors. The traditional diplomacy that had enabled them courteously to escort Vasco Homem's army from their borders in 1573 and permitted them to preserve their effective independence from the domination of the Portuguese in the seventeenth century, the Rozvi in the eighteenth and Nxaba's *impis* in the early nineteenth, was now employed in a juggling act between the rival claims of Sousa, Andrada, the Gaza king and the fledgling British South Africa Company which in 1890 also appeared on the scene with a claim to Manica.

During the dry season of 1888 final military operations were undertaken against the Da Cruz, and Sousa and Andrada planned their long-postponed push into Mashonaland. Meanwhile large numbers of prospectors (as many as 200, according to British sources) had begun searching for gold in Manica. The same year Gungunhana made what was to be his last attempt to hold his position in the north and launched a major raid against Manica. Then in June 1889 after the harvesting of the crops, in a dramatic and unexpected move, he abandoned his capital in the north and moved with tens of thousands of his Nguni and Ndau followers, together with their families and cattle, across the Sabi into the low veldt just north of the Limpopo. By this move he had in effect left Manica and the high veldt of Mashonaland to be contested between Andrada and Sousa and the British South Africa Company.

The reason for Gungunhana's move southwards at a time when the scramble for Africa was nearing its height has naturally given rise to considerable debate. Although there is some evidence that the Portuguese resident may have known of the decision and even approved the shift of the centre of Gaza power from the north, the reason for the move probably lay in the internal politics of Gaza. Gungunhana feared not only that the Limpopo valley had passed out of his control but also that the whole coastal region between the Limpopo and Inhambane, inhabited by the Chopi, would be lost as well. He was aware that the Gaza state now depended increasingly on money brought back by migrant workers and that, with the centre of his kingdom situated in the interior, he would soon lose all control over the migration of people from the southern areas. The lower Limpopo was the old heartland of Gaza where Soshangane's original capital had been and where his body was buried. Gungunhana apparently told the Portuguese resident: 'I am going to Bilene; I go to my home, and where I was born.'[70]

The move south involved the Gaza Nguni in a series of wars with the Chopi, the main objective of which was the acquisition of slaves to provide wives and productive labourers for the Nguni élite whose small numbers had always been a potential source of weakness for the Gaza kings.[71] However, these raids inevitably brought the Nguni into confrontation with the Portuguese of Inhambane and Lourenço Marques as the governors of these *presídios* found the protection they had extended to the low veldt chiefs was now being directly challenged. In November 1889 the Portuguese appointed José Almeida as superintendent of native affairs in Gazaland in the hope that he could restrain the warlike activities of Gungunhana and counter the machinations of foreign concessionaires.[72]

As Gungunhana migrated south with his followers and cattle he was subject to intense pressure from the British South Africa Company to enter into some concession agreement which would enable it to extend its sphere of operations to the sea. Gungunhana had already granted concessions of various kinds to a number of people, contrary to the terms of the 1885 agreement with Portugal, when Aurel Schultz arrived as official envoy of Cecil Rhodes. Rhodes wanted to secure any concession from Gungunhana, whether in the form of land, mineral rights or political protection, as he realised that the negotiations between Britain and Portugal, following the ultimatum in January, might be concluded at any time. In fact the first settlement negotiated in August 1890 was rejected in Portugal, and Rhodes was spurred on to further action. In October Schultz obtained a 'treaty of alliance' from Gungunhana in return for a subsidy and the gift of 1,000 rifles. However, the Portuguese grip on the south of Mozambique was firmer than its presence in Manica. In December Gungunhana again publicly recognised Portugal's sovereignty, and when in February 1891 Rhodes chartered a steamer, the *Countess of Carnarvon*, to run up the Limpopo with the promised rifles, a Portuguese gunboat was on hand to arrest the vessel and give an effective demonstration of Portuguese authority on the coast.[73]

Throughout the first part of 1891 Gungunhana continued to angle for British protection and even sent envoys to London in April. Whether this was a serious attempt to come under British rule or merely an attempt to buy time is not clear, but in June 1891 Britain and Portugal finally concluded a treaty recognising that most of Gaza territory lay within the Portuguese frontiers.[74] In spite of the treaty Gungunhana still saw Gaza as an independent state, and four more years passed before the largest of all the Nguni kingdoms was destroyed.

Drawing the frontiers of Mozambique

The contorted outline of modern Mozambique, locked into an embrace with the former territories of British Central Africa, represents no rational consequence of the needs of a modern state, but immortalises the moment on 11 January 1890 when the music stopped and the missionaries, adventurers, consuls, concession-seekers, white hunters and the whole rabble of 'interested parties' were frozen in postures that an international treaty would soon make unalterable. If the Mozambique that emerged from the subsequent negotiations included the ancient towns of the coast and the Zambesi which had been Portuguese or under Portuguese influence since the sixteenth century, its internal frontiers reflected the most recent activities of adventurers and concession hunters. The most decisive events of the previous five years had been the successful treaty-making of Augusto Cardoso east of Lake Malawi in 1885 and Buchanan and Johnston's treaties made to the west and south in 1889, the failure of Andrada and Sousa to occupy northern Mashonaland when their irregular army was defeated in Mtoko in 1887, and the success of Portuguese as opposed to British adventurers in gaining the ear and some of the trust of Gungunhana in the first five years of his reign. The final drawing of the frontiers, however, was to prove fraught with difficulty, and at one stage in the middle of 1890 it seemed that the music would restart and that the giddy whirl of adventurers and concession hunters would start again.

The immediate Portuguese response to the ultimatum was to seek the support of other European powers for a process of arbitration, evoking Article 12 of the Berlin Congress treaty. Lord Salisbury flatly refused to agree to this, remembering no doubt the outcome of the Delagoa Bay arbitration which had found in Portugal's favour, but discussion of the issue delayed negotiations over the frontier till April when bilateral talks started in Lisbon. Having failed to get

arbitration, Portugal attempted to keep alive its aspirations for a continuous stretch of territory across Africa, and in May proposed the
creation of a sector lying between Angola and Mozambique which
would be jointly administered by Britain and Portugal.

The politics of these proposals is important. The survival of the
Portuguese government and the whole monarchical regime had been
threatened by the ultimatum. The government was in no position to
compromise, although it knew that it could not outface a power such
as Britain which had decided to make an issue of the demarcation of
central African frontiers. The Portuguese therefore advanced claims
they knew would be rejected and waited to have Britain's solution
forced on them. The British government was also under pressure from
Rhodes's British South Africa Company, which was preparing to
occupy its charter territory and was anxious that, if possible, no area
of the high veldt south of the Zambesi should go to Portugal.

On 20 August 1890 a treaty was signed which gave the Shire
Highlands and the Mashonaland high veldt to Britain, though leaving
the Manica highlands in Portugal's sphere. Zumbo was recognised as
the westernmost point of Portuguese influence on the Zambesi;
beyond it there was to be a band of British territory, although Portugal
was granted special rights in a strip along the north bank of the river
where it could build roads and railways and erect telegraph lines. The
treaty was much concerned with freedom of trade and transit rights,
which had caused the diplomatic tensions of the 1880s, and Portugal
undertook not to alienate any of its territory to a third country without
Britain's consent. Finally, Portugal was to lease territory at Chinde
at the mouth of the Zambesi to Britain for the establishment of a port,
and agreed to build a railway from the mouth of the Pungue to the
chartered territory. The treaty threatened to strip away in rude
fashion the fig-leaf covering the embarrassing fact that Portugal was
little more than a client state of Britain.[75]

In the eight months following the ultimatum there had been extraordinary comings and goings in central Africa. Although Salisbury
demanded that the Portuguese abstain from activity in the areas
subject to negotiation, no one prevented Rhodes and his agents
from pushing ahead with their activities. Alfred Sharpe toured the
Luangwa but found the whole area under the Portuguese *chicunda* and
a Portuguese flag flying in Mpezeni's country. In June Rhodes's
'Pioneer Column' entered Mashonaland, and Colquhoun and
Jameson were sent respectively to make treaties in Manica and to
survey a route to the coast. At every point throughout the Manica
highlands they found evidence of the presence and activity of prospectors or officials in the service of the Moçambique Company. In June
the Portuguese established a garrison at the junction of the Kafue and

the Zambesi, and in August an expedition set off for the Lunda country. However, Portuguese attempts to extend their treaty system east of Lake Malawi collapsed when Valadim and his expedition came to grief at the hands of Chief Mataka. Buchanan meanwhile asserted British sovereignty in the Shire Highlands by the rough and ready method of executing two Portuguese *cipais*. At the mouth of the Chinde, unseaworthy Portuguese gunboats with dilapidated engines tried to outface a British naval survey vessel, which responded by running out its guns. During what was in effect a suspension of international law, the 'men on the spot' enjoyed posturing at each other and moving ever closer to actions that might cause a major incident.[76]

By September matters were becoming serious. The Portuguese government, unable to get the treaty accepted in the Cortes, resigned on 16 September; a British gunboat was ordered by the Admiralty to sail up the Zambesi and news arrived of a deliberate piece of buccaneering by Cecil Rhodes. On 15 November some of Rhodes' troopers under Major Forbes arrested Andrada and Manuel António de Sousa at Mutasa's capital and proceeded to occupy Masekesa. Rhodes' intention was to profit by the diplomatic hiatus and the effective rejection of the partition treaty by Portugal to secure as much territory as he could for the Chartered Company, and if possible establish a corridor to the sea. Possession in Africa, he reckoned, was nine-tenths of the law and he anticipated that Salisbury, who had previously been pushed and prodded with effect by Buchanan and Johnston in the Shire area, would prove equally proddable in Manica.[77]

However, the 'men on the spot' had been too slow. On 14 November Portugal and Britain signed an interim agreement (a *modus vivendi*) for six months accepting the territorial limits of the August treaty pending a definitive frontier settlement. The Charter Company decided to stay put and refused to evacuate 'Portuguese' territory, and its troopers were still in occupation of Masekesa in December. During the early part of 1891 the Portuguese tried to assemble an expedition to send to Manica while Rhodes despatched an armed party to the Pungue to open a road from the sea to the high veldt. Almost every day saw some confrontation between Charter Company personnel and the Portuguese, and the Company then shrilly demanded British government intervention to avenge insults to the flag. The most serious incident was in May 1891 when Portuguese and Charter Company troops clashed at Masekesa. After a minor battle the Company's soldiers pursued the retreating Portuguese towards the coast. On 29 May a second battle appeared imminent when an emissary from the British High Commissioner in South Africa unequivocally ordered the Chartered Company forces to withdraw.[78]

On 28 May 1891 Britain and Portugal eventually signed a treaty which somewhat altered the terms agreed the previous year. Events in Manica were reflected in a new frontier to follow the line of the escarpment and leave Mutasa's capital on the British side of the line and Masekesa on the Portuguese side. The original settlement in the Shire and Lake region was not altered, but Portugal had reason to be pleased that Gungunhana's kingdom was finally recognised as being in the Portuguese sphere while extensive territories north of the Zambesi, which the Portuguese *chicunda* had long occupied, were also included in Mozambique. By a secret provision of the treaty, requested by Portugal, Germany was nominated as the power to arbitrate any disagreements. The ultimate satisfaction for Portugal must have been the anger of Rhodes at a settlement which effectively pulled the carpet from under his territorial privateering.

So Mozambique finally emerged from the scattered proposals and counter-proposals, the strident claims of adventurers and the tangle of maps, Rose Coloured or otherwise. Without doubt its frontiers reflected to a certain extent the historical evolution of the region. The ancient seaports from Ibo and Quissanga in the north to Inhambane and Lourenço Marques in the south had been included in the new state with much of the commercial hinterland on which they had depended. However, Delagoa Bay was largely cut off from its hinterland and remained isolated and almost an enclave of the emerging South African state. On the Zambesi the old territories of the *prazos* were included in Portuguese territory, as was the hinterland of Sena in Barue and Manica. Tete and Zumbo found their northern hinterland included but the area to the south restricted to the lower reaches of the Mazoe and Ruenha rivers. The regions west of Zumbo were lost. The final shape of the country showed three salients — Tete and Zumbo, surrounded on three sides by British territory; the British salient of the Shire Highlands hemmed in by Portuguese land; and the salient containing the port of Lourenço Marques, jutting south into South African territory. Mozambique was locked into British South and Central Africa like a piece of a jigsaw puzzle — one which was increasingly to carry the imprinted picture of British capital enterprise and imperial interest.

15

MOZAMBIQUE: THE MAKING OF
THE COLONIAL STATE

The birth of a new state

Astronomers who scan the skies for the birth of a new star are seldom rewarded by witnessing the birth of a whole galaxy. The historian is sometimes more lucky, and those turning their telescopes on to Africa in the last years of the nineteenth century are able to focus on the birth of over fifty new polities. The Scramble for Africa had been conducted largely by diplomats anxious to resolve African disputes before they could disturb the vital interests of states in the rest of the world. As a result the frontiers of Africa often showed more goodwill than knowledge of the African terrain. Frontier lines sometimes followed rivers or watersheds where these were known, but more often the draftsmen in the foreign ministries had to resort to ruling straight lines to bridge the gaps in their scanty real knowledge.

Mozambique is to some extent an exception to this. The frontiers hammered out by British and Portuguese negotiators were the result of a relatively close knowledge of the terrain, and a boundary commission actually surveyed the Manica frontier before the final agreement was signed. Only in northern Zambesia was the frontier not properly marked till the 1930s. However, the drawing of the frontiers of Mozambique did not by itself create a polity. It gave no indication of the type of society, administration or economy that would emerge, or any clue as to how relations with neighbours would develop and how Mozambicans themselves would react to being 'partitioned'. Moreover, although we are now accustomed to the fact that the frontiers drawn in the initial Scramble have remained largely unaltered up to the present, as if ordained by a higher power, it was by no means clear at the time that such rough sketchwork would stand the test of time and not be revised soon and often thereafter.

The colony of Mozambique that had been corralled within frontier lines in the negotiations of 1890–1 had almost none of the characteristics of a modern state. It lacked any unified system of administration or law, was largely unmapped, had little in the way of public revenues or communications infrastructure, and had few of even the most basic services. However, it was not an entirely random creation.

By 1890 fifty years of Gaza overlordship had created a kind of unity in the south of the country. The Gaza kingdom had constantly shifted its centre of gravity, and its rule had been felt throughout the region south of the Zambesi with varying intensity depending on whether the royal capital was in the north or the south. However, the new Mozambique was able to take over more or less directly the tribute-levying role of the Gaza monarchs — to some extent even replicating their methods by instituting a sort of official banditry with armed *cipais* sent on sweeps through the countryside to collect tax.

Overlapping somewhat with Gaza and extending its influence up the coast to Mozambique Island and inland to Lake Malawi and the Luangwa valley was the world of the Zambesi *muzungos*. This region had a common social and political culture and a common experience of Afro-Portuguese domination. It was the north of Mozambique which was almost unknown to the Portuguese in 1890, but even here there was some homogeneity. The peoples of the area were all matrilineal, and dialects of the Makua language were spoken from Cape Delgado to the Zambesi. Moreover it was an area that in the eighteenth and nineteenth centuries had been knit together by the trading caravans of Yao and Makonde and where in the late nineteenth century Islam had spread rapidly.

Overlapping these broad areas of economic, social and political culture were the circles of direct influence radiating from the coastal stations of the Portuguese. These have usually been derided by contemporaries and historians alike who have pointed out that the *presídios* scarcely controlled anything beyond the guns of their little fortresses. In terms of formal colonial administration this was true, but when considering effective influence it is a hopelessly inadequate description. By 1890 the commercial and political influence of the *presídios* had extended deep into the interior so that there were few Mozambicans, except in the far north, who had not had contact with them in one form or another.

Nevertheless, if at its birth Mozambique had more coherence than most of the newly-formed African colonial territories, its future seemed more precarious. The 1890s were a formative decade but for the colony they were chaotic, anarchic years during which it barely survived. There were the international threats, with Britain and Germany openly intriguing to dismember the new entity. These compounded Portugal's difficulty in creating a viable administrative structure while itself under international pressure and experiencing political crisis and bankruptcy.

Continuing international threats

For some years after the initial partition of central Africa, it was widely assumed that there would be further frontier adjustments, and possibly also a further division of territory. For different reasons Germany and Britain both felt themselves increasingly insecure in the 1890s, and central Africa was one of the areas of the world, though not by any means the most important, where this was liable to lead to neurotic over-reaction. Britain was faced with the rising wealth and power of the Transvaal which appeared to be undermining traditional British dominance in southern Africa. To the new imperialists like Joseph Chamberlain, the loss of influence in South Africa could sabotage completely the plans for a closer-knit, more dynamic empire. The clearest formulation of this fear was the notion that the Transvaal would form a close alliance with the Germans, and possibly with the Portuguese, which would threaten Britain's position in South Africa. After the fiasco of the Jameson Raid in 1896, a German-Transvaal link seemed a real possibility. Britain's traditional policy had been to contain the Transvaal by controlling its access to the sea and it was for this reason that Britain had been so anxious to secure control of Delagoa Bay. However, the treaty of 1869 between Portugal and the Transvaal, and the MacMahon award of 1875, had given the Boer republic access to the best port in southern Africa on a free trade basis and without any British control. It remained only to build a railway and this was completed by the end of 1894. Britain had tried to counter these moves diplomatically by negotiating the Lourenço Marques Treaty with Portugal in 1879, and by getting Portugal to sign agreements banning the import of firearms and granting transit rights for British troops. Moreover it seemed at one time as though the railway to the Transvaal would be British-owned. Nevertheless it remained an urgent priority of British policy, directly or indirectly, to gain control of Delagoa Bay, while for the Transvaal it remained equally vital to protect this independent link with the outside world.

Germany's insecurity derived from its position in Europe between Russia and France, rather than from its relatively unimportant African empire. However, its policy-makers increasingly believed that Germany had to assert itself as a great power in various parts of the world as a guarantee of its security in Europe. It was in the 1890s that Tirpitz began to develop the German deep-sea fleet, a move which could only be interpreted as a direct challenge to Britain.

The main thrust of British policy in the 1890s was to remove the threat of a German-Transvaal alliance and secure the diplomatic isolation of the Boers. Essential to this policy was Britain's formal annexation of Pondoland, Zululand and Tongaland, which secured control of the whole of the east coast of South Africa up to the Portuguese frontier. These annexations were completed by 1896 and allowed Britain to compensate the Transvaal by the virtual cession of Swaziland in 1894. However, the completion of the railway from the Rand to Lourenço Marques, also in 1894, made it seem all the more urgent that the long-term future of Mozambique should be settled by international treaty.[1]

In the 1890s all the Portuguese colonial possessions seemed highly unstable. Disorder and anarchy in Angola and Mozambique and the evident incapacity of the Portuguese to control much of the interior, coupled with the financial weakness which had driven Portugal to abandon the gold standard in 1891, suggested to Lord Salisbury that provision should be made for a future crisis in which the powers might have to partition the Portuguese colonies. He began negotiations with Germany to establish the conditions under which Portugal might be offered a loan, secured on its colonies like a kind of mortgage. Eventually in 1898 his diplomacy was successful and Britain and Germany signed a secret accord, known as the Treaty of Westminster, which provided for the partition of the Portuguese empire in the event of Portugal being forced to give up its colonies. Germany and Britain agreed that they would partition Mozambique, giving Germany the north and Britain the south (including, of course, Delagoa Bay). Angola was also to be partitioned with Britain taking a central corridor along which Sir Robert Williams was already planning to build his Benguela railway, and Germany taking territory in the north and south. The southern area would adjoin German South West Africa and give Germany access to the port of Mossamedes — a central ambition of German imperialists at the turn of the century. This treaty has been seen as a cunning hoodwinking of the Germans by the masterly diplomacy of Salisbury, but it was more than a mere paper exercise to exclude the Germans from southern Africa.[2] It had the effect of dividing the Portuguese colonies into spheres of influence for the purposes of commercial activity, investment and even missionary enterprise, and of removing the constant source of friction caused by the mutual suspicions of the great powers.

Although the treaty, the terms of which soon became known, was greatly resented in Portugal, its effect was not to weaken but to strengthen Portugal's hold on its empire. With the two major powers now reasonably confident that their national interests would be safeguarded in the event of any regional crisis, much pressure was removed from Portugal. It was no longer subjected to the intense propaganda and diplomatic harassment it had experienced in the 1880s when Germany and Britain were competing for influence. Moreover, in 1899 Britain signed a secret agreement with Portugal (the Treaty of Windsor) whereby Britain guaranteed the security of Portugal's colonial possessions.

The secret treaty with Germany, renewed in 1913, was a major example of the way in which tension between the great powers could be relieved, and provides a strong argument against the view that imperial rivalry helped to create the conditions for the outbreak of the First World War. Shortly after it was signed, Britain and the Transvaal were involved in the Second Boer War, in which Portugal co-operated fully with Britain: the port of Lourenço Marques remained open for British troop movements but closed for the Boers. With the British occupation of the goldfields in 1900, the signing of the *modus vivendi* over labour and railway matters in 1901 and the formal annexation of the Transvaal in 1902, Britain felt reasonably confident that the Portuguese possession of Delagoa Bay no longer threatened its interests — although the ambitions of certain South African politicians to acquire the Bay remained a factor in regional politics throughout the twentieth century.

The danger of armed intervention from Rhodesia also gradually receded. Briefly, in 1890 and 1891, Mozambique had been menaced by the new buccaneer regime of the British South Africa Company. Portuguese territory had been occupied and armed clashes had taken place. Moreover, Rhodes had surreptitiously encouraged the revolt of Barue against Sousa in 1891 and tried direct negotiations with the still independent and unsubdued Gungunhana, sending guns and even recruiting white mercenaries with the idea of seizing a portion of Mozambique territory. However, Rhodes's credibility in London was ebbing fast and Salisbury had no intention of allowing the carefully negotiated settlement with Portugal to be disrupted. Instead Rhodes was encouraged to proceed by peaceful means to build a railway to Beira and obtain recruitment rights for labour from the Portuguese. With the outbreak of the Mashona rising in 1896 the days of Rhodes' independence were numbered, and after the rebellion was over the government of Rhodesia came under much closer supervision from the British High Commissioner in South Africa. Even so it appears that Rhodes's adventurism lingered on; his agents operated within the unpacified enclave of Barue up till 1902, the year of his death.[3]

Direct military or political intervention from outside gradually receded as a threat to Mozambique's future as a colonial state, but the invasion of foreign capital, however slow to start, soon gathered momentum. By 1900 large areas of Mozambique were controlled by foreign-owned concession companies while others had negotiated extensive rights and privileges for themselves within the country. The reasons for this can best be explained by examining the desperate situation facing the Portuguese in eastern Africa in the aftermath of the partition treaties.

Mozambique and the new imperialism

During the eighteenth century the Portuguese port towns of eastern Africa had been wholly given over to ivory trading. This commerce was dominated by Indian capital, Indians made up the largest and most prosperous section of the population in the ports and the Zambesi settlements, and the whole commercial orientation was in the direction of India. There was no direct trade between Portugal and eastern Africa and barely one ship a year — bringing administrators, convicts and soldiers — linked Mozambique with Lisbon. The growth of the slave trade, however, led to the revival of the commercial interest of metropolitan Portugal in eastern Africa since Portuguese finance had become heavily involved in the Brazilian slave trade.[4]

During the period of liberal ascendancy after 1831 major efforts were made to stimulate economic activity in the African colonies, but this liberal legislation made little real impact in Mozambique, and the growth of Portuguese trade with Africa and investment in it was confined to the West while colonial trade (also almost exclusively with the West African colonies) rose from being barely 1 per cent of Portugal's total overseas trade to 3–6 per cent after 1840.[5]

Metropolitan economic initiatives in Mozambique were fleeting and unsuccessful. In 1824 a trading company called the Companhia Comercial de Feitorias de Lourenço Marques e Inhambane was established, but it was involved in numerous scandals and shady deals and ceased trading in 1835. The attempts to found agricultural settlements under government auspices at Fernão Veloso Bay in 1829 and Pemba in 1856 were likewise unsuccessful, while the 1860s witnessed the spectacular military disasters at Massangano, perhaps the nadir in metropolitan links with eastern Africa.

It was widely appreciated in Lisbon that the backwardness of the metropolitan Portuguese economy was partly the result of the lack of economic infrastructure, and it became the strategy of Portuguese governments during the 1860s and 1870s to try to develop the necessary structures for economic growth. The transference of the colonies to the responsibility of the Navy Ministry in 1859, and the other measures taken in the 1850s to improve colonial administration, should be seen in this light. In 1864 the Banco Nacional Ultramarino (BNU) was founded with a fifteen-year monopoly in colonial banking, and in 1869 the treaty with the South African Republic and the decision to build a road to the high veldt opened an era in which one of the major objectives of Portuguese policy was to develop Lourenço Marques as the principal port serving southern Africa. However, although commerce in Mozambique expanded considerably in the 1870s and 1880s, with French, Dutch and British business interests establishing commercial houses alongside the ubiquitous Indians, Mozambique's share of Portugal's colonial trade actually fell from 3 to 1 per cent.

Nevertheless, the African empire was beginning during the 1880s to assume greater importance in the eyes of the Portuguese business community, and this was reflected in the active imperial policy pursued by the government and the Lisbon Geographical Society throughout that decade. In the second half of the nineteenth century Portugal had begun to industrialise with textiles assuming a leading role. From the start the colonial market was crucial to the success of the industry, and by 1870 three-quarters of textile exports were being absorbed by the colonies. The idea of a great central African empire stretching across the continent appealed strongly to the textile manufacturers who recognised the importance of cloth in African trade. The textile industries were disastrously affected by the European depression of the 1880s and became a vocal pressure group demanding protection for their all-important colonial markets. They were soon to be joined by the wine exporters, who until that time had largely ignored the colonies. The pro-imperial party which was pressing the case for Portuguese settlement in Africa was now increasingly backed by influential sections of the industrial and commercial establishment which wanted to see the economies of the colonies 'nationalised' to a far greater extent.[6]

This was the background to the financial crisis of 1890 which forced the Portuguese government into financial manoeuvres that involved devaluation of the currency and a unilateral rescheduling of foreign debt. The financial crisis came just as Portugal was assuming massive new colonial responsibilities so that, as well as the need to establish some form of administration to fend off the predatory British and Germans, it was now equally urgent to make the colonies pay for themselves and to find some way for them to contribute to the dire problems of the metropolitan economy. This was the background to the policies adopted in the 1890s — the colonial tariff of 1892, the alienation of much of Mozambique to concession companies, the labour agreements with South Africa, and the new land, tax and labour legislation culminating in the labour law of 1899.

The centrepiece of this imperial strategy was the tariff. Its objectives were threefold; to protect Portuguese exports to the colonies, a policy designed to help textile manufacturers and increasingly also wine shippers; to assist Portuguese shipping by means of heavy tariff advantages to both Portuguese and foreign importers using Portuguese ships; and to channel more colonial trade via Lisbon where re-exports could earn much-needed foreign exchange for the Portuguese economy, a policy which undoubtedly saved Portugal from bankruptcy over the next twenty years.[7] The tariff was to be a formative influence in Portugal and throughout its West African colonies, but its influence on Mozambique was marginal. First, large parts of Mozambique were alienated to charter companies which operated their own commercial policy; secondly, most of northern Mozambique came under the regulations governing tariffs which had been agreed at Berlin in 1885 for the conventional basin of the Congo; thirdly, Mozambique had a free trade agreement with the Transvaal and this had far more influence on the growth of its trade than the metropolitan tariff; and finally, no national shipping line operated regular services to Mozambique till 1903 — a situation with ludicrous consequences in the 1880s when Portuguese officers on secret government missions to forestall the dastardly British in Mashonaland or the Shire Highlands had had to travel on British steamers to their points of departure on the Mozambique coast.

More important for Mozambique than the tariff was the general orientation of imperial policy, of which the tariff was merely one aspect. Throughout the 1890s colonial administrators had to give priority to finding the cheapest and most direct means of making the colony pay its way. From the 1870s the economy of Mozambique was expanding as more and more of the interior was opened up and peasant production for the market increased in the coastal zones. The problem therefore for the colonial government was not to stimulate trade but to attract investment. Banking institutions in Portugal operated conservative policies. Domestic interest rates were high and the BNU with its colonial monopoly would only lend at metropolitan interest rates.[8] Investment in the colonies was largely confined to the cocoa plantations of São Tomé. In Mozambique the problem was made worse by insecurity; most of the country was 'unpacified' and even the old-established coastal settlements were threatened from time to time by the semi-independent chiefs or bandit leaders who controlled the immediate hinterland. Here we encounter the cautionary tale of the Opium Company. In 1874 Ignacio de Paiva Raposo, who had made and lost a fortune in ivory trading, took out a concession to grow opium on the lower Zambesi. He was encouraged by the government, recruited Indian poppy-growers, and survived a financial crisis, labour shortages and the Zambesi floods, only to have his poppy fields and company installations burnt in the Massingire rising of 1884.[9]

The story of the Opium Company and of the other early pioneers on the lower Zambesi taught three very clear lessons. First, the lower Zambesi region was geographically suitable for the development of tropical plantations; secondly, there was a need for security for crops and fixed assets; and thirdly, investment would be attracted if supplies of cheap labour could be assured. In the early 1890s the Mozambique government set about resolving these issues and did so through a comprehensive review of its land, labour, taxation and administration policies. The brain and organising ability behind these changes was that of António Ennes whose ideas and creative energy were to be so influential in the development of Mozambique during the 1890s.

The colonial administrators were faced with a policy dilemma. Formal pacification seemed vitally necessary, if for no other reason than that the international community expected it and might consider a repartition if it were not achieved. The rivalry of Britain and Germany would be fed by internal anarchy in Mozambique. However, Portugal's military record was not encouraging. The disasters of the attacks on Massangano in the 1860s were not forgotten, while the more recent humiliations in Manica and the subsequent disintegration of Sousa's empire had removed the most effective of the local private armies. In spite of this it was decided that pacification had to be undertaken.

The Portuguese had little in the way of resources to face these problems. There was no colonial service, and most administrators were career officers from the armed services for whom a posting in Africa was a far from desirable billet. There was no regular emigration of settlers, and the Portuguese community tended to consist of convicts or traders. In most of the settlements, the most important element numerically in the population were the *mestizo* families and Indians and these played a dominant role in the life of the colony. However, they were closely connected with the previous regime of commerce and informal political influence and were far from ideal instruments of the new imperialism. There were numerous foreigners — British, Boers, Germans and others — crowding the port towns of Beira and Lourenço Marques, but they were seen by the struggling colonial administration as a threat rather than as a help. For the metropolitan Portuguese government, with little in the way of funds or manpower at its disposal, a sustained policy of African expansion such as had been undertaken in the 1880s was difficult. The only asset possessed by the Mozambique state which could be immediately realised were the revenues of the port of Lourenço Marques and the earnings from contract labour.

In these circumstances the Portuguese government took what must have seemed to be an inevitable decision. It contracted out the administration, pacification and development of most of Mozambique to private companies, leaving the southern quarter of the country, south of the Sabi, to be exploited directly by the state as a reserve of labour for the South African mines (Map 8).

Developments in the late 1880s had already sketched the outline of such a policy. During that decade, the Portuguese had been forced to recognise the extent to which their African colonial ambitions were at the mercy of the Afro-Portuguese warlords of Zambesia. Augusto de Castilho, the governor-general who had eventually triumphed over the Da Cruz in 1888, had been only too aware that this victory depended on the backing of bandit chiefs no less objectionable than the Da Cruz. He had urged that the *prazo* system be abolished and replaced by a regular administration. Although the minister in Lisbon accepted Castilho's resignation rather than his outspoken ideas, a commission was appointed in November 1888 to review the *prazos*, and from it emerged plans to adapt the ancient institution to the perceived needs of the modern colonial era.[10]

In November 1890 the new secretary of state for the navy and colonies, António Ennes, who had been a member of the *prazo* commission, published a law embodying a comprehensive restructuring of the *prazos* and with them the whole colonial administration of central Mozambique.[11] The *prazos* were, of course, historic institutions, as ancient in their way as English shires or French *départements*, and it was felt that any attempt to construct a new administration in Zambesia had to take account of these traditional divisions of the land and the people. So the intention of Ennes was to make use of the *prazo* system to achieve the pacification and administration of Zambesia and provide the capital and labour to bring about economic development. By this law the *prazos* classified as 'unpacified' were to be leased out for ten years, the lessee having the obligation to pacify the *prazo*, establish an administration and police force, and in return to collect the traditional poll tax (*mussoco*). This was all very much within the traditions of Zambesia, and reading thus far the *muzungo* families would no doubt have thought that for them it would be business as usual. However, in the *prazos* of the lower river, which were deemed already to be pacified and which were to be leased for twenty-five years, it was stipulated that half of the tax had to be collected in the form of labour from the population and that a specified area of the concession had to be cultivated. Clearly Ennes intended that the taxation would pay for administration and police but that the *prazo*-owner would be forced to undertake some economic development in order to make use of the proportion of the tax which the peasants paid in labour.

It is probable that Ennes wanted the *prazos* leased to individuals, thereby encouraging settlement, but in practice, when the law was implemented, almost all the leases were granted to commercial

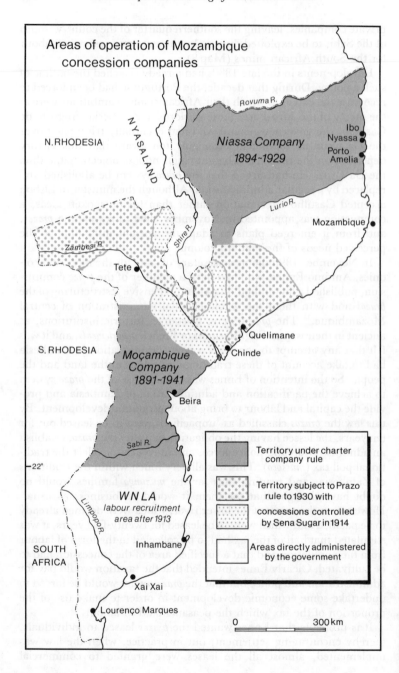

Areas of operation of Mozambique concession companies

NYASALAND

N. RHODESIA

Rovuma R.

Niassa Company 1894~1929

Ibo
Nyassa
Porto Amelia

Lurio R.

Mozambique

Zambesi R.

Shire R.

Tete

S. RHODESIA

Moçambique Company 1891~1941

Quelimane

Chinde

Beira

Sabi R.

—22°

Limpopo R.

WNLA labour recruitment area after 1913

SOUTH AFRICA

Inhambane

Xai Xai

Lourenço Marques

Territory under charter company rule

Territory subject to Prazo rule to 1930 with concessions controlled by Sena Sugar in 1914

Areas directly administered by the government

0   300 km

companies. All the *prazos* on the south bank fell within the concession of the Moçambique Company, which was granted its charter in February 1891, while in the Tete district 126 out of the 134 *prazos* were leased to the newly-formed Zambesia Company which also took out some leases on the lower river.[12] The Zambesia Company was originally dominated by Albert Ochs who had substantial shareholdings in the Moçambique Company and eventually came to control it, and who planned to establish a political and commercial empire which could rival that of Cecil Rhodes. However, the Zambesia Company had taken on a huge, unexplored and wholly unpacified region which it did not have the capacity to administer or occupy. Further down the river a number of consortia, hastily got together, leased blocks of *prazos*. The most important of these were the Boror and Luabo Companies, the Société du Madal and the Moçambique Sugar Company, later to become the famous Sena Sugar Estates.[13]

Initially these companies were largely paper structures. Although on the lower river the development of plantations got under way with the concessionaires recruiting company police, known as *cipais*, to coerce the peasants on their *prazos* into an involuntary labour force, the country above the Lupata gorge was hardly pacified. The Da Cruz had indeed been humbled and the surviving members of their family lived as bandits in the interior. However, the fall of Sousa had led to Barue becoming once again wholly independent, while Sousa's captains had effectively divided up his empire and ruled as bandit chiefs from their strongholds in the interior. Macanga also was totally independent, and the Zumbo *muzungos*, in spite of having lost much of their territory in the partition, still ruled their riverain domains between Tete and Zumbo. The Zambesia Company could do little beyond sub-lease its *prazos* to the actual occupiers and rulers of the land.

Nevertheless the partition of Africa had made some differences. It was no longer possible for the Afro-Portuguese warlords and their *chicunda* armies to raid indiscriminately into the Luangwa and Kafue valleys. British rule effectively closed off this option. There remained a market for slaves in the Ndebele kingdom but this also came under British rule in 1893. Ivory and a little gold could still be traded but the only real resort for the *muzungo* slavers was to turn themselves, almost overnight, into labour recruiters or company police. Labour touts seeking workers for the Rand mines or the Rhodesian farms found willing collaborators among the Afro-Portuguese — the old families of Zambesia adapting their role once again to the new economic climate as they had done in each century since Francisco Barreto arrived in Sena with his army in 1572.

During the 1890s Zambesia was gradually pacified and the

skeleton of an administration was laid out. Company police superseded the *chicunda* as the collectors of tax and the recruiters of labour, and 1902 saw the occupation of Macanga by Zambesia Company police and the end of the independent kingdom of the Caetano Pereiras north of the river.[14] The long resistance of the Afro-Portuguese warlords and their captains from the early days of the Zambesi wars through to 1902 and in some cases beyond, was evidence of the powerfully resilient culture of the Zambesi *muzungos* and their *chicunda*. The peculiar mixture of commerce, banditry and feudal lordship that had marked their survival as a class allowed them to survive whatever attempts the government made to undermine the basis of their power. They were even able to survive the transfer of the *prazos* to company control, many of them enjoying a final decade or two of influence as agents or subcontractors of the concession companies. Seigneurial families fighting to survive as a predatory class have worn the liveries of many different causes — in the history of Europe dissident feudal nobles were associated with Magna Carta and the birth of parliament, and in continental Europe with Protestantism and resistance to absolutism; in more recent times many of them have appeared to fight for liberal or nationalist causes. Likewise the *muzungo* families of Zambesia, essentially fighting for their survival as a class, have been made to carry the banner for those resisting colonial oppression or fighting for the nationalist cause.

Banditry remained endemic in the Zambesi valley and the escarpment even after 1902 — erupting in 1917 into the dangerous and widespread Barue rebellion.[15] During the high noon of colonial rule from 1920 to 1960 banditry as such died down, but company and later state police continued the traditions of the *chicunda*, raiding local villages for labour, military recruits or road workers, and exacting taxation in a more or less violent and predatory manner. It is of little surprise that it was in this area that first Frelimo and then Renamo found the traditions of banditry easy to reawaken in their resistance to remote and centralising governments.

The Moçambique Company

While Ennes sought to remodel the historic institutions of the *prazos* to attract foreign plantation capital and solve the problems of pacification and administration, a somewhat different regime was being created south of the Zambesi. Here the problems of economic development, pacification and administration were being entrusted to a single charter company.

The origin of the Moçambique Company dates from to the mineral and timber concession obtained by Paiva de Andrada in 1878. At that time much of this region was unexplored or in the hands of Afro-Portuguese warlords, and Andrada was to spend the next decade exploring his concession and trying with the help of Manuel António de Sousa to bring it under Portuguese control. Meanwhile his efforts to raise capital to exploit the concession were singularly unsuccessful, and it was not till March 1888 that a body of backers could be found and the first Moçambique Company formed.[16]

The Moçambique Company was originally capitalised at a mere £40,000 sterling, raised by Edmund Bartissol in Paris since Portuguese investors had shown no interest in the venture. The Company's immediate objective was to make money from leasing sub-concessions. Manica was seen as its most valuable asset and although Andrada was not able to get any substantial concession from the Gaza king when visiting his capital in 1888, Gungunhana did agree to co-operate by sending an expedition to Manica. This enabled the Company to begin to grant prospecting licenses throughout the region on the very dubious legal grounds that the chiefs of Manica had in the past recognised the overlordship of Sousa, Andrada's associate.[17]

As the quarrel with Britain developed throughout 1889 and the rival British South Africa Company negotiated for a charter, Andrada and Bartissol pressed for their company to be given a charter as well. The negotiations were completed in February 1891, at a time when Rhodes's men were occupying Masekesa and Portugal was under extreme pressure to assert its 'effective occupation' of the disputed region. The charter granted the Company the right to raise taxes, to grant mineral and land concessions and to issue currency and postage stamps. In return it undertook the administration, pacification and settlement of the region between the Zambesi and latitude 22° south of the Sabi, and agreed to pay the Portuguese government 7.5 per cent of all profits. The term of the charter, originally 25 years, was extended in 1897 so that it would terminate in 1942.[18] The governor of the territory and a majority of the board had to be Portuguese, but from the start the majority of shares in the Company were foreign-owned. The original capital was raised from both French and British investors but in 1893 Albert Ochs, a Jew of Belgian birth, began to buy into the Company and by 1895 had taken financial control.

Although the Company increased its capital through various share issues in the 1890s, it was Ochs's policy that most of this capital should be reinvested outside Africa, thus forcing the Company to provide as best it could from local sources for its rapidly growing expenditure.[19] Its only realisable assets were port revenues, land and minerals rights, and the taxes and labour of the African inhabitants. Mineral and farming concessions were granted in Manica and the lower Zambesi, mostly to non-Portuguese, and work was pushed ahead on developing the port of Beira and on building a railway to Southern Rhodesia. The concession to build the railway was granted to a consortium that was eventually taken over by Cecil Rhodes and the contractor Pauling, and the line was completed in 1898. Revenues from the port of Beira then became the Company's most important asset.

Exploiting the other assets was less straightforward. The collapse of Sousa's power following his capture by the British South Africa police in 1890 had been followed by widespread insurrection, and Sousa was killed in 1892 while trying to reconquer his domain. The Company at that point controlled almost none of its territory and entered into an agreement with Gungunhana whereby he would provide the Company with soldiers and senior *majobos* (officials), impose the joint authority of the king and the Company, and collect tax from the African population. This agreement operated for two years during which time the Company was able, with Gaza aid, to establish some sort of dominance in its territory.[20] The link with Gaza finally collapsed when Gungunhana was defeated at Coolela in 1895, but by that time the Company was in a stronger financial position and able to take over administrative control as heirs of Gungunhana's power.

It took somewhat longer to gain control in Zambesia and the old heartland of Sousa's personal empire. On Sousa's death each of his principal captains set themselves up in *aringas* in different parts of Gorongosa and the Zambesi valley, levying what tribute and services they pleased from the peasantry while Barue reverted to the control of the Macombe. The Company had no funds and no troops of its own and initially sought to co-operate with Cambuemba and Luis Santiago, two of Sousa's principal captains. For five years confusion and anarchy reigned throughout Zambesia and Gorongosa. Warbands raided each other or plundered Company posts, the country witnessing the worst banditry it had experienced since the drought of the 1820s. The captains were incapable of unity among themselves and could not achieve any effective combination with traditional chiefs. The wretched peasant population were harried, plundered and enslaved.[21]

Such a situation would only be ended by an assertion of central authority, and this the Company was unable to make till 1896. In that year its agents began to recruit their own *cipais*, while Gorongosa was subleased to a company which began to collect *mussoco* among the peasantry. In May 1897 the Company's posts were once again attacked by Cambuemba, but this time there was an effective response. João de Azevedo Coutinho, one of the more ruthless and efficient of the Portuguese colonial soldiers, was commissioned to recruit an army north of the Zambesi, and enlisted soldiers from the still independent *chicunda* republic of Maganja da Costa. In June he destroyed Cambuemba's *aringas* and with them his power throughout the Zambesi valley. The Company could now begin to call its concession its own, and in recognition of the changed situation its concession was extended for a further 45 years.[22]

There still remained Gorongosa and Barue to be pacified and occupied, and desultory fighting continued between *cipais* in the pay of the Company and the remnants of the *chicunda* loyal to Cambuemba and Luis Santiago, who increasingly co-operated with the Barue chiefs. Armed raids were launched on Company stores and posts, and collection of taxes or any other assertion of Company authority remained extremely hazardous. Up till 1902, Barue remained independent, the last African chieftaincy south of the Zambesi to do so. This was an extraordinary survival of a Karanga kingdom that had ruled the area continuously since the fifteenth century, but had now come to be surrounded by colonial territory.

The Nyassa Company

The charter to the Moçambique Company was issued in February 1891, and in May Britain and Portugal finally came to an agreement over the frontiers of Mozambique. In September a decree granted a concession for the establishment of a second charter company to control the whole of the 100,000 square miles of territory north of the Lurio River.

Before the 1890s, the Portuguese had done little exploration in the area north of the Zambesi, confining their activities to trading from their *presídios* at Quelimane, which still served as the port of entry to Zambesia, Angoche (conquered in 1862), Mozambique Island and Ibo. Attempts by weak Portuguese forces to conquer areas of the interior had always been disastrously unsuccessful and the Makua chiefs proved far better able to resist the Portuguese than the warlords of Zambesia or the *impis* of Gungunhana.

The first Europeans to travel down the caravan roads that for centuries had run from Kilwa along the Lugenda valley towards the Zambesi were Livingstone and the missionaries of the UMCA. In 1881 Joseph Thompson had made a brief exploration south of the Rovuma; also in that year and again in 1883 the British consul in Mozambique, Henry O'Neill, had travelled widely in the interior exploring the Namuli mountains and reaching Lake Shirwa. He had been followed by an expedition organised by the Royal Geographical Society of London and led by J.T. Last. Last had set out from Lindi in September 1885, travelled to the Lake by the now familiar route of the Lugenda valley and then explored the Namuli mountains before returning to Ibo.[23] Northern Mozambique was at last being explored by the new generation of European geographers and empire-builders.

What is so significant about these expeditions is how easily they passed through the Yao and Makua country. Over the previous three centuries few Portuguese had cared to penetrate the interior, and expeditions setting out from Mozambique Island had had difficulty moving even two or three days' march into the interior. However, in the 1880s it seems that expeditions could move with considerable freedom until they met with the organised Yao or Swahili chieftaincies near the Lake whose attitude was suspicious and sometimes obstructive.

The first serious attempt of the Portuguese to establish their presence in the hinterland of their Cabo Delgado settlements came only in 1885. In that year Serpa Pinto, assisted by the young Augusto Cardoso and accompanied by seventy Nguni soldiers, had set out to march to Lake Malawi. Because of arguments over how the expedition would be supplied and financed, it had shifted its point of departure from Mozambique Island to Ibo, marching with its carriers, *cipais* and stores northwards along the coast. Cardoso had then led the expedition inland to Medo where he made a treaty with Mtarica, the most powerful chief in the area, and proceeded to the Lake where he signed another treaty with Kwirassia, one of the Yao chiefs of the region. These treaties recognised Portuguese sovereignty and bound the chiefs to protect traders and cease raiding.[24]

It was this area, previously explored by Livingstone, the UMCA and Cardoso, that was granted as a fief to the Nyassa Company. The early history of the concession reveals much about the interest of Eurpopean investors in Africa in the late nineteenth century. The Company had originally been granted to a concessionnaire, Bernardo Daupias, who was unable to raise even a deposit of £2,000 and whose associates included at least one bankrupt, two Portuguese peers with royal connections, and a shady Bavarian baron called Merck, who was involved with Rhodes and the Cape government in trying to put together a syndicate to buy the Lourenço Marques railway.[25] However, in 1893 the Companhia do Nyassa was formally constituted, and its charter, similar to that of the Moçambique Company, was granted in 1894 for an extended period of thirty-five years. By 1895 £400,000 had been raised, but the directors of the various syndicates had no intention of investing this money in Africa. Instead they used it to speculate with the stock of their own Company or to invest on the European stock markets. The first managing director was a London concession-broker, called George Wilson, who unilaterally started coining money and printing stamps which he tried to unload on the English philatelic market. A telegram had to be sent to the Company's governor in Africa warning him not to accept either the coins or the stamps.[26] The rival financial syndicates could not agree which of them controlled the Nyassa Company itself. Rival British and French boards both opened offices in Lisbon and began litigation against each other, and it was not till 1897 that a new, united board controlled by British shareholders emerged.

Although the Company's charter had granted it what amounted to almost full government powers, it had only three immediately exploitable assets — taxation of the peasantry, labour and customs dues. Ibo island, the main coastal commercial centre, had not been included in the original concession and was only handed over to the Company in 1897, and the first hut tax collections took place the following year.[27] In 1899 the Company began to occupy the interior of its territory, dispatching three military expeditions which by 1901 had established a line of Company posts connected by a telegraph from the coast to the Lake and had partly surveyed a route for a railway.[28] However, this occupation of the interior remained tenuous as the powerful Yao chief, Mataka, remained actively independent and the Makonde country to the north was still virtually unexplored, let alone occupied. It was only in the coastal area that the Company's writ ran at all and it was there that it registered its one significant achievement, the founding of a town and administrative headquarters at Porto Amelia in 1904.

If lack of resources (or the unwillingness of the directors to use resources in Africa) prevented the establishment of an effective administration, this failure in turn prevented the Company from realising its assets and so increasing its profitability. Very little tax could be collected, trade remained confined to traditional caravan traffic, and when in 1903 the South African labour recruitment organisation WNLA signed a contract to recruit labour in the Company's territory, the results were disappointing.[29] It was only in 1908 that the Company, once again reorganised financially, began to make its presence systematically felt throughout its concession.

The first fifteen years of the Nyassa Company's life were, in so far as economic development or the establishment of a modern state were concerned, a farcical failure. An unedifying band of bankrupts and speculators squabbled in Europe, and an equally unappetising collection of mercenaries and officials tried by terror and extortion, yet inefficiently, to extract money or labour from any African peasants who came into their hands. But seen from another point of view, these fifteen years saw the chiefs of northern Mozambique mostly retaining their independence and the majority of the African population able to continue their traditional pattern of life without incorporation into the colonial state.

Incorporation of the south

The Gaza state had been critically isolated by the partition treaties of 1891. Before that date the Gaza monarchs had been able to play off British and Portuguese traders, missionaries and diplomats, obtaining guns, luxury imports and money without conceding any significant privileges. However, the partition effectively brought to an end this world of double diplomacy and left Gungunhana's state unequivocally in Portuguese territory (although the British South Africa Company maintained an agent at the Gaza court and continued to pay a subsidy till 1893). At first the Portuguese recognised his immediate sovereignty over large sections of the south of the country and the Moçambique Company was prepared to use the structures of the Gaza state to institute a form of indirect rule.[30] However, it was an uneasy relationship as the Gaza state was anyway experiencing severe internal problems.

The decision by Gungunhana to move his capital to the low veldt between the Limpopo and Inhambane had brought him into direct confrontation with the Chopi of that region, and there followed a series of wars as the Gaza king tried to establish firm control of the region. The departure of workers to the South African mines over a twenty-year period had also introduced far-reaching changes. Earnings from the mines were now used to settle brideprice transactions and to subvert the control which chiefs once exercised over cattle herds and the marriage of their young men. Moreover with the disappearance of large numbers of youths to the mines, slaves had been acquired to fill their role in agricultural production, while the army came increasingly to depend on regiments recruited from Tsonga and Ndau rather than Nguni.[31] This had made Gaza society more class-structured and removed the close links that had once existed between the people, the land and military service. The weakening of the Nguni military tradition had been accentuated by the growing restrictions on raiding. The drawing of colonial frontiers closed off the raiding areas to the west while the Moçambique Company's presence in the north effectively prevented raiding there also. There remained only the coastal zone and the presence of the Portuguese *presídios* made raiding the Chopi or the Tonga increasingly a matter of confrontation with the Portuguese authorities. Nevertheless it was the raiding of the Chopi in the final years of the kingdom's existence that generated the supply of female slaves that acted as a sort of demographic blood transfusion for the Gaza kingdom and stimulated a late flowering of the slave trade throughout the whole of southern Mozambique.[32]

In spite of these changes, the Gaza kingdom remained an imposing structure whose needs and modes of operation would sooner or later prove incompatible with those of a modern bureaucratic state. Moreover this state was desperate to unlock the economic resources of the south of Mozambique — to promote the emigration of young men and parcel out the land for plantation development. The building of railways and harbour facilities, the exploitation of minerals and the commercial penetration of the interior all joined the queue as desirable objectives, to achieve which Gaza needed to be fully incorporated into the colonial state. It was widely believed that this could only be done by military conquest.

The agreement made in 1893 between Gungunhana and the Moçambique Company marked an uneasy moment when the interests of a Gaza monarchy struggling to retain some autonomy and the burgeoning colonial state ran in concert. However, almost as soon as the agreement was made, quarrels came to the surface. Significantly it was the drink trade that fermented most of the trouble. In 1891 Gungunhana and the Portuguese had agreed to ban the sale of all alcohol except Portuguese wine and insist that traders had to have a licence issued in Lourenço Marques. In 1893, as a result of the rapid escalation of violence resulting from drink, Gungunhana took action to stop the sale of all alcohol, directly challenging the commercial objectives of the Portuguese.[33] Meanwhile British adventurers were still trying to obtain concessions from Gungunhana, and in 1894 the king made one last attempt to try to deal with the British South Africa Company. These problems brought matters to a head. The Portuguese decision to overthrow the Gaza kingdom had gradually evolved from the realms of fantasy to practical reality. The British South Africa Company's successful conquest of the Ndebele in 1893 had demonstrated how such a conquest might be made and had further isolated Gaza as the only surviving independent African monarchy in southern Africa. Even so, war with Gaza might never have been risked had it not been for the outbreak of hostilities involving Magaia and other Tsonga chiefs south of the Limpopo. These chiefs were nominally subject to the governor of Lourenço Marques and had come increasingly to resent the activities of labour recruiters and traders. The fighting brought Tsonga forces to the outskirts of Lourenço Marques itself between October 1894 and January 1895, and British and German warships arrived in the harbour on the pretext of protecting their nationals in the event of a collapse of Portuguese authority.[34]

In January 1895 António Ennes arrived as the new Portuguese high commissioner. In his mind the reassertion of Portuguese authority and the military defeat of Gaza were immediate necessities and he assembled a large European army of 2,000 men armed with machine-guns. In February Ennes' army won the battle of Marracuene, crushing the hostile Tsonga chiefs, and while J.J. de Almeida spun out further negotiations with Gungunhana, preparations for an invasion of Gazaland got under way. Even as Ennes advanced, negotiations continued and Gungunhana tried to find some way of retaining a limited autonomy for his kingdom. However, Ennes made no serious effort to compromise, and in August, after presenting an ultimatum, he began the invasion of Gaza and defeated some regiments sent against him at Magul. At this stage Gungunhana probably still did not want to fight a war with the Portuguese, and as late as October demobilised a large part of the estimated 40,000 soldiers encamped around the capital at Mandhlakazi.[35] However, the influence of the war party led by Maguiguana triumphed and the regiments were mobilised again. The Portuguese for their part sent forces to Inhambane and invaded Gaza from two directions while an armed flotilla entered the Limpopo. On 7 November eight Gaza regiments were smashed at the battle of Coolela and Mandhlakazi was burned. Gungunhana fled from the battle to Chaimite, the old Gaza capital and burial-place of Soshangane. There he was captured by Mouzinho de Albuquerque on 28 December and, after being paraded through the streets of Lisbon, sent into exile in the Azores (Map 9).[36]

The speed and completeness of this victory by the Portuguese army, reminiscent of the rout of the Ndebele two years earlier, has always surprised historians familiar with the conspicuous lack of success of Portuguese arms in Zambesia and the north. However, by the time the two armies faced each other at Coolela, the Gaza forces were demoralised and all but beaten. Of the eight regiments which faced the Portuguese, five were made up of Ndau or Tsonga little inclined to fight to the death for Gungunhana. There was deep dissension in the immediate entourage of the king, and this together with severe food shortages had undermined the army's morale. The military discipline of the Nguni had always been singularly inappropriate against heavy weapons, and the type of guerrilla warfare practised successfully further north was not something in which the Nguni were experienced. The Gaza monarch, moreover, could not afford to employ different tactics. The cattle-based institutions of the state could not tolerate the loss of its accumulated capital that it would have suffered in a retreat before the colonial forces into the bush, nor would the prestige of the Nguni rulers have survived such a dismantling of their political institutions.[37]

On the Portuguese side, the victories of 1895 greatly enhanced the reputations of a generation of proconsular figures who were to shape the future of Mozambique — Ennes the high commissioner, Freire de Andrade, who led the column invading from the south and who was to be governor-general of Mozambique from 1906 to 1910, Ayres

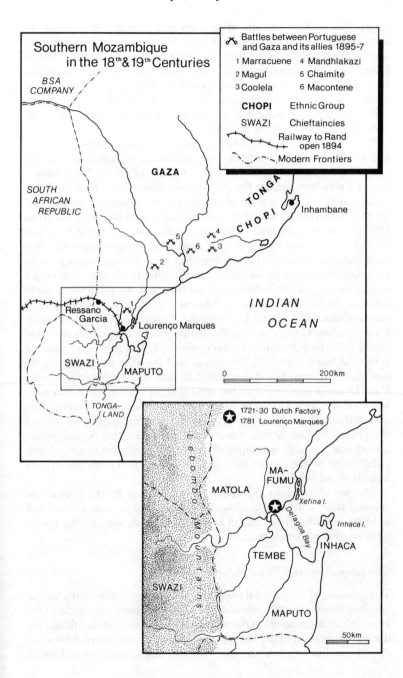

d'Ornellas who carried the ultimatum to Gungunhana and was to become minister for the colonies, and Mouzinho de Albuquerque, who led the force of cavalry that captured Gungunhana and succeeded Ennes as high commissioner in 1896. After the humiliations of the 1890 ultimatum, the imperial party in Portugal badly needed something to raise their prestige. The victors of 1895, and the myths they set about creating for themselves, gave the new colony of Mozambique a vestige of credibility.[38]

Two years later, in 1897, Maguiguana, a man of Tsonga origin who had risen in Umzila's service to command a regiment and under Gungunhana ultimately become commander of all the Gaza forces, staged a rebellion against the Portuguese. After the exile of the king, Gaza had fallen into a state of chaos. The Portuguese conquest had led to widespread destruction, looting and loss of life, and the years 1895-7 saw drought and rinderpest while many of those who had herded royal cattle had lost their livelihood. Maguiguana had not been present at Coolela and, together with Gungunhana's uncle Djambul, became a focus for all the discontent felt after the king's exile. Once again the fighting was decisive and the rebel forces were defeated by the Portuguese at Macontene in July 1897.[39] Maguiguana himself was pursued towards the Transvaal border and killed. This time the Gaza state finally disintegrated. Some irreconcilable chiefs including Pissane, another uncle of Gungunhana, escaped across the border into the Transvaal, and the once imposing empire had ceased to exist. It had also ceased to exist in the eyes of the people. Raúl Honwana recorded in his autobiography 'that when Gungunhana was finally led away by Mousinho de Albuquerque's troops, the crowd shouted. . . . "Away with you, vulture, slaughterer of our chickens".'[40] The destruction of the power of the Nguni ruling houses was probably not unpopular and at the time was regarded with indifference by the people they had conquered and from whom they had obtained tribute.

The end of the Gaza monarchy opened the way for the Portuguese colonial state in the south to achieve some level of organisation and to begin the immediate task of economic exploitation and the longer term process of development.

The administration of Mozambique before 1890

The drawing of the colonial frontiers made it imperative that a formal administrative structure should be created to cover the whole of the area within the frontiers of the new state. At the time of the ultimatum the administration of the Portuguese settlements in eastern Africa had not changed in any fundamental way since the end of the eighteenth century.[41] Zambesia had been divided into three captaincies, Sena, Tete and Quelimane, all responsible to the *Tenente Geral dos Rios*. The capital of the rivers had been moved from Sena to Tete in 1762 and in 1817 the captaincy of Sena was suppressed, the government of the Rivers being divided into two separate governorships based on Quelimane and Tete with Sena included in the latter. In 1829 these were reunited, but in 1853 they were once more separated with Sena this time being attached to Quelimane.[42]

When Francisco Maria Bordalo wrote in 1857, a Portugal dominated by liberal constitutionalists had emerged from thirty years of civil strife. The 595 registered electors of Portuguese East Africa returned two deputies to the Cortes in Lisbon, and the liberal Portuguese penal code had been formally introduced. This, however, was the only sign of liberalism in the settlements. Trial by jury was considered inapplicable and the governor-general presided over a *Junta do Justiça* (court of justice which had replaced the earlier criminal and appeal courts). He also presided over the *Junta da Fazenda* (treasury board) and the *Conselho do Governo* made up of the senior military, judicial and ecclesiastical officials and which stood in for the governor-general if he fell ill or died in office.[43]

During the 1850s efforts were made to create the basic administrative infrastructure which would be needed if the plans for the economic development of the settlements were to be realised. In 1856 a *Junta Geral da Provincia* was set up with 13 delegates from the different settlements. Its terms of reference indicate not so much what this paper organisation actually achieved as the way the government in Lisbon was thinking. It was supposed to 'civilise' the Africans, establish schools, improve commerce, build roads, promote the breeding of horses, camels and sheep, encourage the cultivation of sugar, spices, indigo, cotton and tobacco, see to the cultivation of empty land and the better distribution of the *prazos*, and form mining companies. It was a manifesto for a new capitalist vision of the empire.[44]

In 1854 a public health department was created and in 1858 an official government bulletin began to be published. Up till the 1850s the colonies had been supervised by the old *Conselho Ultramarino*, but in 1859 they were formally brought under the control of the navy ministry, renamed *Ministério da Marinha e Ultramar*. In practice the colonies were administered by service personnel, and the character of the government remained distinctly military. Between 1752 and 1890 there were 46 governors-general, all but two of whom had military or naval rank. Most of the subordinate governorships, too, were filled by military men and only in 1906 was provision made for a professional colonial service with the formation of the *Escola Colonial* in Lisbon.[45]

In the 1870s, as part of Andrade Corvo's plans to improve trade and communications, the government purchased a steamer to connect the coastal ports and a tug to assist ships in and out of Quelimane.[46] In 1862 the capture of the Muslim town of Angoche led to the establishment of a new Portuguese *presídio* and the setting up of a separate administrative district. Then during the 1880s two new administrative districts were created to meet the rapidly expanding Portuguese claims to territory; Manica and Sofala in 1884 and Zumbo in 1889. Other government agencies independent of the governor-general were set up by Lisbon: the treasury fiscals (inspectors) appointed in 1888, the director of public works and the superintendent of the Lourenço Marques railway in 1889 and the secretary-general in 1891.

Reorganisation of the administration after 1890

During the 1890s there was considerable debate about the way that the new colony should develop. Till the 1880s colonial policy had been based on various assumptions, the most important being a sort of liberal, assimilationist doctrine: as far as possible, the colonies should be treated as limbs of the mother-country; metropolitan laws should be enforced, civil rights extended, liberal economic policies pursued, and the labour regime freed. Mozambique sent deputies to the Cortes and the colonial budgets were treated as a single budgetary item, their deficits and surpluses being pooled, and any deficit covered by the metropolitan government.

The generation of colonial administrators who followed Ennes to Mozambique wanted a radical reappraisal. Their approach was summarised by Ennes and Mouzinho de Albuquerque who both wrote books — the one published in 1893, the other in 1899 — which together survey the problems and achievements of the decade.[47] Mouzinho wanted much greater independence for the colonies; the governors should have more authority to act and control all government agencies there; the colonial government must have financial independence from Lisbon and control its own budget; finally the mania for assimilation must end and the colonies be able to introduce legislation suitable for local needs. These changes were less ends in themselves than the means to achieve other ends. Mouzinho greatly admired the British and made no secret of his wish to emulate the development of the British African colonies. To achieve this he wanted an active policy of pacification, the encouragement of white settlement, and policies to force the African population to work within the colonial economy. But he recognised that to achieve these objectives it would be necessary to strengthen the colonial finances, and this rapidly became his top priority.

Once the immediate crisis of the ultimatum and the bankruptcy in Lisbon was over, measures were taken to modernise and strengthen the colonial administration. In 1891-2 António Ennes, who had been responsible for the new *prazo* law in 1890, was sent to Mozambique to recommend administrative changes — a mission which led him to publish his highly influential study, entitled *Moçambique*, in 1893. In 1894 the post of high commissioner was created, with full ministerial rank, to head the government and deal with the emergency created by insurrection in the south. Two of these officials were appointed, Ennes himself (1894-5) and Mouzinho de Albuquerque (1896-7), and together they initiated a policy, followed by their successors, of strengthening the colonial government. In view of the treaties with Britain the jurisdictions of the various *presídios* had to be reorganised. Mozambique was divided into two provinces separated by the Zambesi and named Mozambique and Lourenço Marques after the two principal Portuguese towns. Each province was divided into districts. In Mozambique province the districts were Cabo Delgado (coinciding with the Nyassa Company's concession), Mozambique (absorbing the district of Angoche in 1893) and Zambesia (including the former districts of Tete and Zumbo); in Lourenço Marques province there were the districts of Lourenço Marques, Inhambane, Gaza (made a military district in December 1895) and Manica and Sofala, which coincided with the territory of the Moçambique Company.[48] In 1902, following the reconquest of Barue and its transfer from the control of the Moçambique Company to that of the state, Zambesia was divided and a new Tete district created.[49] As we have seen, the concession companies were entrusted with the task of pacification, economic development and administration within the area of their concessions. Each district had its own governor and administrative council (*concelho administrativo*).

A decree of 20 February 1894 created seven judicial districts (*comarcas*) corresponding with the administrative divisions, except that two *comarcas*, based in Beira and Masekesa, were created for the Moçambique Company's territory. Legal frameworks were also published for health and education.[50]

Pacification campaigns were seen as a high priority and essential if the finances of the colony were to be soundly based and foreign investments attracted. The two most successful military operations were the conquest and incorporation of Gaza in 1895-7 and Barue in 1902. Along with the pacification, a hut tax (or in Zambesia the more traditional *mussoco*, head tax) was introduced, which was raised steadily to 1,200 *réis* in 1894, and eventually to 4,500 *réis* (equivalent at that time to £1 sterling) in 1906 by Freire de Andrade, who later claimed that the conquest of Gaza had amply justified the expense. 'It [the conquest] cost 200 *contos* but this capital has yielded an annual return of 40 to 50 per cent through the imposition of the hut tax made possible that expedition.'[51] The real profit of this colonial policy, however, was not found in hut tax collections but in the mobilisation of a vast army of labour for internal use and to serve the South African gold mines.

The conquest of Gaza and Barue was followed by the removal, death or exile of their ruling dynasties. Military posts were established under Portuguese officers backed by black *cipais*, and these began to collect tax, recruit labour and carry out other rudimentary governmental functions using the *régulos* — petty chiefs or village headmen — as their agents and replacing them if they refused. As more and more of the country became 'pacified', it was recognised that a more formal administrative structure would be necessary. In December 1895 Ennes had divided the territory of the District of Lourenço Marques into five circumscriptions each with its own *administrador*, and this set the pattern for the administrative development of the whole country which was eventually to be incorporated in the Colonial Reform Act of 1907.[52]

Another significant change was the designation of Lourenço Marques as the capital in 1902. With the development of the economic links with South Africa, Mozambique Island had lost its economic significance and was geographically too remote from the all-important southern regions. For a few years the high commissioners divided their attentions between the Island and the growing city in the south, but the formal removal of the government to the latter was only a matter of time. The location of the capital in the extreme south followed the logic of the colony's evolution but it was to have considerable long-term importance for Mozambique's development. Because of its situation almost as an enclave within South Africa, the colonial bureaucracy was far away from the land it ruled and which it tended to view as so many economic concessions rather than as a single country to be united by infrastructure and economic interchange. The city of Lourenço Marques became linked with South Africa, forming part of a dense rail and commercial network that made it part of the South African consumer nexus. It is interesting to imagine how the country might have developed had the capital remained at Mozambique Island or been established at Beira.

Labour legislation: an epitaph for António Ennes

Between 1897 and 1899, another building block of the new colonial state was put in place. In 1897 the South African Republic and Mozambique formalised arrangements for the recruitment and transit of labourers to the gold mines, and in 1899 Ennes, now back in Lisbon, introduced his new colonial labour law, which has rightly been seen as marking a fundamental change of direction in colonial policy.[53]

The imperial party represented by Ennes and Mouzinho had not had their way in everything — indeed Mouzinho had resigned as high commissioner on being refused the plenary powers he sought. However, with the 1899 labour law they witnessed the final burial of the old liberal integrationist colonial principles. Any pretence that metropolitan laws could be applied to colonial populations was now abandoned. From now on, the law would recognise two classes of citizen, *indígena* and *não-indígena*. The *não-indígena* would have full Portuguese citizenship rights and live under metropolitan law while the *indígena* would be formally administered by African law and by the particular laws of the individual colonies. In no field was this to be more important than that of labour and tax obligation.

Between 1850 and 1880 there had been a progressive liberalisation of the colonial labour laws. In 1858, it was decreed that slavery would be abolished twenty years later, in 1878. In 1869 it was decided formally to abolish slavery but to replace it with the intermediate status of *liberto* whereby the ex-slave was contracted to work for his former master till 1878. Then in 1875, as part of Andrade Corvo's efforts to promote free trade and commercial development, *liberto* status was ended too, but the *liberto* was to remain contracted to his former employer till 1878. Already in this crab-like approach to abolition the Portuguese authorities had revealed a remarkable penchant for developing euphemisms. Slave was replaced by *liberto* and *liberto* by contracted labourer — altogether, little had changed.[54]

In 1878, however, forced labour of all kinds officially came to an end in Mozambique and a free labour market reigned. The labour regulation of 21 November 1878 specifically declared that 'no one can be obliged to contract his services, save those individuals who shall be judged vagrants'. Ennes was to consider that this conferred 'the liberty to continue to live in a state of savagery'.[55] This remark was hardly justified since Africans were by that time voluntarily contracting themselves in large numbers with South African labour recruiters, while others were migrating to Lourenço Marques for work on the port and railway, and in regions with easy access to markets peasant cash-crop production was booming.[56] Moreover, the law still provided for penal labour for 'vagrants', which provided colonial officials with a loophole to reintroduce forced labour when it was needed.

What changed this liberal attitude was the realisation that plantation agriculture was the only realistic way of attracting capital to

Africa and that without a cheap labour supply there would be no reason to invest in Mozambique. The *prazo* commission in 1888 envisaged that Africans would be required to pay part of their tax in labour, and this proposal was enshrined in the *prazo* law of 1890. In 1894, for the first time, correctional labour was introduced whereby Africans who defaulted on any law could be made to work as their penalty. Correctional labour was to remain in all the future penal codes adopted by the Portuguese.[57] Then in 1898 the government appointed a commission, chaired by Ennes, to review labour legislation. The report elaborated on the need for cheap labour supplies:

> Portugal needs, needs absolutely and urgently, to make its African inheritance prosper and its prosperity can only come from its productivity. Today the supreme and fundamental problem of the administration . . . is to oblige the overseas provinces to produce and maybe the solution of this most difficult problem will be the single practical solution to the national crisis. Our Africa will not be cultivated except by Africans. The capital which is loaned to exploit it and which is so necessary for it, demands labour for its exploitation, abundant, cheap and resistant labour. . . . The black and only the black can fertilize Africa. . . .[58]

The labour law of 1899 tackled this problem directly:

> All natives . . . are subject to the obligation, moral and legal, of attempting to obtain through work the means that they lack to subsist and to better their social condition.[59]

The law allowed for this 'moral obligation', which applied to all men and women aged between 14 and 60, to be fulfilled by owning capital, practising a profession, farming or producing goods for export, but with the last two it would be for the local authorities to determine whether the condition was being fulfilled. Otherwise the obligation could only be fulfilled by wage labour, and the local authorities had powers forcibly to contract those who did not seek work themselves. It also had powers to impose correctional labour on those breaking the law, including the labour laws.

The law also enshrined certain other principles. The object of making Africans work was not just wealth creation but to allow them to 'improve themselves by work, acquiring through work a happier mode of existence'.[60] Employers were obliged to provide food and accommodation for their workforce and were forbidden to withold pay or force them to buy goods.

The enactment of the labour code on 9 November 1899 was a fitting end to a decade in which Mozambique had been dominated by the ideas, actions and personality of António Ennes. Ennes stands out as one of the greatest figures in the history of Mozambique and one of the great proconsuls in the story of European colonialism. For better or worse Mozambique was forcefully guided along the tracks that he had laid down. Without any realistic expectation of major investment from Portugal, Ennes had shown Mozambique a way of developing through utilising its own resources. The course he adopted attached little importance to individual freedoms or rights, but in a rough and ready fashion it achieved results. The early twentieth century was to see Mozambique develop a productive and expanding economy. Even if the profits were only too often siphoned off into the pockets of foreign concession-owners, the country was far from the basket-case which many had considered it in the early 1890s.

16

MOZAMBIQUE UNDER THE MONARCHY AND THE REPUBLIC

Political evolution

A visitor to the northern Portuguese port of Viana de Castello is charmed to find an ancient Portuguese town complete with Romanesque cathedral, narrow streets, the grand town houses of the aristocracy and rich baroque monasteries. It is a setting suitable for the most romantic conceptions. Cutting right through the centre, however, thrusts a broad boulevard running from the railway station to the sea — the Rua dos Combattentes da Grande Guerra — lined with buildings designed in all the variety of the Art Deco style of the first half of the twentieth century. For those who can read its coded language, art, as always, is ideology. In the early twentieth century Portugal was a country were modern radical ideas tried to find realisation in the framework of a conservative society and a backward economy. The result was to produce tensions and contradictions which, because they were never satisfactorily resolved, resulted in a seemingly endless series of coups and revolutions. The colonies were also to suffer from this uncertainty of values and direction.

The administrative and political history of Mozambique during the last century of Portuguese rule has been seen as a dialogue between centralising and decentralising tendencies. Centralisation has usually meant not only close political control from Lisbon but more or less successful attempts at economic integration and social assimilation. The liberal Monarchy of the mid-nineteenth century had aspired to centralisation, and much of the reforming legislation was passed in that spirit. However, the events of the 1890s had given rise to strong demands for administrative decentralisation and colonial autonomy, and in the reforms of 1907 and other enactments in the last years of the Monarchy an attempt was made to reach a balance of some kind between the two schools of thought. As the preamble to a ministerial order of 1910 stated:

> It is necessary to consider their [the colonies'] just aspirations so that neither an excessive centralisation hampers them, nor, going to the opposite extreme, that we indulge in fleeting adventure and thus find ourselves in a situation for which it would be difficult to find a solution.[1]

The politicians of the Republic, who ousted the king in 1910, were committed to the idea of colonial autonomy, and the Republican period in general was one of decentralisation until a spiral of economic disaster so alarmed ministers that moves to tighten Lisbon's control were instituted once again in the last years of the regime — moves endorsed and strengthened by the New State after 1930.

During the last years of the Monarchy, the opportunities for political and administrative development were severely limited by the terms of the concessions which had been granted to the chartered companies and the *prazos*. The original *prazo* concessions had been for fifteen years, but these had been extended to twenty-five years and most of them were not due to terminate till around 1930. The Nyassa Company's concession was due to expire in 1929, that of the Moçambique Company in 1942. More than half of Mozambique was politically paralysed, while the areas of the country under direct government administration were geographically fragmented. Despite these handicaps the Portuguese slowly set about trying to create a modern state.

The first issue had been to resolve the legal status of the territory and its inhabitants. The nineteenth-century liberal tradition had insisted that the colonies were an integral part of the mother-country and that their inhabitants should enjoy all the rights and privileges of Portuguese citizens. With the great expansion of African territory in the 1890s, the Portuguese abandoned the second of these two liberal tenets. While the colonies were still seen as integral to the mother-country, the inhabitants were now classed as *indígena* and *não-indígena*. The former were not considered 'civilised' and came nominally under tribal law. More to the point, they were subjected to the provisions of the 1899 labour regulations which imposed an obligation to work on all people of *indígena* status. *Indígenas* were placed directly under the administration of a *régulo*, a chief appointed by the administration and responsible for recruiting labour and the collection of poll or hut tax, and could not leave the country without a pass.

One of the most important developments was the establishment of an administration of African affairs. There had been a *curador* with responsibility for Mozambican migrant workers in Johannesburg since 1897, and in 1902 an *Intendência da Emigração* was established. In 1904 a *fiscal* was appointed to Zambesia to oversee emigration arrangements. Then in 1907 a *Secretaria dos Negócios Indígenas* (secretariat for native affairs) was formally established to organise a native justice system, regulate the duties of chiefs, codify African law, organise a civil register of *indígenas*, delineate reserves, control migration, and take responsibility for relief. It also had to organise labour recruitment 'both for the government and for private employment', assist in recruitment of *cipais*, and supervise native labour. Such a list, with its stress on labour questions, makes very clear the way native policy was evolving.[2]

In 1901 an important law was promulgated regulating land ownership and declaring all land not occupied to be state domain. This law recognised African rights to all land in use, but did not set aside specified areas as reserves. In 1918, under the Republic, legal provision was made for the demarcation of reserves but this law was only ever implemented on a very partial basis in the 1940s when pressure on land in the extreme south made it expedient to clarify land rights. In most areas of Mozambique formal reserves were never established because land was plentifully available for all uses. It has been estimated that at independence only between 1 and 3 per cent of the land area of Mozambique was under cultivation.[3]

Except in the areas of the north which remained unpacified, and in the military district of Gaza where military commanders represented the Portuguese government, it was the objective of the government to introduce a regular civil administration. An administrative structure had first been sketched out by António Ennes in the region around Lourenço Marques, and his ideas were elaborated in the reforms decreed by Ayres d'Ornellas in May 1907. The objective of this law was to create a hierarchy of civil administration. The country was divided into five districts or provinces, each with a governor. These were Lourenço Marques, Inhambane, Quelimane, Tete and Moçambique, the military district of Gaza being absorbed into the first two. In addition, of course, there were the territories of the two charter companies. These districts in turn were divided into *circunscriçoēs* and *concelhos*. The *circunscriçoēs* were principally rural areas where there were few people of *não-indígena* status. They were broken down into *postos administrativos* under a *chefe do posto* — roughly the equivalent of the British District Officer. Where the country was still not pacified, as in much of the north, the *circunscrição* was replaced by the *capitania-mor* which was divided into *commandos militares*. The *concelhos* were mostly the urban areas where there was a larger *não-indígena* population. Where there were at least 2,000 'civilised' inhabitants an elected *Câmara* was to be set up, with both official and elected representation, which would be responsible for the operation of local government. The *concelho* was responsible for setting up boards (*juntas*) to provide amenities and to handle local administrative questions. Gradually this structure of government was applied throughout the colony and, with modifications, was to last throughout the whole colonial period.[4]

After Ennes and Mouzinho de Albuquerque no more high commissioners were appointed under the Monarchy, and the colony was ruled by a governor-general. He was assisted after 1907 by a *Conselho do Governo* made up of official members, mostly the heads of the administrative and military services, to whom seven representatives of local chambers of commerce were added in 1917. The *Conselho* had deliberative and consultative functions only. Administrative departments were organised or reorganised to deal with Education, Public Works, Fisheries, Tourism and Agriculture. At the national level Mozambique continued to send deputies to the Cortes in Lisbon, elected by a franchise confined to *não-indígenas*.[5]

Although a regular system of administration was thus created, staffing it remained a major difficulty. The overwhelming majority of senior administrators were still drawn from the armed forces with few appointments only being made from the local settler or Afro-Portuguese populations. However, a school for colonial administrator, the *Escola Colonial*, was established in Lisbon in 1906 and a graded hierarchy of civil administrators created, the higher ranks having to pass examinations to achieve promotion. Gradually civilians took over more and more of the government functions within the colony until Salazar got rid entirely of military personnel from the ordinary administration. The local administrators had a wide range of duties including census taking, tax collection and assessment, and the general operation of the labour regulations. They also had responsibility for public health and relief, and for public works together with supervisory duties over mining, agriculture, roads and bridges, post and telegraph.[6]

The regime that gradually took shape in Mozambique was in essence bureaucratic. Local democracy existed only in the few towns with active town councils — effectively only Lourenço Marques and Beira — and the petty officials who ran the administration were frequently corrupt. The Afro-Portuguese population ceased to provide administrative or military personnel, and although the settler population eventually grew to a size comparable with that of Southern Rhodesia, the two communities were poles apart in their political development. Even when Lisbon devolved autonomy on to the colonies in the 1920s, Mozambique continued to be ruled not by local settlers but by an élite of colonial administrators who were Portuguese in their orientation and loyalty and looked to Lisbon for backing. Government, and hence government policy, in Mozambique was not informed by local opinion in any consistent way, and although local pressure groups could sometimes make themselves felt, they were unable over a long period to dictate government policy or even influence it in any consistent direction.

The failure to develop any organs of settler or indigenous democracy was to have great significance. It meant that the settlers were never able to stage an independent take-over of Mozambique like the white Rhodesian seizure of power in 1965. It also meant that the

Afro-Portuguese, who had been so influential in the earlier phases of Mozambique's history, were altogether excluded from power and no local groupings with political or administrative experience would emerge among any sector of the Mozambique population. This lack of political or even administrative experience was to have serious consequences when Mozambique eventually became independent.

Republican Mozambique

The Portuguese republican governments sought, as a matter of some urgency, to restructure the administration of the empire. They were aware that in many ways the legacy of the Monarchy was a disaster. In Mozambique, although government was in theory highly centralised with budgets controlled by Lisbon and deficits made good by the metropolitan exchequer, the country was in practice administratively and economically fragmented; most of it was controlled directly or indirectly by foreign capital whose concessions — granting quasi-feudal rights over the population — were giving rise to abuses that were becoming increasingly embarrassing and unacceptable.

The Republic wanted to grant the colonies more autonomy and at the same time strengthen the administrative authority of the colonial governments. It drew up a constitution in 1911, Article 67 of which briefly stated: 'In the administration of the overseas provinces there shall predominate the system of decentralisation, with special laws adequate to the state of civilisation of each one of them.'[7]

Each colony was promised an Organic Charter, which would establish the legal framework for devolved government, and the colonies were to become financially autonomous. They were to have power to raise loans and draw up their own budgets while the liability of Lisbon to cover budgetary deficits was removed. The Organic Law for Mozambique, prepared in 1913, was designed to establish the autonomy of the province in policy-making while confirming the administrative structure of 1907. However, the law was not officially promulgated because of the outbreak of the First World War.

In 1911 a Colonial Council was created in Lisbon to represent the interests of the colonies. It was elected indirectly from assemblies of the leading settlers of all the colonies, and had the task of advising the Minister and acting as a judicial tribunal to hear appeals against the administration. During the New State the Council was renamed the '*Conselho Ultramarino*', evoking memories of the empire of the sixteenth and seventeenth centuries, and it survived until the end of colonial rule. Portugal's republican constitution officially separated church and state and removed subsidies from Catholic missions, while in 1914 a new labour code was issued and a far-reaching investigation was begun into the abuses that were rampant on the *prazos*.[8] Before any of these measures could have much effect, Mozambique was plunged into the turmoil of the First World War.

Mozambique, Portugal and the empire

In the late nineteenth century some Portuguese had dreamt of building a new Brazil in central Africa, and although the ultimatum of 1890 had deprived Portugal of the rich region that became the Rhodesias, it had been left with other regions of great potential. By 1900 the importance of the African empire was appreciated by a number of powerful interest groups which, as was the way of the Portuguese establishment, were interlinked through family and political connections. First there were the wine and textile barons for whom Africa was an important market in a world which tended to over-produce these commodities and which had become increasingly protectionist. Then there were the interests which had successfully embarked on plantation agriculture in São Tomé and Príncipe, and less successfully in Angola and Mozambique. Plantation agriculture not only offered Portugal import savings but promised extensive earnings of foreign exchange through re-exports to markets in the industrialised world hungry for sugar, coffee, cocoa, vegetable oils and rubber.

There were also the financial interests which saw great opportunities to milk the colonies for the politically guaranteed profits to be obtained from government monopolies and contracts. Foremost among these groups were the banks, the Banco Nacional Ultramarino (BNU) in particular having already acquired extensive landholdings and mortgages in the colonies as well as the sole right to carry on banking operations and issue colonial currency. The Empresa Nacional de Navegação (ENN) was set up in 1880 with heavy government backing to provide regular steamer services to and from the colonies. Other syndicates received monopolies to run steamers on African rivers, and build railways or port installations. Most of these enterprises looked for substantial profits from acquiring land concessions which would enable them to control commercial activity, land distribution, taxation and labour. There were also individuals who saw in the colonies a way of realising personal ambitions — or of promoting religious or national regeneration. Others again saw Africa as a potential destination for Portuguese emigration and a new source for the remittances which traditionally bridged the gap in Portugal's balance of payments and boosted national gold reserves.[9]

All these interest groups had their counterparts in the other colonial powers — but in this respect there was an important difference between Portugal and the others. In Britain, France and Germany a developed capitalism sought raw materials, markets and investment opportunities in the colonies, and surplus capital and surplus production needed outlets. The industrialised countries imagined at the time of the Scramble that they were going to export their capital, skills and civilisation to the 'dark continent'. For Portugal the whole orientation was the other way round: the wealth of Africa was going to provide the capital to develop the metropole. In the event, however, Portuguese rule in Mozambique during the first thirty years of the twentieth century provided a framework for the development of foreign not Portuguese capitalist enterprise.

The economic crisis of the 1890s left Portugal with an overriding need to earn foreign exchange to cover the huge metropolitan trade deficit which averaged 30,000 *contos* a year between 1905 and 1915.[10] The main instruments for achieving this were the encouragement of the re-export of colonial produce brought to Portugal in Portuguese ships, the substitution of colonial produce for foreign imports in the Portuguese domestic market, and the selling of labour and services to British ruled Africa. At first Mozambique's place in this economic strategy was principally to earn foreign exchange through port, rail and labour fees paid by South Africa and to a smaller extent Rhodesia. However, by 1910 Mozambican sugar had become important in Portugal's trade, filling the annual quota allotted to it and offering major opportunities for import substitution. The Republican government also wanted to promote the import of raw materials from the colonies to help its payments problem, but once again, where Mozambique was concerned, it had success only with sugar, and by steadily increasing the quota of Mozambican sugar allowed into Portugal, it gave impetus to the dynamic growth of J.P. Hornung's sugar empire.

As a result of the 1892 tariff, Portugal's exports to its colonies increased significantly so that by 1914 they were averaging 15 per cent of all exports. In 1914 the tariff was revised and a peak of success was reached in 1915 when 21 per cent of Portugal's exports went to the colonies; Mozambique took 35 per cent of its imports from Portugal.[11] The colonial market was particularly important for the textile industry which before 1892 had suffered badly from foreign competition. Cotton textiles made up 30–40 per cent of exports to the colonies by 1900. However, most of these went to the West African colonies and Mozambique remained a relatively unimportant market for Portugal, dominated as it was by British and British Indian importers. Mozambique did, however, feature largely in the calculations of the Portuguese wine producers, because while Portuguese wine exports sagged in the world glut after 1895, the continually expanding colonial market became all-important. In 1880 just over 2 million litres had been exported to Africa, but by 1901 this had risen to 12.6 million litres. Southern Mozambique played a major part in this expansion. In 1887 only 191,000 litres had been imported through Lourenço Marques but ten years later imports stood at 3.4 million litres, and had risen to 6.96 million litres by 1909, by which time Mozambique made up 43 per cent of the colonial market. The 1892 tariff had begun to put the squeeze on the import of European (mostly German) spirits and the result had been a boom in the production of rum by the expanding Mozambican sugar industry as well as a growth in wine imports. Indeed an increase in alcohol imports and alcohol production was one of the major consequences of the growth of mine earnings in the 1890s. A struggle ensued for the African market, the wine-producers securing limitations on colonial rum production in 1901 and eventually its total abolition. The wine lobby also pressed unsuccessfully for a clause in the Mozambique-Transvaal Convention for the sale of Portuguese wine to Mozambican miners on the Rand.[12]

If Portuguese trade with Mozambique gradually increased, metropolitan investment remained very weak. With the exception of the cocoa plantations of São Tomé, Portuguese capital had been reluctant to invest in the colonies and in order to encourage domestic entrepreneurs the Portuguese government had developed a policy of offering subsidies and monopolistic concessions — a policy which incidentally accounted for some of the hostility shown to Portugal by other powers at the time of the scramble for Africa. Once again Mozambique played little part in this policy. Despite a number of concessions granted in the 1880s, it was not till 1903 that the ENN established a regular shipping service to Mozambique and then only with the backing of expensive subsidies and guarantees; the first railways to the Rand (1895) and Rhodesia (1898) were largely built with foreign capital; the charter companies and the *prazos*, although decked out to look as attractive as possible to Portuguese investors, also largely fell to foreign capital, and when the BNU's banking monopoly ended in 1891 the banking sector was also invaded by foreign banks.[13]

Railways and services

Although in the early twentieth century there were promising signs that profitable plantations were being established in Zambesia, the economy of the colonial state and of the two chartered companies depended overwhelmingly on two factors: the taxation of African peasants and the internal utilisation of African labour, and the provision of labour and services to the British colonies. In the years after the ultimatum government expenditure was largely concentrated on developing those two sectors. Expenditure on pacification campaigns was justified as a form of investment designed to increase the revenues from African tax and labour, and the building of ports and railways as the essential prerequisite to earn British currency through the provision of services.

Two important transit lines crossed Mozambique, the CFLM connecting Lourenço Marques to the Rand via Ressano Garcia, and the railway linking Rhodesia to Beira. The goods traffic carried by the CFLM rose dramatically from 1895, dipped during the Boer War and then enjoyed boom conditions as the Rand mines expanded again after the war. To increase the flow of goods through Lourenço Marques and ease the passage of the rapidly rising numbers of migrants, the Portuguese were eager that a second line should be built across Swaziland, and in 1903 they authorised the construction, at government expense, of the Mozambique section of the railway to the Swazi border. Work began on the line in 1905 and was completed in 1912. The Xinavane-Moamba branch line linking the sugar-growing regions of the Incomati with Lourenço Marques was completed in 1914. The railway employed an array of skilled labour headed by the white railway workers, who became a recognised and not uninfluential group in the society of the capital. The railway yards and locomotive workshops led to the creation of an advanced industrial infrastructure and the Lourenço Marques docks also expanded their facilities to meet the growing demand.[14]

Before 1870 Lourenço Marques had been little more than a trading station 'protected' by a fort with a miserable, fever-stricken garrison. The 1869 treaty with the Transvaal and the growth of traffic resulting from mineral discoveries soon turned Lourenço Marques into one of the most rapidly growing urban centres in Africa. Although Delagoa Bay was an excellent sheltered deep-water inlet, there were no modern port installations and the Portuguese town needed to be extensively rebuilt. During the 1870s a public works department was created under the supervision of the famous railway engineer and future governor-general, J.J. Machado, and the city was equipped with hospital, jail, church and sanitation facilities. To raise the capital to develop the city further, the Portuguese authorities granted monopoly concessions for the operation of services, and between 1885 and 1902 Lourenço Marques was supplied with water and telegraph, and a power system was installed to provide lighting and an electric tram service.[15] Most important of all, the government began to organise the filling-in of swamps so that by the end of the century the coastal flats had been laid out with boulevards, a botanical garden and a beach resort at Polana.

The development of the city was largely carried out with foreign capital. In 1894 only 27 per cent of the nominal capital invested in Lourenço Marques was Portuguese, and as late as 1913 it was estimated that 70 per cent of all residences and business plots were owned by Britons or British Indians.[16] When Britain took over the Transvaal after the South African war, Portugal was afraid that Lourenço Marques would fall either directly or indirectly into British hands and a conscious policy was followed of 'nationalising' the city. Further port works were now paid for by government loans, and in 1903 the city authorities created the Delagoa Bay Development Corporation to take a controlling interest in the city's services — with the result that by the 1920s port operations, power, water and communications were all state- or municipally-owned.

The port and railway of Beira developed in a similar way but on a much smaller scale. A railway, built by a subsidiary of the British South Africa Company, connected Rhodesia with the port of Beira and was opened in 1898. The line cost £2 million to build but was at first constructed to very low engineering standards. The young Kingsley Fairbridge described travelling on this line from Beira before it had been completed:

> This was one of England's gifts to the world. Scores of Englishmen and hundreds of coolies and Kafirs had died in the building of it. It ran through a hundred miles of low-veldt, where dysentery, malaria, and wild beasts had swept off the contractors and their men as the August fires sweep off the long grass. . . . We travelled first, so we had a tarpaulin over our truck, and deck chairs. . . . Our train did not run off the rails but most trains did, and then the passengers had to get out and push them back again.[17]

Work began to convert the line to a broader gauge in 1900. The primary purpose of the line was to serve Southern Rhodesia, and in 1909 only 4 per cent of the receipts of the railway were from local Mozambique traffic.[18] However, as the line passed through the uplands of Manica it did provide an opportunity for a community of white commercial farmers to establish themselves in the region. Beira also developed rapidly until it became the second-most important town in the colony. Between 1896 and 1898 the city enjoyed a building boom with large numbers of businesses being established, and in the latter year its population stood at 4,223 (1,172 of them being European). Between 1898 and 1902 the Moçambique Company raised 2.2 million *milreis*, which was largely spent on infrastructure in the port since the sandy shore and shallow approaches to the harbour required massive engineering works. A stone quay was constructed, cranes and warehouses were improved, and sea defences and a lighthouse were built. Barry Neil-Tomlinson commented that the Company's rule was

> . . . a managerial achievement rare in Africa and unique in
> Mozambique of establishing a colonial administration on a sound
> financial basis within the first five years. . . . Capital was pumped
> into the Company, its turnover increased dramatically and the col-
> onial economy developed into one of the most active and pro-
> sperous in southern Africa.[19]

After about 1903 Beira ceased to expand so rapidly, since it had to
compete with the South African railway system for the rather stagnant
traffic to Rhodesia.[20] By 1910 its population stood at 6,665 (the
European section of the population having actually declined in the
previous ten years to only 860), but the city had now established its
role as the administrative headquarters of the Company and the main
port serving Southern Rhodesia. It had become a city with a distinctive British flavour. Hotels, bars and sporting facilities were developed to serve the British community which, after the Portuguese,
formed by far the biggest element of the European population. The
British character of the town was accentuated by the circulation of
sterling currency issued by the Banco de Beira.

In contrast to the expansion of these two port-cities, the other ports
of Mozambique showed little growth and played a comparatively
minor role in the modern economy. Xai Xai was built up early in the
century as a satellite port of Lourenço Marques, handling much of the
migrant labour and servicing an important hinterland on the lower
Limpopo. A narrow-gauge (0.75 m.) railway was begun in 1909 and
eventually extended inland for 100 km. from the port. Another stretch
of line was built to connect the valley of the Inharrime with the port
of Inhambane, which was also a departure point for migrant
labourers. Both lines were in operation by 1912.[21]

In the late nineteenth century various grandiose railway schemes had
been devised for northern Mozambique by both the government and
the Nyassa Company. Some survey work was even carried out, but
nothing was built apart from 27 km. of narrow-gauge (0.60 m.) railway linking the plantations at Maquival and Madal with Quelimane
in 1901.[22] Proposals to link Nyasaland to a port on the Mozambique
coast were the subject of considerable international manoeuvring.
Portugal was aware that Britain wanted such a line to run through
the Moçambique Company territory to Beira and did not favour the
much shorter route to Quelimane, allegedly because northern
Mozambique was scheduled as an area of German interest. The Portuguese tried to go ahead against the British government's wishes, and
in 1905 authorised the building of a line into the interior from

Quelimane. However, money for it was only voted in 1913 and when, at the end of the 1914–18 war, the line from Beira to the Zambesi went ahead, it was decided that the line from Quelimane should only be built to serve the Boror and Zambesia Company plantations to the north. In the end a short line was completed in 1922 which was never extended in the direction of the borders of British Africa.[23]

Of the other ports, Chinde prospered briefly at the end of the nine-teenth century as the port used by river steamers bound for the Nyasaland Protectorate and then as a company port for Sena Sugar. Sofala had disappeared altogether at the end of the nineteenth cen-tury, being superseded even as a local administrative centre by Chiluane. Angoche remained little more than a harbour for local craft but Mozambique Island was still the second most important port at the end of the century, accounting for about 20 per cent of customs revenue in 1897.[24] Its importance lay in its being the port used by Indian and French traders to export cash crops. However, with the decline of cash crop exports in the twentieth century, Mozambique Island was consigned to a period of picturesque decay. In the Nyassa Company's territory to the north, Ibo had handled a rapidly increas-ing amount of trade in the 1890s, but its difficult and narrow approach made it suitable only for dhow traffic and the Company moved its administrative headquarters to Porto Amelia in 1904. Although Porto Amelia provided an excellent natural harbour, little was done to develop the port and the Company's grandiose plan for a railway to the Lake hardly got beyond the drawing board.

Up till the mid-1920s, therefore, there was considerable govern-ment and private investment in transport infrastructure, but although a network of lines grew up in the region south of the Limpopo, the rest of Mozambique's rail lines remained totally disconnected from each other. They did not link the country together or, with the exception of the Beira-Umtali line, open up the interior. They either served the immediate hinterland of the ports or provided services for British Africa. That a network began to come into existence in the 1920s and 1930s, when the Trans-Zambesia line, the Lower Zambesi bridge and the Moatize line were built, was due to the manoeuvrings of British capital and the policy of the British government which wanted, for its own reasons, to promote the interests of the British-owned Moçambi-que Company. Although the economic activity of Mozambique grew during this period and considerable social change took place, the various parts of the country developed largely in isolation from each other. The modern state and nation of Mozambique were taking shape, but it was a shape characterised by a high degree of dis-integration.

Incorporation of the north into the colonial state

The south of Mozambique had been conquered in the campaigns against Gaza in 1895–7 and incorporated into the world of colonial capitalism by the development of labour migration to South Africa. Zambesia had been largely occupied by colonial forces by 1902 and its economic life was dominated by the plantation system of the *prazos*. There remained the two northern regions, the territory of the Nyassa Company north of the Lurio river and the hinterland of Mozambique Island which was under the direct administration of the colonial government.

The Nyassa Company faced powerful and organised opposition to its advance into the interior from the major Yao chiefs. Its campaigns in 1899 to 1901 had established a line of posts from the coast to the Lake but it had had to abandon efforts to collect tax or obtain labour levies in the interior, and found its garrisons harassed and attacked by the Yao and, in particular, by the most important Yao chief, Mataka, who remained completely independent. In 1908 a consortium of South African mining interests established Nyassa Consolidated which took control of the Company and provided a significant injection of new capital. The Nyassa Company now had the funds to launch a new attempt to occupy the interior. Over a period of four years lines of posts were extended to the north and south of Mataka's territory, and eventually in October 1912 Mataka Chisonga himself was defeated and a fort was built in the ruins of Mwembe. Company administrative posts were now established along the Lake to begin labour recruitment and tax collection. The only region which the Company did not control by the outbreak of the First World War was the Makonde plateau in the far north-east.[25]

South of the Nyassa Company territory was the district of Mozambique, consisting of the old coastal towns of Mozambique Island with its Muslim satellites Sancul and Quitangonha, and Angoche. This was to be the last area in which the Portuguese established effective rule and where they met the most prolonged and determined opposition. Significantly, this resistance came from the leaders of certain Makua confederacies and from members of the coastal ruling families, and not from powerfully organised states with large populations and developed military capacity. Among the Makua, the clan (*nihima*) was the all-important institution, and the head of the clan, the *muene*, was the man who wielded real power. As a result few of the Makua chiefs were able to control the resources or muster the military manpower of the great Yao chiefs, let alone the Gaza in the south. The most tenacious opponents of the Portuguese, therefore, were chieftains and leaders of relatively small warbands who were still deeply involved in the slave trade and whose activities resembled those of the bandits of Zambesia. The Makua proved to be resilient and difficult opponents. They made use of fortified stockades like those in Zambesia, and most of them were armed with rifles obtained through their slaving activities. The unexplored and dense bush of the interior, infested with tsetse, was ideal for guerrilla warfare at which the Makua excelled. Moreover the structure of Makua society made it possible for men to be absent for long periods on military operations. Agricultural work was performed by women who controlled the land and means of production so that men were often excluded from decisions made at village level, though they retained important functions in commerce, war and raiding — raiding both for slaves to sell to the coast and for women to enhance the productive capacity of the clan.[26]

The isolated and somewhat forlorn administrative post which the Portuguese had set up at Parapat in 1862 after the conquest of Angoche managed to survive because it could be supplied by sea and because the chief of the leading Makua clan in the immediate hinterland, the Imbamella, needed Portuguese help against the ruling élites of Angoche. Even so, Parapat was attacked in 1890 by Farelay, great-nephew of Mussa Quanto and leader of the Swahili slaving interests of the Angoche coast. As late as 1900 Farelay levied tolls on traders in Parapat and on caravans coming from the interior. On the mainland opposite Mozambique Island the most direct challenge to any Portuguese pretence of controlling the interior came from chief Mocuto-muno of the Namarral Makua. This group of Makua had moved into the immediate hinterland of Mozambique in the 1860s where they had raided for slaves and levied heavy tolls on the caravans coming from the interior. Henry O'Neill described how the Makua living around Nakala in 1883 'have been subject to periodical attacks from the warlike Makua chief Namaralo, and by him they have been driven across the river towards the sea. Great numbers were killed and others carried off into slavery.'[27] The Portuguese had attempted to use their local allies against the Namarral but instead had seen the firearms they supplied falling into the hands of the network of slavers who dealt with the Namarral, chief among them Suali bin Ali Ibrahimu (usually known as Marave), a Swahili-speaking Muslim who had been to Mecca.

The first attempt to break up this alliance was made when Mouzinho de Albuquerque decided to launch a much-publicised pacification campaign the year after his success in capturing Gungunhana at Chaimite. In fighting which lasted from October 1896 to March 1897 Mouzinho (who, according to the British consul R.C.F. Maugham, had set off into the interior accompanied by a Goanese military band) suffered a number of reverses and had to withdraw from the interior — although the Mocuto-muno did formally submit to the Portuguese in May 1897.[28] However, Marave remained totally defiant, occupying Sancul itself in 1898. There, sometime between 1899 and 1902, he entertained the British consul Maugham, who had been shooting in the Upepe marshes. These had for long been the acknowledged limit of the jurisdiction of the Portuguese in Cabaceira, and on returning to his camp he found it occupied by forty or fifty men:

> All were armed with guns. Their woolly hair, grown long for the purpose, was twisted into innumerable thin, long tails or plaits carried backward and reaching to their shoulder-blades. Their cheeks were slashed with deep longitudinal cicatrizations several inches long, and so deep in some cases, as completely to penetrate the flesh, their upper teeth being visible through the gashes. . . . Slung over their shoulders were bags of monkey or cat skin, which contained their ammunition, snuff and other necessaries.[29]

These were, no doubt, the dreaded *mafridi* on whose military strength Marave depended. Maugham spent a day and night in Marave's town and recorded that 'nothing could have exceeded the dignified courtesy of my reception, or my surprise to find this terrible chief so refined and considerate a host.' He did, however, note the captured field-guns and the bleached skulls stuck on poles lining the entrance to Marave's quarters — relics, he was told, of fights with the Portuguese.

In the early years of the twentieth century the Portuguese were still not able to levy hut tax on the mainland opposite Mozambique Island. The Makua and Muslim chiefs continued to ship slaves to Madagascar and to import firearms for themselves from Nyassa Company territory. As late as 1904 the Portuguese were raided in Mossuril itself and driven to take refuge on Mozambique Island. In 1905, however, the government began the systematic penetration of the interior with armed columns, entering by way of the river valleys. Not until 1910, however, did Pedro Massano de Amorim lead a successful expedition against Farelay who was captured and exiled in Guiné. With this success achieved and with the government's ban on the sale of firearms increasingly effective, the Portuguese began to recruit local Makua forces from chieftaincies hostile to the slaving interests of the coastal warlords and these were used to isolate and hunt down the resisters. Clan heads who did not submit were exiled to Timor and, although guerrilla warfare spluttered on, the region was declared pacified by 1913. However Marave, the greatest of all the bandits, was never captured.[30]

Farelay and Marave were among the last chiefs to resist the

Portuguese. Although connected with the ruling coastal families, they were not the legitimate chiefs of large settled populations like Mataka. Nancy Hafkin described the nature of their resistance:

> The rulers of the sheikhdoms, chiefdoms and sultanates were essentially parasitic in their relationship to the African land and people. Producing little themselves, they had no organic relationship with the regions in which they were situated. The revolts were reactionary, in the sense that they represent the strivings of an elite to preserve a situation in which they alone profited.[31]

They were figures who have remained familiar in Mozambican history up to the present. Leaders of armed bands who obtained access to supplies of arms — in their case through the slave trade — they were able to dominate the fragmented matrilineal society of the Makua and establish a kind of 'protection' over areas of the countryside where they levied tribute and licensed access by Portuguese or Indian traders. Although frequently co-operating with each other against the Portuguese, they were not able to create large or permanent state structures and never struck up alliances with the Yao chiefs further inland. They were bandit leaders exploiting the extreme disintegration of the local population and the weakness of the colonial state.

The Portuguese advance brought an end to the power of the Makua and Muslim chiefs who had led the resistance. These chieftaincies, which had grown in power as a result of the trade which had passed through their country ever since the ivory boom of the eighteenth century, were now systematically destroyed. The Portuguese had no intention of adopting indirect rule, and replaced them with their own *chefes do posto* and, at the purely local level, with appointed *régulos*. 'There arose once again a multitude of small territorial chiefly units based on local lineages.'[32] It was one more example of the process of social and political dis-integration which accompanied the establishment of colonial rule.

The rule of the charter companies to the end of the Republic

By 1895 the Moçambique Company had come under the control of Albert Ochs, who established a committee representing British shareholders in London. It has been argued that Ochs was principally a speculator whose horizons were limited by considerations of how best to create booms in the company's stocks.[33] He treated the huge territory between the Zambesi and the Sabi as a sort of corporate feudal holding. At first his main concern was to make money from African taxation, and even before the territory was pacified he entered into a notorious agreement with Gungunhana whereby the latter's regiments would collect tax for the Company in their old raiding grounds. After the defeat of Gungunhana in 1895 the Company's tax collectors gradually took over and hut tax receipts jumped from barely 11,000 *milreis* in 1894 and 1895 to more than 63,000 *milreis* in 1896.[34]

In 1897 control of the Company briefly passed back into the hands of Edmund Bartissol and the French backers of the original Moçambique Company, but by 1905 Ochs was once more in charge. However, French influence in the Company persisted and only when Libert Oury, also a Belgian with British nationality, replaced Ochs in 1910 with the backing of South African capital did British interests finally dominate the Company's affairs. During the period of disputed control, the Company had proved unable or unwilling to undertake the expense of conquering and occupying Barue, which had remained an independent chieftaincy after the overthrow and death of Sousa in 1892. The Company had to ask the state for aid and after the successful campaign of reconquest in 1902 Barue remained under direct state control and was administered as part of the new Tete District.

As well as collecting tax, the Company was prepared to lease subconcessions. In its first ten years of life a number of mining companies began operations in the Manica area, and by 1902 8,000 claims were registered. By 1910 hydro-electric generating plant had been installed in the mining areas and ten mines were in operation, producing £38,413 of gold.[35] Sugar plantations were also established on the south bank of the Zambesi and on the Buzi, while in the Manica highlands white settlers were granted concessions to establish farms. In 1902 the Company appointed an official to plan agricultural development. Experimental stations were established at Mambone and Chimoio, and attempts to grow cotton were sufficiently successful for the Company to set up a plant for ginning and baling at Beira.[36] The concession to build the railway to Rhodesia was leased to the Beira Railway Company controlled by the British South Africa Company. The railway, which might have earned a considerable income for the Company, therefore passed into the control of the South African railways which tried to manipulate freight rates to divert traffic from the line. In 1898 the Company granted a second railway concession to a consortium to build a line connecting Beira with the Zambesi.[37] Nothing immediately came of this concession except heightened hostility between Britain and Portugal since Portugal favoured a railway from Quelimane to Nyasaland which would serve the plantations of the Zambesia district, and looked with disfavour on another British-dominated line. By the outbreak of the First World War no capital had been raised to build the line to the Zambesi.[38]

These developments, modest as they were, all required labour (6,000 labourers, for example, were employed in building the Beira-Umtali railway). At first the Company simply used military police to round up the labour it needed, but wages rose steadily in the 1890s and it was the consciousness that labour might soon be in short supply that probably explains the Company's policy of refusing outsiders the right to recruit in the Company's territory. Neither WNLA nor the Rhodesia Native Labour Bureau nor the São Tomé planters were given recruiting rights.[39]

The development policy pursued by the Company did not, however, seek to suppress peasant production. Taxes were collected in kind and it became official policy to encourage the growing of cotton and rice and the harvesting of wild rubber. To encourage peasant production, seeds were distributed and arrangements were made for the purchase of the product at fixed prices. Cotton proved moderately successful as a peasant-grown crop. Production rose from 34 tonnes in 1910 to over 600 tonnes by 1925. A cotton concession was then granted to the Belgian-owned Compagnie Cotonière du Moçambique which pushed up production, with fluctuations in bad years, to 3,354 tonnes by 1936.[40] The trade in wild rubber was made a Company monopoly but rubber faded with the collapse of world prices after 1912. By this time a number of sectors of the economy were expanding, notably sugar (Fig. 16.1), and far from having become a labour exporter, the Company was suffering from a severe shortage of labour and began to recruit outside Company territory.[41]

After the end of the war Oury, now firmly in control of the Company, gave priority to developing the port of Beira and the rail network that would feed it. During the war British interests had acquired control of the Nyassa Company, and in 1919 Tanganyika was made over to British control under the terms of the newly-established Mandate system. The British government was now prepared to make positive moves to consolidate its interests in Mozambique, and in the immediate post-war period the British cabinet decided to back Oury's scheme for a railway across Zambesia on the vague assumption that this would in some way bolster Britain's interests in southern Africa. Between 1920 and 1922 the Trans-Zambesia railway was built from Beira to the the banks of the Zambesi, while Oury acquired mineral rights in the Zambesia Company territory in 1919 and negotiated with Katanga copper interests and Sena Sugar to obtain a share of their traffic for the port of Beira.[42]

After the building of the railway, Oury turned to the question of bridging the Zambesi to link both Nyasaland and the mineral concessions he had acquired, in particular the Moatize coalfields, to Beira. After nearly a decade of political manoeuvring, he eventually

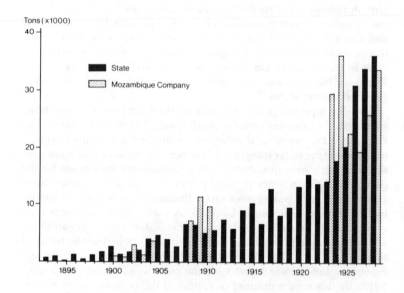

Fig. 16.1. SUGAR EXPORTS

Source: G. Liesegang, 'A First Look at the Import and Export Trade . . .'

persuaded the British government in 1929 to underwrite the loans needed for the building of the Zambesi bridge. The decision was made primarily to provide a stimulus to British industry, then suffering from the depression, but for Oury the bridge was essential if his railway was ever to pay and he was ever to bring the coal fields into production. Opinions differed over whether the bridge would help or hinder the development of Nyasaland, but the interests of the people of the Protectorate were very much a secondary consideration.[43]

Whatever the motives of the actors, the building of the Trans-Zambesia line and of the bridge (completed in 1935) began for the first time to forge links between the different regions of Mozambique. Although the railway to the coalfields was not completed till ten years later, the potential now existed to connect the north of Mozambique with the south, and Tete district with both. However, there was an irony in the building of the Zambesi bridge. This great work of engineering, the second-longest railway bridge in the world at the time, was achieved at a time when road transport was just about to take off. As this great dinosaur of the age of steam was being built, the first lorries were already crossing Tete district picking up migrant workers for transport to Southern Rhodesia, migrants destined never to travel by rail across the river to the south.

Under the Republic, the Nyassa Company became a by-word for all that was worst about colonial rule. After the early boardroom struggles, the Company was run by the Ibo Syndicate, which had been unable to establish control in its territory. In 1908 the Company was taken over by the Nyassa Consolidated Company, backed by Lewis and Marks, the avowed aim of this holding company being to exploit the territory as a labour reserve, primarily for South Africa. At the same time the Company tried to collect hut tax, to operate a monopoly of the rubber trade and to sell firearms to all and sundry. Its officials received a percentage of the tax they collected as pay.

In 1913 Britain and Germany confirmed the treaty of 1898 which had designated areas of the Portuguese colonies as British or German spheres of interest, and when in 1913 recruitment for the South African mines from tropical areas was ended and the world market for rubber collapsed, Lewis and Marks lost all interest in the Nyassa Company and allowed a controlling interest in Nyassa Consolidated to be bought by a German financial consortium. By 1914, as Leroy Vail has written, 'Germany had in effect purchased a colony'.[44] With Portugal entering the war against Germany in 1916, the obvious course of action would have been for it to have cancelled the charter and taken over the administration of the territory. That this did not happen was due to British influence and in particular the machinations of General Jan Smuts whose devious intrigues still had as their objective obtaining control of southern Mozambique for South Africa. So in 1918 the German shares in Nyassa Consolidated were bought at a nominal cost by Owen Philipps of the Union Castle Line. Philipps, who became Lord Kylsant, was the nominee of the British imperial government and apparently had its assurance that after the war diplomatic pressure would be used to extend the Company's charter.[45]

The Nyassa Company's charter was due to run out in 1929, and in the event was not renewed. During its last years there was a stalemate: Kylsant argued that he could not raise capital for development without an extension of the charter, while the Portuguese refused to promise any extension because of the disgraceful state of the territory. Britain was in an embarrassing position, unwilling to back Kylsant at a time when the League of Nations showed concern at labour conditions in Mozambique virtually amounting to slavery, yet unwilling to put serious pressure on its own nominee to change his ways.

Forced labour was widely practised throughout the Company's territory, the main variant on this practice, common in the rest of Mozambique, being that Company officials were frequently owners of plantations themselves and used *chibalo* labour either directly on their plantations or to build roads to them.[46] To the very end the Company continued to extort what tax it could from its subject population and to sell labourers on contract to various clients. Otherwise the income of the Company, which had to pay for its rudimentary administration, consisted in 1927 entirely of hut tax receipts (70 per cent) and customs (21 per cent), most of it duty paid on African cash crops being exported and goods imported for African consumption. When the charter eventually expired, the Nyassa Company — which had never paid a dividend — was effectively bankrupt.

Development of labour and tax policy

During the 1890s it had become clear to the Portuguese that the African population of Mozambique was one of the most easily exploitable resources in their new colony. The products of African agriculture could be exported, Africans could be sold Portuguese wine and textiles, they could be taxed, and their labour could be employed in various ways. Revenues derived from these sources were essential to balance the colonial budgets, while the economic opportunities which they represented were used to try to attract capital investment to the colony. Extracting wealth from African peasant society became the principal objective of colonial policy.

The most direct form of exploitation was to tax the population. The right to collect tribute, usually in kind, had been a traditionally recognised attribute of sovereignty and in Zambesia had been a major source of the wealth of the Afro-Portuguese feudal class. At first tax continued to be collected in kind because many of the African societies did not participate in a monetarised economy and the government was anyway anxious to promote the growth of cash crops. The *prazo* law of 1890, for example, made provision for African tax payments to be made in kind. However, the orientation of colonial policy soon began to change with the growth in demand for African labour. By 1900 three sectors of the economy were requiring large supplies of labour — plantation companies established on the lower reaches of the Zambesi, Buzi and Incomati; the government, which required labour for road, rail and harbour construction, as well as for police and carrier service; and foreign recruiters of labour of which the South

African mines were by far the most important. African tax, instead of being used to promote peasant production, was now used to propel the peasant population on to the labour market.[47]

The most direct device employed was to make part of the annual tax payable in labour, and the *prazo* concessionaires had to employ their peasants for two weeks work a year in lieu of tax. The other device was to require the payment of tax in coin and so force Africans to enter the labour market to earn wages. The taxes thus raised would then become a main source of income for the governments of the districts or for the *prazo* concessionnaires. Collecting tax from the population became an incentive for pushing ahead with pacification campaigns, while the amounts collected became a measure of the success of pacification.

In the early years of the century, raising tax was the most important function of government and sometimes the only one. The Nyassa Company, which originally had grandiose plans for the capitalist development of its territory, soon saw hut tax receipts as its major source of income. In 1898, when its effective government was still confined to a few areas of the coast, it had raised the equivalent of £800. This became £3,105 in 1903 after the first campaigns of occupation, but had risen to £48,232 by the First World War.[48] To supplement this collection of hut tax, the Company decided to promote the export of labour, entering into recruiting agreements with WNLA in 1903 and stepping up recruitment after the takeover of the Company by South African interests in 1908. The number of labourers coming from the Nyassa territory never numbered more than a few thousand, but their earnings were said in 1909 to amount to £20,000, which no doubt partly accounted for the rise in hut tax receipts. Later the Nyassa Company was to try to sell labour to Katanga and even to São Tomé.

On the Zambesi *prazos* the right to collect head tax (*mussoco*) was a privilege of the *prazo* concessionaires but the rate was fixed very low. The *prazo* law of 1890 had fixed the rate at 800 *reis* a year, half of which had to be collected in labour. This amounted to about two weeks' work a year, and although the figures were raised to 1//200 *réis*, or three weeks' work, the *prazo* companies were lumbered with the major task of recruiting and employing huge numbers of workers for very short periods.[49] In order to recruit adequate supplies of labour, the plantation companies leased large numbers of *prazos* to be used simply as labour reserves. The labour regulations of 1899 extended the *indígena*'s obligation to work beyond the period needed simply to clear the tax obligation. As the *prazo* companies constituted the administration within the area of their concessions, they were in effect given a free hand to levy forced labour. In the Tete District, where there were no plantations, Sena Sugar rented the large *prazo* of Angonia, moving its workers by rail through Nyasaland to the lower Zambesi, while the blocks of *prazos* leased by the elephantine Zambesia Company remained for many years effectively under the control of the Afro-Portuguese *senhores* and their *chicunda*.[50] Labour recruitment in these circumstances was little more than a continuation of the slave trade. Crawford Angus, who visited Macanga in 1895-6, recorded:

> The price of slaves averages about 4 s to 6 s each, and children from 3 s to 5 s each; the chief market is Tete, on the Zambizi, the Portuguese headquarters there, where a ready sale is found among the Portuguese police and servants, and among the officers even and other inhabitants.[51]

The reaction of the African inhabitants was widespread evasion, to which the *prazo* companies responded with armed raids to capture fugitive peasants and round up labour gangs.

The Moçambique Company also considered African tax and labour among its principal assets, and by 1900 hut tax had become the second-most important source of the Company's income. The Company was aware that the African population would emigrate if tax policies became too oppressive, and adopted a deliberate policy of keeping its tax rates competitive. Unofficially it let it be known that tax would not be collected from immigrants for two years, and maintained its tax rate significantly below that of surrounding authorities. When in 1904 the Rhodesian authorities raised hut tax to £1, the Company left its tax at only half that figure for the next five years, only raising it to the Rhodesian figure in 1909. This policy paid off and the Company recorded a steady increase in its African population.[52]

The Company also used its *cipais* to round up labour required for public works. In other respects, however, the Moçambique Company policy was different. The Company was anxious to encourage sub-concessionaires to develop plantations, mines and farms, and at an early stage flatly refused to allow labour recruitment by outsiders in its territory, a policy it did not alter throughout the term of its charter. African peasants not required by the labour market within the Company's territories were required to produce cash crops (mainly cotton and rubber), and this policy too the Company continued long after similar policies had been discontinued elsewhere. In 1907 the Company introduced formal labour regulations in line with the colonial labour laws of 1899. Two years later it tried to end the direct recruitment of labour by Company police and handed the task over to a labour supply agency. When this failed to produce enough labourers, the Company established its own *Repartição de Trabalho Indígena* to supervise the recruitment of labour both inside and outside its territory.

It was in the south, however, that taxing the African population proved most profitable. Because of the relatively high cash earnings of returning migrants, the economy of this part of the country was most fully monetarised. Hut tax was continually being raised, standing by 1910 at the equivalent of £1, and arrangements were made for it to be collected directly from miners on the Rand. In the years before the war, hut tax was by far the largest proportion of the income of most of the *circunscrições*. Figures for Marracuene, for example, show it providing on average 74 per cent of the income between 1911 and 1916.[53] Hut tax from the southern districts formed a major part of the income of Mozambique in the years before the 1920s. In 1904-5 it accounted for 28 per cent of state revenue and in 1907-8 for 46.5 per cent. As late as 1917, out of revenue amounting to 7,507,979 *escudos*, 1,170,000 (15.6 per cent) came from this source.[54]

One of the objectives of hut tax had been to push Africans on to the labour market and it undoubtedly had this effect, but the Portuguese colonial government, private employers and the concession companies found themselves in competition with foreign recruiters of labour. In the early twentieth century the Mozambique authorities were under pressure to grant recruitment rights not only to South Africa but to Rhodesia, the French colonies, the São Tomé planters and the Congo Free State. The concession companies either excluded labour recruiters altogether or made special agreements with them to profit by exporting labour. In 1910, for example, a syndicate of São Tomé planters acquired *prazo* Lugella on the Zambesi simply to profit from the resulting access to a labour reserve from which they could recruit for the cocoa islands, and between 1910 and 1917, when recruitment was banned in Angola, Mozambique became a major supplier of labour to São Tomé. According to the *Anuário de Moçambique*, 20,891 labourers were sent to São Tomé between 1911 and 1916 — 2,540 were repatriated during the same period.

In the areas directly administered by the government, competition for labour was even fiercer. The state made agreements with the Rand mines and later with the Southern Rhodesian government, and derived considerable profit from the export of labour, but this threatened to create labour shortages within Mozambique itself and drive up wages. The export of labour was bitterly criticised by the settler press and by pressure groups of white employers, while the government was concerned to meet its own labour requirements as well. For example, up till 1907 the bunkering of coal took place in the Lourenço Marques docks, for which between 4,000 and 5,000 labourers were required daily.[55]

In these circumstances the government simply resorted to *chibalo* — forced labour. *Chibalo* came in two forms: it was either levied directly on the population with the labourers being paid a small wage, or it took the form of penal labour which till 1917 was not paid at all. Penal labour was imposed for all sorts of infringements of the law ranging from failure to pay tax through to being improperly dressed or drunk. Often, however, there was barely any pretence that the labourers rounded up had committed any offence at all. *Chibalo* labour not only provided the government with its basic workforce but was deliberately deployed to dilute the free labour market and so keep wages down. Moreover the police would frequently supply private employers with *chibalo* labour — for a consideration.[56]

Changes to labour law

Ennes's labour law of 1899 had never been formally implemented in Mozambique. Instead a series of local regulations, more or less based on the 1899 law, governed labour recruitment. For example, the Moçambique Company introduced a labour code in 1907, and the Lourenço Marques District adopted its own labour regulations in 1904 and 1906.[57] At the time of the revolution in Portugal in 1910, the demand for labour in Mozambique was at its height. Extreme measures of coercion were being used by the *chefes do posto* to fill the requisitions reaching them from private employers, from the government for its building projects, and from foreign contractors who had agreements with the Mozambique government. Not surprisingly, there were protests at the uninhibited use of forced labour. Some were from interested parties — for example from local employers protesting at the flood of migrants going to South Africa — but there were others prepared to draw attention to the appalling abuses that were taking place and to the flight of the population from many areas. From 1908 the Native Affairs Department began to intervene in the Lourenço Marques area to enforce minimum working conditions.[58] In 1909 the governor-general requested the Secretary for Native Affairs, Francisco Castello Branco, to report on labour conditions on the *prazos*. The result was a catalogue of the crudest abuses by the companies against their semi-servile labourers.[59]

Castello Branco's report had barely appeared when the Monarchy was overthrown; the Republic was prepared, at least on paper, to create a new style of colonial regime. At the time Portugal was under extreme pressure from Britain to reform the system that supplied contract labour to São Tomé. In 1913 the Union government in South Africa took action against the high mortality of Mozambican miners on the Rand and banned all recruitment north of the 22° parallel.

Change was in the air and in October 1914 a decree introduced new labour regulations for the empire. These repeated the main provision of Ennes's law of 1899 but laid down that all labourers forcibly recruited should work under supervised contracts like voluntary labourers, and that penal labour would only be used on state or municipal projects.[60] This was hardly a revolution in labour law, but strong measures were being taken at the same time in Angola and São Tomé to end the worst abuses of forced labour. Portuguese colonial policy was moving away from reliance on crude coercion to a system of recruited labour under relatively long-term supervised contracts.

Further reform was delayed during the First World War when the demands of the armed forces for carriers led to emergency measures to round up the labour necessary, but further significant changes followed. In 1919 the labour regulations of the *prazos* were overhauled, ending forced labour in lieu of tax and expressly permitting freedom of movement for the peasants on the *prazos*. The government now deliberately promoted the idea of work contracts of up to 180 days and the *prazo* companies had to establish recruiting organisations that would compete with other employers of labour.[61]

The African reaction

It is difficult to estimate the impact of tax policies on the population. In some respects the rates of tax were not high. As we have seen, taxes in Zambesia could be paid by three weeks' work, but this was a poll tax, applying to every member of the population over fourteen, and taking no account of the time the workers needed to travel to the plantations, or the violence and poor working conditions they had to suffer. There is evidence that the labour obligation on the *prazos* was resented sufficiently to give rise to extensive population movements as people sought to evade labour and paying tax in one area by moving to another. Early in the twentieth century J.P. Hornung, the owner of the successful Sena Sugar, found that in practice he had to limit the labour obligation of the peasants on his *prazos* if he wanted to prevent their desertion. Instead he raised wages to three times the rates paid in neighbouring Nyasaland and as a result was able to attract substantial immigration and engage workers on six-month or one-year contracts instead of the three weeks to one month he was forced to adopt with his own *colonos*. Meanwhile the Zambesia Company was apparently successful in obtaining voluntary labour from the *nomi* societies — the organisations of unmarried men and women among the Sena.[62]

In the Sul do Save the hut tax was raised to 4//500 in 1908, which was alleged to take 84 days' labour to earn in Lourenço Marques, and the government was fearful that it would cause unrest. However, this sum could be earned on the Rand in ten days, which goes a long way to explain why Africans in the Sul do Save preferred to work off their labour obligation in South Africa rather than locally in Mozambique. However, as an article printed in 1909 in *Africano* explained, some local administrators insisted on collecting the tax in the form of a pound sterling which was worth considerably more than 4//500, and if a peasant had to borrow a pound to pay the tax, he was likely to have to pay as much as 6//500. Anyway, the author of the article continued, 4//500 was exactly what it cost to build an African-style house, and he wondered what people in Portugal would think if they had to pay the cost of their house each year in tax.[63]

In all regions it seems that forced labour rather than taxation was the real grievance. Although on paper Africans were free to contract themselves to any employer and could escape obligatory labour by being engaged in a profession, or by growing crops for sale, none of this applied in practice. Local *chefes do posto* acted arbitrarily using their right to recruit *chibalo* labour to fill labour contracts for private employers. Penal labour was also abused and was used to obtain cheap labour for private as well as public concerns. *Chibalo* itself was the cause of the most bitter complaint. All administrators raised work gangs regularly for road-making, and as areas were pacified a network of wide dirt roads gradually took shape throughout the country. Frequently women were employed on the road gangs. The other main object of *chibalo* was to recruit carriers, until motor transport became general after the First World War. During the war large numbers of carriers were recruited to supply the troops fighting the Germans in the north, and during their absence *chibalo* labour fell particularly heavily on the women who remained behind; this has usually been considered a major cause of the revolt in Barue in 1917. Even so, some groups within the population specialised in being *chibalo* labourers. In Lourenço Marques the jobs of street cleaners and nightsoil workers were monopolised by Chopi who used their status as *chibalo* labourers as a front for running a variety of part-time businesses in the city.

As well as *chibalo* the local *chefes* periodically 'recruited' for the police and the armed forces. The British consul, R.C.F. Maugham, described this procedure as it operated in 1900:

Once or twice a year, a kind of press gang operated. On a given day, a number of military police were sent into the highways and hedges to seize upon any male natives of military age whom they might meet. These were taken, weeping and protesting, before a non-commissioned officer; a nominal roll was drawn up; they were hurried straight on board a steamer and shipped to Angola for service in the native battalions of military police of that or some other colony.[64]

In the south the only escape from *chibalo* was to contract for South Africa, but even then returning migrants often found they had to fulfill local demands for *chibalo* unless chiefs and administrators received substantial bribes.

Nevertheless this conventional catalogue of the abuses of colonial labour is only part of a complex story. At no time was the Mozambican peasant an inert object of oppression. Colonial policy and peasant reaction worked a sort of Hegelian dialectic out of which the Mozambican society inherited by Frelimo was eventually created. The experience of African peasants in Mozambique differed from that of their counterparts in many other parts of Africa in two vital ways. First, labour was not on the whole associated with the loss of land. Its effects therefore have to be assessed as part of the general economic circumstances of village subsistence farming. In some areas contract labour was recruited from populations with a labour surplus in the peasant economy and, however small the wages of the workers, their money income led to an increase in consumption and even an ability to accumulate capital. The second factor was the ability of the Mozambique peasant to emigrate.

Emigration

One of the most formative influences in the lives of Mozambicans in the twentieth century has been emigration. The development of migrant labour from the Sul do Save and Tete district are discussed in Chapter 18, but this was only a small part of a wider migrant movement. Migration had always been a survival strategy for people in times of war and famine, and the major migration movements from Mozambique had all begun before the modern colonial state emerged. Migration continued after 1891, often as a form of resistance to the demands of the colonial state, but paradoxically it was only possible because of the conditions the colonial states themselves created. Migration on such a scale would have been impossible without lorries, railways and shipping and without the element of security which the colonial state provided. Migration was also, of course, the exercise of economic choice. Africans sought access to land or looked for areas where tax and labour demands were less onerous or where more consumer goods were available. There was also the phenomenon of staged migration as Africans whose ultimate destination was the Rand worked their way towards the South African border by seeking employment for a season or two on Mozambican construction projects and plantations or on Southern Rhodesian farms.

Moreover the peculiar circumstances of modern Mozambique enhanced the opportunities for migration. Mozambique itself was divided into different concession areas which lessened administrative control of the population while multiplying the differences between tax and labour regimes. Moreover the country was locked into the jigsaw of Central Africa which made most of the country quite close to the frontiers of British Africa.

If migration began as a search for economic opportunity and as a means of evading colonial oppression, it soon became an essential aspect of the people's life pattern as the social economy of different regions became in one way or another dependent on migration. Migration might be temporary or permanent and the one might lead to the other. Temporary migration was the movement of individuals, seldom whole families, in search of work either in another part of Mozambique or across the borders in British Africa. In theory the migrant intended to return and still thought of himself as belonging to the society left behind. Permanent migration involved the uprooting of whole families into new areas, where they remained.[65]

The most important permanent migrations involved the movement of Shona-speaking peoples into Southern Rhodesia from Tete and Manica e Sofala, of Makonde across the Rovuma into Tanganyika, and of Makua into Nyasaland. The first two involved people moving within their own cultural area since the colonial frontiers had divided Shona and Makonde peoples. The migrants often maintained family links with the communities they left and sometimes returned when local conditions changed. Shona migrants were welcomed into Southern Rhodesia and were encouraged to reside in border areas to swell the tax receipts of the districts and provide a pool of farm labour. Makonde also crossed into Tanganyika in search of work but also to escape the fighting of the First World War and the anarchic and violent administration of the Nyassa Company.

The Makua emigration into Nyasaland was a rather different phenomenon and on a much greater scale. The Lomwe Makua who inhabited the Namuli and Milanje highlands east of the Shire had suffered in the nineteenth century, like so many other Makua communities, from the lack of powerful centralised institutions. They had been raided by Nguni and Yao but the comparative fertility of their area had sustained a relatively dense population, and many of the lesser Lomwe chiefs were able to protect themselves in the mountains. No Portuguese administration was established in the area until 1897-9 when the Lomwe were incorporated into three of the Zambesia Company *prazos*. Already by that time many of them had established contact with the Scottish missions in the Shire Highlands, which opened up a migration route that others were to follow.[66]

Large-scale Lomwe migration into the Shire Highlands, which had been partially emptied of population by a generation of slave raiding, began in the 1890s. The Lomwe tended to come as individual families or small groups and did not establish their own chieftaincies. Instead they sought the protection of Manganja chiefs, more rarely of Yao or Nguni, and sometimes of the white planters. The Lomwe were apparently prepared to accept living and working conditions which local inhabitants would refuse, and they seldom had any problem finding a patron who would allow them to occupy and work land in return for labour services — the so-called *thangata*. Moreover, as migration from Nyasaland to the Rand began to grow there were continual labour shortages which Lomwe were able to fill.[67]

Migration was increased by the passage of the Germans through the Lomwe country in 1918, and by 1921 it was estimated that there were 121,000 Lomwe in the Nyasaland Protectorate. In districts like Mulanje they already made up 30 per cent of the population. However, the main period of migration was only just beginning. The 1920s saw an intensification of the demand for labour on the Zambesi plantations and the demand for forced contract labour reached a peak. This stimulated massive migration and by 1931 the number of Lomwe in Nyasaland was estimated to have doubled to 236,000.[68] In the 1930s and 1940s the pace of migration slowed and became more clearly a response to economic opportunitiy. Lomwe men often came to Nyasaland to seek seasonal work and the relative prosperity of peasant agriculture and opportunities for it became decisive.

Many features make the Lomwe migrations very different from the movement of migrant workers from the Sul do Save. At no stage were they in any way official or legal. The Portuguese did not profit from the migrants. Open recruitment was not allowed, and the Portuguese often tried to prevent migrants from leaving and imposed penalties on those caught. Although the Nyasaland administration and the white planters welcomed migrants and made provision for their settlement, this was throughout a movement inspired and organised by Africans. However, it was so widespread that there can have been few Makua from Moçambique or Zambesia Districts who were not in some way affected.

The First World War and the Barue rebellion

In the years leading up to the First World War Mozambique continued to be a focus for the attention of the other colonial powers. Although the frontiers had been fixed in 1891 and the rivalry of Britain and Germany for influence in the new state had been contained by the secret agreement of 1898, the weakness of the Portuguese administration continued to cause problems. Portugal and Britain became locked in a diplomatic wrangle resulting from the revelations about slavery in São Tomé. Portugal was aware that the great powers that had signed the Berlin Act in 1885 had intervened to remove the Congo Free State from King Leopold's control in 1908. Parts of both Angola and Mozambique fell within the area controlled by the Congo treaties and there was a risk that they might suffer the same fate.

A second cause of concern was the hostility of Southern Rhodesia to the Moçambique Company and the threats it made from time to time that there might be direct intervention; Smuts too openly expressed the desire to acquire Delagoa Bay for the Union. If Britain was able firmly to discountenance intervention by its own colonials, it was less easy to deal with the problem posed by French and German shareholders who threatened British control of the two Mozambique charter companies. Twice French shareholders in the Moçambique Company tried to take control from Ochs and only when Libert Oury appeared on the scene in 1910 were British and South African interests secured. The Nyassa Company, which had early passed under the control of the British-financed Ibo Syndicate and then of a South African consortium, had been taken over by German interests in 1913, and it was partly out of fear of a resurgence of imperial rivalry that Britain and Germany negotiated a fresh agreement in that year which effectively continued the understanding reached in 1898.[69]

When the First World War broke out Portugal remained neutral and was encouraged to do so by Britain, which feared a rapid German occupation of the Portuguese colonies. Indeed early in the war there were clashes on the southern borders of Angola and on the Rovuma frontier of Mozambique which suggested that this was likely to happen. Nevertheless the Portuguese authorities decided to strengthen their position in the north and sent European and African troops and war material to the Nyassa Company's territory. A number of fortified posts were laid out along the Rovuma, and areas of the interior still not securely under Company administration were occupied by the military.

In March 1916 Portugal formally entered the war on the side of the Allies, the main reason being fear that the African colonies might fall to the victor if it remained neutral. The British extended credits to Portugal, promised support for the colonies and persuaded Owen Philipps, director of Union Castle Line, to take over the German assets in the Nyassa Company. Entering the war had no immediate consequences for Mozambique and in April the Portuguese occupied the Quionga triangle, the small piece of German territory south of the Rovuma mouth. Further south, however, the war began to take its toll of the African population. The military operations in the north, where there were few roads and no railways or navigable rivers, meant, as has already been mentioned, that a large number of carriers were required. On the *prazos* throughout Zambesia and in the Sul do Save thousands of men were press-ganged for service by armed police. Black *cipais* were also sent from Zambesia to serve in the north. According to one estimate the Portuguese supplied 30,000 carriers to British forces and 60,000 for their own armies during the war.[70]

Although the *prazos* of the lower Zambesi had been quiet since the 1880s, much of Tete district and Barue had only been formally pacified since 1902. Even after formal administration was established, banditry continued, particularly along the borders with Southern Rhodesia where it was easy for armed bands to pass back and forth across the frontier. The Rhodesian authorities were well known for turning a blind eye to illegal immigrants who swelled the labour force available for white farms. Among these immigrants were members of the Barue ruling aristocracy who had taken refuge after the defeat of 1902. In 1916 the Portuguese began to recruit in Barue; men were taken for the army or for carrier service and women for *chibalo* on road-building projects under the supervision of armed police.[71]

In 1916 opposition to the Portuguese grew but the sons of the previous Macombe Hanga, who had died in exile in 1910, still disputed between themselves who was the rightful successor, and only when the initiative was taken by the Kaguru spirit medium was the decision taken to embark on armed rebellion. Emissaries were sent to chiefs and mediums in the country adjoining Barue to obtain support assisted by the spirit mediums, and in March 1917 the exiled chiefs took control of Barue initiating what soon became a widespread insurrection.[72] The rebellion spread down the south bank of the Zambesi among the population in the Moçambique Company territory, and upstream it engulfed the whole of Tete District as far as Zumbo, including many of the Cewa on the north bank. In many ways this was a revival of the sort of alliance achieved in the 1880s between Barue and the Da Cruz and Pereira factions among the old Afro-Portuguese élite. Indeed, the leaders of the revolt tried to contact descendants of the old Afro-Portuguese *senhores*, enlist Sousa's sons and incorporate former *chicunda* soldiers and disgruntled Afro-Portuguese. The site of Massangano was even occupied by a descendant of one of the Da Cruz *capitães*.[73] No war in Zambesia had ever been fought without the active involvement of the 'bandit classes' — the *chicunda* and their captains, the Afro-Portuguese slavers and elephant hunters, and junior members of chiefly houses who could gather a few men armed with guns into a fortified stockade. As many as 15,000 men may have taken up arms, operating out of fortified stockades in traditional Zambesi fashion, but significantly the rebels failed to gain the co-operation of the Nguni or the inhabitants of the north bank *prazos* of the lower river, an area where Frelimo also had little success in the 1960s.

However, although the revolt attracted massive support from almost all the ethnic groups of the valley, it was still in many ways an insurrection that looked back to the past and relied on traditional beliefs and practices. The fighters were provided with 'medicine' which would turn bullets to water, as in the Maji Maji rising in Tanganyika. In the Tavara country people were urged to kill their pigs before commitment to the rising and this, together with the emergence of a young girl as the medium of Kaguru, brings to mind the circumstances preceding the Xhosa cattle killings in South Africa in 1857. The leaders of the rising were able to unite people in hostility to the Portuguese administration and to the Indian traders who were seen as its agents, but they had no clear long-term objective apart from trying to gain the support of the British authorities in Rhodesia.

The Portuguese north and south of the Zambesi were forced to fall back on three garrisoned strongpoints at Cachomba, Tete and Sena. However, the revolt had reawoken traditions of Zambesi warfare, and the Portuguese response also recalled the last phases of the Zambesi wars. Black auxiliaries were raised by Gustavo Bivar and large numbers of Nguni troops were recruited (according to some reports, as many as 30,000) and these were licensed to hunt down the rebel armies, and to take any plunder, including women and children, that they could lay their hands on.[74] A curious diary kept in Latin by Father Moskopp, the Jesuit missionary in Kapoche, graphically describes the end of the rebellion near Zumbo and its inevitable aftermath — and, incidentally, what must have been the last action of a traditional Nguni regiment:

> 25th September 1917. In the morning lots of people were running on the sands to the Lwangwa. They are fleeing before the Angoni auxilliaries. Near Madzombwe I can see the smoke of burning villages. . . . Some men, and women and children had hardly reached the Lwangwa when the Angoni broke out of the reeds. Many Angoni run along the bank dressed in skins with feathers in the hair, and are armed with lances and large shields. Those who are caught if they are men, are killed, if they are women they are led into capitivity. Only the school at Nhaondo remained intact.
>
> 3rd October 1917 . . . The wives of the natives who had fled before the Angoni came through here on their way to Feira. There they got food and were transferred to Buruma. Madzombwe asked me to write to the Portuguese that he does not want war. . . . He surrendered to the Portuguese at Zumbo. There is famine. The

food stores are burnt and there are no supplies on our side, because in other years we used to buy food on the Portuguese side. In Buruma many have died of hunger.[75]

The war had three phases. A gunboat was sent to the Zambesi and the strategic point of Tambara was captured at the end of May. Portuguese columns defeated the main rebel armies and relieved the threatened towns by the end of 1917.[76] Then, for the next year, fighting took place in the mountains of the escarpment along the Rhodesian border where bands of rebels moved relatively freely in and out of Rhodesia and mounted raids on Portuguese positions. By the end of 1918, however, all the Barue leaders had fled into exile and the war entered a third phase in which small bands of rebel outlaws roamed the country until well into 1920.

The Rhodesian authorities did little to hinder the use of their frontier area for guerrilla operations — an interesting anticipation of the way first Frelimo and then Renamo operated from bases beyond the frontier to destabilise Mozambique. Direct intervention by British forces was confined to the sending of some soldiers to help guard the Beira-Umtali railway — just as Zimbabwean forces were sent in the 1980s to defend the same railway threatened by Renamo in the post-independence wars.[77]

Fighting on the Zambesi was still in progress when a German force commanded by von Stumer crossed the Rovuma and marched south through the Yao country east of the Lake. The Germans were greeted enthusiastically by the Yao, many of whose chiefs rose in revolt. Pursued by British and Portuguese forces von Stumer retreated across the Rovuma, evacuating his final posts in September.[78] Meanwhile the Portuguese military in the north had decided to occupy the Makonde plateau — an operation which lasted from April to September and for which 2,000 Makua irregulars were recruited. It is likely that lingering memories of this campaign created suspicion between Makua and Makonde in the era of the war of liberation.[79]

These campaigns, however, were merely the prelude to a much larger German invasion. A powerful German column retreating before the huge concentration of British, Indian and South African troops in central Tanganyika crossed the Rovuma in November 1917 and headed southwards along the Lugenda valley, the ancient highway between Kilwa and the Lake. The German army consisted of 300 European troops and 1,700 *askari* led by General von Lettow Vorbeck in person. The Germans fanned out through northern Mozambique in four columns, attacking Portuguese garrisons and supplying themselves from arms and food dumps. Everywhere Portuguese forces retreated or were brushed aside and their military posts destroyed. The British, still vainly trying to trap von Lettow, landed troops on the coast at Mozambique and Pemba, as much to secure a presence in northern Mozambique in the event of an armistice finding the area controlled by the Germans as from any hope of actually defeating them. In June the German force invaded Zambesia, capturing and plundering Namacurra on the Quelimane railway before heading north again, recrossing the Rovuma and marching into Northern Rhodesia. There von Lettow Vorbeck eventually surrendered, still undefeated, on the declaration of the armistice in Europe.[80]

Von Lettow Vorbeck with his army of *askari* had marched through Mozambique like the Nguni armies of eighty years earlier and like so many other warlords in the history of the country. His men took with them their women and children and the army lived by plunder, taking not only livestock, food and ammunition but seizing people to act as carriers for the professional fighters. The campaign has usually been seen as a bravura performance, an heroic episode in the history of the First World War, but in the context of Mozambican history it was a phenomenon all too familiar — of the warlord with his professional fighters living from plunder, prepared when necessary to terrorise the local population but carrying among the camp followers the embryo of a new tribe if circumstances should ever allow them to settle.

Although the Portuguese believed that German agents had been at work fomenting the rebellion on the Zambesi, it does not appear that the Germans made any attempt to link up with rebel forces. On the other hand they casually raised revolt among the Yao and Makua by promising an end to taxation and forced labour, and between August and November 1918 there were serious revolts in the coastal regions of Angoche and Sancul.[81] Once von Lettow had left, full attention could be turned to ending the Zambesi rebellion, reoccupying the areas overrun by the Germans, and punishing chiefs throughout the north thought to have collaborated.

If the Portuguese hoped that they would be rewarded at the Versailles peace conference with slices of former German colonies, they were soon disillusioned, and a redrawing of the northern border of Mozambique to include the Quionga triangle was their only territorial gain. The peace conference devised the Mandate system to settle the future of the former German and Turkish empires, and Smuts, one of the originators of the idea, pressed hard for the Mandates to be extended to the Portuguese colonies as well. This demand was clearly motivated by the old South African desire to acquire Delagoa Bay and the Sul do Save, but it was lent credibility by the reports of British officers serving in northern Mozambique which revealed for the first time the weakness, corruption and violence of Portuguese rule in the north. What saved Mozambique was probably the fact that both the

Nyassa and the Moçambique Companies were by this time owned by British capital and had anyway almost become instruments of British colonial rule.[82]

The development of plantation agriculture

The 1890 *prazo* law and the subsequent regulations gave the concessionaires who rented the *prazos* the duty of administering their regions and the right to levy taxation, engage police and exercise a commercial monopoly. The *prazo* concessions also gave them the right to command labour and so control the product of peasant society. Thus the system gave the concessionaires access to labour and capital resources and the ability to create their own system of security. Moreover, it all fitted closely into traditional Zambesian modes of authority and social relations. The *prazo* system of feudal overlordship and patronage had been neatly adapted to the needs of international capital.

The original intention of António Ennes may have been to encourage small-scale Portuguese investment and the immigration of Portuguese entrepreneurs. However, the unsettled state of Zambesia and the harsh conditions that prevailed in the region made it inevitable that only those with large resources would succeed. In the event the *prazos* were leased by six plantation companies: the Mozambique Sugar Company, the Boror Company, the Société du Madal, the Luabo Company, the Lugella Company and the Zambesia Company. The Zambesia Company also leased *en bloc* 126 *prazos* in the Tete region which had been separately classified as unpacified. These companies from the start had substantial foreign backing and all of them were soon controlled by their foreign shareholders.

On the lower Zambesi, both in the Moçambique Company territories and on the state *prazos*, a number of plantation enterprises got under way. Experiments were carried out in all the major tropical staples, including cotton, but only two made any real progress — sugar and copra. Copra was grown primarily in the coastal regions and was the main product of the Zambesia and Luabo Companies, founded respectively in 1893 and 1895. However, it was the Boror Company (it took its name from the large Boror *prazo* north of Quelimane) which, after a number of false starts, became the greatest producer, planting 325,000 trees between 1900 and 1902, but operating for much of the time indirectly through peasant producers who either owned trees on the company concessions or leased them from the company.[83] By the First World War the Boror Company had become one of the world's greatest producers of copra (Fig. 16.2). The Société du Madal, created in 1903, also adopted a dual policy of planting its own trees and allowing the peasants to do likewise and sell their

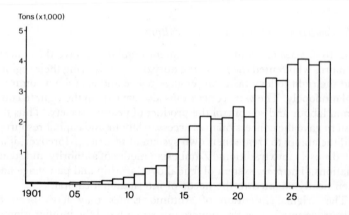

Fig. 16.2. COPRA PRODUCTION OF THE BOROR COMPANY

Source: E. Ribeiro, 'A Zambezia Agricola'.

copra to the company.[84] Thus peasant-grown copra regularly provided more than half the quantity exported from the Zambesi plantations.

Sugar was a much more capital-intensive enterprise than copra and a number of companies began operations towards the end of the nineteenth century. For example, the Companhia do Assucar de Moçambique was founded in 1890 with capital contributed by small Portuguese investors and in 1899 the Sociedade Assucareira de Africa Oriental Portuguesa started a plantation and sugar factory at Marromeu.[85] The main attraction of growing sugar in Mozambique in the 1890s was the production of rum for sale to South Africa. The free trade agreement with South Africa opened the lucrative Rand market to Portuguese rum distillers, and Mozambique spirits flowed into the Transvaal along with the flood of Mozambique workers. It is estimated that by 1896 517,790 litres of spirit were being exported from Mozambique, three-quarters of it from the Mopeia distillery of the Companhia do Assucar de Moçambique.[86] However by the early twentieth century heavy restrictions were being placed on the sale of drink, and Mozambique sugar producers then began to concentrate on invading the South African and Portuguese domestic markets with their sugar. In 1901 the Portuguese government introduced sugar quotas for the first time, allowing 6,000 tonnes of Mozambique sugar into Portugal at preferential rates and in 1909 the Mozambique-Transvaal convention made special provision for it to be imported duty-free into the Transvaal.[87]

By 1910 J.P. Hornung had become the dominant figure in the Mozambique sugar industry, managing or owning most of the plantations on the lower Zambesi, and leasing *prazos* on the north bank as well as in the Moçambique Company territory. In 1911 he leased the Luabo Company *prazos* and *prazo* Angonia in Tete district, and by 1914 had acquired interests in refineries in Lisbon besides controlling the port of Chinde and a fleet of Zambesi steamers (Map 8). Between 1908 and 1914 annual sugar production in Zambesia rose from 13,247 to 28,944 tonnes.[88]

Sena Sugar, as Hornung's companies became known, was the outstanding success story of Mozambique's plantation capitalism. Sugar production depended on a regular flow of labour recruited from all the *prazos* under the company's administration which amounted in 1914 to an estimated 14,000 square miles of Zambesia and Tete districts. As more and more of Zambesi territory came under Hornung's control, his officials and *cipais* formed an administrative network covering much of the central region of the colony. Through his company British capital began to enter that region, leading to the construction of townships, railways, steamer quays, industrial power plants and workshops — all geared to servicing the gigantic sugar industry that was emerging.

Under the Monarchy the sugar quota system had been designed with the idea of encouraging the sugar growers of Angola, who were Portuguese, at the expense of Hornung's Sena Sugar. The Republican government, however, abandoned any attempt to hold back the development of Mozambique sugar. In 1914 it raised duties against foreign imports and abandoned the quotas. By 1925 Mozambique exported three times as much sugar as Angola and by 1933 colonial sugar was supplying 96 per cent of the Portuguese market.[89]

There is no doubt that Sena Sugar's prosperity was built up on its access to what was in effect unfree labour, but the company soon outgrew this crude and inefficient form of exploitation. Gradually wage labour on long-term contracts replaced the short-term service of those working in lieu of taxation. Migrant workers were recruited in Nyasaland, northern Mozambique and wherever Sena Sugar could obtain them, while increasing sums were invested in labour-saving machinery. The success of Sena Sugar was gradually emulated by the other *prazo* companies. Up to the First World War the *prazo* concessionaires had utilised their privileges to the full, extorting labour, forcing Africans to sell cash crops to the companies, and enforcing commercial monopolies. Already by 1914, however, the limits of the *prazo* system had been fully exposed. Moving huge numbers of labourers around Zambesia just to do a few weeks' work was hopelessly inefficient, while the growth of employment opportunities in Rhodesia and South Africa, where work was paid for and the labourer could exercise some form of choice, led to extensive emigration from the *prazos*. A limit had been reached to what could be achieved under such a system. Any further expansion of production would need different arrangements (Figs. 16.3 and 16.4).

Meanwhile attention was being focussed on the internal state of the *prazos*. If the charters of the Moçambique and Nyassa Companies were fairly watertight, the position of the *prazo* companies was less so. Reports of labour scandals stimulated the Portuguese government to use its *prazo* inspectorate to investigate how the companies were operating. A report issued by the Secretary for Native Affairs, Castello Branco, in 1909 gave rise to intense debate over the future of the *prazos*, and the virtues of continuing the system of devolving administrative control to the companies, along with a *de facto* commercial monopoly, were questioned. The debate continued during the war but in 1919 the government introduced measures which removed the commercial monopolies, stopped the collection of *mussoco* in kind, and decreed proper labour contracts, minimum wages and an end to all attempts by the *prazo* concessionaires to control labour migration. They were a signal that the plantation companies would have to move into a more capitalist mode, employing labour on long contracts, paying sufficiently attractive wages and providing minimally acceptable working conditions.[90]

After the First World War prices for agricultural produce rose and remained high till at least 1922. In response the Zambesi plantations were encouraged to increase their output considerably. Sisal, which had begun to be planted before the war, greatly expanded, tea began to be produced by the Lugella Company on the slopes of the highlands towards Nyasaland, and copra showed a dramatic increase reflecting its soaring price (Fig. 16.2). However, it was sugar which once again dominated Mozambique's agricultural export sector. In response to the massive price rises at the end of the war (sugar rose to £91 a tonne) Hornung planned a large expansion of his sugar production. In 1921 he signed a contract with the new high commissioner, Brito Camacho, for an additional 3,000 labourers to be provided by the government from the Mozambique district in return for expanding sugar production by 15,000 tonnes a year. Camacho weakly tried to persuade Hornung to move his operations to the south but this suggestion was

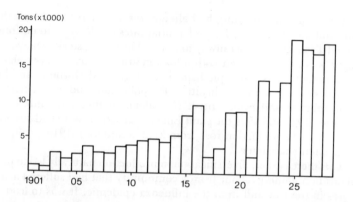

Fig. 16.3. EXPORTS OF COPRA FROM STATE-ADMINISTERED
TERRITORIES

G. Liesegang, 'A First Look at the Import and Export Trade . . .' *Anuário
Estatístico.*

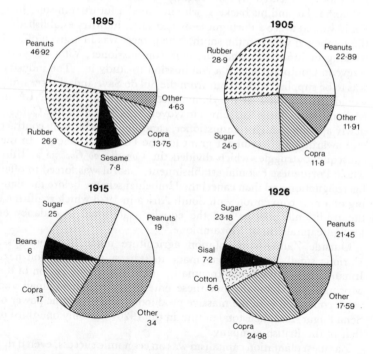

Fig..16.4.   EXPORTS FROM MOZAMBIQUE, 1985–1926 (%)

brushed aside as Hornung had already reached agreement with the Moçambique Company for preferential rates on the soon to be completed Trans-Zambesia railway to Beira. The rolling stock to move his sugar was to be provided with a loan guaranteed by the Nyasaland government. This was capitalism riding high, and Hornung and his associates seemed able to dictate to the politicians and to run central Mozambique and even British Nyasaland in their own interest.[91] Between 1922 and 1924 the giant Luabo plantations were laid out and Sena Sugar's production rose from 27,239 tonnes in 1919 to 69,936 tonnes ten years later.[92]

This increase and diversification in production naturally led to problems·in obtaining labour from a community that had suffered acute losses in the war and from the influenza epidemic. It was to lead in the mid-1920s to a resurgence of the worst excesses of forced labour with the state playing a coercive role hitherto reserved for the *prazo* administrations. It led also to intensified faction fighting within the Portuguese colonial establishment. A rival scheme to the expansion of Hornung's empire had been advanced by certain Mozambican interests represented by the slightly manic Eduardo de Almeida Saldanha. He and his backers, who included a future minister, João Belo, wanted to see a Portuguese-owned sugar industry established in the Umbeluzi valley in the south. The project was first given official backing in June 1925 when the high commissioner, Vitor Hugo de Azevedo Coutinho, set up a commission to study it.[93] The industry was to be supplied with labour from the Sul do Save and, if successful, would strike a blow at the dominance of Hornung and WNLA in Mozambique. Battle was joined in November 1926 when José Cabral, newly appointed high commissioner, cancelled the Hornung contract and awarded a government grant for the Umbeluzi scheme. In the subsequent struggle, which divided the *Conselho do Governo* and the whole Portuguese colonial establishment, Cabral was forced to offer his resignation and then cancel the Umbeluzi scheme before the signing of a new convention with South Africa in 1928 which reaffirmed the traditional policies and the equally traditional ascendancy of foreign capital within Mozambique.[94]

Outside Zambesia plantation agriculture made little progress. Various small attempts were made to start sugar production near Inhambane, on the lower Incomati, and in the coastal region of the Moçambique Company but these enterprises remained small and weak compared with the massive production and economic power of Sena Sugar, and their total output in the 1920s was only one-third of that of the British company.[95]

Zambesi plantation capitalism was an economic success, even if this was the result of following a path of trial and error with the errors predominating. A large export-oriented economy had developed which attracted outside investment, generated considerable foreign earnings and led to the building of a substantial infrastructure network. And it did this without wholly destroying the peasant sector of the economy. It would only be a matter of time before the growth of the plantations would lead to further diversification and industrialisation as service industries and processing plants became increasingly needed. However, the Zambesi plantations undoubtedly imposed a pattern of development on Mozambique which had major disadvantages, the most important of these deriving from the fact that this development was so largely self-contained. The plantations were isolated islands of production linked to the outside world through the nearest port and exporting their product and much of their profits. They perpetuated and intensified the fragmentation of the country. The economic isolation of Zambesia from the rest of the country continued and became ever more deeply ingrained in the institutional and economic life of the country.

The last phase of Republican government

Events in Mozambique during the First World War, the Barue rising and the German invasions certainly emphasised the need for Portugal to make its administration more effective. In the two years following the war, the north, which had been fought over by the Germans, was reoccupied and in the process Portuguese forces finally subdued the Makonde of the Mavia plateau, the last area remaining outside effective administrative control. It was also decided to implement sweeping administrative and constitutional changes. In 1919 new regulations for the *prazos* ended the administrative authority of the companies, and brought the *prazos* directly under the governors of the various districts in which they were situated. However, this was only the prelude to much more far-reaching changes, for in 1920 it was at last decided to establish a new colonial regime based on the Organic Charter. The government of Mozambique was to be separated from Lisbon and made autonomous. A high commissioner, carrying cabinet rank, was appointed with powers to control his own budget, raise loans and administer the country independently of Lisbon. At the same time Mozambique was to be given for the first time a Legislative Council made up of officials but with some elected members. These long overdue measures recognised that Mozambique had to progress towards acquiring the characteristics of a modern unitary state with a locally responsible administration.

However, creating the post of high commissioner and granting autonomy from Lisbon did not in themselves resolve any of the contradictions of the colony, which in the short term were to become intensified. The first high commissioner, Manuel de Brito Camacho, found that while he was autonomous on paper, in practice almost the whole colony was either in the hands of the charter companies and *prazo* concessionaires, or subject to the terms of the Mozambique-Transvaal Convention, while its economy was either controlled by foreign capital or had been mortgaged to the great Portuguese monopolists like the BNU. There was little that could be done immediately about these powerful feudatories whose effective power dwarfed that of the high commissioner. Progress towards the creation of a unified government would have to await the gradual expiry of the concessions. The Convention with the Transvaal was due to expire in 1923, the charter of the Nyassa Company in 1929 and the *prazo* concessions mostly ended in 1930, leaving only the Moçambique Company concession to continue till 1941. In the mean time, however, the colony was plunged into an economic crisis — partly of its own making and partly reflecting global conditions — which involved the high commissioner, like some sixteenth-century monarch, in a prolonged battle with the overmighty subjects who controlled sectors of Mozambique territory and its economy.

At the root of the problem was the BNU, which performed most of the functions of a central bank but was not controlled by the government, and pursued policies that frequently went counter to the state's interests. This encouraged the government to try to take on the bank and operate an independent fiscal policy. When the Banco Nacional Ultramarino was founded in 1864 it was granted a monopoly of banking in the colonies with the sole right to issue paper currency. At first it had paid little attention to Mozambique and contented itself with opening a single branch on Mozambique Island. In 1891 its enemies in Lisbon managed to end its monopoly on banking and British banks began to establish branches in the Mozambique port towns, but the BNU retained its right to issue paper currency, operating in the Moçambique Company territory through a subsidiary, the Banco de Beira. This right was extended in 1901 for a further eighteen years.[96]

The chaotic administrative conditions in Mozambique and the backwardness of its economy did not necessarily imply that the country was financially weak. The labour contracts with South Africa and the earnings of the railways and ports gave it a healthy surplus on its balance of payments for the three decades after 1890. The BNU made its paper issue convertible into gold, which it obtained either from the government or directly from foreign workers returning to the country. Holding to the gold standard allowed both the BNU and the Banco de Beira to issue currency notes in pound sterling denominations. Monetary circulation and the expansion of the economy was therefore paced by the rate at which gold could be earned through providing services and labour supplies to British Africa.

During the First World War the Mozambique government ceased to sell its gold to the BNU, which began to find the backing of its note issue increasingly difficult. When its contract was renewed in 1919 it was with the stipulation that its note issue would be convertible not to gold but to metropolitan Portuguese *escudos*. However, the Portuguese currency was being rapidly devalued, so that by 1924 the *escudo*, worth 5 to the pound sterling in 1914, was changing at 130. When the limits on the BNU's note issue were lifted, the Banco was in a position to flood Mozambique with paper currency in both *escudo* and sterling denominations. The BNU and the Mozambique government then embarked upon a bitter struggle, with each trying to protect its interests, the BNU insisting that foreign notes in circulation were illegal and could only be exchanged for its own notes, and the Mozambique government continuing to refuse to sell gold to the Banco. As a result the economy of Mozambique began to experience intense inflation. Its currency, now linked to that of Portugal and no longer convertible into gold, was discounted at ever-increasing percentages.

Although currency was controlled by the BNU, other economic levers were in the hands of the Mozambique government. With the granting of financial autonomy in 1920, the colonies had separate budgets and could contract loans and administer their own debt. It was open to the high commissioners, at least in theory, to try to negotiate foreign loans, a measure which would accord them some independence from the financial straitjacket of the BNU. By 1926 the colony's accumulated deficits, financed by borrowing, had risen to half a million sterling.[97]

Although they were not able to tackle the administrative chaos and fragmentation inherited from the Monarchy directly, the Mozambique high commissioners tried to stimulate economic growth and development. Immediately after the war there was a boom in world commodity prices, and Brito Camacho was anxious to take advantage of this to boost production in Mozambique. At the same time he wanted to use the new financial autonomy to raise loans to improve infrastructure throughout the colony. In his voluminous writings Brito Camacho explained his desire to develop Mozambique — to encourage peasant production, diversify the plantation sector, and create import-saving industries by stimulating the consumer market.[98] But he found that the deeply imbedded British and South African interests were hostile to his activities as, led on by Smuts, they wanted to obtain closer control over the Lourenço Marques railway and port. Smuts, with co-operation from the British Foreign Office, put endless obstacles in the way of Brito Camacho's attempts to raise a loan on the international money markets, suggesting instead that he should raise his money in South Africa. This encouraged the high commissioner to turn to other possible sources of credit. He found that Sena Sugar was willing to use its good offices to negotiate a loan if he would help meet the company's labour needs. This bargain appealed to the high commissioner and fitted into his plans for economic development.

He therefore concluded an agreement early in 1921, which came to be known by friends and enemies alike as the Hornung Contract, whereby the government would annually supply Sena Sugar with 3,000 labourers recruited in government-controlled territory in Moçambique district, in return for which Sena Sugar would extend its sugar planting, open a new factory and increase its output to 30,000 tonnes a year.[99] The efficient and dynamic Hornung soon moved to fulfill his part of the bargain, and huge new sugar plantations were laid out in the territory of the old Luabo Company. However, the Hornung Contract, successful as it proved to be in the short term, intensified strains elsewhere in the colony. It was bitterly opposed by the Mozambican settlers who believed that Hornung, a foreigner, was creaming off still further the manpower resources of the colony. There was international opposition also and questions were ultimately to be raised in the League of Nations itself about the methods used by the government to recruit the necessary labour, following a report by the American Professor E.A. Ross to the League's Temporary Slaving Commission in 1925.[100] These questions were given some validity by the reports from neighbouring British territory that tens of thousands of peasants from northern Mozambique were fleeing across the borders to avoid recruitment.

This opposition was soon given spurious weight by the economic downturn which began in 1921 with world commodity prices slipping and inflation gathering speed. Together these forces broke Brito Camacho, who left office after only twenty months. Under his successors little apparent progress was made in establishing effective government and economic policy in the colony. Inflation continued, the lack of convertibility of the colonial currency hindered trade and investment, servicing the colonial debt remained a problem, and no loan was negotiated. However, some of the foundations for the more effective policies pursued in the 1930s were already being laid.

During his brief tenure, Brito Camacho had firmly resisted South African pressure for concessions over the control of the port of Lourenço Marques. When the Mozambique-Transvaal Convention lapsed in 1923 a stalemate followed, but this worked in Portugal's favour. Negotiations were resumed in 1928 and a fresh convention was signed confirming all the essential provisions of the earlier conventions and blocking any attempt by South Africa to establish greater control over Lourenço Marques or its railway. Similar stalling tactics were pursued by the Portuguese government in refusing to renew the charter of the Nyassa Company. Here the Portuguese were for once able to 'turn the tables' morally on Britain and pin the blame for the appalling backwardness, corruption and abuse rife in the territory on Lord Kylsant and the British directors of the company. In due time the charter of the company came to an end and a large slice of Mozambique reverted to government control. Time also would solve the problem of the *prazos* as their leases expired in 1930. To some extent, therefore, the long-term future of Mozambique could be secured by waiting.

However, other important initiatives were taken by the Republican government which were to influence the whole future of the country. The last Minister of the Colonies under the Republic was João Belo who had lived in Mozambique for thirty years. He believed that the financial autonomy of the high commissioners had been a disaster and moved to re-establish Lisbon's control while at the same time curbing the powers of the BNU, reducing note issues in circulation and granting the colony a metropolitan loan.[101] As a matter of public policy Belo had wanted to strengthen the commercial and financial ties between Portugal and Mozambique, trying unsuccessfully to stimulate a Portuguese-owned sugar industry in the south which would be supplied with labour diverted from the Rand. He commissioned a study of Belgian compulsory crop-growing and decreed regulations for introducing such a scheme into the Portuguese colonies. Under his auspices also the surveys of the Limpopo were carried out that were to lead to the ambitious and far-reaching plans to develop the Limpopo valley and its water resources. The first steps were also taken to open up the coal deposits of Tete district, the existence of which had been known since the early nineteenth century. The Moçambique Company was interested and plans were laid for a railway to take the coal to a river port. The government set up a statistical department that began to issue regular compilations of statistics in 1926, and ended the experiment of lay instead of religious missions. Finally a full-scale review of the colonies' labour laws was undertaken which resulted in the major revision of the labour code in 1928.

João Belo died prematurely and unexpectedly in January 1928 (the port of Xai Xai was renamed after him to perpetuate his memory in Mozambique).[102] The changes in policy which he had directed were to mean that Mozambique would experience more continuity than change when the New State eventually turned its attention to revising colonial policy.

Social and political development up to 1930

It is difficult to obtain any accurate idea of how the Mozambique population developed in the four decades after 1890. Although the Portuguese administrators loved to produce statistics, these were not systematically collected together until the *Repartição de Statistica* was established in 1926. Various estimates of the African and non-African population were made, but only in 1928 was the first census of non-Africans carried out and in 1930 the first full census of the African population attempted. Counting the African population always presented a major problem. The population itself was highly mobile with numerous migrants absent on work contracts and significant numbers of the population on the move to avoid taxation or *chibalo*. However, official figures are given in Table 16.1. Making full allowance for the impressionistic way they were compiled, it seems

Table 16.1. AFRICAN POPULATION OF MOZAMBIQUE
(including charter company territory)

1908	(1,477,469)[a]
	(2,650,000)[b]
1917	3,652,008[a]
1923	3,530,377[a]
1926	3,523,611[a]
1927	3,479,042[a]
1930	3,960,261[c]

Sources: (a) Mario Costa, 'A População Indígena de Moçambique', pp. 145–6; (b) Sousa Ribeiro (ed.), *Anuário de Moçambique* (1917), p. 50; (c) *Anuário Estatístico* (1930).

reasonable to conclude that the population was at best static and may actually have been declining in the 1920s. Moreover, because of the war, the Barue rebellion and the influenza epidemic, the population had almost certainly been static or declining in the previous decade as well.

The first census revealed considerable differences in population density. A clear pattern is already apparent in the numbers presented in Table 16.2. Inland and frontier areas have low densities and coastal areas high densities. The relevant factors were partly geographical and partly the result of the country's development. Inland areas undoubtedly had higher rates of emigration since access to British Africa was at all times easier. But these population density variations cannot be attributed simply to the ease with which Africans could escape Portuguese oppression. The coastal regions of Mozambique are better watered and more fertile, and include almost all the urban

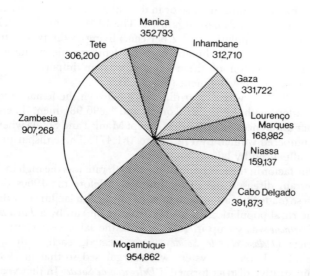

Fig. 16.5. POPULATION BY DISTRICT, 1930

Table 16.2. POPULATION DENSITY AND DISTRIBUTION
OF THE AFRICAN POPULATION, 1930 CENSUS

District	Pop. per sq. km.	† of total
Lourenço Marques	6.8	13.3
Inhambane	5.8	7.7
Quelimane	9.0	22.9
Tete	2.9	9.2
Moçambique	11.5	24.3
Cabo Delgado	4.9	9.9
Niassa	1.4	4.2
Manica e Sofala	2.5	8.4

Source: Anuário Estatístico (1930).

settlements. Indeed some of the areas of greatest density were to be found in Quelimane and Moçambique where demand for plantation labour had been most intense or in the Sul do Save where recruitment for South Africa was best organised. The 1930 census showed nearly half the total population (47.2 per cent) living in the two districts of Moçambique and Quelimane and the demographic strength of the Makua population of these regions was an important factor in Mozambique's development (Fig. 16.5).

In 1930 there was a clear difference between the female and male population, with 2,063,282 women and 1,896,981 men. There were similar differences in all districts except Manica and Sofala where men outnumbered women by 172,835 to 161,471. These disparities were also influenced by labour migration.

One factor in the low population growth rate was the high incidence of certain diseases and of malnutrition. Before the 1960s the Portuguese made little attempt to provide any health facilities for the mass of the rural population. A health department run by a *Junta de Saúde da Província* was set up in 1896, and in the same year eleven health districts (*Delagações de Saúde*) were created, each with its own hospital.[103] Later the system was reorganised so that in 1930 each administrative district formed a *Delegação de Saúde*. In that year there were still eleven town hospitals and a mere forty-four *postos sanitários* in the rural areas, although additional health facilities were provided by missions and by the major plantation companies like Sena Sugar. In 1930 10,582 patients were treated in hospital, 7,809 of them Africans — over half of these attending the hospital in Lourenço Marques. There were 123,555 vaccinations, almost all of them Africans, a figure near to the average for the previous five years.[104]

The missionaries

If colonialism brought the labour recruiter and the tax collector, in many parts of Africa it also brought the missionary. And through the educational networks of the missions there was the hope of acquiring skills that would enable the African peasant to escape both from the narrow confines of traditional society and from the treadmill of *chibalo* and contract labour.

Missionary activity in eastern Africa had all but ceased with the expulsion of the Jesuits in 1759, and any revival of Catholic activity was inconceivable during the civil wars in Portugal since the liberals were anxious to limit the powers of the church. In 1834 the religious orders were abolished altogether. The new missionary orders founded within the Roman Catholic church in the nineteenth century, the White Fathers and the Spiritans, were not attracted to Mozambique, although missions were established in Angola. However, the Portuguese recognised that the lack of a dynamic church was hindering the spread of their influence in Africa, and attempts were made from as early as 1844 to create a seminary for missionaries in Lisbon; this limped along without any conspicuous success. Between 1840 and 1875 twenty-six Goan missionaries served in eastern Africa, after which Portuguese from the Lisbon seminary took over; altogether 109 served in Mozambique before the seminary was closed in 1912.[105]

In 1881 the Jesuits returned to eastern Africa. One of their missions travelled through Gaza in 1879–81 and they rented the *prazo* of Boroma in 1885, building a grandiose mission station from which they planned to evangelise the middle reaches of the Zambesi. Two further Jesuit missions were created at Miruru and in Angonia. Missionaries accompanied the expedition of Cardoso in 1885 as a recognition of the political importance then acceded to 'civilising' activity. Franciscans established themselves in Beira in 1898. However, official figures suggest a low level of church membership — baptisms rose from 1,075 in 1907 (804 Africans) to 8,836 in 1939 (8,017 Africans), while marriages in church rose from 83 to 759.[106] Before 1910 the activity of the Catholic missions was not impressive, and they received a severe blow when the Republic abolished all religious missions in the colonies by a decree of 22 November 1913. The idea was to replace them with secular missions but these either failed to materialise altogether or achieved nothing. In practice the church continued to staff its comparatively few mission stations while remaining as inconspicuous as possible.

Meanwhile Protestant missions had also been active. Livingstone was responsible for planting the first of these, the UMCA mission to the Shire Highlands, in 1861. But it was withdrawn after a year and moved to Zanzibar from where it tried to penetrate Mozambique from the north. W.P. Johnston established a mission at Mwembe in 1875 but this lasted only till 1881, and in 1882 the UMCA moved to Likoma Island in the Lake. Likoma became part of the Nyasaland Protectorate in 1891 but by that time it was already establishing outstations along the eastern shores of the Lake. It continued to be responsible for a modest missionary enterprise among the Nyanja of north-western Mozambique throughout the colonial period.[107] In 1930 the Likoma diocese had three mission stations and two missionaries stationed in Mozambique. The dynamic Scottish missions which established themselves in the Shire Highlands in the 1870s tried to set up outposts in Mozambique among the Lomwe but these were summarily closed down by the Portuguese military who occupied the Namuli region in 1897. Only in the far south did Protestant missions make a lasting impact.

Their entry into southern Mozambique was one of the by-products of mine labour. Churches active in the mining areas often had contact with Mozambican migrants and became interested in establishing stations in the home regions of their converts. It was therefore in the 1870s and 1880s that Protestant missions began to be founded. The earliest and most prestigious was the Suisse Romande mission which established its first stations in 1875. These were followed by the American Board of Foreign Missions, the Methodist Episcopal Church and the Free Methodists, and eventually by Wesleyans, Baptists and Anglicans who created the diocese of Lebombo.[108]

Figures for 1930 show how concentrated was the activity of the foreign Protestant missions in the south: there were 794 foreign mission stations of one kind or another in Mozambique, 783 of them in Lourenço Marques or Inhambane Districts. The Swiss, virtually all of whose activities were in Lourenço Marques District, had 138 stations and employed 195 missionaries and 137 African auxiliaries. In that year the Anglican diocese had 151 mission stations employing 123 missionaries and 102 auxiliaries.[109]

Except in the extreme south, it is difficult to accord the Christian church any major role in social change in the country up to the end of the Republic. Access to employment or recognition within the Portuguese community required the acquisition of the status of *não-indígena*. In practice this meant that the applicant had to be a practising Christian and have some education, which in turn almost inevitably meant attendance at mission schools. But comparatively few people were able to better themselves in this way, and throughout the south emigration to South Africa was overwhelmingly the major cause of social change, bringing the migrants into touch with urban industrial culture and enabling them to earn significant cash incomes. The effects on traditional African society, ranging from the acquisition of consumer goods to changes in agricultural practices and *lobola*, all derived from economic factors linked to migrant labour rather than from cultural ones resulting from conversion. Adherence to a Protestant church was one of the things learnt in South Africa, and the spread of Protestant churches was as much a result of social change as a cause of it. Charles Fuller, estimating the impact of Protestantism among the Gwambe of Inhambane, saw cases of Christian evangelists taking over certain chiefly roles, holding sowing ceremonies at the start of the agricultural year, dispensing medicine and justice, and permitting marriages:

> In Christian villages . . . the distribution of fields is made by the evangelist in charge, though in mixed communities the patriarch or subchief retains his traditional function.[110]

He also writes:

> It is not unnatural that the Africans have associated Christianity with medicine and social control. . . . The Christian evangelist preached, gave out medicines, and acted as judge. In the last function he combined the task of a diviner, for whom he substituted on the religious level, with that of the subchief, in which capacity he acted when the Christian community separated itself from the supervision of hereditary authorities below the chief.[111]

But this social evolution was the result of economic change, to which the Protestant churches were merely helping their members to adjust. If they provided one way by which communities could adapt, there remains little evidence that they played any covert political role — standing between the African and the administration or articulating the grievances of their flock. This may indeed have happened, but little can be said about it at present. Independent African churches grew in Mozambique mostly as offshoots of similar churches in South Africa and Rhodesia and were patronised by migrant workers and their families. There were branches of the important African Methodist Episcopal Church and other churches affiliated to Wesleyanism. Others reflected the prophetic Zionist tradition. One statistic suggests that by the mid-1930s there were over 380 such churches with a membership running to hundreds of thousands.[112]

As elsewhere in Africa, the real importance of the churches in the early period of colonial rule was in providing access to literacy and education and thus opening a pathway, however narrow and restricted, for Africans to play some part in the emerging modern political and economic order.

Islam

While Christianity was largely confined in the nineteenth century to the Afro-Portuguese community (although it may have spread more widely in a syncretistic form among the populations of the Zambesi valley), Islam was making rapid inroads in the north. Although there were Muslim communities along the coast and up the Zambesi valley before the arrival of the Portuguese, there is little evidence that Islam spread beyond the coastal towns till the nineteenth century. It did so once traders from the coast themselves started to operate caravans to the interior. By the 1840s it is clear that many of the Yao and Makua were adopting aspects of the lifestyle of the coastal Muslims and with them some of the tenets of Islam, and the spread of Islam gathered momentum in the 1870s, '80s and '90s when explorers, missionaries and administrators alike commented on the 'fashion' or 'craze' for

Islam throughout the north. By the 1850s Islam was to be found throughout northern Mozambique as far as the Lake (though much more slowly among the Makua than the Yao) and was being carried by the Yao into the Shire highlands. However, it did not appear to spread much south of the Zambesi or west of the Shire where Afro-Portuguese culture was dominant. In practice the Zambesi and Shire had become a religious frontier.

Although Islamic revivalism swept many parts of Africa in the early nineteenth century, there is little evidence that in Mozambique Muslim ideas were deliberately propagated by brotherhoods or preachers. However, Muslim teachers often accompanied caravans from the coast and once a chief had been converted, a Koranic school would be built in his town. The principal attractions of Islam were the trading opportunities it offered and the prestige associated with Swahili culture, dress, building techniques and literacy.[113] It may also have offered a new security to people whose lives were permanently insecure as a result of slaving, Nguni raids or the uncertainties of the European Scramble for Africa, but perhaps most important of all was the fact that Islam — with its patrilineal and patriarchal institutions — offered unique opportunities to men in matrilineal societies to establish new patterns of social and political relations.[114]

Education

Education is essentially the way in which a society prepares the younger generations to perform a useful function in society. It is also a way in which a community perpetuates its mythology and, through that, its system of values and social control. Perhaps only in Western culture has there developed a tension between the main providers of education and the state-society, a tension which has sometimes divorced education from its functional roles and turned it into a process of developing the individual self rather than the individual as a member of a society. Without some discussion of this problem the concept of 'education' can become a source of confusion.

Among the African peoples of Mozambique education had been a tightly controlled process of socialisation. In the patrilineal south as well as in the matrilineal north the education process had been completed by communally regulated initiation rituals, control of which was often an important aspect of political power within the community.[115] But education also involved peer-group associations. These might, like the age-sets of the Nguni, be closely controlled by the chiefs, or less tightly controlled, self-regulating associations like the *nomi* societies of the Sena. In Muslim communities the Koranic school introduced a new element into traditional education. It taught literacy in Arabic and helped to initiate its pupils into the cultural world of the Swahili coast and hence into wider contacts and commercial advantages. Traditional authority watched over it closely.

In the Portuguese community education had been traditionally provided by the church and there are records of church schools in the various Portuguese towns as early as the seventeenth century. However, most Portuguese or Afro-Portuguese of substance would try to get their children educated in Goa or in Portugal itself. This was true also of the African protégés of the religious orders; for example, the Karanga princes entrusted to the care of the Dominicans would be spirited away to Goa.[116] Mozambique had thus never developed major educational institutions. There was no seminary for training priests, all of whom were recruited abroad, nor after the expulsion of the Jesuits in 1759, was there any prospect of a college being established.

In 1869 Lisbon recognised the need to do something about education in the colonies and made provision for *concelhos inspectores de instrução publica*.[117] However, the inspecting council in Mozambique Island did nothing to develop education in the coastal towns, and by the 1890s had virtually ceased to function. The Portuguese found at the same time that they increasingly needed literate manpower. Thus they often had to turn to the Indian trading community, and it became clear that some educational opportunities had to be created for the *não-indígena* population of the towns. Because of the weakness of the Catholic church the government decreed that a girls' and boys' school be set up in Lourenço Marques, and only in 1907 was a legal framework for education provided. Meanwhile the gap in educational provision was being filled by foreign missionaries over whom the government had no control whatever.

The legislation of 1907 reformed the *concelho inspector* in Lourenço Marques, giving it legal powers to enforce standards in private education and in the schools (if any) established by the district governments. All schools were to be authorised and their teachers had 'to submit to an examination in the presence of the governor of the district, administrator of the circumscription, *capitão-mor* or *commandante militar*'.[118] Teaching had to be in Portuguese or the vernacular, but not in a foreign European language; all textbooks had to be approved. The obvious hostility to foreign missions shown in these regulations is mitigated only by the absurdity of ordering school teachers to be examined by the *capitães-mores*, many of whom at this period would have been barely literate themselves.

In 1913 the Republican government replaced all Catholic missions by so-called *missões laicas*, but these were not funded or organised and the governor-general, J.J. Machado, suspended the application of the

Table 16.3. PRIMARY EDUCATION, 1930

	Elementary schools	Rudimentary schools
Government	28	60
Private	6	—
Catholic	19	126
Foreign missions	3	84

Source: *Anuário Estatístico* (1930).

Table 16.4. SCHOOL ENROLMENTS, 1930

	Elementary schools	Rudimentary schools
Government	3,405	8,795
Private	403	—
Catholic	7,812	21,122
Foreign missions	396	8,132

Source: *Anuário Estatístico* (1930).

law. By a decree of 13 October 1926 João Belo abolished the lay missions and officially restored the Catholic church to its role in providing mission education.[119]

Regulations in 1929 divided primary education into 'elementary', designed for *não-indígenas*, and 'rudimentary' designed for *indígenas* — from which it was theoretically possible to progress to 'elementary' schooling or technical training. No official education department was created till 1932.

In 1918 the government set up a secondary school in Lourenço Marques which accepted students between the ages of nine and twenty into seven classes. During the 1920s the number of pupils attending rose from 69 to 208 in 1930, when there were 164 Europeans, 26 Indians, 17 of mixed race and one African girl. There were a total of 326 other schools in the country (excluding the Moçambique Company's territory).

These statistics tell relatively little except that formal education was reaching only a very small part of the population. A more detailed examination reveals that educational provision was overwhelmingly concentrated in the two districts of Inhambane and Lourenço Marques. For example, 75 of the 87 foreign mission schools were in those districts, of 145 Catholic schools 62 were in the south, as were 15 out of 28 government elementary schools and 40 out of 60 government rudimentary schools. Tete district had one elementary school, three rudimentary government schools and one elementary and two rudimentary Catholic schools. Cabo Delgado and Niassa had five elementary schools altogether. The rudimentary schools were only intended for *indígenas* but the elementary schools were for all those of 'civilised' status. For example, those attending the government elementary schools were classified as 1,107 Europeans, 78 Chinese, 208 Indians, 732 mixed and 1,280 Africans.

The varied pattern of development of Mozambique is clearly shown in these figures. The south was where the capital city was located and industrial development was beginning. There too were almost all the foreign mission stations and the greatest educational opportunities, and its population was deeply influenced by the experience of migrant labour in South Africa. Quelimane and Moçambique were the districts where plantation labour demands were heaviest, where forced cotton growing was to be concentrated, and where Islamic influence was most pronounced. The extreme north and Tete were the most backward economically, the least urbanised and also the least populated and least educated.

Class formation and civilised status

The labour and tax regulations that came into force in the 1890s enshrined a distinction between *indígena* (native) and *não-indígena* (non-native). The latter were also sometimes referred to as *civilisado* and naturally included all European-born Portuguese and white-skinned foreigners. The 1928 census of the *não-indígena* population gave the breakdown shown in Table 16.5. Among the European population the great majority were of course Portuguese (14,162) with 2,007 British and, surprisingly, 536 Greeks. (The figures for the mixed population record two Afghan men in Tete. Could these possibly have had the same calling as the Afghan camel-handlers of Western Australia?)

Urban growth had been comparatively slow and was overwhelmingly concentrated in the port cities of Beira, Inhambane and Lourenço Marques (Table 16.6). The *não-indígena* population was almost entirely urban. In the towns Afro-Portuguese owned property, were often partners in business enterprises and played an influential role in local affairs, filling posts in the administration and armed forces or sitting on local councils; for a short time in the 1880s and '90s they were the most important element in the urban middle class.[120] There were also Indians and Afro-Indians whose role was not confined to commerce since they increasingly owned property and provided the literate personnel for the administration as it gradually came into existence.

At first people of Afro-Portuguese and Asian origin automatically escaped the *indígena* net, and for the African population the labour and

Table 16.5. NÃO-INDÍGENA POPULATION, 1928 CENSUS

Europeans	17,842
Yellow	896
British Indians	4,997
Portuguese Indians	3,478
Mixed	8,357
Total	35,570

Source: Anuário Estatístico (1930).

Table 16.6. POPULATION OF THE MAJOR TOWNS, 1928

	European	*African*	*Total*
Lourenço Marques	9,001	28,568	42,779
Inhambane	350	9,274	10,563
Quelimane	348	8,298	9,288
Tete	140	2,307	2,756
Moçambique	486	5,589	6,898
Beira	2,153	19,398	23,694
Porto Amelia	67	1,479	1,633

Source: Anuário Estatístico (1930).

prazo legislation recognised the special status of those practising a profession, chiefs and commercial farmers — everyone else was liable to *chibalo* and contract labour. The Organic Charter drawn up by the Republic for Mozambique before the war defined as citizens (*não-indígena*) those with a knowledge of Portuguese who either practised a profession or some other self-sustaining economic activity, or were in government service. In 1917 the government for the first time established clear procedures for defining status. By the terms of Portaria 317 of 9 January a person could apply for exemption from contract labour and *chibalo*, and would be issued with a so-called *alvará de assimilação*, which confirmed his status as an *assimilado* or *não-indígena*. When the Organic Charter was introduced the *não-indígena* class were issued with *bilhetes de identidade*. However, the 1930 census did not formally recognise any Africans as holding *não-indígena* status. Under the New State the policy was formalised still more. Although Afro-Portuguese (the term *mixtos* was used by the census-takers) continued to be automatically included in the *não-indígena* population, a class of Africans was counted for the first time in the 1935 census of *não-indígenas*.

For an African to acquire *não-indígena* status it was necessary to demonstrate Portuguese culture and a level of education. The administration made the process difficult and only encouraged a limited number of Africans, who for some reason were needed by the regime, to acquire this status. What is perhaps remarkable is that when the colonial economy and administration were expanding so rapidly, there should have been so few skilled Africans required in the modern sector. In fact the expansion of the administration and the modern sector of the economy had been largely staffed by immigrant Portuguese or foreigners. White Portuguese often filled quite lowly posts in the colonial structure — for example, as storekeepers, clerks or mechanics — which restricted the opportunities not only for Africans but also for the *mestizo* class to enter the system. Indeed it is clear that throughout the century the Afro-Portuguese and *assimilado* class suffered a decline in status and were forced into ever more menial roles in the colonial state.[121]

The consciousness that the new colonial state emerging at the end of the nineteenth century was one in which their role would be marginalised stimulated a strong vein of radicalism in the capital's *mestizo* circles. The first important *mestizo* newspaper, *Clamor Africano*, was founded in 1886 by Alfredo Aguiar who had come from Angola where the radical voice was more developed. The paper continued to appear in Quelimane till 1894 and adopted a strong line against the abuses of forced labour. Aguiar's lead was followed by the Albasini brothers, grandsons of the famous João Albasini by an African wife, who represented in their persons the declining status of the great Afro-Portuguese families. Although João Albasini held a government position as overseer of labour recruitment in Lourenço Marques, which naturally associated him with the most hated aspect of colonial rule, this did not prevent him from becoming involved in radical politics.[122] The Albasinis first produced *O Africano* in 1908 as the official voice of a group calling themselves the African Union, and then the more influential *O Brado Africano*. This was founded in 1918 as the voice of the Grêmio Africano, a *mestizo* organisation pressing for reform within the structure of the Republic.[123] An organisation which split from the Grêmio (renamed Associação Africana da Colónia de Moçambique in 1920) was the Associação Africana, and this in turn spawned the Instituto Negrofilio in the late 1930s.[124]

The Afro-Portuguese urban intellectuals were not revolutionaries calling for the end of the colonial state. Like other African intellectuals at the time, they looked for reform within the system and sought to make the colonial powers live up to their professed ideals of assimilation, civilisation and progress. If the criticisms of lack of educational opportunity represent their own class concerns, their highlighting of the issue of forced labour (which did not directly affect them) helped to keep this issue alive not only in Portuguese politics but also in the perception of the outside world. Moreover, the fact that the Albasini brothers published their newspapers in the Ronga language as well as in Portuguese was a clear indication that they wished to speak for, and be read by, the African population of the south.[125]

The *mestizo* voice in Mozambique was not entirely isolated and insignificant. Educated Afro-Portuguese travelled to Portugal and met radicals from the other colonies and from the Cape Verde Islands. More important, they were in touch with the black movements in the New World, with DuBois and Marcus Garvey. Two largely *mestizo* organisations were active in Lisbon, the Liga Africana, founded in in 1910, and the Partido Nacional Africano (PNA) of a more Garveyite persuasion. Both these benefited from the anarchic political freedom of Republican Portugal to voice strong criticism of colonial policies, and the PNA took the labour grievances of Africans in the Portuguese colonies to the ILO and the League of Nations.[126]

17

MOZAMBIQUE AND THE NEW STATE

The advent of Salazar

The New State was a European as well as a Portuguese phenomenon, its very name characteristic of the ideologies of the era. The generals who led the coup which overthrew the Republican government in 1926 were in a conservative tradition of military *pronunciamentos*, clear about what they opposed, clear enough about the values and class interests they wanted to uphold, but without a coherent political or economic programme. Over the next four years, the generals came to be increasingly dependent on Professor António Salazar of Coimbra University whom they called upon in 1928 to deal with the country's financial problems. By 1930 Salazar had taken a grip on the government, insisting that he should have a veto over the budgets of all departments. In 1932 he became prime minister, a post he held without a break until 1968. By that time Salazar and his associates — notably another professor, Marcello Caetano — had produced a new constitution and created an ideological structure that was to control Portuguese affairs for the next forty years.[1]

Salazar and Caetano learnt a great deal from contemporary fascism — the very use of the word 'state' to describe their regime recalled the Italian and German emphasis on the needs of the state as opposed to the rights and freedoms of the individual. Like their fascist contemporaries they were great makers of myths, using history to legitimise their ideology and their political system. They liked to emphasise the chaos and profligacy of the Republic, its lack of order, and the incoherence of its ideas and ideals. For them Mozambique symbolised all that was wrong with the Republican regime — administrative chaos, lack of coherent financial and economic policies, inflation and a worthless currency, foreign domination, and international weakness and humiliation. Reform in the colonies and respect in international affairs would be the touchstone of success for the new regime, quite as much as reform at home in Portugal.[2]

It was one of Salazar's prime aims to establish national autonomy. This was, of course, partly a question of economics. Portugal's own development must be self-financed and the colonies freed from the incubus of foreign concession-holders and capital domination, a policy that before long became the single-minded pursuit of autarky.

However, Salazar also realised that chaotic administration and the recurrence of colonial labour scandals invited foreign interference in Portuguese affairs. Cleaning up the colonies and remedying abuses, on paper and in reality, was an essential part of establishing respect and hence real autonomy in the world. It was necessary to co-operate with Britain, South Africa and later the United States, but it was also necessary to keep them at arm's length in order to end — or at any rate control in the national interest — the privileges they enjoyed and above all to remove overt reasons for them to interfere in Portugal's internal affairs.

The regime was skillful in its use of propaganda. A stream of carefully planned biographies of Salazar, translated into French and English, conveyed the ideas of the prime minister and his own peculiar personality cult. The use of censorship to stifle political opposition was soon felt abroad as well as at home, and sources of information about Portugal and its colonies dried up; the world thereafter fed on, and largely came to accept, the official version.[3] So effective was this censorship that the 1930s and 1940s remain one of the least documented periods of colonial history. The image that Salazar wished to portray was one of a society rebuilt on Catholic principles of authority and family; of financial probity and sound money; of planned economic progress achieved largely from domestic resources; of stern neutrality and national independence; and of a civilising mission in Africa which was stated in its classic form in the new Charter given to Mozambique in 1933:

> It is the essential attribute of the Portuguese nation to fulfill the historic function of possessing and colonising overseas dominions and of civilising the native populations inhabiting them, as also that of exercising the moral influence ascribed to it by the Padroado in the East.[4]

The enemies of the regime, both in Europe and in Africa, were equally determined to respond to this propaganda with a 'black legend'. Salazar was a fascist dictator running a police state which was little more than a front for the big business corporations; in it all freedom was suppressed, poverty was institutionalised, and the African people were systematically reduced to forced labour and servitude. According to this depiction, the forty years of the regime were a long nightmare from which the Portuguese people and their former colonial subjects emerged in 1974 somehow to pick up the threads of their history which they had been forced to drop 1926.[5]

However, it is clear that Salazar was neither as radical in his departures from previous practice nor as successful in realising his objectives as he consistently made out. He was careful to keep

elements of the extreme right at arm's length. Under his rule monar-
chism and the extreme Catholic party were excluded from influence
and dwindled in importance. Instead the regime was built on three
pillars of support — the army, the bureaucracy and the big business
corporations — and there was a close interaction as these powerful
interest groups moulded the state and the state set the parameters for
their action. The army benefited from continually increasing shares
of the national budget, even during the belt-tightening 1930s; the
bureaucracy was accorded a hugely expanded role in administering
the planned growth of the domestic and colonial economies, while big
business, the so-called 'oligopolies', benefited from the regime's
favour in establishing their unique financial and industrial empires
while small business and labour were disciplined by the straitjacket of
official unions and *grêmios*.[6]

Salazar was more the pragmatic politician than the avowed ideo-
logue, and like all people who have successfully held power for very
long periods and survived so many vicissitudes, he was far more flexible and adaptable than he liked to make out. Nor can the period of
his regime be categorised simply as a black hole in history. Portugal,
Angola, Mozambique and the other colonies were transformed over
those forty years almost out of recognition, and the successor-regimes
inherited states which were very much what Salazar had made them.
The unsurprising conclusion of recent scholarship is that the picture
is one of shades of grey, not of stark contrasts.

It would be wrong to think that Salazar came to power with a ready-
made imperial policy. His major preoccupations at first were to deal
with the financial and economic problems of Portugal. These were
partly the result of the failures of Republican policy but were soon
supplemented by the onset of world depression. During the first ten
years of his rule, Salazar evolved a strategy for Portugal's economic
survival which was to become a positive image of economic development for itself and for Africa. This survival strategy drew on orthodox
economic ideas of the pre-Keynesian era, and on thinking about the
empire which had gradually developed over the forty years since the
partition but which took as its starting-point the old monarchist-
imperialist notion that Portugal in Africa could be called into
existence to enable Portugal in Europe to become an industrialised
economy.

At the core of Salazar's strategy were the linked concepts of a sound
convertible currency, surpluses on budgets and balance of payments,
and a cut in international indebtedness. To achieve this the colonies
and the mother-country were to be brought together into an *escudo*
zone which would become to some extent a closed economic system,
aiming to achieve a high degree of self-sufficiency. The colonies were

vital to this strategy in a number of ways. Three of them — Angola, São Tomé and Mozambique — had considerable capacity for earning foreign exchange, and Mozambique was of particular importance because of the hard currency it could earn through providing services and labour to South Africa and Rhodesia. The colonies were also a large potential market for Portuguese products and could supply a wide range of raw materials needed for consumption and industrial growth in Portugal. They were a potential destination for emigrants from Portugal itself and from the increasingly overcrowded and poverty-stricken Atlantic islands, and allowed emigration to remain the regime's answer to the problem of poverty at home. Finally they were a major source of cheap labour.[7] Like the Soviet Union — ideologically at an opposite pole but in practical terms also seeking rapid economic development from within a closed economy — the costs of modernisation were to be borne by the peasant and the peasant sector of production. In Portugal's case the peasantry of Europe, Madeira and the Cape Verde islands, as well as mainland Africa, were all to be squeezed — through taxation, diminutive social budgets, controlled prices for their products, and open or disguised forms of forced labour — to provide the resources for industrial growth.

For Mozambique the New State was to be a rigorous experience, but by no means a wholly negative one. The country was to emerge with a unitary structure and experience nearly four decades of effective unified administration; it was also to face the problems and opportunities of autarkic development. When the Portuguese finally left in 1975, Mozambique had a wide range of industries and a variety of export opportunities which made its economic future appear less fragile than that of many other states in Africa. Moreover, by the time the Portuguese departed, Mozambique no longer exclusively served the needs of the metropolitan economy. It had achieved economic independence from Portugal before the granting of political independence.

The new colonial constitution

Many people had reached the conclusion before Salazar that a thorough overhaul of the constitutional position and public law of the colonies was needed. In their haphazard and instinctive way the politicians of the Republic had already decided to end the position of the foreign concession-holders, and João Belo had initiated a comprehensive series of reforms, publishing the *Bases Orgânicas da Administração Colonial* and the *Estatuto Político Civil e Criminal dos Indígenas*. He also planned the cotton-growing concessions, and tried to renegotiate the labour conventions with South Africa. These measures were taken to end the financial autonomy of the colonies and to reaffirm the traditional policy which distinguished the *indígena*, living under African law and subject to labour and tax laws, from the *não-indígena* or *civilisado* who lived under Portuguese law, paid Portuguese taxes and was exempt from the labour legislation.

Belo also prepared a new comprehensive labour law for the colonies which was promulgated in 1928, after his death. Building on these and other enactments of the monarchical and republican regimes, Salazar's ministers between 1928 and 1932 produced a series of laws which clarified the constitutional position of the colonies and gave each of them a better defined legal structure on which to base their administrations. The most important of these enactments were the *Acto Colonial* of 1930, and the Portuguese Constitution, the *Carta Orgânica* issued to each colony and the Administrative Overseas Reform Act, all of which appeared in 1933.[8]

These enactments ended any administrative or quasi-sovereign rights for concession companies and made the colonies into a single legal entity with Portugal itself, part of the Portuguese state and not separate territories held in some sort of trusteeship. There was to be a common law and citizenship, although the distinction between *indígena* and *não-indígena* remained. Only the *não-indígena* populations enjoyed full citizenship while a responsibility to 'civilise' the *indígenas* and progressively incorporate them into Portuguese culture was recognised. The governments in the colonies were to be closely controlled from Lisbon and autonomy in financial and other matters was to cease. Colonial budgets all had to be submitted to Lisbon for approval. The economies of Portugal and the colonies were to be centrally planned and increasingly integrated. Roman Catholicism was to be the official religion of the state and, most important of all, the framework was laid for all parts of the colonies to come under a uniform administration.

The *Carta Orgânica* was a significant document — in effect the first written constitution Mozambique received. Like all such documents it was a mixture of lofty general principles, provisions of public law, and enactments dealing with specific problems which appeared crucial at the time. The Charter was divided into four parts, entitled 'General Guarantees', 'The Natives', 'The Political and Administrative System', and 'Economic and Financial Guarantees'. The first section defined the new close relations between Portugal and Mozambique.[9]

1. All those provisions of the Political Constitution of the Republic which from their nature do not refer exclusively to the Mother Country, shall be applicable to the colonies. . . .

5. The component parts of the Portuguese Colonial Empire stand together in solidarity with each other and with the Mother Country.

6. The solidarity of the Portuguese Colonial Empire comprises particularly the obligation of contributing in an adequate manner towards securing the aims of all members and interests and defense of the nation.

The concluding section of the Charter is almost obsessively concerned with regulating concessions, beginning with paragraph 7: 'The State shall not alienate in any manner any part of the colonial territories. . . .'

Paragraph 12 declares:

The State shall not grant to individual or collective enterprises in any colony:
(i) the exercise of the prerogatives of public administration;
(ii) the privilege of establishing or fixing any dues or taxes, even though it be in the name of the state;
(iii) the right of possessing lands or mine-prospecting areas with power to grant sub-concessions to other enterprises.

These sentences finally condemned to oblivion the whole sorry episode of charter companies and *prazo* concessions.

The section headed 'The Natives' reads like a bill of rights, but one which is peculiarly conscious of, and virtually acknowledges, the abuses of the previous regime. The state 'guarantees the protection and defence of the natives' and will 'punish in accordance with the law all abuses against the persons and property of the natives'. The 'labour of natives in the service of the State or in that of administrative bodies shall be remunerated'; specifically prohibited are agreements like the Hornung contract 'under which the State undertakes to furnish native labourers to any enterprises working for their own economic development'. Instead 'the system of contracting native labour shall be based on individual liberty and on the right to a fair wage. . . .'

However, some things, like *chibalo*, would not change. 'The State may only compel natives to labour on public works of general benefit to the community', while the old category of *indígena* would stay, attention being paid 'to the stage of evolution of the native people'.

Under section 3, Mozambique is rather surprisingly guaranteed 'administrative decentralisation and financial autonomy . . . so far as these are compatible with the Constitution . . .', but the following sections reveal just how incompatible decentralisation and the Constitution were destined to be. The Portuguese National Assembly alone could alter the constitution, approve treaties or conventions, authorise loans or other guaranteed contracts, and — once again burying the hated concession companies ever deeper — define the powers of the government to grant concessions. Governors could not be directors of any enterprises based in the colony, and their powers were generally limited. 'The legislative function of colonial Governors, within the sphere of their competence, shall always be exercised under the supervision of the Mother Country . . .', while 'executive functions in each colony shall be undertaken subject to the supervision of the Minister for the Colonies.' There would be no more Republican high commissioners!

The section headed 'Economic and Financial Guarantees' emphasised the limits of integration between colony and mother-country. Each colony was to have its own property, its own assets and liabilities, its own legal personality for purposes of contract and its own budget. However, it was made clear that 'the general budget of a colony requires the express approval of the Minister for the Colonies, and expenditure or revenue not within the terms of the legal enactments may not be included'. Moreover, the colonies 'may not contract loans in foreign countries', and 'the rights of the Treasury of the mother country . . . in connection with the past or future debts of the colonies are imprescriptible'. So much for 'decentralisation and financial autonomy'! With a wary eye open to prevent falling into the quagmire of the bitter arguments over Mozambique's economic development, the Charter states:

> The economic system of the colonies shall be established in accordance with the needs of their development, just reciprocity between them and the neighbouring countries and the rights and legitimate requirements of the Mother Country and the Portuguese Colonial Empire.

Under the terms of the Charter and all the associated documents, Mozambique became, for the first time, a unitary state. As the Charter stated, 'political unity shall be maintained by the existence of a single capital and a single general or colonial government.' However, the forty years during which Mozambique had been fragmented not only in its administration but also in the development of its economy and infrastructure had created a situation of dis-integration which it would take more than a high-flown Charter to alter.

A bureaucratic state

Salazar's objective was to give the colonies an administration that would respond promptly and effectively to levers pulled in Lisbon.

The high commissionership had been abolished in 1926 and Mozambique once again had a governor-general directly responsible to ministers in Lisbon. This position was occupied by José Cabral who survived to serve three four-year terms in office, in his person bridging the gap between Republic and New State. The minister could legislate for the colonies by decree, and was responsible for all major appointments and for ratifying concessions. It was a regime which accorded no local initiative to a racial élite of settlers, which had for the time being marginalised the military, which tolerated but did not encourage foreign capitalists, but which gave a free hand to a rapidly growing bureaucracy. The governor-general was a senior civil servant and head of the executive with little policy-making initiative; he was assisted by a council made up of bureaucrats. The regime itself became increasingly bureaucratic as boards and *juntas* proliferated. Statistics were gathered and proformas issued seeking information on every topic from the weather to the number of cars on the road.[10]

Salazar believed in regulating alike people's lives and the operations of the free market. Capitalism was too obviously identified with the great foreign-owned concession companies which had turned huge areas of Mozambique into foreign colonies from which the Portuguese government was almost excluded. Starting from his desire to control colonial indebtedness and inflation, Salazar introduced tight exchange and currency controls and continued to elaborate detailed regulations covering investment and property ownership. Gradually other aspects of national life were regulated: employers' organisations and workers' guilds were established by the state; production quotas and prices were set by the government and production itself was regulated by Boards; and labour regulations prescribed every detail of working conditions covering pay, health, accommodation, food and hours. If Salazar's Portugal was a dictatorship, it was one not so much of the paramilitary or the secret police as of the bureaucrat.

The Legislative Council survived but was remodelled to represent the objects of the regime, ten of its seventeen members being heads of administrative departments and the rest chosen from recognised state organisations and from the *grêmios*, or officially recognised associations of workers and professional people.[11] The franchise remained as restricted as it had been under the Republic, and administrative obstruction was used to limit the number of Africans or people of mixed race who succeeded in acquiring *não-indígena* status.

The structure of *concelhos* and *circunscrições* survived, but at the local level Salazar introduced civilian district officers throughout the country — a professional colonial civil service which would soon be given not only the simple tasks of tax collection and labour recruitment but also elaborate roles in economic planning. In 1935 the colony was divided into three provinces, each in turn divided into districts — Sul do Save (with Lourenço Marques and Inhambane as districts), Zambesia (with Beira, Tete and Quelimane as districts — Beira being the Moçambique Company territory) and Niassa (with Mozambique and Porto Amelia as districts and the capital sited at Nampula).[12]

Gradually throughout the 1930s, Portuguese administration spread to all parts of the country, ending the anachronism whereby many areas, particularly in the north, were only visited spasmodically by bands of armed *cipais* seeking tax and labour. Not that colonial rule in the rural areas immediately became any less oppressive. Although the 1928 labour code specified that administrative officers were not to be directly involved in labour recruitment, the government still let it be known that companies seeking labour must be allowed to obtain what they needed. The state also continued to use the pressgang for the recruitment of colonial troops, and in the 1930s compulsory cotton growing added a new dimension of oppression. But at least the colonial service was now centrally directed and had become more accountable. Scandals were dealt with, corrupt officials could be removed and, particularly under the direct influence of Caetano, standards of administration began to improve.[13] However, the tradition that in Mozambique the concept of the state meant overrule by a predatory ruling class survived. The tribute-collectors of Gungunhana, the *prazo senhores*, the Muslim and Makua sheikhs or the concession companies had given way to a new and more centrally organised predatory class demanding the surplus time, surplus labour and surplus product of the peasant.

Economic policy

The immediate economic measures taken by Salazar were aimed at stabilising the *escudo* and the colonial currencies — measures that became all the more urgent with the onset of the world depression. The policy adopted was one of orthodox conservatism which had the immediate effect of causing considerable hardship and of hastening the onset of the slump. The government ordered all hard currency earned to be centrally deposited, and its allocation to importers was severely rationed. Very little foreign exchange was made available to import luxuries and none at all to import from abroad items produced in Portugal.[14] The colonial currency was made fully convertible only with the Portuguese *escudo*. After an initial loan, no further borrowing was allowed and colonial budgets had to balance.[15] One of the long-term effects of the exchange control policies was to cut back on imports from foreign countries and boost trade with Portugal, but the immediate impact was to create shortages throughout the whole economy, a lack of investment and a rapid decline in production leading to unemployment and a shrinking of government revenue. However, within five years there were signs that the draconian policies had achieved at least some of their objectives as the *escudo* stabilised and the earning capacity of the Mozambique economy again made foreign exchange available.

By 1932 Salazar's ideas for the future of the empire had become much more ambitious. His plan was to strengthen the Portuguese economy using the colonies to perform two vital roles. First, he wished to encourage the colonies to earn foreign exchange which would then be diverted to Portugal through a favourable balance of trade between the mother-country and the African territories. Through careful nurture, Salazar built up Portugal's share of colonial trade. From around 12 per cent of Portugal's exports in the 1930s trade with the colonies rose to nearly a quarter in the 1940s.[16] The colonies paid for their imports by transfers of hard currency. But the colonies had to perform another function in the master plan. Salazar was determined to reduce Portugal's dependence on imports of food, raw materials and industrial goods. While plans were laid for industrial growth at home, plans which presupposed a growing colonial market, the colonies were assigned the role of providing raw materials and foodstuffs.

This was the origin of the planned growth in the production of tropical crops which was to be the centrepiece of economic planning during the twenty-five years after 1935. Unlike the traditional tropical staples — coffee, cocoa and sugar — which had mostly been grown in large, heavily capitalised plantations, a new strategy was to be used for producing cotton and rice. It had long been recognised that price instability was the major factor preventing cotton from becoming established in Mozambique, and in the 1920s plantation-grown cotton had fluctuated wildly with the movement of the world price. The Moçambique Company had experimented with forcing its peasants to grow cotton, and in 1926 João Belo had devised a system for granting concession companies the right to buy African-grown crops, although it was not immediately put into operation. In 1932 a system of guaranteed prices was introduced, and up till the Second World War these were fixed considerably above the depressed world price. Initially the Portuguese government undertook to pay exporters up to 43 per cent above the world price, and this prompted a number of companies to take out concessions.[17] The companies were to be given a franchise for certain areas of the colonies and a free hand to promote the production of cotton by the peasant communities. The relatively high fixed price did not lead to a great expansion of cotton production, partly because barely 40 per cent of this was passed on to the producer, and by 1938 Portugal still obtained only 39 per cent of its cotton from the colonies. So in that year the *Junta de Exportação do Algodão* was established in Lisbon to plan the growth in production, and a new system was introduced whereby the concession companies had to sell their cotton to Portuguese manufacturers who in their turn had to buy the colonial crop. The *Junta* also amalgamated concessions until there were only twelve for the whole of Mozambique, nine of these in the region north of the Zambesi.[18] The crop-growing 'campaigns' that followed were the distinctive feature of colonial life for the next two decades. At first peasants were merely urged to grow cotton, but in 1942 the guaranteed price dipped below the world price for the first time and by 1950 stood 50 per cent lower. Compulsion now took the place of price incentives and, with the appointment of José Tristão de Bettencourt as governor-general in 1940, a tougher policy was pursued. Villages were assigned quotas which they had to meet, and overseers (*capatazes*) were appointed. Initially the support provided to the peasant producer was meagre and went little further than free seed and the visit of the local *chefe* and his police.[19]

By 1944 267,000 hectares were planted with cotton and some 791,000 Mozambican peasants involved in cotton growing, while large numbers were also enlisted in the other crop programmes. The cotton growing campaigns were concentrated in the north of Mozambique — 80 per cent of the cotton came from north of the Zambesi and 48 per cent from the province of Nampula, two *circunscriçoẽs* alone producing 20 per cent of the total. The crop-growing plans were at one and the same time successful and misguided. Their success was such that the colonial output of tropical staples, particularly cotton, rose dramatically. In 1935 Portugal's colonies produced only 2,800 tonnes of the 24,400 tonnes of cotton consumed in Portugal every year; by 1941 the country was able to import virtually all its raw cotton from its colonies. By 1950 Mozambique alone was exporting 25,290 tonnes.[20]

Although peasant-grown cotton had existed in Mozambique for centuries, the large-scale production suitable for marketing in the international economy was really created in the space of ten years.[21] Moreover it was production that did not uproot the peasants from their villages and lead to the disruption and suffering of migrant labour or forced plantation labour. On the other hand, forced cotton growing brought its own problems for the African population. The cotton campaigns led to the growing of expensive and low-grade cotton with much unsuitable land being brought into cultivation simply to meet the targets set by the *Junta*'s officials. The cotton concession companies had to work with narrow profit margins and only succeeded in making substantial profits in areas where peasant labour was not being contracted for other purposes. Sena Sugar, which took out a cotton concession simply to protect its interest in having first call on its traditional labour-recruiting grounds, had to try to get cotton grown by women in ground that was frequently flooded. Not surprisingly it found the cotton concession of dubious value. Moreover, because of the concentration on cotton growing, insufficient land and labour were devoted to food production. As had been proved before, forced labour had very low rates of productivity. Average yields rose from 178 kilos per hectare in 1942 to 470 kilos in 1959, but on properly fertilised and irrigated farms in the Limpopo valley the yields were anything up to 1,600 kilos per hectare. Mozambique was made a great cotton producing state against the natural quality of its geography and its natural capability.[22]

As a result of the obvious hardships caused by the campaigns, new regulations were issued to the concessionaires in 1946 when the cotton concessions came up for renewal. More attention had to be paid to food production in the concession areas, transport had to be provided and technical advice on cotton production given.[23] A cotton research institute (CICA — *Centro de Investigação Científica Algodoeira*) was set up in 1943, and its experts were detailed to survey fields and monitor the rate at which crops were produced. Gradually the planning boards built up cadres of crop experts, soil scientists and even anthropologists who carried out some of the first serious studies of the agricultural and sociological problems of rural Mozambique. Some areas were taken out of cultivation, and the prices paid to registered cotton growers improved. A class of African commercial cotton growers now began to emerge, and in 1955 the government sponsored the creation of peasant co-operatives to handle the sale of cotton. As a result of these developments, productivity increased and in 1960, the last year of compulsory crop growing, 46,000 tonnes were produced — a record cotton crop which constituted a third of all Mozambique's exports.[24]

In 1941, also as a result of war conditions which made the importation of rice from South East Asia impossible, the government set up the *Divisão do Fomento Orizícola* to plan a similar scheme of forced rice cultivation, complete with production quotas and concession companies with the right to purchase the African-grown product. Once again, as with cotton, crude production figures rose from an estimated average of less than 3,000 tonnes in the 1930s to an average of more than over 20,000 tonnes in the decade 1944–54. From being a rice-importing economy, Mozambique was exporting modest amounts in the 1950s. But rice production under the forced concessionary system proved even more unsatisfactory than cotton. Except in a few favoured areas, rice was not a suitable crop for peasant farmers without capital. However, in the late 1950s rice growing began to attract the attention of commercial farmers who by that time were playing an increasingly important role in the Mozambique economy.[25]

Sugar continued to be the other major tropical staple. Building on the system of tariffs and quotas developed under the Republic, Salazar had by 1933 reserved almost the whole of the Portuguese market for colonial sugar. Mozambique, however, which in the last days of the Republic had almost completely filled the Portuguese sugar quota, was guaranteed only half the Portuguese market, the other half being filled by the Angolan sugar industry, which was largely Portuguese-owned. As with cotton, the colonies benefited from controlled prices which throughout the 1930s rewarded them above the world market rates. Moreover, largely as a result of Salazar's mercantilism, although overall production in Mozambique declined between 1930 and 1942, the country escaped the massive cuts in production which international agreement was imposing elsewhere in the world.[26] When in 1937 international quotas were adopted for the world sugar market, Mozambique received additional guarantees for sales of up to 30,000 tonnes of production annually. During the boom conditions of the Second World War, the market situation was reversed and the prices guaranteed by Portugal fell below world levels.

Finding new markets for sugar in a world that overproduced was not easy, but Sena Sugar found that it was able to penetrate the markets of Southern Rhodesia — a development which was one more of the strands linking the economies of Mozambique with central and southern Africa. During the 1930s Libert Oury, who controlled the Moçambique Company and the Trans-Zambesia railway, was also a director of Rhodesian railways and of Sena Sugar. Railway rates were manipulated to enable Sena Sugar to undercut all other producers in the Rhodesian market and ultimately the Nyasaland market as well.[27] By the 1940s the domestic market of Mozambique itself was growing, and in 1957 15 per cent of Mozambique's sugar was sold internally.

Salazar's policies have often been described as neo-mercantilist, but there was no neat complementary relationship between the metropolitan economy and the colonies which produced tropical staples. Crops like maize and sugar were grown in Portugal itself, while there was conflict between the interests of the different colonies, for instance in sugar production, which was hard to reconcile. Measures had sometimes to be taken to limit rather than increase production and to erect barriers against colonial imports into Portugal.[28] Moreover many colonial raw materials could not be absorbed by the Portuguese market at all, and had to find outlets in other parts of the world.

Salazar may have wanted to restrict the colonies as far as possible to importing from Portugal and to producing raw materials for Portuguese consumption, but his economic nationalism was not unbounded. His desire to earn foreign exchange meant that he was anxious to see the colonies earn hard currency by exporting to countries like the United States and South Africa, and in particular he wanted to maintain the flow of sterling from the provision of services to Rhodesia and the Rand. As a result, nothing was done to hinder the recruitment of mine labour and for the New State, as for its republican and monarchist predecessors, the use of the railway and port facilites at Lourenço Marques remained a central part of its colonial policy. These hard currency earnings, transferred to Portugal in payment for imports, provided Salazar with the means to build Portugal's reserves, and turn the *escudo* itself into a hard currency.

Nor did Salazar impede foreign capital investment. Although the regime set its face firmly against the granting of vast concessions such as had been awarded to the *prazo* companies, Salazar was anxious for foreign capital to continue to enter the colony and collaborated closely with the two major foreign capitalists, Oury and Hornung, whose investments included the Moçambique Company, the Trans-Zambesia railway and the vast Sena Sugar complex of the lower Zambesi. However, in developing the quota system for the import of sugar, oil seeds and such like, attempts were made to favour Portuguese-owned production wherever possible. Thus Sena Sugar's dominance in the Portuguese market was pruned back, and during the 1930s the Company had to close two factories, reduce output to 50,000 tonnes and diversify its activities.[29]

In the early 1940s, influenced by the war, which led to temptingly high prices for colonial produce, some steps were taken to establish wider involvement of Portuguese-owned capital in the colonies. Portuguese banks took over some assets owned in countries occupied by the Germans, and in 1943 the *Lei da Nacionalização de Capital* was passed whereby public services and certain strategic industries had to be 60 per cent owned by Portuguese capital. The most striking case of 'nationalisation' as a result of this legislation was the purchase by the state of the Beira port and railway in 1948–9.[30]

As a result of the tight exchange control policy, Portugal steadilly increased its share of Mozambique's imports from the absurdly low figures of the early part of the century. In the 1940s and 1950s, 40–50 per cent of Mozambique's imports came from the mother-country. The most important conquest was in textiles, and half the cloth imported was of Portuguese manufacture. Imports of manufactured goods also grew. Until 1936 Salazar pursued a policy hostile to industrial development in the colonies;[31] however, during the Second

World War a limited policy of industrialisation was begun, with the emphasis as ever on import substitution, and some of the great Portuguese industrial consortia took the lead in establishing factories in the colonies. In Mozambique, for example, António Champalimaud established cement works at Lourenço Marques in 1944 and at Beira in 1951.

Growth of the agricultural sector of the economy under Salazar

The ending of the concessionary powers of the Nyassa Company and the great *prazo* companies in 1929–30 was an important stage in the development of the Mozambique economy. The great concession companies had acted like feudal seigneurs, deriving their profit from direct control of taxation and labour, the possession of commercial monopolies and the right to lease sub-concessions. None of this necessarily involved undertaking any investment or productive enterprise at all. Companies like the Nyassa Company and the Zambesia Company had derived perhaps the majority of their income from these feudal privileges, while firms like the Luabo Company were little more than a letterhead — having rented out all their land and administrative responsibilities. Salazar put an end to corporate feudalism in Mozambique. The state, not the great feudal barons, was now to benefit directly from the manpower and financial resources of its population. The effect of this revolution was to sweep away sections of the feudal class and leave only those enterprises which were productive and undertook genuine investment. Among the Zambesi plantation companies, the Zambesia Company shrank to a fraction of its former feudal grandeur, while the Lugella Company went out of business altogether.[32]

The three companies that dominated the Zambesian plantation sector — Sena Sugar, Boror and Madal — had all expanded production during the days of high prices in the 1920s, making use of their concessionary powers to recruit labour. However, the end of the *prazo* concessions corresponded with the great depression and the precipitous slide in prices for all tropical products. The principal copra producers, Boror and Madal, faced a particular problem in that the great expansion of their planting programme in the 1920s only began to bear fruit as prices fell. Mozambique, one of the world's greatest copra producers, was thus locked into vast overproduction, but copra was not a tropical staple of interest to Portugal and only in the 1940s was an export quota agreed. The companies survived largely by shrinking in size, reducing the labour force and closing installations. The Boror Company, for example, slimmed its labour force from 12,640 in 1930 to 5,978 five years later.[33] An alternative was to find new markets, which Madal did in Scandanavia. The marginal element in the economy of the copra industry was peasant production: by reducing or increasing purchases of peasant-produced copra, the companies could respond to market conditions while leaving the core of their own production relatively unaffected.[34] Sena Sugar also contracted in order to survive, closing its Caia and Mopeia operations and reducing its labour force from 25,000 in 1928 to 13,000 in 1937.

While copra and sugar were experiencing hard times, the Mozambique economy showed a surprising ability to diversify at a most unpropitious time. Tea planting had been pioneered by the Lugella Company in the Milanje highlands, but made no progress till the late 1920s when experts from Nyasaland began to transform production. In the early 1930s tea production boomed at Milanje, where Sena Sugar took over from the Lugella Company and established the highly successful Chá Oriental, and in the Namuli highlands where eventually there were to be no less than ten tea factories in operation. The success of the Mozambique tea industry, unlike earlier plantation investments, was built at first on local demand and then on capturing the Portuguese market. Although Sena Sugar's Chá Oriental became the largest tea company in Mozambique, it was not the only one and the industry included big plantations as well as smallholders. It was a good example of the co-operation of state and private capital, private capital taking the initiatives but the government helping with diplomatic protection, land concessions, loans, distribution of seeds and help with the supply of labour. The tea industry refused to allow itself to be restricted by international agreements, and during the war secured a contract to supply the British Ministry of Food. Moreover, it was a locally processed product, so that more of the value was added in Mozambique than with many other products.[35]

Cashew was the other success story of the 1930s. Up to that time cashew nuts had principally been harvested for distilling into liquor, and it was not till the 1920s that small quantitites began to be exported. In 1924 Mozambique exported 245 tonnes of cashew to India; by 1928 this had risen to 4,000 tonnes and to 11,000 in 1933. In 1935 India began to import in big quantities due to a shortage of domestic production and in 1936 Mozambique exported 28,000 tonnes. Cashew was generally a peasant crop, and rapidly became a major source of peasant income. However in some coastal areas the high prices paid for cashew led to the revival of claims to old estates which had been allowed to lapse, and of an old form of labour tribute called *muta-hanu*. During the Second World War, when shipping to India was interrupted, peasants began to process the cashew themselves and new markets were found in South Africa. Cashew developed as an export entirely outside the mercantilist planning of

Portugal. Already in 1936 it was the fifth most important export and by 1960 it had become the third most important after cotton and sugar.[36]

The rapid growth of cashew production led to one of the most bizarre episodes of popular revolt in the history of modern Mozambique — but perháps not so bizarre to those familiar with popular revolt in early modern France. The landowners of the coastal regions, who included many members of the old Islamic and Afro-Portuguese élites, increased their cashew production by demanding labour services and a proportion of their crops from the peasants living on their land — the so-called *muta-hano*. During the 1930s *muta-hano* began to spread rapidly until in 1936 it was estimated that half the population of the *circunscrição* of Mossuril worked their land under this form of tenure. The labour was unpaid and in their turn the peasants paid no money rent for their land — they also apparently paid no hut tax to the government. The government was anxious to turn the evident wealth being earned from cashew sales into tax revenue, and issued orders that *muta-hano* was to be replaced with wages for labour, rent for land and payment of hut tax (*palhota*). This led to widespread resistance by peasants and landowners, particularly in the immediate hinterland of Mozambique Island, and in August 1939 troops had to be used to collect tax and arrest dissidents.[37]

Further diversification took place as a result of the pressures of the war. In the 1940s South Africa began to manufacture ploughs for sale to African peasant farmers, and these soon became items in which returning African miners in the Sul do Save invested their savings. As a result of spreading plough cultivation, maize production in the south began to increase until in good years at the end of the 1940s the southern districts were producing surpluses.

Between 1939 and 1946 the total value of Mozambique's exports rose fivefold.[38] This was due partly to the high prices paid for raw materials during the war, and partly to the forced crop-growing campaigns and the massivé output of cotton that resulted. However, it was also partly the consequence of the entrepreneurial activity of companies that had led to the expansion of the tea industry and of the peasants who had responded to market opportunities by increasing production of cashew.

Development plans

In 1937 a six-year development plan for Mozambique was published. It was to be funded from accumulated government surpluses and from the profits of the ports and railways. The plan contained provisions for the building of the railway inland from Mozambique Island, the Limpopo Valley and Umbeluzi irrigation schemes, the Tete railway, the development of the port of Nacala, and some agricultural and road investment. The implementation of the plan was interrupted by the war, but in 1947 Portugal granted Mozambique a loan of £10 million to carry out some of the projects.[39] In the 1950s two further six-year plans — always referred to as the First and Second Development Plans — were drawn up covering the years 1953-8 and 1959-64.

The First Development Plan earmarked 1.7 million *contos* of investment which included the rail link between Lourenço Marques and Salisbury; an extension to the Incomati railway and the continuation of the Mozambique railway to the Lake and the building of the Nacala branch; completion of the Limpopo Valley scheme; dams on the Revubwe and Movene rivers and airfield development. Like the schemes in the pre-war plan, those proposed in 1953 almost all involved investment in infrastructure and in fact included many schemes postponed from the pre-war plan.[40] However, the First Plan was also explicit in its objective of promoting white immigration: it called for 'migration from Portugal to establish white population centres which could contribute to the nationalisation of the territory'.[41]

The Second Plan, for the years 1959-64, was drawn up in wholly different circumstances. Decolonisation had begun in British and French Africa, and Portugal was being openly challenged by nationalists to give up its empire. The second six-year plan, therefore, departed from the old Salazarian belief that infrastructural improvement bought opportunity for natural development, and replaced it with a more urgent concern for politically oriented projects. The plan allocated 3.2 million *contos* of investment. First, it envisaged a series of scientific studies of geology, soils and cartography, together with an investigation of the nutrition, education and economic productivity of the African population; then the plan was concerned with developing the massive irrigated farming settlements connected with the Limpopo, Incomati and Revue barrages; there was to be further investment in transport infrastructure; and for the first time a programme was established for health and education, amounting to 14 per cent of the total planned investment. A Third Development Plan was published to cover the years 1968-73, and in the interval (1965-7) an interim plan operated known as the *Plano Intercalar de Fomento*.[42]

Partly because of the plans and partly because of extraneous factors, investment in basic infrastructure in Mozambique gathered pace. In the 1920s and early 1930s British capital had built the Trans-Zambesia railway and the Zambesi bridge, completed in 1935. Mozambique's pre-war development plan made provision for constructing the long-planned branch railway to the Moatise coalfields, and this was eventually completed in 1949.

At the same time, with the Nyassa Company safely wound up, Salazar looked to develop the north and pressed ahead with the creation of ports at Nacala and Pemba Bay, with a railway crossing the north to Lake Malawi. The pre-war plan provided for building a railway from Lumbo opposite Mozambique Island to the Lurio, with a link to the port of Nacala. The work was held up by the war and not completed till 1947; Nacala only came into use in 1951.[43] So, almost exactly eighty years after the British consul, Henry O'Neill, identified the potential of the magnificent harbour of Nacala, the Portuguese authorities made the investment needed to realise one of Mozambique's greatest natural assets. However, the railway planned by the Nyassa Company in the 1890s to run inland from Porto Amelia was never built.

The railways operating to the port of Beira had been built by British capital, but these were bought by the Portuguese government in 1949 and incorporated into the state-administered Railways and Harbours Administration (*Administração dos Serviços dos Portos, Caminhos de Ferro e Transportes*).[44] It remained to link the Lourenço Marques railway system with the north. A railway was planned from Salisbury to Lourenço Marques in the Second Development Plan and this was completed by 1960.

Therefore, although Mozambique's infrastructure was developed and for the first time a network began to be created to link various parts of the country, the economic rationale for these investments remained the provision of services for British Africa. Lines were built to Nyasaland, or to link Salisbury to Lourenço Marques, or to serve the interest of the great British-owned companies like Sena Sugar. Mozambique benefited from this development, but only incidentally.

Road building was becoming increasingly important and the Portuguese continued to use corvée labour through the 1930s and 1940s. The roads they built were excellently engineered and constructed to a higher standard than those in Rhodesia, but they remained dirt roads and the network was only as good as the bridge system of the country. Mozambique is cut by a series of rivers that flow from the interior to the coast, and this has always greatly impeded communications. As late as 1960 it was easier to go from the north of Mozambique to the south by sea or through Nyasaland and Rhodesia than by travelling through Portuguese territory. No road bridge had been built across the Zambesi, and road vehicles either took the ferry at Tete, crossed by rail on the Zambesi bridge at Sena or drove through the Rhodesias, crossing the Zambesi at Chirundu. The failure to develop a modern road system cannot easily be explained, particularly since infrastructural projects ranked highly among those items on which the government was prepared to spend money. As late as 1964 there were only 7,366 miles of national highways, less than 1,000 of which had a tarmac surface — and this in a country·extending more than 1,000 miles from north to south.[45] The lack of roads, of course, had the effect of increasing the isolation of the different regions from each other, emphasising their relationship with nearby countries to which they were linked by railway lines or simply by geographical proximity, and underlining yet again the dis-integration of the country as a whole.

Air services began to be developed in the 1940s. A department of the Railways and Harbours Administration (DETA) was set up to operate internal commercial flights and a network of eighteen airfields was created, three of them (Lourenço Marques, Beira and Lumbo) of international standard. A further fifty landing strips were built in different parts of the country. The development of DETA achieved what railways and even roads had never succeeded in doing — the direct interconnection of all parts of the country.[46]

The Second World War

Salazar remained neutral during the Second World War, determined that neither Portugal nor its colonies would get caught up in the conflict. That the policy of neutrality was cynically angled to look after Portugal's self-interest is undeniable. Early in the war, Portugal clearly favoured the Axis powers and continued to sell wolfram to the German armament industries. However from 1943, as the prospect of an Axis victory receded, Salazar began openly to court the Western Allies and in 1944 allowed the United States air force to use the Azores for their warfare in the Atlantic.[47] After the war Salazar dropped many of the trappings of fascism, and in 1949 Portugal joined NATO. There is no denying that this was agile survival politics, conducted much more successfully than Portugal's ill-conceived intervention in the First World War on the side of the Allies.

For Portuguese Africa the war was a period of great opportunity and even prosperity. The colonies were not affected by the actual conflict, and Portuguese shipping was able to run throughout. The world prices for colonial products soared, and Mozambique and Angola could sell almost any product they could get out of the earth at premium prices. Mozambique particularly benefited in its plantation sector. Sugar and tea production and sales reached new heights and the government promoted the organised growing of cotton and rice. As in previous booms, the population came under pressure with higher demands for labour. In 1942 restrictions on recruitment methods were relaxed and the colonies saw an effective return to forced labour in many areas, with Africans being compelled to contract themselves for up to six months of the year. The prosperity of the war years did, however, lift the finances of Mozambique from their trough in the 1930s. Budgeted revenue rose from 581,839 *contos* in 1938 to 1,336,057 in 1948 and the foreign exchange earned from expanding exports and services enabled Portugal to contemplate a change in imperial policy in the immediate post-war years.[48]

White settlement and the colonatos

Portuguese imperialists had always been keen to divert the stream of migrants from Portugal and the islands to Africa, and the New State was to write another chapter in the long and ambivalent relationship of Portugal with the concept of migration. In some respects Portugal itself resembles an island, like its own offshoot Madeira — it is a community from which people have had to escape to find employment and sometimes even to survive. In the nineteenth century Brazil or the United States were the principal destinations of migrants, whose remittances routinely covered Portugal's balance of payments deficits. There was also emigration from the Atlantic islands, which was particularly a factor in the life experience of Madeirans and Cape Verdeans. However, few of the migrants had gone to the Portuguese territories in Africa except for convicts who till the 1930s continued to be sent to serve their sentences in Angola and Mozambique.[49]

Colonisation schemes and subsidised travel for migrants had been introduced from the end of the nineteenth century, and after the First World War there had been a considerable settlement of hopeful white migrants in both the major colonies. However, these early schemes had not been thought through. Portuguese migrants were unskilled and often illiterate and had no capital, so that the colonial authorities frequently found that they had to be supported from the colonial budget. Those who were established on the land would frequently leave, drift to the towns to become unemployed, or set themselves up as itinerant traders and, later, lorry-drivers, or they would migrate again to South Africa or Rhodesia. As a result, by 1928 there were probably only about 18,000 white Portuguese in Mozambique.[50]

When Salazar first came to power he saw the sums spent on supporting white migrants as providing one of the cuts that would have to be made to balance the colonial budgets. For years white migration was actively discouraged, and in the early 1930s the white population of the colonies probably declined. However, Salazar was to return to the idea of white colonisation with a wholly new eye towards the end of the decade. In the 1920s and 1930s both Spain and Portugal had been faced with the implications of rural poverty and depopulation and developed policies for reviving the countryside based on the construction of dams in the mountains and the laying out of irrigation schemes. Both countries acquired considerable capability in hydraulic technology and it was not long before this began to be applied in Africa.[51]

In the 1920s a hydrographical survey of the Limpopo was undertaken and two plans were produced for extensive development of the valley. The plan eventually adopted was that of A. Trigo de Morais who designed a barrage on the river above Guija which would carry the extension of the railway to Southern Rhodesia. The financial crisis at the end of the 1920s caused the project to be shelved, and a second scheme, proposed by Colonel Balfour, was then investigated. The project initially involved 70,000 hectares of irrigated land, on which 150 farmers would be settled, and a power station, 65 miles of railway, processing plants for rice, cane and cotton, and a distillery would be established. Work was supposed to start in 1935;[52] however, the scheme was eventually incorporated into the 1937 development plan and then postponed during the war years. Plans for the railway to Rhodesia were revived after the war, and Trigo Morais' scheme was once again adopted and Morais himself was put in charge of its operation.[53]

A second barrage scheme was proposed for the Incomati valley to irrigate 95,000 hectares of additional land. The third major scheme involved developing the Revubwe and its tributaries in the highlands on the borders of Rhodesia, where plans to irrigate 30,000 hectares were drawn up. Finally draft plans were laid for a vast settlement project linked to the Cabora Bassa dam on the Zambesi which was built during the 1960s.

These great engineering projects were designed to bring together various aspects of development. The dams and barrages were to provide hyrdroelectric power, some of which could be sold to Rhodesia or South Africa; they were to carry an important transport infrastructure, like roads and railways; they were to impound water for irrigation; and they were flood control measures. However, these schemes were also conceived with social engineering in mind. In planning irrigated agriculture, Salazar also intended to settle Portuguese peasant families on the land. His principal objective was to replicate the Catholic Portuguese peasant family which he believed to be the fundamental strength of his regime. Under a scheme initiated in 1945 settlers were granted free passage, but in the early 1950s with the growth of the *colonatos*, as these irrigated settlements were called, peasant families received extensive loans and grants to get them established.

However, Salazar also wanted to create multi-racial settlements in which African peasants would live and work alongside Portuguese. The idea was partly propaganda — to provide living and tangible evidence for the claim, so frequently made, that the regime was not based on colour distinctions like South Africa, Rhodesia and Kenya; but it was also designed partly to create a class of African peasant farmers who would become supporters of the regime through incorporation into the colonial state. When the Limpopo *colonato* was first set up in 1954 only a few African peasants had been granted probationary status, but in 1959 it was decided to allow selected African farmers to join the *colonato* on the same basis as the Portuguese. In 1961 there were ninety-seven African peasant families established on the Limpopo Valley scheme and by the end of the colonial era approximately one-third of the 1,380 farmers were Africans, with a further 2,584 as probationers.[54]

The *colonatos*, like their successors the state farms of Frelimo, were immensely costly. Huge sums were invested and the peasant farmers who established themselves in these showpiece settlements were heavily subsidised by the state. They were, to say the least, a bizarre experiment. The Portuguese peasants who signed contracts to work the farms were submitting themselves to a closely regulated existence in which every aspect of their lives was supervised. They were not allowed to employ hired labour and had to work their land themselves; initially their farms were limited to 4 hectares. The peasants, most of whom were illiterate, had to work so hard that it was said that local Mozambicans thought this was a form of '*chibalo* for whites'.[55] The *colonatos* never paid their costs or yielded any economic benefit for Portugal, and have been written off as just one more colonial folly. However, it is worth noting that the Portuguese government, whatever its motives, had decided that what Africa needed was not further massive investment in heavily capitalised industries and plantations but thriving peasant agriculture. In a distorted way this was the thinking behind both the *colonatos* and the forced cotton-growing campaigns. It was in the nature of dictatorships that the peasantry could not be just left alone to thrive without interference but had to be forced into a spurious prosperity by government intervention and subsidy. Nevertheless this policy requires more sympathetic consideration with the hindsight provided by Africa's post-independence experience

The *colonatos* were only the flagship enterprise of a wider immigration policy, which saw the white population of Mozambique rise to 48,000 by 1950 and just under 100,000 by 1960, doubling to just under 200,000 by 1974. For one brief period during the 1950s more than half of all Portuguese emigrants were going to Africa.

The beginning of industrialisation in Mozambique

The question of whether the colonies should be encouraged to establish industries was hotly debated in the 1930s, with the Portuguese textile interests strongly opposed to the establishment of factories there. In 1936 the government decided that new industries would all have to have the consent of the Minister of the Colonies and his decision would take into account the interests of Portuguese industry.[56] Nevertheless industrialisation did begin in the 1930s with a limited programme of import substitution. By the outbreak of the Second World War Mozambique produced mineral drinks and syrups, pasta, vegetable oil, candles, soap, salt, cement, ceramics, perfume, furniture, fireworks, tin containers and bus bodies.[57] After the Second World War the relationship between Portugal and its colonies became closer than at any time in the history of the two countries. Portugal now took around 50 per cent of colonial exports and provided Mozambique with 50 per cent of the goods it imported. However, the balance of trade was in favour of Portugal and led to large transfers to Lisbon of hard currency earned by Mozambique through migrant remittances and service industries. In the late 1940s and early 1950s the tough mercantilism of the early years was modified somewhat and industrialisation in the colonies began to be encouraged.

The great expansion in the production of cotton, cashew, rice, tea and other crops during the war led to the establishment of numerous processing plants. Then, in the years between the end of the war and 1960, continued immigration raised the white population to 100,000 and the consumer market within Mozambique began to expand. The First and Second Development Plans allowed for the emergence of local industries. The large Portuguese banks and industrial corporations were encouraged to invest in the colonies and a range of manufactures was created, largely in the two main cities of Lourenço Marques and Beira. Mozambique became a producer of cement, bricks and tiles, asbestos sheeting, electric cables, steel castings, plywood, wire, and such consumer items as umbrellas, cooking pots, household plastics and rubber goods, mattresses, textiles, tyres, radios and bicycles. The chemical industry produced insecticides, tanning materials, paint and pharmaceuticals. There were also widely varied food processing industries. However, the single most important industry was oil refining. A plant at Matola near Lourenço Marques specialised in refining heavy oil for an important export market in South Africa — creating one more vital industrial link between the two countries. Finally, a boom in large-scale construction occurred in the main urban centres.[58]

Alongside secondary industry, hydroelectric power generation and a viable mining sector were developed. The Moatize coalfields had been bought by the Belgian Société Minière et Géologique du Zambèse in 1919. The company built 15 miles of light rail to bring the coal to the Zambesi at Benga, but exploitation was painfully slow and the mines produced barely 8,000 tonnes in 1936, its only customers being Sena Sugar and the Trans-Zambesia railway. In 1949, however, the broad-gauge railway was completed from the coalfields to Mutarara on the north bank opposite Sena, and coal production rose dramatically to more than 200,000 tonnes in 1956 and to 320,000 tonnes in 1961.[59] Geological surveys by the government revealed traces of a large number of minerals, and trials were carried out, in conjunction with foreign companies, with a view to bringing some of them into production. The most important mining enterprises proved to be asbestos in Manica, and in the Alto Ligonha region columbo-tantalite, bismutite and the mining of beryl for the extraction of beryllium, which outstripped even coal in value.[60]

The economy also diversified into tourism. Beira and Lourenço Marques, which had for so long provided port and railway services to the Rhodesias and South Africa and channelled surplus labour into their economies, now began to perform an additional service role. After the war the white population of British Central Africa grew rapidly and Beira beckoned to them as a seaside resort offering water sports and an element of Latin culture. Beira lay within a weekend drive of the white cities of Rhodesia, and soon there emerged hotels, restaurants and yacht clubs. Lourenço Marques saw a similar development, but for slightly different reasons. White South Africans had coastal resorts of their own, but increasingly travelled to Lourenço Marques in search of black prostitutes and the kind of night life officially denied them by the puritanical rigidities of apartheid.[61]

However, if the statistics show the Mozambique economy growing and diversifying, this modern economy nonetheless remained very much confined to the area round two main cities. Outside Beira and Lourenço Marques there was little urban development. A new port town began to grow at Nacala, and Nampula emerged as an important railway junction and administrative centre, but Mozambique mostly remained a country of company towns and small administrative centres, often situated in the historic old trading towns like Quelimane, António Ennes (the former Angoche) or Ibo. Vast areas of the country saw little or nothing of this modern development. Most of the north had no roads, no railways, no airstrips, no telecommunications and no power supplies. Although forced cotton growing continued throughout the 1940s and the plantation companies continued to recruit large numbers of workers for the sugar plantations, the north of Mozambique remained pre-eminently a land of peasant farmers and peasant communities ruled in traditional fashion by the bizarre coming together of matrilineal Makua homesteads with patriarchal Islamic chieftaincies.

The New State's policy towards the African population

The labour scandals of the 1920s had surfaced again and again to affront the self-respect of the Republic and put the whole future of Mozambique in danger. The threat of having its colonies included with those of Germany under the Mandate system was only just avoided at the Versailles Peace Conference, but South Africa continued to put pressure on Lourenço Marques, the deplorable condition of the Nyassa Company territories caused friction with Britain, and the forced labour associated with the Hornung Contract and Ross's report to the League of Nations had once again raised the spectre of foreign intervention. It was believed in Portugal that conditions in Africa were not unconnected with the refusal of the League to grant a loan to the Republic, which in effect delivered the *coup de grâce* to the dying regime.

This is the background to the 'native' and labour policy pursued by the New State. The law had begun to be revised by the Republican government, with the result that a new labour code was introduced in 1928. This contained major changes from the codes of 1899 and 1914.[62] The obligation of all Africans to work was ended; all forced labour for the state had to be paid, and the administration was not allowed to recruit for private companies. On paper these provisions introduced the elements of a free labour system in Mozambique, and they were accompanied, for the first time, by a system of inspection of the provincial administration that was at least capable of bringing transgressors to book. However, continuity, as so often in history, silently triumphed where change had been so loudly trumpeted. Although private plantations and businesses now had to make 'free' contracts with labourers without administrative assistance, in reality the old administrators of the *prazos* and the Nyassa company, often men with notorious reputations, turned themselves into labour contractors. For the African peasant the same man wearing the same uniform, accompanied by liveried 'runners' not easily distinguishable from *cipais*, still came looking for his labour. In Zambesia there was often a direct link with the old seigneurial regime of the *prazos*. Leroy Vail and Landeg White describe one such recruiter, T.A. Rebello, who 'adopted the habit of travelling his bailiwick in a spotless white machilla, carried by six liveried *machileiros*, with parrots attached to each of its four corners'.[63]

In practice, legislation in the Portuguese colonies was always more a landmark of official thinking and a reflection of the changing needs of the local economy than a serious framework moulding social and economic development. The fact was that by the end of the 1920s the need for forced labour was receding. The economic and social evolution of central and southern Africa had created 'natural' labour reserves where the poverty of the soil, increased overcrowding and the lack of any other sort of employment was enough to keep the pulse of migrant and contract labour beating. Year by year it was less necessary to send out the *cipais* to round up labourers or to impose penal taxation — their job was now done for them by poverty and deprivation. Moreover, hut tax was ceasing to be of major significance in colonial finances.

The other major change signalled by the publication of the 1928 code was from forced labour, rounded up and taken to plantations, to a system of forced crop cultivation which required the African to remain in his own village and work his own land. It was no longer appropriate for *cipais* to round up thousands of forced labourers whose absence would undermine the crop-growing campaigns. At first the growing of cotton and rice was seen as a way of getting the African peasant to pay taxes, but as long as taxes were paid no further compulsion was permitted by the law. But in the early 1940s the plantations, eager to expand in response to rising world prices, found difficulty in recruiting workers since one effect of the crop-growing campaigns had been to give African peasants a source of income, however small and hard-earned, which did not require contracting themselves out to work. Although in 1941 a new uniform system of 'native' taxation was introduced which standardised a poll-tax (*capitação*) throughout the country, with women paying at a reduced rate, the old method of using taxation as a regulator of labour supply was ceasing to be effective.

After a tour in the areas of worst shortage, governor-general Bettencourt issued an order in 1942 which would allow the forcible recruitment of peasants not deemed to be fully employed in agriculture, and empowered local *chefes* to decide what acreage of land a man would need to cultivate to be considered fully employed.[64] This regime offered the peasant two options — to join in the cotton and rice programmes or contract with the plantation companies. The system of *cadernetes*, or passes, already in operation in some areas to try to control clandestine migration was now widely extended to keep a check on the peasant's work record.[65]

In 1944 controls over the *indígena* population of the major cities were introduced. Following South African practice, *indígenas* were required to register with the administration and obtain a *livrete* which permitted them to be in town to work. Infringements made an *indígena* liable to penal labour. Like the South African pass system, the *livrete* served a number of purposes. It was a method of controlling the influx into urban areas and of exerting some form of social control over the workforce in the cities, and it helped to seal off yet another means by which the peasant might escape forced labour in rural areas.[66]

In 1953, along with a general overhaul of the public law of the colony, new and elaborate norms were issued for every aspect of 'native policy'. Although in theory a free labour system had been envisaged in 1928, the basic contradiction remained that, no matter what Lisbon might decide, Mozambique remained part of the economy of the southern African subcontinent. A genuinely free labour system would involve competition with South Africa and the Rhodesias for available labour, while in the rural areas of Mozambique some way would have to be found to recruit workers who had the option of migrating to the towns or growing cash crops. Portuguese colonial officials were not blind to this issue. Eugénio Ferreira de Almeida, governor of the Moçambique District, posed the question in a direct way:

> And now it must be asked: Are the wages paid in the district of Moçambique of a level to permit the native to satisfy his wants? Does the amount earned in six months of work satisfy his minimal material ambitions?
>
> No. At the end of six months work in the large agricultural enterprises the native receives about 400//00 in money. After paying his tax he retains 270//00, a quantity which does not allow him to buy the objects with which European industry seduces him. And in such circumstances the voluntary procuring of labour experiences drastic limitations.[67]

The Portuguese were grappling with a problem which would continue to plague Frelimo after independence. How does a relatively poor and underdeveloped country develop itself when the market place for labour, consumer goods and capital is dominated by a much bigger and relatively more developed neighbouring economy?

Another aspect of Portuguese 'native' policy which greatly influenced the development of Mozambique after independence was that of grouping peasant families in large settlements called *aldeamentos*. The objectives of these 'rural concentrations' were many and varied. A concentrated population could be taxed, administered and conscripted with greater ease. It could also be provided with facilities for health and education and with amenities and services. However, the *aldeamento* policy was adopted in the northern districts primarily to aid the supervision of the crop-growing campaigns. It was a policy to which there was a great deal of peasant resistance and frequently, as

Ferreira de Almeida recognised, 'of this chimerical dream there remain only a few ruined huts'.[68] But some had succeeded and in his view the crucial difference between success and failure was the sinking of a well and provision of a water supply. In 1956 he was able to write that more than 30,000 families in the district of Moçambique had been brought into *aldeamentos* and in Cabo Delgado he cited 1,100 families in the *circunscrição* of Montepuez and 300 concentrated in cotton-growing settlements in Marrupa in the Lago district.[69] The *aldeamentos* allowed 6 hectares per family, with 1 hectare set aside for the house, fruit trees and gardens and, of the other 5, half given over to cash crops and half to food crops.

The *aldeamento* policy was intensified during the war of independence when it was seen as the best way of insulating the population from Frelimo propaganda. After independence the Frelimo government adopted the idea and made it the key to its policy of rural development.

Administration of Mozambique in the 1950s and 1960s

With the victory of the Allies in the Second World War, Salazar, as already mentioned, found it expedient to play down the fascist character of the New State and adopt at least the outward forms of liberal democracy. Popular elections were held for the office of President of Portugal and the regime adjusted its public institutions so that they appeared more representative and therefore more acceptable to the West. Salazar was playing for high stakes for he wished Portugal to become a member of NATO; this was achieved in 1949.

In the early 1950s the public law of Portugal and its empire was overhauled, although it was a process of modernisation rather than a radical change of direction. In 1951 the Portuguese Constitution was revised and the term 'colony', used uninhibitedly in the 1930s, was now dropped in favour of the older usage of Overseas Province, emphasising the claim of the regime that the African territories and Portugal formed a single indivisible country. In 1953 the Organic Law of Overseas Portugal was published and in 1955 there followed a Statute for the Province of Mozambique. In 1954 the legislation concerning the African population was updated with the passing of the Native Statute. This was repealed in 1961 when all inhabitants of Mozambique were given full citizenship rights as part of another major overhaul of the public law of the colony, designed to counter the growing international campaign against Portuguese colonial rule.

Mozambique was represented in Lisbon by two members in the 185-man Corporate Chamber, two representatives on the Overseas Council and seven elected members of the National Assembly.[70]

Inside Mozambique the Legislative Council was enlarged to twenty-nine members, sixteen of whom were elected — nine of these by direct suffrage from the enfranchised population. As an additional consultative body an Economic Coordinating Council was created in 1959. On a day-to-day basis the governor-general worked through the *Conselho do Governo* which consisted of the provincial secretaries, the secretary-general, the naval, air and military commanders, the attorney-general, the head of the treasury and two members of the Legislative Assembly. At the local level there were in the early 1960s nine Districts (Lourenço Marques, Gaza, Inhambane, Manica e Sofala, Tete, Zambezia, Moçambique, Cabo Delgado and Niassa), divided into sixty-one *conselhos* and thirty-one *circunscriçoẽs* (see Map 10, p. 518, below). Local democracy existed only in the form of town councils which served provincial capitals and towns with 500 or more electors.[71]

Social and political developments

After remaining static during the 1920s the African population of Mozambique began a relatively slow increase from 3,960,261 in 1930 to 6,430,530 recorded in the 1960 census. These figures appear to show a much faster growth rate in the 1930s than in the next two decades. This may be due to inaccurate counting but it may also be an example of rapid recovery from unusually severe mortality in the previous period. In the early 1960s the growth-rate was running at 1.3 per cent per annum compared with an average for sub-Saharan Africa of 2.4 per cent (Fig. 17.1). By the 1960 census the general pattern of population distribution had not changed greatly since 1930. Population densities were highest in the coastal areas but the percentage of the population in the central districts had dropped from 47.2 per cent to 42.6 per cent (Fig. 17.2).

The gender distribution had also altered little. The average for the whole country was 100 men to 109 women, except in the towns and commercial farming areas where the ratios were reversed. The effect of migrant labour still seemed powerful.

The slow rate of population growth was certainly linked to the lack of adequate health care which marked Mozambique up to the 1960s. Malaria, sleeping sickness, leprosy and bilharzia were all endemic, and a third of all children died in infancy.[72] In 1929 the government had established units to combat malaria and sleeping sickness and after the Second World War bilharzia, tuberculosis and leprosy were added to the list. In 1940 the health department employed 78 doctors, 166 nurses of various grades and 102 African nurses.[73] In addition, there were doctors who practised privately. Provision for improved

Table 17.1 DISTRIBUTION AND DENSITY OF
THE AFRICAN POPULATION, 1960

District	Density per sq. km.	% of total
Lourenço Marques	26.30	6.7
Gaza	7.88	10.3
Inhambane	8.54	8.8
Tete	4.71	7.0
Zambézia	13.28	20.7
Moçambique	18.38	21.9
Manica e Sofala	5.98	11.9
Cabo Delgado	6.99	8.2
Niassa	2.32	4.3

Sources: A.B. Herrick *et al.*, *Area Handbook for Mozambique*, p. 44; D.M. Abshire and M.A. Samuels, *Portuguese Africa*, p. 14.

Table 17.2 NÃO-INDÍGENA POPULATION, 1928–1960

	European	Indian	Chinese	Mixed	Assimilado
1928	17,842	8,475	896	8,357	
1935	23,131	8,304	1,056	13,259	
1940	27,438	9,147	1,449	15,641	
1945	31,221	9,700	1,565	15,784	1,845
1950	48,213	12,630	1,613	26,149	
1955	65,798	15,235	1,945	29,873	4,554
1960	97,245	17,241	2,098	31,455	

Source: *Anuário Estatístico*, 1973.

health care was included in the Second Development Plan which began in 1958. By the early 1960s there were 172 leprosy stations treating the estimated 10,000 lepers and eight sleeping sickness isolation hospitals. In addition the ordinary hospitals were treating 200,000 cases of malaria and 1 million cases of bilharzia a year. These figures merely indicate the extent of a problem which had not been adequately confronted during the colonial period and which certainly affected population growth.

By the end of the colonial period a network of health care had been created covering the whole country based on a total of 395 hospitals and maternity units, but there were only about 400 doctors in all and no medical school existed for training doctors, all of whom had to travel abroad to qualify.[74]

Between 1928 and 1935 the *não-indígena* population grew from 35,570 to 117,405. Thereafter the most important growth was in the

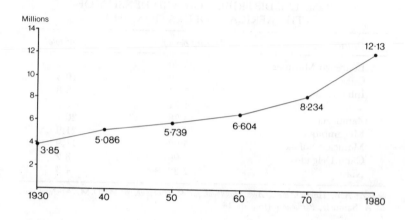

Fig. 17.1   POPULATION OF MOZAMBIQUE, 1930–1980

Source: Anuário Estatístico.

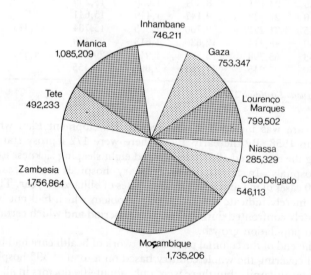

Fig. 17.2   POPULATION BY DISTRICT, 1970

Source: Anuário Estatístico.

European population which reached 100,000 early in the 1960s and had doubled again by the end of the colonial regime. The *não-indígenas* remained primarily an urban class. In 1961 65 per cent lived in urban areas compared with only 7.5 per cent of the *indígena* population and 9 per cent of the population as a whole.[75]

Although Portúguese law had never recognised a colour bar as such and had made provision for people of all races to acquire the status of *não-indígena* or *assimilado*, restrictions of all kinds had been placed in the way of Africans or *mestizos* acquiring posts in the administration or with private firms or developing businesses which might challenge the economic position of whites. The operation of the informal colour bar has been meticulously charted by Jeanne Penvenne who has shown how the New State, in its overriding desire to control labour costs and eliminate all organisations not authorised by the state, imposed a series of hurdles in the way of Africans who sought a role for themselves as *não-indígenas*. Business activities required licenses, promotion required the patronage or support of influential Portuguese, educational opportunities remained absurdly narrow, and the hard-earned status of *assimilado* itself was subject to periodic review. Penvenne has described the farce that sometimes ensued:

> If an inspection visit was anticipated, the subject's circle of friends would contribute whatever material accoutrements (dishes, utensils, chairs, tables, linens etc.) might be necessary to impress the inspector. Informants recalled hilarious community scrambles to fix a soon-to-be-inspected household up to standard.[76]

As the colonial state had developed and its economy grown, almost all the jobs in the modern sector were taken by immigrant Portuguese or Indians. Educated Africans and Afro-Portuguese were required but continued to be marginalised in the state structure. It is difficult not to conclude that the New State made a fundamental error in allowing a small *assimilado* class to emerge and then systematically subjecting it to personal humiliation and depressed status.

The growing effectiveness of the bureaucracy in extending regulation of the economy and of the population in general, and the decline in the status of the *mestizo* and *assimilado* class, are reflected in the fading of political activity and influence. During the Republic years not only had there been a vigorous opposition press in the capital but strikes and demonstrations were common occurrences. The era of close censorship, as in so many other fields, began with the Minister João Belo who introduced a press censorship law in 1926.[77] Although some newspapers tried to avoid the effects of censorship by frequent changes of name, censorship was gradually imposed during the New State on both the Portuguese and the *mestizo* political press and organisations. It was not a censorship that necessarily banned publications or prohibited organisations altogether — that was not the style of the New State — but rather a gradual process of strangulation. The radical journal *O Emancipador* was suspended in 1937 and by the end of the 1930s *O Brado Africano* and the *Grêmio Africano*, though still in existence, were government-sponsored and government-controlled organs.[78] The Associação Africana and the Instituto (renamed the Centro Associativo dos Negros de Moçambique) were also still alive, the latter surviving actively until suppressed in 1965.[79] However, there seems to be general agreement that after about 1933 these organisations adopted an extremely passive stance and gave the authorities little cause for concern.

Labour unrest had been endemic among the port and railway workers of Beira and Lourenço Marques as the system whereby they were hired on a daily basis made their lives precarious in the extreme. The nationalisation of the port operations in the capital in 1929 was followed by the widespread use of *chibalo* labour which all but destroyed the position of the casual dock labourers, while the depression of the early 1930s reduced still further the shipping using the port and with it the employment and wages of the workforce. There were strikes and demonstrations in Beira in March 1932 and in Lourenço Marques in August-September 1933, with some support from the press. But the level of worker organisation remained primitive and the unrest never spread. Political protest in Mozambique remained rudimentary.[80]

Religion and education

The bureaucratic surveillance of the New State was soon extended to the African independent churches. Some of these, like the Igreja Episcopal Luso-Africana, founded as an offshoot of the Swiss mission near Inhambane in 1918, were cajoled by the government to form a religious association with some other churches and concentrate their activities on mutual aid. But others of a more religiously radical nature escaped government control. After the Second World War, as in South Africa, there seems to have been a rapid growth of independent churches, many of them Zionist in their orientation. The police maintained records on thirty such churches in Manica and Sofala, the largest of which, the Igreja Fé dos Apostolos, had 3,000 members. Although they saw these churches as potentially a focus for opposition to the government, the police allowed them to exist, only occasionally resorting to active persecution. In 1953, for example, they banned the Jehovah's Witnesses and exiled its members to São Tomé.[81]

The early history of Catholicism in Mozambique had been entirely dominated by the missionary orders, but in the twentieth century church affairs were directed by the secular hierarchy. In October 1926 João Belo issued his Organic Statute for Missions, bringing some order to the ecclesiastical scene in Mozambique and making the bishop of Mozambique the director of all missions and responsible for the appointment of all mission personnel. Salazar's Colonial Act maintained the formal separation of church and state, but gave the church special recognition as an 'instrument of civilisation and national influence' and channelled state aid to missions for their educational work. Mission education was then regulated further by the *Accordo Missionário* annexed to the Concordat in 1940 and by the *Estatuto Missionário* of April 1941. From then till the war of liberation there was close co-operation between the Catholic establishment and the regime, and Catholicism became in effect the official religion of the state, receiving state aid and many other privileges — including the supply of *chibalo* labour to build Lourenço Marques' cathedral.

The main function of missions was the provision of 'rudimentary' education for the *indígena* population, the state only continuing to perform a role in areas where no missions were yet established. Mission education became official education, and the missions thereby became a branch of the government with an important role in propaganda and social control. The *Accordo Missionário* defined the principal objective of 'rudimentary' education as follows:

> . . . the perfect training of the *indígenas* in national and moral ideals [*nacionalização e moralização*] and the acquisition of habits and aptitudes for work, in keeping with their sex and condition, and the convenience of the regional economy. Moral ideals being understood to include the abandonment of idleness and the training of future rural workers and artisans to produce sufficient for their needs and for their social obligations.[82]

Despite government favour and the central role of the church in African education, it was estimated that in 1964 only 15 per cent of the population were Catholic (a mere 4 per cent were Protestant).[83]

After the Second World War educational opportunity expanded somewhat. In 1942–3 there had been 95,444 pupils registered in mission schools (the more cosmetic term 'Schools of Adaptation' replacing the former 'Rudimentary Schools'). By 1961–2 the number had reached 348,265, of whom 98 per cent were taught in Catholic schools and a mere 7,191 attended foreign mission schools. The relative decline of foreign missions was of course part of government policy, and obstacles were increasingly placed in the way of their operation. African teachers could only gain admission to training institutions if they were Catholic, and access to further education in general likewise depended on subscription to the established state religion. Samora Machel, for example, found that educational progress was barred for him unless he became a baptised Catholic and thus, for the sake of advancement, he joined the church.[84] As Jeanne Penvenne wrote, 'A good education and strong patronage ties emerged as important factors for black mobility.' Access to state education and to patronage within government service came to depend on being Catholic, although Protestants were frequently preferred by foreign companies working in Mozambique and a network of patronage was available for them as well.[85]

The total number of Schools of Adaptation rose from 1,122 in 1951 to 2,563 by 1958. In the same period the numbers of elementary schools (i.e. those intended for Europeans and *não-indígenas*) rose from 139 to 233 and the numbers of pupils from 13,043 to 26,783; by 1962 they had reached 40,063. Even so, barely a quarter of all children of school age were able to get any sort of education.[86] The Schools of Adaptation did not acquire a very impressive reputation, their main purpose being to teach Portuguese and so prepare Africans for elementary education which would be conducted wholly in that language. The level of instruction seems to have been generally low and pupils spent a lot of their time working on the mission farms — another form of cheap labour.[87]

By 1940 Lourenço Marques had a technical college and four other *escolas de artes e ofícios*. A second *liceu* was created in the city in 1954 and by 1961 there were three, and one each in Beira, Nampula and Inhambane. Numbers attending secondary education of all kinds had risen to 12,044.[88] As fees had to be paid for secondary education, very few Africans attended — in 1964 it was estimated that only one African in 12,500 received academic secondary education — although rather more attended technical and professional schools or received in-service education of some kind.

During the 1950s serious educational provision was still only being made for the 'civilised' section of the population, but the attitude of the government to education had begun to change. Although, as has been suggested, the quality of 'rudimentary' education barely allowed even for the acquisition of literacy, it is clear that in the 1950s the first real attempt was made to cover the country with a network of schools, the second six-year plan including a significant element for education.

The gathering momentum of educational provision was partly dictated by the manpower needs of the industrialising economy but was partly also a recognition by the government that it needed to seize the initiative in 'indoctrinating' its citizens. There had always been a concern at the 'denationalising' influence of migrant labour and foreign missionary activity, and early legislation had tried to ensure that education in Mozambique would be Portuguese education; this had been the principle behind the legislation of 1907, 1926 and 1941.

In the early 1960s, not surprisingly, education policy was put into an altogether higher gear. Education was to be centralised and increasingly aligned with metropolitan practice under the direction of a Provincial Directorate. In 1962 a university was established, although it was some years before it taught complete degree programmes. In 1964 school attendance was made compulsory for all those living within 3 miles of a school although this ambitious attempt to spread education was hampered for lack of teachers.[89] This change of pace reflected the educational needs of a settler population which doubled in size in the 1960s. However, it was also a belated response to the demands of African radicals and an attempt to buy time amid the rising tide of nationalism.

18

LABOUR MIGRATION TO SOUTH AFRICA AND SOUTHERN RHODESIA

The perils of migration

Writing in the *Glasgow Herald* in April 1875, David Leslie described a harrowing sight that he had witnessed on the shores of Delagoa Bay four years earlier:

> I saw some miserable-looking wretches seated round a fire, on which there was a pot with some maize in it. There were ten of them, and they, on inquiry, told me that they were the survivors of the sixty men who had passed in good health and high spirits two months before. Poor fellows! I wish some of the diplomatists had seen them as they then were. Emaciated, and covered with wounds. . . .[1]

The sixty men of whom these were the survivors had journeyed from the country in the north-east of the modern Transvaal to seek work on the Natal sugar plantations. Early in 1871 they had begun their journey home travelling through Zululand and along the coast through Tongaland to Delagoa Bay, since it was thought to be too dangerous to cross Swaziland. They carried with them blankets, cloth and money. Having reached the Bay in safety they entered the territory of a minor chief called Matolo and camped only a mile or two from Lourenço Marques. There they were attacked by Matolo's men who killed forty of them and robbed them of everything they possessed. Ten of the survivors fled into the bush and disappeared, the remaining ten encountered by Leslie were helped to return to Natal.

Leslie told this story with a purpose. In part he wanted to show how ineffective Portuguese claims to rule Delagoa Bay really were, but he also wanted to make a case for a more systematic approach to the problems faced by labour migrants — problems that were beginning to intrude themselves with increasing urgency into the normal agenda of colonial politics.

The origins of migrant labour from southern Mozambique

The Tsonga of Delagoa Bay and its hinterland had always interacted with the high veldt communities with whom there were strong ties of culture and kinship. The boom in ivory trading in the early nineteenth century had increased the movement of people along the traditional trade routes, and there is evidence of considerable migration in the 1840s and 1850s between the low veldt and the Zoutpansberg.[2] The 1850s also saw the rapid development of sugar growing in Natal and a sharply increasing demand for labour which could not be met by the local population. Britain landed some consignments of freed slaves who were taken on as wage labour, and in 1860 authorised the import of indentured Indian labour. However, plantation owners soon found that southern Mozambique was the most fruitful area in which to recruit workers.[3]

Much of the low veldt region has a climate which is very susceptible to drought and is made up of poor soils which give low crop yields even in good years. Migration had always been one of the options for survival when times were hard. During the nineteenth century the rise of the Gaza state had been accompanied by the regular and systematic exaction of tribute or booty from the peripheral populations. The Gaza ruling houses demanded payments of cattle, imported goods, women and children, and these exactions, in effect, creamed off much of the surplus produced by the peasant communities. Moreover, intensified ivory hunting had by the 1870s driven the elephant herds from the low veldt and virtually destroyed an important economic resource. On top of this came the civil wars following the death of Soshangane in 1858 which caused widespread destruction, particularly in the extreme south which was devastated year after year by Swazi raids. Large numbers of people became destitute and succumbed to famine and epidemics. Others collected into large fortified settlements or fled to find what protection they could near the Portuguese *presídios*. It was in these circumstances that labour recruiters were able to sign up migrant workers for contracts on the Natal sugar plantations.[4]

The movement of migrants to Natal had already begun when diamonds were discovered in the Orange river in 1867. The diamonds attracted a rush of European prospectors, and with the discovery of the dry diggings in the remote eastern fringes of the Kalahari in 1870, diamond mining turned into a major industrial activity. In the early days the diamond miners were small claim-holders who had no capacity to organise labour supply. They depended on such labour as arrived at the mines, and a free market developed in which wages found their own level. Workers were attracted by the easy availability of firearms in Kimberley, and many chiefs deliberately dispatched parties of young men to the mines so that they could buy guns. However, even when the sale of firearms was stopped and the compound system was introduced to impose a tight control on labour, the relatively high wages still enabled young men to buy consumer goods which increased their personal status or that of their lineage, and to use their cash earnings to meet *lobola* payments.

It has been argued that as a result of thirty years of Gaza raiding, the cattle stocks of the peoples of southern Mozambique had become so depleted that the old *lobola* payments which had been made in cattle, and without which young men could not obtain wives, were no longer possible.[5] At first hoes replaced cattle but with the growth of migrant labour, *lobola* began to be paid in consumer goods or even in money. *Lobola* payments, and hence the possibility of marriage, were now no longer dependent on cattle being provided by the head of the family, and increasingly lineage heads lost the control over their sons which the old *lobola* system had given them. It was alleged that in the Limpopo area in the 1890s *lobola* payments were in the region of £20 in gold sterling, with additional gifts of cloth and a gun to the bride's parents.[6] In this way the wages earned in Natal and at the Kimberley mines initiated a revolution in the social and ultimately also in the political relations of southern Mozambique which gathered momentum as the century advanced.[7]

Migrants heading for Kimberley walked overland for hundreds of miles in circumstances of great hardship and danger, while those on their way to Natal had to cross Swazi and Zulu territory. Both the British and Portuguese colonial authorities were anxious to regulate and regularise this labour supply. The Portuguese appointed a consul in Natal while the Natal government sent a number of unofficial agents, the best known of whom was St Vincent Erskine, to negotiate with the Gaza king, and from 1875 maintained an agent in Lourenço Marques. To avoid the worst horrors of the overland journey, Natal contractors began to use schooners to transport workers to and from Portuguese ports. However, these measures, ostensibly taken to ease the lot of the migrant, soon turned into a means of stripping the labourers of their earnings. In 1872 the governor of Lourenço Marques complained that Africans trying to leave Natal could only obtain a passage from certain stores where they had to make a number of purchases.[8] Three years later he was alleging too that passports could be bought across the counter.[9] The Portuguese, for their part, issued passports to African labourers leaving their ports (for which a fee was charged) and demanded passports and health clearance documents from all Africans returning.[10] In August 1875 Mozambique Island was officially designated a depot for freed slaves, and the export of labour from there and from Lourenço Marques to Natal was put on an official footing. Labourers had to receive official contracts — which would last for three years with a guaranteed free return passage — and pay a passport fee of 2,500 *reis*. In 1876 the

Cape government also reached a labour recruiting agreement with the Portuguese and appointed a superintendent of labour with the task of arranging safe transport and seeing to the proper contracting of workers. In 1885 the Portuguese officially allowed the emigration of workers from Inhambane as well as Lourenço Marques.[11]

This was the situation on the eve of the great gold discoveries on the Witwatersrand in 1886. The development of the Rand mines greatly intensified the need for labour, but the delicate political situation in the area controlled by the Gaza monarchy meant that migrant labour and its recruitment became of increasing political concern to the Portuguese authorities. At first they were mainly anxious to control the supposed political activity of the labour recruiters, but before long they were to realise the possibility of deriving substantial income from encouraging recruitment. They also realised that the flow of labour could substantially aid their plans to develop Lourenço Marques as the major port-city of southern Africa.

The Lourenço Marques railway

Had the British and the Portuguese proceeded to build the Lourenço Marques railway after Britain's annexation of the Transvaal in 1877, the first major freight opportunity would have been the moving of migrant workers from the coast to the high veldt, and there would have been a comforting correspondence between the political and economic needs of the various parties. However, matters did not proceed so smoothly.

The British and Portuguese governments finalised the Lourenço Marques Treaty in May 1879. Britain was to underwrite the building of the railway, and the contract was to be put out to tender. Earlier in the year the Zulu war had broken out, and Portugal co-operated closely with Britain in closing the port of Lourenço Marques to shipments of arms which might reach the Zulus. When the war was over, however, British policy was in full retreat. Zululand was handed back to the Zulu chiefs and dissolved into chaos; the Transvaal too was soon in rebellion and by 1882 Britain had decided to restore it to the control of the local Boer chieftains. While the new Transvaal government reaffirmed the 1869 treaty with Portugal together with the all-important free trade agreement, Britain once again looked with suspicion on the building of a railway which was to become the symbol of Boer independence from British control.

However, the railway soon ran into other problems besides the opposition of the British government. In 1883 the Portuguese engineer Joaquim Machado made a survey of a route which skirted the north of Swaziland; this was accepted by the Boers who feared that any other route would fall under British influence. In 1884 the Portuguese granted a concession to build their portion of the line to an American, Colonel Edward McMurdo,[12] whose company, which was known as the Lourenço Marques and Transvaal Joint Stock Company and had its headquarters in Lisbon, obtained extensive land concessions and the right to fix freight rates. However, the value of this concession was undermined when the Portuguese, under pressure from President Kruger to see rapid progress with the railway, issued a parallel concession to operate a steam tramway over the same route.[13]

McMurdo found difficulty in obtaining financial backing, but eventually did so in London and set up a British-owned company to take over the concession. Much as the Boers must have resented this coup whereby British interests gained control over the Mozambique section of their railway, the Portuguese government appears to have had no objections and work on the Portuguese section of the line eventually started in 1886. However, only part of the line had been built — and to a low standard — when McMurdo died, leaving his concession to his widow. No further progress was made with the line and, since it transpired that no fixed frontier crossing had been agreed where the Portuguese line would meet the Transvaal section and that the contractors were locked in endless arguments over their liability, the Portuguese government moved in June 1889 to revoke the concession. The British company tried to enlist the support of the British government which protested vigorously, nominally against the loss of rights by a British company, but in reality against losing the vital leverage which ownership of a section of the line gave to Britain. An attempt was even made by local officials of the company to resist the take-over. All parties then dug themselves in pending arbitration over the extent of the damages that would be awarded to the company. While the case was being pursued in the courts in Switzerland, Cecil Rhodes put together a syndicate to buy the railway should Portugal be forced to sell to pay the damages. However, Portugal was already extremely sensitive to attempts by South African interests to acquire control of the railway and the port by the back door and a new railway company, the Caminho de Ferro de Lourenço Marques (CFLM), was granted the concession. The same year the Transvaal established the Netherlands Railway Company (NZASM) to control its sector of the line.[14]

Meanwhile the gold strikes on the Rand not only raised the political stakes but greatly increased the level of general economic activity. For the Portuguese in Lourenço Marques this was a unique opportunity. As the industrial complexes grew, the need to import goods of all kind became imperative. Railways began to be built to the Rand from

Natal and from the Cape, but logically it was Delagoa Bay which was bound to play the key role in the Rand's development. Not only was it closer than the other ports but it was the point from which the major flows of labour could be expected, while the free trade treaty of 1873 gave huge incentives to importers to use that port rather than the British ports to the south.

In 1889 Portugal finally took over the railway concession from the heirs of McMurdo, and the 1.067-metre-gauge line along the route surveyed by Machado was completed to the Transvaal border in March 1890.[15] At the same time the Netherlands Railways Company began construction of the route within the Transvaal. The line from the Cape reached the Rand in 1893, giving it a brief overwhelming advantage in southern African trade. However, President Kruger was determined that the line to Lourenço Marques, once built, would carry the bulk of the Rand traffic. In negotiations with the British he insisted that the Natal railway, when completed, would not charge transit duties lower than those of the Portuguese, and the agreement with Natal railways made it impossible for the share of Lourenço Marques to fall below 30 per cent or that of Natal to rise above 50 per cent of rail traffic.[16] Kruger was determined that low railway rates on the Transvaal section of the Delagoa Bay line would be used to compensate importers for the longer sea voyage from Europe to Lourenço Marques and that these rates would be used to promote his political objective of developing a port and railway independent of Britain. The line from Lourenço Marques through to Johannesburg was officially opened on 1 January 1895 and that from Durban to the Rand in December. Between 1896 and the outbreak of the Boer war in 1899 the rail traffic of the Rand was distributed in roughly equal shares between the three rail systems.

Impact of the railway on southern Mozambique

In the first four years of operation Lourenço Marques' share of the Rand traffic rose to only 34 per cent, but the opening of the line at once dramatically affected the whole development of Mozambique. The fragile but effective barrier which the existence of tse-tse fly had presented to the ox-waggon and the horse was now swept aside by the steam engine. The effect was like the pulling of a switch connecting the colonial economy to the powerhouse of the Rand, and the insatiable demand of the new towns and industries began to stimulate every section of the economy of southern Mozambique.

In 1891, the first year of the full operation of the railway to the border, 36,564 passengers were carried. This number had risen to 81,403 by the outbreak of the Boer war and rose again to 125,880 in

1909, the year of the Mozambique-Transvaal Convention.[17] Freight carried rose from 28,129 tonnes to 174,833 in 1899 and 638,294 tonnes in 1909. The line was hugely profitable. Over the period 1889 to 1910 it earned a surplus of 6,189 *contos*. The business of the port grew exponentially. The numbers of ships unloading rose from 228 in 1892 to 503 in 1899 and the value of its commerce rose from 1,656 *contos* in 1892 to 19,247 *contos* in 1900, thus accounting for almost exactly half the total commercial activity of Mozambique.[18] Customs revenue, which had increased from 32.3 *contos* in 1879 to 167.5 in 1889, rose to 730 in 1899 and 1,085 in 1903.[19]

The town, with its port and railway, rapidly attracted a large population — British and South African businessmen, large numbers of African stevedores, construction workers and prostitutes, and Indian traders who moved in to provide a variety of services and retail outlets for the burgeoning city. The port of Lourenço Marques had to be developed to handle international commerce on a big scale. The old ivory trading station had to transform itself. Wharfs were built and equipped with cranes and warehousing facilities. Railway installations followed and the city rapidly grew beyond its old walls. The marshy land by the docks was filled in, and prefabricated buildings of all kinds grew up along newly-built boulevards — perhaps the most remarkable being a large town house consisting entirely of moulded cast-iron plates. The brashness of new construction was never quite to leave the city during the Portuguese period as every decade saw the city grow in one direction or another, but at its core was the elegant nineteenth-century colonial town first laid out in 1890s.[20]

However, the huge and growing market of the Rand was not just supplied with imports which passed through Lourenço Marques in transit. Investors began to see the potential of the free trade agreement between Mozambique and the Transvaal as a way of penetrating the Transvaal market. The opportunity was taken first of all to promote the production of spirits. Mozambique had an infant sugar industry without any well-developed markets and the producers were soon manufacturing rum for export to Johannesburg and for local consumption. Before long, German spirit producers were to take advantage of a loophole in the law by which foreign goods could be landed at Lisbon, 'nationalised' as Portuguese and enter the Transvaal duty-free. German potato spirit then began to arrive in Lourenço Marques to supplement the local rum production and this was closely followed by Portuguese wine. Imports of spirit into Lourenço Marques averaged about 200,000 litres a year between 1894 and 1899 but reached a peak of over 500,000 litres in 1896. The country was soon awash with alcohol, and Indian and Portuguese *cantineiros* competed to attract the unspent wages of the mine and port workers. The problems caused by perpetual drunkenness soon became a preoccupation not only of missionaries and philanthropists but of employers and government officials, and the issue was eventually tackled by international convention in 1899.[21] International concern was echoed by the Portuguese wine producers who had a vested interest in halting the manufacture and sale of spirits in Mozambique. By 1902, as a result of all these pressures, the Mozambique rum industry had been strangled by high excise charges.

If rum casks travelled up the newly-opened line, so did increasing numbers of migrant workers. The 1890s saw the previous flow of workers becoming a regular flood. Labour touts travelled freely about southern Mozambique offering strong incentives to chiefs to cooperate in rounding up young men for the mines, although it was the unsettled political conditions in the southern part of the country that really pushed men into the arms of the labour contractors. With the shift of the centre of the Gaza state south to the Limpopo in 1889, warfare between the Gaza and the Chopi became endemic and Gaza raids on the Tsonga chiefs south of the Limpopo also became more frequent.

These were lawless days. The labour touts fought each other for their recruits, drink flowed, bribery was rife and the authority of the Portuguese administration was openly flouted even in areas where it was nominally effective. Moreover, the process was costly for the mine-owners themselves, who found that compretitve recruiting raised their labour costs ever higher. All parties, including perhaps even the labourers themselves who may have found the advantages of the free market outweighed by the dangers and uncertainties, stood to benefit by a proper regulation of the system. In Johannesburg the Chamber of Mines began to take steps to stop the cut-throat competition between mining houses and in 1893 established the Native Labour Department which in effect became a cartel to fix wages and produce an orderly recruitment operation. In 1894 the Chamber of Mines received a report claiming that up to three-quarters of recruited labour was coming from southern Mozambique but that the supply was being held back by the lawlessness of the region and the lack of facilities for the migrants.[22] The war between the Portuguese and Gaza in 1895 caused the situation to worsen and men began to return home. For a short time at the end of 1895 the movement of migrants all but ceased and the mine-owners faced the prospect of acute labour shortages.[23]

This was the background to the founding of the Rand Native Labour Association in 1896. Officially organised recruiting bases were established in Mozambique but this measure failed to oust the private labour contractor, and the following year the Portuguese and

Transvaal authorities agreed the first set of comprehensive labour regulations. These arranged for the licensing of recruiters, who paid an annual fee; the contracting of workers by the district governors in Mozambique; the payment of a capitation fee for each labourer; and a fee for the issue of a permit (in effect a passport). Recruits were to travel by train and in Johannesburg their permits were deposited with the Portuguese *curador* whose office was established by this accord. The *curador* collected taxes owed in Mozambique by mineworkers and endorsed their labour permits before they returned to show they had fulfilled their labour obligations.[24]

The Portuguese government wanted a systematic control of the labour migration in order to profit from it as much as possible, but it also wanted to ensure that the process of recruitment did not cause local control of the population to pass out of its hands into those of the mining houses and recruiting agencies; it was part of the policy of ensuring that Mozambique remained national territory. And there was another problem. Southern Mozambique itself required workers. Lourenço Marques was growing and labour was needed in general construction work and to operate the docks and the railways. Previously the Portuguese had been able to obtain supplies of labour furnished by chiefs in the neighbourhood of the city, but with the growth of migration to the Rand this source began to fail.[25] Against this background Ennes' new general labour law was drawn up, declaring that all *indígenas* had an obligation to work and that the authorities could forcibly contract those who did not voluntarily sign on. The 1899 labour regulations came in the middle of the Boer war when the movement of migrant labour ceased altogether. However, in the medium term it ensured that there would be a steady flow of recruits for the Rand since the wages paid by the mining houses were always above the minimum rates laid down by the Portuguese government for employers in Mozambique.

The 1899 labour law was never enforced in Mozambique but its general principles underpinned the local labour regulations that were to govern the lives of Mozambicans till the late 1920s.[26] At first there were extensive opportunities for evasion. African villagers became adept at moving their villages, migrating from one area of jurisdiction to another or simply disappearing when the tax collectors and census-takers approached, but this evasion could not take place indefinitely. Gradually the areas to which people could escape became fewer and evasion became a process of making a choice between various types of colonial labour and tax regime. For many Mozambicans, as for Africans in Malawi and elsewhere, the lure of the mines was powerful when compared with the other choices available to them. In the last years of the nineteenth century mine wages, not even taking into account non-cash benefits like food and lodging for the miner, were twice the average local wage in southern Mozambique. By the first decade of the twentieth century direct compulsion as such did not have to be used. Africans made their way to the mines in increasing numbers either signing on at one of the labour recruiting offices or using their own initiative and making their way to the Rand along the many clandestine routes that existed.

The labour conventions

As the vast river of black workers poured in spate towards the Rand, the Mozambique and Transvaal governments sought to harness the flow to drive the turbines of their economies. However, the agreements reached in 1897 with the Republican government were soon overtaken by the Boer war which broke out in the autumn of 1899 and quickly led to the closing of the mines. Many workers were dismissed and made their way back to Mozambique as best they could, while others were interned for the duration of the war. The railway was commandeered for military purposes and Portugal agreed to close the port to Boer arms imports or troop movements. By the summer of 1900, however, the Rand had been occupied by General Roberts and the mining areas were placed under military rule. The question of reopening mining operations at once became urgent. The Mozambique government was approached informally to try to restore the flow of migrant workers as the disorder caused by the war and the heavy demands of the military precluded any serious attempt to recruit black labourers in the South African colonies and protectorates. By December 1901 an agreement had been hammered out which came into immediate effect; this was known as the *Modus Vivendi* since it was not embodied in the form of a final treaty and its terms were supposed to be purely temporary. The *Modus Vivendi* was deeply resented by Cape Colony and Natal, both of which wanted to see the privileged position of the port of Lourenço Marques brought to an end and resented the entry of Mozambique sugar into the Transvaal at what they believed were preferential rates.

The *Modus Vivendi* tried to meet the aspirations of both Portugal and the mine-owners and showed the extent to which Mozambique and South Africa were already married together into one economic region. The main object of the agreement was to continue the recruiting arrangements made in 1897. The same license fees and deposits were reintroduced and a fee of 13 shillings per labourer was to be paid, supposedly to cover administrative charges. Work contracts were given a maximum length of one year with a six-month rest period between contracts. The Portuguese re-established their *curador* in

Table 18.1. MOZAMBICANS EMPLOYED BY W.N.L.A., 1904–19
(*average for year*)

	Mozambicans	Mozambicans as % of total
1904	50,997	66.23
1905	59,284	73.19
1906	57,485	70.97
1907	73,532	69.37
1908	81,920	54.98
1909	85,282	54.32
1910	93,008	51.96
1911	89,766	51.59
1912	91,546	47.93
1913	80,832	52.15
1914	74,428	47.71
1915	83,338	42.09
1916	83,524	43.73
1917	82,597	46.93
1918	81,307	51.46
1919	81,668	46.14

Source: Sheila van der Horst, *Native Labour in South Africa*, pp. 216–17.

Johannesburg. The pre-war rail rates were reconfirmed and Milner agreed to allow the movement of civil freight on the railway once the flow of labourers to the mines began. He rejected Portuguese plans for wine to be sold to workers on the Rand, and the Portuguese appear not to have pressed for their other major objective, the deferrment of pay until workers returned to Mozambique. However, the terms of the 1873 commercial treaty made between Portugal and the South African Republic were upheld.[27]

In one important respect the *Modus Vivendi* went beyond the agreement of 1897. An accord made at the same time as the *Modus Vivendi* granted a recruiting monopoly in southern Mozambique to the Witwatersrand Native Labour Association (WNLA), established the previous year. The founding of WNLA by the Chamber of Mines had as its object the control of labour costs. To achieve this it was essential for all labour to be recruited at a standard rate and according to a standard contract, and WNLA's recruiting monopoly made this an achievable aim.

Under the terms of the *Modus Vivendi* recruitment began again on a large scale. Between 1903 and 1906 154,047 Mozambicans were officially recruited for the mines, and they constituted 60 per cent or more of the total labour force. Although the agreement helped restore normality to the mining industry, it was not immediately the success that had been anticipated. Fewer Africans signed on with WNLA than were needed, since working conditions in the mines were appalling. The Portuguese objected that the WNLA agents were usurping administrative and coercive powers and Portuguese settlers complained about the loss of labour. The whole recruiting operation was endangered when the Moçambique and Nyassa Companies refused to allow WNLA to operate in their concessions. Under Milner's guidance the mineowners tried to bring in Chinese labour and there were experiments with the use of white labour as well.[28] But the *Modus Vivendi* survived all its critics and proved increasingly indispensable. Table 18.1 shows the dependence of the South African mines on Mozambican labour during this period.

It was inevitable that this close dependence of the Rand on Mozambique, and the continued existence of the customs agreement, meant that Mozambique had to be a party to the intercolonial negotiations over the future of the South African colonies. During the period of Milner's rule in South Africa up to 1905, and then during the period of Transvaal self-government in 1907-10, a strong political trend developed for the creation of some formal link between the Transvaal and Mozambique — natural partners in the great mission to extract gold from the earth as cheaply and profitably as possible. Mozambique attended the customs and railway conferences of 1903 and was able to secure the continuation of free trade between itself and the Transvaal in the face of the protests of the other British colonies. In 1904 the customs agreement was modified so that only those goods manufactured from raw materials produced in Mozambique could enter the Transvaal duty-free. In return for what the Portuguese saw as a vital concession Milner promised to build a second railway line across Swaziland to Lourenço Marques. In anticipation of this, the Portuguese authorised the construction of the Caminho de Ferro da Suazilandia in July 1903 and began work on their section of the line which was completed to the frontier at Goba in 1912.

With the election of a new government in the Transvaal in 1907, the question of putting Rand labour on a new footing was immediately raised. The Boer politicians were pledged to end Chinese labour and, having just weathered a serious strike among white miners in 1907, were in no mood for experiments with employing poor whites. The only realistic way ahead was to recruit still more workers from Mozambique. Not having any obligation to consider the interests of the other South African colonies, negotiations were quickly concluded in 1908 and a formal Mozambique-Transvaal Convention was signed in April 1909. This put into treaty form the provisions of the *Modus Vivendi*. The labour-recruiting provisions were confirmed, and despite

long campaigning by Natal and the Cape, the protection of the
amount of freight to be handled at the port of Lourenço Marques was
reconfirmed. This time, instead of charging preferential rates, the
port was to be guaranteed 50–55 per cent of the traffic from the gold-
mining areas, the so-called 'competitive zone'. Labour was to be
traded to secure the rail traffic to the port and the sterling balances of
the Mozambique government. Each side had dismissed the clamours
of its own settlers. In South Africa, Natal and the Cape had pressed
for a revision in favour of their ports; in Mozambique the increasingly
vocal pressure-group of white settlers had demanded an end to the
drain of labour to South Africa which made their own recruitment of
cheap labour so difficult. However, the Mozambique authorities were
precluded once again from achieving two of their major ambitions, the
deferrment of pay and the sale of wine to Portuguese workers at the
mines. Provision for deferred pay was introduced but only on a voluntary basis.[29]

Between 1903 and 1913 WNLA made considerable efforts to recruit
labour in Tete province and in the territory of the Nyassa Company
as well as in the Sul do Save (the area south of the Moçambique Company's concession). This policy had little success till 1908 when Lewis
and Marks bought a controlling share of the Nyassa Company and
began to recruit in earnest. However, northern Mozambique never
became a labour reserve dependent on the Rand industrial complex
because in 1913 the new Union government decided to ban all recruitment north of the 22° parallel — in effect north of the Moçambique
Company's border. This move was ostensibly taken to cut the death-
rate suffered by 'tropical' Africans, which in 1911 ran at the alarming
rate of 6.7 per cent per annum.[30] This move, reflecting a certain
political reality, was a response to the strong criticism of the South
African conventions from plantation-owners and Portuguese business
interests. Within Mozambique the 22° parallel was to become a sort
of economic frontier separating the region dependent on South
African mines in the south from the sphere dominated by the Portuguese plantations further north.

The Act of Union of 1910 went a long way towards establishing a
political form to the interdependent economic region which had
already come into existence. Four British colonies came together to
form a single state; one more, Southern Rhodesia, was lined up for
membership in the future, and the three High Commission Territories — Swaziland, Basutoland and Bechuanaland — were locked
into a customs union and thereby into a future that promised ever
closer integration with their powerful neighbour. Mozambique
entered the second decade of the century with its free trade privileges
intact and its government finances and the prosperity of its ports and

railways dependent on South African traffic, and hence South African goodwill. Southern Mozambique, defined clearly by the 22° parallel, had acquired a status similar in many ways to that of one of the High Commission Territories, economically tied to the Rand while retaining a nominal political autonomy.

The 1909 Convention remained unsatisfactory for the Portuguese, who continued to hold divided and contradictory views about it. On the one hand they wanted shorter contracts, which would mean a higher turnover of labour and more capitation fees, stricter measures against clandestine migrants who travelled to the Rand without going through the WNLA recruitment system, and deferred pay. On the other hand they resented the massive exodus of labourers to the Rand and believed that this labour could be used to better effect within Mozambique.

After the First World War relations between the Union government and Mozambique deteriorated to the point where, in 1922, the Convention was not renewed. The problem would probably never have arisen but for General Smuts who had inherited, along with his growing predilection for the British empire, the old imperial desire to control the port of Lourenço Marques. Smuts, it is now known, had ambitious plans for the expansion of the Union. Already before the War he had secretly sounded the British government about the possibility of a South African strike to seize Delagoa Bay, and during the war, in a secret memo to the War Cabinet, he set out plans for an expansion of the Union which involved taking over southern Mozambique.[31] After the war, although he never entirely abandoned these militaristic plans, he concentrated more on trying to pressurise the Portuguese to hand over the management of the port and the railway (CFLM) to the Union government.

Negotiations over the renewal of the 1909 Convention were held up till the arrival of the new Mozambique High Commissioner, Manuel de Brito Camacho, and Smuts prepared the way by announcing that surveys would begin for the building of a new port on the east coast of South Africa. South Africa also prepared to block Mozambique's attempts to raise loan finance and instead offered South African loans provided the Convention was renegotiated.[32] Smuts then put forward his conditions for a renewal of the Convention; these were that a Board should be appointed to run the railway and port with a majority nominated by the Union. The Portuguese negotiators, Freire de Andrade and then Brito Camacho himself, advanced a series of proposals which included South African financing of the railway across Swaziland and of a line linking Lourenço Marques with Southern Rhodesia, as well as the old demand for a deferred pay clause. Both Brito Camacho and Smuts were disinclined to compromise and the negotiations broke down. Smuts then tried to limit immigration of Mozambicans, but the mines could not replace this labour and after a month or two the flow of mine workers from the Sul do Save resumed and the 1909 regulations concerning labour continued in force.

Smuts fell from power in 1924 and desultory discussions followed during the next three years. However, early in 1926 a serious threat to the South African connection appeared when the new Portuguese Minister for the Colonies, João Belo, and his high commissioner in Mozambique, José Cabral, decided to give their backing to a sugar-growing scheme in the Sul do Save which would be provided with labour from WNLA's traditional recruiting ground.[33] In the acrimonious exchanges that followed, the Portuguese announced that they would withdraw from the labour recruitment agreement. However, with the death of Belo early in 1928, General Hertzog's government acted swiftly and agreed a new Convention. Any South African claim to run the railways and ports of Mozambique was quietly dropped. A ceiling was put on the number of workers who could be recruited — this would stabilise at 80,000 a year by 1933. Lourenço Marques continued to be guaranteed between 50 and 55 per cent of the Rand traffic and deferred pay was at last provided for. The only concession made by Mozambique was that the old free trade arrangements were replaced by a 'most favoured nation' clause with certain specified items being admitted duty free.[34]

The deferred pay provisions introduced in 1928 became a distinctive feature of labour contracts in South Africa. The proportion of deferred pay varied, but in the late colonial period was as much as 60 per cent of pay after the first six months of the contract. The sum accumulated without receiving interest and was paid by WNLA on the return of the worker to Mozambique.[35] The unpopularity of the deferred pay provisions was yet another reason why clandestine migration continued at such a high rate. A proportion of mine earnings went into the payment of tax. In the early days the administration in the Sul do Save was dependent for as much as 80 per cent of its income on African hut tax.[36] After 1940 Mozambique negotiated a special deal whereby the deferred pay of miners was paid in gold. When the two-tier pricing system for gold was introduced in 1969 the Portuguese continued to receive transfers at the official price and sold the gold on the world market. As the free world price for gold increased, the Portuguese government made a large profit amounting to at least R40 million a year on the deal and the Frelimo government was reputed to have netted R150 million in 1975. The two-tier price of gold ended in 1977 and with it the gold 'premium' which had been so lucrative for Mozambique.[37]

Table 18.2. MOZAMBICANS EMPLOYED BY W.N.L.A., 1920–39
(average for year)

	Mozambicans	Mozambicans as % of total
1920	96,188	55.60
1921	88,510	47.08
1922	80.959	44.24
1923	90,728	46.29
1924	87,321	43.88
1925	92,122	47.98
1926	96,506	47.54
1927	107,672	50.08
1928	106,031	49.78
1929	96,657	47.15
1930	82,384	37.11
1931	73,924	32.71
1932	58,483	25.10
1933	55,403	22.34
1934	65,622	24.67
1935	78,773	27.07
1936	88,499	27.83
1937	90,900	30.30
1938	87,771	27.09
1939	84,335	26.11

Source: Sheila van der Horst, *Native Labour in South Africa*, pp. 216–17.

Although a maximum recruitment level of 80,000 a year had been agreed in the 1928 Convention, no one had envisaged any need for a minimum level. However, during the early 1930s the level of activity in the mining industry fell and by 1932 the number of Mozambicans employed on the Rand, which had officially been over 90,000 in 1928, was only 59,000. In 1934, therefore, it was agreed that a minimum of 65,000 would be recruited each year.[38] In 1937 the mines, now expanding and urgently needing more labour, were once more permitted to recruit from areas north of the 22° parallel, supposedly following improvements in preventive medicine, and in 1940 the ceiling on recruitment was again lifted to 100,000 per annum and drifted higher as workers already in South Africa were allowed to recontract (see Table 18.2).[39]

Although WNLA was a smooth-running and professional organisation, the truth had long been apparent that it was in fact steadily losing its grip on migrant labour. Clandestine emigration from the Sul do Save as well as from other regions had existed since the beginning of the century and been connived at by the South African as well as by the Rhodesian authorities. Clandestine emigration allowed the African miner an element of choice as to where and for how long he worked, and of course enabled him to evade the deferred pay arrangements. In 1967 it was estimated that although only 80,000 Mozambicans were working on official contracts in South African mines, there were altogether 300,000 workers in South Africa and a further 150,000 in Rhodesia.[40]

WNLA's monopoly of recruitment in the Sul do Save was ended in 1965 when the colonial administration licensed three other recruiting agencies to recruit for agricultural work and for mines not affiliated to the South African Chamber of Mines. These three together were responsible for recruiting between 12 and 25 per cent of the Mozambican workers employed in South Africa.[41]

Migrant labour from independent Mozambique

In general the mutual interest that had tied Mozambique and South Africa to each other since the opening of the first mines waned in the 1970s. The removal of controls on the price of gold altered the whole economic basis of the gold-mining industry the profits of which now enabled it to mechanise to a greater extent and to pay wages high enough to attract the local workforce. The proportion of workers recruited inside South Africa rose perceptibly from a mere 28 per cent in 1970 to 63 per cent by 1979. This rather dramatic shift in the recruitment policy of the mines was triggered by the embargo Malawi imposed on all recruitment in 1974, the year of the Portuguese revolution. This move made the South African mines suddenly heavily dependent on Mozambique for labour and in 1975 a record 113,000 Mozambicans were recruited. By this time the mines were becoming alarmed lest the rhetoric of the new Frelimo government might lead to an end to recruitment as sudden as that of Malawi, and in 1976 the mines began a policy of not re-employing Mozambicans once their contracts were ended. The mines had already adopted contingency plans when Frelimo closed seventeen of the twenty-one WNLA recruiting stations in Mozambique. In 1976 and 1977, recruitment fell to 32,648 and 36,447, the lowest levels since records began. The old Transvaal-Mozambique alliance changed in other ways too. In 1969 the provisions guaranteeing traffic to Lourenço Marques, which had been scaled down from 55 to 40 per cent by 1964, were abandoned altogether. In 1976–7 South Africa brought into use two new ports, at Richards Bay and Saldanha Bay, capable of handling bulk cargoes, thus cutting still further the country's dependence on Delagoa Bay.[42]

Although these were pre-eminently economic developments, there was a political background. Independent Mozambique was in no position to give up its earnings from migrant labour and port traffic, yet is clearly resented its dependence on South Africa and talked openly of policies that would make its economy more autonomous. In the past the Portuguese authorities had been able to use considerable leverage in their dealings with South Africa, as the events of the 1920s showed; there was a clear relationship of mutual need. In the 1970s the balance of advantage swung heavily the other way. South Africa now actively sought to make itself more self-reliant and this meant loosening some of the close economic ties with its neighbour. As a result independent Mozambique found that its port, railway and labour services were no longer urgently required and could, if politics so dictated, be dispensed with.

Annual recruitment of labour from Mozambique remained below 38,000 till 1984 when the signing of the Nkomati Accord was followed by both the South African and Mozambique governments trying to revive migrant labour. Mozambique wanted the quota raised to 120,000 and agreed to remove restrictions on recruitment. In 1984 these moves were backed by the South African government and the number of Mozambicans recruited rose briefly in 1985 to 52,410. In 1986 the South African government switched tack and threatened to expel all foreign workers. As a compromise new recruitment was banned and only those recontracting were allowed to enter South Africa. As a result recruitment fell back somewhat to 44,015 in 1989, by which time Renamo banditry was disastrously dislocating the Mozambique economy.[43]

The experience of mine labour

From 1901 WNLA established a network of receiving stations and depots throughout the Sul do Save region. In 1914 there were 75 recruiting stations employing 200 'runners' who went out into the villages.[44] Recruits wishing to go to the mines would present themselves at a receiving station where there would be a preliminary assessment to see if they were able-bodied and of the right age. They would then be sent to the depots. Those from the northern districts would travel by steamer from Inhambane or Xai Xai to Lourenço Marques and from there they would be taken by rail to Witbank and the Rand. As the labour requirements of the mines fluctuated from year to year, the WNLA's recruiting officers used a number of devices to restrict or expand the number of miners signing on. The easiest regulating device was the medical examination, the standards of physical fitness being relaxed when there was a need to increase recruitment. At other times WNLA would hold *batuques* (parties) in villages or hand out soap or bags of salt as inducements.[45]

The novice going to the mines had little choice and was easily exploited by the system. More experienced miners returning for renewed contracts had some measure of choice and knew which mines to avoid. As early as 1911, when an inquiry was held into WNLA's operations in Mozambique, less than 10 per cent of recruits were first-timers and this remained a fairly constant figure (in the last ten years of colonial rule an average of 12 per cent of annual recruits were novices).[46] One way of exercising choice was to avoid recruitment by WNLA and to travel on a pass issued by the authorities in Lourenço Marques, or to go overland and enter South Africa secretly over some section of its land frontier. Another way was to take advantage of the special category status whereby WNLA allowed experienced miners and their 'brothers' to return to a mine where they had worked before.[47] In the 1960s and 1970s the mines issued 'bonus cards' recording the employment details of individual miners and these gave preferential treatment to those seeking re-employment at the same mines.[48] After independence in 1975 recruitment was scaled down and for a time was restricted only to those holding 'bonus cards'.

In general, however, the system operated to make sure that all mines, good and bad, received their supplies of labour, and from the mine-owners' point of view the great advantage of the Conventions with Mozambique and the monopoly of recruiting these bestowed on WNLA was the ability to direct labour to where it was needed. The coal mines, for example, were always unpopular and as late as 1925 between 80 and 90 per cent of their labour force was recruited by WNLA from Mozambique.[49] Some mines acquired an evil reputation for accidents, and even after the ending of 'tropical recruitment' annual mortality remained high. Between 1921 and 1930, for example, an average of 1,400 miners died of disease every year and a further 200 from accidents.[50] Pneumonia was the main cause of death, followed by tuberculosis and meningitis.

Throughout the century the standard length of a contract was officially twelve months with a possibility of six months' renewal. Most miners tended to serve the additional period, but a significant group managed to renew their contracts again and again, remaining on the Rand for six years or more. Official Portuguese statistics indicate that in the twelve months between July 1913 and June 1914 12 per cent went home after a year, 73 per cent served one renewal but 6.4 per cent served up to three years, 4 per cent more than three and 1.7 per cent more than six years. In 1930 15.8 per cent were serving up to three years and 2.3 per cent more than six years.[51] From their surveys of the migrant miners in the 1970s, Ruth First and her team showed that they had spent on average 42 per cent of their working lives on the mines and by the age of sixty this might have covered up to fourteen separate contracts.[52]

Migrant labour became a factor of central importance in the life of the African peasantry of the Sul do Save. It affected almost every family and cumulatively had a profound effect on the community. In the 1940s between 26 and 31 per cent of the active male population of Inhambane province were away on migrant labour at any one time, and in earlier periods the figure had been even higher. Clearly it deprived the peasant economy of a significant proportion of its labour force which, in theory or least, might have been employed to raise levels of subsistence and produce cash crops for the market. However, mine labour developed in a context where the colonial state was also concerned to profit from the labour of the peasantry. Under the terms of the 1899 labour legislation, and in the codes published in 1911 and 1928, Africans had to seek wage labour for a proportion of the year and in addition were liable for *chibalo* or forced labour on government projects. The wages paid by the state and by private Mozambican employers were significantly below those paid in the mines. The existence of mine labour, of course, had the effect of prolonging the systems of forced labour employed by the state. Because the local economy could not pay wages comparable to the mines, and therefore could not compete for labour in a free market, so it had to resort to various methods of compulsion. Migration to the mines, therefore, was not so much a consequence of *chibalo* as a cause of it.[53] Moreover, when compulsory crop-growing was introduced after about 1935, mine wages were essential for some families to buy the food they were no longer able to grow for themselves. Mine labour was thus a relatively highly paid source of employment and in the course of the century the peasant economy of the Sul do Save came to depend on miners' remittances.

Mine earnings operated in two ways. First they were a means of survival for peasant families in hard times. Mine labour enabled taxes to be paid, years of drought to be endured, crop failures to be ameliorated. They were what kept poorer peasants afloat through the hardest of times. For others it was a way of accumulating capital with which to rent land or purchase cattle, ploughs, cashew trees and ultimately even tractors. Samora Machel's father provides an example of this process. He went to the mines for the first time in 1912 and up till 1926 served several contracts. In 1917 he married and in 1921 bought an ox plough. Eventually he acquired enough capital to build up a herd of several hundred head of cattle and to work 30 hectares of land. The considerable growth in peasant production in the last colonial years was only possible because of this investment in ploughs and cattle. The deferred payment regulations had the effect desired by the government and stimulated consumption within Mozambique itself, so that mine wages were the mainstay of the commercial economy of the villages right up till independence. The full importance of the mine earnings was only appreciated when South Africa cut down and eventually stopped recruitment after 1975, precipitating a disastrous depression in the economy of southern Mozambique.[54]

On the other hand it can be argued that the siphoning off of so much agricultural labour led to the very low peasant agricultural output in the Sul do Save, Inhambane in the late colonial period having the lowest levels of production of both peasant and settler agriculture. Once compulsory crop-growing was abandoned in the 1960s there was a marked growth of other less labour-intensive forms of cash cropping like the production of coconut and cashew, and in the last years of colonial rule there was a considerable increase in peasant prosperity. The 1960s not only saw a growth of peasant cash cropping but also a decline in the numbers departing for the mines. This in turn was related to higher wage-levels in the South African mines so that declining numbers of recruits did not lead to a decline in income from the mines. At the time of independence, income from cash cropping was fast overhauling income from mine labour as the main source of peasant cash. In 1967 in Inhambane province mine earnings had been three times as much as crop earnings; in 1974 they were less than twice as much.[55] It is ironic that the development of peasant-based cash cropping in the nineteenth century had been cut short by the imposition of the colonial plantation and forced labour system. When, in the 1960s, conditions in the colonial economy at last favoured the peasant again, this development was to be cut short by the Frelimo state concentrating all investment in collective farms at the expense of the peasant farmer.

Over a hundred years of emigration to the mines certainly worked major social changes not least in the structure of the family, the monetarisation of the economy and the growth of a relatively prosperous 'middle peasantry'. Mine earnings had formed part of *lobola* payments even before colonial rule was established in the Sul do Save, and it seems that in the twentieth century they were one of the causes of the steady inflation of *lobola* and of the entire replacement of traditional transactions by money payments.[56] Many miners also acquired a taste for consumer goods or joined independent churches of which they established branches in Mozambique. However, in general migrant labour has generally been considered a conservative force. Migrants tend to seek money to maintain or improve their status within a traditional society, and are often more concerned with preserving the traditional hierarchies and structures than those who stay behind. It seems that the miners of the Sul do Save did not become involved in radical or nationalist politics to any significant extent and that Frelimo did not find particularly fertile ground in this region.

The Southern Rhodesian connection

While the people of the Sul do Save migrated to South Africa and so locked the development of their part of Mozambique firmly into the industrial complex of the Rand, the people of Tete district were beginning a similar relationship with Southern Rhodesia.

Tete had been formed into a separate District after the administration of Barue had been taken over by the government in 1902, and by 1910 it had become something of an island surrounded by developing capitalist economies. In Nyasaland the British authorities had tried to promote plantation agriculture by making huge land grants to companies and planters who experimented with cotton and tobacco. On the lower Zambesi the *prazo* companies were producing sugar, sisal and copra. The Moçambique Company had leased out sugar concessions and was recruiting for its mines and public works. Mining had begun in both Northern and Southern Rhodesia and the white farmers of Southern Rhodesia were producing tobacco, maize and cattle. All these enterprises were seeking large numbers of workers and were aware that they would have to compete with various other major consumers of labour — the colonial governments, the São Tomé cocoa planters, the Benguela railway and the giant capitalist enterprises of the Rand.

The *prazo* laws of 1890 had divided most of Tete district into *prazos* of which the majority were leased to the Zambesia Company — which also owned a number of plantations on the lower river. Before 1902 most of the area had been subleased to various individuals, often connected with the old *prazo* élites, who collected tax from the peasants and recruited labour for various clients. These sub-contractors operated with bands of armed *cipais* and their exploitation of their concessions was more or less a continuation of the traditional forms of Zambesian armed extortion. Gradually the sub-contractors were replaced by agents of the companies and the recruitment of labour for work on the lower Zambesi plantations became more systematic. Meanwhile a different regime had been established in the area round Tete and in Barue south of the River. Here direct rule by the Mozambique government had opened the way for the collection of head tax and the recruitment of labour for government purposes, as well as for the export of labour under government license. This posed a threat alike to the peasantry of the district, who regularly moved informally into Rhodesia for seasonal work, and to the Rhodesian farmers who valued their access to clandestine supplies of migrant labour.

The Rhodesian government had strongly objected to the 1901 *Modus Vivendi* since it wanted access to migrant labour from Mozambique, and eventually WNLA had agreed to allow a proportion of the labour it recruited to be employed in Rhodesia. However, this was not seen as satisfactory by the Rhodesians and in 1906 the Rhodesian Native Labour Bureau (RNLB) was formally established to recruit labour for the Southern Rhodesian mines. At an early stage this form of labour acquired an evil reputation, and Africans seeking work in the south were usually anxious to avoid falling into the hands of RNLB agents. Working for Rhodesian farmers thus became a way of moving south by stages and avoiding the clutches both of the RNLB and the WNLA.[57] Tete Africans entering Rhodesia took out work passes from the nearest Native Commissioner, and if they wished to remain in Rhodesia all they had to do was go to the Native Commissioner and announce their wish to stay, whereupon they would be certified as 'indigenous natives'.

By the second decade of the century, considerable numbers of Africans from Tete crossed into Rhodesia either for seasonal work, or to set up villages for the temporary production of crops, or as a stage on their way south. The Mozambique authorities were concerned at this situation and wanted to establish a more regular and productive tax regime and more formal control over labour. Above all they wanted to prevent clandestine emigration, and if possible regain some of the population that had already permanently migrated south. Formal recruiting agreements with repatriation clauses were seen by the Portuguese as the way of combating clandestine migration, and since compulsory repatriation was being demanded of the Portuguese planters themselves by the British in the increasingly bitter disputes over 'slavery' in São Tomé, it seemed appropriate to propose this solution to the British authorities in Central Africa.

The Rhodesian authorities believed that the RNLB was losing out in the uncontrolled scramble for labour taking place in Mozambique. Agents of the Rand mines, of the lower Zambesi planters and increasingly also of the São Tomé cocoa barons received preferential treatment from the Mozambique authorities and offered incentives to Africans which the RNLB felt it could not match in the absence of any formal presence in the country. The Rhodesian government knew that although the *prazos* were closed to outsiders the Mozambique government was prepared to allow foreign recruitment officially within the areas it directly administered, and this encouraged it to approach the Portuguese for a formal agreement to cover recruitment in Tete district.

Negotiations began in 1912. The Portuguese government wanted to strengthen its administration in the area and saw a formal agreement as a way of reasserting control over the population. For this reason it insisted on compulsory repatriation and deferred pay clauses. Repatriation was to be made retrospective and enforced on all who had crossed the frontier since 1903, although eventually the term 'compulsory' was cut out of the wording of the agreement that came into force. The Rhodesians were to be able to recruit annually up to 15,000 labourers whose affairs would be supervised by a *curador* in Salisbury. The so-called Tete Agreement was eventually signed in August 1913, the same year the Rand mines officially ceased recruiting 'tropical' Africans and WNLA abandoned its formal recruiting activities in the district.[58]

For both signatories the Tete Agreement was a disappointment. Although the recruitment of 15,000 labourers a year was envisaged, the RNLB was scarcely ever able to recruit even one-tenth of that number and Rhodesian employers continued to rely on, and actively encourage, the independent 'clandestine' migrant. As a means of controlling the Mozambican population the Agreement also failed. It only covered Tete district and the *curador* in Salisbury had no jurisdiction over Africans from other parts of Mozambique. Moreover, in practice he was dependent on the Rhodesian Native Commissioners to collect the annual passport fee and, if the experience of the Native Commissioner of Darwin is typical, the immediate effect of the Agreement was to dry up completely the numbers of Africans coming forward to seek passes. No doubt rumours of compulsory repatriation and deferred pay circulated swiftly.[59]

However, in 1917, before any new assessment of the situation could be made, the Barue rebellion broke out. During the fighting much of Tete district was overrun by rebel bands and by the raiding parties of Nguni recruited by the Portuguese to suppress the rebellion. Although Portuguese control was re-established in most areas by the middle of 1918, guerrilla activity continued in some remote areas as late as 1920. The rising was to be significant for the development of Tete district for a number of reasons. First, it gave a huge impetus to population movement as large numbers of people fled across the borders to safety. The frontier areas of Southern Rhodesia were inundated with refugees who were eagerly absorbed into the Rhodesian economy as cheap labour. Moreover the rebellion gave the Rhodesian authorities good reasons not to operate the clause of the Tete Agreement which had required repatriation. They declared that they would not repatriate people who had fled for political reasons, a category that could be expanded to cover any clandestine migrant. Finally it led to semi-official measures by the Nyasaland and Rhodesian authorities to assist and protect migrant workers passing through Tete district.

Patterns of labour migration through Tete district, 1920–50

The development of African migration from Tete district cannot be separated from the migration of Africans from Nyasaland, partly because Nyasalanders had to pass through Mozambique on their way south, but also because there was a deliberate attempt by all migrants to hide their identity as a way of evading official controls.

The African population of Nyasaland had been highly mobile even before the establishment of colonial rule but this mobility increased rapidly after 1890. In parts of Nyasaland the African population was pressurised into virtual serfdom under the *thangata* labour system; rates of taxation were high and there was recruitment of forced labour for road building, carrier service and the police. Like Tete District, Nyasaland was strongly affected by the powerful capitalist economies of the south where the lure of high wages and consumer goods was an undoubted attraction for men, many of whom were anyway somewhat marginalised in the traditional matrilineal societies.

The Rand was the favoured destination of Nyasalanders. Although some tried to reach South Africa in a single journey, it became increasingly common for them to move south by stages. For many the first stop was to seek employment in Mozambique. Conditions often seemed better in Portuguese territory where rates of taxation were actually lower and the possibility of evading forced labour greater. The lower Zambesi plantations, like those of Sena Sugar, were already a favoured stop-over location when the legislation of the South African government intervened to make staged migration almost a necessity. The regulation of 1913 which prevented WNLA recruiting 'tropical' Africans hit particularly at recruitment in Nyasaland. It provided the African population with yet one more colonial regulation which had to be evaded. The First World War and the Barue rebellion then intervened, but once these were past and movement again became relatively secure, a regular pattern of migration developed. Nyasalanders would enter Mozambique to work for Sena Sugar or on the Trans-Zambezia railway. After a season or two they would work their way south to a point where they could cross the border into South Africa or be formally recruited by the WNLA. The process was described by the Native Commissioner in Umtali:

> Nyasaland Natives come over in considerable numbers to work on the Sugar Estates on the Zambesi. They work there for some time when they proceed further in and obtain work when they want food

and a rest. Apparently Nyasaland Natives can travel throughout Portuguese territory on their Nyasaland Passes. The Portuguese authorities do not require them to take out Portuguese passes. The Nyasa natives collect in gangs at or near Amatongas, and from there they proceed to the Transvaal. . . . They cut in and out of this territory until they reach the Sabi. . . . From there they travel in Portuguese Territory crossing the Limpopo at or near Chiqualquala. On the Transvaal border they are met by labour touts, who I have no doubt inform the natives what is required of them. I am told all passes are destroyed before going over. This no doubt is done to evade the 22 degrees south latitude rule.[60]

In the process of moving south many Nyasalanders would change their identity and pose as natives of Mozambique, thus evading not only the ban on the recruitment of 'tropicals' but also tax obligations and other irksome restrictions of the colonial government.[61] This southward movement of Nyasalanders using Mozambique as a staging post caused a variety of problems for the colonial administrations. In 1916 it had been reported that the Portuguese were instituting medical checks, trying to impose a charge of 2 shillings on all Africans in transit and demanding a license for all *capitâes* in charge.[62] Migrants were often attacked and robbed on the road or press-ganged by Portuguese *cipais* looking for forced labour. Nyasalanders, for their part, were accused of spreading propaganda as they went and of encouraging the local Tete population to emigrate. 'It is natural', Francisco de Melo Costa wrote in 1938, 'that on their way they should spread propaganda, getting Portuguese natives to accompany them and to emigrate secretly', and he advised that 'the ferries crossing the Zambesi should be inspected to make sure that only bona fide British Africans should cross'.[63]

Although the ultimate destination of the Nyasalanders may have been the Rand, the Rhodesian farmers and mine-owners were anxious to intercept as many of them as possible. Between 1913 and 1922 the proportion of 'indigenous' farm workers employed on Rhodesian farms fell from an estimated 71 per cent to 34 per cent of the total employed, and migrants from Nyasaland and Tete were urgently required to make up the difference.[64] To give protection and some assistance to migrants the Rhodesian authorities started to provide food depots and lorries which met travellers on the road and transported them safely to the borders and the clutches of the waiting employers. During the 1930s increasingly large numbers of the Tete population took advantage of the lorries to pose as Nyasalanders and cross the border to seek work. The mass evasion of colonial regulations and the constant changes of identity that Africans resorted to made this clandestine migration difficult to monitor and almost impossible to control.

During the 1920s the plantation economy of Mozambique enjoyed boom conditions. Sugar production increased substantially and Tete district became a major recruitment ground for plantation workers. *Prazo* Angonia, for example, was leased by Sena Sugar, which annually recruited thousands of workers for its plantations.[65] Other major demands on labour were railway construction and later the building of the Zambesi bridge which required a workforce of 20,000 men. These works between them lasted till 1935. The pressures on a Tete population disrupted and depleted by war and rebellion were considerable. The Portuguese government still insisted on its right to demand *chibalo* labour and to recruit for the colonial police and military.[66] In the areas of the *prazo* concessions the government was in direct competition with the *prazo* companies. Many Africans who lived near British territory used to escape into the hills or across the borders when it was known that the colonial authorities were recruiting; they planned to return to their villages later. According to J.C. Abrahams, 'at certain seasons, many Portuguese natives do come across into our country but this is to avoid compulsory recruitment for military service at Mocambique — *not* to avoid work on the Sena Sugar Plantations.'[67] To counter this tactic the Portuguese colonial police kept their recruiting activities secret and mounted what amounted to full-scale raids on the villages to obtain their recruits. They also pursued fugitives into British territory or kidnapped their wives or families and held them hostage for the return of the men. In April 1925 the Rhodesian authorities were receiving reports that recruitment of forced labour with all its attendant abuses threatened to lead to another insurrection.

The 1920s, therefore, saw the forced labour system pushed to greater lengths than ever before, providing the African peasant with further incentives to migrate — migration being the most effective way of resisting the grasping tentacles of the colonial bureaucracy.

Revisions of the Tete Agreement

It is in the light of the quickening pace of emigration that the revisions of the Tete Agreement have to be seen. The Agreement first came up for renewal in 1919. The Portuguese still wanted their *curador* in Salisbury to have the right to register and issue passes to all Portuguese Africans, not just those from Tete district, and they pressed for repatriation to include the refugees from the rebellion. The Rhodesians would grant neither of these, and the Agreement was renewed for one year only. However, the main concern of the

Portuguese was to tighten their administrative control over the African population, and in 1920 they eventually won a concession from the Rhodesians that free passports would be issued to all Africans from Portuguese territory other than Tete district where passport fees would still be charged. On these terms the agreement was renewed for five years. Since the Nyasaland government was also issuing free passes in order to keep some administrative control over emigration, this was a standardisation of practice throughout the region.

The Agreement as it operated in 1920–5 identified three categories of Tete African in Rhodesia: those recruited by the RNLB who paid no tax but were due for repatriation and deferred pay; new arrivals not recruited by RNLB who paid a £1 passport fee; and domiciled Africans, who paid an annual passport 'renewal' of £1, half of which was retained by the Rhodesians.[58] In the early 1920s the numbers wishing to cross the borders into Rhodesia strained the working of the Tete Agreement to breaking-point. In 1923 the acting Native Commissioner in Darwin reported:

> Whilst I was on patrol 105 adult males asked for permission to settle and pay tax. The (proportionately) enormous number of women and children in some of the kraals is a clear indication that the transfer has in fact taken place, although the husband and father takes care to evade capture.[69]

He suggested that these illegal immigrants should be allowed to settle but should pay an annual passport fee equivalent to the tax they would have paid in Tete, and the Portuguese *curador* eventually accepted this idea. Settlement across the frontier now continued on a legal basis and early in 1924 the British South Africa Police reported 'thousands of alien natives entering the territory to seek work'.[70] Not surprisingly, when the Agreement came up for renewal again in 1925, it was decided to end all charging for passports but instead to collect tax from Portuguese Africans domiciled in Rhodesia, a proportion of which would then be paid to the Portuguese authorities.[71] The Agreement was renewed once again in 1934 after the demise of the RNLB when the Portuguese were guaranteed that the amount paid to them would not fall below a 'floor' of £4,500.

This completed the change in the whole nature of the Tete Agreement from the Portuguese point of view. Originally it had been seen as a way of controlling clandestine emigration; Africans would have to get passes to migrate whereas those without passes would be repatriated and face punishment. Gradually this had been changed, first to a system where everyone was issued with a passport for which payment had to be made, and then to one where only free passports were issued and instead taxes were collected by the Rhodesians. The

Agreement no longer even purported to control migration and had become a purely fiscal measure whereby Tete district's revenues were subsidised with an annual payment in return for allowing emigration to continue unchecked. The Rhodesian authorities were happy with a system that guaranteed their supply of cheap labour, but the chief beneficiaries were Africans whose evasion of colonial regulations had triumphed. The colonial authorities had been forced by their over-riding desire to register and tax their inhabitants to concede almost complete freedom of movement. Tete district had become simply a labour reserve of Southern Rhodesia.

Emigration to Southern Rhodesia in the 1930s and 1940s

During the 1920s the pattern of migration had fully established itself. Intense labour recruitment by the state and the plantation companies had led to the press-gang and various severe abuses. The population, particularly of the border areas, had responded by fleeing as indivi-duals or as whole families into Rhodesia and Nyasaland, often pur-sued by the Portuguese police. The revisions of the Tete Agreement now meant that the Rhodesian authorities did not attempt to repatriate these 'clandestine immigrants' but merely collected taxes from them. At the same time lorries and launches were being orga-nised to help the flow of Nyasaland migrants, and their passage through Tete district attracted yet more Africans from Portuguese ter-ritory to make the journey south.

In 1928 the new Portuguese labour code abolished forced labour, except for work on government projects, and it was replaced by inten-sified methods of recruitment and by compulsory crop-growing. Tete District, however, was not formally included in the areas of the cotton-growing concessions since geographical conditions were unsuitable. Instead it became the target for recruiting campaigns by licensed agents. As well as the lower Zambesi plantations, which remained hungry for labour, the biggest demands came from the Zambesi bridge project and from the Moatize coalfields north of the river which had begun production in a small way in the 1920s and whose output was steadily rising throughout the 1930s. In Southern Rhodesia labour recruited by the RNLB continued to decline as a percentage of the labour force and in 1934 the Bureau itself was closed. The Rhodesian economy also came to rely increasingly on voluntary migrant labour.

The statistics in Tables 18.3, 18.4 and 18.5, incomplete as they cer-tainly are, show clearly that there was a huge increase in the numbers of Mozambicans entering and residing in Southern Rhodesia during the 1930s. Numbers officially resident rose in the decade from just over 13,000 to 68,000. Although the numbers working in the Rhodesian mines more than doubled (Table 18.3), the main part of the increase was absorbed by agriculture, the frontier districts in particular obtaining the main benefit from the clandestine migration (Table 18.4).

At first sight it may seem paradoxical that this great increase in emigration occurred during a decade when forced labour in Mozambique showed a marked decline. However, both the increase in emigration and the abandonment of forced labour has to be seen against a background of the great depression and the collapse of commodity prices. Wages were forced steadily down and the freedom to contract one's labour voluntarily was a freedom to be exercised in a world of shrinking economic opportunities. Moreover once the RNLB had been abolished and there was no danger of their being handed over to RNLB agents, Mozambican migrants showed a greater willingness to register themselves. The effect was to inject masses of cheap unskilled labour into the Southern Rhodesian economy and to cushion the economic position of the white settler enterprises.

Although reasonably satisfied with the financial provisions of the agreements with Rhodesia, the Mozambique authorities continued to see clandestine migration as a major problem standing in the way of any long-term economic development of Tete district. By the 1930s the Salazar government was firmly in control in Portugal and was devising new policies for development of the colonies. Initially these entailed widespread reorganisation of the colonial administration. The new labour laws of 1928 were followed in 1930 by the ending of the leases of the *prazo* companies, administrative control of the *prazos* reverting to the colonial government. This was an important development in Tete district which now for the first time came under a single administrative regime. The colonial administration itself was strengthened and reformed and regular visits by the colonial inspectorate began to enforce higher standards of conduct on local officials. The reports of the colonial inspectorate during the 1930s and 1940s focus overwhelmingly on the problem of migration. They show the Portuguese colonial service grappling with a problem beyond its powers to control but forcing it to a greater degree of self-knowledge and self-analysis.

Underlying the whole problem were deep-rooted administrative failures. The new labour laws had determined that all males aged over eighteen resident in the colony should be obliged to have a *cadernete de identificação e de trabalho*, a sort of pass. *Cadernetes* were in the African's interest, it was claimed, because if he possessed one and was injured in the mines, he could receive compensation. In practice they were only issued where there were official recruiting offices

Table 18.3. MIGRATION FROM PORTUGUESE AFRICA
TO SOUTHERN RHODESIA, 1929–45

	Entering SR	Leaving SR	Estimated total in SR
1929	4,711	1,747	13,145
1930	5,120	2,019	16,169
1931	4,125	2,234	17,975
1932	4,597	2,138	20,370
1933	6,062	3,911	22,447
1934	6,333	2,635	26,068
1935	10,286	3,541	32,730
1936	11,331	11,337	32,577
1937	16,940	7,437	41,930
1938	10,749	2,507	49,976
1939	12,895	5,845	56,867
1940	11,437	5,764	68,304
1941	12,858	3,613	75,247
1942	9,431	4,199	80,858
1943	8,993	3,274	85,601
1944	15,495	3,563	97,740
1945	10,292	3,829	104,289

Source: Sousa Ribeiro (ed.), *Anuário de Moçambique*, p. 315; *Anuário Estatístico Ano de 1946*.

Note: These are official figures compiled by the *Curadoria* in Salisbury which in turn depended on returns by Rhodesian Native Commissioners; they almost certainly underrepresent the numbers. Almost all these workers were thought to have come from Tete District.

Table 18.4. MOZAMBICAN MIGRANTS WORKING
IN RHODESIAN MINES

	Numbers working in mines	% of total migrants
1931	4,010	22.30
1938	9,868	19.74
1939	10,833	19.04
1940	11,277	16.51
1941	11,706	15.55
1942	11,130	13.76
1943	11,219	13.10
1944	11,746	12.01
1945	11,022	10.56

Source: Anuário Estatistico Ano de 1946.

Table 18.5. MOZAMBICANS AS A PROPORTION OF
THE RHODESIAN LABOUR FORCE (%)

Districts	1931	1936	1941	1946
Hartley	9.9	10.8	15.1	17.9
Lomagundi	11.5	14.6	23.6	29.5
Makoni	17.7	25.7	28.9	30.5
Marandellas	10.8	14.2	14.0	27.1
Mazoe	13.7	16.8	26.7	35.1
Salisbury	6.9	9.8	16.8	24.5
Umtali	21.1	25.4	43.0	51.4
Total	10.5	13.6	20.7	26.6

Source: Richard Hodder-Williams, *White Farmers in Rhodesia, 1890–1965*, p. 166.

and in three *circunscricões* — Zumbo, Maravia and Chicoa — there was no recruitment at all. Evasion was on a massive scale. As one government inspector, Francisco de Melo Costa, observed in a letter to the governor-general:

There is a great number of natives either without documents at all or with insufficient documentation — many with *cadernetes* issued three years ago or more, many no longer residing in the circumscriptions where they were issued — which makes their identification and hence their recruitment very difficult.[72]

One cannot help observing that 'making their identification and hence their recruitment very difficult' was the major objective of the African population itself in its clandestine activities.

The failure of the administration to keep a check on the population was hardly suprising. As Melo Costa observed:

I noticed [while inspecting Chicoa] that the native populations live far removed and divorced from the administrative authorities, not appearing at the secretariats either to pay the tax which is imposed on them by the native authorities, or to call for the intervention of the authorities in the resolution of their *milandos*. I called the attention of the respective authorities to these facts which are evidence of a bad native policy which is greatly to be censured. [. . .] Today the censuses are not taken every year and are carried out along the roads where cars can pass and are made on the move, the census official not seeing more than a part of the population.[73]

Small wonder then that he had earlier recommended that villages be built near the roads where they could benefit from the 'civilising' influence of the census-takers. Finally, Melo Costa concentrated in some detail on the Rhodesian lorry system as a factor in migration. As we have seen, this dated from the mid-1920s and was designed to help Nyasaland Africans cross Tete district in safety. Melo Costa was convinced that not only did Tete Africans join the parties of Nyasalanders but that the Rhodesian lorry operators deliberately recruited Tete workers as part of their operation.

The report of Melo Costa is interesting in that it combines traditional Portuguese interpretations of emigration and the sinister activities of the Rhodesians with an assessment of their own administrative failings that was on the way to becoming realistic and was characteristic of the bureaucratic reformism of the Salazar regime.

After the Second World War

During the Second World War demand for labour in Mozambique soared as the colony was able to take advantage of the rapidly rising prices for tropical products. There was a resurgence of forced recruitment of labour and a coincidental rapid increase in the amount of migration from Tete district. Numbers of Mozambicans resident in Rhodesia rose from 56,867 to 104,289.

This growth in migration kept the subject high on the official agenda. In June 1945 Horténsio de Sousa, district superintendent of Tete, penned a report on the problem of *emigração clandestina*. The issue had arisen again because of the publication of the development plans for the colony and Sousa pointed out that no development plan could even be contemplated with the emigration of labour as it was. The census had shown that adult males aged between eighteen and fifty-five had numbered 68,841 throughout the district but the Rhodesian authorities had estimated there were 69,000 in Rhodesia from Tete district alone: 'The authorities are not lying when they declare that in the land there are only old men, women and children.'[74]

'Why do they emigrate?' he asked.

There is no doubt that the native emigrates because he feels better off in a foreign country than in his own. Because they (the authorities and settlers in the land where he emigrates) treat him better than us? We cannot believe this. In my opinion the problem is essentially an economic one. The native emigrates, above all because his life is easier abroad. His wages are higher. Higher prices are paid for his produce than would be paid in our country. The articles which he likes, and which constitute his *chiquismo* — cloth, clothes and secondhand coats, blankets, coloured shirts, shoes, hats, bicycles, trunks, mirrors and every sort of quincaillerie — he can find abroad at lower prices while in our country he can either not find them at all or finds them at prices which he cannot afford.

In addition women pay no tax abroad and there are leisure activities which attract the men — 'the *casas de chá* [tea houses] and the bars which are scattered throughout the bush and which exist there but not here'.[75]

He recommended that these causes of migration should be remedied, taxes should be brought into line with those in British territories, and taxation of women abolished. The problem of polygamy could be resolved by giving monogamous men tax remission. Better prices should be paid for African produce; duties on goods for African consumption should be lowered; and more entertainment should be provided by 'each *regedoria* establishing a football team'.

Once again there are elements of fantasy in this report, the *casas de chá* spread throughout the bush being on a par with the electric light in the locations as images of the Shangri-La beyond the frontier, in which even the Portuguese officials had come to believe. But there are elements of realism also. Africans did migrate mainly for economic reasons — better wages, lower prices, lower taxes.

In the same year, 1945, the government received a report on clandestine emigration from the *inspector administrativo*, Júlio Augusto Pires. The extent of the problem was illustrated by the fact that 32,009 people had crossed the border post at Changara in 1944 but only 1,479 of these were officially designated Portuguese nationals. The traditional explanation that Africans were emigrating because somehow they were 'lazy' had now been officially abandoned. The reasons were more complex:

> What the black detests, what revolts him and makes him disrespectful and irreverent is the [work] contract. It is work for a determined length of time and direction to this or that form of work. He likes to be free to work when he likes, where he likes and for the wage that suits him. The native does not like impositions. It is for this reasons that he emigrates; for this he frequently deserts the work to which he is contracted and goes abroad; for this he abandons family, lands, village, children and wives and leaves for a foreign country, carried also by a modicum of the spirit of adventure. The black from Angonia does more still. He brings his sons and young brothers to cook for him and other emigrants. When the stay is prolonged and the boy grows to puberty he in his turn becomes an emigrant also.[76]

Throughout his tour of inspection, Pires came across numerous examples of Africans who had worked on the railway or for the *Obras*

Públicas who had not been paid punctually or who had not been paid at all. Largely the shortage of labour was due to bad administration, and bad conduct and the lack of propaganda by employers. He contrasted the situation in Mozambique with that in Nyasaland which had successfully attracted thousands of Mozambican Africans to settle.

Once an African had decided to emigrate, he thought, no propaganda or advice or good treatment could influence him:

> One can cross huge areas and only see women and children. Even when the native has not emigrated, he lives in hiding so that he can consider emigrating. For the greater convenience of the emigrant, recruiters for various employers are not lacking on the other side of the frontier, and the black from Angonia who wants to emigrate to the Transvaal stays in Southern Rhodesia for sufficient time to earn some money, even at the cost of the hardest work and privation. And when he feels ready to undertake the journey to the Rand mines, although he cannot legally leave that territory, he goes to the nearest station of the Transvaal railways and buys a train ticket to his destination.[77]

The Rhodesians encouraged migration not only by providing the '*uleres*' (lorries) but by establishing near the frontier stores where tea, sugar, bread and beer could be obtained cheaply. The Tete Agreement, he said like so many before him, had been set up to control clandestine emigration but had actually promoted it, because the African workers wished to avoid the taxes and travel deductions laid down in the Agreement. Pires' report confirms that the pattern of migration that had grown up early in the century was continuing. Africans were following a well understood staged migration, working a season or two in Rhodesia before going south to the Rand. The reason for this was quite explicit — to evade controls over labour recruitment and so exercise choice, and evade contract labour within Mozambique.

19

THE WAR OF LIBERATION

Portugal opts for war

The war that broke out in September 1964 with a raid on a military base in the north of Mozambique had been clearly signalled from a long time before by both sides. Usually a war is preceded by some kind of contact or negotiation between the combatants but in this case the two sides did not recognise each other's existence. When they communicated at all it was through the world's media, or occasionally through intermediaries. Before its outbreak there had been no discussion or negotiation, although each side had conducted a fierce internal debate before the die was eventually cast.

Before the 1960s Portugal experienced little challenge to its African empire. The rather futile activities of the weak and divided opposition movements seldom referred to colonial issues and, with the lone exception of Henrique Galvão, no responsible or knowledgeable Portuguese had spoken out in opposition to the regime's colonial policies. The sole pressure was perceived as being external. Portugal had joined the United Nations in 1955 and, as a result, the Committee for Decolonisation had begun to take note of Portugal's colonies, brushing aside the semantic device which had named them Overseas Provinces in 1951. However, during the 1950s the main challenge to the empire came not from the UN but from India, which in 1956 stirred up nationalist riots in Goa and whose claim to the three Portuguese enclaves in India was being pressed with some vigour.

The beginnings of decolonisation in Africa were watched by Portugal with some scepticism. Publicly it maintained that this issue was irrelevant since the African colonies were part of the mother-country. Pragmatically Portuguese policy-makers watched, and tried to draw lessons from, the actions of other colonial powers — the French and Americans in Indo-China and Algeria, the British in Kenya and Malaya. The lessons did not unequivocally point one way. The Indo-Chinese nationalists were bound to win because they were fighting Western powers which had no settlers and clearly did not intend to stay indefinitely; in Algeria France had allowed too much power to fall into the hands of the *colons* and was trapped into fighting an urban guerrilla war; in Malaya and Kenya, however, the British had

517

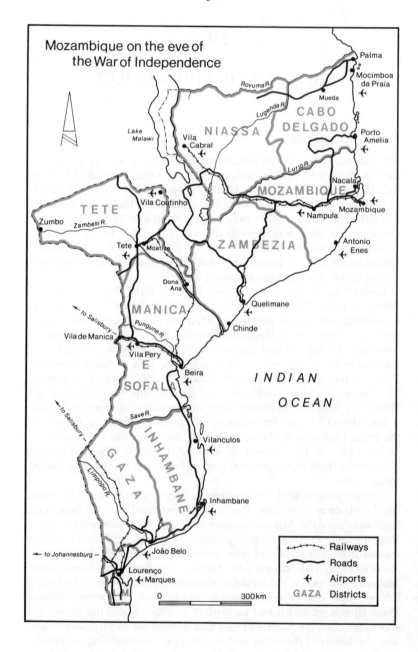

Mozambique on the eve of the War of Independence

Railways
Roads
✈ Airports
GAZA Districts

0 ____ 300km

successfully fought rural insurgency through the device of concentrating the rural population and isolating it from nationalists.

While publicly expressing its belief that insurrection was unlikely in either Angola or Mozambique, the Salazar regime took precautionary measures during the 1950s. PIDE (the state security police) established itself in the colonies in 1956 and began systematically bringing under surveillance people known to be hostile to the regime. Under the influence of Kaulza de Arriaga, a network of airforce bases was created throughout Mozambique, with a number concentrated in the north, and in 1960 Arriaga had 1,000 regular paratroopers stationed there as a mobile task force. Naval facilities were improved in Porto Amelia and military roads were constructed elsewhere in the country. In 1962 plans were even drawn up for a local militia (the OPUDC) in which the white settlers and *civilisados* would serve.[1]

These low-profiled preparations were highly successful. When in February 1961 a violent rural rebellion broke out in Baixa de Cassange in Angola, evidently catching the government by surprise, it was widely thought that similar rural uprisings would take place in Mozambique. However, the country remained quiet. Nor, apart from a few strikes, were there any disturbances among the urban black population — or among disgruntled settlers, as occurred during the Luanda insurrection of 1961. PIDE had done its work, and throughout the war the cities of Mozambique remained almost wholly, indeed quite strangely, quiet.

The principal challenge to the regime during these years in fact came from within the ruling élite of Portugal itself. It was a challenge which for the first time made the colonies an issue in Portuguese domestic politics. The late 1940s had seen a certain amount of political turbulence centred around certain venerable Republican politicians, but the early 1950s had been very quiet with the various factions of Salazar's supporters apparently reconciled. In 1958, however, Salazar decided to replace Craveiro Lopes as president with a more trustworthy member of the armed forces, Américo Tomás. The presidential elections were contested by General Humberto Delgado, who succeeded in forming a united front among all the opponents of the regime; he enlisted the support of monarchists and communists and almost everyone in between. Delgado was a man of great personal energy and charisma and he made the continued rule of Salazar the issue of the election. His campaign achieved widespread popular support and, although he had little to say about colonial issues, he won the electoral contest among the voters in both Mozambique and Angola, highlighting for Salazar the high level of discontent among the white settlers and no doubt helping to convince him that these settlers were not to be trusted.[2]

Delgado's weakness was his lack of support in the military high command and in the Portuguese business community, and after his electoral defeat his attempts to organise traditional Iberian-style *pronunciamentos* failed and in 1959 he fled the country. In 1961, however, a serious threat to the regime emerged in the conspiracy headed by the Defence Minister, Botelho Moniz. Moniz appears to have enlisted the support of the heads of the armed forces and a galaxy of ministers and establishment figures. Early in 1961 revolt broke out in Angola. A settler conspiracy in Luanda coincided with the melodramatic hijacking of the cruise liner *Santa Maria* by Henrique Galvão in January. In February rural insurrection flared up in the Baixa de Cassange. Moniz was on record as having advised Salazar against a military solution to the problems in Africa. American sources even believed that Moniz was thinking of a phased decolonisation. Whatever the truth might have been, African issues were now introduced for the first time into Portuguese domestic politics. The Moniz coup collapsed on 13 April, the conspirators having made no effort to widen the movement to enlist popular backing or even to seek the support of the lower ranks of the armed forces. Further splutterings of opposition occurred for another nine months. In November a hijacked airliner scattered a democratic manifesto over Lisbon; in December India seized the enclaves of Goa, Damão and Diu; and in January 1962 a mutiny in the Beja barracks took on the appearance of yet another failed coup.[3]

Faced with a challenge which had put African issues high on the agenda, Salazar emerged triumphant but with the flag of his regime firmly nailed to the mast of the empire. From then on the regime was in a position where it could not back down or admit of any compromise over African affairs. It prepared both militarilly and ideologically to face a war in Africa and outwardly presented an inflexible face to the world.

The emergence of Frelimo

The Portuguese had tried to insulate Mozambique from the changes happening elsewhere in Africa. A centralised bureaucratic state backed by an increasingly effective security police made sure that the population, white as well as black, was dis-integrated and disorganised within itself. It was helped in this by the low level of literacy and education, and by the lack of trades unions or of any of the forms of African organisation that had given birth to nationalism in other parts of Africa. However, certain aspects of Mozambique's evolution worked the other way. A large part of the population had been affected by migrant labour; there was scarcely an African family in Tete

District, the Sul do Save or the far north without members who had
worked abroad. The more densely populated central belt was the area
from which the mass emigration to Nyasaland had taken place, so that
here too most families had relatives living beyond the frontier in
British territory.

Mozambicans abroad were exposed to all the tides of politics and
modern thought and many of them responded by becoming involved
in the political affairs of their host-country. They agitated in the mines
of the Copper Belt and the Rand, joined political movements or
independent churches, and sought education of a kind they could not
obtain at home. It was the same for those lucky enough to be able to
get to Europe or the United States, where they could enjoy the luxury
of free intellectual discussion, tune in to the latest ideas and become
involved in the latest political movements. The young Eduardo
Mondlane, having been involved in 1948 in founding Nesam, a
radical student organisation in Lourenço Marques, was able to continue his studies in Lisbon. There he met the men who later led the
nationalist movements in Angola and the Cape Verde Islands.[4]

It was abroad that Mozambican nationalism was effectively born.
Again and again PIDE and the authorities snuffed out independent
African organisations inside Mozambique, so that only expatriate
Mozambicans were able to respond to the first wave of decolonisation
in the late 1950s by forming independence movements among their
own countrymen in the neighbouring countries. Only three of these
early movements are now remembered since they were the ones that
came together to form Frelimo: Udenamo, founded in Bulawayo in
1960; Unami, established in Malawi; and Manu, founded among
Makonde emigrants in Kenya and Tanzania. These organisations
were located in specific groups of expatriates who in turn tended to
come from specific areas of Mozambique. Of these movements only
Manu attempted to work inside Mozambique, and it was a crowd of
its supporters who gathered to petition the local Portuguese administrator at Mueda in June 1960. The administrator met the demonstrators by calling out the troops, who shot down large numbers of
demonstrators in a Mozambican version of Sharpeville. This experience showed that the Portuguese were committed to using troops in
civil disturbances and proved the futility of pitting unarmed peasants
in demonstrations against a ruthless regime. Mueda also helped to
politicise the Makonde people and therefore greatly influenced the
way in which Frelimo and its campaign developed.[5]

These early movements achieved little except the mere fact of
existing, but for the first time they allowed a black Mozambican
leadership to emerge and were a forum where the initial ideas about
the future of the country could be tested. But before any of these

movements had developed very far, they were cajoled and bullied by
Kwame Nkrumah of Ghana and Julius Nyerere of Tanzania into
coming together. They were encouraged also by CONCP, the committee formed to co-ordinate the independence movements in the five
Portuguese-ruled territories in Africa whose secretary was the
Mozambican Marcelino dos Santos. As a result, in June 1962,
Frelimo (Frente de Libertação de Moçambique) was formed in Dar
es Salaam. Frelimo was a front of largely expatriate Mozambicans
and, as if to underline this characteristic, it was headed by Eduardo
Mondlane, the most distinguished black Mozambican academic and
an official at the United Nations in New York, but a man who had
lived abroad almost without a break for the previous ten years.[6]
Frelimo's beginnings were not auspicious. Of its first congress, held
in September 1962, Frelimo itself stated officially that it 'defined the
basic role played by unity in the process of national liberation; it
showed that division was the major cause of the weakness of the
historical resistance of our people to colonialism. The First Congress
is the Congress of *unity*.'[7] Resolutions of a fairly general nature were
passed and Mondlane returned to his post in the United States, leaving Frelimo to be run by a black American called Aldridge who had
somehow gained his confidence and who masqueraded as a Mozambican exile.[8] Mondlane's American connections, the fact that his
wife was a white American, and the poor judgement that he frequently
displayed in his choice of confidants were to lead to accusations that
he was unduly influenced by the United States and that Frelimo was
in the pay of, or at least infiltrated by, the US Central Intelligence
Agency (CIA). Mondlane and his supporters quarrelled almost from
the start with other elements in Frelimo and until his murder in 1969
the movement was endlessly torn by strife and divisions.

However, if Mondlane was always a controversial figure, he was in
many ways a powerful leader who helped to turn Frelimo into what
it became after his death, a remarkably cohesive and effective guerrilla
movement. During his leadership crucial issues were faced which
were to have a profound impact on the struggle and on the whole
future of the country. Not surprisingly many of these reflected issues
currently being hotly debated within other black political movements
in southern Africa. Was Frelimo to be an Africanist party, along the
lines of the South African PAC, or was it to embrace people of all
races? Was it to be socially radical, or merely a front to unite all
elements anxious to see the end of Salazarism? Was Mondlane, in
other words, to be Mozambique's General Delgado? Was Frelimo to
commit itself to armed struggle or was it to operate through agitation,
propaganda, public opinion and civil disobedience? What stance was
Frelimo to adopt in wider world issues.[9]

It was not surprising that issues as fundamental as these should have split Frelimo, just as they were to divide the ANC and other political movements. Mondlane's success was not that he avoided conflict and held the movement together with a spurious and unsustainable façade or unity, but that he led the party to make choices that ultimately enabled it to emerge strong, united and successful and which, for the time being at any rate, isolated and marginalised his opponents.

War and internal conflict

When Frelimo was formed there was no agreement among its constituent members that it was about to embark on armed insurrection, and many within the party wanted a political campaign and to avoid armed conflict. Even among those who believed that war was inevitable there were deep divisions over the tactics to be adopted, some wanting an urban insurrection which had proved so formidable in Algeria, others calling for popular rebellion, and only a minority believing that a low-intensity, prolonged guerrilla campaign offered the best chance of success. Nor at this stage was there any clear ideological understanding of the nature of the movement, with opinions ranging from those who saw Frelimo as a broadly-based movement for national independence to those committed to turning it into a movement for social revolution.

The first conflicts within the front occurred when Mondlane returned from the United States to find that Aldridge had dismissed a number of key party workers. Aldridge's influence lasted at least till August 1964, and opposition to the 'Americans' led to some of the old leaders, Gumane and Gwambe among them, leaving Frelimo. By this time the decision had been taken to launch the military campaign. This action was certainly precipitate and was forced on Frelimo by the evident fact that sporadic outbursts of violence and banditry were occurring in Mozambique, to which the Portuguese had responded by declaring a state of emergency.[10] Fearing that, as in Angola, spontaneous insurrection might break out at any time, Frelimo decided to launch its own campaign. This it did on 25 September 1964 by attacking the Portuguese base at Chai in northern Mozambique, at the same time issuing a proclamation and a call to arms. Frelimo began operations with only 250 trained combatants.

The crucial questions over the nature of the campaign were not yet answered and there is evidence that Frelimo at this time was preparing for some kind of major campaign in the south based in the capital. If this was the case, then the PIDE action of December 1964 not only destroyed the possibility of insurrection but resolved the debate within

Frelimo. In December, in a number of sweeps, PIDE arrested some 1,500 Frelimo activists and effectively destroyed the party's organisation in the south. From this time the option of a *putsch* based in the capital had disappeared.[11]

The early uncertainties paralysed and threatened to destroy Frelimo. During the first part of 1965 there were attempts to bring the defecting leaders back into the movement, culminating in a meeting in Lusaka in June when there was a final break and the defectors proceeded to form Coremo, a rival 'front' based in Zambia. Gwambe, its first leader, was soon exposed as a Portuguese agent, but Coremo continued to exist under Gumane throughout the period of the war. Militarily it was active only briefly in 1971, but it remained a potentially alternative focus for nationalist sentiment.[12]

The internal divisions were in part a response to military failure. There is some indication that Frelimo was hoping that early successes in the north would be followed by a mass insurrection.[13] However, an attempt by Frelimo early in 1965 to infiltrate the Zambesian plantations failed, and the fronts which had been announced in Zambesia and Tete had to be abandoned with Hastings Banda taking action to stop Frelimo using Malawi as a supply route.[14] In Lourenço Marques PIDE action led to the banning of Nesam and of the Centro Associativo dos Negros de Moçambique and the arrest of Domingos Arouca, one of the few black Mozambicans with an international profile.[15] The following year PIDE picked up and detained a number of other leading intellectuals including Luis Honwana and the outstanding Mozambican artist Malangatana.[16]

However, in contrast to its failure on the central and southern fronts, Frelimo scored some rapid success in the north. By the end of 1965 much of the Makonde area in the extreme north had become Frelimo-held territory, and Frelimo was acting effectively down the shores of Lake Malawi among the Nyanja-speaking population, at one point briefly threatening the railway town of Novo Freixo.

The successes in the north undoubtedly strengthened the hand of the Makonde and the former Manu leaders within Frelimo. It was the support of the Makonde population, alienated by the Mueda massacre and politicised by the to-and-fro migration across the Tanzanian border, which had allowed Frelimo to keep the Portuguese confined to their bases and to 'liberate' the territory. The Makonde country was won for Frelimo by enlisting the help of traditional chiefs, many of whom were made party 'chairmen' in the areas of their chieftaincies.[17] However, the Makonde leaders showed no interest in social revolution. Many of them, and notably their leader Lazaro Nkavandame, were not radicals but traditionalists who wanted a more vigorous prosecution of the war and a less intensive political campaign. Many of Nkavandame's supporters had become 'chairmen' in the liberated zones and, according to the Frelimo official account, they formed a pressure-group which attempted to take over the party and the running of the war. To try to halt the conflict between the 'chairmen' and the guerrilla fighters, it was decided in October 1966 to end the division of authority between Frelimo's Department of Internal Affairs and the Department of Defence.[18]

The successes of late 1965 were soon reversed. Although the Portuguese had expected a guerrilla war to start after the outbreaks in Angola and Guiné, they were taken somewhat by surprise by the first attacks. Their armed forces in the north were scarcely impressive, and it appears that the northern command only had five aircraft and two patrol boats in operation. In 1966 the Portuguese counter-attacked — encouraged, or so it appears, by the hostile reception Frelimo was receiving from the Yao and Makua, the most Islamised ethnic groups and traditionally hostile to the Makonde. Along Lake Malawi Frelimo's campaign had resulted in widespread disruption and starvation, and it was easy for the Portuguese to drive the guerrillas back.[19] In Cabo Delgado a policy of grouping the population in *aldeamentos* got under way, and some 250,000 people were resettled in 150 villages by 1966.[20] These setbacks settled another argument within Frelimo: it was decided that political 'softening up' would be necessary before they launched offensives in future. In October 1966 Frelimo's commander, Filipe Magaia, was murdered and Samora Machel was appointed in his place. Reorganisation took place and in 1967 an attack was launched on the airbase in Mueda. The Portuguese meanwhile responded with increased patrols on Lake Malawi.

The ineffectiveness of the military campaign increased the ideological and ethnic tensions in Frelimo and was to lead directly to confrontations and virtual 'civil war' in 1968–9. Early in 1968 Frelimo reopened the Tete front, partly to meet Makonde criticisms that the war was being fought almost exclusively in their country, and partly to counter Coremo propaganda in the area. Plans were announced to hold a Second Party Congress inside Mozambique; it was thought this would isolate the Makonde 'chairmen' who believed that if the Congress was held in Tanzania their supporters would dominate it, but it was also thought that holding the congress in liberated territory would be seen as a propaganda victory.[21] In the run-up to the Congress faction fighting intensified. Makonde loyal to Nkavandame raided Frelimo offices in Dar es Salaam in May and killed a party official. In the Mozambique Institute (the secondary school set up by Frelimo in Tanzania) students influenced by the newly-recruited priest, Father Gwenjere, rioted and closed it down. Support for

Gwenjere also came from Mozambican students in the United States. None of this prevented the Congress from being held.

The Second Congress, held inside Mozambique in July 1968, was a triumph for Mondlane. The Central Committee was expanded to include more of the younger radicals who backed the twin concepts of social revolution and a prolonged guerrilla campaign based on politicising the peasantry and establishing co-operatives. The Congress also approved the concept of working with like-minded international movements and adopted the analysis that the war was against class enemies not race enemies. These propositions placed Frelimo ever more clearly at the socialist end of the spectrum of world political opinion.[22] In spite of the undoubted success of the Congress, Frelimo was not able to establish a base for any of its operations within Mozambique, and till the end of the war operated wholly from organisational headquarters outside the country.

Nkavandame, who boycotted the Congress, was now isolated and in a minority. He and his followers met Mondlane at Mtwara in Tanzania in August to try to resolve their differences, and when this failed Nkavandame tried to take over the liberated areas of Cabo Delgado and close the frontiers to loyalist Frelimo, 'using groups of bandits and other lumpen characters who comprised the ''chairmen's'' so-called Frelimo Youth League'.[23] As a result he was stripped of his party posts in January 1969 and defected to the Portuguese. He was later accused of having been involved in planning the assassination of Mondlane in February 1969.

Nkavandame believed that he and his followers were the true representatives of traditional Makonde and Mozambican values and that, with his long history of work within the country, he was a leader whose ideas were more attuned to those of the people than those of the 'American' Mondlane. The struggle between the two was largely personal, but a number of issues of policy came to hinge on the struggle. Nkavandame was socially conservative and opposed the revolutionary stance of Mondlane's followers; he became increasingly an Africanist, and a traditionalist, and even contemplated federal solutions in which a Makonde state would emerge from the destruction of the Portuguese regime. It also appears that Nkavandame, who held important Frelimo posts in the Central Committee and Cabo Delgado province, was involved, with other Makonde chiefs, in financial and commercial corruption and profiteering; he may also have been involved in the assassination of political opponents. After he lost the struggle for power within Frelimo, he became its most outspoken opponent.[24]

At first Nkavandame's defection only stimulated more infighting. Mondlane was murdered with a parcel bomb in February, almost certainly by dissidents in the party with the assistance of PIDE agents.

A struggle for the leadership of Frelimo followed. Uria Simango was the vice-president and should have succeeded Mondlane but the rest of the leadership did not trust him and a Council of Presidency, consisting of Dos Santos, the military commander Machel and Simango himself, was elected. The struggle for power continued throughout 1969. Casal Ribeiro, the Tete provincial secretary, defected, which led to the collapse once again of work in the Tete District, and in November, after issuing a manifesto against his opponents, Simango was expelled from the party and left to join other disappointed leaders in Coremo. Machel was eventually installed as party leader in May 1970.[25]

The propaganda war and the Cabora Bassa dam

Since the second half of 1965 when Frelimo appeared to have made swift advances, the war had ebbed to a very low-intensity affair. Frelimo contented itself with minor ambushes and with mine-laying. This was enough to persuade the Portuguese to keep within their bases and not try much in the way of hot pursuit. Portuguese tactics were mostly political. PIDE infiltrated Frelimo, encouraged the defection of leaders and played on ethnic rivalries. Inside Mozambique successful propaganda kept traditional authorities largely loyal to Portugal's cause, while PIDE prevented any disruption in the towns. Less easy to explain is the failure of Frelimo to win any serious support from the Zambesian plantation workers or, it appears, from migrant mine workers in South Africa.[26] More than one commentator has referred to this phase as being a 'phoney war' in which propaganda was as important as bullets.

Frelimo held on to small areas of the Makonde country and to some of the interior of Niassa district. Although the population of these regions was rather low, at most 200,000, this was enough for Frelimo to embark on a programme of social and economic reconstruction: peasants were grouped 'for protection' into communal villages, production and marketing co-operatives were set up and education and health campaigns were mounted. These developments were important for the evolution of Frelimo as a radical social movement and provided much effective propaganda for outside consumption. However, such developments reached comparatively few of the Mozambique population, and it appears that a number of Frelimo's model co-operative communities which were shown to the foreign press were actually located in Tanzania![27]

The Portuguese countered with their own version of a 'hearts and minds campaign'. Important changes to key colonial legislation had taken place before the outbreak of fighting. The old distinction

between *indígena* and *não-indígena* was removed with the repeal of the
1954 Native Code and legal equality was established; forced labour
and forced cotton-growing were officially and publicly prohibited
when a new labour code was introduced in 1962; and in the Interim
and Third Development Plans which ran from 1965, social expenditure was stepped up with greatly increased budgets for education
and health provision, mobile health units being operated by the army.
In the zones threatened with Frelimo infiltration, fortified villages
(*aldeamentos*) were established, and to cultivate religious support
money was spent on building churches and mosques. Parallel to this
was the policy of bringing in large numbers of white settlers: during
the decade of the war the white settler population doubled.[28]

International propaganda concentrated on maintaining the backing
of NATO and on building a strong local alliance with Rhodesia and
South Africa. By the end of the 1960s joint defence operations with
the Rhodesians were a regular feature of the anti-guerrilla campaign.[29] Both sides enlisted academics and politicians in the West to
argue their case, and the battle for Mozambique was sometimes
fiercer in the Western media than on the ground. Journalists loyal to
Frelimo would be taken inside the liberated areas while those disposed
to support the Portuguese would be taken on tours to show that the
country was still firmly in Portuguese control. Gradually, however,
the propaganda battle came to focus on one key issue — the giant
Cabora Bassa dam.

That one of the world's greatest civil engineering projects should
have been undertaken in the dying days of colonialism in one of the
remotest and most backward regions of Africa is an astonishing aspect
of Mozambican, indeed of African history. The Cabora Bassa rapids
on the Zambesi had already played their part in forming European
perceptions of Africa. Livingstone, on his descent of the Zambesi in
1856, had made a detour which prevented him seeing the rapids,
thereby leading him to believe that the Zambesi was navigable from
the sea to the Victoria Falls. Later he was to realize how disastrously
wrong this estimate was, and his plan to blast away the rocks that
formed the rapids was from the first a futile suggestion. Various plans
to dam the Zambesi emerged during the late 1950s but the dam at
Kariba was finished first, in 1961, and this confirmed the logic of
building a second dam to harness the vast flows of the Zambesi floods.
Work began on putting together a consortium just as guerrilla warfare
broke out in Mozambique. The Cabora Bassa dam, the fifth largest
in the world, was designed to produce 3.6 million kilowatts of
electricity. South Africa was clearly the biggest client for its power
but there were plans also for major agricultural and industrial
developments in Tete and Zambesia and talk of large-scale European

settlement. It was also hoped that the lake which filled behind the dam would place a significant barrier in the way of the Frelimo guerrillas operating from bases in the north.[30]

From then on the building of the dam became a contest of wills and propaganda. Frelimo exerted itself diplomatically and militarily to prevent the dam being built, trying to discourage potential participants and mounting its 'dam busters' campaign in the West. Portugal continued to assert that the building of the dam was the main guarantee that it was to continue in Africa. Work started on the dam in 1969 with a construction town being built at Songo. Frelimo's claims that it would stop the dam were too ambitious and its attacks on the fortified construction sites were expensive failures. Nor was the flow of material to the dam site seriously interrupted. However, the 'dam busters' campaign was not without its importance in the war. The protection of the dam absorbed a great deal of Portuguese military effort and for the first time in the war an important economic target was in the firing line. Defending the dam also made the armed forces very static and if Frelimo failed in its attacks on the dam itself, it was able for the first time to outflank the defences and begin operations south of the river. Moreover the campaign to stop the dam undoubtedly caught the world's imagination and raised the international profile of the struggle.[31]

Portugal's counter-offensive

The announcement that work was to start on the dam coincided with the decision taken in Lisbon to go on to the offensive against Frelimo. In 1968 Salazar had a stroke and was succeeded by Marcello Caetano who had been associated with him almost from the start of the New State. The appointment of a new prime minister was an occasion to reassess the policies pursued by the old dictator. Caetano showed a willingness to bring in new men, and to listen to those who wanted to modernise the Portuguese state and its economy as well as those who argued for a new approach to the African colonies. However, the reassessment of policy took place within the context of the regime's overall character and objectives, and Caetano's room for manoeuvre was soon shown to be limited as the old president, Tomás, represented a powerful bloc of conservative military and social forces at the heart of the regime opposed to significant reform.[32]

Up to the death of Salazar, Portugal's policy in Africa was to contain insurgency within the sparsely populated areas in the north and play on ethnic rivalries and personal animosities to split the nationalist movement. It was a tactic which worked to perfection in Angola and up till about 1969 showed every likelihood of success in Mozambique.

Frelimo was deeply divided, splits were appearing almost every month, and ethnic hostility to Frelimo seemed to have been aroused in various parts of the country; it had not been able to threaten any economically significant part of the country and Portuguese confidence was boosted by the decision of the international consortium to go ahead with the construction of the dam. However, Frelimo still occupied stretches of country in the north and had been able to hold its Second Party Congress on Mozambican soil. It was this annoying fact, along with the apparent success of the policy of containment elsewhere in the country, which convinced Caetano's military advisers that the war in Mozambique could now definitively be won, with all the incalculable advantages that this would bring to the regime at home and abroad.

The man chosen to deliver the knock-out blow was General Kaulza de Arriaga, who for so long had urged a hard-line military solution. His military career, like the careers of many other senior Portuguese figures, was interspersed with senior political, diplomatic and administrative appointments, and he seemed to move with ease in the governing circles in Lisbon. Aged fifty-five at the time of his appointment, he had founded the army's engineer corps and in the early 1950s as Secretary of State for Aviation was entrusted with developing the air defences of the colonies, which included planning a series of air bases in Mozambique. In the early 1960s he became known as a supporter of the hard line in Africa; he opposed Botelho Moniz's plans for a negotiated settlement there, and it seems that he may have been the officer who betrayed the coup attempt to Salazar. After the coup, and somewhat late in his career, he attended the Centre for Strategic Studies and rose to be its director in 1966.[33]

In this role he studied the classic counter-insurgency campaigns of the British and French, and concluded that PIDE's success in rooting Frelimo out of the towns made the French experience in Algeria irrelevant while Britain's campaigns in Kenya and Malaya had been fought before the development of the helicopter. He also got to know the leading American commanders involved in Vietnam and had Portuguese officers sent to the United States for training.[34] In common with so many influential Americans at that time, he became convinced that it was necessary to check the communist advance in the world and believed that this could be done by an effective combination of military and civil measures.

Arriaga believed that Portugal's passive policy of containment had lowered military morale and that the war effort had been unnecessarily hampered by divided command both in Portugal and in Africa. Caetano, on coming to power, revived the Supreme Defence Council and tried to form a joint general staff; in this Arriaga backed him and demanded that there should be effective joint command in Mozambique.[35] In July 1969 he was made commander of land forces in Mozambique and in March 1970 took over as commander-in-chief. He was aided by the appointment of a new governor general, Pimentel dos Santos.

Arriaga planned a massive sweep in the north of Mozambique in which proper reconnaissance and airborne assault would search out and destroy Frelimo bases and units. He wanted to combine this with offensive operations against Frelimo bases inside Tanzania and attempts to destabilise the country, but Caetano vetoed this plan. Arriaga launched his famous operation, codenamed 'Gordian Knot', in May 1970, allocating 35,000 troops to the operation backed by 100 helicopters and other aircraft. During May he cleared the lowland areas round Mueda and then moved on the Frelimo sanctuaries on the Mueda plateau. In all, his men undertook forty separate operations and he claimed that sixty-one bases had been destroyed, with large numbers of Frelimo fighters defecting. Ten operations were also undertaken in Niassa. As the country was cleared, the Makonde population who did not flee the fighting were resettled in *aldeamentos*. Official Portuguese casualties were announced to be 132 dead and 260 wounded. By September almost the whole of Cabo Delgado was back in Portuguese hands, although the main damage inflicted on Frelimo was the loss of stores and equipment and disruption to their political campaign in the region. Arriaga and the government developed long-term plans for the north. In the border area a network of tarred roads was to connect a series of modern towns to be built inland from the coast. *Colonatos* were laid out and white settlers brought into the region. In the north the principal *colonato* was at Montepuez and in Niassa at Nova Madeira.[36]

Frelimo was taken by surprise by the scale of the Portuguese operation, which was far greater than anything attempted by the army before. Rather than try and hold on to the north and fight Arriaga, Frelimo countered the offensive with what proved to be a masterstroke. Guerrilla forces were rapidly withdrawn before the advancing Portuguese and transferred through Malawi to Tete district, a move made possible by the tacit support offered by Hastings Banda during one of his tortuous changes of political direction. By September 1970 Frelimo was mounting an increasing number of attacks north of Tete, and Arriaga had to switch the scene of his operations to the Zambesi, mounting in all 20 operations in the northern part of Tete district before the onset of rains put an end to his campaign. In spite of this development, Arriaga himself was delighted with the success of his operations and spent Christmas with his wife in a former Frelimo base in the north. Caetano was less delighted at the rapidly escalating cost in money, military hardware and soldiers' lives. Further offensives were halted on orders from Lisbon.

After the completion of 'Gordian Knot', Arriaga implemented another of his ideas. He believed that greater use should be made of African troops in the campaigns and he was instrumental in building up the *Grupos Especiais* (GE) and the *Grupos Especiais Paraquedistas* (GEP), while the *Flechas* (black commandos) were developed as a paramilitary unit within the *Direcção Geral de Segurança* (DGS), as PIDE was now called.[37] By the time Arriaga left Mozambique at the end of 1973 more than half the strength of the security forces consisted of locally recruited black troops, whose use in colonial wars was very much part of Portugal's tradition. Arriaga's black units were to be one of the elements of continuity linking the early history of Mozambique with the civil wars in the post independence era.

In its way 'Gordian Knot' was a well conducted operation, but it was probably a serious misuse of limited resources. The Portuguese counter-insurgency operation had been crippled through lack of intelligence and inadequate policing of the population. The resources devoted to the operation could almost certainly have been better used in establishing a more effective internal police network.

Final phase of the war

The reopening of the Tete front proved to be a breakthrough for Frelimo, although two previous attempts in this area had failed. It seems that Frelimo received enthusiastic backing from the Cewa north of the Zambesi, which enabled attacks to be mounted against the Cabora Bassa dam and the main Salisbury-Blantyre road. The attacks on the dam proved a failure and served to bring Rhodesian and South African forces into active service in Tete. Rather than retreat, however, Frelimo moved units south of the river in 1971 and in July 1972 guerrilla activity began in the Manica area, threatening for the first time an important section of the settler population. The Beira-Tete railway was attacked in 1972 and early in 1974 a train was derailed on the Beira-Umtali line. The ease with which Frelimo moved south of the Zambesi surprised the Portuguese since the frontiers there were well protected by the Rhodesian regime. It is likely that Frelimo found it easy to operate in what was classic bandit country, the old kingdom of Barue where resistance to colonial authority had been endemic. However, the support of the Shona for Frelimo at this stage needs further analysis since these were the same people who later opposed the Frelimo government and formed the main cadres of Renamo.[38]

Frelimo's Tete and Manica campaigns were psychologically

successful and in the period 1972–4 contributed to a rapid crumbling of the colonial structure. Of equal importance, however, were economic and political developments within Portugal itself. While Gordian Knot was being planned and executed, a major reorientation of Portuguese economic policy towards the colonies was being put into action. The Lisbon government had continued to finance the high spending in the colonies through loans and export credits but early in the 1970s it changed this policy and introduced a tighter economic regime. Lisbon now demanded payment for goods and services in foreign or metropolitan currencies and began to shift the burden of financing the war to Mozambique itself.[39] At the same time Portugal was negotiating for entry to the EEC. Associate status was granted in July 1970 but this required Portugal to dismantle the structures which had reserved colonial markets exclusively for Portuguese exports. Restrictions on foreign investment were also lifted.[40] The result was a sharp decline in trade with the colonial territories — notably Mozambique — while the major Portuguese corporations began to liquidate their investments and sell out. South African business eagerly stepped into Portugal's place. South Africa overtook Portugal as Mozambique's major trade partner in 1971 and by 1974 had also become the principal source of external capital.[41] With this orientation of Portugal's economy towards Europe and Mozambique's towards South Africa, the groundwork was being laid for a reasoned withdrawal from Africa which a few years later was to be backed by most of the moguls of Portuguese business.

In the last years of the colonial regime, there was quite rapid economic development inside Mozambique, which in retrospect can be seen as complementary to the withdrawal of metropolitan influence. High government expenditure led to rising inflation but also to impressive rates of growth in the economy. As an increasing number of white immigrants went to the cities, a belt of agricultural and industrial enterprises grew up to supply the settler consumer market. In the region round Lourenço Marques and Beira private farms produced European-style foods, and light industries supplied the consumer market with a range of manufactured goods. Mozambique was at last beginning to enjoy import-saving, though not yet export-led, industrial growth.

Economic disengagement was followed by tentative political moves. As early as 1971 General Spínola is said to have suggested negotiating a settlement in Guiné, making use of the good offices of President Senghor of Senegal as mediator.[42] Caetano rejected this, but although few members of the regime were contemplating a complete withdrawal from Africa, its élite were beginning to abandon the idea of integrating Africa with metropolitan Portugal. Caetano himself came to accept, in principle at least, the need to dismantle the integrated Portuguese state. In Mozambique Portuguese business-men were calling for more financial autonomy, and settler opinion increasingly expressed resentment at the tight control still exerted from Lisbon.

Caetano edged slowly towards meeting these demands for local autonomy. In 1972 Mozambique formally ceased to be a province of Portugal and became a 'state', implying the sort of local autonomy enjoyed by 'states' of the American union. The old nominated Legis-lative Assembly was enlarged, and twenty of its now fifty members were to be elected. When the first and last elections were held in 1973, a majority of non-European delegates were returned.[43] In the last years of the regime, also, there were signs of a lifting of political con-trols with the settlers being encouraged to form political organisations, and in September 1973 members of GUMO, a moderate settler organisation which Caetano had allowed to be formed, had a meeting with the prime minister.[44] However, these moves came when the military situation was already deteriorating, and were anyway so ten-tative that they scarcely amounted to the emergence of a viable alter-native policy.

A further weakening of the regime, and a clear indication that the old alliances which had held it together were breaking up, came with the rapidly deteriorating relations with the Catholic church. Salazar's Concordat with the Pope in 1940 had given the church a major role within the colonies as the only recognised church and the main pro-vider of education. Salazar maintained that Portuguese rule upheld Christian Catholic values, and his regime received papal endorsement as late as 1967 when the Pope visited the shrine at Fatima on the fif-tieth anniversary of the vision of the Virgin which had led to its foun-dation. By 1970, however, the Vatican's position was changing. In that year Pope Paul VI accorded the leadership of Frelimo, MPLA and PAIGC a formal audience, after which he is reported to have said: 'We are on the side of those who suffer. We are for the peace, the freedom, and the national independence of all peoples, particularly the African peoples.'[45] By 1971, however, a serious division had grown within the church in Mozambique between the senior Por-tuguese clergy and some of the missionaries, notably the White Fathers. Disagreements in the 1960s had led to the expulsion of six priests, and now a number of new issues appeared to have arisen including disagreements over church appointments as well as the attitude of the church to African nationalism. As a result of these disputes, the Order withdrew its personnel from Africa completely. Further difficulties arose with the Spanish Burgos Fathers, who were alleged actually to have helped Frelimo and who made a series of accusations of massacres and ill-treatment by Portuguese soldiers. Two of their number were imprisoned in Lourenço Marques for 'treason' and it was from two others back in Spain that Father Adrian Hastings learned the details of the 'Wiriamu Massacre'.[46]

This massacre was said to have been perpetrated by GEPs near Tete in December 1972. Although the Vatican reported its information to Portugal early in the year, Hastings published his information in *The Times* in London to coincide with the state visit of Caetano to Britain in July 1973. Further accounts of massacres and ill-treatment of the population by the Portuguese army followed. There is no doubt that the revelations of the missionaries were immensely damaging to the regime and its credibility among its friends in the West. However, it is perhaps not entirely a coincidence that the major revelations that proved so embarrassing to the Portuguese occurred after the Vatican's change of political stance.

Revolution in Portugal and decolonisation

Between 1974 and 1976 Portugal severed its African connections with comparatively little trauma to itself. The African empire had always possessed a dual reality — there was the empire of government ideology and that of economic reality. The empire was of great propaganda value to the Salazar regime and, particularly in the regime's later years, the notion of the historic Lusitanian civilising mission formed a significant part of its self-image. The fraudulent nature of these claims was ruthlessly exposed during the ideological battles that accompanied the wars of liberation and by 1974 the propaganda war had been lost as decisively in the minds of the Portuguese people themselves as in the minds of foreigners.

It has only recently become clear to what extent the empire of economic opportunity had also lost credibility by the early 1970s and declined to the point where it was no longer worth fighting for.[47] In the 1930s and 1940s Africa had assumed great economic importance as Portugal struggled to modernise itself and survive the great depression by constructing an economic autarky linking Africa and the metropole. Africa was essential to this process since it produced raw materials at controlled prices which supported Portugal's industrialisation, and became, even if only briefly, the main focus for Portuguese emigration. Moreover, Africa took increasing proportions of the country's exports, which were paid for by the transfer of hard currency earned through migrant labour, the provision of services for the South African economy or through the direct sale of raw materials to other developed economies. The ability of the colonies to earn surpluses for the *escudo* zone persisted to the end, and as

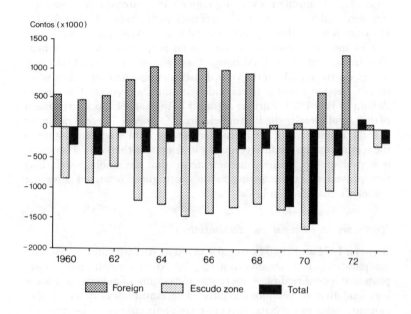

Fig. 19.1. BALANCE OF PAYMENTS

Source: J. Mittelman, *Underdevelopment and the Transition to Socialism*, p. 54.

late as 1973, they still amounted to 5 per cent of Portugal's GNP (Fig. 19.1).

However, there were already signs by the 1950s that the African empire had passed the peak of its importance for Portugal. In that decade the Portuguese economy rapidly industrialised and expanded, but the significant development was the increase of foreign investment and the growth of trade with Europe rather than Africa. This trend was intensified after 1960; in that year Portugal joined EFTA and in 1961 controls on foreign investment were partly lifted, resulting in major capital inflows from Western Europe and the United States. At the same time the tide of emigration began to flow to France and Germany rather than to traditional areas like Brazil and the United

States, or to the colonies.[48] In 1971 these migrant remittances were the equivalent of nearly half the total value of Portuguese exports.

By the early 1970s Portugal's eyes were firmly turned to Europe. After 1968 trade with the African colonies declined, and between 1970 and 1974 the proportion of its exports taken by the colonies fell from 24 per cent to 11 per cent, with the government having to make large loans to the colonies to help them pay for even this amount.[49] In the same period there was actually large-scale disinvestment in the colonies by major Portuguese banks and corporations, which sold out to South African concerns. By 1973 South Africa and not Portugal was the major trading partner and source of investment capital for Mozambique, and in the early 1970s 89 per cent of all new capital invested in Mozambique came from South Africa.[50] Already before the events of April 1974 economic logic had drawn a line under Portugal's imperial experiment. It simply required some act of will or vision to dismantle the now hollow and expensive structure.

It was widely felt at the time that the pressure of the African wars, which began in 1961, were somehow critical in bringing about the revolution and topped the list of reasons for the coup drawn up by the MFA (Movimento das Forças Armadas) in April 1974. Initially, however, the wars led to modernisation in Portugal and a general energising of the regime, as Tom Gallagher has noted.[51] The military opened their ranks to new elements from the bourgeoisie; the state became more active in economic planning and in addressing social questions; new men were recruited into the officer corps, the administration, and ultimately the government itself. For much of the 1960s foreign investment and heavy government expenditure induced quasi-boom conditions and wages moved well ahead of prices.[52] The economic growth enabled Portugal to pay without much difficulty for the African wars which between 1965 and 1970 took an average of 8.1 per cent of GNP.

Modernisation and economic growth may act as catalysts for revolutionary change just as effectively as discontent, but as the wars continued discontent grew along with the prosperity. By 1974 one million Portuguese men had served in the armed forces in Africa and conscription was affecting one adult male in every four. The African wars politicised the Portuguese middle classes in an unprecedented way, not through the direct conversion of large numbers to the revolutionary ideology of Amilcar Cabral or Samora Machel, but through forcing conscripts and their families to ask questions about the nature of the state and the purpose of the colonial wars. The leading generals — some of whom, like António de Spinola, had close links with the major industrial and banking corporations — were also becoming discontented with a war that was not being won and were encouraged by their business associates to look for a political, post-colonial answer to the African problems. The extent to which the large business corporations withdrew their support from Caetano before April 1974 was a significant cause of the collapse of the regime.

Handover of power in the colonies

The MFA, which made the revolution in April 1974, was determined to end the wars in Africa and to find what it called political not military solutions. These solutions were not defined or agreed in advance and a commitment to self-determination for the colonies was left out of the MFA programme eventually published in April 1974.[53] Ideas ranged from instant withdrawal to the continuation of a federal Portuguese community which was advocated by Spínola and which clearly appealed to the Portuguese business corporations which backed him.

The decolonisation process in Guiné, São Tomé, Cape Verde and Mozambique took place while the outcome of the revolution in Portugal itself was still far from resolved, and the decolonisation of these territories in turn influenced what happened in Angola. During the year and a half that followed the coup of April 1974, a strong bid was made by extreme left-wing elements to control the revolution in Portugal, and the future of Africa and Portugal became inextricably entwined. A radical outcome in Africa was seen as essential for a radical regime in Portugal. The leftist officers of the MFA identified strongly with the nationalist movements in Africa and shared with them a belief that Salazarism was the common enemy. However, when negotiations opened with the colonies, Portugal was nominally under the presidency of António de Spínola, a conservative general intent on pursuing his own private diplomacy in Africa while trying to impose a conservative hue on developments within Portugal itself. The decolonisation process, therefore, became an aspect of the struggle for power in Portugal itself. While Spínola tried to pursue his own plans for the future of the African colonies, the MFA officers opposed to him also resorted to private diplomacy with the objective of hastening the complete transfer of power. With the Portuguese side not only divided but presenting factions working in secret against each other, it was not difficult for PAIGC, MLSTP and Frelimo to brush aside talk of referendums or pre-independence elections.[54]

Inside Mozambique the April revolution brought confusion and chaos. The army and the civil government were uncertain of what role they were to play and even from whom they were to take orders. General Costa Gomes, the Portuguese chief of staff, visited the colony in May to strengthen the position of the MFA within the army in Mozambique, but he did little to clarify the direction events were taking.[55] Military units began to refuse to fight and fraternisation with Frelimo took place in many areas. Frelimo, however, continued the war, pushing into Zambesia province and southwards towards the Sabi. It met no resistance. In Lourenço Marques the DGS was abolished, political prisoners were released and the governor-general was recalled to Lisbon.

Political movements of all complexions emerged in the new-found freedom. Before the revolution Jorge Jardim, a wealthy Mozambican businessman and former confidant of Salazar, had tried to obtain Lisbon's support for a coalition to negotiate independence, using President Kenneth Kaunda of Zambia as an intermediary.[56] Now GUMO, the settler organisation approved by Caetano in the last days of the regime, joined in August with the old Coremo leadership — with Simango and Gwenjere — to form the PCN which was based in Beira. Groups purporting to represent the interests of the Makua emerged; one of them, Frecomo, was led by Joana Simião. Conservative white settlers formed Fico, and radical white liberals reformed the Mozambican Democrats (under the acronym MUDM) and actively campaigned on behalf of Frelimo. The new governor of Mozambique was a former MUDM member.[57]

In June 1974 the first negotiations took place between the Portuguese and Frelimo. The Portuguese wanted a ceasefire which Frelimo would not grant. As a result order began to disintegrate throughout Mozambique; there were numerous attacks on white settlers and on Portuguese property, and in August Frelimo belatedly called a halt to its military campaign. On 7 September 1974, after private meetings in Tanzania between MFA officers and Frelimo, the Lusaka Accord was signed allowing for the rapid and unequivocal transfer of power to Frelimo without prior elections and with only nine months of transitional government. The transitional government was to be headed by Joaquim Chissano, the future president and successor to Machel.[58]

It has been argued that there was no realistic alternative to this precipitate transfer of power. Frelimo refused to accept a cease-fire and the colonial army in Mozambique would certainly not have continued the war. There was no way in which Frelimo's demands could seriously have been resisted. However, its continuation of the war for three months after the revolution helped to create the feeling among the settlers that a Mozambique ruled by it would have no place for them. Frelimo for its part feared, with some justification, that there might be a settler coup of some kind which would immensely complicate the independence process. It is now clear that in the last months of the colonial regime moves were made, centred on the city of Beira, to try to create settler-based organisations to resist a handover. Jorge Jardim conducted secret diplomacy with Malawi in order to create some local backing for a settler take-over. On 9 September 1974, just two days after the Lusaka Accord, there was an abortive settler rising in Lourenço Marques, with further disturbances in the following month; in both there was considerable loss of life. Conceivably, given time, some rival front to Frelimo, some rallying of rightist forces, could have been put together. Both Frelimo and the Portuguese MFA, each for their own reasons, were anxious to prevent this and to end quickly a transition period which in practice would have seen chaos and uncertainty offering opportunities for right-wing forces to organise.

The agreement granting Mozambique independence was signed on 28 September shortly before Spínola was forced to resign. It marked, and to some extent helped to cement, the temporary supremacy in Portugal of the MFA, which went on in January 1975 to sign the Alvor agreement for the handover of power in Angola. For the radical African nationalists these agreements were made only just in time. Already by the summer of 1975, when the flag of independent Mozambique was at last hoisted, the settlers were returning in angry mood from Angola and the nationalisation of private banks was giving the Portuguese state a new interest in controlling the future of huge colonial assets. Moderate centre-right politicans were in the ascendant and Portuguese politics had once again reached a turning-point. Frelimo had secured its independence at the moment most favourable for an untrammelled transfer of power.

The Lusaka Accord left many matters unsettled. The position of the settlers and their property received no guarantees; no decisions were made about Portuguese assets or about compensation; and the whole question of the colonial debt was unresolved. Eventually some of these matters were cleared up but not before lasting damage had been done to the post-colonial relations between Mozambique and Portugal. It can only be considered a complete abdication of responsibility by both sides that conditions under which skilled Portuguese and Mozambican workers could have stayed on were not negotiated, and that no commercial or financial arrangements were made which would have guaranteed a continued harmonious relationship between former colony and metropole.

20

AFTER INDEPENDENCE

Frelimo

The Lusaka Accord handed over power to Frelimo almost uncondi-
tionally. There were no elections, no referendum and only nine
months of interim administration before the independence celebra-
tions of July 1975. Many Mozambicans were unfamiliar with the new
rulers who took power from the Portuguese, and Frelimo was
relatively unfamiliar with much of the country it was to rule. What
was the nature of Frelimo and what qualities did it bring to the task
of ruling the newly-independent state?

As has already been described, Frelimo was founded in Tanzania
and owed much to the friendship and help of Julius Nyerere. Its
origins lay in three small ethnically based parties brought together in
1963 to form a 'front' (*frente*). At first it was made up largely of exiles
drawn from Mozambicans being educated abroad and migrant
workers residing in neighbouring countries. It also drew considerably
on the Makonde, the ethnic group located astride the Mozambique-
Tanzania frontier. The early quarrels in the party led to the expulsion
of northern Makonde from the leadership and to the consolidation of
control of the party in the hands of educated southerners.

So, almost from the start, Frelimo was an intellectuals' party.
Mondlane himself had a doctorate and wrote an excellent book on the
birth of the independence struggle.[1] Machel, who succeeded him in
1970, had no higher education but was a man of great intelligence who
assimilated and interpreted the key ideas of the movement and
became one of its most articulate exponents.[2] Educated black and
mestizo Mozambicans were attracted to the party which assimilated
and absorbed the creative talents of many writers, poets and
academics. There was also, from the start, an enthusiastic band of
foreign supporters including brilliant Western academics like Allen
Isaacman, the talented team who staffed the Eduardo Mondlane
University, and South African exiles like Ruth First and Albie Sachs.
Few political parties can have attracted such a distinguished battery
of intellectual firepower.

The intellectual orientation of the party was to be of fundamental
significance. From the start great importance was attached to understanding the country that Frelimo was going to rule. The history,

social structure and economic development of Mozambique were all carefully studied so that Frelimo's policies would be founded on the best possible intellectual base. The leaders believed that policy had to be founded on a correct analysis and form an integrated and rationally constructed whole — otherwise it would founder.

At first there was no particular orientation of Frelimo towards Marxist thought, and the dominant ideas of Mondlane were little different from those of other African nationalists. However, following the power struggle which ousted Nkavandame and Simango in 1969–70, the party moved sharply to the left. From then on its leadership became much influenced by the pragmatic Marxism of Amilcar Cabral with his classic identification of neo-colonialism, as well as colonialism, as the enemy to be confronted.[3] When it took power in 1975, Frelimo was already armed with a range of policies and an analysis of the task to be done which reflected the revolutionary ideologies of the 1960s, of Cuba and Vietnam as well as those of Cabral and the PAIGC. However it was only in 1977, at its Third Party Congress, that it declared itself to be a Marxist-Leninist Party.[4]

This declaration was more than just the adoption of a label. During the war of liberation Frelimo had paid close attention to mass mobilisation of the peasantry. It had shared Cabral's belief that the structures of the colonial state had to be analysed on a class not an ethnic basis and it identified the peasantry as the most oppressed class under the old regime. Believing that ordinary people could be mobilised to support the revolution, it set about creating a mass membership, enlisting traditional leaders like chiefs and heads of co-operatives as well as obviously oppressed groups like labourers and women. Attention was given to setting up schools, stores and clinics in the rural areas, and to creating communal villages to protect the population. But Frelimo had only been able to organise at all extensively in three of the country's nine provinces, and it took power without having any formal party organisation in most of the country. Only after 1977 were serious attempts made to remedy this. Party 'cells' were created throughout Mozambique, their number having allegedly reached 4,200 by 1983.[5]

After independence, however, the party changed its nature. Mass mobilisation was still thought essential but it was to take place outside the party structure, through organisations like the OMM (Organização das Mulheres Moçambicanas) and the OJM (Organização da Juventude Moçambicana), but the party itself was to become a so-called 'vanguard' with a relatively restricted membership. It also retained a tight control over the newly-created democratic institutions. For instance, the members of the Popular Assembly, the country's law-making parliament, were nominated by the Central Committee of the party. At the same time the party officially shifted from regarding the peasantry as the main revolutionary force to putting their trust formally in the proletariat that had been, and would be, created by the expansion of the modern sector of the economy.[6]

This tighter party organisation led to a more managerial approach to politics, and arguably this was necessary as the problems of independence crowded in on the new rulers. Whereas previously the party had often been prepared for lengthy popular debates on important issues before decisions were reached, after 1975 these popular democratic procedures tended to be circumvented. Party members gradually changed their role from dynamising, motivating and creating political consciousness in a newly liberated people, to issuing orders and carrying centrally decided party diktats to the provinces. At the same time control of state enterprises by workers' co-operatives was discouraged.[7] The commitment to centralised planning and to the dynamic role of state-owned productive resources became the hallmark of a practical revolutionary ideology.[8]

At first the party and the state were not easily distinguishable. The collapse of the Portuguese administration and the flight of bureaucrats and managers meant that the party had to fill many of these posts with its own personnel. As Sonia Kruks was to write, 'positions such as locality administrator and locality Party secretary are frequently vested in one person.'[9] The *Grupos Dinamizadores* (GDs — dynamising groups), created soon after independence with the intention of mobilising the population to support the policies of the new government, clearly performed both political and administrative functions. In many areas the GDs acted as popular tribunals until a new legal system could be created. Later a greater distinction was to emerge between party, state and industrial management, but it had not been a satisfactory way to begin the new social and economic order.

The convergence of these trends in the evolution of Frelimo was dangerous. The influence of intellectuals in the party appears to have encouraged the adoption of policies rooted in theory rather than in a sound knowledge of the country and the people, a tendency made worse by the way the party increasingly distanced itself from ordinary people and ceased genuinely to listen to what they and their traditional leaders were saying. Barry Munslow, a committed supporter of the regime, commented:

> The more articulate and educated members of the petty bourgeoisie were quick to present themselves as longstanding sympathisers. Within the colonial hierarchy, they occupied the junior grades but still enjoyed a social superiority in relation to the

overwhelming proportion of black Mozambicans who were workers or peasants. The latter let them take over control of many [GDs] in part as a result of deference to their superior wealth, education and social standing.[10]

In particular, by attributing ethnic differences to the evil of divide-and-rule policies of the Portuguese, and substituting a class analysis of social and economic problems, Frelimo allowed ethnic tensions to be buried out of sight. It refused to see that, however unjustifiably, it was viewed as a 'southern' party with a 'southern' leadership, a problem made all the worse by the physical location of the capital in the far south of the country.

Nevertheless Frelimo retained many characteristics of a responsible and democratic political movement. It was well aware of the dangers of a one-party system that became isolated from popular opinion, and understood the tyranny that a bureaucracy could wield, even after the end of formal colonial rule. One of Frelimo's most imaginitive creations had been the cartoon character of 'Xiconhoca' who epitomised the continuity between the petty tyrannies of the colonial era and those of post-independence bureaucrats.[11] To counter these dangers a pyramid of popular assemblies was created at the national, provincial, district, city and local levels. Elections to these assemblies — some 1,341 in all — were held in 1977 and involved genuine popular participation. Frelimo would present a list of candidates and the suitability of these nominees would then be discussed and debated by public gatherings, with unpopular or unsuitable persons being struck off. However, certain people were barred from election, among them traditional chiefs and *régulos* who had held posts under the colonial regime; great tension was created in some areas where the 'natural' leaders of the community were replaced by party nominees with no local standing whatever.[12]

Frelimo also adopted the procedure of self-examination and self-criticism. At its Congresses the party regularly went through a public self-examination in which many 'mistakes' were identified and past policies criticised. This procedure should not be despised — it represented a genuine willingness to admit errors and enabled 'opposition' to exist within a one-party state organisation. However, it has been pointed out that public self-criticism is a clever and subtle political device. By allowing some areas of policy to be publicly criticised and overturned, the Frelimo leadership was able to deflect attention from other areas of policy that it did not want challenged. It also deflected any challenge from the leadership itself. Self-criticism became a legitimising process in which the admission of mistakes and the willingness to change failed policies proved the party's fitness to rule. The outstanding example of this use of self-criticism to reinforce the party's authority and leadership came with Machel's campaign against corruption in 1980. In this, as in other presidential 'campaigns', the president and leader of the party was seen as leading the nation, the people, in person against a faceless, corrupt bureaucratic 'them'.[13]

The presidential 'campaigns' were Machel's preferred method of introducing reform and change. There was the 1976 production offensive; the 1978 campaign to build the party organisation; the 1980 presidential offensive against corruption; in 1981 two ministers, Jorge Rebelo and Marcelino dos Santos, were given the job of dealing with illiteracy and corruption within the party; 1982–3 was the year of preparation for the party Congress; 1983 was the year of production.[14] These campaigns were opportunities for changes of direction and for focusing attention on particular problems or issues, but they were not always accompanied by significant changes to structures in the party, the bureaucracy or the state enterprises.

Whatever the explanation, Frelimo remained a remarkably cohesive party which managed major changes in policy without changes in leadership.[15] It did not suffer from serious internal disputes or from schisms. Its ability to create a consensus within the ruling group was outstanding. There may have been disgruntled intellectuals or disillusioned party members, but it is remarkable how few they were and how ineffectual in mobilising dissent. Part of this success lies in the remarkably united and cohesive group of people who have led Frelimo since its beginning. In the first fifteen years of independence the membership of the Political Bureau, the inner cabinet, did not change except to add Oscar Monteiro, the former Secretary-General of CONCP and one of the inner group who made the revolution, to its number in 1983.[16]

The Frelimo leadership

Samora Machel dominated Frelimo from the time he took over as its principal military commander in 1966 till his death in a plane crash twenty years later. He was born in 1933 and — like the other two leaders of Frelimo, Mondlane and Chissano — was a southerner. He was the son of a peasant farmer who, like so many other men from the southern provinces, had been to the mines and used his earnings to invest in oxen and a plough. His eldest son had also gone to the mines and died there. Machel's father had joined the Free Methodist Church and Samora was brought up in the tradition of the African independent churches. However, he had to attend a local school run by the Catholic church, which he joined in order to be allowed to sit examinations. Subsequently he was frustrated in his attempts to go on to secondary school and trained to be a nurse at the Miguel Bombarda hospital in Lourenço Marques. After a meeting with Mondlane, he became involved in the work of Frelimo and in 1963 left to join the movement in Dar es Salaam.

Machel's main concern was to help in the organisation of armed rebellion, and he was sent to Algeria for training. On returning he became involved in the earliest military action and was soon promoted to a position where he was the natural successor as commander of Frelimo forces in 1966. From then on he was a power in the party, helping to steer it to the left and turning it into a revolutionary movement as well as one aiming for national independence. On Mondlane's death he was elected to the three-man *junta* that took over and in 1970 became sole president of Frelimo.[17]

Machel was immensely energetic and hard-working. He set high personal standards for members of the movement and under his influence it became almost puritanical in its demands for personal sacrifice and commitment; Machel himself devoted his life to the cause. Like the other leaders of the Portuguese resistance movements he realised the importance of ideas, and although not educated like Mondlane, Neto or Cabral, he acquired a wide grasp of their ideas and those of men like Giap, Mao, Fanon and the other intellectual founders of Third World revolutionary politics. He was soon to give a distinctive flavour to the Mozambican revolution in a series of speeches and addresses to the party on important occasions.

The social revolution

Frelimo came to power determined to end social as well as political oppression. The hated colonial rulers had been defeated, and now it was necessary to liberate the people from internal oppression. This was defined partly in class terms — the existence of feudal and capitalist social relations that had exploited ethnic differences — and partly in terms of the oppression of ignorance. Feudal and capitalist social relations dominated the lives of a population 80 per cent of whom were still rural; they had emphasised ethnic divisions, installed traditional chiefs as agents of the colonial government with power over people's lives, placed wealthy polygynous males in a position to control the productive and reproductive capacity of women, and subjected the male population to ill-paid wage labour. The radical wing of Frelimo feared that independence would not necessarily change this situation. The Report to the Third Congress described what, in its view, had happened in liberated zones:

The administrative and economic presence of colonialism had disappeared from these areas, but feudal structures remained and with them the anti-democratic authority of the chiefs, the oppression of women and youth, and tribal divisions. On the other hand, there arose new exploiters, elements who began to show that they were intent on replacing the colonialists in the exploitation of the people.[18]

Ignorance was the other form of oppression. Not only did illiterate people lack political consciousness, but they were at the mercy of traditional knowledge and practices which condemned them to poverty, made them superstitious and perpetuated the tyranny of customs like *lobola*, polygamy and initiation.

Frelimo's programme of social reform was to cover all these issues, and its prime purpose was to create the social integration which colonial rule had failed to achieve. Its foundation was to be universal literacy. A campaign to that end was mounted throughout the country, on the state farms and co-operatives, in towns and villages. Women as well as men were to be encouraged to become literate, without which other reforms would be pointless. But literacy was to be a means as well as an end. It was to be the means by which Mozambicans would enter into modern social relations in a modernised economy. Frelimo believed that the future of the country lay in building up a modern economy based on mechanised farming and a spread of industries which would increasingly be served by Mozambicans trained in the necessary managerial and technical skills. To this end science was to replace tradition, a transformation to be carried out by the locomotive of the state industrial and agricultural corporations and by the communal villages where people could receive the services and the education of a modern state.

What would the new society be like? At every stage Frelimo stressed the existence of a single Mozambican nation. Portuguese was adopted as the national language and, ironically, greater efforts were made to widen the knowledge of it and to make people literate in the language of Camoēs and Caetano than the Portuguese themselves had ever made. People would be encouraged to take responsibility for their own lives in the context of a wider community. In rural areas the communal village or township would replace the older lineage-based villages. In the workplace and in the community there would be consultative or democratic structures in which all would participate. Access to health and educational services would be extended and equalised. At the village level chiefs would be replaced by presidents and secretaries, symbols of the new social order. Expressions of ethnicity were discouraged and the old chiefs' and elders' tribunals would be replaced by Local Justice Tribunals to which all people could come to seek for justice. The institutionalised power of religions would be removed. The churches, for example, would lose their property, their role in education and their control over marriage.

The most important transformation would take place in the role of women, and Machel's speech at the founding conference of the OMM in 1973 is a useful summary of the social objectives of the Frelimo revolution:

> The emancipation of women is not an act of charity, the result of a humanitarian or compassionate attitude. The liberation of women is a fundamental necessity for the revolution, the guarantee of its continuity and the precondition of its victory. The main objective of the revolution is to destroy the system of exploitation and build a new society which releases the potential of human beings, reconciling them with labour and with nature. This is the context within which the question of women's emancipation arises.[19]

Machel was convinced of women's supreme importance as educators of the young and used to refer to the family as 'the first cell of the party'.[20]

Frelimo was committed to encouraging women to take a full part in society on an equal basis with men. To achieve this the OMM was founded with the aim of mobilising women to support the revolutionary changes and to represent women's interests at the centre. In 1976 the OMM and Frelimo discussed a new Family Law, finally implemented in 1981, establishing monogamous marriage, making provision for joint ownership of property and joint decisions about place of residence, allowing women access to courts for maintenance, and establishing the duties of fathers to maintain their children.[21] Machel delivered a number of speeches on the subject of women's revolution. The key to emancipation was to be education, political mobilisation and entry into the modern sector of the economy. Through the OMM women were encouraged to bring their children for immunisation, attend literacy classes and put themselves forward for election to assemblies. The institutionalised prostitution of the cities was ended, and polygamy, which was seen as a way in which men commandeered the labour of women, was strongly discouraged, with active discrimination against those who practised it. Campaigns were also mounted against *lobola*.

Frelimo's ideas were clear, integrated and undoubtedly humane and progressive in their orientation. On the whole few people could have quarrelled with the necessity or desirability of steering society in this general direction. However, social engineering on this scale is extremely difficult to realise. Deconstruction of the social relations of the colonial era was needed along with the formulation of alternatives. Frelimo was well aware of this need, but it believed that the traditional society could be allowed to wither away, and that this would happen once the modern sector developed and absorbed a new generation in its operation. In practice what happened was often much more violent and disruptive.

In the years immediately after independence, changes were begun on all fronts. In the first six years primary school enrolment doubled from 700,000 to 1,376,000, while the numbers in secondary education rose from 20,000 to 135,000.[22] The adult literacy campaigns achieved some results. In 1981 half a million people were enrolled in such schemes (in 1979, 40 per cent of all those attending literacy classes were women) but they stalled for lack of trained manpower to run the campaigns, while the demands of the subsistence economy left people without enough time to attend classes.[23]

Communal villages developed only slowly and were treated with great suspicion by the peasants involved who found that they fitted ill with the continued pattern of family farming. By 1984 about 1,500 Communal Villages had been established, but over half of these were ones that had been set up during the war of liberation and 600 of them were to be found in Cabo Delgado in the extreme north.[24] The idea of the Communal Village can be traced in the history of Mozambique directly to the *aldeamentos* planned, particularly in the north, as part of the cotton-growing campaigns — but it is not too fanciful to see them as rooted in a much older Iberian tradition, in the attempts by the Spaniards to eradicate the religion of the Incas by concentrating the rural population of Peru in the sixteenth century, and in the planned Jesuit settlements in Brazil and Paraguay designed to 'civilise' and Christianise the Indian population. Seen in this light, the Communal Village has always had two purposes: to bring about a measure of co-operation and a pooling of resources in peasant agriculture and to indoctrinate the peasantry in the political or religious ideology of the rulers of the time. The Communal Villages met with opposition above all because they involved the forcible movement of peasants from land they had traditionally farmed, and which was controlled by their own lineage, into large semi-urban settlements where they depended on the village commune for access to land. Many peasants relocated to Communal Villages simply returned to their old houses leaving the new settlements empty, and they were encouraged in this by their lineage chiefs who had been displaced by party officials and elected deputies. Although Communal Villages may have had many advantages on paper, they represented what one French observer described as '*une violence culturelle*'.[25]

Women were brought into national life only by slow degrees. Traditional relationships and the hostility of males meant that they were reluctant to put themselves forward for classes, for wage employment or for public office. Those women who did take steps along the Frelimo road found the burden of trying to fulfill traditional wifely roles at the same time heavy. Even so, 28 per cent of those elected to popular assemblies in 1977 were women — a percentage which would probably compare favourably with participation rates in any other country in the world.[26]

Health was a high priority, and Frelimo emphasised preventive, social medicine. Most Portuguese doctors left after independence, and the new health campaign depended largely on expatriate medical personnel. However, by 1979 a national campaign of immunisation against smallpox, tetanus and measles had reached an estimated 90 per cent of the population, and infant mortality had already fallen by 20 per cent.[27]

The main problem for Frelimo was that the modern sector of the economy grew too slowly to be the locomotive of change. Frelimo was trying to coax new social relations into existence in a society where more than 80 per cent of the people still participated in traditional family farming. Not only did the economic infrastructure not allow for rapid social change but there was a more insidious way in which Frelimo's policies were undermined. Although the reforms were intended to produce an integrated concept of a new society, they were not based on any particular sectional interest. On the contrary, traditional interests of all kinds found themselves threatened by the changes — ethnic identity, institutionalised religion, the family, the traditional village leadership, traditional law and marriage, and the ability of the subsistence peasant to enter the consumer economy through marketing his surpluses were all attacked. This left few people who could identify strongly with Frelimo and see themselves as benefiting unequivocally by the proposed changes. The groups most clearly targeted, women and *chibalo* labourers, at best found mixed benefits in the changes — women experiencing the problems of double employment and *chibalo* workers suffering unemployment and poverty.

The census of 1980 showed that progress had been slow, with much of the traditional social structure still intact albeit under threat. However, what the census did not show was that the pace of change, instead of gathering momentum, was about to slow down, and Mozambican society was about to suffer a renewed dis-integration. The key to this development lies in the story of the economy in the first five years after independence.

The economy

The immediate effect of independence was to plunge Mozambique into a deep recession. According to various indicators there was already a down-turn in progress before the Portuguese left, and the effects of the 1973 Arab-Israeli war soon fed through into a deepening world recession which hit the prices paid for tropical raw materials. This alone would have created serious problems for Frelimo, but three other factors helped to create an emergency situation. During the year after independence there was a mass exodus of white settlers and skilled black and Indian workers and professionals, precipitated by the confusion and violence accompanying Frelimo's take-over. The continuation of the war after the Portuguese offered a ceasefire and the massacre of over 9,000 people after the abortive settler *putsch* in September 1974 was followed by the nationalisation of housing, health and education.[28] As early as February 1975 the interim government issued a decree allowing control of private enterprises to be transferred if economic sabotage was suspected.[29] As the exodus gathered momentum further nationalisation measures helped to create a snowball effect. The retreating settlers cashed whatever assets they could. Vehicles were driven out of the country, bank balances were emptied, consumer goods were purchased and taken along. Portuguese companies used a variety of devices to get their assets repatriated including sending money abroad as payment for phantom orders. As the banks in Portugal were nationalised, the Lisbon government suddenly had an interest in seeing balances repatriated and did little to prevent the drain on resources.[30] The settler exodus also deprived the country of most of its skilled personnel, so that the back-up services for the industrial sector largely collapsed. For example, the port and railway complex lost 7,000 skilled workers.[31]

At the same time South Africa started to lay off Mozambican workers and the cash flows from earnings on the Rand began to dry up. In 1975 113,488 Mozambicans had been officially recruited by the South Africans but in 1976 the figure was only 32,648. In 1978 the South African government refused to renew the deferred pay agreement.[32] Declining cash incomes from migrant workers coincided with a collapse of Mozambique's service industries such as tourism with its large employment of domestic labour. The third factor which hit the economy was climatic. Heavy rains in 1977 and 1978 led to flooding in some vital agricultural areas including the Limpopo valley, and these years were followed by the onset of drought which lasted at least till 1982 and brought the population in much of the country to the edge of starvation.

The effects of the depression were to create a corkscrew of economic decline which threatened to spiral ever downwards. Mozambique's export-earning sector, the plantations and peasant-grown cash crops (chiefly cashew), suffered severely. *Chibalo* finally ended with the revolution of 1974 and plantations were unable to get workers. The Portuguese managers began to leave and decline in output was matched by decline in world prices. At the same time the government, faced with a huge influx of unemployed into the cities, introduced price controls over food. Unable to pay for consumer goods, country stores soon ran out of stock, and the family farms, no longer having to fulfill quotas and with nothing to buy with their cash earnings which anyway were fixed artificially low, ceased to grow cash crops. This virtual collapse of the agricultural economy affected all sectors. Between 1974 and 1976 production of export crops fell by 40 per cent, peasant-grown maize by 20 per cent, cassava by 61 per cent, and settler agricultural production by 50 per cent. Industrial production fell in the same period by 36 per cent.[33]

Meanwhile the same factors were helping to push up the import bill. Unemployed workers from the agricultural sector and unemployed miners from South Africa moved into the cities to find work. In five years the population of the capital doubled, and had to be fed with imported food since most of the Portuguese farmers who had supplied the cities had left by 1977. Between 1975 and 1982 there was a fourfold increase in food imports and a tenfold increase in their cost, until they constituted 60 per cent of all consumer goods imported and 21 per cent of all imports.[34]

Frelimo's immediate response to these challenges was to nationalise Portuguese businesses that had been abandoned and install managerial teams to run them. The state soon controlled a huge sector of the economy ranging from major plantations and factories down to local village stores and retail outlets. It has been estimated that by 1978 50 per cent of all businesses had come under state control and that by 1981 65 per cent of industrial production, 85 per cent of transport and 90 per cent of construction was within the state sector.[35] It has been pointed out that this 'nationalisation' was forced on Frelimo by the need to take urgent action to prevent a collapse and that it should not be taken as indicating a predetermined plan to socialise the economy. The same point has been made about the nationalisations carried out by the new government of São Tomé and Príncipe at the same time — a government which never claimed to be a Marxist one. This interpretation is valid up to a point but it is fairly clear that the pressure to nationalise huge sectors of the economy was welcome to many in Frelimo and still more to its expatriate advisers. It justified pragmatically action which Frelimo wanted to take for ideological reasons.

The early days of trying to run a modern economy when all the technicians had fled was chaotic but led to an enthusiasm at home and abroad which Frelimo skilfully harnessed. Aid began to arrive from Eastern Bloc countries, and crowds of *cooperantes* speaking a multitude of languages tried to replace the departed Portuguese. Gradually some kind of order returned to the state and Frelimo began to institute plans for the economy. It was clear that there was a long-term need to create an integrated and balanced economy to replace the variously developed and force-fed sectors which had contributed to the needs of the *escudo* zone. In one respect this was achieved for, as Fig. 20.1 shows, one of the results of independence was the striking decline of trade with Portugal.

In the short term there was a pressing need to feed the population and to generate some export earnings. After the Third Party Congress in 1977 Frelimo created a National Planning Commission to co-ordinate the planning of the various ministries. A highly centralised national development plan was produced which identified the modern sectors of the economy under state control as the locomotives for the growth of the economy as a whole. This modern sector was to receive major investment, and its growth was supposed to generate the resources to bring ever more aspects of the economy within its scope. But, as with the colonial development plans before it, investment seldom reached the planned levels and the state enterprises were unable to contribute significantly to the resources available for the national plan, which came to depend exclusively on external finance.[36]

The most important part of this modern state sector consisted of the state farms, which by 1982 worked 140,000 hectares of land. Frelimo divided the agricultural sector into four distinct parts — family farms, private farms, co-operatives and state farms. The state farms were created partly from the abandoned estates of the Portuguese, and pre-empted any possibility that these would be distributed to peasant families or turned into co-operatives. Some state farms were former plantations, but others were formed by grouping the smallholdings of the *colonatos* into huge state-managed concerns. An example of the latter was the massive Complexo Agro-Industrial do Limpopo (CAIL), consisting of 16,000 hectares and including a rice-dehusking factory, a sausage and cheese factory and tomato and tobacco processing plants. To create CAIL Frelimo had to thwart the aspirations of many hundreds of peasant farmers who had hoped either to regain land lost to the original *colonato* or to acquire one of the irrigated farms as a probationer or a *colono*.[37]

Plans were drawn up to run the state farms using high technology and the latest scientific farming methods. They were to produce the

% of imports to:-

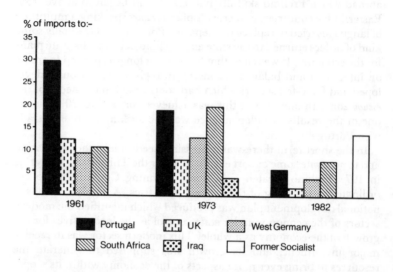

Portugal   UK   West Germany   South Africa   Iraq   Former Socialist

% of exports from:-

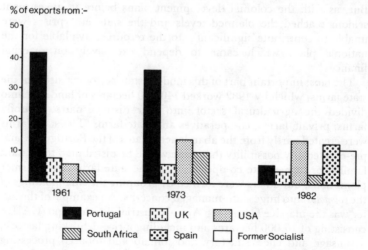

Portugal   UK   USA   South Africa   Spain   Former Socialist

Fig. 20.1. TRADE PARTNERS, 1961, 1973, 1983

Source: J. Hanlon, *Mozambique: The Revolution under Fire*, p. 286.

food to feed the cities, while their surpluses earned exchange for the government. Under the guidance of Eastern bloc managers, investment was poured into the state farms. Huge consignments of machinery were imported to replace what the Portuguese had removed or destroyed, and it has been estimated that the state farms received over 90 per cent of all agricultural investment during the first five years after independence — CAIL alone taking 50 per cent in 1977. More significantly they continued to rely on seasonal wage labour and thereby, as Michel Cahen has phrased it, 'preserved the social relations of colonialism'.[38]

There was the same concentration on technological investment in the modern industrial sector. By 1981 the state-owned industries accounted for 65 per cent of industrial production, 85 per cent of transport, 90 per cent of construction and 40 per cent of commerce; and within the agricultural sector, state enterprises accounted for 85 per cent of sugar, 90 per cent of tea and 80 per cent of rice production (Fig. 20.2).[39] After the collapse of 1974–6, the Mozambique economy had grown overall by 11.6 per cent between 1977 and 1981 and in some key sectors had returned to the production level of 1970.[40] This was a considerable achievement given the post-1974 collapse and the disastrous circumstances in which the government subsequently tried to operate. What soon became clear, however, was that the high levels of production had been obtained by massive and uneconomic inputs of investment and by sucking in imports of machinery, chemicals etc. which could not be paid for. Far from the economy taking off, the large and cumbersome enterprises were threatening to drag the whole of Mozambique down into bankruptcy. However, the full impact of the policies pursued in those years cannot be seen because catastrophe was soon to overtake the country and regular economic activity in most sectors ceased. The statistics that should have provided a picture of what was happening had little meaning.

Nevertheless, what appears to have been happening to the economy is this. The state enterprises had been receiving the major share of all investment. This took the form of importing advanced technology and heavy machinery which proved expensive to run because of the high price of fuel, and rapidly became uneconomic because the ability to service this machinery and provide spare parts did not exist. After 1976 paying for these capital goods became increasingly difficult, and consumer imports (except for food) had to be cut back, so that retail outlets soon collapsed as they had nothing to sell (Fig. 20.3). Shortages of consumer goods were exacerbated by the steady rise of wages in monetary terms. The lack of goods in the shops led to rapid inflation, a black market and a spreading web of corruption. Eventually it forced more and more people out of the cash economy altogether

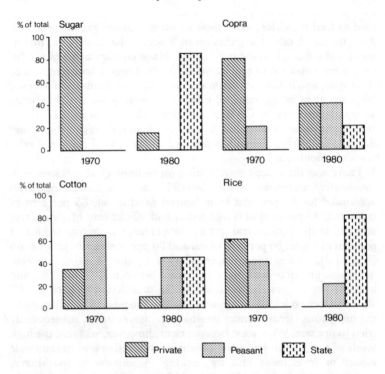

FIG. 20.2. CROP PRODUCTION BY SECTOR, 1970 and 1980

Source: J. Hanlon, *Mozambique: The Revolution under Fire*, p. 286.

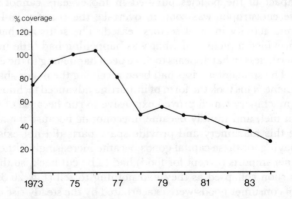

FIG. 20.3. IMPORTS COVERED BY EXPORTS, 1973–1983

Source: Marc Wuyts, 'Accumulation, Social Services and Socialist Transition. . . .',
p. 143.

and back into subsistence farming. This was the reverse of what had been intended, which was that an expanding modern economy would draw people out of the subsistence sector.[41].

The state farms laboured to maintain their levels of output and achieved what they did only by inputs on a vastly uneconomic scale. The state farm policy had focused on continuing to produce high-quality food characteristic of the settler market before independence. The state farms were given no autonomy in what they produced or how they produced it. Central planning set production targets which were worked out according to supposedly scientific norms for rates of productivity, with local managers and accountants being given little discretion. Real output seldom came anywhere near what had been planned.[42] Production levels were achieved by applying very heavy inputs of fertiliser, pesticide and machinery, and after a few years' experience most observers concluded that the output of state farms was less, in monetary value, than the input.[43] One estimate for CAIL suggested that in 1982 it took 2.86 *meticais* of inputs to produce 1 *metical* of rice.[44]

The other sector to receive some attention from the government was that of the cooperatives. These were regulated by the 1979 Cooperative Law which established a structure for their organisation and government and by 1984 17 per cent of communal villages had a cooperative although these involved only 2.7 per cent of the population.[45] During the first eight years the cooperatives received only 2 per cent of government agricultural investment, and the impression that they were considered the poor relation in the family of state enterprises is correct. Their managers and accountants received little training, and cooperatives took second place to the state farms in obtaining machinery and other imports; also, they were only able to pay workers a fraction of the wages offered by the state farms.[46] Not surprisingly the cooperatives that proved most successful were those that attracted experienced and relatively wealthy farmers who found the front of a cooperative a useful way of obtaining state aid that was denied to the private sector.

During the first seven or eight years after independence Frelimo wholly neglected the peasant family sector, believing that it would in time be fully absorbed into the system of cooperatives and state enterprises. But the family sector, dwelling in what Marc Wuyts called 'its underworld of subsistence production', was not marginal to the Mozambique economy.[47] The family farm provided, and continued to provide, the pool from which seasonal labour was drawn by large agricultural enterprises. Moroever, at independence this sector had been responsible for 30 per cent of marketed (including exported) agricultural production.[48] However, it had suffered from the decline in migrant labour and urban employment since such capital inputs as it could afford, like the purchase of oxen and ploughs, came from migrant remittances and urban wages. Frelimo noted the dwindling output from the family farm sector and tried to counter it by introducing a system of bartering whereby consumer goods were made available only in return for cash crops.[49]

By the early 1980s all indicators suggested that the gamble of achieving growth led by the state sector was failing. Not only were investment and production targets for state enterprises not being met but the attempt to obtain external finance and import capital goods for the state farms had opened up a huge trade and payments deficit.

Foreign policy

Newly-independent Mozambique was born into a dangerous part of the world. The 'white laager' of the 1960s had provided protection for white South Africa, for white rule in Namibia and for the rebel regime of Ian Smith in Rhodesia. The falling away of Angola and Mozambique left Namibia and Rhodesia dangerously exposed and led to a direct escalation of the independence struggle in those countries. The collapse of Portuguese rule also soon led to a major reorientation of South African policy, of which the invasion of Angola in 1975–6 was a foretaste. At the same time Frelimo had debts to pay. The solidarity of the CONCP states with each other and with the SWAPO-ZANU-ANC alliance in southern Africa was one of the fixed points in its political universe.

Outside the southern African region, Frelimo's relations with Portugal remained tense for some years after 1975. Up till 1978 Frelimo was pursuing a policy of nationalising businesses and property that had belonged to Portuguese settlers, and as late as 1979 Portugal withdrew an official delegation to Maputo (as Lourenço Marques was now named) when a Portuguese supporter of Renamo was executed.[50] Numerous contentious issues were still unresolved and the interests of the former settlers were espoused by right-wing politicians like Sá Carneiro. However, with Sá Carneiro's death in 1980 the ascendancy in Portuguese politics passed to the centre-left politicians, Soares and Eanes, and relations with the former colonies soon improved. Eanes visited Maputo in 1981 and in 1982 Portugal signed a military aid agreement involving arms, training and intelligence to help Mozambique in the fight with Renamo.[51]

If relations with Portugal were difficult, Frelimo felt it had firm friends in a number of minor Western countries like Sweden and the Netherlands, and could look to the Eastern bloc and its surrogates in Cuba for practical as well as diplomatic assistance. Enemies seemed rather remote. Britain had failed to resolve the Rhodesian dispute but maintained a posture, under its Labour government (1974–9) at any rate, that was nominally friendly to the liberation movements. The United States, wrestling with the Watergate scandal and unwilling to back South Africa's attempt to intervene in Angola, was soon to see the sunburst of liberalism associated with the presidency of Jimmy Carter, which brought Andrew Young to the United Nations as US ambassador. And with the *verligtes* (moderate nationalists) in the ascendant in South Africa, Frelimo did not feel unduly threatened.

After the fiasco of the intervention in Angola, the *verligtes* in South Africa urged a policy of friendship and co-operation with newly-independent Mozambique; it was argued that the old close relationship built on economic interdependence would continue and keep Mozambique from political extremism. South Africa offered technical assistance to help run and improve the ports and railways, and recruitment of Mozambican miners continued. Maputo continued to get its electricity from South Africa and to supply South Africa with heavy fuel oil from its refinery. Above all, the powerlines of the Cabora Bassa dam strode across Rhodesia carrying Mozambican-generated electricity to the Rand industrial complex. In turn Frelimo recognised the extreme vulnerability of Maputo to South African pressures and abstained from direct confrontation with Pretoria; for example, it refused to allow the ANC to set up military bases in Mozambique.

Nevertheless, Frelimo felt free to take a fairly radical and exposed stand in world and regional affairs. It expressed strong support for the liberation movements in southern Africa, and in 1974 joined the alliance of front-line states in support of the ANC and SWAPO, closed its borders with Rhodesia, and helped to tighten the UN sanctions. The ANC were allowed to set up offices in Mozambique. Eastern-bloc missions began to arrive, and after 1977 Marxist slogans appeared on the walls and public buildings in Maputo. Mozambique joined the Non-Aligned Movement, which it saw not as a posture of neutrality in world affairs but as a positive commitment to fight 'imperialism' throughout the world, particularly in southern Africa.[52] In the UN it voted with the PLO and did what it could to support South American guerrilla movements in El Salvador and Nicaragua. At the same time it sought bilateral aid agreements with Libya, India, Algeria and Iraq.[53]

This was a foreign policy which repaid debts and asserted the right to an independent line in world and regional affairs. Its greatest success was undoubtedly a relatively speedy end to the Rhodesian rebellion. Mozambique allowed ZANU and ZAPU to operate from its territory and helped to support an estimated 150,000 refugees from the fighting in Rhodesia. By 1978 the white Rhodesians were looking for a way out of their difficulties and in 1979 independence was finally negotiated and power transferred to ZANU which, unlike Frelimo, had been wise enough to agree to seek a mandate at the polls. Machel is supposed to have urged Mugabe to take positive measures to encourage the white settlers to stay to prevent an economic collapse similar to that experienced in Mozambique.[54] The new government in Harare was to have warm and close relations with Mozambique which were to complement the still close relations with Tanzania to the north. In 1980 Mozambique was in the forefront of negotiations for the formation of SADCC, the association of southern African states, which was formed to counter South Africa's economic dominance in the subcontinent.

The fall of the white Rhodesian regime precipitated what was tantamount to a revolution in South Africa. In 1978 John Vorster was ousted from the leadership of the Nationalist Party as a result of the 'Muldergate' scandals. Under his successor, P.W. Botha, South African policy was to veer away from the co-existence advocated by the *verligtes* and become dominated by the military and by the last phase of the Cold War ushered in by the election of Ronald Reagan to the United States presidency. Regional co-operation was replaced by frequent direct attacks by the South Africa Defence Force (SADF) on Mozambique, culminating in the raid on Maputo in 1981. Mozambique's response to this change was to move closer to Eastern bloc countries. Soviet warships visited Maputo after the South African raid, and trade and aid agreements were signed with Bulgaria, East Germany and the Soviet Union. However, Mozambique was never absorbed into the Eastern bloc of states: it was refused entry to COMECON in 1981 and in turn refused to allow the Soviet Union to establish a naval base on the Mozambique coast.

Initially Frelimo was hostile to the NATO countries, and the US consulate in Maputo was closed soon after independence. However, as early as 1978, while the war in Rhodesia still continued, Machel visited the United States and began to seek Western aid for the development of the country. He and his foreign minister, Joaquim Chissano, who succeeded him as President in 1986, always maintained that the regime had not been hostile to Western interests and had welcomed Western investment when this was offered.

South Africa's destabilisation policy

Mozambique's existence had always been closely linked with that of the other states and peoples of central and southern Africa, and thus it is not surprising to find the root-cause of the catastrophe that overtook the country in the 1980s to lie in this region. South Africa's embattled stance towards the rest of Africa had arisen during the period of decolonisation when the white settler regimes in South West Africa, South Africa, Rhodesia and the Portuguese colonies tried to hold out against decolonisation and form a block of white-ruled territories in the southern part of the continent. This 'white laager' was breached in 1975 with the withdrawal of the Portuguese. There was then a battle within the South African cabinet between those who wanted to pursue a policy of friendship towards newly-independent states to the north, with the long-term objective of spreading South African influence through making them economically dependent, and those, impressed by Israel's policy towards the Arabs, who wanted to maintain South Africa's ascendancy by military means with or without — though preferably with — the backing of the United States. Behind these rival policies were certain economic assumptions. The *verligtes* looked to expand South African investment and the markets for South African goods in black Africa, rightly seeing that South Africa could not compete in world markets with the industrial superpowers. The hard-line *verkramptes* believed South Africa could survive by attracting outside investment and becoming, like Israel, a high-technology outpost of the Western economies.

The fall of the Portuguese colonial regime led to the immediate ascendancy of the *verkramptes*, who launched an attack on Angola in October 1975. But the United States would not back this forward policy and the subsequent withdrawal of the SADF, the arrival of the Cubans in Angola and the installation of the MPLA in Luanda marked a major defeat for the *verkramptes*. By 1980, however, the balance of forces had changed, with P.W. Botha replacing Vorster as head of the South African government in 1978, the collapse of Ian Smith's settler regime in 1979, and the formation in 1980 of the SADCC with Mozambique and newly-independent Zimbabwe among its most important members. However, the decisive factor in the change in policy was the arrival of Reagan at the White House in 1980. With his coming to power, those interested in promoting the Cold War, whatever their real motive, were given their head. South Africa was now free to play the role of Israel in the southern part of the African continent.

In spite of being a strong politician who for ten years kept firm control of power in South Africa, P.W. Botha relied from the first on the backing of the armed forces, and the inner cabinet which dealt with security matters was the country's real government during this period. The foreign policy pursued in the 1980s has usually been described by the term 'destabilisation'. The SADF began a series of direct attacks on neighbouring countries, allegedly striking at ANC bases, but in fact gaining a psychological ascendancy by

After Independence

demonstrating the impunity with which South Africa could attack the independent states to the north. It stepped up the direct war on the Angolan border, permanently occupying a part of southern Angola just as Israel did in southern Lebanon. However, the most striking and effective aspect of destabilisation was the support given to dissident and rebel movements in neighbouring — and in some rather less than neighbouring — countries, and the creation of these where, as in Mozambique, they had not existed before.

The objectives of this policy were never clearly stated and may not have been fully articulated by the South Africans themselves. It seems that at times different policies were pursued by various government agencies, which would explain this uncertainty over final objectives. However, it has been alleged that the principal object of 'destabilisation' was to prevent the SADCC becoming an economic force in the region. With that aim in view, the railways and ports which linked the SADCC countries to the outside world and were not under South African control had to be put out of action. This was effectively accomplished when the railways to Beira and Lobito were destroyed by sabotage in the early 1980s. Once the SADCC countries had been made dependent on South African railways and ports, the government in Pretoria was able to tighten the economic screws as and when it pleased.[55]

The second objective has always been held to be the destruction of the external bases of the ANC and SWAPO, a carbon copy of Israel's relentless war against the Palestinians, and a third objective appears to have been to weaken the surrounding states politically so that they would not be able to act effectively in a united way against South Africa. Destabilisation meant that the economies of the surrounding states were undermined, their budgets had to make ever-increasing provision for security, and internal dissension was fomented. South Africa does not appear to have wished to replace the neighbouring governments with its own clients, and it made no serious attempt to topple the rulers of the frontline states. It has been argued that its interests were best served by having weak, nominally Marxist or left-wing regimes because this guaranteed the continued backing of the Reagan administration, or at least of the rabidly anti-communist agencies within the administration which the President himself backed.

A final aspect of South African foreign policy at this time was its interventions outside the southern African region. Of these the best documented were its attempt to stage a coup in the Seychelles, its diplomatic offensive in Madagascar and the strong backing it gave to the French mercenaries who took over the Comoro Islands in 1978. These policies represented a South African offensive against diplomatic and economic isolation. They were accompanied by attempts to find investment outlets, and served to keep open the route by which oil and arms could continue to reach South Africa. They enabled South Africa to create friendships of expediency and interest in the world by forging links with Iran, France, Israel and their clients. The Comoro Islands were also seen as a useful base for possible South African attacks on northern Mozambique and Tanzania.[56]

This classic analysis of South African policy does not bring out the real contradictions that lay embedded in it. The policy of destabilisation was pursued in Angola and Mozambique with a venom and ruthlessness which did not so much weaken as virtually destroy the economies of those two countries and threaten to destroy the economy of the whole region. Yet South Africa's own wellbeing was ultimately linked with the prosperity of Mozambique and Angola. South Africa obtained water and electricity from Mozambican and Angolan dams, it needed Mozambican labour, obtained its heavy fuel oil from a refinery in Mozambique, and still depended on the port of Maputo and the rail link with it to serve the Rand industrial complex. Moreover South African business had heavy investments in Mozambique which were threatened by destabilisation. It was never clear how South Africa's economic interests or even its long-term political interests were served by the scale of the destruction which destabilisation unleashed. However, South Africa's responsibility for wreaking this destruction on its neighbours cannot be doubted.

The rise of Renamo

In the fifteen months between the Portuguese revolution of 1974 and the raising of the flag of independent Mozambique there were a number of attempts to put together a viable opposition movement against Frelimo. Although there were some African dissidents who had either been expelled from Frelimo or who had been associated during the war of liberation with marginal and shadowy movements like COREMO, the most determined efforts to organise opposition came from some settlers. Their efforts came too late and did not rally significant support from the white population, which had never been used to organising itself and controlled none of the levers of power. Moreover all such moves were firmly opposed by the Portuguese army and by the left-wing politicians in Lisbon who increasingly controlled events during the crucial months between April 1974 and July 1975.

Those principally involved in the opposition to Frelimo fled abroad, taking with them a determination to sabotage the new regime. The government of Ian Smith was the first to give dissident Mozambicans some haven. Jorge Jardim and his agent Orlando Cristina are supposed to have escaped with some of the DGS files and helped the Rhodesians found Renamo, recruiting elements from the black military and paramilitary units that had fought for the Portuguese. Firmly under the control of the Rhodesian security organisation, Renamo developed as a military unit and not a political movement. It was given the task of leading raids into Mozambique to disrupt communications, divert the attention of the government and act in support of Rhodesian forces on special operations against ZANLA guerrillas. In this capacity Renamo forces helped the Rhodesians in their commando raid on the Beira oil storage depots in March 1979.[57]

The fall of Ian Smith's government deprived Renamo of its patron, and in October 1979 its only significant presence in Mozambique was destroyed when a Frelimo security operation captured its headquarters in Gorongosa. At this stage Renamo was simply a mercenary unit of a white colonial army. After Jardim's death in 1976 it had had no political aspirations and it would probably have disappeared along with other agencies of Smith's rule had the SADF not decided to take it over as a going concern. In 1980 Renamo was transferred with much of its equipment to South Africa and given training facilities and a base in the northern Transvaal.

At about the same time Renamo's original leader, Matsangaissa, was killed in action and Afonso Dhlakama won a violent contest to succeed. From this time Renamo, directed by the SADF, became the main instrument for destabilising the Frelimo government. At first it had no permanent bases in Mozambique and its units were supplied either by sea or by air from South Africa. Its orders were not to attack well-defended military targets or towns but to sabotage the economic infrastructure and the basis for the rural economy. Its attacks were levelled against the roads and railways — its most sensational act of sabotage being the blowing-up of the Zambesi rail bridge in 1983. It also attacked foreign *cooperantes* — killing or kidnapping 100 in the five years up to 1985. However, its principal targets were the rural population. It struck at communal villages and cooperatives, at social infrastructure like hospitals, schools and government buildings, and at the installations of the rural economy like plantation buildings and warehouses.[58]

Although Renamo's leaders were largely from the Shona-speaking Ndau, its rank and file were increasingly recruited by kidnapping young men and boys from rural areas. By 1984 its numbers had increased to between 15,000 and 20,000 and it was able to operate in all parts of Mozambique, though concentrating in the central band, destroying the plantation economy of Zambesia and the Beira-based rail network.

At the same time Renamo began to develop as a political organisation. Offices, purporting to represent the movement overseas, appeared in Lisbon, in West Germany and in the United States, and it was alleged that in 1984 Renamo held a 'congress' which produced a statement of policy. That Renamo had any existence as a political movement in the early 1980s is doubtful. For their own political purposes South Africa and the Reagan administration needed Renamo to have at least as much credibility as an anti-communist movement as UNITA, the vehicle of US and South African policy in Angola. But Dhlakama and his agents were not likely to produce anything which would prove acceptable even to the unexacting standards of right-wing opinion in South Africa and the United States. So various non-African individuals were recruited to provide a European and American front for Renamo. The best known of these was Evo Fernandes, a Goanese, who ran Renamo's Lisbon office until his murder in 1981. There is no evidence that these front organisations and their self-appointed leaders had any influence on Renamo within Mozambique, or that they represented any coherent political organisation based in the country. Most of Renamo's officials in Europe and the United States appear to have been freelance operators playing the right-wing political scene in search of funding.[59]

In 1984, however, there was a significant development in South African policy which proved of the utmost importance in the evolution of Renamo and of Mozambique as a whole. On 16 March Machel and Botha signed the Nkomati Accord.

Frelimo's response to Renamo

It was some time before Frelimo acknowledged, even to itself, that Renamo was a serious threat to its plans and to the stability of the whole state. The problem was partly psychological. Since its founding in 1963, Frelimo had never been seriously challenged; dissident individuals and breakaway movements had all been isolated and withered for lack of support. Because Frelimo had never been elected to office, it was doubly important to show that no other movement commanded any popularity or support, and that it had unchallenged control of the country. It was difficult for Frelimo's leaders even to be seen to be taking seriously a phenomenon like Renamo, which by 1980 appeared to have gone the way of all other movements which had attempted to challenge Frelimo; its international support had collapsed and its only base in Mozambique had been captured. How could the regime explain the re-emergence of the Renamo in new and revived form?

By the early 1980s there were other factors besides Renamo that

caused Frelimo to try to reassess its policies and its stance in international affairs. The natural disasters of flood and drought came to a
head in the early part of the decade with widespread starvation and
the collapse of the rural economy. With them came a realisation that
the state farms and cooperatives were not producing enough to support the country's population. The decline in living standards was
affecting all sections of the population, but most serious was the
alienation of the peasantry whose support was so essential to the
regime in combating rural guerrilla activity like that of Renamo.
Moreover, severe balance of payments difficulties and growing
foreign debt forced Mozambique to face the realities of its international position while the newly-emergent SADCC, of which Mozambique was a founder-member, was as a matter of policy trying to court
Western aid.

Therefore Machel began in the early 1980s consciously to mend
relations with Western countries, typically claiming that Frelimo had
always been open to foreign investment and favourably disposed to
the West. In 1980 Mozambique joined the African Development
Bank and in 1982 the government took the decision to court Western
aid and apply to join the International Monetary Fund (IMF). At
the same time Mozambique sought bilateral aid agreements from
Western countries including Britain and the United States. The latter
insisted on the condition that all aid should be channelled towards the
private sector and in its Fourth Party Congress in 1983 Frelimo
adopted a radical change of policy, immediately associated with
another presidential 'campaign' — the campaign for production. In
1984 it joined the Lome Convention and in September was accepted
as a member of the IMF, at once beginning negotiations for a
rescheduling of the country's debts which by that time amounted to
eighteen times its annual exports. In 1987 agreement was reached
with the IMF on a package of measures.[60]

The main change of direction in internal policy affected agriculture.
There was to be no expansion of the state farm sector; its management
was to be decentralised and greater resources would be channelled to
the private and family farms. At the same time, some price controls
were lifted. One immediate consequence of the new policy was the
breaking-up of the great state enterprises like CAIL into smaller units
and the distribution of some state land to private farmers. At the same
time the Mozambique government, assisted by foreign aid donors,
began to set up support services for peasant and private farmers. The
results were impressive. Irrigated rice production in the Chokwe area,
for example, rose from 12,000 tonnes in 1982 to 50,000 tonnes in
1986–7 despite the difficulties caused by the civil war and the lack of
foreign exchange.[61] However, some of the economic and political

measures taken after the 1983 Congress smacked of desperation. To boost agricultural production there was a round-up of urban unemployed, and youths were recruited into the army and others forcibly deported to the rural areas. The formation of communal villages was pushed ahead, sometimes at gunpoint, until about 20 per cent of the population could be said to have been communalised, and production quotas were once again demanded from the peasantry within the 'family sector'.[62] In 1984 a Private Investment Code was adopted to try to lure significant private funds into the country, and in May 1985 price and wage controls were lifted in a major retreat from the idea of a planned economy. There were also appeals to Portuguese businessmen to return.[63]

In spite of these significant changes in policy, Renamo depredations and the effects of seasons of drought had, by the beginning of 1984, wrought such destruction to the economy that Machel was forced into a political gamble which was seen by some as a measure of desperation and by others as politically daring and courageous. He entered into discussions with Botha for a security agreement which was eventually to be signed at Nkomati in March 1984. The Nkomati Accord attracted much international attention and was widely interpreted as a triumph for South African policy. Machel, the wicked Marxist leader, was seen to be coming to beg for terms from the hated apartheid regime, which he had denounced with such vigour. At Nkomati both sides agreed not to support armed insurrection in each other's countries and to adopt measures of mutual co-operation. On South Africa's side the Accord formed part of a pattern of diplomatic activity designed to force the front-line states into a client relationship with South Africa that would be publicly recognised in a series of formal bilateral agreements.[64]

Most observers saw Mozambique's signing of the Accord as a symptom of desperation and political weakness. However, one should perhaps place it in the wider context of Machel's long-term diplomatic initiative aimed at Western countries. Shortly after Nkomati, Machel made a number of important visits abroad including a much-heralded meeting with Margaret Thatcher: pictures of the slight figure of Machel inspecting a contingent of scarlet-coated guardsmen in London were displayed outside the British Embassy in Maputo and continued for some time to attract favourable attention. This diplomatic campaign had a considerable if quiet success. Machel was an impressive public figure and his wooing of the West led to important results. The government of Margaret Thatcher became favourably disposed, sending a military mission to train Mozambican officers while in the United States a Congressional inquiry into Renamo produced a report devastating in its revelations of the extent and nature of its atrocities. This stopped in its tracks what had threatened to become a Renamo bandwagon in right-wing American circles. At the same time relations with Portugal became much closer. Eanes visited Maputo and Machel visited Lisbon, and Portugal extended export credits to help the Mozambique economy.[65] Machel also sought to rebuild relations with the Vatican; as part of a campaign to win back the support of Catholics, he restored confiscated church property in 1983 and allowed churches once again to run their own schools.

Nearer home Machel and the leaders of the other front-line states moved closer together to confront the threat of Renamo. Tanzania and Zimbabwe sent troops in 1984 to help the Frelimo forces, and there were concerted efforts to persuade Malawi to withdraw its clandestine support for Renamo-related activities. In December 1985 the Beira Corridor Authority was set up to concentrate international influence and aid on the reopening of the vital rail and port link which Zimbabwean troops were to defend. This campaign culminated in the fateful summit of September 1986.

Was Machel deceived by South Africa at Nkomati? Did South Africa gain all the publicity advantages without altering its policy? At first sight this appears to have been so: Renamo's attacks continued and when one of its bases in Gorongosa, Casa Banana, was taken in 1985, it was clear from documents discovered there that South African agencies were continuing their support. Nevertheless certain things did change as a result of Nkomati. South Africa once again began to recruit Mozambican labourers and its traffic tried to use the port of Maputo. A joint South Africa-Mozambique commission began to examine the Cabora Bassa power-lines and a plan was drawn up to rebuild the pylons. It has been argued that the main outcome of Nkomati was to make Mozambique once again economically dependent on South Africa as in colonial times,[66] but if this was so, it is difficult to see the commitment to restore the power-lines being undertaken by a government which was knowingly and by design planning to sabotage its own infrastructure.

It appears that after Nkomati, support for Renamo ceased to be official South African policy. However, certain agencies of the South African security services continued to provide it with support, and the government did nothing to prevent this happening. It became diplomatically more convenient that Renamo should not operate out of South Africa itself, and from 1984 Malawi became the principal channel for foreign support reaching the bandits. It seems likely also that SADF agents based in the Comoro Islands used this obscure Islamic state, which after 1978 was effectively controlled by French mercenary adventurers, as another route for the reinforcement of Renamo fighters. Nkomati appears to have opened up something of a gap bet-ween the official public policy of the South African Foreign Affairs Ministry and the activities of Magnus Malan and the military hierarchy.[67]

The events of 1986 can best be undertstood in these terms. In September 1986 Machel flew to Malawi with Robert Mugabe and Kenneth Kaunda in order to persuade President Banda to close Malawi as a route for South African penetration. Banda was reportedly convinced by the pressure put on him. Before any action could be taken, however, Machel had gone from the scene. As his plane returned from the Lilongwe summit, it lost course, diverted by a radio beam from South Africa. The plane crashed just inside South Africa, killing the President and a number of his ministers and aides. It is fairly certain that elements inside South Africa brought about the crash, but the motivation for this crime remains obscure. It is not clear that any South African interest was served by Machel's death, and it can only be assumed that elements in the SADF acted independently on the assumption that Frelimo would thus be thrown into disar-ray.[68] If this was the calculation, exactly the opposite occurred. The resulting shock gained Mozambique great international sympathy and helped to unite many Mozambicans. Joaquim Chissano, one of the inner group of Frelimo leaders, succeeded to the presidency without any internal divisions or conflict.

In December John Tembo, the heir-apparent of Hastings Banda, came to Maputo to sign a mutual security arrangement. Malawi was henceforward to withdraw all official or even clandestine support for Renamo, and plans were laid for the reopening of the railway across Mozambique to the coast. Before the pact was signed, however, Renamo had launched a massive invasion of central Mozambique, ushering in a new and disastrous phase of the conflict.

Renamo and the catastrophe

The Renamo campaign in Mozambique which followed the expulsion of the organisation from Malawi in 1986 led to some of the darkest moments in the history of any African country. Up to 1986 there were some signs that Renamo was under the control of foreign masters. However hideous its methods, there was at least some hope that these masters could be persuaded to end the devastation and call back the dogs of war. After 1986 Renamo was increasingly based inside Mozambique itself, and although it continued to receive supplies, help and support from outside organisations, it was less under their control and for the first time had to evolve ways of existing and surviv-ing within the country.

For the first half of the 1980s Renamo fighters had moved from one part of the country to another. When they entered an area their prime target consisted of personnel and any building or installation associated with the government. The choice of these targets was aimed at destroying all trust or belief in the government as an effective, protective or beneficent organisation. Their secondary targets were economic installations ranging from bridges, power-lines and railways to factories, workshops and plant of all kinds. These would be systematically smashed and destroyed, often with meticulous care being taken to damage every piece irreparably. If there was any thought-out long-term objective, it was to drive the population back into a subsistence life in the bush, which was the final negation of all that Frelimo stood for. But much of Renamo's activity was simply the tactics of terror. Men, women and children were massacred or mutilated, and young men and boys were frequently kidnapped and made to commit horrific crimes in order to initiate them into the mentality of the Renamo bands.[69]

These terror tactics were documented in detail not only by Frelimo but also by the US government which, along with its British ally, refused to treat Renamo as a *bona fide* anti-communist movement in spite of pressure from influential right-wing and church quarters in the United States. This had the effect of opening the way to extremist organisations in the United States, Germany, Portugal and South Africa, and elements within the Portuguese and South African military intelligence, to attempt to manipulate Renamo for their own purposes. These purposes began to seem increasingly complex. Renamo had always received support from elements within the Malawi establishment, but in the late 1980s the government of Kenya began to provide aid too. Renamo units became active outside Mozambique, making raids into Zambia and Zimbabwe and allegedly involving themselves in the fighting in Natal only a short step from their old base in the northern Transvaal.[70]

The alliance between Renamo and extreme religious organisations in the West is one of the strangest developments of the post-Nkomati period. Once again this development was orchestrated by elements in South Africa which realised the potential that missionary organisations had for obtaining resources and personnel and channelling them to organisations like Renamo and UNITA. The so-called Frontline Fellowship was the best known of these missionary front organisations. However, playing on the supposed 'religious dimension' of the conflict in Mozambique was also seen as a way of tapping a rich vein of support in the United States. Bizarre extremist organisations, like Christ for the Nations Inc. (CFNI), the Believers Church and the End of Time Handmaidens, raised money there and channelled funds to

Renamo, often making use of a front organisation called Shekinah Missions based in Zimbabwe. The public representation of Renamo fighters as religious revivalists going into battle carrying Bibles provided by god-fearing anti-communist Americans stretches the imagination almost beyond belief.[71]

The result of Renamo's activity was destruction on a massive scale. Generally accepted figures show that by 1990 100,000 people had lost their lives as a result of the fighting and up to 4 million (one-third of the entire population) had been made refugees or been displaced. According to many reports the number of people affected was much larger than these figures suggest. The surrounding countries all received tens of thousands of Mozambican refugees and the government presence was effectively eliminated from large areas of the country.

Once it was compelled to exist for long periods within the borders of Mozambique, Renamo began to change its tactics. Permanent armed camps were set up with fortified villages as outliers. The camps were supported by requisitions on the surrounding population and by kidnapping people as a form of enslaved workforce. The Communal Villages and cooperatives set up by Frelimo were systematically destroyed and the peasantry told to disperse into small villages in the bush. *Mujeebas* were installed in the villages; these were agents of Renamo who acted as overseers, denouncing government collaborators and maintaining the atmosphere of terror and subservience.[72] Gradually Renamo consolidated its hold on areas of the country and, while not abandoning its tactics of terror, began to use other measures against the population. It noted that in many areas there was latent hostility between Frelimo and various traditonal authorities, and Renamo commanders apparently took sides on numerous occasions with local interest groups hostile to Frelimo.

This appears to suggest that the rise of Renamo can be seen as an articulation of rural opposition to Frelimo. It is certainly true that by the early 1980s opposition to Frelimo's policies was widespread. Many families had lost influence and control over their affairs by being moved into Communal Villages, where they were effectively under the control either of party officials or of the lineages on whose land the village was built. Traditional chiefs had also lost influence to party officials or to the new People's Tribunals. This process was documented by the French anthropologist Christian Geffray, working in the district of Eráti north west of Nacala: he noted the extreme disaffection of the local population with the Communal Village programme, so that when Renamo warbands were reported to be in the area whole sectors of the population, often led by lineage heads, would leave the villages and move to areas under Renamo 'protection'.[73]

Frelimo had also denounced many traditional religious practices and was on bad terms with churches and with Islam. Most serious of all, steadily declining living standards had alienated the peasantry. Monetary inflation and a famine of consumer goods had been accompanied by price controls for produce, compulsory bartering and a decline in employment opportunities in migrant labour. After the Fourth Party Conference in 1983 Frelimo decided to pay more attention to the peasant sector, but in giving it a new role in the national economy there was a visible return to hated practices of the colonial era. Production targets were set for peasant families, government officials were sent to villages to enforce production, and there were even reports of corporal punishment being reintroduced.[74] Although these practices were hardly comparable to the crude and brutalising terror of Renamo, they produced a disaffected and apathetic peasantry who were more easily dominated and exploited by Renamo.

The suggestion that some of Renamo's success could be attributed to internal conditions in Mozambique and even to Frelimo's own policies towards the peasantry was deeply resented since it diverted world indignation from South Africa's role in bringing about the disaster, but it seems that these allegations forced Frelimo into reassessing its policies. Luis Honwana, the distinguished Mozambican writer, summed up this realisation when he wrote:

> We didn't realise how influential the traditional authorities were. We are obviously going to have to harmonize traditional beliefs with our political project. Otherwise we are going against things that the vast majority of our people believe; we will be like foreigners in our own country.[75]

Although Renamo offered to hold talks in 1987, this was resisted by Frelimo, which understandably refused to recognise that the people who could perpetrate such appalling massacres were representatives of a *bona fide* political movement. However, by 1990 the situation in southern Africa was changing. The accession to power of F.W. De Klerk and the unbanning of the ANC gave real promise of an end to confrontation and destabilisation. Magnus Malan lost his job in charge of the SADF and the South Africans were deprived of their power-base in the Comoros when French commandos expelled the mercenaries. Encouraged by the new *verligte*-dominated South African government, various mediators emerged who sought to find a basis for peace between Renamo and the Frelimo government, among them the private Lonrho corporation and the Italian government.

Frelimo was now ready to consider alternative ways of bringing about peace, and its overseas aid donors were demanding that it enter into formal negotiations with Renamo. During 1990 Frelimo prepared far-reaching constitutional changes to end one-party rule. The new constitution introduced in November 1990 allowed multi-party elections, freedom of the press and a legal right to strike. The constitution had been brought in against a backdrop of unofficial negotiations with Renamo in which Dhlakama demanded a power-sharing agreement and Frelimo, shrewdly bidding for Western backing, stood out for multi-party elections. In December a limited agreement was signed. Renamo agreed not to attack the rail corridors from Zimbabwe to the sea in return for the withdrawal of Zimbabwean troops to those corridors. As this limited ceasefire became effective, the railway corridors were crowded with refugees seeking a haven of peace.[76]

The change of tactics gave Renamo the advantage of recognition, but by forcing it into the world of diplomacy threatened to rob it of the kind of brutal initiative it had been able to sustain for the previous decade. Frelimo, for its part, was forced to recognise the need for multi-party elections and to seek the mandate of the ballot-box which it had scornfully rejected in 1975. Thus one of Frelimo's major weaknesses over the previous fifteen years, the fact that it had never been voted into power, would be remedied. The ceasefire agreement with Renamo also left the railway corridors free and in this world of murky political compromise the freeing of the rail routes proved a victory for SADCC against one of the few discernible objectives of the original sabotage campaign.

Throughout 1991 Renamo refused to sign a ceasefire or agree to take part in elections. Although the US government and South Africa were now working for a settlement in Mozambique, as they were in Angola, Renamo was being encouraged to resist by private backers in the US, in Portugal and even in Britain, while Kenya had emerged as a powerful regional supporter. Meanwhile Frelimo began to counter Renamo more effectively on the ground among the peasant communities. During 1991 the government cause was helped by the emergence of the *Naparama* — the armed followers of a charismatic leader called António: he claimed to be immune from Renamo bullets and under his inspiration local militias were formed. Renamo suffered some significant defeats and there was a mass return of refugees to their villages throughout much of central Mozambique. By early 1991 it looked as though Frelimo was succeeding in turning the tide on Renamo, not through the conventional means of a modern state but by enlisting those very traditional beliefs which it had been determined to uproot. However, António was killed in clashes with Renamo forces, and by the end of 1991 the brutal stalemate had returned with Frelimo confined to the coastal cities and a few garrisoned towns, and Renamo more or less randomly terrorising the countryside.[77]

During 1992 it became clear that the progress of talks, which were hosted in Rome by the Italian government, depended on the parallel developments in Angola. As MPLA and UNITA agreed a ceasefire and moved towards free elections in October 1992, so there was increasing pressure on Dhlakama to take the same path. After many attempts to stall the negotiations, a ceasefire agreement pending elections was signed in Rome on 15 October 1992.

As the possibility of some settlement became more realistic, the full weakness of Frelimo's government came under international scrutiny. The latter part of the 1980s had seen not only economic collapse but also the collapse of the machinery of government. Officials were not paid, and at every stage corruption was rife. Consignments of foreign aid mysteriously disappeared or else simply could not be distributed. The army was demoralised, unpaid and unequipped. It even had difficulty maintaining its numbers, and the pressgang regularly rounded up likely youths for military service. Moreover, army discipline broke down. Bands of armed soldiers played their part in terrorising the countryside and robbing communities, so that observers were often left in doubt whether atrocities were being committed by Renamo, the army or by groups of freelance bandits. Early in 1990 there was a series of strikes in the public services and in industry, which the government met with increases in bonuses and pay. A drought, more severe than any of those in the previous decade, returned in 1992 to compound the suffering and starvation caused by war and the breadown of government. This breakdown in government authority was partly the result of the aid organisations themselves. Western aid channelled through Western-controlled agencies bypassed the Frelimo government. Health programmes paid for by donors were often not coordinated with the government officials, and some aid organisations stated explicitly that their objective was to change the policy of the Frelimo government.[78]

However, by the early 1990s foreign aid of one kind or another constituted 70 per cent of GNP and donors and agencies which had kept the country afloat for nearly a decade were agreed that peace represented a last chance before a final collapse of the structures of a settled society.[79]

Conclusion

The savage destruction wrought by Renamo can be seen purely as a consequence of South Africa's cynical desire to destabilise its neighbour and reduce to impotence the radical Frelimo government that had so often expressed support for the ANC. The weight of known facts about Renamo's origins and development make it clear that this is at least part of the truth. More recently Renamo's success, if not the very existence of the organisation, has been attributed to the failures of Frelimo's first ten years of government. In some distorted way Renamo is seen as a protest movement sweeping up the grievances of peasants, traditional authorities, religious and ethnic groups and even, more generally, 'youth'. It is even represented as a flag-carrier for capitalism, born-again Christianity and 'the West'. Although grievances against the Frelimo government were many, such an interpretation can only be held by people who are politically motivated and know relatively little about either the history of Mozambique or latter-day conditions in the country.

In reality Renamo must be understood, as this book has continually argued, in the context of Mozambican history. Most of the peoples of Mozambique have lived in small, dis-integrated social and political units. The matrilineal societies north of the Zambesi have always experienced tension between the local control of the matrilineage over land and resources and the political power wielded by males through war, commerce, slave trading and slave owning. South of the Zambesi the patrilineal Shona, Tsonga and Nguni have found it difficult to maintain large chieftaincies because of the unsuitability of much of lowland Mozambique for cattle rearing. In these circumstances forms of banditry have become endemic. Communities competed not so much to own cattle as to swell their numbers through slave raiding and the acquisition of women. Because of the relatively small and dis-organised political units in much of the country, there has always been the opportunity for bandit leaders, warlords, mercenaries and the like to carve out domains for themselves. Banditry and warlordism have always become more serious during the frequent periods of drought and famine when the frail agricultural base of the peasantry in the drier areas collapses and starving people are driven either to become bandits themselves or to submit to the domination of the warlords.

Banditry of this kind is so common in the history of Mozambique that it is pointless even to begin to list examples. Suffice it to say that such bandit leaders might be local men (enterprising hunters or traders, younger sons of chiefly families and so on), or foreigners (Indians, Portuguese, Muslims), or invaders from the African interior (Maravi chiefs, Yao, Makololo or Nguni). Whatever their origin, the Mozambican warlords have used similar methods. A nucleus of armed men, often using terror tactics, establishes itself in an area of the country and exacts plunder, tribute and labour services from the peasants, seizing young men and women to swell its numbers. Classically the invaders operate from fortified stockades from which they can dominate a large area of the countryside and extend their raiding into new and untouched areas.

By their very nature warbands have frequently destroyed each other, but those that survived have in time become absorbed into traditional African patterns of life. Through marriage they acquire an interest in the land and come under the influence of local rain-making or spirit cults. Raiding often gives way to commerce. The warlords become chiefs and increasingly adopt the traditional trappings and practices of chieftaincy. The bandit leader's followers acquire a distinct identity as a recognisable ethnic group. When better ecological conditions return, the stability of the 'small society' triumphs over the destructiveness of the warband.

However hideous its methods and however suspect the motives of the Western businessmen, church leaders and academics who have espoused its cause, Renamo was essentially a Mozambican phenomenon, comprehensible only in terms of the history of the country — a history which has etched patterns of action and reaction which modern Mozambican society finds itself unconsciously repeating.

It has been argued that the resurgence of banditry was aided by the particular way in which independent Mozambique developed. Although the newly-independent state strove to provide greater integration at the social, political and economic levels, this proved only partly successful. The creation of Communal Villages in rural areas led to bitter local strife. Geffray recorded how fighting broke out between rival lineage villages even before Renamo appeared. Some villages declared for the government, others for Renamo and

> . . . .the men organised themselves into groups of fighters and went to pillage, kill and rape in the territory of their neighbours where they were able to recover some of the women kidnapped in the earlier fighting. In this way a deadly war fought with spears and axes (*armas brancas*) broke out between the civil population of two old chieftaincies, outside the control of and without the direct intervention of the organised forces of either the government or of Renamo.[80]

Meanwhile the economic measures of the government, all of which seemed to marginalise the peasant farmers, soon undermined the patterns of production and consumption on which peasant families depended. As the peasants became increasingly marginalised, there remained the choice, as one commentator put it, 'to live from alms or from robbery'.[81] Robbery, or confiscation, became a way of life not only for Renamo bands but for everyone in Mozambique. As the economy became more and more dominated by aid, so those who could redistribute the aid for their own personal gain or that of their friends, family or network were the survivors. In the capital, political power became the route to control the redistribution of state resources; in the countryside banditry performed that role.

Such an interpretation makes it extremely doubtful that banditry and social violence in Mozambique can be ended by diplomacy. Renamo was never a coherent political movement, and the leaders, like Dhlakama, who appeared at the negotiating table almost certainly did not possess much authority over the warbands active in the countryside. War, as Geffray noted, 'is the condition for the reproduction of Renamo as an armed institution and constitutes in itself its own objective'.[82] The warbands that formed the armies of the Thirty Years War in Europe were just as little susceptible to persuasion and control by their nominal political masters. War provided their *raison d'être*, their means of livelihood and their very identity as human beings.

However, the sad story of the collapse of independent Mozambique raises other issues. The irresponsibility of the protagonists of the Cold War in fighting their ideological battles through surrogates in Africa has been savagely revealed. The government structures and civil society of Africa were not secure enough to stand the pressures of Cold War politics. Older forms of organisation, based on the 'tribe', the clan or the warlord have proved better able to wield power on the ground and command the loyalty or fear of the people. In many African countries the destruction of ordered government and society has been frighteningly rapid, the collapse escalating as a result of drought and famine. With the Cold War ended, the international community must be prepared to make firmer commitments to rebuilding not only the economies of the damaged countries but also their basic security and their civil and political institutions. The United Nations must face up to the need for a greater level of intervention where the very fabric of society itself is in danger of collapse. Nor should it be any longer acceptable for Western academics, churchmen or business leaders to adopt some African warlord and make him the flag-carrier for interests which ultimately have no relevance to Africa. Mozambique and Angola will be test-cases for the viability of a new international order.

REFERENCES

Chapter 1. The Mozambique Channel Region in the 16th Century

1. 'Letter from [João Velho] former Factor of Sofala to the king' (post 1547), *Documents on the Portuguese in Mozambique and Central Africa* (hereafter *Documents on the Portuguese. . . .*), vol. 7, pp. 168–83.
2. Letter from [João Vellio], former Factor of Sofala, to the King (Goa 4 Nov. 1548), *Documents on the Portuguese*, vol. 7, pp. 184–9.
3. 'Letter from Diogo de Alcaçova to the king' (Cochin 20 Nov. 1506), *Documents on the Portuguese. . . .*, vol. 1, pp. 388–401.
4. Gerhard Liesegang, 'Archaeological Sites on the Bay of Sofala', *Azania*, 7 (1972), pp. 147–59. R.W. Dickinson, 'The Archaeology of the Sofala Coast', *South African Archaeol. Bull.*, 30 (1975), pp. 84–104.
5. That the ruler of Mozambique was a *sharif* see 'Extracts from the Book written by Duarte Barbosa', G.M. Theal (ed.), *Records of South Eastern Africa* (hereafter Theal, *Records*), vol. 1, p. 16.
6. 'Letter from Diogo de Alcaçova to the king' (Cochin 20 Nov. 1506), *Documents on the Portuguese. . . .*, vol. 1, pp. 388–401.
7. 'Extracts from the Book written by Duarte Barbosa', Theal, *Records*, vol. 1, p. 93.
8. *Ibid.*, p. 95. Barbosa thought that the process of interweaving imported cloth with locally made thread was developed only after the Portuguese interfered with imports from Asia.
9. João dos Santos, *Ethiopia Oriental*, p. 245.
10. *Ibid*, p. 252; 'Account of the Voyage of D. Francisco de Almeida, viceroy of India, along the East Coast of Africa', *Documents on the Portuguese. . . .*, vol. 1, p. 539.
11. These ideas are developed in Raymond Kent, *Early Kingdoms in Madagascar*.
12. 'Extracts from the Navigation of Pedro Alvares Cabral', Theal, *Records*, vol. 1, p. 48. Cabral met a Melinde ship off Sofala on board of which was a 'cousin' of the king of Melinde.
13. João de Barros, 'Da Asia', Theal, *Records*, vol. 6, p. 284.
14. Extracts from many traditional histories of the coast were published in G.S.P. Freeman-Grenville, *The East African Coast*. The traditional histories of the Comoros are only now being researched and published for the first time. For examples see Georges Boulinier *et al.*, *Traditions d'une Ligne Royale des Comores*, and its bibliography.
15. João de Barros, 'Da Asia', Theal, *Records*, vol. 6, p. 216.
16. M. Newitt, 'The Southern Swahili Coast in the First Century of European Expansion', *Azania*, 13 (1978), pp. 111–26.
17. For Arab geographical knowledge of the East African coast see G.R. Tibbetts, *Arab Navigation in the Indian Ocean before the Coming of the Portuguese*, and T.A. Chumovsky, *Tres Roteiros Desconhecidos de Ahmed Ibn-Majid*.
18. Sena and Tete are not mentioned by name in documents till the second half of the sixteenth century but it seems clear from António de Saldanha's correspondence in 1511 that trading towns existed on the Zambesi at that time. This makes their existence, and perhaps foundation, in the fifteenth century very probable. See

'Summary by António Carneiro, Secretary of State, of letters from António da Saldanha, captain of Sofala and Mozambique, to the king, 1511', *Documents on the Portuguese.* . . ., vol. 1, pp. 11-19.

19. The standard histories of the the Portuguese in eastern Africa in the sixteenth century are: Alexandre Lobato, *A Expansão Portuguêsa em Moçambique de 1498 a 1530*; Eric Axelson, *Portuguese in South-East Africa, 1488-1600*.

20. 'Instructions to the Captain-major D. Francisco de Almeida' (Lisbon 5 March 1505), *Documents on the Portuguese.* . . ., vol. 1, pp. 156-261.

21. João de Barros, 'Da Asia', Theal, *Records*, vol. 6, p. 212.

22. For Mozambique Island see ch. 6.

23. 'Letter from Pero Ferreira Fogaça, captain of Kilwa to the King' (Kilwa 22 December 1506), *Documents on the Portuguese.* . . ., vol. 1, pp. 754-61.

24. Lobato, *Expansão Portuguêsa.* . . ., vol. 3, p. 166.

25. Portuguese raids on the East African coast are described in João de Barros, 'Da Asia', Theal, *Records*, vol. 6; Walter de Gray Birch (ed.), *Commentaries of the Great Afonso Dalboquerque*; of Axelson, *Portuguese in South-East Africa*.

26. 'Pedro Vaz Soarez, factor of Sofala to the king Dom Manuel' (Sofala 30 June 1513), Theal, *Records*, vol. 1, pp. 80-5.

27. Axelson, *Portuguese in South-East Africa*, p. 96.

28. 'Summary of a Letter from Pero Ferreira Fogaça, Captain of Kilwa, to the King', (Kilwa, 31 August 1506), *Documents on the Portuguese.* . . ., vol. 1, pp. 616-21.

29. Lobato, *Expansão Portuguêsa.* . . ., vol. 3, pp. 9, 124, 186; Axelson, *Portuguese in South East Africa.* . . ., p. 137.

30. E.A. Alpers, *Ivory and Slaves in East Central Africa*.

31. Lobato, *Expansão Portuguêsa.* . . ., vol. 3, p. 104.

32. M.Newitt, 'The Southern Swahili Coast. . . .', *op. cit.*, and 'The Early history of the Sultanate of Angoche', pp. 397-406.

33. For the employment of black divers see 'Summary of a letter from Pero Ferreira Fogaça, Captain of Kilwa to the King' (Kilwa 31 August 1506), *Documents on the Portuguese.* . . ., vol. 1, pp. 616-21.

34. João dos Santos, *Ethiopia Oriental*, p. 347.

35. For a discussion of the location of Maluane see M. Newitt, 'The Southern Swahili Coast . . .', p. 116, note 17; for lists of the cloths stocked by the Sofala factory see 'Receipt and Expenditure Book kept by Cristovão Šalema, Factor of Sofala, 1516', *Documents on the Portuguese.* . . ., vol. 4, pp. 296-501.

36. See the lists of maintenance payments for the fort of Sofala printed in *Documents on the Portuguese.* . . ., vol. 3.

37. 'Letter from Pero Ferreira Fogaça, Captain of Kilwa, to the King' (Kilwa 21 December 1506), *Documents on the Portuguese.* . . . , vol. 1, pp. 754-61.

38. João dos Santos, *Ethiopia Oriental*, pp. 186, 209, 305, 409.

39. William Foster (ed.), *The Voyages of Sir James Lancaster*, p. 5.

Chapter 2. The Interior South of the Zambesi in the 16th Century

1. João dos Santos, *Ethiopia Oriental*, p. 274; the first mention of Botonga occurs in 'Letter from Diogo de Alcaçova to the King', *Documents on the Portuguese . . .* , vol. 1, pp. 388-401.

2. João dos Santos, *Ethiopia Oriental*, p. 292; António Bocarro, 'Livro do Estado da India', extracts printed in Theal, *Records*, vol. 3, p. 424.

3. Allen Isaacman, 'Madzi-Manga, Mhondoro and the use of oral traditions — a chapter in Barue religious and political history', pp. 395-409.

4. David Beach, *The Shona and Zimbabwe, 900–1850*, p. 185.

5. The reference to Otonga is contained in 'Summary by António Carneiro, secretary of state, of letters from António de Saldanha, captain of Sofala and Mozambique, to the king', 1511, *Documents on the Portuguese* . . ., vol. 3, pp. 10–19. Reports of António Fernandes' travels are contained in two documents: 'Notes made by Gaspar Veloso, clerk of the factory of Mozambique, and sent to the king', 1512, *Documents on the Portuguese* . . ., vol. 3, pp. 180–9, and 'Letter from João Vaz de Almada, captain of Sofala, to the king' (Sofala 26 June 1516), *Documents on the Portuguese* . . ., vol. 3, pp. 274–95. The reference to Onhaquoro occurs in the second of these, p. 286.

6. P.S. Garlake, *Great Zimbabwe*.

7. *Ibid.*, p. 164; a similar conclusion was reached about Manekweni. See G. Barker, 'Economic Models for the Manekweni Zimbabwe, Mozambique', pp. 71–100.

8. João dos Santos, *Ethiopia Oriental*, p. 274.

9. David Beach, *The Shona and Zimbabwe*, pp. 62–3, 80. A recent detailed attempt to make sense of the'traditions about the origin of the Monomotapa state is contained in S.I. Mudenge, *A Political History of Munhumutapa c 1400–1902*, chapter 2. Like so many other accounts of the Monomotapa state it relies heavily on the research papers of Donald Abraham and accepts almost without question the notion that there was a vast 'empire of Monomotapa' sometime in the fifteenth century.

10. 'Letter from Diogo de Alcaçova to the king', *Documents on the Portuguese* . . ., vol. 1.

11. João de Barros, 'Da Asia', Theal, *Records*, vol. 6, pp. 267–8.

12. P.S. Garlake, 'An Investigation of Manekweni, Mozambique', pp. 25–47; G. Barker, 'Economic Models . . .'

13. João dos Santos, *Ethiopia Oriental*, p. 273.

14. David Beach, quoting the famous 'Descrição Corográfica' AHU Moç Cx 17, estimates that Manica had a population of 14,000 in the eighteenth century, a figure which, however speculative, creates a sense of reality in discussions about the size of the Karanga chieftaincies.

15. João dos Santos, *Ethiopia Oriental*, pp. 290–1.

16. For Barue and its institutions see Isaacman, 'Madzi-Manga . . .'

17. Garlake, 'An Investigation . . .'; Barker, 'Economic Models. . . .'

18. For the account of Inhamunda's followers herding cattle, 'An Order from João Vaz de Almada, provost of the Fortress of Sofala, to the Factor, Cristovão Salema' (Sofala 15 January 1517), *Documents on the Portuguese* . . ., vol. 5, pp. 10–17; João dos Santos, *Ethiopia Oriental*, p. 206.

19. António Bocarro, 'Livro do Estado da India', pp. 355–6.

20. *Ibid.*, p. 377.

21. Anne Hilton, *The Kingdom of Kongo*.

22. António Bocarro, 'Livro do Estado da India', p. 377; António Bocarro and Pedro Barreto de Resende, 'Do Estado da India', Theal, *Records*, vol. 2, p. 416; Isaacman, 'Madzi-Manga . . .', pp. 399–400.

23. João dos Santos, *Ethiopia Oriental*, p. 194.

24. *Ibid.*, p. 222.

25. *Ibid.*, p. 192–4; Gerhard Liesegang (ed.), *Reposta das Questoens sobre os Cafres*, p. 20.

26. António Nogueira da Costa, *O Caso do Muenemutapa*, pp. 25–6, describes the reciprocal exchange of imported goods on which the power of the Karanga aristocracy was based. This stimulating essay is flawed, in my opinion, by its assumption that there was at one time an 'empire' of Monomotapa. There is a discussion of the relationship of the Monomotapas to the *mhondoros* and rain-making cults in Avital Livneh, 'Precolonial Polities in Southern Zambesia and their Political Communications', pp. 203–5; Beach, *The Shona*. . . ., p. 118, and Mudenge, *A Political History*. . . ., pp. 127–34.

27. João dos Santos, *Ethiopia Oriental*, p. 225.
28. Father Monclaro, SJ, 'Account of the Journey made by the Fathers of the Company of Jesus with Francisco Barreto in the Conquest of Monomotapa in the Year 1569', Theal, *Records*, vol. 3, p. 246.
29. 'Letter from Pero Vaz Soares, factor of Sofala, to the king' (Sofala, 30 June 1513), *Documents on the Portuguese.* . . ., vol. 3, pp. 458-69.
30. António Bocarro, 'Livro do Estado da India', p. 355.
31. 'Inquérito em Moçambique no anno de 1573', Alcantara Guerreiro (ed.), *Studia*, no. 6, pp. 7-19.
32. João dos Santos, *Ethiopia Oriental*, p. 212.
33. Monclaro, 'Account of the Journey. . . .', Theal, *Records*, vol. 3, p. 235.
34. Documents describing the Silveira mission were printed in Theal, *Records*, vol. 2; *Documents on the Portuguese.* . . ., vols 7 and 8; the standard biography of Silveira is Bertha Leite, *D. Gonçalo da Silveira*.
35. The sources for the Barreto-Homen expedition have been collected together and published by João C. Reis in *A Empresa da Conquista do Senhorio do Monomotapa*. The best general account of the expedition is contained in Axelson, *Portuguese in South-East Africa*, pp. 157-64.
36. R.S. Whiteway (ed.), *The Portuguese Expedition to Abyssinia*.
37. Monclaro, 'Account . . .', Theal, *Records*, vol. 3, p. 225.

Chapter 3. Mozambique North of the Zambesi to the mid-17th Century

1. The story of cannibalism is contained in João dos Santos, *Ethiopia Oriental*, p. 314.
2. *Ibid.*, p. 319.
3. G. T. Nurse, 'The people of Bororo: a lexicostatistical enquiry', pp. 123-8.
4. João dos Santos, *Ethiopia Oriental*, pp. 254-5.
5. H.L. Dames (ed.), *The Book of Duarte Barbosa*, vol. 1, p. 16.
6. Monclaro, 'Account of the Journey. . . .', Theal, *Records*, vol. 3, pp. 220-1.
7. João dos Santos, *Ethiopia Oriental*, p. 309.
8. *Ibid.*, pp. 306-8.
9. A. Rita-Ferreira, *Fixação Portuguêsa e História Pré-colonial de Moçambique*, p. 127.
10. António Gomes, 'Viagem que fez o Padre António Gomes, da Companhia de Jesus ao Imperio de Manomotapa; e assistencia que fez nas ditas terras de algus annos', p. 165. I am grateful to David Beach of the University of Zimbabwe for letting me use a copy of H. de Noronha's translation of this text.
11. *Ibid.*, p. 170.
12. *Ibid.*, p. 169.
13. *Ibid.*, p. 170.
14. *Ibid.*, p. 163.
15. João dos Santos, *Ethiopia Oriental*, p. 305.
16. António Gomes, 'Viagem. . . .', p. 164.
17. Monclaro, 'Account of a Journey. . . .', Theal, *Records*, vol. 3, pp. 238-9.
18. M. Schoffeleers, 'M'Bona the Guardian Spirit of the Manganja', unpubl. B. Litt. thesis, Univ. of Oxford, 1966, pp. 5-8.
19. João dos Santos, *Ethiopia Oriental*, pp. 309-12; Diogo do Couto, 'Décadas da Asia', Theal *Records*, vol. 6, pp. 392-8.
20. João dos Santos, *Ethiopia Oriental*, pp. 299-304.
21. *Ibid.*, pp. 290-1.
22. Axelson, *Portuguese in South-East Africa*, pp. 176-7.
23. Diogo do Couto, 'Décadas da Asia', Theal, *Records*, vol. 6, p. 393.

24. António Bocarro, 'Livro do Estado da India', Theal, *Records*, vol. 3, p. 363.
25. For a discussion of the importance of M'Bona in the history of the peoples of the Shire and the Mozambique lowlands, see M. Schoffeleers, 'M'Bona the Guardian Spirit of the Manganja'; M. Schoffeleers, 'Symbolic and Social Aspects of Spirit Worship among the Mang'anga'; T. O. Ranger, 'Territorial Cults in the History of Central Africa', pp. 581–97; M. Schoffeleers, 'The Zimba and the Lundu State in the Late Sixteenth and Early Seventeenth Centuries', pp. 337–55; C. Wrigley, 'The River-God and the Historians: Myth in the Shire Valley and Elsewhere', pp. 367–83.
26. M. Newitt, 'The Early History of the Maravi', pp. 145–62. See esp. note 31.
27. Schoffeleers, 'The Zimba. . . .', p. 349; Alpers, *Ivory and Slaves*, pp. 51–2.
28. For early references to Maravi chiefs see Newitt, 'Early History. . . .', pp. 156–62.
29. *Ibid.*, pp. 158–62.
30. For the origin of the Kalonga chieftaincy see the views of Newitt, *ibid.*, pp. 159–60; Schoffeleers, 'The Zimba. . . .', where it is argued that Muzura's chieftaincy was centred some way south of Lake Malawi while Kalonga's capital was on the lake shore. However, the famous letter of the Jesuit Luís Mariano makes it clear that Muzura's capital in 1624 was only half a league from the Lake shore, see 'P. Aloysius Mariana ad Praepositum provinciae goanae', *Rerum Aethiopicarum Scriptores*, pp. 112–14. It still seems probable that Muzura was the founder of the Kalonga chieftaincy. For the reference to Manuel Godinho see A. C. P. Gamitto, *King Kazembe*, vol. 1, p. 64; Kalonga is referred to as Caronga in 1667 by Manuel Barreto, 'Informação do Estado e Conquista dos Rios de Cuama', Theal, *Records*, vol. 3, p. 481.
31. António Francisco Cardim, *Relacam da Viagem do Galeam Sam Lourenco e sua Perdicam nos Baixos de Moxincale em 3 de Septembro de 1649*.
32. António Bocarro, 'Livro do Estado da India', Theal, *Records*, vol. 3, p. 418.
33. A. C. P. Gamitto, *King Kazembe*, vol. 1, pp. 772–3.
34. Ranger, 'Territorial Cults. . . .', p. 586.
35. Manuel Barreto, 'Informação do Estado e Conquista dos Rios de Cuama', Theal, *Records*, vol. 3, pp. 468–72.
36. For the history of Undi and the Cewa, see H. Langworthy, 'A History of Undi's Kingdom to 1890: Aspects of Chewa History in East Central Africa'; K.Phiri, 'Chewa History in Central Malawi and the Use of Oral Tradition'.
37. Alpers, *Ivory and Slaves*, p. 56.

Chapter 4. The Portuguese Conquest and Loss of the High Veldt

1. Paul Schebesta, *Portugals Konquistamission in Südost-Afrika*, p. 104.
2. António Bocarro, 'Livro do Estado da India', Theal, *Records*, vol. 3, p. 364.
3. *Ibid.*, p. 362.
4. *Ibid.*, pp. 364–5.
5. *Ibid.*, p. 366.
6. The most carefully constructed narrative of events in seventeenth-century Mozambique is still Eric Axelson, *Portuguese in South-East Africa 1600–1700*. The other detailed accounts of the period are Paul Schebesta, *Portugals Konquistamission in Südost-Afrika*; W. G. L. Randles, *L'Empire du Monomotapa du XVe au XIXe siècle*; and S. I. Mudenge, *A Political History of Munhumutapa*. D. P. Abraham, 'The Early Political History of the Kingdom of Mwene Mutapa, 850–1589', and 'The Monomotapa Dynasty', are undoutedly seminal works which should still be consulted, though with due caution.

7. António Bocarro, 'Livro do Estado da India', Theal, *Records*, vol. 3, pp. 368–70.
8. S.I. Mudenge, *Christian Education at the Mutapa Court*, pp. 14–15.
9. António Bocarro and Pedro Barreto de Resende, 'Do Estado da India', Theal, *Records*, vol. 2, p. 418.
10. Bocarro, 'Livro do Estado da India', Theal, *Records*, vol. 3, p. 373; 'King to viceroy' (Lisbon 24 March 1612).
11. Axelson, *Portuguese in South-East Africa* . . . ., pp. 52–8.
12. Bocarro, 'Livro do Estado. . . .', p. 385.
13. Axelson, *Portuguese in South-East Africa* . . . ., pp. 37–9.
14. The Portuguese began their search for silver mines with the Barreto expedition of 1569–75, and alleged discoveries of silver ore were still being talked about in the mid-eighteenth century. At different times during this 200-year period silver ore, supposed to come from Zambesia, was professionally assayed and found to be silver-bearing. However, no deposits of silver ore are known to exist anywhere in the region. Portuguese belief in the existence of the silver mines was partly the wishful thinking of those jealous of the wealth from the South American mines and partly deliberate fraud by those who stood to gain from a royal 'conquest' of the interior.
15. 'King to viceroy' (Lisbon 24 March 1612), Theal, *Records*, vol. 4, pp. 83–7.
16. Axelson, *Portuguese in South-East Africa*. . . ., pp. 52–8; the source for almost all that is known about Madeira is António Bocarro, 'Livro do Estado da India', Theal, *Records*, vol. 3.
17. Bocarro and Barreto de Resende, 'Do Estado da India', Theal, *Records*, vol. 2, p. 415. Throughout I have used the Portuguese version of the Monomotapa's name which is Caprasine or Kapransine.
18. Frei Luís Cacegas, 'Extractos da História de S.Domingos', Theal, *Records*, vol. 1, pp. 355–406.
19. 'Letter from Frei Luís do Espírito Santo to Provincial' (3 Feb. 1630), Theal, *Records*, vol. 2, pp. 427–8.
20. Frei Luís Cacegas, 'Extractos da História de S.Domingos', Theal, *Records*, vol. 1, p. 400.
21. 'Advices from Goa', Theal, *Records*, vol. 2, pp. 429.
22. 'Regent to viceroy, enclosing a summary of a letter of Diogo de Sousa de Meneses' (Lisbon, 28 March 1636), Theal, *Records*, vol. 4, pp. 473–81. For the Muslim chief 'Xarife' see 'Declaration made by Father Frei Gaspar de Macedo' (Sena 21 July 1633), *Livros dos Monções*, no. 41. I am indebted to David Beach for lending me the translation of this document by H. de Noronha.
23. Axelson, *Portuguese in South-East Africa*. . . ., pp. 129–43.
24. Manuel Barreto, 'Informação do Estado e Conquista dos Rios de Cuama' (Goa 11 December 1667), Theal, *Records*, vol. 3, p. 488.
25. Bocarro and Barreto de Resende, 'Do Estado da India', Theal, *Records*, vol. 2, p. 411.
26. Allen Isaacman, 'Madzi-Manga, Mhondoro and the use of oral traditions — a chapter in Barue religious and political history'.
27. João dos Santos, *Ethiopia Oriental*, p. 380.
28. Diogo do Couto, 'Decadas da Asia', Theal, *Records*, vol. 6, pp. 387–8.
29. For the relations of Rodrigo Lobo with Kiteve see João dos Santos, *Ethiopia Oriental*, pp. 225–7.
30. 'Declaration made by Father Frei Gaspar de Macedo' (Sena 21 July 1633), *Livros dos Monções*, no. 41.
31. For the history of the *prazo* of Cheringoma see M. Newitt, *Portuguese Settlement on the Zambesi*, chapter 9 and the sources quoted therein. For Bayão see also C.R. Boxer, 'Sisnando Dias Bayão: Conquistador da "Mãe de Ouro"' '

32. 'Prince to viceroy' (Lisbon 24 March 1681), Theal, *Records*, vol. 4, p. 404. For the power struggles in Kiteve and the intervention of Portuguese *sertanejos* see 'Noticias que se me pedirão no anno de 1677 de Lxa dos Rios de Cuama e da forma que devia ter pa poder concervasse entrando na companhia que se determina fazer pa este Estado', in Orbe Lusitano, Ajuda Library, 50 v 37 fol. 482.
33. 'King to viceroy' (Lisbon 15 March 1702), Theal, *Records*, vol. 5, p. 7.
34. Bocarro and Barreto de Resende, 'Do Estado da India', p. 412.
35. 'Breve Informação dos Rios de Cuama, que da o Pe Frey Philipe de Asumpção por andar nas ditas Terras quatorze annos, e estado em todas as feiras e ter larga noticia dos vios e costumes dellas', Ajuda Library, 51.ix.3, fol. 38.
36. H. H. K. Bhila, *Trade and Politics in a Shona Kingdom*, chapter 2.
37. For what may be the beginning of the Zimbabwe garrison see 'King to viceroy' (Lisbon, 1 November 1613), Theal, *Records*, vol. 4, pp. 113–16.
38. For Maramuca see D. P. Abraham, 'Maramuca: An Exercise in the combined use of Portuguese Records and Oral Tradition', pp. 213–25.
39. S. I. Mudenge, *Christian Education at the Mutapa Court*; Anne Hilton, *The Kingdom of Kongo*.
40. 'Proposta que o Rey Monomotapa offerece ao V Rey da India pelo seu Procurador, o Padre Frey Manuel da Purificação Religioso da Ordem de São Domingos', 12 April 1645, *Livros dos Monções*, no. 60, fols 233–5.
41. Hilton, *The Kingdom of Kongo*.
42. D. P. Abraham, 'Maramuca: An Exercise in the combined use of Portuguese Records and Oral Tradition'.
43. For the origin of the Rozvi see S. I. Mudenge, 'The Rozvi Empire and the Feira of Zumbo', pp. 52–86.
44. For the last days of the Karanga fairs see the classic account of António da Con-ceição, 'Tratado dos Rios de Cuama', *O Chronista de Tissuary*.

Chapter 5. Government of Mozambique

1. Eric Axelson, *Portuguese in South-East Africa* . . . ., p. 54.
2. 'King to viceroy' (Lisbon 26 March 1612), Theal, *Records*, vol. 4, p. 88.
3. Axelson, *Portuguese in South-East Africa*. . . ., pp. 48–9.
4. *Ibid.*, pp. 50–1; 'Report made by the governor-general Diogo da Cunha Castelbranco' (Goa 7 Feb. 1619), Theal, *Records*, vol. 4, pp. 155–62.
5. 'King to viceroy' (Lisbon 12 Feb. 1622), Theal, *Records*, vol. 4, pp. 175–6; 'King to viceroy' (Lisbon 15 April 1626), Theal, *Records*, vol. 4, pp. 195–6.
6. M. N. Pearson, *The New Cambridge History of India: The Portuguese in India*.
7. The households maintained by the great Portuguese *fidalgos* in the East are described in A. Gray (ed.), *The Voyage of François Pyrard de Laval*, vol. 2, pp. 85–8, 127; M. Newitt, 'Plunder and the Rewards of Office in the Portuguese Empire', pp. 10–28.
8. John Villiers, 'The Estado da India in South East Asia', pp. 37–68.
9. 'Regulations for Sofala', *Documents on the Portuguese*. . . ., vol. 6, pp. 304–424; 'Expenditure in the Fortresses of Sofala, Mozambique and Sena', Theal, *Records*, vol. 4, pp. 2–9.
10. 'Summary by António Carneiro of letters from Afonso de Albuquerque to the King', 1511, *Documents on the Portuguese*. . . ., vol. 3, pp. 4–9.
11. See chapter 1.
12. 'Letter from Simão Botelho, Vedor da Fazenda of India to the King' (Cochin 30 January 1592), *Documents on the Portuguese*. . . ., vol. 7, pp. 262–97; extract Theal, *Records*, vol. 3, p. 149.

13. Father Monclaro, 'Account of the Journey made by the Fathers of the Company of Jesus with Francisco Barreto in the Conquest of Monomotapa in the Year 1569', Theal, *Records*, vol. 3, p. 209.
14. 'Livro das Cidades e Fortalezas que a Coroa de Portugal tem nas Partes da India
  • e das Capitanias e mais Cargos que nelas ha e da Importancia delles', F.P. Mendes da Luz (ed.), *Studia*, vol. 6, pp. 351–63 with facsimile of text, fols 37–9.
15. 'King to viceroy' (28 March 1613), Theal, *Records*, vol. 4, p. 108.
16. 'King to viceroy' (Lisbon 18 March 1614); 'Alvará' (Lisbon March 1614); 'Alvará' (Lisbon 20 March 1614), Theal, *Records*, vol. 4, pp. 125, 126, 128.
17. 'King to viceroy' (Lisbon 26 March 1612), Theal, *Records*, vol. 4, p. 88.
18. Axelson, *Portuguese in South-East Africa. . . .*, p. 72.
19. 'Record of the Orders carried with them by the Captains of the Fortresses of Mozambique and Sofala', Theal, *Records*, vol. 4, p. 27.
20. *Ibid.*
21. 'King to viceroy' (Lisbon 24 March 1612), Theal, *Records*, vol. 4, pp. 83–9.
22. The Portuguese calculated money in *cruzados*, *pardãos*, *xerafins* and *milreis* (1,000 *reis*). The *cruzado* was worth 400 *reis*; the *pardão* and the *xerafin* were each worth 360 *reis*. There was, therefore, a considerable difference between 40,000 *cruzados* and 40,000 *xerafins/pardãos*. The equivalent in *milreis* was 16,000 as opposed to 14,400.
23. Manuel Barreto, 'Informação do Estado e Conquista dos Rios de Cuama', Theal, *Records*, vol. 3, p. 465.
24. 'King to viceroy' (Madrid 22 January 1607), Theal, *Records*, vol. 4, p. 59.
25. Axelson, *Portuguese in South-East Africa. . . .*, pp. 94, 108.
26. Barreto, 'Informação. . . . .', Theal, *Records*, vol. 3, p. 480.
27. *Ibid*, p. 506.
28. António Gomes, 'Viagem que fez o Padre António Gomes, da Companhia de Jesus ao Imperio de Manomotapa; e assistencia que fez nas ditas terras de algus annos'.
29. Bocarro and Barreto de Resende, 'Do Estado da India', Theal, *Records*, vol. 2, pp. 405–6.
30. 'Letter of Dom Andres Vides y Albarado Administrator and Assayer of the Gold and Silver Mines' (Sena 22 July 1633), *Livros dos Monçoẽs*, no. 41, fols 13–14 (transl. H. de Noronha).
31. Axelson, *Portuguese in South East Africa. . . .*, p. 101.
32. M. Newitt, *Portuguese Settlement on the Zambesi*, p. 43.
33. 'Extracts from the Account of the Wreck of the Ship Santiago', Theal, *Records*, vol. 1, p. 342.
34. Barreto de Resende, 'Do Estado da India', Theal, *Records*, vol. 2, p. 403–6.
35. *Ibid.*, p. 412.
36. *Ibid.*, p. 414.
37. *Ibid.*, pp. 417–8; Barreto, 'Informação. . . .', Theal, *Records*, vol. 3, p. 482.
38. *Ibid.*, pp. 468–9.
39. 'Extract from a letter dated 24 March 1608', Theal, *Records*, vol. 4, p. 74; Barreto, 'Informação . . .', Theal, *Records*, vol. 3, p. 469.
40. Extract from Dominican document dated 28 June 1631, Theal, *Records*, vol. 2, pp. 432–40.
41. For accounts of priests leading warbands see 'Letter from Friar Louis to his Provincial', 3 Feb. 1630, Theal, *Records*, vol. 2, p. 427; Barreto, 'Informação. . . .', Theal, *Records*, vol. 3, p. 475.
42. Alexandre Lobato, *Evolução Administrativa e Económica de Moçambique, 1752–1763*, pp. 29–49.
43. Fritz Hoppe, *Portugiesisch-Ostafrika in der Zeit des Marquês de Pombal, 1750–1777*, pp. 12–22; José Joaquim Lopes de Lima and Francisco Maria Bordalo, *Ensaio sobre a Estatística das Possessões Portuguezas no Ultramar*, pp. 100–1.

44. Lobato, *Evolução*. . . . ,?

45. The colourful lives of Frei Pedro da Trindade and Frei João de Moraes are described in chapters 8 and 9.

46. For an account of a visitation by the Inquisition see 'Edital da Inquisição de Goa', *O Chronista de Tissuary*, 2, pp. 273–5.

47. Sousa Ribeiro (ed.), *Anuário de Moçambique* (1940), p. 188; the first prelate to reside in Mozambique appears to have been D. Frei Bartolomeu dos Martires, bishop of São Tomé, who was nominated in 1819, arrived in Mozambique in 1820 and died in 1828. He was the author of an important account of the colony. See Bartolomeu dos Martires, 'Memória Chorografica da Provincia ou Capitania de Mossambique na Costa d'Africa Oriental conforme o Estado em que se achava no ano de 1822', edited by Virginia Rau in 'Aspectos etnico-culturais da ilha de Moçambique em 1822', pp. 123–65.

Chapter 6. Afro-Portuguese Society and Town Life

1. *A Ilha de Moçambique em Perigo de Desaparecimento*.

2. Dames (ed.), *The Book of Duarte Barbosa*, vol. 1, p. 16.

3. C.R. Boxer, 'Moçambique Island as a Way-station for Portuguese East-Indiamen', pp. 3–18.

4. Father Monclaro, 'Account of the Journey made by the Fathers of the Company of Jesus with Francisco Barreto in the Conquest of Monomotapa in the Year 1569', Theal, *Records*, vol. 3, p. 208.

5. João dos Santos, *Ethiopia Oriental*, pp. 316–1.

6. 'Mozambique in 1688', extract printed in Theal, *Records*, vol. 4, pp. 436–45.

7. Prior's description of Mozambique Island is contained in James Prior, *Voyage along the Eastern Coast of Africa to Mosambique, Johanna, and Quiloa . . . in the Nisus Frigate*, pp. 31–8.

8. Bartolomeu dos Martires, 'Memória Chorografica da Provincia ou Capitania de Mossambique na Costa d'Africa Oriental conforme o Estado em que se achava no ano de 1822', edited by Virginia Rau in 'Aspectos etnico-culturais da ilha de Moçambique em 1822', pp. 123–65.

9. For the commercial struggles of the Mozambique *moradores* see E.A. Alpers, *Ivory and Slaves in East-Central Africa*, pp. 55–6; for a statement of their rights see 'Alvará do gor. Manoel de Sousa Coutinho pa. q̃ os Casados e mores. de mossabiq̃ possão hir commerciar na ilha de São Lourenço e toda a costa de moss . . . etc', *Monções do Reino*, nos 29 and 30.

10. Bocarro and Barreto de Resende, 'Do Estado da India', Theal, *Records*, vol. 2, p. 404.

11. 'Brief resumé of an account given by Custodio de Almeida e Souza on the situation of the Rivers of Senna and Sofalla', Ajuda 51.viii.40, fols transl. H. de Noronha, pp. 271–2.

12. Inácio Caetano Xavier, 'Notícias dos Domínios Portugueses da Costa de Africa Oriental 1758', A.A. de Andrade (ed.), *Relações de Moçambique Setecentista* (hereafter *Relações*) p. 154.

13. João dos Santos, *Ethiopia Oriental*, p. 220.

14. *Ibid.*, p. 225.

15. 'Treatise of the Misfortune that Befell the Great Ship São João Baptista' in C.R. Boxer (ed.), *The Tragic History of the Sea*, p. 266.

16. M. Newitt, *Portuguese Settlement on the Zambesi*, pp. 209–10; 'King to viceroy', (Lisbon 24 February 1635), Theal, *Records*, vol. 4, pp. 253–62.

17. Bocarro and Barreto de Resende, 'Do Estado da India', Theal, *Records*, vol. 2, p. 406.

18. João dos Santos, *Ethiopia Oriental*, p. 304
19. Bocarro and Barreto de Resende, 'Do Estado da India' Theal, *Records*, vol. 2, p. 406.
20. António Pinto de Miranda, 'Memória sobre a Costa de Africa', Andrade, *Relações*, p. 256.
21. *Ibid.*
22. João Baptista de Montaury, 'Moçambique, Ilhas Querimbas, Rios de Sena, Villa de Tete, Villa de Zumbo, Manica, Villa de Luabo, Inhambane', Andrade, *Relaçõẽs*, p. 355.
23. Anon, 'Descripção da Capitania de Monsambique, suas povoações e produções, 1788', Andrade, *Relaçoẽs*, p. 394.
24. João dos Santos, *Ethiopia Oriental*, p. 388.
25. Barreto de Resende, 'Do Estado da India', Theal, *Records*, vol. 2, p. 409.
26. António Gomes, 'Viagem que fez o Padre António Gomes, da Companhia de Jesus ao Imperio de Manomotapa; e assistencia que fez nas ditas terras de algus annos', p. 181.
27. Manuel Barreto, 'Informação do Estado e Conquista dos Rios de Cuama', Theal, *Records*, vol. 3, p. 472.
28. A. Rita-Ferreira, *Fixação Portuguesa e História Pré-colonial de Moçambique*, pp. 117, 149.
29. Anon., 'Descripção da Capitania de Monsambique, suas povoações e produções, 1788', Andrade, *Relações*, p. 397.
30. *Ibid.*
31. António Pinto de Miranda, 'Memória sobre a Costa de Africa', Andrade, *Relações*, p. 260.
32. Anon., 'Descripção da Capitania de Monsambique, suas povoações e produções, 1788', Andrade, *Relações*, p. 399.
33. Pinto de Miranda, 'Memória. . . .', Andrade, *Relações*, pp. 262.
34. Montaury, 'Moçambique. . . .', Andrade, *Relações*, p. 356.
35. Pinto de Miranda, 'Memória. . . .', Andrade, *Relações*, p. 262.
36. Anon., 'Descripção da Capitania de Monsambique, suas povoações e produções, 1788', Andrade, *Relações* p. 396, 398; Anon., 'Memórias da Costa d'Africa Oriental e algumas reflexões uteis para estabelecer melhor, e fazer mais florente o seu commércio, 1762', Andrade, *Relações*, p. 190.
37. *Ibid.*, pp. 190–1.
38. Montaury, 'Moçambique. . . .', Andrade, *Relações*, p. 357.
39. Caetano Montez, 'Sena. Forte de S. Marçal', pp. 41–8; A.N. de B. de Villas-Boas Truão, 'Plano para um Regimento ou Nova Constituição Económica e Política da Capitania dos Rios de Senna', p. 408.
40. António da Conceição, 'Tratado dos Rios de Cuama', *O Chronista de Tissuary*, para. 35.
41. Caetano Montez, 'Apontamentos para o Roteiro dos Monumentos Militares Portugueses: Praça de S. Tiago Maior; Forte de S. Tiago Maior', pp. 67–73.
42. Bocarro and Barreto de Resende, 'Do Estado da India', Theal, *Records*, vol. 2, p. 413.
43. 'Instrucção que o Illmo e Exmo Sr Governador e Capitão General Baltazar Manuel Pereira do Lago deo a quem lhe suceder neste Governo', Andrade, *Relações*, p. 328.
44. Pinto de Miranda, 'Memória. . . .', Andrade, *Relações*. . . ., pp. 265.
45. Anon., 'Descripção da Capitania de Monsambique, suas povoações e produções, 1788'; Andrade, *Relações*, p. 403.

Chapter 7. Southern Mozambique

1. Most of the accounts of Portuguese shipwrecks on the coasts of southern Africa which have been used in this book have been published in translation and can be found in: Theal, *Records*; C.R. Boxer (ed.), *The Tragic History of the Sea*, 'Narrative of the Shipwreck of the Great Ship São Thomé in the Land of Fumos, in the year 1589', pp. 52–104; 'Shipwreck of the Great Ship Santo Alberto, and Itinerary of the People who were saved from it, 1593', pp. 107–86; 'Treatise of the Misfortune that befell the Great Ship São João Baptista, 1622', pp. 189–271; C.D. Ley (ed.), *Portuguese Voyages, 1498–1663*; 'Account of the very notorious loss of the great galleon, the São João', pp. 239–59.
2. David Hedges, 'Trade and Politics in Southern Mozambique and Zululand in the Eighteenth and early Nineteenth Centuries', pp. 67–90.
3. *Ibid.*, p. 83.
4. Alan K. Smith, 'The Peoples of Southern Mozambique: an Historical Survey', p. 572; Patrick Harries, 'The Roots of Ethnicity: Discourse and the Politics of Language Construction in South-East Africa', discusses the origins of ethnic distinctions in the Bay region.
5. Boxer, 'Narrative of the Shipwreck . . .', p. 92.
6. *Ibid.*, pp. 75, 89.
7. Ley, *Portuguese Voyages*. . . ., 'Account of the very notorious loss. . . .', pp. 250–1.
8. Boxer, 'Narrative of the Shipwreck . . .', p. 98.
9. Caetano Montez, *Descobrimento e Fundação de Lourenço Marques*, pp. 37–40; Boxer, 'Narrative of the Shipwreck. . . .', p. 73; João dos Santos, *Ethiopia Oriental*, p. 367.
10. Ley, 'Account of the very notorious loss. . . .', p. 258.
11. Hedges, 'Trade and Politics. . . .', pp. 111–14.
12. *Ibid.*, pp. 115–18.
13. João dos Santos, '*Ethiopia Oriental*', p. 331.
14. Smith, 'The Peoples of Southern Mozambique. . . .'
15. Caetano Montez, *Descobrimento*, p. 62; 'Rodrigo da Costa, viceroy, to King', Goa, 24 January 1687, enclosing 'Miguel de Almeida, captain of Mozambique to the viceroy' and 'Copy of the decision of the council of Mozambique concerning the trading ship for Cape Correntes', Mozambique, 6 August 1686, Theal, *Records*, vol. 5, pp. 295–7.
16. Montez, *Descobrimento*. . . ., p. 63.
17. 'A Relation of three Years Sufferings of Robert Everard upon the Island of Assada near Madagascar, in a Voyage to India, in the Year 1686', Theal, *Records*, vol. 5, pp. 407–8.
18. 'The ship Little *Josiah*, Capt Dering, at St Lawrence', Bodleian Library, Oxford, MS Rawl. A 336.
19. Montez, *Descobrimento*. . . ., p. 65.
20. *Ibid.*, pp. 69–77; Hedges, 'Trade and Politics. . . .', p. 122.
21. Alexandre Lobato, *História da Fundação de Lourenço Marques*, pp. 39–47.
22. Hedges, 'Trade and Politics. . . .', p. 129.
23. *Ibid.*, pp. 149–52.
24. 'Description of the Situation, Customs and Produce of some Places of Africa', *c*.1518, *Documents on the Portuguese*. . . ., vol. 5, pp. 355–7; Paul Sinclair, 'Chibuene — an early trading site in southern Mozambique', pp. 149–64.
25. 'Chapters relating to East Africa in the Account of Martin Fernandez de Figueroa', *Documents on the Portuguese*. . . ., vol. 3, p. 593.
26. 'King to viceroy', Lisbon, 18 February 1709, Theal, *Records*, vol. 5, p. 15; 'King to viceroy' (Lisbon 11 September 1710), *ibid.*, pp. 26–7.

27. Alan K. Smith, 'The Struggle for Control of Southern Moçambique', 1720-1835', p. 97.
28. Anon., 'Memórias da Costa d'Africa Oriental e algumas reflexões uteis para estabelecer melhor, e fazer mais florente o seu commércio, 1762', Andrade, *Relações*. . . ., pp. 219-20.
29. AHU Moç Cx 6 Pedro Rego Barretto to the king, 10 Nov. 1745.
30. 'Instrucção que o Illmo e Exmo Sr Governador e Capitão General Baltazar Manuel Pereira do Lago deo a quem lhe suceder neste Governo', Andrade, *Relações*. . . ., pp. 320-2.
31. Fritz Hoppe, *Portugiesisch-Ostafrika*. . . ., p. 74.
32. Smith, 'The Struggle for Control. . . .', p. 117.
33. *Ibid.*, p. 129; for a contemporary description of the Hlengwe attacks in the region of Inhambane see AHU Moç Cx 6 M. Correa Monteiro de Mattos to governor general, Inhambane, 11 June 1761.
34. Sr Ferão, 'Account of the Portuguese Possessions within the Captaincy of the Rios de Senna', Theal, *Records*, vol. 7, p. 381.
35. Anon., 'Memórias da Costa d'Africa Oriental. . . .'; Andrade, *Relações*, p. 212.
36. 'Instrucção que o Illmo e Exmo Sr Governador e Capitão General Baltazar Manuel Pereira do Lago deo a quem lhe suceder neste Governo', Andrade, *Relações*, pp. 320-2.
37. *Ibid.*, p. 321.

Chapter 8. International Relations and Coastal Commerce, 1600-18

1. Sir William Foster (ed.), *The Voyages of Sir James Lancaster to Brazil and the East Indies 1591-1603*, pp. 5-6.
2. M.Newitt, 'The East India Company in the Western Indian Ocean in the Early Seventeenth Century', p. 20.
3. Eric Axelson, *Portuguese in South-East Africa* . . . ., pp. 15-29.
4. António Bocarro, *Década 13 da História da India*, ch. 155.
5. Newitt, 'The East India Company. . . .', p. 21.
6. Axelson, *Portuguese in South-East Africa*. . . ., pp. 121-3.
7. Newitt, 'The Comoro Islands in Indian Ocean Trade before the 19th Century', p. 148.
8. *Ibid.*, p. 148.
9. *Ibid.*, p. 150, and sources quoted.
10. 'Pedro da Costa's Voyage to Madagascar with Luis Marianno and Pedro Freire', vol. 2, pp. 1-79, in A. and G. Grandidier (eds), *Collections des Ouvrages Anciens concernant Madagascar*.
11. For the English in Madagascar see Axelson, *Portuguese in South-East Africa*, pp. 121-2, and Newitt, 'The East India Company. . . .', pp. 23-5, and the sources quoted.
12. Axelson, *Portuguese in South-East Africa*, p. 141.
13. *Ibid.*, pp. 139-42.
14. 'Prince to viceroy' (Lisbon 3 April 1675), Theal, *Records*, vol. 4, pp. 375-7; 'Concelho Ultramarino to Prince' (Lisbon 6 August 1677), AHU Moç Cx 3 doc. 33
15. E.A.Alpers, *Ivory and Slaves in East Central Africa*, p. 56.
16. *Ibid.*, p. 55.
17. *Ibid.*, pp. 42-5.
18. João dos Santos, *Ethiopia Oriental*, pp. 300-1.

19. Details of Gaspar Bocarro's journey are contained in António Bocarro, 'Livro do Estado da India', pp. 416–19.
20. For a detailed discussion of the commercial regime in Mozambique see Hoppe, *Portugiesisch-Ostafrika*, pp. 12–22, and for a summary see José Joaquim Lopes de Lima and Francisco Maria Bordalo, *Ensaio sobre a Estatística das Possessoẽs Portuguezas no Ultramar*, pp. 100–2.
21. Alpers, *Ivory and Slaves*. . . ., pp. 122, 126–7.
22. 'Inquérito em Moçambique no anno de 1573', Alcantara Guerreiro (ed.), *Studia*, vol. 6, pp. 7–19.
23. António Gomes, 'Viagem que fez o Padre António Gomes, da Companhia de Jesus ao Imperio de Manomotapa; e assistencia que fez nas ditas terras de algus annos', *Studia*, vol. 3, p. 241.
24. Miguel de Almeida to governor of Moçambique (Sena 23 June 1687), *Livros dos Monções*, no. 52, fols 403–403v (transl. H. de Noronha).
25. Manuel Barreto, 'Informação do Estado e Conquista dos Rios de Cuama', Theal, *Records*, vol. 3, p. 480.
26. António da Conceição, 'Tratado dos Rios de Cuama', *O Chronista de Tissuary*, paras 55, 115; Francisco de Sousa, *Oriente Conquistado a Jesu Christo pelos Padres da Companhia de Jesu da Provincia de Goa*, ch. 30; 'King to viceroy' (Lisbon 20 March 1690), Theal, *Records*, vol. 4, pp. 449–52.
27. Alpers, *Ivory and Slaves*. . . ., pp. 86–94.
28. *Ibid.*, pp. 113–6.
29. *Ibid.*, pp. 76–85.
30. João Baptista de Montaury, 'Moçambique, Ilhas Querimbas, Rios de Sena, Villa de Tete, Villa de Zumbo, Manica, Villa de Luabo, Inhambane', Andrade, *Relações*. . . ., p. 348.
31. Inacio Caetano Xavier, 'Notícias dos Domínios Portugueses da Costa de Africa Oriental', Andrade, *Relações*. . . ., p. 153.
32. Barreto, 'Informação. . . .', Theal, *Records*, vol. 3, p. 462.
33. António Cabral, *Dicionário de Nomes Geográficos de Moçambique*, p. 24.
34. 'King to viceroy' (Lisbon, 7 April 1727), Theal, *Records*, vol. 5, pp. 153–5.
35. Barreto, 'Informação. . . .', Theal, *Records*, vol. 3, p. 464.
36. António Francisco Cardim, *Relacam da Viagem do Galeam Sam Lourenco e sua Perdiçam nos Baixos de Moxincale em 3 de Septembro de 1649*, fol. 114.
37. *Ibid.*, fol. 114.
38. A. Rita-Ferreira, *Fixação Portuguesa e História Pré-colonial de Moçambique*, pp. 157–8.
39. *Ibid.*, pp. 156–7.
40. M. Newitt (ed.), *Account of a Journey made overland from Quelimane to Angoche in 1752*, by F.R. Moraes Pereira, p. 25.
41. *Ibid.*, p. 30.
42. *Ibid.*, p. 22.
43. *Ibid.*, p. 27; Alpers, *Ivory and Slaves*. . . ., p. 128.
44. M. Newitt, 'The Southern Swahili Coast in the First Century of European Expansion'; João dos Santos, *Ethiopia Oriental e Varia História de Cousas Notaveis do Oriente*, p. 81.
45. 'Letter from D. Pedro de Castro to the king' (Mozambique 8 July 1523), *Documents on the Portuguese*. . . ., vol. 6, pp. 173–9.
46. João dos Santos, *Ethiopia Oriental*, p. 79.
47. 'Livro das Plantas de Todas as Fortalezas, Cidades e Povoaçoẽs do Estado da India' by António Bocarro, *Arquivo Portugues Oriental*, A.B. de Bragança Pereira (ed.), tom. iv, vol. 2, pt. 1. pp. 40–3.
48 'Copea do assento feito em vertude de hũa Carta do sor. Governador Antonio de mello de Castro na fortza. nos apozentos do Capitão e Govor. Dom Mel. maz., e

mais deputados adjuntos, cujo theor he o seguinte', Monções do Reino, nos 29 and 30, fol. 130.
49. C.R. Boxer, 'The Querimba Islands in 1744', pp. 343–54.
50. Jeronimo José Nogueira de Andrade, 'Descrição em que ficaram os Negocios da Capitania de Moçambique em Fins de 1789 e considerações sobre a decadencia do seu Commércio', *Archivo da Colonias*, p. 123; Newitt, *Portuguese Settlement*. . . ., p. 214.
51. Anon., 'Memórias da Costa d'Africa Oriental e algumas reflexoës uteis para estabelecer melhor, e fazer mais florente o seu commércio, 1762', Andrade, *Relações*. . . ., p. 220.
52. Alpers, *Ivory and Slaves*. . . ., p. 128.
53. Newitt, *Portuguese Settlement*. . . ., p. 213.

Chapter 9. The Gold Fairs

1. P.S. Garlake, 'Excavations at the seventeenth-century Portuguese site of Dambarare, Rhodesia'.
2. S.I. Mudenge, *A Political History of Munhumutapa*, pp. 166–7, 178–88; I. Phimister, 'Alluvial Gold-mining and Trade in Nineteenth Century South Central Africa', pp. 447–9.
3. 'Notes made by Gaspar Veloso, clerk to the factory of Mozambique, and sent to the king', *Documents on the Portuguese*. . . ., vol. 3, pp. 181–9.
4. 'Inquérito em Moçambique no anno de 1573', Alcantara Guerreiro, ed., *Studia*, vol. 6, pp. 7–19.
5. António Bocarro and Pedro Barreto de Resende, 'Do Estado da India', Theal, *Records*, vol. 2, p. 412.
6. J.M. de Souza Monteiro, *Diccionário Geographico das Provincias e Possessões Portuguezas*; H.H.K. Bhila, *Trade and Politics in a Shona Kingdom*, p. 81.
7. 'King to viceroy' (Lisbon, 21 March 1608), Theal, *Records*, vol. 4, pp. 69–74; M. Newitt, *Portuguese Settlement on the Zambesi*, pp. 41–7.
8. 'Brief resumé of an account given by Custódio de Almeida e Souza on the situation of the Rivers of Senna and Sofalla', Ajuda 51.viii.40, fols 271–2.
9. Manuel Barreto, 'Informação do Estado e Conquista dos Rios de Cuama' (Goa 11 December 1667), Theal, *Records*, vol. 3, p. 482.
10. Garlake, 'Excavations. . . .', p. 23.
11. 'Brief resumé of an account given by Custódio de Almeida e Souza. . . .', *loc. cit.*.
12. António da Conceição, 'Tratado dos Rios de Cuama', *O Chronista de Tissuary*, vol. 2, paras 53–7.
13. 'João de Sousa Freire to king' (Sena 12 June 1673), *Livros dos Monções*, no. 38A.
14. 'Caetano de Mello e Castro to viceroy' (Sena 26 June 1684), *Livros dos Monções*, no. 49.
15. *Ibid.*
16. 'Brief resumé of an account given by Custódio de Almeida e Souza. . . .', *loc. cit.*.
17. S.I. Mudenge, 'The Rozvi Empire and the Feira of Zumbo', p. 73.
18. Bhila, *Trade and Politics*. . . ., pp. 93–7.
19. Mudenge, 'The Rozvi Empire. . . .', pp. 42–3.
20. David Beach, *The Shona and Zimbabwe, 900–1850*, p. 142.
21. For the *munhai* see *ibid.*, p. 150–1, and 'Artigos do Tratado de Reconcilhação entre of Emperador de Moanamotapa e o Estado dos dominios de S. Mage . . .', Zimbaoe, June 1783, AHU Moç Cx 20; 'Instrucção que o Illmo e Exmo Sr Governador e Capitão General Baltazar Manuel Pereira do Lago deo a quem lhe suceder neste Governo', Andrade, *Relações*, p. 328; 'Inacio de Mello Alvim, to governor general'

(23 Jan. 1770), in Caetano Montez, ed., *Inventário do fundo do Século XVIII*.

22. For the refounding of the Manica fair see AHU Moç Cx 17 'Descripção Corografica do Reino de Manica seus Costumes e Leis'; H.H.K. Bhila, *Trade and Politics in a Shona Kingdom*, p. 98; AHU Moç Cx 3 'Memorial do que tenho obrado nestes Rios no Serviço de S. Magestade que Deus Guarde' (7 Dec. 1751).

23. Mudenge, 'The Rozvi Empire. . . .', p. 168; J. Desmond Clark, 'The Portuguese Settlement at Feira', pp. 275-86.

24. *Ibid.*, p. 183.

25. E.C. Tabler (ed.), *The Zambezi Papers of Richard Thornton*, vol. 1, p. 161.

26. Mudenge, 'The Rozvi Empire. . . .', p. 183-4; W.F. Rea, *The Economics of the Zambezi Missions, 1580-1759*, pp. 32-7; A. de F. de Mesquita e Solla, 'Apontamentos sobre o Zumbo', pp. 252-3.

27. Rea, *The Economics*. . . ., p. 133.

28. Mudenge, 'The Rozvi Empire. . . .', p. 260.

29. *Ibid.*, p. 197.

30. *Ibid.*, p. 190.

31. N. Sutherland-Harris, 'Zambian Trade with Zumbo in the Eighteenth Century', pp. 233-7.

32. Mudenge, 'The Rozvi Empire. . . .', pp. 322-4; J. Desmond Clark, 'The Portuguese Settlement at Feira', pp. 286-92.

33. Mauriz Thoman, SJ, *Reise und Lebensbeschreibung*, chapter 9.

34. Frei Francisco de Santa Caterina, 'A Dominican Account of Zambesia in 1744'; Dionízio de Mello e Castro, 'Notícia do Império Marave e dos Rios de Sena', in Luiz Fernando Carvalho Dias ed., *Fontes para a História, Geografia e Comércio de Moçambique (sec xviii)*.

35. A.C.P. Gamitto, *King Kazembe*, vol. 1, p. 43.

36. Newitt, *Portuguese Settlement*. . . ., pp. 82-5; Rea, *The Economics*. . . ., p. 136; AHU Moç Cx 23, 'Relação de dez amostras de ouro de outras tantas minas de Rios de Senna' by Mattheus Ignacio de Almeida, Mozambique 3 December 1786.

37. Gamitto, *King Kazembe*, vol. 1, pp. 58-61.

38. *Ibid.*, p. 58; Mauriz Thoman confirms that only women dug gold and he says they were guarded by men while they did so to prevent their being kidnapped: *Reise und Lebensbeschreibung*, chapter 9.

39. Francisco José de Lacerda e Almeida, *Travessia de Africa*, p. 184.

40. Gamitto, *King Kazembe*, vol. 1, p. 40.

41. AHU Moç Cx 5 'David Marques Pereira to viceroy' (30 May 1755).

42. Newitt, *Portuguese Settlement*. . . ., chap. 14, for the Caetano Pereira family; Francisco José de Lacerda e Almeida, *Travessia de Africa*, pp. 156-7, 182-4.

43. AHU Moç Cx 17 'Descripção Corografica do Reino de Manica seus Costumes e Leis'.

44. Bhila, *Trade and Politics*. . . ., p. 123.

45. AHU Moç Cx 17 'Descripção Corografica do Reino de Manica seus Costumes e Leis'.

46. Caetano Montez (ed.), *Inventário do fundo do Século XVIII*. For *mussitos* see, 'Inacio de Melo e Alvim to governor general' (Tete 23 Jan. 1770), p. 113, and for the wars with Barue and the treaty signed in 1769 see 'Inacio de Melo e Alvim to governor general' (Sena 16 July 1769), p. 104; 'Record of a meeting with the ambassadors of Macombe' (3 Oct. 1768), p. 168.

47. AHU Moç Cx 17 'Descripção Corografica do Reino de Manica seus Costumes e Leis; H.H.K. Bhila, *Trade and Politics*. . . ., p. 126.

48. Manuel Galvão da Silva, 'Diário das Viagens, feitas pelas terras de Manica', in Luiz F. de Carvalho Dias (ed.), *Fontes para a História, Geografia e Comércio de Moçambique (sec xviii)*, p. 323.

49. *Ibid.*, pp. 324–5.
50. *Ibid.*, p. 326.
51. Bhila, *Trade and Politics*. . . ., p. 123.
52. *Ibid.*, p. 132.
53. *Ibid.*, pp. 146–58.
54. *Ibid.*, p. 157.
55. Beach, *The Shona*. . . ., p. 178.

Chapter 10. The *Prazos*

1. By far the best book on the *prazos* is Allen Isaacman, *Mozambique*. For their origins see M. Newitt, *Portuguese Settlement on the Zambesi*, ch. 4; Alexandre Lobato, *Colonização Senhorial da Zambézia*, pp. 97–116.
2. For the origins of the ecclesiastical *prazos* see W.F. Rea, *The Economics of the Zambezi Missions*, pp. 27–32.
3. João dos Santos, *Ethiopia Oriental*, p. 82; and Theal, *Records*, vol. 7, p. 338.
4. Manuel Barreto, 'Informação do Estado e Conquista dos Rios de Cuama', Theal, *Records*, vol. 3, pp. 467–9.
5. Declaration of 'Dom Sebastião por graça de Deus Emperador deste Imperio do Quiteve . . .', 23 Oct. 1644, *Livros dos Moções*, no. 60, fols 231–2.
6. *Ibid.*
7. Barreto, 'Informação . . .', Theal, *Records*, vol. 3, pp. 491–2.
8. *Ibid.*, p. 483.
9. Lobato, *Colonização*. . . ., p. 9.
10. Eric Axelson, *Portuguese in South-East Africa 1600–1700*, pp. 99–101.
11. *Ibid.*, chapter 10.
12. Lobato, *Colonização*. . . ., p. 105.
13. Newitt, *Portuguese Settlement*. . . ., pp. 2–3.
14. 'King to viceroy', (Lisbon 12 Dec. 1646), *Livros dos Monções*, no. 57, fol. 65.
15. Barreto, 'Informação. . . .', Theal, *Records*, vol. 3, p. 468.
16. 'Carta de Aforamento for Mabunga', issued by João Moreira Pereira, Tete 25 October 1772, in Caetano Montez (ed.), *Inventário do Fundo do Século XVIII, Introdução, Inventário, Sumarios e Transcrições*.
17. Newitt, *Portuguese Settlement*. . . ., pp. 87–90.
18. Dionízio de Mello e Castro, 'Notícia do Império Marave e dos Rios de Sena', in Luiz Fernando Carvalho Dias (ed.), *Fontes para a História, Geografia e Comércio de Moçambique (sec. xviii)*, pp. 144–9.
19. Newitt, *Portuguese Settlement*. . . ., p. 142.
20. *Ibid.*, pp. 140–1; Fritz Hoppe, *Portugiesisch-Ostafrika in der Zeit des Marquês de Pombal, 1750–1777*, pp. 71–5.
21. Newitt, *Portuguese Settlement*. . . ., p. 117.
22. *Ibid.*, p. 148.
23. AHU Moç Cx 6, 'Pedro da Saldanha de Albuquerque to the King', Mozambique, 27 December 1758.
24. Newitt, *Portuguese Settlement*. . . ., pp. 87–8, and chapter 9.
25. For Francesca Josepha de Moura e Meneses see M. Murias, ed., *Travessia da Africa*, pp. 157–8; A.C.P. Gamitto, *King Kazembe*, vol. 1, p. 42.
26. Augusto de Castilho, *Relatório da Guerra da Zambézia em 1888*, pp. 39–40.
27. António Pinto de Miranda, 'Memória sobre a Costa de Africa', Andrade, *Relações*, p. 254.
28. For a wider discussion of these issues, see, M. Newitt, 'Mixed Race Groups in the Early History of Portuguese Expansion'.

29. E.A. Alpers, 'Trade, State and Society among the Yao in the Nineteenth Century', p. 412.
30. Bronislaw Stefaniszyn and Hilary de Santana, 'The Rise of the Chikunda "Condottieri" ', p. 362.
31. Charles E. Nowell, *The Rose-Coloured Map*, pp. 66, 235.
32. Newitt, *Portuguese Settlement*. . . ., pp. 170–4.
33. *Ibid.*, chapter 11.
34. Pinto de Miranda, 'Memória. . . ., pp. 266–68.
35. A.C.P. Gamitto, 'Escravatura na Africa Oriental', p. 399.
36. *Ibid.* Pinto de Miranda, 'Memória. . . ., pp. 266–68.
37. Rea, *The Economics*. . . ., p. 127.
38. *Ibid.*, p. 129.
39. 'Mapas das Terras da Gorungosa e da Chiringome, e seus costumes', in Luiz F. Carvalho Dias (ed.), *Fontes para a História, Geografia e Comércio de Moçambique (sec. XVIII)*, pp. 333–57.
40. Rea, *The Economics*. . . ., pp. 91–8.
41. *Ibid.*, pp. 94–5.
42. Newitt, *Portuguese Settlement*. . . ., p. 116.
43. Gamitto, *King Kazembe*, vol. 1, p. 55.
44. Rea, *The Economics*. . . ., pp. 126–7.
45. A.N. de B. de Villas-Boas Truão, 'Plano para um Regimento ou Nova Constituição Econômica e Política da Capitania dos Rios de Senna', p. 451.
46. A.N. de B. de Villas-Boas Truão, *Estatística de Capitania dos Rios de Senna do Anno de 1806*, p. 14.
47. Rea, *The Economics*. . . ., p. 124.

Chapter 11. Time of Troubles: Drought, the Slave Trade and the Nguni Invasions

1. For the raids of the Betsimisaraka see Barbara Dubins, 'A Political History of the Comoro Islands 1795–1886', chapter 4; James Prior, *Voyage along the Eastern Coast of Africa*, pp. 62–5.
2. E.A. Alpers, *Ivory and Slaves in East Central Africa*, pp. 94–8.
3. E.A. Alpers, 'The French Slave Trade in East Africa 1721–1819', pp. 92–4.
4. *Ibid.*, pp. 101–2.
5. Alpers, *Ivory and Slaves* . . ., p. 112.
6. Prior, *Voyage*. . . ., p. 33.
7. António Carreira, *O Tráfico Português de Escravos na Costa Oriental Africana nos Começos do Século XIX*.
8. A.N. de B. de Villas-Boas Truão, 'Plano para um Regimento ou Nova Constituição Econômica e Política da Capitania dos Rios de Senna', p. 414.
9. Carreira, *O Tráfico* . . ., p. 35.
10. M. Newitt, 'Drought in Mozambique 1823–1831', p. 22; figures for slave exports are contained in Gerhard Liesegang, 'A First Look at the Import and Export Trade of Mozambique, 1800–1914', p. 463.
11. A.C.P. Gamitto, 'Escravatura na Africa Oriental', p. 370.
12. Charles Ballard, 'Drought and Economic Distress: South Africa in the 1800s'; Newitt, 'Drought. . . .', pp. 15–22.
13. AHU Moç Cx 225, 'M.J.M. Vasconcellos e Cirne to Conde de Basto' (Quelimane 6 Dec. 1829).
14. AHU Moç Cx 224, 'A.M. da Cunha to P.J.M. de Brito' (Quelimane 24 Sept. 1829).

15. Newitt, 'Drought. . . .'
16. F. Santana (ed.), *Documentação Avulsa Moçambicana do Arquivo Histórico Ultramarino*, vol. 1, p. 269.
17. AHU Moç Cx 251 'P.J.M. de Brito to Duque de Cadaval' (Mozambique 8 Nov. 1831).
18. AHU Moç Cx 249, 'M. da Silva Gonçalves to P.J.M. de Brito' (Fernão Veloso 3 Aug. 1831).
19. For the ill-fated fair on the Luangwa see José Manuel Correa Monteiro, 'A Feira do Aruangoa do Norte'.
20. David W. Hedges, 'Trade and Politics in Southern Mozambique and Zululand in the Eighteenth and early Nineteenth Centuries'; Elizabeth Eldridge, 'Sources of Conflict in Southern Africa, *ca.* 1800-30: The "Mfecane" Reconsidered'.
21. Jeff Guy, 'Ecological Factors in the Rise of Shaka and the Zulu Kingdom'.
22. Gerhard Liesegang, 'Nguni Migrations between Delagoa Bay and the Zambesi, 1821-1839', p. 321.
23. A. Rita-Ferreira, *Fixação Portuguesa e História Pré-colonial de Moçambique*, p. 205.
24. Quoted in Liesegang, 'Nguni Migrations. . . .', p. 325.
25. Rita-Ferreira, *Fixação.* . . ., p. 206.
26. David Beach, *War and Politics in Zimbabwe, 1840-1900*, p. 20.
27. Rita-Ferreira, *Fixação.* . . ., p. 188.
28. *Ibid.*, pp. 207-13.
29. AHU Moç Cx 249, doc. 67 'J.X.D.Costa to P.J.M. de Brito' (Mozambique 5 Feb. 1831).

Chapter 12. Expansion in the Nineteenth Century

1. José Manuel Correa Monteiro, 'A Feira do Aruangoa do Norte', pp. 207-8.
2. Gervase Clarence-Smith, *The Third Portuguese Empire, 1825-1975*, pp. 5-8.
3. José Capela, *Escravatura*, p. 229.
4. *Ibid.*, pp. 240-5.
5. Leroy Vail and Landeg White, *Capitalism and Colonialism in Mozambique*, pp. 16-29.
6. José Capela, *Escravatura*, p. 251.
7. F.L. Barnard, *A Three Years Cruize in the Mozambique Channel*, p. 153.
8. *Ibid.*, p. 41.
9. W. Cope Devereux, *A Cruise in the Gorgon*, p. 62.
10. *Ibid.*, p. 64.
11. *Ibid.*, p. 72.
12. Nancy J. Hafkin, 'Trade, Society and Politics in Northern Mozambique', pp. 191-2.
13. *Ibid.*, pp. 191-8.
14. *Ibid.*, pp. 122-43; M. Newitt, 'Drought in Mozambique 1823-1831'.
15. M.Newitt, 'Angoche, the Slave Trade and the Portuguese, c. 1844-1910', pp. 659-61.
16. For Angoche and the career of Mussa Quanto see João de Azevedo Coutinho, *As Duas Conquistas de Angoche*; Eduardo do Couto Lupi, *Angoche*; Hafkin, 'Trade, Society. . . .', chapter 6.
17. Newitt, 'Angoche. . . .', pp. 663-5; M. Newitt, *Portuguese Settlement on the Zambesi*, chapter 16.
18. M. Schoffeleers, 'M'Bona the Guardian Spirit of the Manganja'.
19. E.A. Alpers, *Ivory and Slaves in East Central Africa*, pp. 250-1.
20. W. Basil Worsfold, *Portuguese Nyasaland*, p. 94
21. E.A. Alpers, 'Towards a History of the Expansion of Islam in East Africa: the

Matrilineal Peoples of the Southern Interior'; 'Trade State and Society among the Yao in the nineteenth century'.

22. W.P. Johnson, *My African Reminiscences, 1875-1895*, chapter 5.
23. Alpers, 'Towards a History. . . .', pp. 184-5.
24. R.B. Boeder, *Silent Majority: a History of the Lomwe in Malawi*.
25. For first-hand published accounts of Mozambique by British writers see Henry Salt, *A Voyage to Abyssinia . . . in the Years 1809 and 1810*; James Prior, *Voyage along the Eastern Coast of Africa to Mosambique, Johanna, and Quiloa . . . in the Nisus Frigate*; Capt. Thomas Boteler, *Narrative of a Voyage of Discovery to Africa and Arabia*; Capt. W.F.W. Owen, *Narrative of Voyages to Explore the Shores of Africa, Arabia and Madagascar*; Barnard, *A Three Years Cruize*. . . .
26. Landeg White, *Magomero*, part 1; Owen Chadwick, *Mackenzie's Grave*.
27. Correa Monteiro, 'A Feira. . . .'
28. E.C. Tabler (ed.), *The Zambezi Papers of Richard Thornton*, vol. 1, p. 137.
29. *Ibid.*, p. 134.
30. David Beach, *War and Politics in Zimbabwe 1840-1900*, pp. 24-5, 34-5; for the refounding of Zumbo see 'Tavares de Almeida to Secretaria Geral (Tete 1 Feb 1861), AHM Tete Codice 2-446 FE2 no. 35 and other correspondence in the same register; Albino Manuel Pacheco, 'Uma Viagem de Tete a Zumbo'.
31. Bronislaw Stefaniszyn and Hilary de Santana, 'The Rise of the Chikunda "Condottieri" '.
32. Alpers, *Ivory and. . . .*, p. 252.
33. *Termos de Vassalagem nos Territórios de Machona, Zambézia e Nyasa, 1858-1889.*
34. Matthews, 'Portuguese, Chikunda and the Peoples of the Gwembe Valley: the impact of the 'Lower Zambezi Complex' on Southern Zambia', pp. 31-2.
35. Gerhard Liesegang, 'Notes on the Internal Structure of the Gaza Kingdom of Southern Mozambique, 1840-1895', p. 193.
36. H.H.K. Bhila, *Trade and Politics in a Shona Kingdom*, p. 185.
37. Tabler (ed.), *Zambezi Papers*, vol. 1, p. 171.
38. Beach, *War and Politics. . . .*, p. 23.
39. For standard accounts of Sousa's life see João de Azevedo Coutinho, *Manuel António de Sousa, um Capitão-mor da Zambezia*; M. Newitt, *Portuguese Settlement on the Zambesi*, ch. 18.
40. H.H.K. Bhila, *Trade and Politics. . . .*, pp. 216-22.
41. K.D. Dhliwayo, 'External Traders in the Hinterland of Sofala, 1810-1889', pp. 84-5.
42. *Ibid.*, pp. 96, 102-5; José Joaquim Lopes de Lima and Francisco Maria Bordalo, *Ensaio sobre a Estatística das Possessões Portuguezas no Ultramar* (Lisbon, 1859), II serie, book 4: *Província de Moçambique*, pp. 239-41.
43. René Pélissier, *Naissance du Mozambique*, vol. 1, pp. 79-80.
44. José Joaquim Lopes de Lima and Francisco Maria Bordalo, *Ensaio. . . .*, p. 265.
45. Pélissier, *Naissance. . . .*, vol. 1, pp. 79, 87; for a description of Inhambane in the 1850s see Lyons McLeod, *Travels in Eastern Africa*, vol. 1, pp. 197-201.
46. Patrick Harries, 'Slavery, Social Incorporation and Surplus Extraction: The Nature of Free and Unfree Labour in South-East Africa', pp. 312-18.
47. Roger Wagner, 'Zoutpansberg: The Dynamics of a Hunting Frontier, 1848-67', p. 326.
48. A. Rita-Ferreira, *Fixação Portuguesa e História Pré-colonial de Moçambique*, p. 191.
49. Gerhard Liesegang, 'Dingane's Attack on Lourenço Marques'.
50. Diocleciano Fernandes das Neves, *Itinerário de uma Viagem a Caça dos Elephantes*, pp. 6-9; for the slave trade at Lourenço Marques in the 1850s see McLeod, *Travels. . . .*, pp. 120-5.

51. Fernandes das Neves, *Itinerário*. . . ., pp. 11-16; McLeod, *Travels*. . . ., p. 179, records 30 tons of ivory from Zoutpansberg exported in three months in 1859.
52. Wagner, 'Zoutpansberg:. . . .,' p. 325.
53. Pélissier, *Naissance*. . . ., vol. 1, pp. 82-3, vol. 2, pp. 537, 540, 543; Wagner, Zoutpansberg. . . .
54. Pélissier, *Naissance*. . . ., vol. 2, p. 542.
55. Rita-Ferreira, *Fixação*. . . ., p. 188.
56. S. Young, 'Fertility and Famine: Women's Agricultural History in Southern Mozambique', p. 73.
57. Liesegang, 'Notes on the Internal Structure. . . .', pp. 188-9.
58. *Ibid.*, pp. 194-5.
59. Rita-Ferreira, *Fixação*. . . ., p. 199.

Chapter 13. Zambesia and the Zambesi Wars

1. João Joaquim Lopes de Lima and Francisco Maria Bordalo, *Ensaio sobre a Estatística das Possessões Portuguezas no Ultramar* (Lisbon, 1859), II series, book 4, *Província de Moçambique*, p. 288. For conditions in the region of Cabo Delgado in the mid-nineteenth century see Jeronymo Romero, *Memória acerca do Districto de Cabo Delgado*.
2. 'Decreto de 6 de Novembro de 1838', *Regimen dos Prazos da Coroa*, p. 12.
3. 'Decreto de 22 de Dezembro de 1854', *Regimen dos Prazos da Coroa*, pp. 12-14.
4. E.C. Tabler (ed.), *The Zambezi Papers of Richard Thornton*, p. 70.
5. Victor Courtois, SJ, 'Terras de Macanga'; Emile Durand, *Une exploration française au Zambèze*, ch. 16.
6. For descriptions of Massangano see M. Newitt and P.S. Garlake, 'The "Aringa" at Massangano'; Augusto de Castilho, *Relatório da Guerra da Zambézia em 1888*, pp. 17-18.
7. Tabler, *Zambezi Papers* . . . ., pp. 70, 80.
8. Bronislaw Stefaniszyn and Hilary de Santana, 'The Rise of the Chikunda "Condottieri"', p. 363.
9. Tabler, *Zambezi Papers* . . . ., p. 70; Emile Durand, *Une exploration*. . . ., p. 82, tells of an Afro-Portuguese, Cristovão Xavier, who had called his son Vasco da Gama.
10. A.P. Miranda, *Notícia acerca do Bonga da Zambézia*, p. 7; Emile Durand, *Une exploration* . . . ., p. 95.
11. Ayres d'Ornellas, *Collectanea das suas Obras Militares e Coloniais*, vol. 2, p. 317.
12. João de Azevedo Coutinho, *Memórias de um Velho Marinheiro e Soldado de Africa*, ch. 8.
13. For the rule of Sousa's captains on the lower Zambesi *prazos* after 1890 see Barry Neil-Tomlinson, 'The Mozambique Chartered Company 1892-1910'.
14. Quoted in Newitt, *Portuguese Settlement*. . . ., p. 236.
15. For the Vas dos Anjos see M. Newitt, 'The Massingire Rising of 1884'; René Pélissier, *Naissance du Mozambique*, vol. 1, p. 65.
16. Coutinho, *Memórias* . . . ., ch. 8; Newitt, *Portuguese Settlement* . . . ., ch. 16.
17. Filipe Gastão de Almeida de Eça, *História das Guerras no Zambeze: Chicoa e Massangano (1807-1888)*, vol. 1, ch. 2.
18. Miranda, *Notícia* . . . ., p. 6.
20. Almeida de Eça, *História das Guerras* . . . ., vol. 1 pp. 249-91.
21. Augusto de Castilho, *Relatório da Guerra da Zambézia em 1888*, p. 30.
22. Almeida de Eça, *História* . . . ., vol. 1, pp. 274-91.
23. Miranda, *Notícia* . . . ., p. 8.
24. Almeida de Eça, *História* . . . ., vol. 2, pp. 17-45.

25. Newitt, 'The Massingire Rising of 1884'.
26. For the attack on Shamo see Tabler, *Zambezi Papers* . . . ., pp. 68–80 and Reginald Foskett (ed.), *The Zambesi Journal and Letters of Dr John Kirk*, vol. 1, pp. 71–4.
27. Almeida de Eça, *História* . . . ., vol. 2, pp. 153–203.
28. *Ibid.* pp. 203–491.

Chapter 14. Mozambique and the Scramble for Africa, 1879–1891

1. C.S. Nichols, *The Swahili Coast*; E.A. Alpers, 'Gujerat and the Trade of East Africa, c. 1500–1800'; L.J. Sakaraj, 'Indian Merchants in East Africa: the Triangular Trade and the Slave Economy'.
2. R.C.F. Maugham, *Zambezia*, p. 276; W.P. Johnson, 'Seven Years' Travel in the Region East of Lake Nyasa', p. 533.
3. M. Newitt, 'Drought in Mozambique, 1823–1831', p. 22.
4. Gerhard Liesegang, 'A First Look at the Import and Export Trade of Mozambique, 1800–1914', p. 467.
5. A. Rita-Ferreira, 'A Sobrevivência do mais fraco. . . ., pp. 304–6; Arlindo Chilundo, 'Quando começou o comércio das oleaginosas em Moçambique?' pp. 512–13.
6. *Ibid.*, pp. 512–3.
7. Rita-Ferreira, 'A Sobrevivência. . . .', p. 313.
8. Arlindo Chilundo, 'Quando começou. . . .', pp. 516–20.
9. Rita-Fereira, 'A Sobrevivência. . . .', p. 310.
10. Leroy Vail and Landeg White, *Capitalism and Colonialism in Mozambique*, p. 65.
11. Jeanne Marie Penvenne, 'A History of African Labour in Lourenço Marques. . . .', pp. 14–15; A. Rita-Ferreira, *Fixação Portuguêsa e História Pré-colonial de Moçambique*, p. 46.
12. Quoted in W. Basil Worsfold, *Portuguese Nyasaland*, p. 151.
13. *Ibid.*, p. 144.
14. *Ibid.*, p. 148.
15. Maugham, *Zambezia*, p. 273.
16. J. Mouzinho de Abuquerque, *Moçambique*, pp. 139–40.
17. For Indian-African marriages see Maugham, *Zambezia*; Johnson, 'Seven Years' Travel. . . .', p. 533.
18. Barbara D. Dubins, 'A Political History of the Comoro Islands 1795–1886', ch. 4.
19. Lyons McLeod, *Travels in Eastern Africa*.
20. Henry Faulkner, *Elephant Haunts*; E.D. Young, *The Search after Livingstone*.
21. Axelson, *Portugal and the Scramble*. . . ., pp. 20–3.
22. *Ibid.*, pp. 164.
23. *Ibid.*, pp. 174, 176.
24. Simon Katzenellenbogen, *South Africa and Southern Mozambique*, p. 10.
25. Roger Wagner, 'Zoutpansberg: the Dynamics of a Hunting Frontier, 1848–67'.
26. A. da Silva Rego, 'Relações entre Moçambique e a Africa do Sul', p. 66.
27. *Ibid.*, p. 69.
28. *Ibid.*
29. Marquês do Lavradio, *Portugal em Africa depois de 1851*, pp. 53–66; for a flavour of the debate over Delagoa Bay see the articles of David Leslie collected in *Among the Zulus and Amatongas*.
30. Axelson, *Portugal and the Scramble*. . . ., pp. 10, 12; St Vincent Erskine, 'Journey to Umzila's, South-East Africa, in 1871–1872' and 'Third and Fourth Journeys in Gaza, or Southern Mozambique'.

31. For the Confederation scheme see Norman Etherington, 'Labour Supply and the Genesis of the South African Confederation in the 1870s'.

32. Axelson, *Portugal and the Scramble*. . . ., p. 21; R.J. Hammond, *Portugal and Africa 1815–1910*, ch. 3.

33. Axelson, *Portugal and the Scramble*. . . . .; Marquês do Lavradio, *Portugal em Africa depois de 1851*, ch. 4; Hammond, *Portugal and Africa*, ch. 3; R.T. Anstey, *Britain and the Congo in the Nineteenth Century*.

34. For the Portuguese economy in the late nineteenth century see Gervase Clarence-Smith, *The Third Portuguese Empire*; Ramiro da Costa, *O Desenvolvimento do Capitalismo em Portugal*.

35. Charles E. Nowell, *The Rose-Coloured Map*, pp. 21–2.

36. *Ibid.*, p. 22.

37. *Ibid.*, p. 51.

38. *Ibid.*, p. 77.

39. *Ibid.*, ch. 6.

40. Vail and White, *Capitalism and Colonialism*. . . ., pp. 73–6.

41. 'Decreto de 27 de Outubro de 1880', *Regimen dos Prazos da Coroa*.

42. Axelson, *Portugal and the Scramble*. . . ., p. 160.

43. For Paiva de Andrada and the origins of the Moçambique Company see *ibid.*, p. 120; D.N. Beach, 'The Origins of Moçambique and Zimbabwe: Paiva de Andrada, The *Companhia de Moçambique* and African Diplomacy 1881–91', section 4.

44. AHM Manica Codice 2-1389 Ga8, J.J. Fereira to Secretaria Geral, 28 December 1890, no 35; Axelson, *Portugal and the Scramble*. . . ., pp. 140–1; Beach, 'The Origins. . . .', pp. 8–9; João de Azevedo Coutinho, *Manuel António de Sousa, um Capitão-mor da Zambézia*; Newitt, *Portuguese Settlement*. . . ., ch. 18.

45. Vail and White, *Capitalism and Colonialism*. . . ., pp. 78–82; Newitt, 'The Massingire Rising of 1884'.

46. Beach, 'The Origins. . .', section 6.

47. *Ibid.*, p. 19; Newitt, *Portuguese Settlement*. . . ., pp. 323–5.

48. Joaquim Carlos Paiva de Andrada, 'Campanhas de Zambesia, 1887'.

49. Axelson, *Portugal and the Scramble*. . . ., p. 144.

50. Hammond, *Portugal and Africa*. . . ., p. 103.

51. Marquês do Lavradio, *Portugal em Africa depois de 1851*, p. 146; Nowell, *The Rose-Coloured Map*, p. 128.

52. Hammond, *Portugal and Africa*. . . ., p. 114; Nowell, *The Rose-Coloured Map*, p. 149.

53. Nowell, *The Rose-Coloured Map*, ch. 10.

54. Carlos Wiese, 'Expedição Portuguesa a M'Pesene'.

55. For the last campaign against Massangano see Augusto de Castilho, *Relatório da Guerra da Zambézia em 1888*; Newitt, *Portuguese Settlement*. . . ., pp. 272–4.

56. For Vitor Cordon's expedition and its consequences see *ibid.*, pp. 156–62; Beach, 'The Origins. . . ., pp. 30–40; Albino Lapa, *Vítor Cordon*.

57. Nowell, *The Rose-Coloured Map*, pp. 165–6; Beach, 'The Origins. . . .', section 11.

58. *Ibid.*, pp. 152–6.

59. Axelson, *Portugal and the Scramble*. . . ., pp. 182–3.

60. *Ibid.*, pp. 198–200; Hammond, *Portugal and Africa*, p. 115.

61. Axelson, *Portugal and the Scramble*. . . ., p. 204.

62. *Ibid.*, p. 206.

63. *Ibid.*, pp. 223–32.

64. Rita-Ferreira, *Fixação*. . . ., pp. 190–1.

65. Axelson, *Portugal and the Scramble*, p. 119.

66. Douglas L. Wheeler, 'Gungunyane the Negotiator: A Study in African Diplomacy', p. 586.

67. Axelson, *Portugal and the Scramble.* . . ., p. 128.
68. Wheeler, 'Gungunyane. . . ., p. 586.
69. Axelson, *Portugal and the Scramble.* . . ., pp. 129–30.
70. Wheeler, 'Gungunyane. . . ., p. 588.
71. Patrick Harries, 'Slavery, Social Incorporation and Surplus Extraction; the Nature of Free and Unfree Labour in South-East Africa'.
72. Axelson, *Portugal and the Scramble.* . . ., pp. 246–7.
73. P.R. Warhurst, *Anglo-Portuguese Relations in South-Central Africa, 1890–1900,* ch. 3.
74. Wheeler, 'Gungunyane. . . .', p. 572.
75. Axelson, *Portugal and the Scramble.* . . ., pp. 289–97.
76. *Ibid.,* pp. 284–9; Warhurst, *Anglo-Portuguese Relations.* . . . ., ch. 2.
77. Axelson, *Portugal and the Scramble.* . . ., pp. 266–7.
78. *Ibid.,* p. 288; Warhurst, *Anglo-Portuguese Relations.* . . ., ch. 2.

Chapter 15. Mozambique: The Making of the Colonial State

1. D.M. Schreuder, *The Scramble for Southern Africa, 1877–1895.*
2. J. Willequet, 'Anglo-German Rivalry in Belgian and Portuguese Africa', p. 265.
3. P.R. Warhurst, *Anglo-Portuguese Relations in South-Central Africa,* 1890–1900, ch. 5.
4. Clarence-Smith, *The Third Portuguese Empire.* . . ., pp. 22–5; António Carreira, *O Tráfico Português de Escravos na Costa Oriental Africana nos Começos do Século XIX.*
5. Clarence-Smith, *The Third Portuguese Empire.* . . ., p. 64.
6. *Ibid.,* pp. 67–8.
7. *Ibid.,* pp. 85–6.
8. G. Pirio, 'Commerce, industry and empire: the making of modern Portuguese Colonialism in Angola and Mozambique, 1890–1914', p. 67.
9. Vail and White, *Capitalism and Colonialism.* . . ., pp. 76–19.
10. *Ibid.,* pp. 87–90.
11. *Regimen dos Prazos da Coroa,* 'Decreto de 18 de Novembro de 1890', pp. 85–94; for discussion of this law see Vail and White, *Capitalism and Colonialism.* . . ., pp. 131–4; Newitt, *Portuguese Settlement.* . . ., pp. 353–61.
12. Vail and White, *Capitalism and Colonialism.* . . ., p. 110.
13. *Ibid.,* pp. 114–28.
14. The continuing bandit activity of the Da Cruz and the position of the *muzungo capitães-mores* cut off in British territory are dealt with in the correspondence of A. de F. de Mesquita e Solla to the Secretaria Geral in AHM Codice 1122 2-Ga3, no. 129, 26 Dec. 1892; no. 130, 28 Dec. 1892; no. 131, 29 Dec. 1892; no. 4, 13 Jan. 1893. For Macanga see René Pélissier, *Naissance du Mozambique,* vol. 2, p. 484.
15. Allen Isaacman and Barbara Isaacman, *The Tradition of Resistance in Mozambique.*
16. Barry Neil-Tomlinson, 'The Mozambique Chartered Company. . . ., pp. 19–20; Beach, 'The Origins. . . .'
17. Beach, 'The Origins. . . .', p. 30.
18. Aurélio Rocha, Carlos Serra and David Hedges (eds), *História de Moçambique,* p. 174.
19. Neil-Tomlinson, 'The Mozambique Chartered Company. . . .', pp. 34–7.
20. *Ibid.,* pp. 51–7.
21. João de Azevedo Coutinho, *Memórias de um Velho Marinheiro e Soldado de África,* chs 4 and 7.

22. *Ibid.*, chs 4 and 7; Neil-Tomlinson, 'The Mozambique Chartered Company. . . .', pp. 84–99.
23. W. Basil Worsfold, *Portuguese Nyasaland*, pp. 103–5.
24. Charles E. Nowell, *The Rose-Coloured Map*, p. 85.
25. R.J. Hammond, *Portugal and Africa 1815–1910*, p. 215; Warhurst, *Anglo-Portuguese Relations*. . . ., pp. 122–6.
26. Hammond, *Portugal and Africa*. . . ., p. 216.
27. Barry Neil-Tomlinson, 'The Nyassa Chartered Company, 1899–1929', p. 115.
28. Pélissier, *Naissance*. . . ., vol. 1, pp. 277–81; Worsfold, *Portuguese Nyasaland*, pp. 82, 139.
29. Vail, 'Mozambique's Chartered Companies. . . .', p. 398.
30. Douglas L. Wheeler, 'Gungunyane the Negotiator: A Study in African Diplomacy', p. 594.
31. Patrick Harries, 'Slavery, Social Incorporation and Surplus Extraction: The Nature of Free and Unfree Labour in South-East Africa', pp. 318–22.
32. *Ibid.*, pp. 324–5.
33. Rocha, Serra and Hedges, *História*. . . ., pp. 226–7.
34. *Ibid.*, p. 228; Pélissier, *Naissance*. . . ., vol. 2, pp. 579–88.
35. A. Rita-Ferreira, *Fixação Portuguesa e História Pré-colonial de Moçambique*, p. 196.
36. Wheeler, 'Gungunyane. . . .', p. 599.
37. Pélissier, *Naissance*. . . ., vol. 2, pp. 607–21.
38. James Duffy, *Portuguese Africa*, pp. 232–2.
39. Rocha, Serra and Hedges, *História*. . . ., p. 232; Rita-Ferreira, *Fixação*. . . ., p. 199.
40. Raúl Honwana, *The Life History of Raúl Honwana*, p. 43.
41. Alexandre Lobato, *Evolução Administrativa e Económica de Moçambique, 1752–1763*.
42. José Joaquim Lopes de Lima and Francisco Maria Bordalo, *Ensaio sobre a Estatística das Possessões Portuguezas no Ultramar* (Lisbon, 1859, II series, book 4, *Província de Moçambique*, p. 59.
43. *Ibid.*
44. *Ibid.*, pp. 94–5.
45. Sousa Ribeiro (ed.), *Anuário de Moçambique*, pp. 25, 163.
46. M.E. Lobo de Bulhões, *Les Colonies Portugaises: Court Exposé de leur Situation Actuelle*, p. 113.
47. J. Mouzinho de Albuquerque, *Moçambique*; António Ennes, *Moçambique*.
48. Worsfold, *Portuguese Nyasaland*, p. 53; Ennes, *Moçambique*, pp. 293–316, contains his blueprint for an administrative structure.
49. Sousa Ribeiro (ed.), *Anuário de Moçambique* (1940), p. 499.
50. Ernesto, J. de C. e Vasconcellos, *As Colónias Portuguezas*, pp. 319–20.
51. Quoted in José Capela, *O Imposto de Palhota e a Introdução do Modo de Produção Capitalista nas Colónias*, pp. 66–7; A. Rita-Ferreira, *O Movimento Migratório de Trabalhadores entre Moçambique e a Africa do Sul*, p. 53.
52. 'Remodelando a organisação administrativa das terras da districto de Lourenço Marques', *Providencias publicados pelo Comissário Regio na Provincia de Moçambique desde 1 de Janeiro até 18 de Dezembro de 1895.*
53. J.M. da Silva Cunha, *O Trabalho Indígena*, pp. 151–98; 'Relatório e Projecto da Commissão presidida pelo conselheiro António Ennes', *Relatório, Propostas de Lei e Documentos relativos as Possessões Ultramarinas.*
54. Duffy, *Portuguese Africa*, pp. 152–6.
55. Cunha, *O Trabalho*. . . ., p. 148.
56. Duffy, *Portuguese Africa*, pp. 151–3; Cunha, *O Trabalho*. . . ., pp. 145–9.
57. Rocha, Serra and Hedges, *História*. . . ., p. 89.
58. *Ibid.*, p. 90; Cunha, *O Trabalho* . . . ., p. 158.

59. Cunha, *O Trabalho*. . . ., p. 151; Duffy, *Portuguese Africa*, p. 155; 'Relatório e Projecto. . . .'
60. Cunha, *O Trabalho*. . . ., p. 157.

Chapter 16. Mozambique under the Monarchy and the Republic

1. Alfredo Héctor Wilensky, *Trends in Portuguese Overseas Legislation for Africa*, p. 29.
2. For the Native Affairs Department see Sousa Ribeiro (ed.), *Anuário de Moçambique* (1940), pp. 301–15; Ayres d'Ornellas, *Collectanea das suas Obras Militares e Coloniais*, vol. 3; Jeanne Marie Penvenne, 'A History of African Labour in Lourenço Marques: Mozambique 1877–1950', pp. 104–7.
3. Narana Coissoró, 'O regime das Terras em Moçambique'; A.B. Herrick *et al.*, *Area Handbook for Mozambique*, pp. 202, 216.
4. João Villas-Boas Carneiro de Moura, *Os Ultimos Anos da Monarquia e os Primeiros da República em Moçambique*, pp. 11–15.
5. Ribeiro (ed.), *Anuário de Moçambique* (1940), pp. 169–71.
6. Carneiro de Moura, *Os Ultimos Anos*. . . ., p. 15.
7. Wilensky, *Trends*. . . ., p. 58.
8. Herrick *et. al.*, *Area Handbook*. . . ., p. 73.
9. For the economy of Portugal and its empire at the end of the nineteenth century see G. Pirio, 'Commerce, industry and empire: the making of modern Portuguese Colonialism in Angola and Mozambique, 1890–1914'; Clarence-Smith, *The Third Portuguese Empire*. . . .; Ramiro da Costa, *O Desenvolvimento do Capitalismo em Portugal*; A. Torres, 'Le rôle du capitale bancaire dans les colonies portugaises de l'Angola et de St. Tomé de 1864 au début du xxe siècle'.
10. Clarence-Smith, *The Third Portuguese Empire*. . . ., p. 87.
11. *Ibid.*, p. 118.
12. *Ibid.*, pp. 89–94; Penvenne, 'A History of African Labour. . . .', pp. 129–45.
13. *Ibid.*, pp. 96–7.
14. *Estatística nos Caminhos de Ferro das Colónias Portuguesas de 1888 a 1911.*
15. Kingsley Fairbridge, *The Autobiography of Kingsley Fairbridge*, p. 9.
16. Aurélio Rocha, Carlos Serra and David Hedges (eds), *História de Moçambique*, p. 254.
17. Neil-Tomlinson, 'The Mozambique Chartered Company. . . ., pp. 140, 143.
18. *Ibid.*, pp. 196–200.
19. *Estatística nos Caminhos de Ferro das Colónias Portuguesas de 1888 a 1911*, p. 43.
20. *Ibid.*, p. 63.
21. Leroy Vail, 'The Making of an Imperial Slum: Nyasaland and its Railways, 1895–1935', pp. 89–104.
22. Situação Económica das Diversas Possessões Ultramarinas, *Relatório, Propostas de Lei e Documentos relativos as Possessoês Ultramarinas*, p. 34.
23. Penvenne, 'A History of African Labour. . . .', pp. 37, 51.
24. *Ibid.*, p. 41.
25. Rocha, Serra and Hedges, *História*. . . ., pp. 109–29; Neil-Tomlinson, 'The Nyassa Chartered Company, 1891–1929'; Pélissier, *Naissance du Mozambique*, pp. 277–301.
26. For a detailed explanation of the mechanics of the matrilineal society of the Makua see Christian Geffray, 'Travail et Symbole dans la Société des Makhuwa'; A.J. de Mello Machado, *Entre os Macuas de Angoche*, pp. 173–224; Rocha, Serra and Hedges (eds), *História*. . . ., p. 112.
27. Henry O'Neill, 'Some Remarks upon Nakala (Fernão Veloso Bay) and other

ports on the Northern Mozambique Coast', p. 374; Rocha, Serra and Hedges, *História*. . . ., p. 110.

28. J. Mouzinho de Albuquerque, *A Campanha contra os Namarrais*; R.C.F. Maugham, *Africa as I have known it*; Pélissier, *Naissance*. . . ., pp. 195-202.

29. Maugham, *Africa as I have known it*, pp. 240-3.

30. Rocha, Serra and Hedges (eds), *História*. . . ., p. 114; Pélissier, *Naissance*. . . ., pp. 220-38; Pedro Massano de Amorim, *Relatório sobre a Occupação de Angoche*.

31. Nancy J. Hafkin, 'Trade, Society and Politics in Northern Mozambique', p. 400.

32. Rocha, Serra and Hedges, *História*. . . ., pp. 114-5.

33. Barry Neil-Tomlinson, 'The Mozambique Chartered Company, 1892-1910', p. 45.

34. *Ibid.*, p. 65.

35. *Ibid.*, p. 212.

36. *Ibid.*, p. 216; M. Anne Pitcher, 'Sowing the Seeds of Failure: Early Portuguese Cotton Cultivation in Angola and Mozambique, 1820-1926', p. 55.

37. Vail, 'The Making of an Imperial Slum. . . .', p. 95.

38. *Ibid.*, p. 100.

39. Neil-Tomlinson, 'The Mozambique Chartered Company. . . .' pp. 128-32.

40. *Report on Economic and Commercial Conditions in Portuguese East Africa* (1938); Pitcher, 'Sowing the Seeds. . . .', p. 59.

41. Rocha, Serra and Hedges (eds), *História*. . . ., p. 202.

42. Leroy Vail, 'Mozambique's Chartered Companies: The Rule of the Feeble', p. 412.

43. The bridge was 3,677 metres long, and 17,000 tonnes of steel and 73,202 cubic metres of concrete were used in its construction. For the building of the Zambesi bridge see Leroy Vail, 'The Making of an Imperial Slum. . . .', F.W.A. Handman, *The Lower Zambezi Bridge*, and G.E. Howorth, *The Construction of the Lower Zambezi Bridge*; *Le Port de Beira et le Pont sur le Zambèze* (no author given).

44. Vail, 'Mozambique's Chartered Companies:. . . .', p. 407.

45. Neil-Tomlinson, 'The Nyassa Chartered Company,. . . .', p. 121.

46. *Ibid.*, p. 122.

47. The linkage between tax and labour is the theme of José Capela, *O Imposto de Palhota e a Introdução do Modo de Produção Capitalista nas Colónias*.

48. Neil-Tomlinson, 'The Nyassa Chartered Company,. . . .', p. 118.

49. Vail and White, *Capitalism and Colonialism*. . . ., p. 134.

50. M. Newitt, 'Labour Migration from the Tete District', p. 13, and sources quoted.

51. H. Crawford Angus, 'A Year in Azimba and Chipitaland: The Customs and Superstitions of the People', p. 317.

52. Neil-Tomlinson, 'The Mozambique Chartered Company. . . .', pp. 184-7.

53. These figures come from Ribeiro, *Anuário de Moçambique* (1917), p. 351; also Capela, *O Imposto*. . . ., p. 84.

54. *A Manual of Portuguese East Africa*, pp.150-1.

55. Penvenne, 'A History of African Labour. . . .', p. 108.

56. *Ibid.*, pp. 109-20.

57. *Ibid.*, p. 94.

58. *Ibid.*, p. 106.

59. *Boletim Official de Moçambique*, 'Relatório das Investigações a que procedeu o Secretario dos Negócios Indígenas, sobre Emigração dos Indígenas, nos Districtos de Quelimane e Tete, e sobre outros Assumptos mencionados na Portaria Provincial no. 268 de 13 de Maio de 1908', Relatório Annexo ao Boletim Official (1909); for the reply of the *prazo* concessionaires see *Protesto de Arrendatarios de Quelimane e Tete contra o Relatório do Secretario dos Negócios Indígenas*.

60. J.M. da Silva Cunha, *O Trabalho Indígena*, pp. 199-201.

61. Pitcher, 'Sowing the Seeds. . . .', p. 55; Vail and White, *Capitalism and Colonialism.* . . ., pp. 191–2, 211.
62. Vail and White, *Capitalism and Colonialism.* . . ., pp. 176, 181.
63. Capela, *O Imposto.* . . ., p. 92.
64. Maugham, *Africa as I have known it*, p. 232.
65. Newitt, 'Labour Migration. . . .'
66. R.B. Boeder, *The Silent Majority*, ch. 2.
67. *Ibid.*, pp. 25–6.
68. *Ibid.*, p. 31.
69. J. Willequet, 'Anglo-German Rivalry in Belgian and Portuguese Africa'; J. Vincent Smith, 'Britain, Portugal and the First World War, 1914–1916'; J. Vincent Smith, 'The Portuguese Republic and Britain, 1910–1914'; Katzenellenbogen, *South Africa.* . . ., pp. 120–5.
70. Pélissier, *Naissance.* . . ., p. 684.
71. Allen Isaacman and Barbara Isaacman, *The Tradition of Resistance in Mozambique*; T.O. Ranger, 'Revolt in Portuguese East Africa'.
72. Isaacman and Isaacman, *The Tradition of Resistance.* . . ., p. 162.
73. Pélissier, *Naissance.* . . ., p. 670; E.A. Azambuja Martins, *Operações Militares no Barué em 1917*, p. 14.
74. Rocha, Serra and Hedges, *História.* . . ., p. 184; Martins, *Operações Militares.* . . ., p. 17.
75. Father Moskopp, SJ, 'The PEA Rebellion of 1917: Diary of Rev. Father Moskopp, SJ', pp. 159–60.
76. Martins, *Operações Militares.* . . .; for a comment on Martins' pamphlet see Pélissier, *Naissance.* . . ., p. 653 n.
77. Isaacman and Isaacman, *The Tradition of Resistance.* . . ., p. 169.
78. Pélissier, *Naissance.* . . ., pp. 695–9.
79. *Ibid.*, pp. 700–4.
80. The most careful modern assessment of the war in Mozambique is undoubtedly that of Pélissier in *Naissance.* . . . See also Leonard Mosley, *Duel for Kilimanjaro*, chs 10 and 11.
81. Pélissier, *Naissance.* . . ., pp. 714–16.
82. G. Curry, 'Woodrow Wilson, Jan Smuts and the Versailles Settlement'.
83. Vail and White, *Capitalism and Colonialism.* . . ., p. 120; Pitcher, 'Sowing the Seeds. . . .', p. 55.
84. Vail and White, *Capitalism and Colonialism.* . . ., pp. 155, 160.
85. *Ibid.*, p. 106.
86. *Ibid.*, p. 127.
87. *Ibid.*, p. 149.
88. *Ibid.*, p. 152.
89. Clarence-Smith, *The Third Portuguese Empire.* . . ., p. 151.
90. Vail and White, *Capitalism and Colonialism.* . . ., pp. 190–2. The most important protagonists who went into print on the future of the *prazos* were A. de Portugal Durão, 'O Districto de Quelimane'; Pedro Alvares, 'O Regime dos Prazos'; and Ernesto de Vilhena, *Regime dos Prazos da Zambezia.*
91. *Ibid.*, p. 215.
92. *Ibid.*, p. 213.
93. Eduardo d'Almeida Saldanha, *O Sul do Save*, pp. 120–1.
94. Vail and White, *Capitalism and Colonialism.* . . ., pp. 236–7.
95. Clarence-Smith, *The Third Portuguese Empire.* . . ., p. 133.
96. Katzenellenbogen, *South Africa.* . . ., p. 127; Clarence-Smith, *The Third Portuguese Empire.* . . ., p. 118.
97. Clarence-Smith, *The Third Portuguese Empire.* . . ., pp. 97–8, 118.

98. Manuel de Brito Camacho, *Moçambique: Problemas Coloniais*.
99. *Ibid.*, pp. 79–87; Vail and White, *Capitalism and Colonialism*. . . ., pp. 215–16.
100. E.A. Ross, *Report on the Employment of Native Labour in Portuguese Africa*, is discussed in James Duffy, *Portuguese Africa*, pp. 166–8 and Vail and White, *Capitalism and Colonialism*. . . ., pp. 222–4.
101. *Ibid.*, and Eduardo d'Almeida Saldanha, *João Belo e o Sul do Save*, for a general appreciation.
102. Saldanha, *João Belo*. . . ., p. lxxxv.
103. Ribeiro, *Anuário de Moçambique* (1940), p. 283.
104. *Anuário Estatístico: Ano de 1930*, ch. 20.
105. Ribeiro, *Anuário de Moçambique* (1940), p. 190.
106. *Ibid.*, p. 201; Ribeiro, *Anuário de Moçambique* (1917), p. 512–13.
107. A.E.M. Anderson-Morsehead, *The History of the Universities Mission to Central Africa*, vol. 1, ch. 9.
108. C. Fuller, 'An Ethnohistoric Study of Continuity and Change in Gwambe', pp. 38–9; for the cultural impact of the Swiss see Patrick Harries, 'The Roots of Ethnicity: Discourse and the Politics of Language Construction in South-East Africa'.
109. *Anuário Estatístico: Ano de 1930*, ch. 15.
110. C. Fuller, 'An Ethnohistoric Study. . . .', p. 159.
111. *Ibid.*, p. 196.
112. Allen Isaacman and Barbara Isaacman, *Mozambique: from Colonialism to Revolution, 1900–1982*, p. 72.
113. W.P. Johnson, 'Seven Years' Travel in the Region East of Lake Nyasa', p. 513.
114. E.A. Alpers, 'Towards a History of the Expansion of Islam in East Africa: the Matrilineal Peoples of the Southern Interior', p. 188.
115. *Ibid.*, pp. 188–89.
116. S.I. Mudenge, *Christian Education at the Mutapa Court*.
117. Ribeiro, *Anuário de Moçambique* (1940), p. 291.
118. *Ibid.*, p. 291.
119. Manuel Dias Belchior, 'Evolução Política do Ensino em Moçambique'.
120. Penvenne, 'A History of African Labour in. . . .', pp. 209–50.
121. *Ibid.*, pp. 215, 240; Penvenne, 'Taxation, Registration, Unionization, Licensing and Conscription: African Accomodation of New State Labour Policies: Lourenço Marques, 1932–1962'; Aurélio Rocha, 'O Estado Colonial em Moçambique: a Política de Assimilação Portuguesa', 1930–1974', p. 2, n. 5.
122. Isaacman, *Mozambique: from Colonialism*. . . ., pp. 52, 73–4, 2–09 n. 52.
123. Thomas H. Henriksen, *Mozambique: a History*, p. 156.
124. Rocha, Serra and Hedges, *História*. . . ., p. 288.
125. *Ibid.*, p. 29–4.
126. Henriksen, *Mozambique: a History*, p. 158; Rocha, Serra and Hedges, *História*. . . ., pp. 288–9.

Chapter 17. Mozambique and the New State

1. Richard Robinson, *Contemporary Portugal*, pp. 41–4.
3. The classic of this genre is António Ferro, *Salazar: Portugal and her Leader*. But see a critique of the book in Ralph Fox, *Portugal Now*.
4. The text of the Mozambique Colonial Charter was published in *The Times* (London), 5 July 1935.
5. António de Figueiredo, *Portugal's Fifty Years of Dictatorship*.
6. For the corporative structure of the regime see Robinson, *Contemporary Portugal*,

ch. 2; also the essays in Lawrence S. Graham and Harry M. Makler, *Contemporary Portugal*.

7. For Salazar's economic strategy see Gervase Clarence-Smith, *The Third Portuguese Empire*. . . . , pp. 146-57; Robinson, *Contemporary Portugal*, pp. 128-36.

8. For the constitutional reforms see Robinson, *Contemporary Portugal*, pp. 96-101; James Duffy, *Portuguese Africa*, ch. 11.

9. Mozambique Colonial Charter, *The Times*, 5 July 1935.

10. The *Anuário Estatístico* for 1930, for example, runs to 436 pages and contains statistics on agriculture, health, education, finance, population, migration and the courts but also tables dealing with the weather, tourism, hunting licenses, prices and the number of reported fires. The central administration sent regular question-naires to the District governors covering matters of particular concern at that moment. The report of the District Governor of Zambezia in May 1947, for exam-ple, included reports on 'native policy', 'health', 'agriculture', 'schools', 'tax col-lection', 'labour', 'African crop growing', 'administrative authorities', and 'white settlement'. *Respostas ao Questionário por Sua Exa o Governador-Geral da Provincia da Zambézia*.

11. *Report of the Commercial, Economic and Financial Condition of Portuguese East Africa* (1927).

12. *Report on Economic and Commercial Conditions in Portuguese East Africa*, (1938), p. 1.

13. Vail and White, *Capitalism and Colonialism*. . . . , pp. 325-9. From the late 1930s the government inspector's reports on local administration show a readiness to recognise frankly the abuses that were being practised and recommended the dismissal of officials as well as paying lip-service to reform. A good example is 'Relatório e Documentos referentes a Inspeção Ordinária ao Districto de Tete', by Francisco de Melo Costa, 1938-1939, AHM Inspeção dos Serviços Adminis-trativos e dos Negócios Indígenas.

14. *Report on Economic and Commercial Conditions in Portuguese East Africa*, (1938) p. 14; Clarence-Smith, *The Third Portuguese Empire*. . . . , p. 147, 153-5.

15. Clarence-Smith, *The Third Portuguese Empire*. . . . , p. 147.

16. *Ibid.*, p. 158.

17. *Ibid.*, p. 150; Anne Pitcher, 'Sowing the Seeds of Failure: Early Portuguese Cotton Cultivation in Angola and Mozambique, 1820-1926', p. 61; Anne Pitcher, 'Is State Intervention worth the Price?', p. 10.

18. Vail and White, ' "*Tawani, Machambero!*"': Forced Cotton and Rice Growing on the Zambezi', p. 274; Pitcher, 'Is State Intervention . . .', pp. 11-12.

19. 'A Restruturação do colonialismo em Moçambique, 1938-1944', p. 46.

20. Vail and White, ' "*Tawani, Machambero!*". . . .' Pitcher, 'Is State Interven-tion. . . .', p. 17.

21. Pitcher, 'Sowing the Seeds. . . .'

22. Vail and White, ' "*Tawani, Machambero!*". . . .'

23. C.F. Spence, *Moçambique: East African Province of Portugal*, pp. 78-9.

24. *Ibid.*, p. 81; A.B. Herrick *et al.*, *Area Handbook for Mozambique*, p. 216; Pitcher, 'Is State Intervention. . . .', pp. 21-2.

25. Vail and White, ' "*Tawani, Machambero!*". . . .'

26. Vail and White, *Capitalism and Colonialism*. . . . , pp. 259-60.

27. *Ibid.*, p. 261.

28. Clarence-Smith, *The Third Portuguese Empire*. . . . , p. 148.

29. *Ibid.*, pp. 170-2.

30. *Ibid.*, p. 175.

31. *Ibid.*, p. 164.

32. Vail and White, *Capitalism and Colonialism*. . . . , p. 253.

33. *Ibid.*, p. 254.

34. *Ibid.*, p. 256-7.

35. *Ibid.*, pp. 265-72.

36. *Report on Economic and Commercial Conditions in Portuguese East Africa* (1938), pp. 57-8; Spence, *Moçambique:. . . .*, pp. 72-3; David Hedges and Aurélio Rocha, 'Moçambique face á Crise Económica Mundial e o Reforço do Colonialismo Português', p. 18.

37. 'A Restruturaçao do colonialismo. . . .', pp. 63-4; for an account of *muta-hano* see Michel Cahen, 'Mossuril (1939): La Révolte ambigue des "Naharras".

38. *Ibid.*, pp. 54-5; *Portuguese East Africa* (1948), appendix VII.

39. *Report on Economic and Commercial Conditions in Portuguese East Africa*, p. 8; *Portuguese East Africa* (1938), p. 3.

40. Spence, *Moçambique. . . .*, p. 100.

41. A.B. Herrick *et al.*, *Area Handbook for Mozambique*, p. 53.

42. *Ibid.*, pp. 197-8; D.M. Abshire and M.A. Samuels, *Portuguese Africa*, pp. 226-30.

43. Spence, *Moçambique. . . .*, p. 47.

44. *Ibid.*, p. 30.

45. Herrick *et al.*, *Area Handbook. . . .*, p. 19. In 1963 I travelled from Salisbury to Mozambique Island by road. It was necessary to cross the Zambesi by ferry at Tete and travel via Zomba in Malawi. On the return I travelled along the coast to António Ennes (Angoche). The roads were passable only by trucks, and the bridges were sometimes suicidally precarious. To cross the Zambesi to Sená, I had to pay £5 sterling for the hire of a steam locomotive and truck to take my Landrover across the Zambesi bridge.

46. Spence, *Moçambique. . . .*, p. 52; *Portuguese East Africa* (1948), p. 28.

47. Hugh Kay, *Salazar and Modern Portugal*, ch. 7.

48. *Portuguese East Africa* (1948), p. 45.

49. A decree of 1881 established a convict settlement in eastern Africa and in 1884 Fort São Sebastião on Moçambique Island was designated for that purpose. Between 1905 and 1916 365 convicts from all parts of the empire (116 of them murderers) served their sentences in Mozambique. Time-served convicts could remain in the colony. Ribeiro, *Anuário de Moçambique* (1917), pp. 546-9.

50. For white colonisation policies see José Maria Gaspar, 'A Colonização Branca em Angola e Moçambique'.

51. For example, J. Naylon, 'An Appraisement of Spanish Irrigation and Land Settlement Policies since 1939'.

52. *Economic Conditions in Portuguese East Africa* (1935), p. 22.

53. Spence, *Moçambique:. . . .*, p. 104.

54. *Ibid.*, pp. 101-8; Merle L. Bowen, 'Peasant Agriculture in Mozambique: the Case of Chokwe, Gaza Province', pp. 360-1.

55. Kenneth Hermele, *Land Struggles and Social Differentiation in Southern Mozambique*, p. 38.

56. David Hedges and Aurélio Rocha, 'Moçambique face á Crise Económica Mundial e o Reforço do Colonialismo Portuguese', p. 10.

57. *Economic Conditions in Portuguese East Africa* (1935), p. 17; *Report on Economic and Commercial Conditions in Portuguese East Africa* (1938), p. 25.

58. *Portuguese East Africa* (1948), pp. 20-1; Spence, *Moçambique:. . . .*, ch. 13.

59. *Ibid.*, p. 70.

60. *Ibid.*, pp. 61-71.

61. Before the revolution prostitution was a major industry in Lourenço Marques. It was common for visiting 'clients' to stay in the house of a prostitute who would cook, clean and generally provide accomodation during his stay.

62. J.M. da Silva Cunha, *O Trabalho Indígena*, pp. 210-46.

63. Vail and White, *Capitalism and Colonialism. . . .*, p. 289.

64. Vail and White, ' "*Tawani, Machambero!*":. . . .'.
65. 'A Restruturação do colonialismo. . . .', p. 49.
66. *Ibid.*, p. 52.
67. Eugénio Ferreira de Almeida, *Governo do Districto de Moçambique: Relatório*, vol. 1, p. 61.
68. *Ibid.*, vol. 1, p. 21.
69. *Ibid.*, p. 26.
70. Herrick, *Area Handbook*. . . ., pp. 144–7.
71. *Ibid.*, p. 154.
72. *Ibid.*, p. 117.
73. Ribeiro, *Anuário de Moçambique* (1940), p. 286.
74. Abshire and Samuels, *Portuguese Africa*, pp. 192–3.
75. Herrick, *Area Handbook*. . . ., p. 46.
76. Jeanne-Marie Penvenne, 'Taxation, Registration, Unionization, Licensing and Conscription: African Accomodation of New State Labor Policies: Lourenço Marques, 1932–1962', p. 4.
77. Rocha, Serra and Hedges, *História*. . . :, p. 289.
78. Hedges and Rocha, 'Moçambique face á Crise. . . .', p. 14.
79. Henriksen, *Mozambique*. . . ., p. 159.
80. Hedges and Rocha, 'Moçambique face á Crise. . . .', pp. 12–14.
81. Anne-Sophie Arnold, 'Missions, African Religious Movements and Identity in Mozambique, 1930–1974', pp. 17–19.
82. Quoted in Aurélio Rocha, 'O Estado colonial em Moçambique: A Política de Assimilação Português, 1930, 1974', p. 6.
83. Robinson, *Contemporary Portugal*, p. 115. The 1970 census counted 1,824,721 Catholics, 368,139 Protestants and 1,107,113 Muslims (*Anuário Estatístico*, 1973).
84. Barry Munslow (ed.), *Samora Machel: An African Revolutionary*, p. x; John Paul, *Mozambique: Memoirs of a Revolution*, p. 29.
85. Jeanne-Marie Penvenne, 'A History of African Labour in Lourenço Marques, Mozambique, 1877–1950', p. 214.
86. Allen Isaacman and Barbara Isaacman, *Mozambique: from Colonialism to Revolution, 1900–1982*, p. 51.
87. Munslow, *Samora Machel*. . . ., p. x.
88. Manuel Dias Belchior, 'Evolução Política do Ensino em Moçambique'.
89. Herrick, *Area Handbook*. . . ., p. 92.

Chapter 18. Labour Migration to South Africa and Southern Rhodesia

1. David Leslie, *Among the Zulus and Amatongas*, p. 268.
2. Roger Wagner, 'Zoutpansberg: the Dynamics of a Hunting Frontier, 1848–67', pp. 324–5.
3. Luís António Covane, 'Considerações sobre of Impacto da Penetração Capitalista no Sul do Moçambique, 1850–1876'.
4. David Webster, 'Migrant Labour, Social Formation and the Proletarianization of the Chopi of Southern Mozambique', pp. 161–2.
5. A. Rita-Ferreira, *O Movimento Migratório de Trabalhadores entre Moçambique e a Africa do Sul*, pp. 42–3; Jeanne-Marie Penvenne, 'A History of African Labour in Lourenço Marques, Mozambique, 1877–1950', pp. 9–16.
6. Rita-Ferreira *O Movimento*. . . ., p. 44.
7. For a wide-ranging discussion of the writing on migrant labour see Ruth First, *Black Gold: The Mozambican Miner, Proletarian and Peasant*, pp. 241–6.

8. AHM, J.A. de Sá e Simão to Portuguese vice-consul in Natal, 17 Dec. 1872, Caderno para Registo da Correspondência expedida para o Consul Português em Natal e Cabo, Codice 301 2-Fd 9, fol. 16.

9. AHM, Governor of Lourenço Marques to Walter Peace, Portuguese consul in Natal, 28 Oct. 1875, Caderno para Registo da Correspondência expedida para o Consul Português em Natal e Cabo, Codice 301 2-Fd 9, fol. 22.

10. AHM, J.A. Sá e Simão to Frederick Elton, British Consul in Mozambique, 23 Oct. 1871, Caderno para Registo da Correspondência expedida para o Consul Português em Natal e Cabo, Codice 301 2-Fd 9, fols 11-13.

11. AHM, 'Governor of Lourenço Marques to Portuguese Consul General at the Cape', 6 June 1878, Caderno para Registo da Correspondência expedida para o Consul Português em Natal e Cabo, Codice 301 2-Fd 9, fol. 29; *Boletim Official*, no. 32, 7 Aug. 1875, Portaria 152; Rita-Ferreira, *O Movimento Migratório*. . . ., p. 13; Luís António Covane, 'Considerações sobre of Impacto da Penetração Capitalista no Sul do Moçambido, 1850-1876'.

12. Axelson, *Portugal and the Scramble*. . . ., pp. 99-100.

13. *Ibid.*, p. 111.

14. R.J. Hammond, *Portugal and Africa 1815-1910*, pp. 224-44; Katzenellenbogen, *South Africa*. . . ., pp. 19-24.

15. *Estatística nos Caminhos de Ferro das Colónias Portuguesas de 1888 a 1911*, pp. 15-21.

16. Katzenellenbogen, *South Africa*. . . ., p. 28.

17. *Estatística nos Caminhos de Ferro*. . . ., p. 16.

18. Ernesto J. de C. e Vasconcellos, *Colónias Portuguezas*, p. 291.

19. Gerhard Liesegang, 'A First Look at the Import and Export Trade of Mozambique, 1800-1914', p. 473.

20. Penvenne, 'A History of African Labour. . . .', pp. 51-7.

21. On the alcohol question see Hammond, *Portugal and Africa*. . . ., pp. 304-23; Rita-Ferreira, *O Movimento*. . . ., p. 15; Vail and White, *Capitalism and Colonialism*. . . ., pp. 127; Charles van Onselen, 'Randlords and Rotgut'.

22. Rita-Ferreira, *O Movimento Migratório*. . . ., p. 15.

23. *Ibid.*, p. 63.

24. Katzenellenbogen, *South Africa*. . . ., p. 40; Rocha, Serra and Hedges (eds), *História de Moçambique*, pp. 236-7.

25. Penvenne, 'A History of African Labour. . . .', pp. 91-3; Rocha, Serra and Hedges (eds), *História de Moçambique*, p. 224.

26. Penvenne, 'A History of African Labour. . . .', p. 96.

27. Katzenellenbogen, *South Africa*. . . ., pp. 49-54.

28. *Ibid.*, pp. 58-60.

29. *Ibid.*, pp. 95-8.

30. Sheila van der Horst, *Native Labour in South Africa*, p. 221.

31. Katzenellenbogen, *South Africa*. . . ., pp. 120-3.

32. *Ibid.*, pp. 128-9; Vail and White, *Capitalism and Colonialism*. . . ., pp. 200-5.

33. The Umbeluzi scheme and its relation to the South African connection is discussed at length in Eduardo d'Almeida Saldanha, *O Sul do Save*, and more succinctly in Vail and White, *Capitalism and Colonialism*. . . ., pp. 234-7.

34. Katzenellenbogen, *South Africa*. . . ., ch. 9.

35. Ruth First, *Black Gold: The Mozambican Miner, Proletarian and Peasant*, p. 25.

36. *Ibid.*, p. 118.

37. *Ibid.*, p. 49; Jonathan Crush, Alan Jeeves and David Yudelman, *South Africa's Labor Empire*, pp. 221-2, n. 25.

38. Katzenellenbogen, *South Africa*. . . ., p. 155.

39. Crush, Jeeves and Yudelman, *South Africa's Labor Empire*, p. 71; van der Horst, *Native Labour*. . . ., pp. 220, 222.

40. Herrick *et al.*, *Area Handbook for Mozambique*, pp. 51–2.
41. First, *Black Gold.* . . . , p. 23.
42. Crush, Jeeves and Yudelman, *South Africa's Labor Empire*, pp. 109–10.
43. *Ibid.*, pp. 112–13.
44. J. Serrão de Azevedo, *Relatório do Curador Ano Económico de 1913–1914*, p. 162.
45. First, *Black Gold*, pp. 34–5; Katzenellenbogen, *South Africa.* . . . , pp. 107–8.
46. First, *Black Gold*, p. 56; Katzenellenbogen, *South Africa.* . . . , p. 106.
47. First, *Black Gold*, pp. 58–9.
48. van der Horst, *Native Labour in South Africa*, p. 229.
49. Sousa Ribeiro (ed.), *Anuário de Moçambique* (1940), p. 376.
50. *Ibid.*; Azevedo, *Relatório do Curador.* . . . , p. 21.
51. First, *Black Gold*, p. 70.
52. Penvenne, 'A History of African Labour. . . .', p. 109.
53. Kenneth Hermele, *Land Struggles and Social Differentiation in Southern Mozambique*, p. 37; First, *Black Gold*, pp. 111–35.
54. *Ibid.*, p. 127.
55. *Ibid.*, p. 118.
56. Van Onselen, *Chibaro*, pp. 110–14.
57. P.R. Warhurst, 'The Tete Agreement'.
58. Native Commissioners' Reports, Darwin, 30 Sept. 1914; ZNA S670.
59. Native Commissioner, Umtali to Chief Native Commissioner, 8 Feb. 1927; ZNA S/138 4 1923–8.
60. Van Onselen, *Chibaro*, p. 232.
61. Chief Native Commissioner to Governor, 7 Jan. 1916; ZNA S1542 T7.
62. Dr Francisco de Melo Costa, 'Relatório e documentos referentes a inspecção ordinária ao Districto de Tete, 1938–1939', section III, p. 104; AHM, Inspecção dos Serviços Administrativos e dos Negócios Indígenas.
63. Ian Phimister, *An Economic and Social History of Zimbabwe 1890–1948*, p. 85.
64. Governor of Nyasaland to Secretary of State for the Colonies, Zomba, 8 August 1921; NAM S1/1970/21.
65. A.C. Jennings, Southern Rhodesia Chief Road Engineer, reported in 1929 that gangs of 200 were working on the Southern Rhodesia to Tete road and a further 500 on the Tete to Fort Jameson road; ZNA S481/818.
66. Minute by J.C. Abraham, 24 Jan. 1927; NAM S1/2/5/7.
67. Secretary to the Treasury to Chief Native Commissioner, 'Short Precis on the Tete Agreement', Salisbury, 26 July 1924; ZNA S138 65.
68. N.H. Wilson Acting Native Commissioner to Native Commissioner, Darwin, 30 May 1923; ZNA S1542 T7 1915–1934.
69. Staff Officer BSA Police to Chief Native Commissioner Salisbury, Salisbury, 29 Jan. 1924; ZNA S1542 T7.
70. Treasurer to Premier, Salisbury, 3 April 1925; ZNA S138 65. The arrangement suggested was that the Portuguese would receive all the tax collected in Salisbury, and half that collected in the rest of the country.
71. Costa, 'Relatório e documentos. . . .', section III, p. 116; AHM, Inspecção dos Serviços Administrativos e dos Negócios Indígenas.
72. *Ibid.*, pp. 117–18.
73. Horténsio de Sousa, 'Contribuição para o Estudo da Emigração Clandestina no Districto de Tete: Ano de 1945', AHM, p. 30.
74. *Ibid.*, p. 31.
75. Julio Augusto Pires, 'Relatório da Inspecção Ordinária aos Postos Administrativos . . . do Districto de Tete, realizada em 1945'; AHM Fundo Governo Geral, Relatórios 191, p. 269.
76. *Ibid.*, p. 271.

Chapter 19. The War of Liberation

1. G.E. Monks, 'Operation Gordian Knot — a Survey of Portuguese Counter-Insurgency — Mozambique', p. 33; Thomas H. Henriksen, *Revolution and Counterrevolution: Mozambique's War of Independence, 1964–1974*, p. 111.
2. Richard Robinson, *Contemporary Portugal*, pp. 73–9.
3. Tom Gallagher, *Portugal: a Twentieth Century Interpretation*, pp. 150–3; Robinson, *Contemporary Portugal*, pp. 74–7.
4. Eduardo Mondlane, *The Struggle for Mozambique*, ch. 5.
5. Henriksen, *Revolution and Counterrevolution:* . . . , p. 19; Henriksen, *Mozambique.* . . . , pp. 163–8; Mondlane, *The Struggle.* . . . , ch. 5.
6. Anon., *Eduardo Mondlane*, p. 24.
7. *Central Committee Report to the Third Congress of Frelimo*, p. 4.
8. Henriksen, *Mozambique.* . . . , pp. 174–5.
9. For ideological debates within Frelimo see Barry Munslow, *Mozambique: The Revolution and its Origins*, chs 9 and 11; Isaacman and Isaacman, *Mozambique.* . . . , pp. 79–100.
10. Henriksen, *Mozambique.* . . . , pp. 187.
11. Monks, 'Operation Gordian Knot. . . . ,'
12. On COREMO see Henriksen, *Mozambique.* . . . , pp. 176–7.
13. *Ibid.*, p. 187.
14. For Malawi's relations with the Portuguese and Frelimo, see David Hedges, 'Notes on Malawi-Mozambique Relations'; Monks, 'Operation Gordian Knot. . . . ', pp. 64–5.
15. Henriksen, *Mozambique.* . . . , p. 208.
16. *Ibid.*, p. 185.
17. Henriksen, *Revolution and Counterrevolution:* . . . , p. 74.
18. *Central Committee Report to the Third Congress of Frelimo*, pp. 5–6.
19. Henriksen, *Mozambique.* . . . , p. 186; Munslow, *Mozambique.* . . . , p. 94.
20. Henriksen, *Revolution and Counterrevolution.* . . . , p. 155.
21. Munslow, *Mozambique.* . . . , p. 107.
22. Anon., *Eduardo Mondlane*, pp. 103–8; *Central Committee Report to the Third Congress of Frelimo*, pp. 9–10.
23. *Ibid.*, p. 11.
24. For Lázaro Nkavandame see Henriksen, *Mozambique.* . . . , pp. 179–81; Vail and White, *Capitalism and Colonialism.* . . . , pp. 394–8; and for a Frelimo view, Isaacman, *Mozambique.* . . . , pp. 96–9.
25. Munslow, *Mozambique.* . . . , pp. 110–12.
26. Vail and White, *Capitalism and Colonialism.* . . . , pp. 272–3.
27. Henriksen, *Revolution and Counterrevolution.* . . . , pp. 150–1.
28. For social expenditure during the war, see D.M. Abshire and M.A. Samuels, *Portuguese Africa: a Handbook*, ch. 9.
29. Henriksen, *Revolution and Counterrevolution.* . . . , pp. 178–81.
30. Keith Middlemas, *Cabora Bassa: Engineering and Politics in Southern Africa*.
31. Henriksen, *Revolution and Counterrevolution.* . . . , pp. 34–6; *Cabora Bassa and the Struggle for Southern Africa*.
32. Gallagher, *Portugal.* . . . , pp. 161, 165–6.
33. Monks, 'Operation Gordian Knot. . . . ,' pp. 82–5.
34. *Ibid.*,
35. *Ibid.*, p. 87.
36. *Ibid.*, ch. 4, pp. 50–2.
37. *Ibid.*, pp. 60–2.
38. *Ibid.*, pp. 37–8.

39. Clarence-Smith, *The Third Portuguese Empire.* . . ., pp. 192–7.
40. *Ibid.*, p. 195.
41. *Ibid.*, pp. 200, 208.
42. Robinson, *Contemporary Portugal*, p. 179.
43. Henriksen, *Revolution and Counterrevolution.* . . ., p. 167.
44. *Ibid.*, p. 218.
45. Robinson, *Contemporary Portugal*, p. 172.
46. Adrian Hastings subsequently turned his accusations into a book called *Wiriyamu*.
47. Clarence-Smith, *The Third Portuguese Empire.* . . ., pp. 195–6.
48. Jorge Carvalho Arroteia, *A Emigração Portuguesa — suas Origens e Distribuição*; Robinson, *Contemporary Portugal*, pp. 154–8.
49. Clarence-Smith, *The Third Portuguese Empire.* . . ., p. 199.
50. James H. Mittelman, *Underdevelopment and the Transition to Socialism*, p. 47.
51. Gallagher, *Portugal.* . . ., pp. 158, 172.
52. *Insight on Portugal*, p. 63.
53. *Ibid.*, p. 50.
54. Kenneth Maxwell, 'Portugal and Africa: The Last Empire'; for a Portuguese version of the last days of the war see Manuel Pereira Crespo, *Porque Perdemos a Guerra*.
55. *Ibid.*, 'A Derrota'; Robinson, *Contemporary Portugal*, p. 208.
56. *Ibid.*, p. 181.
57. *Ibid.*, pp. 208–10.
58. *Acôrdo de Lusaka e Lei Constitucional no. 8/74*; for a detailed study of the situation during the interim government, see A. Rita-Ferreira, *Moçambique post-25 de Abril: Causas do Exodo da População de Origem Europeia e Asiática*.

Chapter 20. Mozambique after Independence

1. Eduardo Mondlane, *The Struggle for Mozambique*.
2. Barry Munslow (ed.), *Samora Machel: An African Revolutionary*.
3. Patrick Chabal, *Amílcar Cabral*.
4. Barry Munslow, *Mozambique: The Revolution and its Origins*, ch. 4; Allen Isaacman and Barbara Isaacman, *Mozambique: From Colonialism to Revolution, 1900–1982*, pp. 121–2; *Central Committee Report to the Third Congress of Frelimo*.
5. Catherine Scott, 'Socialism and the "Soft State" in Africa: An Analysis of Angola and Mozambique', p. 30.
6. Sonia Kruks and Ben Wisner, 'The State, the Party, and the Female Peasantry in Mozambique', p. 110.
7. Michel Cahen, *Mozambique. La révolution Implosée*, p. 28.
8. Tom Young, 'The Politics of Development in Angola and Mozambique', p. 170.
9. Kruks and Wisner, 'The State, the Party. . . .,' p. 108.
10. Munslow, *Mozambique: The Revolution.* . . ., p. 153.
11. Isaacman and Isaacman, *Mozambique: From Colonialism.* . . ., p. 114.
12. Cahen, *Mozambique. La Révolution.* . . ., p. 76; Christian Geffray, *A Causa das Armas*, p. 18.
13. Young, 'The Politics of Development. . . .', p. 173.
14. Isaacman and Isaacman, *Mozambique: From Colonialism.* . . ., p. 125; Cahen, *Mozambique. La Revolution.* . . ., p. 74–5.
15. Marina Ottway, 'Mozambique: From Symbolic Socialism to Symbolic Reform', p. 211.
16. *Ibid.*, p. 215; Young, 'The Politics of Development. . . .', p. 168.
17. Munslow, *Samora Machel.* . . ., Introduction.
18. *Central Committee Report to the Third Congress of Frelimo*, p. 5.

19. Quoted in Stephanie Urdang, 'The Last Transition? Women and Development in Mozambique', p. 90.
20. Quoted in *ibid.*, p. 31.
21. Kruks and Wisner, 'The State, the Party. . . .', p. 119.
22. Isaacman and Isaacman, *Mozambique: From Colonialism*. . . ., p. 139.
23. *Ibid.*, p. 139; Kruks and Wisner, 'The State, the Party. . . .', p. 116.
24. Cahen, *Mozambique. La Revolution*. . . ., p. 52.
25. *Ibid.*, p. 53; Maureen Mackintosh and Marc Wuyts, 'Accumulation, Social Services and Socialist Transition in the Third World: Reflections on Decentralised Planning based on the Mozambican Experience', pp. 139–40; Geffray, *A Causa das Armas*, pp. 20–1.
26. Kruks and Wisner, 'The State, the Party. . . .', p. 117.
27. Isaacman and Isaacman, *Mozambique: from Colonialism*. . . ., p. 139; Mackintosh and Wuyts, 'Accumulation. . . .', pp. 150–1.
28. Richard Robinson, *Contemporary Portugal*, p. 210; A. Rita-Ferreira, *Moçambique post-25 de Abril: Causas do Exodo da População de Origem Europeia e Asiática*, pp. 145–8.
29. Marc Wuyts, 'Money, Planning and Rural Transformation in Mozambique', p. 185.
30. *Ibid.*, p. 185.
31. Isaacman and Isaacman, *Mozambique: from Colonialism*. . . ., p. 145; the Portuguese census of 1981 recorded 168,000 people who had been living in Mozambique ten years earlier and who were therefore *retornados*. In addition, thousands more had fled to South Africa and Brazil, Rita-Ferreira, *Moçambique post-25 de Abril*. . . ., pp. 122–3.
32. Cahen, *Mozambique. La Révolution*. . . ., p. 16.
33. Wuyts, 'Money, Planning. . . .', p. 186.
34. Philip Raikes, 'Food Policy and Production in Mozambique since Independence', pp. 94, 101.
35. Cahen, *Mozambique. La Révolution*. . . ., p. 28; Mackintosh and Wuyts, 'Accumulation, Social Services. . . .', pp. 140.
36. Wuyts, 'Money, Planning. . . .', p. 196.
37. Anna Wardman, 'The Co-operative Movement in Cokwe', p. 297; Kenneth Hermele, *Land Struggles and Social Differentiation in Southern Mozambique*, pp. 46–53.
38. Cahen, *Mozambique. La révolution*. . . ., p. 62; Mackintosh and Wuyts, 'Accumulation, Social Services. . . .', p. 144.
39. Wuyts, 'Money, Planning. . . .', p. 188.
40. *Ibid.*, p. 188.
41. *Ibid.*, p. 199; Joseph Hanlon, *Mozambique: The Revolution under Fire*, pp. 190–201.
42. Wuyts, 'Money, Planning. . . .', pp. 190, 195.
43. Raikes, 'Food Policy. . . .', pp. 102–5.
44. Wardman, 'The Co-operative Movement. . . .', pp. 295–304.
45. Cahen, *Mozambique. La révolution*. . . ., p. 59; Kruks and Wisner, 'The State, the Party. . . .', p. 111, says 37,000 people were involved in cooperatives.
46. Wardman, 'The Co-operative Movement. . . .', p. 301; Mackintosh and Wuyts, 'Accumulation, Social Services. . . .', p. 149.
47. Wuyts, 'Money, Planning. . . .', p. 194.
48. *Ibid,*, p. 182.
49. *Ibid.*, p. 201.
50. Norman Macqueen, 'Portugal and Africa: The Politics of Re-engagement', pp. 46–7.
51. Isaacman and Isaacman, *Mozambique: from Colonialism*. . . .', p. 187.
52. *Ibid.*, p. 180.
53. *Ibid.*, p. 181.

54. *Ibid.*, p. 172.

55. For SADCC and the policy of destabilisation see Robert M. Price, 'Pretoria's Southern African Strategy'; Douglas G. Anglin, 'SADCC after Nkomati'; Joseph Hanlon, *Beggar your Neighbour*.

56. For South Africa and the Comoro Islands see M. Newitt, 'The Perils of being a Microstate: São Tomé and the Comoros Islands since Independence', in Helen Hintjens and Malyn Newitt (eds), *The Political Economy of Small Tropical Islands*, pp. 76–92.

57. Alex Vines, *Renamo: Terrorism in Mozambique*, ch. 2.

58. Steven Metz, 'The Mozambique National Resistance and South African Foreign Policy'; Vines, *Renamo:. . . .*, pp. 17–31.

59. *Ibid.*, pp. 32–52.

60. *Ibid.*, pp. 42–50; Norman Macqueen, 'Portugal and Africa:. . . .'; Cahen, *Mozambique. La Révolution. . . .*, pp. 35–9; Hermele, *Land Struggles. . . .*, pp. 31–4.

61. Merle L. Bowen, 'Peasant Agriculture in Mozambique: The Case of Chokwe, Gaza Province'.

62. Cahen, *Mozambique. La Révolution. . . .*, p. 59.

63. *Ibid.*, p. 36.

64. For the Nkomati Accord see *Africa Contemporary Record*, 1983–4, pp. A84–85, B670–73.

65. On international backing for Machel see *Africa Contemporary Record*, 1984–5, pp. B676–97.

66. Cahen, *Mozambique. La Révolution. . . .*, pp. 46–7.

67. Vines, *Renamo:. . . .*, pp. 24–31; Metz, 'The Mozambique National Resistance. . . .'.

68. *Samora: Why he Died.*

69. Vines, *Renamo:. . . .*, ch. 4.

70. David Beresford, 'Renamo behind Natal violence', *Guardian*, 30 Oct. 1992.

71. Steve Askin, 'Mission to Renamo: The Militarization of the Religious Right'; see also review by Margaret Hall of Vines, *Renamo:. . . .*, *African Affairs*, 1992.

72. Vines, *Renamo:. . . .*, ch. 4.

73. Geffray, *A Causa das Armas*, pp. 24, 34.

74. Cahen, *Mozambique. La Révolution. . . .*, esp. pp. 50–9; G. Derluguian, 'Les têtes du monstre. Du climat social de la violence armée au Mozambique', pp. 105–7.

75. Quoted in Tom Young, 'The MNR/Renamo External and Internal Dynamics', p. 507.

76. Paul Vauvet, 'Mozambique's radical changes slowed by war and inertia', *Guardian*, 12 Dec. 1990; Andrew Meldrum, 'Mozambicans put faith in ceasefire', *Guardian*, 15 Feb. 1991.

77. Vines, *Renamo:. . . .*, ch. 4, pp. 118–9; Ruth A. Ayisi, 'Back to the Stone Age'.

78. Mackintosh and Wuyts, 'Accumulation, Social Services. . . .', pp. 157–9; review by Margaret Hall of Vines, *Renamo:. . . .*, *African Affairs*, 91(1992), pp. 285–7.

79. 'Foreign Extra: Mozambique's Famine', *Guardian*, 8 June 1991; Julie Flint, 'Race to rescue disaster-struck Mozambique', *Observer*, 4 Oct. 1992; Tom Carver, 'Starvation kills appetite for war', *New Statesman and Society*, 2 Oct. 1992.

80. Geffray, *A Causa das Armas*, p. 40.

81. Derluguian, 'Les têtes du monstre. . . .', p. 106.

82. Geffray, *A Causa das Armas*, p. 26.

BIBLIOGRAPHY

This bibliography consists only of works referred to in the notes at the end of each chapter.

MANUSCRIPT SOURCES

Ajuda Library, Lisbon

'Notícias que se me pedirão no anno de 1677 de Lxa dos Rios de Cuama e da forma que devia ter pa poder concervasse entrando na companhia que se determina fazer pa este Estado', in *Orbe Lusitano*, 50. v. 37, fol. 482.

Brief resumé of an account given by Custódio de Almeida e Souza on the situation of the Rivers of Senna and Sofalla, 51. viii. 40, fols 271-2 (transl. H. de Noronha).

'Breve Informação dos Rios de Cuama, que o Pe Frey Philipe de Asumpção por andar nas ditas Terras quatorze annos, e estado em todas as feiras e ter larga noticia dos vios e costumes dellas', 51. ix. 3.

Arquivo Histórico do Estado da India, Goa

Monções do Reino
'Alvará go gor. Manoel de Sousa Coutinho pa. q̃ os Casados e mores. de mossabiq̃ possão hir commerciar na ilha de São Lourenço e toda a costa de moss. (excepto a do contrato) na de milinde de Cabo delguado e todas corrẽtes the o da boa esperança e mandarẽ a elles suas embarçãois sem lhes ser prohibido por pessoa algũa como se te assentado na relação com pareceres dos desembargadores della', 20 July 1663, nos 29 and 30, fols 128-128v.

'Copea do assento feito em vertude de hũa Carta do sor. Governador Antonio de mello de Castro na fortza. nos apozentos do Capitão e Govor. Dom Mel. maz., e mais deputados adjuntos, cujo theor he o seguinte', nos 29 and 30, fol. 130.

Arquivo Histórico de Moçambique, Maputo

'Relatório e Documentos referentes a Inspecção Ordinária ao Districto de Tete', by Francisco de Melo Costa, 1938-1939, Inspecção dos Serviços Administrativos e dos Negocios Indígenas.

Horténsio de Sousa, 'Contribuição para o Estudo da Emigração Clandestina no Districto de Tete: Ano de 1945'.

615

Julio Augusto Pires, 'Relatório da Inspecção Ordinária aos Postos Administrativos . . . do Districto de Tete, realizada em 1945', Fundo Governo Geral, Relatórios 191.

Caderno para Registo da Correspondencia expedida para o Consul Português em Natal e Cabo, Codice 301 2-Fd 9
J.A. Sá e Simão to Frederick Elton, British Consul in Mozambique, 23 Oct. 1871, fols 11–13.
J.A. de Sá e Simão to Portuguese vice-consul in Natal, 17 Dec. 1872, fol. 16.
Governor of Lourenço Marques to Walter Peace, Portuguese consul in Natal, 28 Oct. 1875, fol. 22.
Governor of Lourenço Marques to Portuguese Consul General at the Cape, 6 June 1878, fol. 29.

Manica Codice 2-1389 Ga8
J.J. Fereira to Secretaria Geral, 28 Dec. 1890, no. 35.

Tete Codice 2-446 FE2 no. 35
Tavares de Almeida to Secretaria Geral', Tete, 1 Feb. 1861.

Tete Codice 1122 2-Ga3
A. de F. de Mesquita e Solla to Secretaria Geral', 26 Dec. 1892, no. 129; 28 Dec. 1892, no. 130; 29 Dec. 1892, no. 131; 13 Jan. 1893, no. 4.

Arquivo Histórico Ultramarino, Lisbon

Moç Cx 3 Concelho Ultramarino to Prince, Lisbon, 6 Aug. 1677.
Moç Cx 3 'Memorial do que tenho obrado nestes Rios no Serviço de S. Magestade que Deus Guarde', 7 Dec. 1751.
Moç Cx 5 David Marques Pereira to viceroy, 30 May 1755.
Moç Cx 6 Pedro Rego Barretto to the king, 10 Nov. 1745.
Moç Cx 6 Pedro da Saldanha de Albuquerque to the King, Mozambique, 27 Dec. 1758.
Moç Cx 6 M. Correa Monteiro de Mattos to governor general, Inhambane, 11 June 1761.
Moç Cx 17 'Descrição Corográfica do Reino de Manica seus Costumes e Leis' (transl. H. de Noronha).
Moç Cx 20 'Artigos do Tratado de Reconcilhação entre of Emperador de Moanamotapa e o Estado dos dominios de S. mage . . .', Zimbaoe, June 1783.
Moç Cx 23, 'Relação de dez amostras de ouro de outras tantas minas de Rios de Senna' by Mattheus Ignacio de Almeida, Mozambique, 3 Dec. 1786.
Moç Cx 224, A.M. da Cunha to P.J.M. de Brito, Quelimane, 24 Sept. 1829.
Moç Cx 225, M.J.M. Vasconcellos e Cirne to Conde de Basto, Quelimane, 6 Dec. 1829.

*These numbers may have been changed since 1973 when the files were consulted.

Moç Cx 249, J.X.D. Costa to P.J.M de Brito, Mozambique, 5 Feb. 1831.
Moç Cx 249, M. da Silva Gonçalves to P.J.M. de Brito, Fernão Veloso, 3 Aug. 1831.
Moç Cx 251 P.J.M. de Brito to Duque de Cadaval, Mozambique, 8 Nov. 1831.

Bodleian Library, Oxford

'The ship Little Josiah, Capt Dering, at St Lawrence', MS. Rawl. A 336.

National Archives of Malawi, Zomba

Governor of Nyasaland to Secretary of State for the Colonies, Zomba, 8 Aug. 1921; S1/1970/21.
Minute by J.C. Abraham, 24 Jan. 1927; S1/2/5/7.

Torre de Tombo, Lisbon

Livros dos Monçoës
João de Sousa Freire to king, Sena, 12 June 1673, no. 38A.
Letter of Dom Andres Vides y Albarado Administrator and Assayer of the Gold and Silver Mines, Sena, 22 July 1633, no. 41, fols 13–14 (transl. H. de Noronha).
Declaration made by Father Frey Gaspar de Macedo, Sena, 21 July 1633, no. 41 (transl. of H. de Noronha).
Caetano de Mello e Castro to viceroy, Sena, 26 June 1684, no. 49.
Miguel de Almeida to governor of Moçambique, Sena, 23 June 1687, no. 52, fols 403–403v (transl. H. de Noronha).
King to viceroy, Lisbon, 12 Dec. 1646, no. 57, fol. 65.
Declaration of 'Dom Sebastião por graça de Deus Emperador deste Imperio do quiteve . . .', 23 Oct. 1644, no. 60, fols 231–2.

Zimbabwe National Archives, Harare

Native Commissioners' Reports, Darwin, 30 Sept. 1914; S670.
Chief Native Commissioner to Governor, 7 Jan. 1916; S1542 T7.
N.H. Wilson Acting Native Commissioner to Native Commissioner, Darwin, 30 May 1923; S1542 T7 1915–34
Staff Officer BSA Police to Chief Native Commissioner Salisbury, Salisbury 29 Jan. 1924; S1542 T7.
Secretary to the Treasury to Chief Native Commissioner, 'Short Precis on the Tete Agreement', Salisbury, 26 July 1924; S138 65.
Treasurer to Premier, Salisbury, 3 Apr. 1925; S138 65.
Native Commissioner, Umtali to Chief Native Commissioner, 8 Feb. 1927; S/138 4 1923–28.
Report by A.C. Jennings, Southern Rhodesia Chief Road Engineer, S481/818.

Repostas ao Questionário formulado por Sua Exa o Governador-Geral ao Governador da Província da Zambézia, May 1947 (in possession of M. Newitt).

UNPUBLISHED THESES

Dhliwayo, K.D., 'External Traders in the Hinterland of Sofala, 1810–1889', M.Phil., London, 1977.

Dubins, Barbara. D., 'A Political History of the Comoro Islands 1795–1886', Ph.D., Boston, 1972.

Fuller, C., 'An Ethnohistoric Study of Continuity and Change in Gwambe', Ph.D., Northwestern, 1955.

Geffray, Christian, 'Travail et Symbole dans la Société des Makhuwa', Ph.D., Ecole des Hautes Etudes en Sciences Sociales, Paris, 1987.

Hafkin, Nancy J., 'Trade, Society and Politics in Northern Mozambique', Ph.D., Boston, 1973.

Hedges, David. W., 'Trade and Politics in Southern Mozambique and Zululand in the Eighteenth and early Nineteenth Centuries', Ph.D., London, 1978.

Langworthy, H., 'A History of Undi's Kingdom to 1890: Aspects of Chewa History in East Central Africa', Ph.D., Boston, 1969.

Livneh, Avital, 'Precolonial Polities in Southern Zambesia and their Political Communications', Ph.D., London, 1976.

Monks, G.E., 'Operation Gordian Knot — a Survey of Portuguese Counter-Insurgency-Mozambique', M.A., York, 1990.

Mudenge, S.I., 'The Rozvi Empire and the Feira of Zumbo', Ph.D., London, 1972.

Neil-Tomlinson, Barry, 'The Mozambique Chartered Company 1892–1910', Ph.D., London, 1987.

Penvenne, Jeanne Marie, 'A History of African Labour in Lourenço Marques: Mozambique 1877–1950', Ph.D., Boston, 1982.

Phiri, K., 'Chewa History in Central Malawi and the Use of Oral Tradition', Ph.D., Wisconsin, 1975.

Pirio, G. 'Commerce, industry and empire: the making of modern Portuguese Colonialism in Angola and Mozambique, 1890–1914', Ph.D., California, 1982.

Schoffeleers, J. M., 'M'Bona, the Guardian Spirit of the Manganja', B.Litt., Oxford, 1966.

——, 'Symbolic and Social Aspects of Spirit Worship among the Mang'anga', Ph.D., Oxford, 1968.

Smith, A., 'The Struggle for Control of Southern Moçambique, 1720–1835', Ph.D., California, 1970.

UNPUBLISHED PAPERS

Beach, D.N., 'The Origins of Moçambique and Zimbabwe: Paiva de Andrada, the *Companhia de Moçambique* and African Diplomacy 1881–91', Dept. of History, Univ. of Zimbabwe.

Papers read at the II Colóquio Internacional em Ciencias Sociais sobre a Africa de Língua Official Portuguesa, Bissau, 1991:

Arnold, Anne-Sophie, 'Missions, African Religious Movements and Identity in Mozambique, 1930-1974'.

Cahen, Michel, 'Mossuril (1939): La Révolte Ambigue des "Naharras"'.

Newitt, M., 'Labour Migration from the Tete District'.

Penvenne, Jeanne-Marie, 'Taxation, Registration, Unionization, Licensing and Conscription: African Accommodation of New State Labour Policies: Lourenço Marques, 1932-1962'.

Pitcher, Anne, 'Is State Intervention worth the Price? Mozambique's Cotton Regime under Salazar'.

Rocha, Aurélio, 'O Estado Colónial em Moçambique. A Política de Assimilação Portuguesa, 1930-1974'.

NEWSPAPERS '

Guardian (London)

Paul Vauvet, 'Mozambique's radical changes slowed by war and inertia', 12 Dec. 1990.

Andrew Meldrum, 'Mozambicans put faith in ceasefire', 15 Feb. 1991.

'Foreign Extra: Mozambique's Famine', 8 June 1991.

David Beresford, 'Renamo behind Natal violence', 30 Oct. 1992.

New Statesman and Society (London)

Tom Carver, 'Starvation kills appetite for war', 2 Oct. 1992.

Observer (London)

Julie Flint, 'Race to rescue disaster-struck Mozambique', 4 Oct. 1992.

The Times (London)

Mozambique Colonial Charter, 5 July 1935.

PRINTED DOCUMENTS

Arquivo Histórico de Moçambique. Inventário do Fundo do Século XVIII, Introdução, Sumários e Transcrições, Caetano Montes (ed.), Lourenço Marques, 1958, separate from *Moçambique*, nos 72-92.

Inacio de Melo e Alvim to governor general, Sena, 16 July 1769, p. 104.

Inacio de Mello Alvim to governor general, Tete, 23 Jan. 1770, p. 113.

Record of a meeting with the ambassadors of Macombe, 3 Oct. 1768, p. 168.

Carta de Aforamento for Mabunga, issued by João Moreira Pereira, Tete, 25 Oct. 1772, p. 88.

Arquivo Português Oriental, A.B. de Bragança Pereira (ed.), 11 vols (Bastora, 1936-40).

'Livro das Plantas de Todas as Fortalezas, Cidades e Povoações do Estado da India' by António Bocarro, vol. 4, part 1.

Boletim Official do Governo de Moçambique:

Portaria 152, no. 32, 7 Aug. 1875.
'Relatório das Investigações a que procedeu o Secretario dos Negócios Indígenas, sobre Emigração dos Indígenas, nos Districtos de Quelimane e Tete, e sobre outros Assumptos mencionados na Portaria Provincial no 268 de 13 de Maio de 1908', Relatório Annexo ao Boletim Official (1909).

Collections des Ouvrages Anciens concernant Madagascar, A. and G. Grandidier (eds), 9 vols (Paris, 1903-20):

'Pedro da Costa's Voyage to Madagascar with Luis Marianno and Pedro Freire', vol. 2, pp. 1-79.

Documents on the Portuguese in Mozambique and Central Africa, A. da Silva Rego, T.W. Baxter and E.E. Burke (eds), 8 vols, Centro de Estudos Históricos Ultramarinos and National Archives of Rhodesia [and Nyasaland] (Lisbon, 1962-75):

Vol. 1
'Summary by António Carneiro, secretary of State, of letters from António da Saldanha, captain of Sofala and Mozambique, to the king, 1511', pp. 11-19.
'Instructions to the Captain-major D. Francisco de Almeida', Lisbon, 5 March 1505, pp.156-261.
'Letter from Diogo de Alcaçova to the King', Cochin, 20 Nov. 1506, pp. 388-401.
'Summary of a Letter from Pero Ferreira Fogaça, Captain of Kilwa, to the King', Kilwa, 31 Aug. 1506, pp. 616-21.
'Letter from Pero Ferreira Fogaça, captain of Kilwa to the King', Kilwa, 22 Dec. 1506, pp. 754-61.

Vol. 3
'Summary by António Carneiro of letters from Afonso de Albuquerque to the King', 1511, pp. 4-9.
'Summary by António Carneiro, secretary of state, of letters from António de Saldanha, captain of Sofala and Mozambique, to the King', 1511, pp. 10-19.
'Notes made by Gaspar Veloso, clerk to the factory of Mozambique, and sent to the King', 1512, pp. 181-9.
'Letter from João Vaz de Almada, captain of Sofala, to the King', Sofala, 26 June 1516, pp. 274-95.
'Letter from Pero Vaz Soares, factor of Sofala, to the King', Sofala, 30 June 1513, pp. 458-69.
'Chapters relating to East Africa in the Account of Martin Fernandez de Figueroa', pp. 586-632.

Vol. 4
'Receipt and Expenditure Book kept by Cristovão Salema, Factor of Sofala', 1516, pp. 296-501.

Vol. 5
'An Order from João Vaz de Almada, provost of the Fortress of Sofala, to the Factor, Cristovão Salema', Sofala, 15 Jan. 1517, pp. 10–17.
'Description of the Situation, Customs and Produce of some Places of Africa', *c.* 1518, pp. 355–71.

Vol. 6
'Letter from D. Pedro de Castro to the king', Mozambique, 8 July 1523, pp. 173–9.
'Regulations for Sofala', Lisbon, 20 May 1530, pp. 304–424.

Vol. 7
'Letter from [João Velho], former Factor of Sofala to the king', post 1547, pp. 168–83.
'Letter from [João Velho], former Factor of Sofala, to the king', Goa, 4 Nov. 1548, pp. 184–9.
'Letter from Simão Botelho, Vedor da Fazenda of India, to the King', Cochin, 30 Jan. 1592, pp. 262–97.

Fontes para a História, Geografia e Comércio de Moçambique (sec xviii) ed. Luiz Fernando Carvalho Dias, *Anais*, vol, ix, tom. 1, Junta de Investigações do Ultramar, Lisbon, 1954.
De Mello e Castro, Dionízio, 'Notícia do Império Marave e dos Rios de Sena', pp. 119–50.
Galvão da Silva, Manuel, 'Diário das Viagens, feitas pelas terras de Manica', pp. 323–32.
'Mapas das Terras da Gorungosa e da Chiringome, e seus costumes', pp. 333–57.

O Chronista de Tissuary, J.H. da Cunha Rivara (ed.), 4 vols, Nova Goa, 1866–9:

Vol. 2
António da Conceição, 'Tratado dos Rios de Cuama'.
'Edital da Inquisição de Goa', vol. 2, pp. 273–5.

Portuguese Voyages 1498–1663, C.D. Ley (ed.), London: J.M. Dent, 1947, repr. 1960.
'Account of the very notorious loss of the great galleon, the São João', pp. 239–59.

Providencias publicados pelo Commissário Regio na Província de Moçambique desde 1 de Janeiro até 18 de Dezembro de 1895, Lisbon: Imprensa Nacional, 1896.
'Remodelando a organisaçaão administrativa das terras da districto de Lourenço Marques', 7 Dec. pp. 211–18.

Records of South Eastern Africa, G.M. Theal (ed.), 9 vols, Cape Town, 1898–1903, repr. C. Struik, Cape Town, 1964:

Vol. 1
'Extracts from the Account of the Wreck of the Ship Santiago', p. 342.
Frei Luís Cacegas, 'Extractos da História de S. Domingos', pp. 355–406.

Vol. 2

António Bocarro and Pedro Barreto de Resende, 'Do Estado da India', pp. 378–426.
'Advices from Goa', p. 429.

Vol. 3

'Account of the Journey made by the Fathers of the Company of Jesus with Francisco Barreto in the Conquest of Monomotapa in the Year 1569' by Father Monclaro SJ, pp. 157–253.
António Bocarro, 'Livro do Estado da India'.
Manoel Barretto, 'Informação do Estado e Conquista dos Rios de Cuama', Goa, 11 Dec. 1667, pp. 436–508.

Vol. 4

'Expenditure in the Fortresses of Sofala, Mozambique, and Sena', pp. 2–9.
'Record of the Orders carried with them by the Captains of the Fortresses of Mozambique and Sofala', pp. 11–28.
'King to viceroy', Madrid, 22 Jan. 1607, p. 59.
'King to viceroy', Lisbon, 21 March 1608, pp. 69–74.
'King to viceroy', Lisbon, 26 March 1612, p. 83–9.
'King to viceroy', Lisbon, 28 March 1613, p. 108.
'King to viceroy', Lisbon, 1 Nov. 1613, pp. 113–6.
'King to viceroy', Lisbon, 18 March 1614, p. 125.
'Alvará', Lisbon, 20 March 1614, p. 126.
'Alvará', Lisbon, 20 March 1614, p. 128.
'Report made by the governor-general Diogo da Cunha Castelbranco', Goa, 7 Feb. 1619, pp. 155–62.
'King to viceroy', Lisbon, 12 Feb. 1622, pp. 175–6.
'King to viceroy', Lisbon, 15 April 1626, pp. 195–6.
'King to viceroy', Lisbon, 24 Feb. 1635, pp. 253–62.
'Regent to viceroy; enclosing a summary of a letter of Diogo de Sousa de Meneses', Lisbon, 28 March 1636, pp. 273–81.
'Prince to viceroy', Lisbon, 3 April 1675, pp. 375–7.
'Prince to viceroy', Lisbon, 24 March 1681, p. 404.
'Mozambique in 1688', pp. 436–45.
'King to viceroy', Lisbon, 20 March 1690, pp. 449–52.

Vol. 5

'King to viceroy', Lisbon, 15 March 1702, p. 7.
'King to viceroy', Lisbon, 18 Feb. 1709, p. 15.
'King to viceroy', Lisbon, 11 Sept. 1710, pp. 26–7.
'King to viceroy', Lisbon, 7 April 1727, pp. 153–5.
'Rodrigo da Costa, viceroy, to King', Goa, 24 Jan. 1687, pp. 295–7, enclosing 'Miguel de Almeida, captain of Mozambique to the viceroy' and 'Copy of the decision of the council of Mozambique concerning the trading ship for Cape Correntes', Mozambique, 6 Aug. 1686.
'A Relation of three Years Sufferings of Robert Everard upon the Island of Assada near Madagascar, in a Voyage to India, in the Year 1686', pp. 407–8.

Vol. 7
Ferão, Sr., 'Account of the Portuguese Possessions within the Captaincy of the Rios de Senna', pp. 371–86.

Regimen dos Prazos da Coroa, Ministério da Marinha e Ultramar (Lisbon, 1897).
'Decreto de 6 de Novembro de 1838', p. 12.
'Decreto de 22 de Dezembro de 1854', pp. 12–16.
'Decreto de 27 de Outubro de 1880', pp. 19–24.
'Decreto de 18 de Novembro de 1890', pp. 85–94.

Relações de Moçambique Setecentista, A.A. de Andrade (ed.), Lisbon: Agência Geral do Ultramar, 1955.
Xavier, Inacio Caetano, 'Notícias dos Domínios Portugueses da Costa de Africa Oriental, 1758', pp. 139–89.
Anon., 'Memórias da Costa d'Africa Oriental e algumas reflexoēs uteis para estabelecer melhor, e fazer mais florente o seu commércio, 1762', pp. 189–224.
Pinto de Miranda, António, 'Memória sobre a Costa de Africa', pp. 231–312.
'Instrucção que o Illmo e Exmo Sr Governador e Capitão General Baltazar Manuel Pereira do Lago deo a quem lhe suceder neste Governo', pp. 317–38.
Montaury, João Baptista de, 'Moçambique, Ilhas Querimbas, Rios de Sena, Villa de Tete, Villa de Zumbo, Manica, Villa de Luabo, Inhambane', pp. 339–74.
Anon., 'Descripção da Capitania de Monsambique, suas povoaçoēs, 1788', pp. 375–406.

Relatório, Propostas de Lei e Documentos relativos as Possessoēs Ultramarinas, A. Eduardo Villaça, 2 vols, Lisbon: Imprensa Nacional, 1899.
Portaria sobre o Trabalho dos Indigenas, pp. 5–6.
Relatório e Projecto da Commissão presidida pelo conselheiro António Ennes, pp. 7–50.
Situação Económica das Diversas Possessoēs Ultramarinas, pp. 13–75.

Rerum Aethiopicarum Scriptores, C. Beccari (ed.), Rome, 1912, vol. xii 'P. Aloysius Mariana ad Praepositum provinciae goanae', pp. 112–4.

Segundo Congresso da Associação Histórica Internacional do Oceano Indico (Lisbon, 1963) and published as *Océan Indien e Mediterrané*, Paris: SEVPEN, 1964.
Bartolomeu dos Martires, 'Memória Chorografica da Provincia ou Capitania de Mossambique na Costa d'Africa Oriental conforme o Estado em que se achava no ano de 1822', edited by Virginia Rau in 'Aspectos etnico-culturais da ilha de Moçambique em 1822', pp. 123–65.

Studia
'Inquérito em Moçambique no anno de 1573', Alcantara Guerreiro (ed.), no. 6 (1960), pp. 7–19.
'Livro das Cidades e Fortalezas que a Coroa de Portugal tem nas Partes da India e das Capitanias e mais Cargos que nelas ha e da Importancia delles', F.P. Mendes da Luz (ed.), with facsimile of the text, vol. 6 (1960), pp. 351–63.

The Tragic History of the Sea, C.R. Boxer (ed.), Cambridge: Hakluyt Society, 1959:
'Narrative of the Shipwreck of the Great Ship São Thomé in the Land of Fumos, in the year 1589', pp. 52–104.
'Shipwreck of the Great Ship Santo Alberto, and Itinerary of the People, who were saved from it, 1593', pp. 107–86.
'Treatise of the Misfortune that befell the Great Ship São João Baptista, 1622', pp. 189–271.

PUBLISHED WORKS

Abraham, D.P., 'The Monomotapa Dynasty', *NADA*, 36 (1959), pp. 59–84.
——, 'The Early Political History of the Kingdom of Mwene Mutapa, 850–1589', *Historians in Tropical Africa*, proceedings of the Leverhulme Intercollegiate History Conference held . . . September 1960 (cyclostyled), Salisbury, 1962, pp. 61–91.
——, 'Maramuca: An Exercise in the combined use of Portuguese Records and Oral Tradition', *J. of African History*, 2 (1961), pp. 213–25.
Abshire, D.M., and M.A. Samuels, *Portuguese Africa*, London: Pall Mall, 1969.
Acôrdo de Lusaka e Lei Constitucional No 8/74, pamphlet distributed by Centro de Informação e Turismo, Lourenço Marques, 1974.
Africa Contemporary Record, New York: Africana Publishing Co., 1983–4 and 1984–5.
Albuquerque, J. Mouzinho de, *A Campanha contra os Namarrais*, Lisbon: Imprensa Nacional, 1897.
——, *Moçambique*, Lisbon, 1899.
Almeida, Eugénio Ferreira de, *Governo do Districto de Moçambique: Relatório*, 2 vols, Lisbon: Agência Geral do Ultramar, 1957.
Almeida de Eça, Filipe Gastão de, *História das Guerras no Zambeze: Chicoa e Massangano 1807–1888*, 2 vols, Lisbon: Agência Geral do Ultramar, 1953–4.
Alpers, E.A., 'Trade, State and Society among the Yao in the Nineteenth Century', *J. of African History*, 10 (1969), pp. 405–20.
——, 'The French Slave Trade in East Africa 1721–1819', *Cahiers d'Etudes Africaines*, 37 (1970), pp. 80–124.
——, 'Towards a History of the Expansion of Islam in East Africa: the Matrilineal Peoples of the Southern Interior', in T.O. Ranger and I.N. Kimambo (eds), *The Historical Study of African Religion*, London: Heinemann, 1972, pp. 172–201.
——, *Ivory and Slaves in East Central Africa*, London: Heinemann, 1975.
——, 'Gujerat and the Trade of East Africa, *c.* 1500–1800', *Int. J. of African Historical Studies*, 9 (1976), pp. 22–44.
Alvares, Pedro, 'O Regime dos Prazos', *Boletim da Sociedade de Geografia de Lisboa*, April–June (1916), pp. 137–213.
Amorim, Pedro Massano de, *Relatório sobre a Occupação de Angoche*, Lourenço Marques: Imprensa Nacional, 1911.

Anderson-Morsehead, A.E.M., *The History of the Universities Mission to Central Africa*, 3 vols, rev. edn, London: UMCA, 1955.

Anglin, Douglas, 'SADCC after Nkomati', *African Affairs*, 84 (1985), pp. 163–81.

Angus, H. Crawford, 'A Year in Azimba and Chipitaland: the Customs and Superstitions of the People', *J. of the Royal Anthropological Institute* (1898), pp. 316–25.

Anon., *Eduardo Mondlane*, London: Panaf, 1972.

Anstey, R.T., *Britain and the Congo in the Nineteenth Century*, Oxford University Press, 1962.

Anuário Estatístico: Ano de 1930, Lourenço Marques: Repartição Estatística da Colónia, 1931.

Askin, Steve, 'Mission to Renamo: the Militarization of the Religious Right', *Issue*, 18 (1990), pp. 29–38.

Arroteia, Jorge Carvalho, *A Emigração Portuguesa — suas Origens e Distribuição*, Lisbon: Biblioteca Breve, 1983.

Axelson, Eric, *Portuguese in South-East Africa 1600–1700*, Johannesburg: Witwatersrand University Press, 1960.

——, *Portugal and the Scramble for Africa*, Johannesburg: Witwatersrand University Press, 1967.

——, *Portuguese in South-East Africa 1488–1600*, Cape Town: C. Struik, 1973.

Ayisi, Ruth. A., 'Back to the Stone Age', *Africa Report*, 36 (1991), pp. 37–9.

Ballard, Charles, 'Drought and Economic Distress: South Africa in the 1800s', *J. of Interdisciplinary History*, 17 (1986), pp. 339–78.

Barker, G., 'Economic Models for the Manekweni Zimbabwe, Mozambique', *Azania*, 13 (1978), pp. 71–100.

Barnard, Lt. F.L., *A Three Years Cruize in the Mozambique Channel*, London: Richard Bentley, 1848.

Beach, David, *The Shona and Zimbabwe, 900–1850*, London: Heinemann, 1980.

——, *War and Politics in Zimbabwe 1840–1900*, Gweru: Mambo Press, 1986.

Belchior, Manuel Dias, 'Evolução Política do Ensino em Moçambique', *Moçambique: Curso de Extensão Universitária Ano Lectivo de 1964–1965*, Lisbon: Instituto Superior de Ciências Sociais e Política Ultramarina, 1965, pp. 635–74.

Bhila, H.H.K., *Trade and Politics in a Shona Kingdom*, Harlow: Longman, 1982.

Birch, Walter de Gray (ed.), *Commentaries of the Great Afonso Dalboquerque*, 4 vols, London: Hakluyt Society, 1875–84.

Bocarro, António, *Década 13 da História da India*, Lisbon, 1876.

——, 'Livro do Estado da India', extracts published in G.M. Theal (ed.), *Records of South Eastern Africa*, vol. 3.

Boeder, R.B., *Silent Majority: a History of the Lomwe in Malawi*, Pretoria: Africa Institute of South Africa, 1984.

Boteler, Capt. Thomas, *Narrative of a Voyage of Discovery to Africa and Arabia*, 2 vols, London, 1835.

Boulinier, Georges, B.A. Damir and P. Ottino, *Traditions d'une Ligné Royale des Comores*, Paris: L'Harmattan, 1985.

Bowen, Merle L., 'Peasant Agriculture in Mozambique: the Case of Chokwe, Gaza Province', *Canadian J. of African Studies*, 23 (1989), pp. 355-79.

Boxer, C.R. (ed.), *Sisnando Dias Bayão: Conquistador da "Mãe de Ouro"*, I Congresso da História da Expansão Portuguesa no Mundo, 4 Secção, Lisbon, 1958.

—— (ed.), *The Tragic History of the Sea*, vol. 1, Cambridge: Hakluyt Society, 1959.

——, 'Moçambique Island as a Way-station for Portuguese East-Indiamen', *The Mariner's Mirror*, 48 (1962), pp. 3-18.

——, 'The Querimba Islands in 1744', *Studia*, 11 (1963), pp. 343-54.

Cabora Bassa and the Struggle for Southern Africa, London: World Council of Churches, 1971.

Cabral, António, *Dicionário de Nomes Geográficos de Moçambique*, Lourenço Marques: Empresa Moderna, 1975.

Cahen, Michel, *Mozambique: La Revolution Implosée*, Paris: L'Harmattan, 1987.

Camacho, Manuel de Brito, *Moçambique: Problemas Colóniais*, Lisbon: Guimarães, 1926.

Capela, José, *Escravatura*, Edições Afrontamento, Oporto, 1975.

——, *O Imposto de Palhota e a Introdução do Modo de Produção Capitalista nas Colónias*, Oporto: Edições Afrontamento, 1977.

Cardim, António Francisco, *Relacam da Viagem do Galeam Sam Lourenco e sua Perdiçam nos Baixos de Moxincale em 3 de Septembro de 1649*, Lisbon, 1651.

Carreira, António, *O Tráfico Português de Escravos na Costa Oriental Africana nos Começos do Século XIX*, Lisbon: Junta de Investigações Científicas do Ultramar, 1979.

Castilho, Augusto de, *Relatório da Guerra da Zambézia em 1888*, Lisbon: Imprensa Nacional, 1891.

Central Committee Report to the Third Congress of Frelimo, London: Mozambique, Angola and Guiné Information Centre, 1978.

Chabal, Patrick, *Amílcar Cabral*, Cambridge University Press, 1983.

Chilundo, Arlindo, 'Quando começou o Comércio das Oleaginosas em Moçambique? Levantamento estatística da produção e exportação no periodo entre 1850 e 1875', *1 Reunião Internacional de História de Africa; Relação Europa-Africa no 3o Quartel do Século XIX*, Lisbon: Instituto de Investigação Científica Tropical, 1989, pp. 511-23.

Chumovsky, T.A., *Três Roteiros Desconhecidos de Ahmed Ibn-Majid*, trans. M. Malkiel-Jirmounsky, Lisbon: Comissão Executiva das Comemorações do V Centenário da Morte do Infante D. Henrique, 1960.

Clarence-Smith, Gervase, *The Third Portuguese Empire, 1825-1975*, Manchester University Press, 1985.

Clark, J. Desmond, 'The Portuguese Settlement at Feira', *Northern Rhodesia Journal*, 6 (1963), pp. 275-92.

Coissoó, Narana, 'O regime das Terras em Moçambique', *Moçambique: Curso de Extensão Universitária ano lectivo de 1964-5*, Lisbon: Instituto Superior de Ciências Sociais e Política Ultramarina, 1965, pp. 367-436.

Costa, Ramiro da, *O Desenvolvimento do Capitalismo em Portugal*, Lisbon: Cadernos Peninsulares, 1975.

Courtois, Victor, SJ, 'Terras de Macanga', *Boletim da Sociedade de Geografia de Lisboa*, 8 (1885), pp. 502–20.

Coutinho, João de Azevedo, *As Duas Conquistas de Angoche*, Pelo Império no. 11 (Lisbon, 1935).

——, *Manuel António de Sousa, um Capitão-mor da Zambezia*, Lisbon: Pelo Império no. 20, 1936.

——, *Memórias de um Velho Marinheiro e Soldado de Africa*, Lisbon: Livraria Bertrand, 1941.

Couto, Diogo do, 'Da Asia', G.M. Theal (ed.), *Records of South Eastern Africa*, vol. 6, pp. 307–411.

Covane, Luís António, 'Considerações sobre of Impacto da Penetração Capitalista no Sul do Moçambique, 1850–1876', *1 Reunião Internacional de História de Africa*; *Relação Europa-Africa no 3o Quartel do Século XIX*, Lisbon: Instituto de Investigação Científica Tropical, 1989, pp. 525–33.

Crespo, Manuel Pereira, *Porque Perdemos a Guerra*, Lisbon: Abril, 1977.

Crush, Jonathan, Alan Jeeves and David Yudelman, *South Africa's Labor Empire*, Boulder, CO: Westview Press, 1991.

Curry, G.W., 'Woodrow Wilson, Jan Smuts and the Versailles Settlement', *American Historical Review*, 66 (1961), pp. 968–86.

Dames, M.L. (ed.), *The Book of Duarte Barbosa*, 2 vols, London: Hakluyt Society, 1918.

Derluguian, G., 'Les têtes du monstre. Du climat social de la violence armée au Mozambique', *Année Africaine* (1989), pp. 89–127.

Devereux, W. Cope, *A Cruise in the Gorgon*, London, 1869, repr. Dawsons of Pall Mall, London, 1968.

Dickinson, R.W., 'The Archaeology of the Sofala Coast', *South African Archaeological Bulletin*, 30 (1975), pp. 84–104.

Duffy, James, *Portuguese Africa*, Cambridge, MA: Harvard University Press, 1961.

Durand, Emile, *Une Exploration Française au Zambèze*, Paris: Challamel, 1888.

Economic Conditions in Portuguese East Africa, by S.E. Kay for the Department of Overseas Trade, London: HMSO, 1935.

Eldridge, Elizabeth, 'Sources of Conflict in Southern Africa, *ca.* 1800–30: the "Mfecane" Reconsidered', *J. of African History*, 33 (1992), pp. 1–36.

Ennes, António, *Moçambique*, Lisbon, 1893, repr. Sociedade de Geografia de Lisboa, Lisbon, 1913.

Erskine, St Vincent, 'Journey to Umzila's, South-East Africa, in 1871–1872', *J. of Roy. Geogr. Soc.* 45 (1875).

——, 'Third and Fourth Journeys in Gaza, or Southern Mozambique', *J. of Roy. Geogr. Soc.*, 48 (1878), pp. 25–56.

Estatística nos Caminhos de Ferro das Colónias Portuguesas de 1888 a 1911, Lisbon: Ministério das Colónias, 1913.

Etherington, Norman, 'Labour Supply and the Genesis of the South African Confederation in the 1870s', *J. of African History*, 20 (1979), pp. 235–53.

Fairbridge, Kingsley, *The Autobiography of Kingsley Fairbridge*, London: Oxford University Press, 1927.

Faulkner, Henry, *Elephant Haunts*, London: Hurst and Blackett, 1868, repr. Blantyre, Society of Malawi, 1984.

Ferro, António, *Salazar: Portugal and her Leader*, London: Faber and Faber, 1935.

Figueiredo, António de, *Portugal: Fifty Years of Dictatorship*, Harmondsworth: Penguin: 1975.

First, Ruth, *Black Gold: The Mozambican Miner, Proletarian and Peasant*, Brighton: Harvester Press, 1983.

Foskett, Reginald (ed.), *The Zambesi Journal and Letters of Dr John Kirk*, 2 vols, London: Oliver and Boyd, 1965.

Foster, Sir William (ed.), *The Voyages of Sir James Lancaster to Brazil and the East Indies 1591–1603*, London: Hakluyt Society, 1940.

Freeman-Grenville, G.S.P., *The East African Coast*, Oxford University Press, 1962.

Fox, Ralph, *Portugal Now*, London: Lawrence and Wishart, 1937.

Gallagher, Tom, *Portugal: A Twentieth Century Interpretation*, Manchester University Press, 1983.

Gamitto, A.C.P., 'Escravatura na Africa Oriental', *Archivo Pitoresco*, 2 (1858-9), pp. 369–73, 397–9.

—— *King Kazembe*, trans. Ian Cunnison, 2 vols, Lisbon: Junta de Investigações do Ultramar, 1960.

Garlake, P.S., 'Excavations at the seventeenth-century Portuguese site of Dambarare, Rhodesia', *Proceedings and Transactions of the Rhodesia Scientific Association*, 54 (1969), pp. 23–60.

——, *Great Zimbabwe*, London: Thames and Hudson, 1973.

——, 'An Investigation of Manekweni, Mozambique', *Azania*, 11 (1976), pp. 25–47.

Gaspar, José Maria, 'A Colonização Branca em Angola e Moçambique', *Colóquios de Política Ultramarina Internacionalmente Relevante*, Lisbon: Junta de Investigações do Ultramar, 1958.

Geffray, Christian, *A Causa das Armas*, Oporto: Edições Afrontamento, 1991.

Gomes, António, 'Viagem que fez o Padre António Gomes, da Companhia de Jesus ao Imperio de Manomotapa; e assistencia que fez nas ditas terras de algus annos', *Studia*, 3 (1959), pp. 155–242.

Graham, Lawrence S. and Harry M. Makler, *Contemporary Portugal*, Austin: University of Texas Press, 1979.

Gray, A. (ed.), *The Voyage of François Pyrard de Laval*, 2 vols, London: Hakluyt Society, 1887-90.

Guy, Jeff, 'Ecological Factors in the Rise of Shaka and the Zulu Kingdom', in S. Marks and A. Atmore (eds), *Economy and Society in Pre-Industrial South Africa*, Harlow: Longman, 1980, pp. 102–19.

Hall, Margaret, Review of Alex Vines, *Renamo: Terrorism in Mozambique*, in *African Affairs*, 91 (1992), pp. 285–7.

Hammond, R.J., *Portugal and Africa 1815–1910*, Stanford University Press, 1966.

Handman, F.W.A., *The Lower Zambezi Bridge*, London: Institution of Civil Engineers, 1936.

Hanlon, Joseph, *Mozambique: the Revolution under Fire*, London: Zed Books, 1984.

——, *Beggar your Neighbours*, London: James Currey, 1986.

Harries, Patrick, 'Slavery, Social Incorporation and Surplus Extraction; the Nature of Free and Unfree Labour in South-East Africa', *J. of African History*, 22 (1981), pp. 309–30.

——, 'The Roots of Ethnicity: Discourse and the Politics of Language construction in South-East Africa', *African Affairs*, 87 (1988), pp. 25–52.

Hastings, Adrian, *Wiriyamu*, London: Search Press, 1974.

Hedges, David, 'Notes on Malawi-Mozambique Relations', *J. of Southern African Studies*, 15 (1989), pp. 617–44.

Hedges, David and Aurélio Rocha, 'Moçambique face á Crise Económica Mundial e o Reforço do Colonialismo Português, 1930–1937', *Cadernos da História* (Maputo), 4 (1986), pp. 5–20.

Henriksen, Thomas H., *Mozambique: A History*, London: Rex Collings, 1978.

——, *Revolution and Counterrevolution: Mozambique's War of Independence 1964–1974*, Westport, CN: Greenwood, 1983.

Hermele, Kenneth, *Land Struggles and Social Differentiation in Southern Mozambique: a Case Study of Chokwe, Limpopo 1950–1987*, Research Report No. 82, Uppsala, Scandanavian Institute of African Studies, 1988.

Herrick, A.B. *et al.*, *Area Handbook for Mozambique*, DA Pam no 550–64, Washington, DC, 1969.

Hilton, Anne, *The Kingdom of Kongo*, Oxford: Clarendon Press, 1985.

Hintjens, Helen and Malyn Newitt (eds), *The Political Economy of Small Tropical Islands*, Exeter University Press, 1992.

Hodder-Williams, Richard, *White Farmers in Rhodesia, 1890–1965*, London: Macmillan, 1983.

Honwana, Raúl, *The Life History of Raúl Honwana*, ed. Allen Isaacman, Boulder, CO: Lynne Rienner, 1988.

Hoppe, Fritz, *Portugiesisch-Ostafrika in der Zeit des Marquês de Pombal 1750–1777*, Berlin: Colloquium Verlag, 1965.

Howorth, G.E., *The Construction of the Lower Zambezi Bridge*, London: Institution of Civil Engineers, 1936.

A Ilha de Moçambique em Perigo de Desaparecimento, Oporto: Fundação Calouste Gulbenkian, 1983.

Insight on Portugal, by the Insight Team of the *Sunday Times*, London: André Deutsch, 1975.

Isaacman, Allen, *Mozambique: the Africanisation of a European Institution, the Zambesi Prazos, 1750–1902*, Madison: University of Wisconsin Press, 1972.

——, 'Madzi-Manga, Mhondoro and the use of oral traditions — a chapter in Barue religious and political history', *J. of African History*, 14 (1973), pp. 395–409.

—— and Barbara Isaacman, *The Tradition of Resistance in Mozambique*, London: Heinemann, 1976.

——, *Mozambique: From Colonialism to Revolution, 1900–1982*, Boulder, CO: Westview Press, 1983.

Johnson, W.P., 'Seven Years' Travel in the Region East of Lake Nyasa', *Proceedings of the Royal Geographical Society*, 6 (1884), pp. 512–36.

——, *My African Reminiscences, 1875–1895*, London: UMCA, 1924.

Katzenellenbogen, Simon, *South Africa and Southern Mozambique*, Manchester University Press, 1982.

Kay, Hugh, *Salazar and Modern Portugal*, London: Eyre and Spottiswood, 1970.

Kent, Raymond, *Early Kingdoms in Madagascar*, New York: Holt, Rinehart and Winston, 1970.

Kruks, Sonia, and Ben Wisner, 'The State, the Party, and the Female Peasantry in Mozambique', *J. of Southern African Studies*, 11 (1984), pp. 105–27.

Lacerda e Almeida, Francisco José, *Travessia de Africa*, M. Murias ed., Lisbon: Agência Geral das Colónias, 1936.

Lapa, Albino, *Vítor Cordon*, 2 vols, Lisbon: Pelo Império nos 50 and 51, 1939.

Lavradio, Marquês do, *Portugal em Africa depois de 1851*, Lisbon: Agência Geral das Colónias, 1936.

Leite, Bertha, *D. Gonçalo da Silveira*, Lisbon, 1946.

Leslie, David, *Among the Zulus and Amatongas*, W.H. Drummond ed., Edinburgh: Edmonston & Douglas, 1875, repr. Negro Universities Press, New York, 1969.

Liesegang, Gerhard (ed.), *'Reposta das Questoens sobre os Cafres ou Notícias Etnográficas sobre Sofala do Fim do Século XVIII*, Lisbon: Junta de Investgações do Ultramar, 1966.

——, 'Dingane's Attack on Lourenço Marques', *J. of African History*, 10 (1969), pp. 565–79.

——, 'Nguni Migrations between Delagoa Bay and the Zambesi, 1821–1839', *African Historical Studies*, 3 (1970), pp. 317–37.

——, 'Archaeological Sites on the Bay of Sofala', *Azania*, 7 (1972), pp. 147–59.

——, 'A First Look at the Import and Export Trade of Mozambique 1800–1914', in *Proceedings of the Symposium on the Quantification and Structure of the Import and Export and Long Distance Trade of Africa in the 19th Century (c. 1800–1913)*, St Augustin, 1983, pp. 452–523.

——, 'Notes on the Internal Structure of the Gaza Kingdom of Southern Mozambique 1840–1895', in J.B. Peires (ed.), *Before and After Shaka*, Grahamstown: Institute of Social and Economic Research, 1983.

Lobato, Alexandre, *História da Fundação de Lourenço Marques*, Lisbon: Edições da Revista 'Lusitana', 1948.

——, *A Expansão Portuguêsa em Moçambique de 1498 a 1530*, 3 vols, Lisbon: Centro de Estudos Históricos Ultramarinos, 1954.

——, *Evolução Administrativa e Económica de Moçambique, 1752–1763*, Lisbon: Agência Geral do Ultramar, 1957.

——, *Colonização da Zambézia*, Lisbon: Junta de Investigações do Ultramar, 1962.

Lobo de Bulhoẽs, M.E., *Les Colonies Portugaises: Court Exposé de leur Situation Actuelle*, Lisbon: Imprensa Nacional, 1878.

Lopes de Lima, José Joaquim and Francisco Maria Bordalo, *Ensaio sobre a Estatística das Possessões Portuguezas no Ultramar*, II serie, book 4: *Provincia de Moçambique*, Lisbon, 1859.

Le Port de Beira et le Pont sur le Zambèze, Portugal 1937 Exposition de Paris, Lisbon: Neogravura, 1936.

Lupi, Eduardo do Couto, *Angoche*, Lisbon, 1907.

Mackintosh, Maureen, and Marc Wuyts, 'Accumulation, Social Services and Socialist Transition in the Third World: Reflections on Decentralised Planning based on the Mozambican Experience', *J. of Development Studies*, 24 (1988), pp. 136–79.

Macqueen, Norman, 'Portugal and Africa: the Politics of Re-engagement', *African Affairs*, 23 (1985), pp. 31–51.

A Manual of Portuguese East Africa, Admiralty Naval Intelligence Division, London: HMSO, 1920.

Martins, E.A. Azambuja, *Operações Militares no Barué em 1917*, Revista Militar, Lisbon, 1937.

Matthews, T.I., 'Portuguese, Chikunda and the Peoples of the Gwembe Valley: the impact of the "Lower Zambezi Complex" on Southern Zambia', *J. of African History*, 22 (1981), pp. 23–41.

Maugham, R.C.F., *Zambezia*, London: John Murray, 1910.

——, *Africa as I have known It*, London: John Murray, 1929.

Maxwell, Kenneth, 'Portugal and Africa: the Last Empire', in K. Maxwell (ed.), *Transfer of Power in Africa*, New Haven, CN: Yale University Press, 1983.

McLeod, Lyons, *Travels in Eastern Africa*, 2 vols, London: Hurst and Blackett, 1860.

Mello Machado, A.J. de, *Entre os Macuas de Angoche*, Lisbon: Prelo, 1968.

Mesquita e Solla, A. de F. de, 'Apontamentos sobre o Zumbo', *Boletim da Sociedade de Geografia de Lisboa* (1907), pp. 247–57, 274–87, 319–27, 340–56, 382–91, 436–56.

Metz, Steven, 'The Mozambique National Resistance and South African Foreign Policy', *African Affairs*, 85 (1986), pp. 491–507.

Middlemas, Keith, *Cabora Bassa: Engineering and Politics in Southern Africa*, London: Weidenfeld and Nicolson, 1975.

Miranda, A.P., *Notícia acerca do Bonga da Zambézia*, Lisbon: Typographia Lisbonense, 1869.

Mittelman, James H., *Underdevelopment and the Transition to Socialism*, New York: Academic Press, 1981.

Mondlane, Eduardo, *The Struggle for Mozambique*, Harmondsworth: Penguin, 1969.

Monteiro, José Manuel Correa, 'A Feira do Aruangoa do Norte', *Annaes do Concelho Ultramarino*, parte não official (1859–61), pp. 203–8.

Montez, Caetano, *Descobrimento e Fundação de Lourenço Marques*, Lourenço Marques, 1948.

——, 'Sena. Forte de S. Marçal', *Monumenta*, 5 (1969), pp. 41–8.

——, 'Apontamentos para o Roteiro dos Monumentos Militares Portugueses: Praça de S. Tiago Maior; Forte de S. Tiago Maior', *Monumenta*, 6 (1970), pp. 67–73.

Moura, João Villas-Boas Carneiro de, *Os Ultimos Anos da Monarquia e os Primeiros da República em Moçambique*, Lourenço Marques: Imprensa Nacional, 1965.

Moskopp, Father, SJ, 'The PEA Rebellion of 1917: Diary of Rev. Father Moskopp, SJ', *Northern Rhodesia J.*, 4 (1961), pp. 154–60.

Mudenge, S.I., *Christian Education at the Mutapa Court*, Harare: Zimbabwe Publishing House, 1986.

——, *A Political History of Munhumutapa*, Harare: Zimbabwe Publishing Co., 1986.

Munslow, Barry, *Mozambique: the Revolution and its Origins*, Harlow: Longman, 1983.

—— (ed.), *Samora Machel: an African Revolutionary*, London: Zed Books, 1985.

Naylon, J., 'An Appraisement of Spanish Irrigation and Land Settlement Policies since 1939', *Iberian Studies*, 2 (1973), pp. 12–17.

Neil-Tomlinson, Barry, 'The Nyassa Chartered Company: 1891–1929', *J. of African History*, 18 (1977), pp. 109–28.

Neves, Diocleciano Fernandes das, *Itinerário de uma Viagem a Caça dos Elephantes*, Lisbon: Typographia Universal, 1878.

Newitt, M. (ed.), 'Account of a Journey made overland from Quelimane to Angoche in 1752' by F.R. Moraes Pereira, Local Series 4, Salisbury: Central African Historical Association, 1965.

—— and P.S. Garlake, 'The "Aringa" at Massangano', *J. of African History*, 8 (1967), pp. 133–56.

——, 'The Massingire Rising of 1884', *J. of African History*, 9 (1970), pp. 87–105.

——, 'The Early history of the Sultanate of Angoche', *J. of African History*, 13 (1972), pp. 397–406.

——, 'Angoche, the Slave Trade and the Portuguese, *c.* 1844–1910', *J. of African History*, 4 (1972), pp. 659–72.

——, *Portuguese Settlement on the Zambesi*, Harlow: Longman, 1973.

——, 'The Southern Swahili Coast in the First Century of European Expansion', *Azania*, 13 (1978), pp. 111–26.

——, 'Plunder and the Rewards of Office in the Portuguese Empire', in M. Duffy (ed.), *The Military Revolution and the State, 1500–1800*, University of Exeter Press, 1980, pp. 10–28.

——, 'The Early History of the Maravi', *J. of African History*, 23 (1982), pp. 145–62.

——, 'The Comoro Islands in Indian Ocean Trade before the 19th Century', *Cahiers d'Etudes Africaines*, 23 (1983), pp. 139–65.

——, 'The East India Company in the Western Indian Ocean in the Early Seventeenth Century', *J. of Imperial and Commonwealth History*, 14 (1986), pp. 5–33.

——, 'Drought in Mozambique 1823–1831', *J. of Southern African Studies*, 15 (1988), pp. 15–35.

——, 'Mixed Race Groups in the Early History of Portuguese Expansion', in T. Earle and Stephen Parkinson (eds), *Studies in the Portuguese Discoveries I*, Warminster: Aris and Phillips, 1992, pp. 35–52.

Nichols, C.S., *The Swahili Coast* London: Geor. Allen and Unwin, 1971.

Nogueira da Costa, António, *O Caso do Muenemutapa*, Maputo: Cadernos Tempo, 1982.

Nogueira de Andrade, Jeronimo José, 'Descrição em que ficaram de Negocios da Capitania de Moçambique em fins de 1789 e considerações sobre a decadencia do seu Commércio', *Archivo da Colónias* (Lisbon, 1917–18).

Nowell, Charles E., *The Rose-Coloured Map*, Lisbon: Junta de Investigações Científicas do Ultramar, 1982.

Nurse, G.T., 'The people of Bororo: A lexicostatistical enquiry', in B. Pachai (ed.), *The Early History of Malawi*, Harlow: Longman, 1972.

O'Neill, Henry, 'Some Remarks upon Nakala (Fernão Veloso Bay) and other ports on the Northern Mozambique Coast', *Proceedings of the Royal Geographical Society*, 7 (1885), pp. 373-7.

Ornellas, Ayres d', *Collectanea das suas Obras Militares e Colóniais*, 3 vols, Lisbon, 1934-6.

Ottway, Marina, 'Mozambique: from Symbolic Socialism to Symbolic Reform', *J. of Modern African Studies*, 26 (1988), pp. 211-26.

Owen, Capt. W.F.W., *Narrative of Voyages to Explore the Shores of Africa, Arabia and Madagascar*, 2 vols, London, 1833.

Pacheco, Albino Manuel, 'Uma Viagem de Tete a Zumbo', *Boletim do Governo de Moçambique*, (1883), nos 17-19, 21-24, 28-3.

Paiva de Andrada, Joaquim Carlos, 'Campanhas de Zambesia, 1887', *Boletim da Sociedade de Geografia de Lisboa*, 11 (1887), pp. 713-38.

Paul, John, *Mozambique: Memoirs of a Revolution*, Harmondsworth: Penguin, 1975.

Pearson, M.N., *The New Cambridge History of India: the Portuguese in India*, Cambridge University Press, 1987.

Pélissier, René, *Naissance du Mozambique*, 2 vols, Orgeval: Pélissier, 1984.

Phimister, Ian, 'Alluvial Gold-mining and Trade in Nineteenth Century South Central Africa', *J. of African History*, 15 (1974), pp. 445-56.

——, *An Economic and Social History of Zimbabwe 1890-1948*, London: Longman, 1988.

Pitcher, M. Anne, 'Sowing the Seeds of Failure: Early Portuguese Cotton Cultivation in Angola and Mozambique, 1820-1926', *J. of Southern African Studies*, 17 (1991), pp. 43-70.

Portugal Durão, A. de, 'O Districto de Quelimane', *Boletim da Sociedade de Geografia de Lisboa*, 5-6 (1914), pp. 139-89.

Portuguese East Africa by C.W. Andrews for the Board of Trade, London: HMSO, 1948.

Prior, James, *Voyage along the Eastern Coast of Africa to Mosambique, Johanna, and Quiloa . . . in the Nisus Frigate*, London, 1819.

Protesto de Arrendatários de Quelimane e Tete contra o Relatório do Secretario dos Negócios Indígenas, Lourenço Marques: Imprensa Nacional, 1909.

Raikes, Philip, 'Food Policy and Production in Mozambique since Independence', *Review of African Political Economy*, 29 (1984), pp. 95-107.

Randles, W.G.L., *L'Empire du Monomotapa du XVe au XIXe siècle*, Paris: Mouton, 1975.

Ranger, T.O., 'Revolt in Portuguese East Africa', *St Antony's Papers*, 15 (1963), pp. 54-80.

——, 'Territorial Cults in the History of Central Africa', *J. of African History*, 14 (1973), pp. 581-97.

Rea, W.F., SJ, *The Economics of the Zambezi Missions, 1580-1759*, Rome: Institutum Historicum SJ, 1976.

Reis, João C., *A Empresa da Conquista do Senhorio do Monomotapa*, Lisbon: Heuris, 1984.

Report of the Commercial, Economic and Financial Condition of Portuguese East Africa, by J. Pyke for Dept. of Overseas Trade, London: HMSO, 1927.

Report on Economic and Commercial Conditions in Portuguese East Africa, by C.N. Ezard for Dept. of Overseas Trade, London: HMSO, 1938.

'A Restruturação do Colonialismo em Moçambique 1938-1944' (Esboço do 3 Capítulo da *História de Moçambique*), *Cadernos da História* (Maputo), 5 (1987), pp. 41-74.

Ribeiro, Estolano, 'A Zambézia Agrícola', *Boletim da Agência Geral das Colónias*, 50 (1929), pp. 59-73.

Ribeiro, Sousa (ed.), *Anuário de Moçambique*, Lourenço Marques: Imprensa Nacional, 1917 and 1940.

Rita-Ferreira, A., *O Movimento Migratório de Trabalhadores entre Moçambique e a Africa do Sul*, Lisbon: Junta de Investigações do Ultramar, 1963.

——, *Fixação Portuguesa e História Pré-colonial de Moçambique*, Lisbon: Junta de Investigações Ciêntificas do Ultramar, 1982.

——, *Moçambique post-25 de Abril. Causas do Exodo da População de Origem Europeia e Asiática*, extract from *Moçambique: Cultura e História de um Pais*, Coimbra: Instituto de Antropologia, 1988.

——, 'A Sobrevivência do mais fraco. Moçambique no 3o Quartel do Século XIX', in *Reunião Internacional de História de Africa*; *Relação Europa-Africa no 3o Quartel do Século XIX*, Lisbon: Instituto de Investigação Científica Tropical, 1989, pp. 299-347.

Robinson, Richard, *Contemporary Portugal*, London: Geo. Allen and Unwin, 1979.

Rocha, Aurélio, Carlos Serra and David Hedges (eds), *História de Moçambique*, vol. 2, Maputo: Cadernos Tempo, 1983.

Romero, Jeronymo, *Memória acerca do Districto de Cabo Delgado*, Lisbon: Imprensa Nacional, 1856.

Ross, E.A., *Report on the Employment of Native Labour in Portuguese Africa*, New York, 1925.

Sakaraj, L.J., 'Indian Merchants in East Africa: The Triangular Trade and the Slave Economy', *Slavery and Abolition*, 1 (1980).

Saldanha, Eduardo d'Almeida, *O Sul do Save*, Lisbon: Tipografia Formosa, 1928.

——, *João Belo e o Sul do Save*, Lisbon: Tipografia Formosa, 1928.

Salt, Henry, *A Voyage to Abyssinia . . . in the Years 1809 and 1810*, London, 1814.

Samora: Why he died, Maputo: Mozambique News Agency, 1986.

Santa Caterina, Francisco de, 'A Dominican Account of the Zambezi in 1744', C.R. Boxer (ed.), *Boletim da Sociedade de Estudos de Moçambique*, 29 (1960).

Santana, F. (ed.), *Documentação Avulsa Moçambicana do Arquivo Histórico Ultramarino*, 2 vols, Lisbon: Centro de Estudos Historicos Ultramarinos, 1964-7.

Santos, João dos, *Ethiopia Oriental e Varia Historia de Cousas Notaveis do Oriente* Evora, 1609.

——, *Ethiopia Oriental*, extracts printed in G.M. Theal, *Records of South Eastern Africa*, vol. 7.

Schebesta, Paul, *Portugals Konquistamission in Südost-Afrika*, St Augustin: Steyler, 1966.

Schoffeleers, M., 'The Zimba and the Lundu State in the Late Sixteenth and Early Seventeenth Centuries', *J. of African History*, 28 (1987) pp. 337–55.

Schreuder, D.M., *The Scramble for Southern Africa, 1877–1895*, Cambridge University Press, 1980.

Scott, Catherine, 'Socialism and the "Soft State" in Africa: An Analysis of Angola and Mozambique', *J. of Modern African Studies*, 26 (1988), pp. 23–36.

Serrão de Azevedo, J., *Relatório do Curador Ano Económico de 1913–1914*, Lourenço Marques: Curadoria dos Indígenas Portugueses no Transvaal, 1915.

Shepherd, Gill, 'Trading Lineages in Historical Perspective', *Africa and the Sea*, proceedings of a colloquium at the University of Aberdeen, Aberdeen, 1985, pp. 152–77.

Silva Cunha, J.M. da, *O Trabalho Indígena*, Lisbon: Agência Geral das Colónias, 1949.

Silva Rego, A. da, 'Relações entre Moçambique e a Africa do Sul', *Moçambique: Curso de Extensão Universitária, Ano Lectivo de 1964–5*, Lisbon: Instituto Superior de Ciências Sociais e Política Ultramarina, 1965, pp. 57–76.

Sinclair, Paul, 'Chibuene — an early trading site in southern Mozambique', *Paideuma*, 28 (1982), pp. 149–64.

Smith, Alan K., 'The Peoples of Southern Mozambique: an Historical Survey', *J. of African History*, 14 (1975), pp. 565–80.

Sousa, Francisco de, *Oriente Conquistado a Jesu Christo pelos Padres da Companhia de Jesu da Provincia de Goa*, Lisbon, 1710.

Souza Monteiro, J.M. de, *Diccionário Geographico das Provincias e Possessões Portuguezas*, Lisbon, 1850.

Spence, C.F., *Moçambique: East African Province of Portugal*, Cape Town: Howard Timmins, 1963.

Stefaniszyn, Bronislaw, and Hilary de Santana, 'The Rise of the Chikunda "Condottieri"', *Northern Rhodesia J.*, 4 (1960), pp. 361–8.

Sutherland-Harris, N., 'Zambian Trade with Zumbo in the Eighteenth Century' in R. Gray and D. Birmingham (eds), *Pre-Colonial African Trade*, London: Oxford University Press, 1970, pp. 231–42.

Tabler, E.C. (ed.), *The Zambezi Papers of Richard Thornton*, 2 vols, London: Chatto and Windus and Rhodes-Livingstone Museum, 1963.

Termos de Vassalagem nos Territórios de Machona, Zambézia e Nyasa 1858–1889, Lisbon, 1890.

Theal, G.M. (ed.), *Records of South Eastern Africa*, 9 vols, Cape Town: Government of Cape Colony, 1898–1903, repr. C. Struik, Cape Town, 1964.

Thoman, Mauriz, SJ, *Reise und Lebensbeschreibung*, Augsburg, 1788.

Tibbetts, G.R., *Arab Navigation in the Indian Ocean before the Coming of the Portuguese*, London: Luzac 1971.

Torres, A., 'Le Rôle du Capitale Bancaire dans les Colonies Portugaises de l'Angola et de St. Tomé de 1864 au début du xxe siècle', *African Economic History*, 12 (1983), pp. 227–40.

Urdang, Stephanie, 'The Last Transition? Women and Development in Mozambique', *Review of African Political Economy*, 27/28 (1984), pp. 8–32.

Vail, Leroy, 'The Making of an Imperial Slum: Nyasaland and its Railways, 1895-1935', *J. of African History*, 16 (1975), pp. 89-112.

Vail, Leroy, 'Mozambique's Chartered Companies: the Rule of the Feeble', *J. of African History*, 17 (1976), pp. 389-416.

—— and Landeg White, '"Tawani, Machambero": Forced Cotton and Rice Growing on the Zambezi', *J. of African History*, 19 (1978), pp. 239-63.

——, *Capitalism and Colonialism in Mozambique*, (London: Heinemann, 1980).

Van der Horst, Sheila, *Native Labour in South Africa*, London: Oxford University Press, 1942.

Van Onselen, Charles, *Chibaro*, London: Pluto Press, 1976.

——, 'Randlords and Rotgut, 1886-1903', *History Workshop Journal*, 2 (1976), pp. 33-89.

Vasconcellos, Ernesto J. de C., *As Colónias Portuguezas*, Lisbon, 1903.

Vilhena, Ernesto de, *Regime dos Prazos da Zambézia*, Lisbon: Imprensa Nacional, 1916.

Villas-Boas Truão, A.N. de B. de, 'Plano para um Regimento ou Nova Constituição Económica e Política da Capitania dos Rios de Senna', *Annaes do Conselho Ultramarino*, parte não official, December (1857), pp. 406-17.

——, *Estatística de Capitania dos Rios de Senna do Anno de 1806*, Lisbon, 1889.

Villiers, John, 'The Estado da India in South East Asia', *The First Portuguese Colonial Empire*, in M. Newitt (ed.), University of Exeter Press, 1986, pp. 37-68.

Vincent J. Smith, 'Britain, Portugal and the First World War, 1914-1916', *European Studies Review*, 4 (1974), pp. 207-38.

——, 'The Portuguese Republic and Britain, 1910-1914', *J. of Contemporary History*, 10 (1975), pp. 707-27.

Vines, Alex, *Renamo: Terrorism in Mozambique*, London: James Currey, 1991.

Wagner, Roger, 'Zoutpansberge: the Dynamics of a Hunting Frontier, 1848-67', in Shula Marks and Anthony Atmore (eds), *Economy and Society in Pre-industrial South Africa*, Harlow: Longman, 1980.

Wardman, Anna, 'The Co-operative Movement in Cokwe', *J. of Southern African Studies*, 11 (1985), pp. 295-304.

Warhurst, P.R., *Anglo-Portuguese Relations in South-Central Africa, 1890-1900*, Royal Commonwealth Society Imperial Studies XXIII, London: Longman, 1962.

——, 'The Tete Agreement', *Rhodesian History*, 1 (1970), pp. 31-42.

Webster, David, 'Migrant Labour, Social Formation and the Proletarianization of the Chopi of Southern Mozambique', *African Perspectives*, 1 (1978), pp. 157-74.

Wheeler, Douglas L., 'Gungunyane the Negotiator: a Study in African Diplomacy', *J. of African History*, 9 (1968), pp. 583-602.

White, Landeg, *Magomero*, Cambridge University Press, 1987.

Whiteway, R.S. (ed.), *The Portuguese Expedition to Abyssinia*, Hakluyt Society (Kraus Reprint, 1969).

Wiese, Carlos, 'Expedição Portuguesa a M'Pesene', *Boletim da Sociedade de Geografia de Lisboa*: (1891) pp. 235-73, 297-321, 331-412, 415-30, 465-97; (1892) 373-431, 435-516.

Wilensky, Alfredo Héctor, *Trends in Portuguese Overseas Legislation for Africa*, Braga: Editora Pax, 1971.

Willequet, J., 'Anglo-German Rivalry in Belgian and Portuguese Africa', in P. Gifford and W.R. Louis (eds), *Britain and Germany in Africa*, New Haven, CT: Yale University Press, 1967, pp. 215–44.

Worsfold, W. Basil, *Portuguese Nyasaland*, London: Sampson Low, 1899, repr. Negro Universities Press, New York, 1969.

Wrigley, C., 'The River-God and the historians; Myth in the Shire Valley and Elsewhere', *J. of African History*, 29 (1988), pp. 367–83.

Wuyts, Marc, 'Money, Planning and Rural Transformation in Mozambique', *J. of Development Studies*, 22 (1985), pp. 180–207.

Young, E.D., *The Search after Livingstone*, London: Letts, 1868, repr. Blantyre: Society of Malawi, 1984.

Young, S., 'Fertility and Famine. Women's Agricultural History in Southern Mozambique' in R. Palmer and R. Parsons (eds), *The Roots of Rural Poverty in Central and Southern Africa* (London, 1977).

Young, Tom, 'The Politics of Development in Angola and Mozambique', *African Affairs*, 87 (1988), pp. 165–84.

——, 'The MNR/Renamo External and Internal Dynamics', *African Affairs*, 89 (1990), pp. 491–507.

Willis, Roy de Heston, *Towa Indians as Queens*, Ipsarian Shaftans, Brugo Editions, Paris 1971.

Wilmsen, J., *Anglachment Rituals in Bedouin and Paraguayan Areas*, in P. Gifford and W. R. Louis (eds), *Britain and Germany in Africa*, ed. OTP Yale University Press, 1967, pp. 313–343.

Wombcke, V., *Death Ceremonies Around the World*, Chicago, Jorgensen and Nemo Universities Press, New York, 1993.

Wrigley, C., "The Kimera Cult and the Interlacustrine Myth in the Agra Valley and Elsewhere," *Uganda Journal*, 29 (1988), pp. 387–392.

Wynne-Morse, Mickey, "Farming and Ritual," *Anthropology Notebook,* quest. 27 of *Omnipotent Sudan*, 22 (1982), pp. 150–170.

Young, D., *Rites of Passage*, Longmans, London Lane, 1863, repr. Bloomington Society at Midwest, 1988.

Young, S., "Fertility and Farming: Women, A tradition of History in Southern Mozambique," in S. Palmer and R. Parson (eds), *The Roots of Rural Poverty in Central and Southern Africa*, London, 1977.

Young, Tom, "Theory, History of Development in Angola and Mozambique," *African Affairs*, 87 (1988), pp. 165–84.

——, "The MNR/RENAMO: External and Internal Dynamics," *African Affairs*, 69 (1990), pp. 491–507.

INDEX